THE FOREST SERVICE

Fighting for Public Lands

Gerald W. Williams

Understanding Our Government

Greenwood Press
Westport, Connecticut • London

Library of Congress Cataloging-in-Publication Data

Williams, Gerald W.
   The Forest Service : fighting for public lands / Gerald W. Williams.
        p. cm.—(Understanding our government, ISSN 1556–8512)
   Includes bibliographical references and index.
   ISBN 0–313–33794–2 (alk. paper)
   1. United States. Forest Service—History. 2. Forest policy—United States. 3. Forests and
forestry—Environmental aspects—United States. 4. Forest reserves—United States. I. Title. II.
Series.
   SD565.W55 2007
   333.750973—dc22   2006025380

British Library Cataloguing in Publication Data is available.

Library of Congress Catalog Card Number: 2006025380

ISBN: 0–313–33794–2
ISSN: 1556–8512

First published in 2007

Greenwood Press, 88 Post Road West, Westport, CT 06881
An imprint of Greenwood Publishing Group, Inc.
www.greenwood.com

Printed in the United States of America

The paper used in this book complies with the
Permanent Paper Standard issued by the National
Information Standards Organization (Z39.48–1984).

10 9 8 7 6 5 4 3 2 1

Contents

Series Foreword

Since the founding of our country in 1776, the U.S. government has been transformed significantly. Changing societies and events, both domestic and international, have greatly affected the actions and development of our country. The Industrial Revolution, World War II, the civil rights movement, and the more recent "war on terrorism" are just a few of the events that have changed our government and its functions. Depending on the needs of our country at any given time, agencies are developed or terminated, their size and/or budget increased or decreased, their responsibilities perhaps even transferred to another department within the government, in order to meet policymakers' objectives. Whether an independent agency or one of the 15 executive-branch departments overseen by the president and the cabinet, each is given specific responsibilities, and all are formed to fulfill an important role for the country and its people.

The Understanding Our Government series was developed to offer an in-depth view of the most powerful, controversial, and misunderstood agencies of the U.S. government and how they have changed American society and, in some cases, the world. Well-known agencies frequently in the media spotlight, such as the Central Intelligence Agency and the National Aeronautics and Space Administration, are included, as well as lesser-known, but important, agencies such as the Bureau of Indian Affairs and the Forest Service. Written by experts on the particular agencies, including former employees or advisory committee members, each volume provides a historical overview of an agency and includes narrative chapters describing such aspects as organization, programs, significant events, controversies, key people, and influence on society, as well as additional topics tailored to the particular agency. Subjects vary greatly among the different titles. Depending on readers' interests or needs, some will be able to find information on subjects such as the Central Intelligence Agency's role in the Cuban missile crisis, as well as its history of covert operations, while others may be interested in the Environmental Protection Agency's response to environmental disasters such as the *Exxon Valdez* oil spill and the Three Mile Island nuclear accident. Still others may be curious to learn about the Federal Communication Commission's role in communications policy and regulation of the media and the fine line between censorship and freedom of speech or the Drug Enforcement Administration's enforcement of drug laws and methods of combating drug trafficking and how the legalization of certain illegal drugs would affect the agency and the country in general.

Whether readers are students conducting research on a specific agency for a high school or college assignment or just want to learn more about one agency or how the government works, our hope is that each reader will gain further knowledge about the U.S. government and its employees. We want readers to comprehend our nation's significant achievements, yet also understand its failures and how we can learn from them. Over the years, our country has performed great feats, from creating lifesaving drugs to space exploration, but it has also experienced tragedies, including environmental catastrophes and terrorist attacks. Readers will learn how such events shape legislation and public policy and how they affect everyday life for the citizens of this country. While many agencies have been portrayed in certain ways in newspapers, on television, and in films, such representations have not always been realistic or impartial. This series attempts to offer fair, objective views of U.S. government agencies and to allow readers to think about them and to form their own opinions.

Steven Vetrano

Preface

The Forest Service is one of the oldest agencies in the U.S. Department of Agriculture. In 2005, the agency celebrated 100 years of managing the national forests and grasslands and also changed its name from the Bureau of Forestry. The 100 years have not been easy; managing the national forests has been fraught with controversy from the day the Forest Service began. This controversy continues to this day. Although there have been a number of books and hundreds of articles about Forest Service and the national forests, few have tried to place the agency in context vis-à-vis other federal agencies.

The agency manages 193 million acres of national forests and grasslands. Almost every state has one or more of these unique places. One state, Hawaii, has only one acre under Forest Service control; Alaska, on the other hand, has almost 22 million acres. The three agency branches each have their own functions—management of the national forest system, research and development, and state and private forestry. The Forest Service employs around 30,000 people, including administrators, airplane and helicopter pilots, archaeologists, carpenters, civil rights, economists, engineers, fish biologists, foresters, historians, landscape architects, law enforcement, legal advisors, mechanics, planners, public relations, silviculturalists, sociologists, support staff, wildlife biologists, and many more specialists and generalists. The fact that the national forests exist today is a testament to the forces at play at the end of the nineteenth century and a handful of individuals who were committed to saving and managing forestlands for the public—forever. It was not an easy task then, nor is it now.

I came to write this book after almost three decades of working inside the agency on two national forests (Umpqua and Willamette) in western Oregon, in the Pacific Northwest Region, in Portland, and then in the national headquarters, in Washington, D.C. My last assignment was to serve as the national historian for the

Forest Service. I retired on July 1, 2005, exactly 100 years after the Forest Service was "born" as a newly named agency in the Department of Agriculture. Moving back to my home state of Oregon has allowed me the opportunity to continue researching and writing even more that I was able to in my other jobs. Writing from my home office has been a challenge, since when I worked for the agency it was easy to just walk down the hall and talk with an expert. But with the Internet, e-mail, and even old-fashioned telephones, it has been relatively easy to talk with friends and to gather information used in this book. Of course, I have an extensive library on federal forestry to draw upon, as well. The advent of digital imaging, as well as the ability to digitize existing photos, has been a godsend for this book.

This book will give the reader, whether an academic scholar, researcher, student, or the interested general reader, an inside look at the USDA Forest Service, how it operates in the federal government and within the overview by Congress and the people. It is beyond the scope of this book to look with any detail into how other federal agencies, states, and the private sector operate or how they interact or are influenced by the Forest Service. This unique book looks at the rich history of the agency. It also covers the three branches of the agency, as well as international and cooperation with the states. The mission of the Forest Service is "caring for the land and serving people," which summarizes the role the agency plays in American culture and in the federal government.

The Forest Service operates in a political environment that is shaped by the president, the Congress, the federal courts, interest groups, and agency expertise. Sometimes it is a messy business, which is the way a democracy must operate. The Forest Service is fully committed to the utilitarian idea of "the greatest good, for the greatest number, in the long run." The difficulty facing the Forest Service is to determine what constitutes the greatest good. Ask any person, or a thousand people, and you will get a multitude of answers. When an issue or opportunity comes to the table, the Forest Service can bring many experts to sort through the problem and develop a resolution and decision. Not all decisions are universally liked, but the public has many opportunities to be involved and even to challenge both the analyses and the decisions.

Several decades ago, I drove a Chinese graduate student from my workplace in Roseburg, Oregon, to her home in Eugene. I was trying to explain to her what it was that I did for the Forest Service and how the national forests fit into the landscape of western Oregon. The drive took about an hour. Explaining the relations between the federal national forests, national parks, Bureau of Land Management lands, and national wildlife refuges was difficult at best. But then I had to throw into the discussion the various state forests and parks, the county parks, and industrial private forestlands, as well as the small woodlots. Also added to this was the fact that every agency that manages the land has different administrators, laws, and implementing regulations to follow. She explained that, in China, everything was federal. What a difference—from the most simple to the most complex!

Chapter 1, "The Forest Service: Fighting for Public Lands," is a brief history of the Forest Service from the very beginning in the late 1800s until 1990. The chapter discusses the early days, when there were few laws governing the use of the national public domain and how the early leaders, like Gifford Pinchot, were able to expand the size and number of the national forests, although not without controversy and great struggles. This chapter documents the many challenges in establishing management of the national forests and building the agency—the Forest Service. In part, this chapter follows the outline of agency history contained in my book, *The USDA Forest Service: The First Century*, printed by the Forest Service in 2000 and reprinted in 2005. Chapter 2, "The 1990s and Early Twenty-first Century," covers the period from the early 1990s to 2006. This was a significant era as management of the national forests fully matured. The past 15 years have seen a huge change in societal values toward the management of natural resources from the nation's forestlands. Much of the current management of the national forests, and even other forestlands, was led by Forest Service researchers to better take into account the many natural resources on the forests.

Chapter 3, "Structure and Functions of the Forest Service," concentrates on how the three branches of the agency—the national forest system, research and development, and state and private forestry—operate. Managing the massive 193 million acres of the national forest system has always been problematic as values and social conditions, needs, and expectations change. The Forest Service is unique among the federal agencies in that it has a strong internal research unit that has several thousand employees working on pure and applied forest research questions that apply equally to federal, state, and private lands. The state and private forestry branch assists landowners in both the utilization and the restoration of their forestlands. This branch also serves as a "pass through" of funds authorized by Congress to the state foresters for local programs in every state. Several subthemes are also discussed in this chapter, including international programs, roadless and wilderness, and forest fires and firefighting.

Chapter 4, "Challenges for the Twenty-first Century," includes discussion of the major issues or challenges that will face the Forest Service over the next hundred years. These challenges include fire in the forests; water protection/restoration and water use; recreation on the national forests and grasslands; ways to involve the public in federal land and natural resource management decisions; and fish and wildlife preservation. Each of these concerns has a number of significant subissues that are briefly discussed. Chapter 5, "Organization of Forest Service Management," includes information on how the agency is organized into the national headquarters, 9 regional offices, 110 national forest supervisors' offices, and 506 ranger districts. Another part of Chapter 5 concerns attempts to reorganize the agency by the executive branch, Congress, and the Forest Service itself. The chapter ends with a discussion about future options for reorganizing the agency and the management of the national forests.

Chapter 6, "Selected Biographies of Persons Associated with the USDA Forest Service," covers biographical information about 75 interesting people who either have worked for or are currently working for the Forest Service. The biographies include every chief forester from 1876 to present, women, minorities, and even non–Forest Service personalities like John Muir and several administrators of the Department of the Interior and the Department of Agriculture. Chapter 7, "Relationships with Other Federal Agencies," includes discussions of each of the major federal agencies that are important partners with the Forest Service. The list includes the General Land Office (today the Bureau of Land Management), the U.S. Geological Survey, the National Park Service, the Bureau of Land Management, the Fish and Wildlife Service, the National Marine Fisheries Service, and the Natural Resources Conservation Service. Chapter 8, "Chronology of Key Events and People," is essentially a timeline of conservation from 1799 to the present.

Several appendices cover information that would generally too long or specific to be included in the eight chapters of the book. These appendices include the national forests by name, state, and current acreage; a discussion of the eight American Forest Congresses that have met between 1873 and 2005; Forest Service badges, patches, and chinaware; game refuges on the national forests; timber sales from 1905 until 2002; and the 13 major laws affecting Forest Service management. In addition, there is a lengthy bibliography or reference list, and an index.

My wife, Joyce, and my kids, Colin, Maggie, Justin, and Tristan, have often wondered what I was doing in my office (playing computer games or tracking eBay). They have supported me in many ways during this project. Even when the kids were at school and my wife at work (for the Forest Service), I've had two wonderful golden retrievers—Sandy and Barlow—as constant companions. I hope you, the reader, enjoy reading about this fascinating agency as much as I've enjoyed writing about it.

Introduction

The Forest Service is the largest agency in the Department of Agriculture. It manages almost 193 million acres of national forests and grasslands. The Forest Service officially began operations in 1905, when the first forest reserve was only 14 years old. New forest reserves were being established by presidential proclamations in many parts of the West, and by 1905 there were some 59 reserves encompassing 62.6 million acres. At this time, roads were but a pipe dream; in fact, the age of automobiles was still quite young. But the nation was moving westward, changing everything in the way. Prairies became cities, forests became farms and ranches, rivers became reservoirs.

Battles over these early forest reserves were fought in Congress and at the local level. It was not an easy task, for representatives and senators from the western states generally opposed the new reserves, while the eastern delegations generally preferred them. The situation is not very different today. Regardless, the early forest reserves and national forests were authorized by a single long sentence in a related bill that was signed into law in 1891. What today is known as the national forest system was almost thrown out in 1897 when a congressional move to eliminate the reserves was pocket-vetoed by the president. Actions later that year authorized the reserves and set up a system of management through forest rangers. In 1905, at the insistence of President Theodore Roosevelt, the reserves were transferred from the Department of the Interior to the Bureau of Forestry in the Department of Agriculture. On July 1, 1905, the Bureau was renamed the Forest Service, the name that remains attached to the agency today.

The new Forest Service then began a long battle to manage the national forests. The Forest Service, at a time when political opponents were everywhere, strove to introduce scientific forestry and conservation to the federal forests. It was very successful in this enterprise, but the job took years to accomplish. The agency remained noncontroversial from around 1910 to the 1950s, as the Forest Service was building infrastructure and friends. But, after World War II, when the national forests were opened in order to meet the nation's demand for timber, the agency began to lose its luster. It was still the most popular of the federal agencies, but times were changing.

By 1960, a new era was beginning. The Forest Service was still efficient in its work, but now the work and the national forests were being viewed less as the ultimate timber supply and more as places for recreation. This transition would take another 40 years to reach fruition, and many battles with special-interest groups, Congress, agency employees, and the public. Since the 1980s, the Forest Service has tried to regain its lost luster, but the efforts have been not as rewarding as hoped. By the turn of the twenty-first century, the agency was changing faster than ever before, but it still had a long way to go.

In recent years, Congress has set the management agenda through a wide variety of laws, while interest groups have used the courts to impose their ideas of proper management. The agency is sometimes caught in a crossfire between Congress and the courts, and the agency must sometimes change its policies or suggest changes to the laws.

Will the Forest Service and the national forests be relevant in the twenty-first century? It is hard to tell. A lot depends on the ability of the agency to change. With the "baby boom" generation retiring over the next 10 years, the agency will have the opportunity to hire new people who reflect the new societal values. I expect that the Forest Service will still be around, but probably merged, along with the Bureau of Land Management and perhaps the Natural Resources Conservation Service, into a massive new Department of Natural Resources. The national forests and grasslands will become truly the "nation's playground." There will be much less dependence on the extraction of natural resources.

But this emphasis will not totally vanish. Some organizations wish that the Forest Service would cut no more timber. It seems unlikely that this will come to pass, but certainly it will be necessary to lower production levels. Grazing, a traditional use of the forests and grasslands, will be challenged as never before. Mining on the national forests will, I hope, be reduced, but this will require that the General Mining Law of 1872 be changed, as well. Recreation will play an increasing role, but with that will come problems of overcrowding and damage to the forests.

But this clouds the fact that the Forest Service continues to manage the national forests and grasslands for a multitude of general and special purposes. The users of the national forests take advantage of the opportunities for mining; for recreational activities such as camping, driving, fishing, hunting, and skiing; for timber harvesting; for utilizing water resources for municipal drinking water and irrigation; for wilderness activities; and many others. The concepts, set in law, that multiple use of these lands sometimes come into conflict when some uses are in opposition to others about how to use one parcel of land.

Some people believe that the Forest Service is a century-old dinosaur that needs to be replaced. Other want it moved into a new department of natural resources.

There are those who believe that the federal government should not own or manage any land and that the federal lands should be sold off to the public or transferred to the states. At least one academic, speaking to a crowd 20 years ago, at Oregon State University, wondered aloud whether federal ownership of land and resources was an anomaly in history and whether in the future these lands would be placed in private ownership. These options have been discussed for more than 100 years, but Congress and the people continue to support leaving things as they are. That could change in the future, but that is the democratic process. For now and well into the twenty-first century, the Forest Service and the national forests and grasslands will remain under public management and ownership.

The Forest Service: Fighting for Public Lands

The founding of the national forest system and the Forest Service, an agency of the U.S. Department of Agriculture, has its roots in the last quarter of the nineteenth century and the beginning of the twentieth century. Visionary men of the era profoundly influenced thinking about the remaining public lands and the resources they contained, as well as about proposals for saving, preserving, and managing these important lands. It was not an easy task. The preference of some Americans then, and even today, was to transfer the public land to the private sector either by selling or granting. Thinking in the late 1800s and early 1900s was rooted in the Jeffersonian notion that farmers and farming would make the country great. The common people were by far the most important asset, followed by what they could make from or take off the land. We were a nation of farmers. But that early-nineteenth-century ideal of Thomas Jefferson's agricultural America was changing rapidly. The year 1890 has often been assumed to mark the "end of the frontier." The homestead acts of the middle 1800s were wildly successful, and the land in the West was filling up fast, the population was growing, and cities were rising.

In the late 1800s, several influential writers began a campaign to save the public forest areas for both national parks and forests. The first national park, Yellowstone, was established in 1872. It took almost two decades for the idea of forest protection to gain a foothold. The forest effort was greatly enhanced in 1891 with passage of the Forest Reserve Act, which allowed the president to establish public forests from unclaimed public lands. The Forest Service at the end of the 1890s provided expert forestry knowledge to landowners who were interested in managing their forestland and preventing land erosion. The national forest crusaders were so successful in their battle for protection of public forest domain land that the United States today has a system of 155 national forests, 20 national grasslands, and 20 research and experimental forests, as well as other special areas, covering a

President Theodore Roosevelt. (Gerald Williams Personal Collection)

total of 193 million acres of public land. The Forest Service has evolved into a 31,000-employee agency that manages the forests for a number of multiple uses, including timber harvesting, wilderness activities, recreation, mining, water use, grazing, and wildlife refuges.

A GROWING CONCERN ABOUT NATURAL RESOURCES, 1873–1905

Following its devastating Civil War, the United States experienced tremendous growth and change, especially in the West. American Indians, buffalo, trappers, and pioneers had already given way to miners, timber cutters, and other people bent on exploiting the land and resources of our quickly growing, resource-rich nation. Hard-rock and hydraulic mining quickly became major industries in the Sierra Nevada, the Cascades, and the Rocky Mountain ranges. Mining extracted valuable minerals but often severely eroded the land. Herds of cattle and sheep soon spread over the grasslands of the Great Plains and Southwest. Yet, even these uses were beginning to be replaced by homesteading farmers who broke the sod and sowed grain and corn over the prairies and plains.

Railroads had just finished linking the far West (California) with the rest of the nation, and plans were being made to connect all of the West's major population centers by rail. Congress gave massive land grants to many railroads, especially along the northern tier of states (from Minnesota to Washington state) to encourage the railroads to build rail lines to connect cites and towns, as well as to spawn growth and provide cheap rail shipping in the West. Timber companies, which had exhausted the standing forests of the East, were quickly clearing the great pine forests of the Lake States (Minnesota, Wisconsin, and Michigan) and were contemplating moving their operations to the South and the far West.

Acquisitiveness and exploitation were the spirit of the times, with little regard for the ethics of conservation or the needs of the future. The reaction to the abuse of the nation's natural resources during this period gave rise to America's forestry and conservation movement. The beginning of America's concern about the conservation of land for the people can be traced to George

Perkins Marsh, who, in 1864, wrote the book *Man and Nature: Or Physical Geography as Modified by Human Action*. This influential book drew on the past to illustrate how human actions had harmed the earth, leading to the demise of earlier civilizations. Marsh wanted not only to warn his contemporaries against this fate but also to initiate actions to prevent it. One measure that Marsh advocated was the protection of forests, yet few heeded his important message. For during this era of unbridled exploitation, any notion of preserving anything was almost universally ignored. After all, there were more trees, gold and silver, and water "just over the next hill." Develop what you can, then move on to the next piece of land—the American way.

Painters and Photographers

Two other influential persons in the early conservation movement were Ferdinand V. Hayden, who made several important investigations of the Rocky Mountains with the King, Powell, and Wheeler surveys—especially the Yellowstone area—for the U.S. Geological and Geographical Survey, and John Wesley Powell, who surveyed and reported on large portions of the arid West and its major rivers for the U.S. Geophysical and Geological Survey (predecessor of the U.S. Department of the Interior's Geological Survey). Interestingly, Powell advocated the removal of forests to increase the water supply. This notion ran contrary to the ideas that trees were needed to hold back the water/floods and erosion. These contradictory ideas would spawn research for decades to come. In the end, both notions would prove to be correct, but for different reasons.

The "Hudson River school" painters in the 1825–1875 period were important in generating a new imagery of the East and the West that, for the first time, showed U.S. landscapes that rivaled those found in Europe. Included were the paintings of Thomas Cole, Albert Bierstadt, Worthington Whittredge, Jasper Cropsey, Sanford Gifford, Frederick Church, and others. They portrayed the natural world, sometimes fanciful and inspired, for the patrons of the arts. Few were available to the general public. Frederick Remington and George Catlin produced hundreds of paintings and sketches that were often reproduced as illustrations in magazines and books and that are still widely collected. These paintings led to a greater appreciation of the natural wonders of America.

But another form of imagery had the potential to reach the masses—photography. The most influential in the late 1800s were the landscape photographers—especially Timothy H. O'Sullivan, William Henry Jackson, and Carlton E. Watkins. They were important in generating concern about the marvelous and unusual features present in the largely unpopulated West. The impressive, large format images they produced gave photographic visions of the stark beauty and startling majesty that abounded in the western mountains and valleys. Hayden's scientific reports of the Yellowstone area in northwest Wyoming and its remarkable features, accompanied by O'Sullivan's spectacular photographs, moved Congress to establish Yellowstone National Park in 1872—the first such park in the world.

Erosion effects of deforestation in Colorado, 1915. (USDA Forest Service)

First Federal Forestry Expert

Others became convinced that the more ordinary forest areas, which were still in public ownership, also needed protection. This effort was spearheaded by Dr. Franklin B. Hough, a physician, historian, and statistician. He noticed that timber production in the East would build up, then fall off in some areas, while building up again in different areas, which to him indicated that timber supplies of the United States were being exhausted. As a result of his observations, Hough presented a paper, "On the Duty of Governments in the Preservation of Forests," to the annual meeting of the American Association for the Advancement of Science (AAAS), held at Portland, Maine, in August 1873. The following day, AAAS passed a petition to Congress "on the importance of promoting the cultivation of timber and the preservation of forests." It sought congressional action, but no legislation was passed for three years.

On August 15, 1876, a rider (amendment) was attached to the free-seed clause of the Appropriations Act of 1876. This amendment provided $2,000 to fund a person with "approved attainment, who is practically well acquainted with methods of statistical inquery [sic], and who has evinced an intimate acquaintance with [forestry matters]." This was the first federal appropriation devoted to forestry. Dr. Hough was appointed to the position. Thus, a new governmental "organization" was formed that consisted solely of Dr. Hough, as the first forestry agent, who was placed under the supervision of the Commissioner of Agriculture. He was directed to undertake a study to encompass forest consumption, importation, exportation, national wants, probable supply for the future, the means of preservation and renewal, the influence of forests on climates, and forestry methods used in other countries. In 1878, his 650-page report, titled simply "Report on Forestry," so impressed the Commissioner (later the Secretary) of Agriculture and Congress that they authorized the printing of 25,000 copies.

However, the forestry agent did not have any authority over timbered areas that remained in public domain. In 1881, the Division of Forestry was *temporarily* established to study and report on forestry matters in the United States and abroad; Hough was named its "chief." In Hough's 1882 report, he recommended "that the principal bodies of timber land still remaining the property of the government … be withdrawn from sale or grant." His idea was that federal timber could be cut under lease and that young timber growth would be protected for the future. In 1883, Nathaniel H. Egleston, who was very active role in the American Forestry Association (AFA), replaced Hough. Spending much of his time with AFA matters, Egleston was not the leader of federal forestry that Hough had been.

Leaders after Hough

Egleston served uneventfully until the spring of 1886, when he was replaced by Dr. Bernhard E. Fernow, who was trained in forestry in his native Germany (there were no American forestry schools at the time). Fernow was a leader in the new field of forestry and a founder of the American Forestry Association. As chief of the Division of Forestry, he brought much-needed professionalism to the job. He set up scientific research programs and initiated cooperative forestry projects with the states, including the planting of trees on the Great Plains. On June 30, 1886, the Division was given permanent status as part of the Department of Agriculture. This provided the needed stability for the fledgling government forestry organization.

In early 1889, Charles S. Sargent, professor of arboriculture at Harvard and editor of *Garden and Forest*, wrote an editorial for his magazine that took to heart Hough's 1882 recommendation to not permit the sale or grant of government timberland. Sargent proposed three things: the temporary withdrawal of all public forestlands from sale or homesteading; the use of the U.S. Army to protect these lands and forests; and the presidential appointment of a commission to report to Congress on a plan of administration and control of forested areas. As Gifford Pinchot pointed out, "the first suggestion was politically impossible, the second practically unworkable, but the third, in the end [some seven years later], put Government forestry on the map."

In April of the same year, the law committee of the American Forestry Association, consisting of Fernow, Egleston, and Edward Bowers, of the U.S. Department of the Interior's General Land Office (GLO), met with President Benjamin Harrison. The committee recommended that the nation adopt a new forestry policy. In 1890, after the president took no action on the matter, the American Forestry Association petitioned Congress to create forest reservations and provide a commission to administer them. Again, no noticeable action took place, but there was a strong groundswell to retain the forest covered public domain for the people. The Boone and Crockett Club rallied around the issue of protecting Yellowstone National Park, as well as other forested areas in the West. This sportsmen's club was founded in 1887 with such distinguished members as Theodore Roosevelt, Gifford Pinchot, George Bird Grinnell, Henry Cabot Lodge, and Henry L. Stimson. Their influence in national politics substantially helped the fledgling national forest and conservation movement in the early 1890s and the decades to follow.

It was apparent to many that the remaining forests on the public domain represented a great, but vulnerable, national asset that needed to be protected from unbridled despoliation for the sake of posterity. The weight of the data complied by Hough and others, as well as the recommendations of Hough, Fernow, Sargent, the Boone and Crockett Club, the American Forestry Association, and an aroused citizen-led effort, led to the creation of the national forest system as we know it today.

Forest Reserves Established

In early 1891, Congress was debating the issue of land frauds (the illegal purchase or use of deceit in the homesteading of federal land) related to the Timber Culture Act of 1873 and several homestead acts. A bill to rectify at least the most blatant of the transgressions was presented to Congress. A rider, or amendment, was attached to the bill, which was signed into law on March 3, 1891. This one-sentence amendment (section 24), afterwards referred to as the Forest Reserve or Creative Act, allowed the president to establish forest reserves from public domain land:

> SECTION 24—The President of the United States may, from time to time, set apart and reserve, in any state or territory having public land bearing forests, in any part of the public lands, wholly or in part covered with timber or undergrowth, whether of commercial value or not, as public reservations; and the President shall, by public proclamation, declare the establishment of such reservations and the limits thereof.

The Forest Reserve Act (see further discussion in Appendix 6) was used by President Benjamin Harrison on March 30 of the same year to set aside the first forest reserve—the Yellowstone Park Timberland Reserve (now part of the Shoshone National Forest). By the end of Harrison's term as president, in the spring of 1893, he had created 15 forest reserves containing 13 million acres. These forest reserves were the White River Plateau, Pikes Peak, Plum Creek, South Platte, and Battlement Mesa, all in Colorado; the Grand Canyon, in Arizona; the San Gabriel, Sierra, Trabuco Canyon, and San Bernardino, in California; the Bull Run, in Oregon; Pacific, in Washington; and the Afognak Forest and Fish Culture Reserve, in Alaska. On September 28, 1893, his successor, President Grover Cleveland, added two forest reserves—the huge Cascade Range Forest Reserve and the tiny Ashland Forest Reserve, a total of 5 million acres, in Oregon. Cleveland did not add any more forest reserves for almost four years, until Congress was willing to pass legislation to allow for the management of the public forests.

National Academy of Sciences Commission

Meanwhile, there were efforts in Congress to change the procedure for establishing federal forest reserves. In the summer of 1896, Congress, through the National Academy of Sciences, funded the national forest commission to study the forest situation and report back to Congress on its findings. The commission, which consisted of Charles Sargent (chair), Henry L. Abbot, William H. Brewer, Alexander Agassiz, Arnold Hague, Gifford Pinchot (secretary), and Wolcott Gibbs (member ex officio), traveled throughout the West on a tour of the forest reserves and areas where new reserves were proposed. John Muir and Henry S. Graves accompanied the commission on parts of the forest reserve investigations. Although members of the commission disagreed with one another much of the time, they did agree on the need for Mt. Rainier and Grand Canyon National Parks and on a number of new and expanded forest reserves.

Management of the Reserves

On February 22, 1897, President Grover Cleveland, as a result of the commission's recommendations, proclaimed 13 new or expanded forest reserves in the West, totaling some 21 million acres. These new reserves were known thereafter as the "Washington's birthday reserves." These were the San Jacinto and Stanislaus, in California; Uintah, in Utah; Mt. Rainier (renamed from Pacific and enlarged) and Olympic, in Washington; Bitter Root, Lewis and Clarke, and Flathead, in Montana; Black Hills, in South Dakota; Priest River, in Idaho; and the Teton and Big Horn, in Wyoming. The furor of opposition—mostly from state and congressional delegations—to these new or expanded forest reserves was unprecedented. Many wanted the new reserves, and even the older reserves, to be abolished, as they believed that the reserves would hinder grazing and timbering (both illegal at the time), as well as slow future growth of the affected states. But the outcries also rallied supporters of forest reserves. Congress passed the Sundry Civil Appropriations Act—the yearly act that provides funding for the federal government. One amendment to the bill would have eliminated the old and new reserves, but Cleveland pocket-vetoed the bill just before he left office. The incoming President McKinley would have to deal with the highly volatile situation.

Congress, in the spring of 1897, passed the revised Sundry Civil Appropriations Act. President William McKinley signed the act on June 4, 1897. The act contained several important amendments to mollify critics of the forest reserves. One of the amendments, the so-called Pettigrew amendment (later referred to as the "Organic Act") provided that any new reserves would have to meet the criteria of forest protection, watershed protection, and timber production, thus providing the charter for managing the forest reserves, later called national forests, for more than 75 years. The act also suspended the "Washington's birthday reserves" for nine months, except for those in California. This suspension, designed to allow homesteading of farmland inside the forest boundaries, was seen as a clever tactic to overcome western demands for elimination of the new forest reserves. However, scores of "land looters" took advantage of the law and illegally homesteaded several hundred thousand acres of heavily tree-laden forest areas, claiming that they were valuable farm or grazing lands. Most all these "homesteads" were immediately transferred to timber companies and land speculators.

Basically, the Organic Act (see further discussion in Appendix 6) allowed for the proper care, protection, and management of the new forest reserves and provided for an organization to manage them. One of the first General Land Office employees, if not the first, was Gifford Pinchot, who was hired in the summer of 1897 as a special forestry agent to make further investigations of the forest reserves and recommend ways to manage them. The Department of the Interior's GLO was able to appoint superintendents in each state that had forest reserves. The following summer, 1898, saw the appointment of forest reserve supervisors and forest rangers to patrol the reserves during the fire season, usually July 1 to October 1, after which they were furloughed for the year.

From 1897 until 1905, forest reserve superintendents, supervisors, and rangers were appointed by the U.S. senators—who were themselves appointed by the state legislatures, since there was no direct election of senators until the Seventeenth Amendment passed in 1913—and by the GLO through the Department of the Interior. No forest reserve rangers were appointed from the Department of Agriculture, where all the forestry experts were located. The first GLO forest ranger was William Kreutzer, appointed in the summer of 1898. Kreutzer rode into Denver and met with Colonel May on August 8, 1898, with the idea to become a forest ranger. The Colonel was impressed by this young man and hired him on the spot, without talking to anyone else. This first forest ranger was given the following instructions: "go back to the Plum Creek Reserve, ride as far and as fast as the Almighty will let you, and put out those forest fires." Another very early ranger was Frank N. Hammitt, a native of Denver, Colorado. He also went to work in the summer of 1898, on the Yellowstone Park Timberland Reserve. Prior to his appointment with the GLO, he had been chief of the cowboys in Colonel William F. Cody's Wild West Show. Like many of the old-time GLO rangers, he was selected from the local area, but he had no knowledge of forestry. Yet he was a "rough-and-ready," practical man with great knowledge of the mountains. He stayed with rangering until his untimely death in the summer of 1903 after falling from a cliff on that reserve (now the Shoshone National Forest).

Smith Bartrum, who was appointed as forest ranger in 1899 on the Cascade Range Forest Reserve in Oregon, wrote somewhat optimistically that

> the requirements at this time was; That a Ranger was to equip himself with one saddle horse, one pack horse, with riding and pack saddles, saddle bags for pack-horse, one axe, one shovel, provisions for at least six weeks or two months, adequate cooking utensils, all at his own expense, his salary was $60.00 per month. The Forest Ranger at that time must be prepared to range alone in the mountains in any and all kinds of weather, to know the general compass directions, legal sub-divisions of surveyed lands. To be able to find himself and go anywhere without loosing [sic] your direction; To be able to spot a fire and go to it at the earliest possible moment, night or

day, and suppress it, never leaving a fire until safe. Estimate the acreage of the burned over area. Make an estimate of the amount in board feet, of merchantable timber destroyed, and its value. To be familiar with the names of the different species of timber, to be able to operate a compass, to know the strip and circle method of cruising timber, and to have had experience in logging operations.

Yet another ranger at the same time was a man of no experience, as was typical of the GLO rangers—"In 1899, 1900 and 1901 Capt. C.V. Dodd, a Civil War Veteran, represented the Forest Service [actually the GLO]. His equipment consisted of two horses, a pistol with four shells, a large badge and a full beard." His firefighting experience, apparently, consisted of throwing another log in the fireplace at the Log Cabin Inn, in McKenzie Bridge, Oregon.

At the national level, Bernhard Fernow performed his duties as chief of the Division of Forestry with great distinction until April 15, 1898, when he resigned to become the director of Cornell University's new forestry school. In the 25 years since Hough had presented his AAAS paper, the nation had made significant progress in its movement from the frontier exploitation of the natural resources in the forested areas toward a policy of wise use and conservation.

Gifford Pinchot

Fernow's replacement was Gifford Pinchot—America's first native-born professional forester. He had been schooled at Yale, then spent about a year in France and Germany studying forestry, gained experience in managing George Vanderbilt's Biltmore estate in Asheville, North Carolina, and became personally familiar with many of the new forest reserves while serving as secretary on the national forest commission in 1896–1897. As the new and charismatic chief of the Division of Forestry, Pinchot was in charge of 60 enthusiastic and dedicated employees. The headquarters consisted of offices on the third floor and a small place in the attic of the old Department of Agriculture building in Washington, D.C. Pinchot had his title changed from "chief" to "forester," as there were "many chiefs in Washington, but only one forester."

Pinchot was instrumental in obtaining full bureau status for the Division of Forestry. It became the Bureau of Forestry on March 2, 1901. In 1902, the Minnesota Forest Reserve was the first reserve created by Congress rather than by presidential proclamation. Strong support by the Federation of Women's Clubs, which had 800,000 members in 1905, made the establishment of this forest reserve possible.

THE EARLY FOREST SERVICE AND CUSTODIAL MANAGEMENT ERA, 1905–1933

From 1897 until 1905, the administration of the federal forest reserves was divided between the supervisors and rangers of the GLO and the surveyors and mappers of the Geological Survey (USGS), both in the Department of the Interior. The forestry experts in the Department of Agriculture's Bureau of Forestry were limited to

Forest Service National Headquarters in Washington, D.C., 1901–1938. (USDA Forest Service)

providing technical forestry advice and assistance. Franklin B. Hough, Bernhard E. Fernow, and Gifford Pinchot contributed years of their lives, strong leadership, and assistance to the new field of forestry and especially federal forestry. Their expertise helped to create millions of acres of forest reserves (now called national forests) in the West. They also laid the foundation for the development of the new Forest Service in the Department of Agriculture. These visionaries, along with willing presidents (especially Teddy Roosevelt), scientific and conservation organizations, and newly trained forestry professionals, led the successful effort to retain millions of acres of federal forestland for future generations.

Forest Service Established in 1905

Pinchot was the primary advocate (with the strong concurrence from his friend President Theodore Roosevelt) of moving the responsibility of forest management away from the Department of the Interior. On February 1, 1905, Pinchot was able to unify all government forest administration under the Department of Agriculture's Bureau of Forestry (see Appendix 2 and Appendix 6). The main premise for the unification of forest reserve management with forestry expertise was Pinchot's strong belief that the USDI General Land Office was too politically charged and that rangers and even supervisors had little or no training in or understanding of forestry. In addition, there was evidence of political favoritism, land fraud, and malfeasance by the GLO. The Forest Service was established on July 1, 1905, when the name of the Bureau of Forestry was changed (see further discussion in Appendix 6). The creation of the Forest Service was followed by a change—the custom of GLO forest rangers gaining employment via political appointments ended, and selections were made through comprehensive field and written civil service examinations. These new standards helped create a workforce that was well qualified, satisfied, and inspired by Pinchot's leadership.

The Forest Service's early years were a period of pioneering in practical field forestry on the national forests in the West, as there were none in the East at the time. Forest rangers were directed from Washington, D.C., and by local national forest supervisors. A *Use Book* was written in 1905 and updated almost every year; it contained all the Forest Service laws and regulations used by the rangers. Today, the laws require a book of 1,163 pages, while the regulations required to manage the national forests fill several bookshelves. The Forest Service manuals and handbooks are now available on the Forest Service's computer system and Web site.

Much of the ranger's activity centered on creating a forest management infrastructure in forests where, in many cases, the only occupants for thousands of years had been American Indians. Getting to these locations required days spent on horseback, and the often backbreaking work involved mapping the national forests, marking the forest boundaries, building trail shelters, constructing ranger and guard stations, establishing fire lookout sites, stringing miles and miles of telephone lines, providing trail access, converting older trails into roads, building bridges, administering sheep and cattle permits, and protecting the forests from wildfire, game poachers, timber and grazing trespass, and other exploiters. In other words, the rangers acted as custodians of the national forests during this "Stetson hat" era.

Management Challenges

An important but controversial land management decision was made to charge user fees for sheep and cattle grazing on the national forests, which raised the ire

Arkansas National Forest supervisor's office, 1908. (USDA Forest Service)

of many sheep and cattle owners. Several challenged the law but lost in the courts, including the Supreme Court. A law was passed in 1906 to transfer 10 percent of the forest receipts (through grazing fees and some timber sales) to the states that had national forests to support public roads and schools. Two years later, payments to the states were increased to 25 percent. Often these funds are referred to as "payments in lieu of taxes," as federal land cannot be taxed by state or local authorities. It was one way to placate the states, to keep them from trying to eliminate the national forests and to encourage them to see the forests as revenue sources.

As some of the forest reserve boundaries had been hastily drawn, the Forest Homestead Act of June 11, 1906, allowed homesteading inside the reserve boundaries on land that was considered primarily agricultural. However, there were many instances of land fraud on agricultural and state school lands within the national forests. To meet the intent of the law, unscrupulous speculators would pay people to fraudulently claim that they were making a home on the land. After such "ownership" was established, when the homesteaded land was transferred from the federal government, the new owners would immediately transfer their ownership to a land speculator, timber, or mining company. The terms "land-office business" and "land-office rush" came about during this period, reflecting the people lining up to secure legitimate and not-so-legitimate land claims at the local General Land Offices.

Sheep on the way to their summer range on Beaverhead National Forest in Montana, 1945. (USDA Forest Service)

Federal investigations about land fraud were started in several states, and a few elected officials were indicted. The first successful fraud prosecutions, involving land speculators and various state, county, and GLO employees, occurred in Oregon between 1905 and 1910. GLO head Binger Hermann resigned after having been indicted, but he was later found innocent; Oregon's Senator John Mitchell was convicted. Many minor federal and state officials spent time in jail over such wrongdoings.

In January 1907, there was considerable opposition to a presidential proclamation that reserved thousands of acres of prime Douglas-fir timberlands in northern Washington state. The local press, chambers of commerce, and the congressional delegation protested that the reserve would cause undue hardship on residents by taking away homestead and "prime" agricultural lands (it was heavily forested), as well as impeding the future development of the state. After considerable pressure, Pinchot and President Roosevelt relented, saying that the reserve had been a "clerical error." Soon thereafter, Senator Charles W. Fulton, of Oregon, who had been implicated in the land frauds in that state, introduced an amendment to the annual agricultural appropriations bill. This amendment prohibited the president from creating any additional forest reserves in the six western states of Washington, Oregon, Idaho, Montana, Wyoming, and Colorado. It also gave Congress alone the authority to establish reserves, taking away the presidential power to proclaim reserves, as given by the Forest Reserve Act of 1891. However, before this bill could be signed into law, on March 7, 1907, Gifford Pinchot and the president came up with a plan.

On the eve of the bill's signing, Chief Forester Pinchot and his assistant Arthur C. Ringland used heavy blue pencils to draw many new forest reserves on maps from the affected six western states. As soon a map was finished and a proclamation written, the president signed the paper to establish another forest reserve. On March 1–2, Roosevelt established 17 new or combined forest reserves containing more than 16 million acres. Included were the Bear Lodge, in Wyoming; Las Animas and Ouray, in Colorado; Little Rockies and Otter, in Montana; Cabinet, Lewis and Clark, Palouse, and Port Neuf, in

A forest ranger camp in Logan Canyon, Cache National Forest in Utah, 1914. (USDA Forest Service)

Idaho; Colville and Rainier, in Washington; and the Blue Mountains, Cascade, Coquille, Imnaha, Tillamook, and Umpqua, in Oregon. These have been since referred to as the "midnight reserves." The president defended his actions by claiming that he had saved vast tracts of timber from falling into the hands of the "lumber syndicate." The Fulton amendment, at the suggestion of Pinchot, also changed the name of the "forest reserves" to "national forests" to make it clear that the forests were to be used and not preserved. The first national forests established east of the Mississippi River were the Ocala and the Choctawhatchee National Forests, in Florida, in November 1908.

Establishing Regional Offices

During the same month, six district offices were established in various sections of the country: Denver, Colorado; Ogden, Utah; Missoula, Montana; Albuquerque, New Mexico; San Francisco, California; and Portland, Oregon. They were part of a successful effort to decentralize or push decision making from Washington, D.C., down to the districts, which were closer to and more familiar with local and regionwide problems. These new districts were staffed the following December and January by employees from the Washington office and from various supervisor's offices.

Decentralization was carried further with the creation of the Ogden (Utah) Supply Depot in 1909. This new depot was centrally located in the West and took advantage of the reduced shipping costs and the shortened time that it took remote ranger outposts to receive supplies. To respond to local conditions, local national forest supervisors were given greater fiscal responsibilities. A seventh district, covering the administration of the national forests in Arkansas and Florida, was added in 1914. Alaska was made a separate district in 1921; a new district was created in 1929 to cover the eastern states. All the districts were renamed regional offices on May 1, 1930. (Region 7 was eliminated in 1966, leaving nine regions today.)

Pinchot recognized the need to continue cooperation with the states and the private sector when, in 1908, he organized the Division of State and Private Forestry (S&PF). The new division immediately began a cooperative study with the states to look at forest taxation issues. With the passage of the Weeks Act of 1911, the S&PF focused on working with state forestry and fire prevention associations—a cooperative relationship that continues to this day.

The first forest experiment station was established in 1908 at Fort Valley on the Coconino National Forest, Arizona, followed by other research stations in Colorado, Idaho, Washington, California, and Utah. Primarily focused on watershed studies, the Fort Valley station provided the first long-term research on the effects of precipitation on water flow in forested ecosystems. Today, there are 20 research and experimental areas in the national forest system.

Prior to 1910, the Forest Service undertook major efforts to evaluate sites on the national forests for possible on-the-ground forest management camps called ranger stations. Ranger stations, which were often small, windowless, floorless log

Perry Davis on an early speeder fire patrol, Pisgah National Forest, North Carolina, 1923. (USDA Forest Service)

structures, in remote areas, were established because of the need to have local control of the national forests. It was only in the 1920s that more modern, wood-frame stations were built along the edges of the national forests so that visitors could easily interact with the rangers. About the same time, many of the larger forests were divided into smaller, easier-to-manage national forests.

The Conservation Movement

The height of the nationwide conservation movement occurred between 1907 and 1909, just before and after Theodore Roosevelt's national conference of governors met at the White House in May 1908 to consider America's natural resources. The president told the conference attendees that "the conservation of natural resources is the most weighty question now before the people of the United States." The conference recommended that the president appoint a national conservation commission to "inquire into and advise me as to the condition of our natural resources." The commission returned with a three-volume report, which Roosevelt used in the effort to conserve the nation's natural resources. Roosevelt left office in 1909 and was succeeded by William Howard Taft, Roosevelt's handpicked successor. Pinchot ran into problems with the new Secretary of the Interior, Richard A. Ballinger, over coal leasing in Alaska. After months of national debate and personal attacks from both men, Taft fired Pinchot for insubordination, in January of 1910. Pinchot was replaced as forester by Henry Graves, his long-time associate and personal friend, then director of the Yale School of Forestry in New Haven, Connecticut.

During this era, the Forest Service also began several important programs to better manage the national forests, including an extensive program of basic and applied research, timber management, recreational planning, and highway construction to better provide access to the forests. This era was also the beginning of a system for detecting and fighting forest fires. During the summer of 1910, when extremely dry conditions prevailed in the West, widespread fires flared in the Northwest and the northern Rocky Mountains, burning more than 3 million acres in Idaho and Montana alone. Seventy-eight forest firefighters lost their lives nationwide trying to protect the national forests and remote communities from these devastating fires. Soon the federal government made firefighting funds available to combat such fires. As a result of the 1910 fires, as well as the Weeks Act of 1911, cooperation between the various state foresters and the Forest Service became a driving force.

Henry Graves, chief of the Forest Service, noted that with the forest practices of this era, loggers were typically leaving as much as 25 percent of the trees on the stump or ground and more than half of the trees that reached the mill were either discarded as waste products or burned on the site. The Forest Products Laboratory (FPL) was established in 1910 at Madison, Wisconsin, in cooperation with Wisconsin State University (now the University of Wisconsin). The FPL was to be a "laboratory of practical research" that would study and test the physical

The result of a fire along St. Joe River, Coeur d'Alene National Forest, Idaho, 1910. (USDA Forest Service)

properties of wood; develop and test wood preservation techniques; study methods to reduce logging waste, improve lumber production methods in sawmills and devise new uses for wood fiber; distribute wood product information to the public; and cooperate with the wood products industry. FPL research made utilization of forest products an important element in the greater use and production of wood from public and private forests.

The Weeks Act of 1911 (see further discussion in Appendix 6) allowed the government to purchase important private watershed land on the headwaters of navigable streams that might have been cut over, burned over, or farmed out. As a result, this act indirectly supported the creation, though land purchases, of new national forests in the eastern United States, where there was little public domain land left. It also provided cooperation with, and federal matching funds for, state forest fire protection agencies. By 1920, more than 2 million acres of land had been purchased under the Weeks Act; by 1980, more 22 million acres in the East had been added to the national forest system.

The Forest Service research branch, known earlier as the office of silvics, was established, in 1915, to investigate better ways to manage the national forests, to study the hundreds of tree species, and to explore methods to reseed and re-plant forests. This period saw a great expansion of the number of national forest timber sales, the construction of numerous ranger stations, lookout, trails, and trail shelters, and the first use of telephones on national forests.

In the Forest Service's early days, it was against legislation to create a National Park Service (NPS) to manage the national parks (the act passed Congress in 1916). To counter the recreation component of the new NPS, the Forest Service initiated an extensive outdoor recreation program, including the leasing of summer home sites and the building of campgrounds on many national forests. The first Forest Service campground was developed in 1916 at Eagle Creek, on the Oregon side of the Columbia River Gorge, on the Mt. Hood National Forest. The first cooperative campground was constructed in 1918 at Squirrel Creek, on the San Isabel National Forest, near Pueblo, Colorado. At the time, federal funding was lacking, and communities saw the need for better camping and picnicking facilities on the national forests.

When the Southern Pacific Railroad Company failed to live up to the terms of its nineteenth-century land grant to the Oregon and California (O&C) Railroad (purchased by Southern Pacific), the U.S. Supreme Court ruled that the remaining unsold grant land must be returned (revested) to the federal government. Extensive congressional hearings in 1916 resulted in the revesting of 2.4 million acres of the heavily forested O&C lands, which today are managed by the Bureau of Land Management and several national forests in Oregon. The O&C lands in California did not come under the same scrutiny and were not revested to the government. The Northern Pacific Railroad land grant, across the northern tier of states from Minnesota to Washington, was also investigated by Congress, but ownership remained with the railroad. Interestingly, when Mount St. Helens exploded in 1980, the top of the mountain was owned by the railroad—part of the old land grant—and it was traded to Forest Service land to establish the Mount St. Helens National Volcanic Monument in 1982.

The Pisgah National Forest, the first national forest comprised almost entirely of purchased or donated private land, was established on October 17, 1916. The core portion of the new forest came from the privately owned Biltmore Forest (once managed by Gifford Pinchot). Land purchases for the Pisgah began in 1911, soon after the passage of the Weeks Act.

World War I: The War to End All Wars

Two U.S. Army Engineer Regiments (10th and 20th Forestry) were formed in 1917 and 1918 to fight in Europe during World War I. Many Forest Service employees joined and, after arriving in France, were assigned to build sawmills in England and France to provide timbers for railroads and to line the miles and miles of trenches. One of their leaders, Lt. Colonel William B. Greeley, later became the third chief of the Forest Service. Greeley, like other officers after the war, kept the title Colonel. Another unique organization formed during the war was the U.S. Army Spruce Production Division. Some 30,000 army troopers were assigned to Washington and Oregon to build logging railroads and to cut Sitka spruce trees for airplanes and Douglas-fir for ships. The reason for this operation was that the unions, especially the IWW and the AFL, slowed and stopped lumber production in the West during the summer and fall of 1917, just as the U.S. entered the war. Lumber became quickly a necessary war commodity. The army also created a new, patriotic "union" composed of workers and timber/mill owners, called the Loyal Legion of Loggers and Lumbermen (LLLL). Although the Spruce Division lasted only one year (1918–1919), it affected private and public logging operations and unions for the next two decades. Remnants of the spruce railroads can still be found on the Siuslaw National Forest, in Oregon, and the Olympic National Park, in Washington State, which was then part of the Olympic National Forest.

While the men were off fighting the war in Europe, women were employed outdoors as fire lookouts on many national forests. Women had worked in clerical positions for many years, but working outdoors was an unusual occupation for them. A few of the women lookouts stayed with the Forest Service after the war was over.

Fire Cooperation

In 1919, soon after the war, cooperative agreements between the Forest Service and the Army Air Corps led to experiments using airplanes to patrol for forest fires in California; this use was quickly expanded to the mountainous areas of Oregon, Washington, Idaho, and Montana. Army pilots flew the planes during the summer fires season, while Forest Service spotters looked for fires. The system worked quite well for several decades, until the aerial patrol was replaced by lookout houses and towers atop the mountain peaks. In the past few decades, most of the lookouts have been removed, replaced by electronic lightning detection systems, satellites, and aerial reconnaissance after major lightning storms.

Before and for a while after World War I, there were no radios, and communications between the lookouts and the ranger station were limited to messages delivered on foot, on horseback, and by carrier pigeon. Soon, however, an extensive (and expensive) system of field telephones, connected by miles and miles of telephone wires, was used to communicate between the lookouts atop the mountain peaks and the ranger stations in the valleys below. Because trees often fell on the No. 9 wire, breaking the connections, these phone systems along major forest roads and trails needed continual maintenance and repair. Many new forest fire lookout houses and towers using standardized construction plans were built during the 1920s. Two-way radios were invented near the end of World War I, and there were a number of experiments after the war with using them in fire detection. These radios eventually made communication much easier and less costly.

Helen Dowe, one of the first female lookouts, Pike National Forest in Colorado, c. 1920. (USDA Forest Service)

In the mid-1920s, there was an unusual overlap between the Forest Service and the military. National forests are usually thought of as having been established on the public domain in the West or purchased from private landowners in the East and South. There were, however, for a short period national forests established on military reservations, usually army bases. The enabling legislation, the Clarke-McNary Act, was passed in 1924. All told, there were 16 new national forests established in various parts of the country. New executive orders were issued in 1927 that returned these national forests to the military in the 1927–1929 period, although one forest wasn't canceled until 1954 and two more later became part of existing national forests.

Increasing Demand for Products and Services

The economic boom of the Roaring Twenties vastly increased need for wood products. Many extensive national forest timber sales were authorized, including a 1921 sale of 335 million cubic feet of pulpwood on Alaska's Tongass National Forest. Within a few years, scores of huge timber sales were being made, including a 1922 sale on the California's Lassen National Forest that topped 1 billion board feet. Previously, most timber sales had been for rather small volumes; many of them were for timber beams for mining and ties for railroads. Most of the new, large timber sales were for large railroad logging operations that were geared to lengthy harvesting periods of several decades or longer. The national forests began to play an increasing role in providing timber for the United States.

In the early 1920s, there was an increasing need for improved recreational facilities on the national forests. A good part of this need was caused by the increasing use of the forest roads and trails by recreationists' automobiles. As cars became cheaper, more reliable, and more numerous, an increasing number of people were willing to spend their free time in mountains, at lakes, and along streams—as long as these areas were easily accessible. Existing roads and highways had to be improved. The U.S. Bureau of Public Roads was instrumental in proving funding to develop and improve major highways across national forests. In this same era, the Forest Service began to use trucks and automobiles—a significant change from the days of the horse, packhorse, and mule. But there were still vast areas of unimproved and unroaded forestlands.

Numerous special-use recreation resorts, which provided for developed recreation facilities in popular areas, began operations on the national forests in the 1920s. Long-term summer home leases were allowed to give people greater use of the national forests and to provide a group of supporters for the national forests. Many of these early summer homes are now being considered for historic status. Hundreds of new campgrounds were opened. A number of so-called organizational camps were built to assist larger groups, such as the Boy Scouts, with their desires to hold large summer camping operations for their membership. Small ski areas were

Campers at Peralta Canyon, Tonto National Forest, Arizona, 1938. (USDA Forest Service)

developed in many national forests, but they were usually restricted to the lower mountain areas because of road closures due to deep snow at higher elevations. Most of these ski areas were slopes with trees removed and perhaps a rope tow to carry skiers from the bottom to the top of the ski run. Many thousands of people now owned or had access to automobiles, which made recreation in the national forests easier, while new roads got people to the forests quicker.

Wilderness

One of the Forest Service's first wilderness advocates was Arthur H. Carhart, a landscape architect. In the late 1910s and early 1920s, his innovative ideas, which involved leaving some forest areas intact (no-development) for recreational use, received limited support. He was sent to study an area around Trapper's Lake, on Colorado's White River National Forest, for which there was a proposal calling for the development of a road system and cabins next to the picturesque lake. After his study, he recommended that the area remain roadless and that summer home applications be denied. He then developed a functional plan to preserve the area's pristine conditions around the lake and convinced his superiors to halt plans to develop the area. Later, he recommended that the lake region of the Superior National Forest in northern Minnesota be left in primitive condition and that travel be restricted to canoe. This plan was approved in 1926, and the Boundary Waters Canoe Area (now part of the national wilderness preservation system) was dedicated in 1964. Carhart, however, frustrated by what he felt was a lack of support from the Forest Service, resigned in December 1922. During his later years, Carhart became a dedicated outdoor writer.

Aldo Leopold, author of the *Sand County Almanac*, took up where Carhart left off. In 1922, Leopold made

Forest Service ranger boat, Tongass National Forest, Alaska, c. 1940. (USDA Forest Service)

21

an inspection trip into the headwaters of the Gila River, on New Mexico's Gila National Forest. He wrote a wilderness plan for the area but faced opposition from his own colleagues, who thought that development should take precedence over preservation. However, his plan was approved in June 1924, and the 500,000-acre area became the first Forest Service wilderness—the Gila Wilderness. Leopold transferred to the Forest Products Laboratory the same year, then resigned from the Forest Service in 1928, five years later he began teaching at the University of Wisconsin, where he had a profound influence on students and the public as a proponent of wildlife management and the notion of a "land ethic."

In 1929, the Forest Service published the L-20 Regulations concerning primitive areas that were basically undeveloped and unroaded areas, many of which would later become wildernesses. Regional offices were requested to nominate possible "primitive areas" that would be maintained in a primitive status without development activities—especially roads. Within four years, 63 areas comprising 8.7 million acres were approved. By 1939, the total acreage in primitive classification had increased to 14 million acres. Most of these areas became administrative wilderness, while others were added to the national wilderness preservation system by the Wilderness Act of 1964.

Gila Wilderness sign, New Mexico, Gila National Forest, 1960. (USDA Forest Service)

Fire Control

Many new forest fire lookouts (houses and towers) were built in the early 1920s, while two-way radios were becoming more practical and were used extensively to communicate during forest fires. These lookouts were often staffed during the summer fire season by schoolteachers, writers, and others who enjoyed the mountaintop solitude. Of the thousands that were built, today only a few are still standing. Scores of them are available as rentals. The Clarke-McNary Act of 1924, an extension of the Weeks Act, greatly expanded federal-state cooperation in fire control on state and private lands. Many states formed fire-protection associations that still operate today.

Forestry research came into full swing with the establishment of two new experiment stations in 1922. Today there are seven experiment stations scattered across the country, with 72 research work unit locations (see Chapter 3).

The natural resource controversy of the early 1920s arose over a huge increase in the number of mule deer on the Grand Canyon Federal Game Preserve (established in 1906) on Arizona's Kaibab National Forest. In 1906, the deer herd numbered only about 3,000, but after almost 20 years without being hunted and with predator control, the herd exploded to more than 100,000 animals. The Forest Service sought to reduce the number of deer on the refuge to prevent many from starving. In 1924, the case went to the Supreme Court; its ruling allowed the Forest Service to remove excess deer to protect wildlife habitat.

THE GREAT DEPRESSION AND WORLD WAR II, 1933–1945

The Great Depression (previously called "panics") is generally thought to have started in the fall of 1929 with the New York stock market crash. It did not take long for the entire country to be hard hit by the devastating economic downturn. Because of low wood prices and lack of demand, timber sales declined, hundreds of timber companies went bankrupt, and tens of thousands of employees lost their jobs. Federal government workers took pay cuts but remained working.

Civilian Conservation Corps

President Franklin D. Roosevelt came into office in March 1933. One of the first goals of his "New Deal" was to put Americans back to work through various programs. The most significant of these programs was the Civilian Conservation Crops (CCC), which was aimed at reviving the lagging economy and which marked a renewed interest in the conservation of natural resources through work in the outdoors. The CCC was authorized by Congress within days, provided work for millions of young unemployed men, and later was expanded to include World War I veterans and American Indian tribal members. The first CCC camp, appropriately named Camp Roosevelt, began operation late in the spring of 1933 on Virginia's George Washington National Forest. Thousands of other camps were established in national and state parks and refuges, national monuments, soil conservation districts, and other areas.

Fortunately, the Forest Service was prepared for these conservation workers. The massive 1,677-page *National Plan for American Forestry* (also called the Copeland Report), published a few months previously, had suggested a comprehensive plan for more intensive management of all the national-forest-system lands. Included in the report was the call for hundreds of projects that needed money or people to complete them. The CCC program was the ideal opportunity for young men (there were no women's camps) to be engaged in outdoor projects that would help improve the recreation potential and management of the national forests. Through the entire nine-year program, more than 3 million men enrolled for six months or longer in more than 2,600 camps (200 men per camp). Each national forest had at least one CCC camp, and many had as many as four or five camps. That enabled hundreds of work projects to begin, many of which were intended to develop recreational facilities, especially trails, trail shelters, campgrounds, and scenic vistas. The CCCs also worked on truck trails (roads), guard and ranger stations, lookouts, and telephone lines, and members fought many forest fires (nearly 6.5 million person days).

In response to the "Dust Bowl" conditions in the Great Plains between Texas and North Dakota during the early 1930s, the cooperative prairie states forestry (shelterbelt) project was developed. This unique windbreak project, also an idea of the New Deal, began in 1934 under the leadership of Raphael Zon from the Forest Service. In March 1935, the first tree was planted, on a farm in Mangum, Oklahoma. The project involved extensive cooperation between the USDA Soil Conservation Service, various state, county, and local agencies, and hundreds of farmers. Legions of Works Progress Administration (WPA) relief workers, many of whom were unemployed farmers, accomplished the work. In the spring of 1938, they planted approximately 52,000 cottonwood trees in one severe sand-blown area south of Neligh, Nebraska.

The Taylor Grazing Act of 1934 ended unregulated grazing on the national forests and remaining General Land Office–administered land. The act authorized the creation of 80 million acres of grazing districts and the establishment of a U.S. Grazing Service, which was combined with the GLO in 1946 to form the Bureau of Land Management in the Department of the Interior. In 1935, the title "chief" of the Forest Service came back into use.

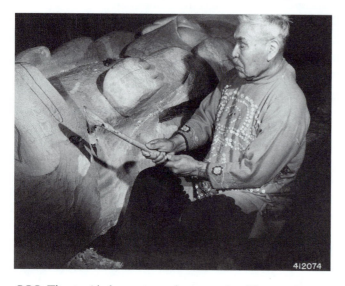

CCC Tlingit Alaska native pole carver Joe Thomas, Tongass National Forest, Alaska, 1941. (USDA Forest Service)

Ranger and permittee in Gifford Pinchot National Forest, Washington, 1949. (USDA Forest Service)

Robert Marshall, founder of the Wilderness Society and author of the recreation portion of the national plan for American forestry, worked for the Forest Service in the mid-1930s. He proposed that the Forest Service inventory the national forests for large unroaded areas that might be suitable for designation as wildernesses or primitive areas. Shortly before his untimely death in 1939, Marshall and several others made a tour of the western national forests, performing this inventory and making recommendations to the regional foresters to greatly increase the number of wilderness and primitive areas.

Timber sales, which had practically disappeared during the Great Depression, started again just before World War II. Millions of trees were blown down by the Great New England hurricane of September 1938. The Forest Service directed massive salvage operations on national forest, state, and private lands. More than 50 CCC camps and 15,000 WPA enrollees worked feverishly to salvage the downed trees to prevent insect and disease infestations and to prevent fires from starting in the dried trees. During the three years that followed, the Northeastern Timber Salvage Administration was able to salvage 700 million board feet of timber.

Because many of the forest fires in the West were started by lightning in inaccessible locations, the Forest Service experimented with having firefighters parachute to fires before they became large and out of control. The first experimental "jumps" began in 1939, at Winthrop, Washington, on the Okanogan National Forest. By the summer of 1940, the smokejumpers, as they became known, were operating out of Winthrop and the Moose Creek Ranger Station on Montana's Bitterroot National Forest and made their first jump on a fire on the Nezperce National Forest, in Idaho. The successful operation proved that smokejumping into remote, rugged areas was feasible. During World War II, the lessons learned from smokejumper training methods and actual jumping into heavily forested areas would prove useful to the new military paratrooper units like the 101st Airborne.

National Defense

National defense became important in the late 1930s and early 1940s. World War II started for the United States on December 7, 1941. In early 1942, the CCCs were disbanded because fewer men were signing up and national attention (and money) was being diverted to the war effort. The war years, 1941–1945, intensified the need to establish priorities for the national forests—one of which was increasing national forest wood outputs through the timber production war project. The biggest single wood use was for packing crates to ship military supplies, but other important uses included the construction of bridges, railroad ties, gunstocks, ships, docks, barracks, other buildings, and aircraft. The Forest Service's Forest Products Laboratory greatly expanded its research to fulfill military needs.

The Forest Service also was called on to lead a high-priority project—producing a rubber substitute from the guayule plant, a shrub native to the Southwest. A pilot project was begun in Salinas, California, and by 1944, more than 200,000 acres of guayule were under cultivation—producing 3 million pounds of rubber substitute for use on airplanes, ships, and vehicles, especially for tires. The project was abandoned after the war, when rubber from Southeast Asia again became available.

Forest Fire Protection during the War

Recreation was deemphasized nationwide during the war; forest fire protection became quite important, especially along the West Coast. To warn of impending air attacks on the West and East Coasts, the Aircraft Warning Service (AWS), established lookout stations at selected forest lookouts in 1942. The Forest Service, as well as the War Department, believed that the Japanese, especially, could and probably would attack the West Coast, or at least set fire bombs in the forests to divert thousands of citizens and soldiers to extinguish the blazes. These AWS sites were required to be staffed 24 hours per day. The AWS often employed husband-and-wife teams on this unusual duty in the forests. With the advent of radar in the 1943–1944 period, AWS sites were gradually phased out. Almost 2,000 Forest Service employees joined the armed forces.

On February 6, 1941, President Franklin D. Roosevelt signed an executive order creating the Civilian Public Service (CPS) program as a way for conscientious objectors (COs) to serve their nation without directly contributing to war. More than 10,000 men entered the CPS program, and the first conscientious objector camps were established at abandoned CCC camps in 1941. The majority of the COs were members of one of five religious denominations: Amish, Brethren, Hutterites, Mennonites, and Quakers. Some came from other religious denominations, and a few had no church affiliation. Most of the COs believed, even insisted, that they should not be forced to violate the Fifth Commandment, "Thou shalt not kill," even if their nation was attacked or invaded. In 1943, many conscientious objectors at home volunteered for smokejumper duty. Sixty were chosen for this very dangerous work. As during World War I, women were again employed as fire and aircraft lookouts, while civilian volunteers and outdoor groups were encouraged to form "Forest Service reserves," composed of men above or below the draft age, to help with lookout and firefighting work on the national forests.

The cooperative forest fire prevention campaign—a joint venture of the Forest Service and state forestry officials—was organized during the war, when it became vitally important to protect the nation's timber supply. In 1944, this program became the Smokey Bear campaign, which became the official fire prevention symbol of the nation. The first Smokey poster was distributed the following year. On June 27, 1950, a badly burned young bear cub—the only survivor from a massive fire on the Lincoln National Forest—was moved to the National Zoo in Washington, D.C., where he became the symbol of Smokey Bear In May 1975, the original Smokey Bear was retired from public duties. He died quietly the following January, Smokey II took his place. In the summer of 1990, Smokey II died. There are no more living Smokey Bears at the National Zoo.

Just before the end of the war, a unique fire situation floated across the Pacific Ocean. During the waning years of the Second World War, the Japanese, in a desperate attempt to forestall the coming invasion of their homeland, deployed hydrogen-filled paper balloons carrying bombs against the United States. The balloons bombs were, in retrospect, a slight diversion in the Pacific war front, but they were significant as the first instance of intercontinental bombing in recorded history. The fire balloons, with suspended incendiary magnesium bombs, as well as regular bombs, were sent aloft from Japan to float on the newly discovered high-altitude wind currents (the jet stream) across some 6,000 miles of the North Pacific Ocean to the West Coast of North America. Upon arrival over the western U.S. and Canada, the balloons were designed to drop their bombs, which, it was hoped, would start huge forest fires. It was thought that soldiers would be diverted from military operations to fight the massive forest fires and that the bombs would demoralize the civilian population. It never happened. Of the estimated 6,000 fire balloons that were sent aloft, probably 2,000 actually arrived. They have been found in Alaska, Canada, the continental United States, and Mexico. The majority floated over the United States and western Canada. Most of the balloons found were in British Columbia, Canada, with 58 landings discovered, followed by Oregon, with 54 and Alaska with 38. A number of others were shot down by military aircraft over the Pacific before they made landfall. Two balloons floated as far east as Michigan. One even landed in the Cicero district of Chicago! Only one documented forest fire was started from the thousands of attempts.

Near the end of World War II, the Forest Service was beginning to plan for the postwar era. One of the overriding issues, which the agency felt was an opportunity, was to rachet up timber harvesting on the national forests. This was helped by the fact that many private and corporate lands by this time had been severely over-cut—and they were not capable of providing the needed timber for the postwar and post-Depression market. The agency was a strong supporter of a piece of new legislation to more closely tie national forests to communities and timber companies.

The Sustained-Yield Forest Management Act of 1944 authorized the establishment of two classes of sustained yield timber units. Cooperative sustained yield units were to combine the management of federal timberland with private land to stabilize communities. Federal units, the other category, reserved national forest timber for only one geographic area—usually one community and one mill. The act was first heralded as protecting mills and jobs in the communities, but soon other companies and towns that were not included in the agreements thought them to be monopolistic, noncompetitive, and exclusionary. The Shelton (Washington) Cooperative Sustained-Yield Unit agreement was signed in 1946—the only cooperative unit ever established—and is still in operation today. Five federal sustained yield units were established: Vallecitos, New Mexico (Carson National Forest); Grays Harbor, Washington (Olympic National Forest); Flagstaff, Arizona (Coconino National Forest); Lakeview, Oregon (Fremont National Forest); and Big Valley, California (Modoc National Forest). Only the Lakeview unit is actively operating today.

TIMBER MANAGEMENT AND MULTIPLE USE, 1946–1970

In part because of the vastly increased demand for wood products and the construction of new homes, the postwar national forest managers were active in opening vast forest areas to timber management. Until then, the timber industry had viewed the national forests as huge sources of timber that should be kept off the market so that they could keep private timber prices high. The timber industry now sought cheap national forest timber to supplement or replace heavily cut private forestlands. The opening of the national forests to timber harvesting and road development after World War II would have consequences that we are still feeling today.

The technology of extracting timber from the woods changed dramatically. Before the Depression and the Second World War, much lumbering was done with axes and crosscut saws, but, after the war, everyone was using the new, highly efficient chainsaws. Log transportation evolved from the use of horses, oxen, and railroads and the floating of logs down rivers to the new systems of roads and trucks, and even balloons and helicopters by the 1970s. With the increased emphasis on timber production after the war, the number of timber sales jumped dramatically (see Appendix 5). Forestry schools around the nation were training thousands of new foresters who were dedicated to finding more efficient and intensive methods

Sawmills benefiting from the Shelton Cooperative Sustained-Yield Unit, Shelton, Washington, c. 1950. (USDA Forest Service)

of managing the national forests. The Forest Service was entering what has been called the "hard-hat era." Intensive forest management was beginning in earnest. Congress passed the Tongass Timber Act on July 27, 1947. It authorized four 50-year timber sales on Alaska's Tongass National Forest, which years later were at the heart of controversies over timber cutting in Alaska.

During the same period, national forest research came of age: Research stations and new experimental forests conducted studies to find better ways to harvest trees, construct new roads, and measure the effects of logging and roads on streams and watersheds. A system of multifunctional research centers was established in 1946, with each center concerned about its own assigned research territory, and a new program was designed to address local forest and range problems, with applications to regional and national issues.

The Bureau of Land Management (BLM) in the Department of the Interior was formed in 1946 from the Grazing Service and the General Land Office. The BLM currently manages some 264 million acres of federal land—mostly grazing land, except the old O&C Railroad Grant land in western Oregon, which is heavily timbered.

The Forest Pest Control Act of 1947 paved the way for increased protection from pest outbreaks. The act encouraged the federal, state, and private cooperation in the prevention, control, and even eradication of forest insects and diseases that reduced tree growth or killed trees. In 1948, the Forest Service became involved in the Yazoo-Little Tallahatchie flood prevention project—the largest tree planting program the country has ever known—with some 621,000 acres planted. The project was designed to rehabilitate severely eroding lands—with some gullies as much as 50 feet deep—in Mississippi. The USDA Soil Conservation Service (now called the Natural Resources Conservation Service), as well as other federal, state, county, and local agencies cooperated in this extensive project until it ended in 1985. New technology in every field became very important in managing the forests.

During the 1950s, forest engineers, landscape architects, and silviculturists became common in the Forest Service. In 1954, the agency became responsible for managing approximately 4 million acres of "land utilization projects" (referred to as LU lands), which were basically grazing lands on the Great Plains. These lands, acquired by the federal government during the Depression years of the 1930s, were in many cases relinquished or abandoned farms. In 1960, many of the earlier land utilization projects became the first national grasslands in the Forest Service. In 1953, the Department of Agriculture transferred forest insect and disease research and control work from other department agencies to the Forest Service.

In 1955, the Multiple-Use Mining Act helped prevent abuses of mining laws on the national forests. An important feature of this law was that, after proper notice, mining claimants could be requested to prove the validity of their claims. This procedure quickly eliminated many thousands of abandoned mining claims on the national forests.

An old B-17 air tanker dropping retardant on fire, c. 1960. (USDA Forest Service)

The year 1956 saw the first practical airplane tanker airdrop of water and chemicals on a forest fire. Many of the airplanes were converted World War II bombers, now with their bomb bays full of Borate and other mixtures, rather than bombs. Over the years, this would develop into sophisticated operations involving air tankers, helicopter tankers, smokejumpers, and ground firefighters. Firefighting became similar to a combat operation, this time against forest fires.

Recreational demands on the national forests were increasing; millions of new visitors used the national forests and parks. In 1956, the Park Service launched its Mission 66 program that was designed to restore and improve the national parks over a 10-year period. The Forest Service, feeling a sense of competition with the Park Service over recreational opportunities, began "Operation Outdoors" in 1957. It was a five-year program designed to improve and replace many of the older CCC-built structures and to expand the recreation facilities and opportunities to meet the increasing recreational demand on the national forests. The program also provided for the creation of a recreation program in the Forest Service research branch.

In 1958, the Forest Service issued the results of the nationwide timber resource review, "Timber Resources for America's Future." This extensive national study, begun six years earlier, and prepared with the assistance of other federal, state, and private agencies, found that the nation needed to grow more timber to meet expected demands. The study was a preview of more extensive timber resource assessments that would be made in the future.

At the same time, there was a growing concern that the Forest Service was clearcutting too many areas that were also used for recreation. This issue and others about resource priorities would involve many outdoor groups, timber industry organizations, the Forest Service, and Congress and would result in the Multiple-Use Sustained-Yield Act of 1960.

Most of the national forests were opened up for timber, recreation, and protection activities by an extensive network of roads. Many of the older trails were replaced by the growing road system used to access remote forest areas.

In the early 1960s, a new wave of national concern about the conservation of natural resources began. It resulted in several controversies over the management of the national forests and in the passage of many environmental protection laws. The first was the Multiple-Use Sustained-Yield Act (MUSY) of 1960. Its purpose was to ensure that all possible uses and benefits of the national forests and grasslands be treated equally. The "multiple uses" included outdoor recreation, range utilization, timber harvesting, and watershed, wildlife, and fish protection in combinations that would best meet and serve human needs.

This act was necessary because many members of Congress and many interest groups felt that the Forest Service was giving too much attention to timber harvesting on the national forests—just 15 years after the huge postwar development push to open the national forests for timber to be used in the national housing boom. Multiple-use forestry was in full swing, with an increasing emphasis placed on nontimber resources, while timber production increased to the maximum in the private sector and approached that in the national forests. However, the act was

Wildlife biologist Bernie Carter measuring seed production, Umatilla National Forest, Oregon, 1964. (USDA Forest Service)

never fully implemented, at least with regard to the agency. Many employees believed that multiple use was simply a restatement of what the agency had been doing since Pinchot's time and that there was no need to change. After that act, the agency was trying to say that many multiple uses or benefits came from timber production, including insect and disease control, firefighting, road access to remote areas, hunting and fishing access, hiking trails, and, of course, jobs in the local economy.

However, members of the pessimistic environmental groups still saw only a road through the forest leading to a clearcut. MUSY did not satisfy the public as much as it did the agency. In reality, it was just putting a new name on current management, which allowed more words and catchphrases to be added to management actions. Little changed on the ground. Chief Ed Cliff noted, in an oral history, that he believed that MUSY did not make any "substantial changes in the way we were trying to do business" and that MUSY "reflected what we thought we should be doing." Real change on the ground, mandated by Congress, would have to wait until passage of the National Forest Management Act of 1976.

In the early 1960s, the Forest Service became involved with a nonnational forest property in eastern Pennsylvania. Cornelia Pinchot, wife of Gifford Pinchot, donated to the Forest Service the family home—Grey Towers—and surrounding land in Milford, Pennsylvania. Extensive stabilization and repair work were needed on the magnificent building, although for years it was looked at as a "white elephant." Grey Towers is listed as a national historic landmark, one of three Forest Service building with that designation—another being Timberline Lodge on the south face of Oregon's Mt. Hood, on the Mt. Hood National Forest, and the third is called the Rabideau Civilian Conservation Corps Camp, located on the Chippewa National Forest, in Minnesota. The newly formed Pinchot Institute for Conservation Studies was dedicated at Grey Towers by President John F. Kennedy on September 24, 1963, less than two months before his assassination. The Pinchot Institute currently is based in Washington, D.C., with a small staff at Grey Towers. Today, after some $10 million in major renovations, Grey Towers has been transformed into the outstanding structure that it was in the 1940s. It plays an increasingly important role in early conservation, providing a grounding in Forest Service history and hosting important conferences and seminars on the future of the agency and conservation.

Work programs for youths once again became important for the nation and the national forests in the 1960s. In 1963, the Forest Service became involved with the national Accelerated Public Works (APW) program that was designed to put unemployed men (there were no women in the program) to work on projects to develop or improve national forest resources. The 1963–1964 program provided immediate work for more than 9,000 men on more than 100 national forests in 35 states. It also brought increased business to numerous communities adjacent to the national forests, providing much-needed boosts to their economies. APW tasks included working on camp and picnic areas, planting

President Kennedy and Chief Ed Cliff at the Pinchot Institute dedication, Milford, Pennsylvania, 1963. (USDA Forest Service)

trees, thinning timber stands, improving fish and wildlife habitat, and constructing or improving roads, trails, fire lookouts, and other facilities.

A new work program for young, unemployed youth, called the Job Corps, began in 1964. The Job Corps was designed to give young men (young women were admitted later) ages 16–24 from deprived backgrounds basic schooling, training in skills, and valuable job experience before they returned to their home communities. It resembled the older CCC program of the Great Depression; participants were involved in firefighting, community work, building construction, and forestry activities on the national forests. Many of the enrollees were black and Latino. Most of the original Job Corps center sites were run by the Forest Service and the Park Service, in cooperation with the Department of Labor's employment and training administration. In the 1980s, there was a successful effort to remove most of the Job Corps centers from control of the agencies and to turn operations over to private control. In 1989, the Job Corps program celebrated its twenty-fifth anniversary, having served more than 1.4 million youths. By early 2006, there were 122 Job Corps centers, but most of the government centers had gone private. The federal government and tribes operate 30 centers, with the USDI Bureau of Reclamation managing 5; USDI National Park Service, 2; Indian tribes, 2 more; USDI Fish and Wildlife Service, 2; and 18 currently under Forest Service management.

After years of struggle, the Wilderness Act of 1964 was signed into law. This unique law established a national wilderness preservation system of more than 9 million acres, incorporating the existing Forest Service wilderness areas and creating several new ones. One provision in the Wilderness Act called for an evaluation of any national forest areas that were without roads (hence the name "roadless areas") that might be considered for wilderness status. In 1967, the Forest Service undertook a roadless area review and evaluation (RARE) to identify and study

An Ojibway job corps enrollee and Forest Service fish biologist taking water samples, Ottawa National Forest, Michigan, 1967. (USDA Forest Service)

these "de facto wildernesses." The RARE results would be shrouded in controversy that still affects the agency today. See the discussion later in this chapter.

A controversy erupted in the mid-1960s in the Sierra Nevada mountain range of California. As early as 1949, the Sequoia National Forest advertised that there was an opportunity for a ski development in the Mineral King area, which has possibly the best snow conditions in the country. The area could accommodate a 3,700-foot vertical drop, with ski runs as long as four miles. It was believed the new development would attract a huge skiing crowd in the winter and vacationing people in the summer. The Sequoia wanted a destination resort hotel that would accommodate at least 100 people, a mile-long chairlift and a 2,100-foot T-bar. The Forest Service received no bids. Walt Disney, a downhill skier himself, had visited Mineral King not long after the original prospectus was offered. Apparently, in the early 1960s, he asked the Forest Service if the offer of development was still open.

In early 1965, the Forest Service published another ski area prospectus for the U-shaped valley. This time, the prospectus increased the size of the proposal to house double the number of people, upgrade the roads into the valley, and construct easier access roads across the Sequoia National Park. Disney died in 1966, but the development plans continued. However, the proposed project soon became mired in legal battles. Several organizations fought the development (which would have also affected the adjacent Sequoia National Park). A lawsuit was filed by the Sierra Club (*Sierra Club v. Morton*), but the organization eventually lost the case in the U.S. Supreme Court in 1972. Nonetheless, the whole imbroglio set precedent for the use of litigation by organizations to settle disputes with the Forest Service. The ski area was never developed, and the Mineral King area was added by Congress to the Sequoia National Park in 1978.

The Wild and Scenic Rivers Act of 1968 applies, in many instances, directly to management of the national forest system. Section 1(b) of the act states that it will be the policy of the United States that "certain selected rivers of the Nation which ... possess outstandingly remarkable scenic, recreational, geologic, fish and wildlife, historic, cultural, or other similar values, shall be preserved in free-flowing condition, and that they and their immediate environments shall be protected for the benefit and enjoyment of present and future generations." The act authorizes a number of important, distinctive rivers to be classified as wild, scenic, or recreational. These categories are defined in the act: (1) wild rivers—"Those rivers or

John Muir Wilderness, Sierra National Forest, California, 1963. (USDA Forest Service)

sections of rivers that are free of impoundments and generally inaccessible except by trail, with watersheds or shorelines essentially primitive and waters unpolluted. These represent vestiges of primitive America"; (2) scenic river areas—those rivers or sections of rivers that are free of impoundments, with shorelines or watersheds still largely primitive and shorelines largely undeveloped, but accessible in places by roads; (3) recreational river areas—those rivers or sections of rivers that are readily accessible by road or railroad, that may have some development along their shorelines, and that may have undergone some impoundment or diversion in the past.

The act specified that more than 140 rivers or segments would be designated as wild and scenic rivers, along with another 135 river segments to be studied for possible inclusion. Since many of the wild and scenic rivers, or segments thereof, flow from the forested headwaters, it is logical that many of the designed rivers are on national forests. Several of the wild and scenic rivers designated by the act on national forest system lands included Clearwater (Idaho), Feather (California), Rogue (Oregon), Salmon (Idaho), Chattooga (North Carolina, South Carolina, and Georgia), Snake (Idaho and Oregon), Flathead (Montana), St. Joe (Idaho), Verde (Arizona), and the Skagit (Washington). Today, the Forest Service manages more than 4,000 miles of such wild and scenic rivers on nearly 100 rivers or river segments.

PUBLIC PARTICIPATION AND ENVIRONMENTALISM, 1970–1990

Beginning in the 1970s, there was growing, widespread public concern that new laws and regulations were needed to preserve and protect the environment. Several of these laws derived from a new environmental awareness brought about by Rachel Carson's book *Silent Spring,* published in 1962, which documented the overuse of pesticides, especially DDT. The use of chemicals, such as herbicides and pesticides on the national forests, came into contention, leading to numerous demonstrations, lawsuits, and occasional violence by those in favor and those opposed. These controversies led the Forest Service to reconsider many of its land management practices, including the use of herbicides.

The National Environmental Policy Act of 1969 (NEPA), signed into law January 1, 1970, mandated the comprehensive analysis of environmental impacts of proposed federal projects. An important part of the act made it mandatory for agencies to seek public participation on projects—from the planning stage to the review-of-documents stage. These requirements were quickly incorporated into the many projects already under way on the national forests. Earth Day, on April 22, 1970, foreshadowed the beginnings of a new and fundamentally different conservation-environmental movement.

Youth Employment Programs and Other Acts

In 1970, a three-year pilot Youth Conservation Corps (YCC) program began; it became fully established in 1974. It was designed to further the development and maintenance of natural resources by America's youth ages 15–19. The young male and female YCC members, from all parts of the country and all walks of life, spent the summer months working on conservation projects on the national forests.

During 1977, another new youth employment program arrived—the Young Adult Conservation Corps (YACC). This program was intended to further the development and maintenance of natural resources by America's young adults (both male and female) ages 16–23. The Forest Service provided many opportunities for enrollees to work on important projects on the national forests. This program was short-lived because its funding was eliminated in 1981.

Woodsy Owl, who symbolizes antipollution and the wise use of the environment, was introduced in 1971 with the slogan "Give a Hoot, Don't Pollute." Just as with Smokey Bear, the Woodsy symbol and slogan are protected by law except as authorized for antipollution programs. In 1997, Woodsy's image was updated, and his message became "Give a hand, Care for the Land" (see Chapter 3).

President Jimmy Carter signed the Alaska Native Claims Settlement Act of 1971 (ANCSA), which authorized the transfer of 44 million acres of land in Alaska from the federal government to various Alaska Native corporations in exchange for the extinguishing of aboriginal title to the remaining lands traditionally used and occupied by Alaska Natives. The agency then began a long process of analyzing lands in Alaska for possible national forests (see the planning section later in this chapter).

The Volunteers in the National Forests Act of 1972 authorized the Forest Service to recruit and train volunteers to help manage the national forests. It has been a highly successful and visible program. Many of the volunteers are retired people who enjoy working outdoors and with the public in a wide variety of capacities ranging from serving as campground hosts to assisting with archaeological digs. Often a hundred or more volunteer opportunities are available each summer in most parts of the national forest system.

As the Wilderness Act of 1964 provided, the draft roadless area review and evaluation (RARE) report was completed in 1972. This very controversial wilderness review process evaluated some 55.9 million acres of land and 1,449 roadless areas for possible inclusion in the national wilderness preservation system. The final report was published in 1973, with 274 of the roadless areas (12.3 million acres) selected for possible wilderness designation by Congress. The decision became immediately embroiled in controversy. A lawsuit in California (*Sierra Club v. Butz*) over a roadless area that had not been selected resulted in the Assistant Secretary of Agriculture and the chief of the Forest Service ordering a new study of all roadless areas, called RARE II, in 1977 (see further discussion in Chapter 3).

The Endangered Species Act of 1973 provided for protection of rare, threatened, and endangered animal and plant species. It established federal procedures for identifying and protecting endangered plants and animals in their native, critical habitats and declared broad prohibitions against taking, hunting, harming, or harassing the listed species. The intent of the act was to restore endangered species to a level where protection would no longer be needed. Implementing this act would have drastic consequences on the management of national forest timber and road construction programs during the 1980s and 1990s (see further discussion in Chapters 3 and 6).

The Planning Process

Although the Forest Service began planning efforts as early as the 1910s, there was nothing to compare with the new planning efforts in the 1960s, 1970s, and 1980s. The Multiple-Use Sustained-Yield Act of 1960 started many major national forest planning efforts, and, by the mid-1970s, unit plans (ranger district level) and several forest plans were developed. Nationally, hundreds of these plans, usually one for each resource (e.g., a timber plan, a recreation plan, a grazing plan) were completed. However, there was obvious overlap of multiple resources within one area. In the management aftermath of these many plans, decisions had to be made about which of the plans would take precedence in any given area. Usually the timber plan was selected as the "trump card" of plans, overriding the interests of recreation and other resource plans. Many national forests created planning teams to assist in the multiple use planning of their many resources. New Forest Service specialists were hired because of the planning needs—wildlife biologists, soil scientists, landscape architects, and hydrologists.

Northern Spotted Owl in an old growth forest, Pacific Northwest, c. 1990. (USDA Forest Service)

In 1974, the Forest and Rangeland Renewable Resources Planning Act (RPA) came into effect. The act provided that, beginning in 1976, the Forest Service would develop a program or assessment every five years that outlined the proposed expected national forest production of various resources. With the RPA program in hand, the Forest Service would go to Congress to obtain the necessary money to implement its program. RPA represented Congress's first legislative recognition that management of our natural resources could occur only with long-range planning and funding—not planning and funding on a year-to-year basis. However, the RPA process never met expectations, even though millions of dollars and many people were assigned to assess the national situation and come up with a reasonably funded plan. In fact, former Chief Dale Robertson said that the best way to fund the agency was to use the budget allocation of the previous year, not start the process anew each year. Also, a five-year funding of the agency was never in the cards from Congress, since the political priorities of Congress and the president change every two to four years, thus throwing cold water on the long-range funding idea.

The National Forest Management Act of 1976 (NFMA) amended RPA and also repealed major portions of the Organic Act of 1897. Congress had many concerns when writing the act, but probably the most controversial aspect was how specific to make the legal requirements—too little specificity would allow the Forest Service to carry on with management as it had for 75 years, while too many legal requirements would bog the agency down with paperwork. NFMA mandated intensive long-range planning for the national forests—the most comprehensive planning effort in the western world. NFMA specifically incorporated public involvement

Monitoring fish populations, Ouachita National Forest, Arkansas, c. 1990. (USDA Forest Service)

and advisory boards, various natural resources, transportation systems, timber sales, reforestation, payments to states for schools and roads, and reporting on the incidence of Dutch elm disease.

A committee of scientists wrote the draft implementation regulations for NFMA, which became final in 1979 after a public comment period. At the same time, an intensive NFMA forest planning effort began on the national forests. To address the various provisions of NFMA, the Forest Service hired new specialists, many of them women, including public affairs specialists, economists, archeologists, sociologists, geologists, ecologists, and operations research analysts. The Forest Service began an extensive public involvement effort to prepare the new plans. In the early 1980s, each national forest was required to use the computer FORPLAN model to test alternatives under consideration in the plan. FORPLAN model was written by Norm Johnson, of Oregon State University, and tested at the Forest Service computer and planning facility at Ft. Collins, Colorado. Millions of dollars and several years of time by the operation research analysts were spent in collecting, analyzing, and inputting data into the FORPLAN model. In 1997 and 1998, a new committee of scientists met to evaluate and recommend changes to NFMA and the revised forest planning regulations.

Much of the long-range forest management planning was placed in the hands of forest specialists. Public controversy erupted over management requirements for wildlife, water and soils, old growth timber, disposition of remaining roadless areas, road construction costs, and below-cost timber sales in the NFMA planning process. The latest round of forest planning, in which every Forest Service region and national forest developed comprehensive, NFMA-directed forest plans, was basically completed by the end of 1990; however, numerous appeals and lawsuits by the timber industry and by environmental and other groups delayed the implementation of many of these plans. On some national forests, the appeals and lawsuits have been successfully resolved through a negotiation process in which the contending parties sat down and discussed options and eventually came to an agreement.

The Alaska Native Interest Land Conservation Act of 1980 (ANLICA) set aside many millions of acres of Alaska public land for national parks and preserves, as well as national wildlife refuges. Initially, the Forest Service sent teams out across the state to evaluate and complete EIS reports on as many as 10 new national forests. The proposed expansion of the national forest system in Alaska failed to materialize. Instead of many new national forests in the state, ANILCA made only small additions to the Chugach and Tongass National Forests and transferred the old Afognak Forest and Fish Culture Reserve (established in 1902), then part of the Chugach National Forest, to the Alaska Native corporations. The National Park Service, on the other hand, gained as national parks and/or national preserves all of the 1978 national monuments made by President Jimmy Carter, as well as new national park status for Aniakchak and Cape Krusenstern, and national park recognition for two older national monuments at Glacier Bay and Katmai. The act also designated as wilderness the core of the Admiralty Island and Misty Fiords National Monuments on the Tongass National Forests.

Roadless Area Reviews

In the late 1970s, RARE II was launched, putting the Forest Service once again into the public arena. The draft RARE II report, published in 1978, led to many public demonstrations and massive letter-writing campaigns from both environmentalists and the timber industry. The final RARE II report, published in January 1979, recommended that Congress add 15 million acres (only 12.3 million acres were recommended in the original RARE) to the national wilderness preservation system. However, the roadless decisions and wilderness legislation would have to wait until Congress acted as the "agency proposes and Congress disposes." Beginning in 1984 with the Oregon and Washington Wilderness Acts, which contained much-sought-after "release language" for remaining roadless areas, a number of state-by-state wilderness bills passed Congress (16 additional statewide wilderness bills were passed in 1984). Still long awaited are wilderness bills for the important states of Idaho and Montana, which contain millions of acres of unroaded lands. Today, after a series of congressional acts that established new wildernesses, the Forest Service today manages more than 35 million acres of wilderness. This is approximately 18.4 percent of the entire national forest system.

Timber Bidding

Bidding for national forest timber reached an all-time high in 1979 and 1980, just before a wood-products "depression" hit the timber industry. Because of very high interest rates, the new-home market and home remodeling industries became very depressed, with the demand and price for lumber products falling to lows that had not been experienced for decades. Timber companies could not economically harvest the timber that they had purchased at high prices. Chief Peterson, USDA Assistant Secretary John Crowell, and the Office of Management and Budget argued against any bailout of the companies—let the free market reign—but the timber industry began lobbying. The Timber Relief Act of 1984 was a godsend for companies that still held large amounts of high-priced federal timber. Nationally, a number of timber companies struggled, some going bankrupt, until the economy picked up in the mid- to late 1980s.

The Forest Service experimented with a lighter-than-air balloon and tethered four-helicopter mix, which was referred to as a "helistat," to transport logs from remote areas. After many attempts and millions of dollars spent, the effort failed when the innovative system crashed at Lakehurst, New Jersey, with the loss of one pilot on July 1, 1986. The project was not renewed.

Law Enforcement

In the late 1970s and early 1980s, the illegal growing of marijuana on the national forestlands caused numerous management problems. Many of the national forests responded to this problem and other lawlessness by hiring law enforcement specialists, who have worked closely with other federal, state, and local authorities. There were a new series of problems with the law enforcement personnel. For at least 20 years, law enforcement personnel were assigned to the respective manager—a district ranger, forest supervisor, or regional forester. At times there arose jurisdictional conflicts between the law enforcement agencies and the Forest Service. After much acrimony, early in the 1990s, law enforcement was "stove-piped" to the chief of the Forest Service. That is, law enforcement and special investigations officers were responsible to the public and their law enforcement managers, rather than to local managers.

Volcanoes

In the Pacific Northwest, Mount St. Helens, on Washington State's Gifford Pinchot National Forest, rumbled to life with a huge volcanic explosion on May 18, 1980, that sent ash around the world. President Jimmy Carter visited the Forest and was instrumental in establishing the Mount St. Helens National Volcanic Monument in 1982. There was a short-lived controversy about which agency should manage the monument—the Forest Service or the National Park Service—but the Forest Service won. One primary goal of the monument is to study recovery processes in

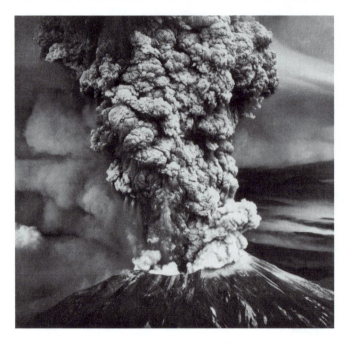

Mount St. Helens during the May 18, 1980 eruption, Gifford Pinchot National Forest. (USDA Forest Service)

the area, rather than to return the area to timber production. Much of the research work is carried out by the Pacific Northwest Research Station and a bevy of university researchers. Many reports have been produced on the recovery.

The Forest Products Laboratory designed a new, strong, lightweight system for wood construction. Called the timber truss-frame, the system has been widely used by the home construction industry since the 1980s. Many other wood products have been studied and improved, including recyclable postage stamp adhesive developed for the U.S. Post Office.

Women in the Forest Service

Although women has been employed as clerks and some field and research positions from the start of the agency, a growing number of women employees believed that they were being discriminated against in both hiring and promotions. On June 29, 1972, Gene Bernardi, a female former employee of the Forest Service, filed a complaint alleging that the agency had discriminated against her because she was a woman in direct contravention of the Civil Rights Act of 1964. Bernardi, a sociologist at the Pacific Southwest Forest and Range Experiment Station (PSW), alleged that she was denied promotion because of her sex. She also alleged that discrimination on the basis of sex was a common practice in the Forest Service. This case did not go to trial. Instead, the attorneys for the parties settled the case through negotiation. In August 1979, the parties agreed to a proposed settlement, known as a "consent decree." In consent decrees, a voluntary agreement is worked out by the parties involved in the litigation, but no blame or responsibility is assigned; the affected parties agree to specific changes to remedy the complaints rather than proceed with costly, lengthy litigation.

Almost two years later, on July 1, 1981, the parties signed the consent decree (*Bernardi v. Madigan*, C-73–110-SC (N.D. Cal.)) that established certain hiring goals and affirmative action requirements to be undertaken by the Pacific Southwest Region and the Pacific Southwest Research Station The decree accelerated advancement of women and minority employees into management and line officer positions. The women's settlement agreement concluded on January 8, 2006. In 1985, Geri B. Larson was named the Forest Supervisor of the Tahoe National Forest in California—the first female forest supervisor in Forest Service history.

Reorganization and the Sagebrush Rebellion

Budget cuts in the mid-1980s reduced the number of Forest Service employees and eliminated a number of positions that had been created in the late 1970s. In the 1990s, reducing the national deficit became a priority of the Clinton administration. There had been several attempts over the years to reorganize the agency, but little had come of them. The most recent attempt aimed at revamping most of the regions, as well as reducing organizational complexity and the number of employees. The reorganization of the regions was not accomplished because of congres-

Charles "Chip" Cartwright, the first black district ranger, Gifford Pinchot National Forest, Washington, 1983. (USDA Forest Service)

sional opposition, while other aspects were implemented (see Chapter 5). Today, the Forest Service has around 31,000 permanent employees, down from 35,400 in 1992 (see Figure 1.1a, b).

The Forest Service adopted the Data General computer system, which electronically linked all agency locations—the Washington office, research stations, regions, national forests, and ranger districts. Ten years later, the Forest Service adopted an IBM/UNIX-based system to replace the Data General system.

In 1985, to stall the so-called Sagebrush Rebellion, the Reagan administration proposed that the Forest Service and the Bureau of Land Management interchange certain lands in the West for ease of management. Chief Max Peterson said that one Montana congressman noted that there was a "big cloud of dust that you see in eastern Montana every morning [which] is the Forest Service and BLM people driving past each other to go to their land." In 1986, the Forest Service and the BLM produced a 250-page legislative environmental impact statement (LEIS) on the proposal. An LEIS differed from a regular EIS in that it did not allow for a public comment period. But comment they did, with a great outcry. The preferred action was the exchange of 24 million acres of land and 204 million acres of mineral jurisdiction between the two agencies. It was hoped that some 350 jobs would be eliminated and as many as 71 offices combined at a savings of $13 million annually. Opposition focused on three factors, according to former Associate Chief George Leonard: (1) the agencies tried too hard to balance land swaps, (2) user groups "tended to favor the status quo," and (3) the two agencies used different formulas to share receipts, especially in the timber-rich western Oregon area. Leonard continued by saying that "there was simply no significant constituency for government efficiency, [but there] were strong constituencies for maintaining the status quo." This proposal, even after a major revision, was tabled by Congress.

FIGURE 1.1a National Forest System Growth from 1891 to Present

Year[1]	Fr/NF[2] Number	Gross[5] Acres	Net[6] Acres	Year	NF Number	Gross Acres	Net Acres
1891	2	2,437,120		1915	154	184,505,602	162,773,280
1892[3]	10	5,353,040					
1893	17	17,564,800		1920	150	181,299,776	156,032,053
1897	29	18,993,280		1925	159	184,125,912	158,395,056
1898	33	40,719,474					
1899 (6/30)	37	46,021,889		1930	149		160,090,817
1899	38			1935	142		163,310,002
1900 (6/30)	38	46,772,129		1940	160		174,769,543
1900	38			1945	155		177,641,903
1901	41	46,410,209					
1902	54	60,175,765		1950	151		179,685,328
1903	55	62,354,965		1955	149		180,302,398
1904	62	62,763,494	c56,000,000				
				1960	151		180,843,513
1905	96	85,852,229	75,352,175	1965	154		182,138,750
1906	137	106,994,018	94,159,492				
1907 (3/4)	153			1970	154		182,571,102
1907	164	150,832,665	132,731,865	1975	155		183,280,072
1908	146	167,976,886	147,819,660				
1909	152	194,505,325	172,230,233	1980	155	220,090,852	183,060,464
				1985	156	229,979,210	186,315,499
1910	154	192,931,197	168,028,752				
1911	163	190,608,243	168,165,163	1990	156	231,098,504	187,083,200
1912(6/30)[4]	157	187,406,376	165,027,163	1995	155	231,745,585	191,614,904
1912	164						
1913	164	186,616,648	165,516,518	2000	155	232,443,534	192,383,077
1914	163	185,321,202	163,848,524	2004	155	232,488,901	192,857,908

Notes: [1] End of calendar year through 1950, then fiscal year, unless otherwise noted; [2] Forest reserve names changed to national forests on March 4, 1907; [3] Excludes Afognak Forest & Fish Culture Reserve (Alaska); [4] Reductions from 1911 to the early 1920s reflect the timberlands on Indian reservations that were not national forestlands, elimination of national forest system lands for land claims, transfer to new national parks, and other purposes; [5] Gross acres refer to both the *net acres* along with *other lands*, including private, *within the proclaimed national forest boundaries*; [6] Net acres refer to the total acres of national forests, purchase units, national grasslands, land utilization projects, research and experimental areas, other areas, and national preserves.

FIGURE 1.1b Foresters and Chiefs of the USDA Forest Service

Division of Forestry (1881–1901) Then the Bureau of Forestry (1901–1905)

Franklin B. Hough [1]	1876–1883
Nathaniel H. Egleston	1883–1886
Bernhard E. Fernow	1886–1898
Gifford Pinchot [2]	1898–1905

Forest Service (1905–Present)

Gifford Pinchot	1905–1910
Henry S. Graves	1910–1920
William B. Greeley	1920–1928
Robert Y. Stuart	1928–1933
Ferdinand A. Silcox	1933–1939
Earle H. Clapp (Acting)	1939–1943
Lyle F. Watts	1943–1952
Richard E. McArdle	1952–1962
Edward P. Cliff	1962–1972
John R. McGuire	1972–1979
R. Max Peterson	1979–1987
F. Dale Robertson	1987–1993
Jack Ward Thomas	1993–1996
Michael P. Dombeck	1997–2001
Dale N. Bosworth	2001–Present

Notes: [1] Dr. Franklin B. Hough was originally given the title of "Forestry Agent" in 1876. When the Division of Forestry was temporarily established in 1881, he was given the title of "Chief"; [2] When Pinchot became Chief of the Division, he requested that his title be changed from "Chief" to "Forester," as there were many Chiefs in Washington, but only one Forester. The "Forester" title remained in effect until 1935, when the title "Chief" was readopted.

In the 1990s, the new "wise-use" or "property-rights" or "county-supremacy" movement replaced the Sagebrush Rebellion. The words are all different, but county commissioners from Nye County, Nevada, and Catron County, New Mexico, put new emphasis on local control of federal land. There were also a rash of bombings and threats to Forest Service employees and facilities. However, following the bombing of the Murrah Federal Building, in Oklahoma City, in 1995, as well as the events of September 11, 2001, this violent extremism has seemingly cooled.

Wildlife Concerns

There has been growing public concern over unique wildlife, several species of which were threatened or endangered, that lived or nested on national forests around the country. In the West, spotted owls, marbled murrelets, grizzly bears, caribou, Pacific salmon, and wolves caused concern, while Texas and the Southeast were concerned about the red-cockaded woodpecker. In other regions, different species of wildlife and plants are unique to certain areas. In 1987 and 1988, various environmental groups sought to have the northern spotted owl listed with the Department of the Interior's U.S. Fish and Wildlife Service as a threatened or endangered species. A judge later declared that the Fish and Wildlife Service did not provide sufficient information about its decision not to list the bird. Subsequently, the U.S. Fish and Wildlife Service declared its intent to restudy the issue, and in June 1990, it declared the spotted owl threatened in western Washington, western Oregon, and northern California.

Other plant and animal species inhabiting the national forests have joined the spotted owl as species to be considered for threatened or endangered status. Considerable controversy has arisen over the reintroduction of the wolf into the Yellowstone ecosystem. Other concerns have been expressed over many animal and plant species in various parts of the national forests, including the bald eagle, the peregrine falcon, the eastern timber wolf, the Puerto Rican parrot, the Mount Graham red squirrel, the Pacific salmon, the steelhead trout, the bull trout, and other species.

As a result of the terrible fires that spread through Yellowstone National Park and adjacent national forests in the summer of 1988, the Forest Service and the National Park Service were under considerable public pressure to change their policies of letting some fires burn naturally (the so-called let-burn policy). After much public and scientific debate about the proper role of fire in the environment and after viewing the subsequent "rebirth" of the park and adjacent national forests, the agencies have modified their policies to put out fires more quickly but to continue to allow natural fires to burn under strictly controlled conditions.

Cooperation

A series of new programs was developed at the national level of the agency in the late 1980s and early 1990s. The "Challenge Cost-Share Program," established by Congress in 1986, provided the means for the Forest Service and the private sector to share management and financial costs for projects on the national forests. Currently, the Forest Service, other federal and state agencies, and nonprofit organizations, such as Ducks Unlimited, the Rocky Mountain Elk Foundation, and many others, carry out several thousand cooperative wildlife habitat enhancement projects in the national forests. The habitat enhancement program grew from $2.5 million in fish and wildlife habitat improvements in 1986 to more than $17 million in federal funds that were matched by $23 million from partners in 1996, accomplishing 2,135 projects.

"America's Great Outdoors" program, a presidential initiative, was designed to encourage cooperation between the Forest Service and the private sector in developing and improving recreational facilities and opportunities for the public. Another popular program, in conjunction with other federal agencies, is the "Scenic Byways" program, which has designated about 7,700 miles of roads and highways that are on the national forests for recreational pleasure—often scenic roads that have ample opportunities for scenic vistas, unusual geologic and forest features, bicycle and hiking trails, rest stops, picnic areas, campgrounds, boating, fishing, and wildlife viewing. In Alaska, the Alaska Marine Highway (the Alaska Ferry System) has also been designated a scenic byway.

Several other initiatives have been developed to encourage recreational pursuits on the national forests, as well as to improve the natural resources. One of these has been the successful "Rise to the Future," which was designed to enhance fish production and encourage fishing on the forest lakes and rivers. Others include "Taking Wing," a waterfowl and wetland program to enhance habitats on national forests and support the North American waterfowl plan; "Animal Inn," designed to communicate the importance of managing dead standing timber and fallen trees for wildlife habitat; and "Join Us," an initiative to strengthen public-private partnership in fisheries and wildlife management.

The past 15 years—1990s through 2005—are covered in greater detail in the following chapter, which discusses the increasing involvement of presidents and the increasing agency oversight by Congress. It also touches on the growing public disenchantment with Forest Service decisions.

---- ☆ **②** ☆ ----

The 1990s and the Early Twenty-first Century

The focus of the 1990s and the early twenty-first century can be thought of as managing natural resources for sustainability, seen as the key to conserving and restoring the health of the land. Management of the national forests and grasslands involves working with scientists, managers, and the private sector to produce sustainable ecosystems. Sustainable resource management is the Forest Service's commitment to landscape-level management across ecosystems and ownerships, in accordance with sound science. The foundation for ecosystem management, based on the ecology of the land, air, water, plants, animals, and people, was introduced by Chief Dale Robertson in 1992. It was the logical conclusion to the earlier management ideas called "new forestry" and "new perspectives." Although the ideas had been talked about for decades, this was the first concerted effort to apply the principles to the national forest system of 193 million acres.

The national forest system was founded in part "for the purpose of securing favorable conditions of water flows" (Organic Act of 1897). By 2000, watersheds in the national forests and grasslands supplied about 60 million Americans with their drinking water. Moreover, Forest Service research had shown that healthy watersheds were the foundation for sustainable forest and grassland ecosystems, which in turn supported prosperous rural communities. But, by the 1980s and 1990s, the agency was also in the midst of great controversies over any and all management of the national forests and grasslands.

ECOSYSTEM MANAGEMENT

F. Dale Robertson as Chief

Soon after his appointment as chief, in 1987, Dale Robertson had to face a public that was wary of anything the Forest Service had to say or proposed to do. Especially troubling was a growing controversy about the harvest of old growth (ancient forest) trees in the Pacific Northwest and several species of animals and plants that fell under the protection of the Endangered Species Act of 1973. Robertson appointed several task forces to consider all options, but when the decisions were made, they did not satisfy everyone. Robertson also led efforts by the Forest Service to find new and creative ways to manage the national forests, especially by emphasizing the noncommodity (nontimber) resources and three successive management approaches, dubbed "new forestry," "new perspectives," and ecosystem management. In 1992, he spoke before Congress on the need for the agency to move into ecosystem management and reduce reliance on clearcutting techniques.

In 1990, nearly 300,000 acres of wilderness were designated in the Tongass National Forest in Alaska. The Colorado RARE II act established 611,000 acres of wilderness plus an additional 173,000 acres designated for special protection in that state. Other RARE II acts designated 38,000 acres of wilderness in Illinois and Maine.

International forestry took a new direction in the early 1990s. Congress passed two pieces of legislation in 1990—the Global Climate Change Prevention Act and the International Forestry Cooperation Act—that greatly expanded the role of the Forest Service in international resource management. The Global Climate Change Prevention Act directed the Secretary of Agriculture to establish an office of International Forestry under a new and separate deputy chief in the Forest Service under the leadership of Jeff Sirmon. In 1997, the position of deputy chief for International Forestry was eliminated, and International Forestry became the office of international programs, reporting directly to the chief. The program continues to work with countries on natural resource management issues internationally.

Earth Summit in 1992

The United Nations Conference on Environment and Development (UNCED)—called simply the Earth Summit—met in June 1992, in Rio de Janeiro, Brazil. The summit brought together leaders from 172 governments to discuss many areas of mutual concern in the world environment. The Earth Summit was unprecedented, in terms of both its size and the scope of its concerns. Hundreds of thousands of people from all walks of life were drawn into the Rio process.

The Earth Summit, among other outcomes, adopted Agenda 21, a wide-ranging blueprint for action to achieve sustainable development worldwide. Although Agenda 21 had been weakened by compromise and negotiation, it was still the most comprehensive and effective program of action ever sanctioned by the international community. The 1992 Earth Summit called upon all nations to ensure sustainable development, including the management of all types of forests. The summit produced a "statement of forest principles," conventions on biodiversity, climate change, and desertification, and a plan of action for the twenty-first century, all of which have implications for forest management. The forestry component was led by the Forest Service. Unexpected opposition arose from several developing nations that did not want the larger, more developed countries to tell them how to manage their resources. One outcome of the forestry portion was the following statement:

Non-Legally Binding Authoritative Statement of Principles for a Global Consensus on the Management, Conservation and Sustainable Development of All Types of Forests

> States have the sovereign and inalienable right to utilize, manage and develop their forests in accordance with their development needs and level of socio-economic development and on the basis of national policies consistent with sustainable development and legislation, including the conversion of such areas for other uses within the overall socio-economic development plan and based on rational land-use policies. (b) Forest resources and forest lands should be sustainably managed to meet the social, economic, ecological, cultural and spiritual needs of present and future generations. These needs are for forest products and services, such as wood and wood products, water, food, fodder, medicine, fuel, shelter, employment, recreation, habitats for wildlife, landscape diversity, carbon sinks and reservoirs, and for other forest products. Appropriate measures should be taken to protect forests against harmful effects of pollution, including air-borne pollution, fires, pests and diseases, in order to maintain their full multiple value. (c) The provision of timely, reliable and accurate information on forests and forest ecosystems is essential for public understanding and informed decision-making and should be ensured. (d) Governments should promote and provide opportunities for the participation of interested parties, including local communities and indigenous people, industries, labor, non-governmental organizations and individuals, forest dwellers and women, in the development, implementation and planning of national forest policies.

Following UNCED, Canada convened in Montréal an international seminar of experts on sustainable development of boreal and temperate forests. This seminar, held in 1993, focused specifically on criteria and indicators and how they can help define and measure progress toward sustainable development of forests. European countries decided to work together under the framework of the ministerial conference on the protection of forests in Europe (Pan-European Process). Another initiative was launched among non-European temperate and boreal countries to develop and implement internationally agreed criteria and indicators for sustainable forest management.

The Montréal process, as it became known, began in June 1994, in Geneva, with the first meeting of the working group on criteria and indicators for the conservation and sustainable management of temperate and boreal forests. The regional and international criteria and indicators for sustainable forest management now involve the cooperation of more than 150 countries. These international criteria and indicators address sustainability at the national scale. They are also used to monitor national or regional trends in sustainability of forestry efforts. Criteria are categories of forest values that society wishes to maintain, and indicators are quantitative or qualitative aspects of these criteria. There are also criteria and indicators that address forest operations at the local level. These criteria and indicators are used to monitor the quality of forest management activities and may result directly or indirectly in the process of certifying field operations. Certification of sustainable forest products has been the goal, and it appears to be working as more and more lumberyards across the world are selling certified wood to developers and remodelers. It is a growing market segment.

The General Agreement on Tariffs and Trade (GATT) is a multilateral trade agreement that establishes a common set of ground rules for world trade. The completion of the most recent iteration of the GATT negotiations—the Uruguay Round—has created the largest, most comprehensive set of trade agreements in history. The Uruguay Round of talks was formally completed on December 15, 1993. The proper way to handle international environmental problems, GATT officials assert, is through international agreements. The Uruguay Round also established the World Trade Organization (WTO) to facilitate the implementation of the trade agreements reached by bringing them under one institutional umbrella, requiring full participation of all countries in the new trading system and providing a permanent forum to address new issues facing the international trading system.

President Clinton, not long after he took office, in January 1993, called for and attended the forest conference in Portland, Oregon. In early April 1993, President Clinton and Vice President Al Gore, along with five cabinet members, met representatives of the public in Portland, Oregon, to discuss the spotted owl and the timber harvest situation in the Pacific Northwest and northern California. Never in the history of the agency had the administration put such emphasis on resolving problems in the national forests and adjacent BLM districts. The result of the forest conference was a call to top forest researchers to develop a credible scientific solution for managing the spotted owl habitat in western Washington, western Oregon, and northwestern California. Researchers from the Pacific Northwest Research Station led the massive undertaking. The president gave the Forest Service and the BLM, in cooperation with the USDI Fish and Wildlife Service, 60 days to come up with a scientifically sound plan. After a 30-day extension, the forest ecosystem management assessment team (FEMAT) prepared an extensive report and an accompanying EIS team and had the draft environmental impact statement documents "on the street" by July. By the following spring, the Northwest Forest Plan was approved and implemented. The public was not especially happy with the selected outcome—often called Option 9—which severely reduced timber harvest in the affected areas.

New Forestry, New Perspectives, and Ecosystem Management

Jerry Franklin, formerly with the Forest Service, and Chris Maser, formerly with the Bureau of Land Management, are often considered the "gurus" of the "new forestry" approach to forest management. The findings of decades of important scientific forest research have provided much-needed clues to the long-term health and productivity of the coniferous forests of the Northwest. Because of extensive research carried out on the H. J. Andrews Experimental Forest (part of the Willamette National Forest), Franklin and Maser were able to make some preliminary conclusions that indicated that there was more to the forest than the trees. They led the Forest Service into "new forestry" as a search for alternative ways to manage the federal forests. Interestingly, this push for change has come from inside the agencies, rather than from external pressure from interest groups or Congress.

There were a number of significant changes from old- to new-forestry practices: leaving large logs on the ground after harvest to help replenish the soil with nutrients rather than leaving the clearcut area laid bare to mineral soil; leaving dead trees standing in clumps or scattered for wildlife refuge and nest building rather than falling every snag for safety; creating wildlife snags by blasting commercially valuable green trees rather than taking every green tree; leaving large strips of trees to connect with other areas as travel ways (corridors) for animals rather than clearcutting until the entire drainage is cut over; leaving trees along creeks and rivers and in stream headwall areas to protect the water and fisheries rather than taking every tree except in critical soil areas; using cool or no burning for site preparation rather than burning down to mineral soil; replanting mixed species rather than creating a monoculture of evergreens or hardwoods. A revolution in management practices was taking place on the basis of research from within the agencies.

In the summer of 1990, the Forest Service embraced a new concept called "new perspectives" as a "top-down" idea that would be complementary to the new forestry "bottom-up" idea. "New perspectives" set a new goal for the national forests that was more philosophical and that addressed the larger societal questions and values surrounding the management of the national forests. "New forestry" and "new perspectives" were replaced in 1992 with the more comprehensive term "ecosystem management." The historian Harold Steen explained how the whole concept originated in 1992:

> EPA administrator William Riley led the U.S. delegation to the "Earth Summit" in Rio de Janeiro. … President Bush was to speak during the last day, and Reilly was explaining by phone to Chief of Staff [Clayton] Yeutter that the president needed to defuse the [about the "terrible" U.S. forestry practices] criticism and "say great things." Yeutter then asked Robertson for a statement "to eliminate clearcutting that the president can announce in Rio. Boy, the lights went on." Robertson well understood that new policies had to be formulated but could not be adopted and implemented without "working the process" in Washington that included his political bosses and Congress. "There was my chance to get the official policy." Not only would the president announce the end of clearcutting as a standard practice on national forests, with some exceptions, but he would also explain that it was all part of a new policy called Ecosystem Management. He drafted the message, and Yeutter took it to the president who agreed to the language. Chief Robertson made the announcement on adoption of Ecosystem Management at home, and the president confirmed it in Rio. "That was really something to get it through the Republican administration." There had been a glitch; Secretary of Agriculture Madigan "was not in the loop." It had all happened so rapidly that there had been no opportunity to brief the secretary. Before he made his public announcement on Ecosystem Management, he first went to Assistant Secretary John Beuter, who agreed to the "need for a major change" in policy. Beuter and Robertson then went with the secretary's public relations officer to explain the situation to a secretarial aide who exclaimed, "What's this ecosystem stuff!" He hoped that there would not be "any words like that in the press." The public relations officer

assured the aide that "clearcutting" will be the headline. The next day, the *Washington Post* headlined "Ecosystem," using clearcutting as a secondary title.

Today, the Forest Service, the Bureau of Land Management, the Fish and Wildlife Service, the National Park Service, and other land management and regulatory federal agencies are embracing ecosystem management as a new paradigm for management into the next century.

Northwest Forest Plan of 1994

Since the 1970s, the management of federal forests in the Pacific Northwest has been controversial and contentious. By 1992, there were more than a dozen lawsuits and three court injunctions involving the northern spotted owl, the marbled murrelet, and timber harvest in old growth forest.

In October 1993, coordination began with the signing of the memorandum of understanding to establish a regional framework for cooperative planning, decision making, and implementation of a northwest forest plan. About 30 percent of the area covered by the plan already had special congressional designations (such wilderness areas and wild and scenic river areas). Under the plan, the remaining 70 percent was classified into late-successional reserves (30 percent), adaptive management areas (6 percent), managed late-successional areas (1 percent), administratively withdrawn areas (6 percent), riparian reserves (11 percent), and matrix (16 percent). Each allocation had accompanying standards and guidelines that work together to form a comprehensive management strategy. The strategy included protection measures, restoration activities, and commercial timber harvest. Ongoing monitoring helped determine the plan's effectiveness in promoting habitat for northern spotted owls and marbled murrelets, protecting and restoring watersheds, and promoting a sustainable level of goods and services from federal forests.

The resulting Northwest Forest Plan, signed in 1994, was declared sufficient by the courts to settle the then-ongoing lawsuits. The Northwest Forest Plan represented the first time that the Forest Service and the BLM, in conjunction with the USDC National Marine Fisheries Service, the Fish and Wildlife Service, and the Environmental Protection Agency, developed a common management approach for an entire ecological region. Science contributions provided federal land managers with crucial scientific information for environmentally sound management decisions of complex and varied ecological systems throughout the region. The comprehensive ecosystem management strategy developed under the plan served as a prototype for similar regional initiatives in other parts of the United States.

Jack Ward Thomas as Chief

In 1993, after years of controversy surrounding national forest management, the Forest Service was demoralized, with the public deeply suspicious of agency motives and initiatives. Jack Ward Thomas, a Forest Service wildlife researcher his entire career, had led successful efforts to resolve conflicts over management, especially related to spotted owls in the Pacific Northwest. In the spring and summer of 1993, he was appointed as the leader of the forest ecosystem management assessment team (FEMAT) that became the Northwest Forest Plan in 1994. Dale Robertson, although responsible for moving the Forest Service into ecosystem management, was felt by the Clinton administration to be moving too slowly in making changes. Robertson, after months of administration indecision, was transferred (many would say fired) to the USDA. He was replaced by Jack Ward Thomas. After his appointment as chief in late 1993, Thomas moved quickly to implement an ecosystem-based approach to managing all national forestlands. One of the first messages as chief was a message that he sent to all employees: "obey the law and tell the truth." It was the first step of many in reestablishing trust among employees and the public.

Interior Columbia Basin Ecosystem Management Project

After completing the Northwest Forest Plan, the administration focused on federal lands in the eastern portion of the Pacific Northwest. In July 1993, the Forest Service and the BLM were directed to "develop a scientifically sound and ecosystem-based strategy for management of eastside forests." In response, the two agencies initiated the Interior Columbia Basin ecosystem management project (ICBEMP). The ICBEMP was designed to provide a long-term, comprehensive strategy for managing public lands on a landscape level, addressing forest and grassland health, fish and wildlife habitat, and regional social and economic issues.

The project included completion of a framework for ecosystem management based on a scientific assessment of the interior Columbia River Basin. The assessment examined the status of ecosystems within the basin, including their historic trends, current status and trends, and projected future outcomes and conditions. The ICBEMP science team gathered information from a multitude of sources throughout the basin, including more than 20 databases and 180 geographic information system layers for mapping. Forty expert panels and workshops were convened and more than 130 reports were contracted from independent scientists. Scientists focused on the need to reduce the threat of wildland fire, the spread of noxious weeds, and damage to forest health from disease and insects while remaining sensitive to local communities that rely on natural resources. Public participation began with scoping meetings to encourage public participation. Beginning in March 1994, the public was invited to periodic project update meetings. Project staff gave more than 70 special presentations. Two far-reaching video teleconference broadcasts were held to solicit public comments and provide information. The broadcasts reached more than 87 communities in 6 states, eliciting thousands of public comments.

In 1997, the ICBEMP released two draft environmental impact statements (EISs), one for the eastside of the Cascades in Washington and Oregon and the other for the upper Columbia River basin. During the ensuing 335-day public comment period, there were more than 100 meetings, and more than 83,000 comments were generated. Project staff met with interested citizens, resource advisory councils, provincial advisory committees, special interest groups, and Forest Service and BLM employee groups. The executive steering committee participated in several tribal summits with American Indian tribes. In October 1998, Secretary of Agriculture Dan Glickman and Secretary of the Interior Bruce Babbitt directed the ICBEMP team to develop a new approach for the project and to issue a supplemental draft EIS for public comment. The supplemental draft EIS was to focus only on critical, broad-scale issues—landscape health, aquatic and terrestrial habitat, and socioeconomics within the project area. Released in May 2000, the supplemental draft EIS received about 500 public comments. The project released a final EIS and proposed decision in December 2000. In January 2003, the regional executives for the Forest Service, the Forest Service research branch, the Bureau of Land Management, the Fish and Wildlife Service, the National Marine Fisheries Service, and the Environmental Protection Agency signed a memorandum of understanding (MOU) completing the project. The regional federal managers decided that instead of a formal, basinwide decision on management of the basin, they would adopt a strategy of incorporating the science learned from the decade-old assessment into ongoing land use planning efforts. In making this decision, as opposed to the FEMAT process, the decision makers believed that it would lead to greater flexibility on federal, state, and private lands in the basin.

The ICBEMP scored several notable successes. It completed the first comprehensive, landscape-level scientific assessment of its size in the United States. It was the first major federal resource management planning process to include, from the beginning, a multistate coalition of counties, making it a model for county involvement in other regions. It prepared a subbasin review guide to help users consistently apply the project's broad scientific findings and decisions to smaller areas.

Sierra Nevada Framework for Conservation and Collaboration

The Sierra Nevada ecosystem project (SNEP) was requested by Congress in the conference report for Interior and related agencies in the 1993 Appropriations Act. SNEP was to assess or study the vast area along the spine of California and was directed not to prepare a plan or a range of options or alternatives for possible implementation, as the FEMAT report had done. The Forest Service established a steering committee that included representatives from the Forest Service, the Department of the Interior, the National Park Service, the University of California, the California Academy of Sciences, and the National Academy of Sciences. A science team was then selected and began meeting in the summer of 1994.

At the same time, an EIS team was begun to provide a scientific study of remaining old growth in the national forests of the Sierra Nevada for the California spotted owl and related species. A draft EIS, with alternatives for management, was released in January 1995. In the summer of 1996, a revised draft EIS (RDEIS) was completed but was withdrawn by USDA Under Secretary Jim Lyons as the SNEP project was nearing completion.

In 1998, the Forest Service initiated the Sierra Nevada framework for conservation and collaboration. The new framework was designed to integrate the latest science from the earlier SNEP and RDEIS into a collaborative approach to national forest management. It included developing an EIS to update forest plans for national forests in the Sierra Nevada and on the Modoc Plateau for managing 11 national forests and 11.5 million acres of national forestland. Even before the framework process began, the Forest Service invited the public to participate in formulating a proposed action. Another round of public meetings came after the draft EIS was published in May 1999. The EIS addressed five problem areas: old forest ecosystems; aquatic, riparian, and meadow ecosystems; fire and fuels management; noxious weeds; and lower westside hardwood ecosystems. The EIS also considered access and recreation opportunities, subregional differences, and socioeconomic impacts on communities. Special teams updated analyses in the EIS on the basis of scientific review and public comment, working closely with Fish and Wildlife Service biologists to develop conservation strategies.

Recommendations for a final decision were developed with advice from scientists and resource specialists from state and other federal agencies and from forest supervisors and their staffs. Before completion of the final EIS, an independent team of scientists reviewed the scientific information in the EIS for consistency with current research findings and scientific methods. The most visible and difficult task was developing an effective conservation strategy for old forests and associated wildlife species while at the same time reducing forest fuels and losses from wildland fire. The final EIS was printed December 2000.

In January 2001, the Pacific Southwest Region adopted the Sierra Nevada forest plan amendment (SNFPA). The Forest Service received more than 200 appeals to the SNFPA decision. In November 2001, the chief of the Forest Service affirmed the decision but expressed concerns about the flexibility of the program; its compatibility with other important programs, such as fire and fuels treatments, the national fire plan of 2000, and the Herger-Feinstein Quincy Library Group (HFQLG) forest recovery pilot project; and the effects of the SNFPA on grazing, recreation, and local communities. A year-long review provided specific recommendations for improving the SNFPA.

In January 2004, the Forest Service amended the Sierra Nevada forest plan (framework) to improve protection of old forests, wildlife habitats, watersheds, and communities in the Sierra Nevada and Modoc Plateau. The new plan is designed to reduce the acres burned by severe wildfires by more than 30 percent within the next 50 years. It will double the acres of large, old growth trees and California spotted owl nesting habitat over the next 50 years. Around communities, fuels will be reduced on about 700,000 acres over the next 20 years, helping to protect them from severe wildfires. The plan will reduce forest fuel buildup on nearly 115,000 acres per year. Under the 2001 SNFPA rule, effective fuels treatments could not be accomplished on that much area because of the complex and overly restrictive standards and guidelines. It is assumed that the placement of fuel treatments in specific patterns will help reduce severe wildfires over an area approximately three times that directly treated. The new plan maintains a cautious approach to protecting old forests and wildlife habitat by treating about 1 percent of the land each year. Appeals of the decision were made to the chief and to Mark Rey, USDA Under Secretary, but in both instances the appeals were turned down in early 2004. But controversy still lingers over the decisions.

Southwest Strategy

The southwestern states of Arizona and New Mexico have unique cultures and ecosystems, partly because of the region's special climate. In the 1990s, federal agencies in the region recognized the need for a landscape-level, ecosystem-based approach to natural resource management to help conserve the region's social and natural heritage.

In November 1997, the Secretaries of Agriculture and the Interior, together with the Deputy Under Secretary of Defense (for environmental security), directed their respective land management agencies to develop an interagency strategy for conserving the values unique to the Southwest. The "southwest strategy" was designed to maintain and restore the region's cultural, economic, and environmental quality of life in a manner that was collaborative, scientifically based, legally defensible, and implementable. Federal land managers were directed to manage natural resources in Arizona and New Mexico for sustainability, with sensitivity to the unique social, economic, and cultural diversity of the region. That included meaningfully engaging stakeholders in resolving issues affecting their lives.

A regional executive committee, with representatives from federal agencies and the states and tribes, was formed to implement the "Southwest strategy." The committee chartered issue-based work groups to develop seamless, current, and accessible information for resolving issues of concern. Work groups devised policy recommendations, coordinated with other interorganizational efforts, and explored ways to improve public service. For example, a priority for the "scientific information work group" was to list research and monitoring needs for the Southwest that were not being addressed.

"Rise to the Future" and Other Fish and Wildlife Programs

For many decades, the agency thought of wildlife as big game, upland and waterfowl bird species, and various salmon, trout, and warm-water species of fish. The notion was that in order to have value, the species must bring in recreation dollars to the agency or local communities. It was only in the 1980s and especially the 1990s that these notions changed. The Endangered Species Act of 1973 helped to speed the change from the listing of a few key species—like the bald eagle and peregrine falcon—to the inclusion of more controversial species such as the much-debated northern spotted owl and snail darter fish, as well as the Canada lynx, bull trout, and several species of salmon in the Pacific Northwest.

Traditionally, the Forest Service has managed national forest habitat for wildlife and fish, leaving population management, including reintroductions, up to state and other federal agencies. Challenges for the Forest Service in wolf reintroduction include sustaining habitat (for example, fire use to stimulate forage for prey species); helping to manage wolf encounters with humans and livestock; and helping to address deep-rooted, culturally ingrained public fears through educational programs. Once hunted nearly to extinction, the wolf has been reintroduced in several parts of the United States by the USDI Fish and Wildlife Service. The red wolf, native in the Southeast, has been reintroduced on national forests in eastern Tennessee and North Carolina; the gray wolf, native throughout most of the North and West, has been reintroduced onto national forests in the Southwest, the northern Rockies, and the Great Lakes region. The reintroduced wolves have been nearly doubling their population annually. Wolf conservation and recovery in the Southwest took a major step forward in spring 2000 with the release of captive-bred Mexican wolves in Arizona and New Mexico.

Wildlife Programs

The USDI Fish and Wildlife Service (USF&WS) has completed the planning process for reintroducing grizzly bears into the Bitterroot Mountains of Idaho and Montana. Under the plan, there will be a minimum introduction of 25 bears over five years into the 5,785 square miles of the Selway-Bitterroot and Frank Church-River of No Return Wildernesses. The wilderness areas are surrounded by more than 15,000 square miles of additional public land. The recovery goal for the Bitterroots ecosystem is about 280 grizzly bears in 50 to 100 years. An estimated 50,000 grizzly bears lived in the contiguous United States prior to European settlement. Grizzlies have been eliminated from about 98 percent of their historic range in the lower 48 states. Roughly 1,000 to 1,100 bears remain in five scattered populations in Idaho, Montana, Washington, and Wyoming. Only two of the populations have more than 50 bears. Today, there is an active discussion by the Fish and Wildlife Service to "delist" the grizzly bears in at least some parts of their habitat.

By 1990, money spent on fishing outnumbered dollars spent on both hunting and nonconsumptive uses. The Forest Service has initiated a number of significant fish and wildlife programs, including protection and improvement of the Kirtland's warbler habitat in Michigan, bats in the Southwest (through installation of "bat-gates"), and red-cockaded woodpecker in the Southeast. Wildlife resource initiatives included cooperative programs to manage and improve healthy ecosystems and high-quality wildlife habitat for terrestrial and semiaquatic wildlife, provide food, cover, and water supplies for quail, and many others. For fish, there is the iniative called "Fish Watch," an education program designed to elevate the importance of fish and clean water, that was started by presidential executive order in 1995. Other fishing efforts include "Pathway to Fishing," "Adopt a Watershed," and "Future Fisherman's Foundation" that are all led by key fish and wildlife organizations and federal agencies.

In the mid-1990s, the Forest Service entered signed a collaboration with three other federal agencies regarding the importance of native plants and plant communities. The resultant program, called "Celebrating Wildflowers," is designed to promote the conservation and management of native plants and plant habitats, while emphasizing the aesthetic, recreational, biological, medicinal, and economic values of wildflowers.

ALASKA ISSUES

Alaska Contract Cancellations

Established in 1917, the Tongass National Forest covers some 17 million acres, making it the largest unit in the national forest system. Its borders include about 85 percent of southeastern Alaska, a region 500 miles long and 100 miles wide. After World War II, the government vigorously promoted wood-pulping facilities in southeastern Alaska to utilize the vast wood supply and to provide stable, year-round employment. In 1951, the Forest Service awarded a 50-year contract for some 8.5 billion board feet of Tongass timber to a company operating a pulp mill in Ketchikan, Alaska. In 1957, the Alaska Lumber and Pulp Company, Inc. (now the Alaska Pulp Corporation) closed a similar deal for operating a pulp mill in Sitka, Alaska. In 1980, Congress bolstered the timber supply through the Alaska National Interest Lands Conservation Act (ANILCA), directing the Secretary of Agriculture to offer 4.5 billion board feet of Tongass timber per decade.

However, Alaskan lumber companies steadily lost market share in the Pacific Rim. From 1980 to 1987, the Forest Service prepared and offered an annual average of 467 million board feet of Tongass timber, whereas the volume sold and harvested averaged only 280 million board feet. The disparity precipitated the Tongass Timber Reform Act of 1990, repealing the ANILCA provisions. In 1994, continued losses forced Alaska Pulp Corporation to close its Sitka mill, and the Ketchikan mill followed suit in 1997. After negotiations, the Forest Service terminated the long-term timber supply contracts for both companies. Although the Forest Service continued to support a stable timber program, the agency was finally free from statutory and contractual obligations to manage the Tongass National Forest just like the rest of the national forest system—for the long-term health of the land.

Tongass National Forest Plan

By the 1990s, a new forest plan for the Tongass National Forest was long overdue. The existing plan dated from 1979 and called for an annual timber sale level of 520 million board feet to feed the two large pulp mills in Sitka and Ketchikan, Alaska. Moreover, it contained only minimal protections for wildlife habitat. In

1991, a committee of scientists commissioned by the forest planning team warned that unless the pace of logging was slowed, at least nine wildlife species, including the brown bear, the Queen Charlotte goshawk, and the Alexander Archipelago wolf, could disappear from the Tongass National Forest. The scientists recommended establishing large old growth reserves to maintain habitat blocks for wildlife.

The forest plan drafted in 1993 did not adequately reflect the scientific findings and was shelved. In May 1994, Chief Thomas directed the regional forester to obtain a scientifically credible, legally defensible land management plan for the forest. A team of scientists from the Pacific Northwest Research Station assembled the best information available on the key issues addressed in the new plan—wildlife viability, fish habitat, caves and karst (sensitive to logging), alternatives to clearcutting, and social and economic issues.

The closing of the mills in Sitka and Ketchikan facilitated the forest planning process by freeing the Forest Service from its contractual obligations for high levels of timber harvest. In 1997, after repeated revisions to strengthen its scientific foundations, the Tongass National Forest land and resource management plan was signed. However, to address 33 challenges filed against the plan by special interests, the Forest Service made further modifications, primarily to reduce the annual allowable timber sale quantity and to add more protections for old growth. In 1999, USDA Under Secretary Jim Lyons signed a record of decision finalizing the modified plan.

In the final plan, the annual allowable sale quantity of 187 million board feet provided a sound commercial basis for Alaska's timber-dependent communities. In 42 separate wildlife areas scattered throughout the forest, the plan established timber harvest rotations of 200 years, with 234,000 acres of old growth permanently shielded from harvest. The plan ensured the long-term health of the land by protecting old growth, headwater areas, stream and beach buffers, caves and karst, and habitat for species viability. Perhaps most important, the planning process could serve as a national model for integrating science into natural resource management planning.

THE SALVAGE RIDER

In 1994, more than 1.4 million acres burned on the national forests. The fires left large areas of dead and dying timber, raising the risk of insect infestation and future large fires. On July 27, 1995, the Rescission Act (Salvage Rider) was signed into law. It contained provisions for an emergency salvage timber sale program that essentially meant logging unhealthy forests. The program was designed to reduce the risk to forest health by salvaging timber from burned areas. A provision in the Rescission Act gave it primacy over other laws, specifically federal laws for environmental protection. President Clinton and the heads of the agencies affected by the Rescission Act strongly believed that they should follow the environmental laws circumvented by the Act, even though there was no legal requirement to do so. They were confident that salvage could be accomplished in accordance with environmental standards. Accordingly, the president directed the affected agencies to implement the Act's salvage provision, in accordance with the Northwest Forest Plan, other existing policies and plans, and existing environmental laws, except for actions expressly prohibited by the Rescission Act.

The various agency heads signed an interagency memorandum of agreement. The memorandum reaffirmed the agencies' commitment to comply with existing environmental laws while conducting the salvage-related activities authorized by the Rescission Act. In fulfilling their commitment, the signatories agreed to build upon ongoing efforts to streamline procedures for environmental analysis and interagency consultation and cooperation. Interagency collaboration received a vital boost. The Rescission Act provoked a divisive national controversy. Environmental groups branded the Act as an attempt to allow "logging without laws," and many suspected that the real purpose of the Rescission Act was to cut old growth timber.

The Act, in addition to prohibiting appeals by the public and providing for salvage sales, also contained a provision about "318" sales, which pertained to old growth sales delayed by lawsuits and by new listings of threatened and endangered species. The 318 provision, as Pete Steen mentioned in his oral history with Jack Ward Thomas, said:

> Section 318 of the 1990 Appropriations Act for Interior and Related Agencies instructed the Forest Service to make two old-growth timber sales in each national forest that was within the range of the owl. "Most of the 318 sales were harvested in short order, but some of them were not cut and went into limbo over time." The salvage rider said that the in-limbo sales "would be released to the original buyers under the original conditions." The Forest Service was able to trade out of some of the sales—"we did everything we could to spare these areas"—but some of them were cut. "The enviros yelled, 'See what the Forest Service is doing under the guise of salvage—they are cutting old growth forests!' Salvage and the 318 sales were two very different things, and they damn well knew it. But, boy, they used the circumstance most adroitly as a propaganda tool. The Forest Service was the big loser."

Salvage sales in roadless areas also became a contentious issue. Secretary Glickman directed the Forest Service to allow salvage sales in roadless areas only where the risk of fire was high in the vicinity of homes and communities or where trees were susceptible to insect attack within three years. Harvest of green trees during timber salvage raised further concerns. The Forest Service directed managers to subordinate the harvest of green trees to the salvage of dead and dying trees, limiting green-tree harvest during timber salvage to areas where it was necessary for safety and stand improvement.

In testimony before the Senate Committee on Energy and Natural Resources, on August 1, 1996, Secretary Glickman went straight to the heart of the matter. Excluding the public, he said, from its right to consultation on public policies for managing public lands "has created an atmosphere of misinformation and even mistrust between the Government and the people." Noting that litigation had risen to unprecedented levels, the Secretary invoked the words of Gifford Pinchot, first chief of the Forest Service, who argued that the American people must know all about their national forests and take an active part in their management. "After guiding Forest Service policy and implementing this emergency program," added Secretary Glickman, "I wholeheartedly agree."

The timber target level under the Rescission Act was to offer 4.5 billion board feet of salvage timber, plus or minus 25 percent. The Forest Service achieved that goal while observing the letter and spirit of environmental laws designed to protect the nation's natural resources for the benefit of future generations. However, the Act and the Forest Service response brought nightmares to the environmental community. Even some higher levels of the Forest Service look back at the Act as a law that was forced on the agency. The timber was removed, but the agency once again walked away with a black eye.

Mike Dombeck Appointed as Chief in 1997

Chief Jack Ward Thomas retired from the agency for personal reasons. In January 1997, Secretary Glickman called on Mike Dombeck, then acting director of the BLM, to serve as Forest Service chief. Dombeck created a long-term vision for improving the health of the land through a natural resource agenda focusing on healthy watersheds; sustainable forest ecosystems; dispersed recreation opportunities for all Americans; and a sound system of forest roads, including special protections for roadless areas. Dombeck worked to implement the Forest Service's natural resource agenda through collaborative stewardship, helping to restore confidence in the Forest Service as a conservation leader.

NATURAL RESOURCE AGENDA

Not long after his appointment, Chief Dombeck received a letter from Congress threatening to fund the Forest Service at a diminished, "custodial" level because the agency was allegedly not producing commodities commensurate with its level of funding at the time. The letter reflected widespread concern among Congress, the public, and even the agency itself that the Forest Service had lost sight of its mission. The Forest Service faced a crisis of confidence. "We have two very basic choices," said Chief Dombeck. "We can sit back on our heels and react to the newest litigation, the latest court order, or the most recent legislative proposal. This would ensure that we continue to be buffeted by social, political, and budgetary changes. Or we can lead by example. We can lead by using the best available scientific information based on principles of ecosystem management to advance a new agenda. An agenda with a most basic and essential focus—caring for the land and serving people."

Formulated in 1997, the Forest Service's natural resource agenda was designed to regain the initiative for the agency in the debate over public land and resource management. At its core were four focal areas, each chosen as a basis for consensus among the contending parties. The first agenda item was *watershed health*. The national forest system was founded in part "for the purpose of securing favorable conditions of water flows" (Organic Act of 1897). By 2000, watersheds in the national forests and grasslands supplied about 60 million Americans with their drinking water. Moreover, Forest Service research had shown that healthy watersheds were the foundation for sustainable forest and grassland ecosystems, which in turn supported rural communities. A second focal area was *managing natural resources for sustainability,* seen as the key to conserving and restoring the health of the land. The third natural resource agenda was *recreation.* Long before the 1990s, recreation had become the dominant use of the national forests and grasslands, eclipsing commercial resource extraction. Recreation provides forest visitors with a variety of developed and dispersed recreation opportunities while protecting the wildland values that draws visitors and supports the fast-growing tourism trade. The fourth focal area was *roads management,* including the provision of protecting the remaining roadless areas as well as the decommissioning of unneeded roads. Sustainable forest management and recreation both depend on a dependable forest road system. However, the road system is in growing disrepair and is underfunded for proper maintenance and reconstruction.

Recreation Agenda

After World War II, the number of recreational visits to the national forests soared. From just 18 million visitor-days in 1946, it climbed to almost 1 billion in 1999—nearly 50 times as many. By the 1990s, recreation dwarfed all other uses of the national forests and grasslands, contributing billions of dollars to the gross national product.

In 1997, the Forest Service acknowledged the central role of recreation by making it a major focal area in the new natural resource agenda. A growing number of visitors placed potential strains on the land; three-quarters of the nation's outdoor recreation occurred within half a mile of a stream or water body. The Forest Service faced daunting challenges in meeting visitor expectations for enjoyable access to recreational activities while conserving the high quality of the wildland experience—the very thing visitors came for. The agency's first priority remained conserving and restoring watershed health.

To meet the challenge, the Forest Service crafted a recreation agenda to protect and maintain the essential wildland character of the national forests and grasslands. Like the natural resource agenda, the recreation agenda abandoned old ways of doing business in favor of new approaches. Good social science became the basis for recreation management decisions. The agency adopted a customer-driven approach, relying on sound marketing to deliver the right services in the right way. That included collaborating with the private sector to enhance revenues while improving customer service. By managing business relationships strategically, the Forest Service sought to become a better business partner.

The agenda included a new commitment to reaching youth and underserved populations, thereby building future constituencies and extending the benefits of outdoor recreation to all Americans. Another focal area was to increasing the quantity and quality of conservation education and interpretive programming, thereby expanding the agency's support base while reducing the adverse effects of recreation on ecosystems. By managing and using information more effectively, the Forest Service would improve accountability, efficiency, and responsiveness. Finally, the agenda included national design standards for facilities to create a strong sense of place.

The recreation agenda was designed to guide Forest Service recreation programs into the twenty-first century, helping the Forest Service live within the limits of the land while increasing visitor satisfaction. Partnership was key; projects would be prioritized on the basis of feedback from partners and local communities and in accordance with sound science. It is expected that by focusing on core competency—offering outstanding natural settings for dispersed recreation—the recreation agenda will improve customer service, expand conservation education and interpretation, and build community relationships and partnerships.

Wilderness Values

America's love affair with its wilderness has always been troubled. By the 1990s, only 5 percent of the original American forests and prairies remained protected in designated wilderness areas. Much of the remaining American wilderness was rock and ice, located in high-elevation areas with little or no commercial potential. Challenges to wilderness had grown to include wildland fire management as well as the maintenance of water and air quality; the popularity of new technologies, such as motorized vehicles; an increasingly urban society often out of touch with the wilderness idea; a growing tendency to use wilderness for temporary release from urban pressures, without regard for its special values; and habitat loss through encroachment by invasive nonnative species.

Wilderness values are unique. Wilderness provides the cleanest water and air; critical habitat for many native plants and animals, often their last, best hope for refuge; quiet venues of unmatched scenic splendor for solitary enjoyment; and economic benefits to communities through tourism and recreation. Responsible wildland stewardship is predicated on conserving the remaining wilderness for the benefit of future generations.

In 1994, the Forest Service rededicated itself to effective wilderness management. The agency's wilderness agenda was designed to address problems facing wilderness management, guiding the wilderness program into the twenty-first century. The agenda committed the Forest Service to outreach, education, and training to increase public support for wilderness, including designation of new wilderness areas in underrepresented ecosystems, such as old growth and bottomland forest. To help the agency better understand the threats to wilderness, the agenda called for a comprehensive program of wilderness inventory and monitoring and a common wilderness information-delivery system shared across agencies. The value of wilderness as a baseline for scientific research would be enhanced by incorporating wilderness areas into national forest inventorying and monitoring processes.

Theodore Roosevelt once stood on the rim of the Grand Canyon and said, "Leave it as it is. The ages have been at work on it and man can only mar it." The same can be said about every remaining acre of American wilderness. The wilderness agenda was designed to address the challenges to America's remaining wilderness by working in the spirit of Theodore Roosevelt to help inspire in all Americans an awe and a reverence, a love for the land.

Recreation Fee Demonstration Program

All receipts on federal lands were traditionally returned to the U.S. Treasury and could not be invested in the projects, facilities, and services that generated them. By the 1990s, many underfunded federal facilities were deteriorating. The Forest Service joined other federal agencies in working with Congress to address the problem. In FY96, Congress authorized a test: fees collected from recreational users at a number of sites would be retained by federal agencies for investment at those sites. The recreational fee demonstration program was born.

From October 1, 1995 to September 30, 2001, the Forest Service retained all project revenues and at least 80 percent of the revenues at 100 specially chosen recreation sites in 38 states and Puerto Rico. In FY99, the Forest Service collected $26.5 million. The fees were used to maintain thousands of miles of trails, retrofit hundreds of facilities and sites for accessibility, refurbish hundreds of campsites, upgrade signs and information for visitors, expand office hours for improved visitor services, and more. The Forest Service reinvested at least 90 percent of revenues at the project or site where it was collected. The remainder was distributed to fee projects within the region, at the discretion of the regional forester.

The Forest Service began by testing many kinds of fees to see what the public might best accept. On the basis of public comments, changes were made to projects. Free days or areas were instated to accommodate low-income visitors; volunteers were rewarded with free passes; and annual pass systems were designed to reduce per-visit costs. The Forest Service worked to ensure that the program did no damage to relationships with concessionaires and permittees and that the program was fairly administered to all user groups.

National Recreation Reservation Service

In the 1980s, the Forest Service opened a campsite reservation service because of the growing recreational use of the national forests and grasslands. In a 1996 survey, the overwhelming majority of campground respondents welcomed the idea of a reservation service. The national recreation reservation service (NRRS) emerged from a 1995 memorandum of understanding among major federal providers of outdoor recreation opportunities. Launched in 1999, the NRRS included nationwide recreation facilities managed by the Forest Service and the U.S. Army Corps of Engineers, which maintains campgrounds on federal reservoirs across the country. The system was set up for other providers of recreation services to join, if they chose.

The NRRS was designed to provide seamless, one-stop shopping for federal recreation opportunities while achieving management efficiencies for the participating agencies. Through the NRRS, customers benefited from enhanced recreation information and reservation services through multiple sales channels for more than 50,000 recreation sites and facilities.

Olympics on the National Forests

Only once in the 100-year history of the Forest Service did the Olympic games have a venue on the national forest system. In 1960, the winter Olympics were held at Squaw Valley, on the Tahoe National Forest, in California. More than 25 years would pass before another Olympic event would be scheduled on the national forests. The Cherokee National Forest served as a venue for the 1996 Olympic Games in Atlanta, Georgia. The Forest Service collaborated with the Tennessee Valley Authority, the state of Tennessee, and local communities to promote economic development in the Ocoee River watershed, including promotion for the world's greatest whitewater facility. The result was an unparalleled accomplishment; this was first Olympic Games whitewater slalom event ever on a natural river.

Federal Lakes Recreation Demonstration Program

The federal lakes recreation demonstration program was founded as a laboratory for the national partnership for reinventing government. The Forest Service chief is a member of the Federal Lakes Recreation Leadership Council, an eight-agency group formed in October 1999 to implement recommendations by the president's National Recreation Lakes Study Commission. The federal lakes recreation demonstration program was designed to showcase improvements to recreation opportunities on federal lakes. The purpose is to better serve the public, protect natural resources, and create a healthier social and economic environment.

Projects chosen for the program had a high level of community and interagency support but faced regulatory challenges to their lake management plans. Demonstration projects were designed to show how the regulatory or contracting authority could be improved or how partnership funding could be obtained. Six nominated projects were accepted and added to the pilot list of 30 lakes.

The natural resource agenda became the basis for a series of Forest Service initiatives, some involving partnerships across ownership boundaries, others entailing the most extensive public consultations in Forest Service history. Initiatives included large-scale watershed restoration projects and new rules for roads management and roadless area conservation.

National Heritage Strategy

Heritage connects people to the land. For thousands of years, the forests and grasslands have been home to communities who depended upon their mountains, rivers, and canyons for food, shelter, and spiritual well-being. The same applies today. The Forest Service's national heritage strategy was designed to deepen the agency's understanding of the lands that it manages and the communities that are served and to ensure that future generations will have an opportunity to discover the human story etched into their public landscapes. Awaiting discovery in the hollows, mountains, and valleys of our national forests and grasslands are the remnants of past cultures, of a centuries-old relationship between people and the land. Heritage resources hold clues to past ecosystems, add richness and depth to the national forest landscapes, provide links to living traditions, and help transform a beautiful walk in the woods into an unforgettable encounter with history.

Through the national heritage strategy, the Forest Service gained a framework for enhancing the cultural value of the public lands. It has helped the agency make the past come alive as a vibrant part of people's recreational experiences and community life. The strategy helped move the Forest Service's heritage program more firmly into the arena of public outreach, seeking to define the program in terms of stewardship, public service, and a context for natural resource management. The strategy focused efforts on prioritizing and protecting the most important heritage sites; developing more effective ways to inventory, evaluate, and protect heritage resources; expanding partnerships with researchers and scholars; and building stronger relationships with tribes on the basis of mutual heritage goals.

NATIONAL FOREST MANAGEMENT ACT PLANNING RULE

The Forest Service is required, under the Forest and Rangeland Renewable Resources Planning Act of 1974 (RPS) as amended by the National Forest Management Act of 1976 (NFMA), to establish and maintain sound regulations for national forest management planning. The existing NFMA planning rule was adopted in 1979 and amended in 1983. By the 1990s, the public was demanding more involvement in policy planning, and new ecological insights were revolutionizing natural resource management through ecosystem-based approaches. A planning rule revision was overdue.

For more than 10 years, the Forest Service worked on revising the NFMA rules. Secretary of Agriculture Dan Glickman facilitated the process by appointing the committee of scientists, a group of eminent specialists commissioned to review and evaluate the Forest Service's planning procedures. The committee published its report and recommendations in March 1999. On the basis of these, the Forest Service released the proposed rules in October 1999. To discuss the proposed rules, the agency held 23 national public workshops; more than 10,000 public comments were received. The agency analyzed the comments and used them in preparing the final NFMA rules, released in November 2000.

The final rules affirmed ecological, social, and economic sustainability as the overall goal for managing the national forest system. Maintaining and restoring ecological sustainability became was confirmed the highest priority. In the spirit of Gifford Pinchot, first chief of the Forest Service, the rule also facilitated greater public collaboration in all phases of the planning process. "National Forests are made for and owned by the people," wrote Pinchot in *Uses of the National Forests* (1907)—the public version of the Forest Service's *Use Book* of laws and administrative procedures. "They should also be managed by the people." Under the new rule, national forest management was to be based on cooperatively developed landscape-level goals. The postdecisional appeal process was replaced with a predecisional objection process to increase public input into the decision making.

The final NFMA rules placed greater emphasis on the use of science in planning, partly by promoting the use of regional ecosystem assessments in planning and decision making. The rules also emphasized monitoring and evaluation of resource conditions and trends over time so that management can adapt to changing conditions. Under the new rules, science advisory boards were to be established to update planners on the latest scientific information and analysis. The rules affirmed the Forest Service's commitment to the viability of all species in the national forest system. Finally, the rules established a framework for identifying and responding to emerging problems. It remains to be seen as to how effective the new rules will be to sustain the health, biological diversity, and productivity of the national forests.

INTERNATIONAL COOPERATION AND RESEARCH

Research and Development Programs

Forest Service scientists at the Forest Products Laboratory completed research that demonstrated that low-cost, fiber-based water filtering technology can remove organic and inorganic toxic materials, pesticides, and herbicides from both point and non-point sources. Field research trials have been initiated in the New York City and the Catskill Watershed Corporation (which provides potable water to over 9 million people), and in the Wayne National Forest to clean up contaminated water from old, abandoned mines.

The first map of land cover in Puerto Rico since 1978 was completed by the International Institute of Tropical Forestry. Accuracy assessments and further research on advanced mapping algorithms are continuing.

Forest Service scientists have developed guidelines for the application of cutting-edge science on contentious management issues. These guidelines will be used by the Forest Service and other land management agencies to defend management decisions on millions of acres of public forest and rangelands. Forest Service scientists in the Pacific Southwest Research Station distributed a revised software package through the national interagency fire center to firefighting agencies throughout the United States for assessing the relative merits of alternatives for fighting escaped wildfires. This software has resulted in saving millions of dollars by guiding more cost-effective fire management decisions.

In June 1999, the Department of Agriculture, the Department of the Interior, and Mexico's Secretaria De Medio Ambiente, Recursos Naturales Y Pesca signed a wildfire protection agreement. The purpose of the agreement was to enable wildfire protection resources originating in the territory of one country to cross the United States–Mexico border in order to suppress wildland fires on the other side of the border.

The Forest Service and the Department of the Interior led an interagency effort to develop the working draft of the unified federal policy for the clean water action plan. The Forest Service distributed copies of the working draft to governors, tribal leaders, members of Congress, and stakeholder groups in response to President Clinton's direction to federal agencies to adopt a comprehensive strategy under the plan to better safeguard rivers and other bodies of water on federal lands. "Survey and manage species," that is, those that are not listed under the Threatened and Endangered Species Act, yet are sensitive and/or indicators of how well an ecosystem is functioning, have been ruled by the courts as requiring extensive studies by the Forest Service.

On February 16, 2000, President Clinton assigned Secretary of Agriculture Dan Glickman to study a possible new national monument to protect the remaining 38 Sequoia groves and surrounding areas on the Sequoia National Forest. A Forest Service team was given 60 days to recommend or reject national monument status for the area of more than 400,000 acres. It was not widely known that if the Forest Service did not agree to establish a national monument, the president would recommend that the land be transferred to the National Park Service for management, much as what occurred in the aftermath of the Mineral King decision in the 1970s. On April 15, on a visit to California, President Clinton proclaimed a 328,000-acre Giant Sequoia National Monument on the Sequoia National Forest. The new monument is in two sections that protect about half of the remaining Sequoia groves. On October 24, the president signed an act to establish a new national monument—the Santa Rosa and San Jacinto Mountains National Monument, in southern California. The new monument contains 272,000 acres of federal, state, county, Indian, and private lands. In one of President Clinton's last days in office, on January 17, 2001, he set aside about 1,103,437 acres as new national monuments in California, Montana, Arizona, New Mexico, and Idaho.

ROADS AND ROADLESS AREAS

Road Management Rule and Policy

The national forest transportation system mushroomed in the postwar period to meet the rising demand for timber harvest from the national forests. The system grew to some 380,000 miles of forest roads—enough to circle the earth about 15 times; only about a fifth of those roads were suitable for passenger cars. In the 1990s, with the Forest Service's shift in emphasis to sustainable forest management, timber harvest declined to a fraction of its former level. The agency was left with a road system that was designed primarily for a vastly diminished use.

As a result, the Forest Service was no longer able to afford its vast road system. Congressional funding for forest roads declined from $600 million in 1980 to less than $200 million in 2000. The agency received only about 20 percent of the funding needed to maintain existing roads, and its funding backlog for roads reached $8.4 billion—more than twice its entire FY2000 budget. Deteriorating forest roads were causing landslides, soil erosion, and stream siltation, destroying habitat for sensitive species and reducing safe public access.

In 1997, the natural resource agenda made a sound system of forest roads a top Forest Service priority. The agency began the process of revising its road management rule and policy. The intent was to ensure that new and existing roads were essential for resource management and use; that construction, reconstruction, and maintenance of roads minimized adverse environmental impacts; and that unneeded roads were decommissioned and natural processes restored.

In February 1999, the Forest Service announced an interim rule that temporarily suspended road construction and reconstruction in certain unroaded areas on national forests and grasslands. The interim rule gave the agency 18 months to draft a new road policy and to develop new analytical tools. On March 2, 2000, the Forest Service outlined a proposed road management policy. The policy would rely on scientific analysis and public involvement at the local level. It was designed to help the Forest Service determine how best to manage the more than 380,000 miles of roads in the national forest roads system. The 77-day comment period generated 5,900 public responses used in preparing the final rule and policy. The final rule, released in January 2001, requires a science-based analysis of the forest road system as a basis for all future decision making.

The new policy was designed to help the Forest Service prioritize its road maintenance and reconstruction work so the national forest road system will be more affordable to manage in the future. With the new policy, all roads are to meet standards designed to ensure their efficient management within the capabilities of the land. Standards included compliance with resource objectives and sustainability at likely funding levels. All adverse environmental effects associated with road construction, reconstruction, and maintenance were to be minimized. Unneeded roads were to be identified for decommissioning, starting with those that posed the greatest risk to public safety or environmental health. Public involvement in forest road management will be ensured through coordination with state, county, local, tribal, and other federal authorities. Additionally, the final rule includes interim prescriptions for new road construction in sensitive unroaded and roadless areas until a comprehensive forest-scale, science-based analysis of the road system is incorporated into forest plans.

Roadless Area Conservation Rulemaking

The 1995 salvage rider controversy highlighted a lingering problem: the lack of special protections for roadless areas on national forest lands. Following passage of the 1964 Wilderness Act, the Forest Service began inventorying roadless areas for possible designation by Congress as wilderness. Many of these areas were chosen for the national wilderness preservation system. By 1998, remaining inventoried roadless areas covered some 58.5 million acres, or about 31 percent of the national forest system.

Many inventoried roadless areas do not meet the strict criteria for wilderness designation, even though they share many wilderness characteristics. Roadless areas provide values unique to a tiny and dwindling portion of the increasingly developed American landscape. They are a biological refuge for native plant and animal species and a bulwark against the spread of nonnative invasive species. As a baseline for natural habitats and ecosystems, roadless areas offer rare opportunities for study, research, and education. In addition, they provide unique opportunities for dispersed recreation, sources of clean drinking water, and large undisturbed landscapes that offer privacy and seclusion.

In late 1998, recognizing the unique value of roadless areas, the Forest Service began to formalize a vision for their long-term protection. On October 13, 1999, President Clinton formally announced his support during a speech at Reddish Knob, in Virginia's George Washington National Forest. He directed the Forest Service to undertake an open and public process to "provide appropriate long-term protection for most or all of these currently inventoried 'roadless' areas, and to determine whether such protection is warranted for any smaller 'roadless' areas not yet inventoried."

The Forest Service issued a project plan to complete rule making for roadless area protection within 14 months. On October 19, 1999, in a formal notice of intent published in the *Federal Register*, the Forest Service proposed to immediately restrict certain activities in roadless areas, such as road construction. In addition, the agency proposed to develop procedures to guide roadless area management but to treat Alaska's Tongass National Forest separately because of its unique social and economic conditions.

The initial rule-making process included 187 public meetings attended by about 16,000 people and an interactive Web site that scored more than 11 million hits in its first six months. In all, the Forest Service's notice of intent elicited more than 517,000 responses, an unprecedented number for any federal rule making. A special team analyzed the comments, and the Forest Service used the analysis to help formulate alternatives for roadless area conservation to propose for public discussion.

In formulating the alternatives, the Forest Service analyzed the environmental, social, and economic impacts of each, conducting in-depth scientific research and using innovative analysis techniques. For example, the agency developed the most complete and accurate maps of roadless, wilderness, and other national forest areas to date. In addition, the agency compiled the first complete national database of threatened and endangered species on national forest lands and the first analysis on the effects of fire in inventoried roadless areas. To improve the environmental analysis, the Forest Service consulted with representatives from 17 other agencies.

The Forest Service released its Draft Roadless Area Conservation Environmental Impact Statement on May 9, 2000, and held a public comment period of the draft that closed on July 17, 2000. The proposed rule included a prohibition on road construction and reconstruction in all roadless areas except in the Tongass National Forest, where a decision would be deferred until the next forest plan review and made by local forest officials. Following release of the proposed rule, the Forest Service held 445 public meetings, attended by more than 23,000 people. About 7,000 chose to make oral comments at sessions specifically designed for that purpose. The proposed rule generated more than 1.6 million public responses. Again, a special team analyzed the responses, and the Forest Service used them to modify the alternatives, strengthen the analysis, and select a preferred alternative. The final EIS was released in November, with the publication of the final rule following, in January 2001. One change between draft and final was the inclusion of the Tongass National Forest in the analysis and a ban on new road construction.

The roadless rule of 2001 fundamentally changed the Forest Service's long-standing approach to management of inventoried roadless areas by establishing nationwide prohibitions generally limiting, with some exceptions, timber harvest, road construction, and road reconstruction within these areas of the national forest system. These nationally applied prohibitions superseded the management prescriptions for inventoried roadless areas applied through the development of individual land management plans and would not have been subject to change through subsequent plan amendments or revisions.

The roadless rule has been the subject of nine lawsuits in federal district courts in Idaho, Utah, North Dakota, Wyoming, Alaska, and the District of Columbia. As part of the legal challenge to the roadless rule by the state of Wyoming, the U.S. District Court for the District of Wyoming issued a permanent injunction and set aside the roadless rule on July 14, 2003. The court found that the roadless rule was promulgated in a manner that was illegal, both procedurally and substantively. The court ruled against the government on five of six claims under the National Environmental Policy Act and also found that the roadless rule violated the Wilderness Act of 1964 because the timber harvest and road construction prohibitions constitute establishment of de facto wilderness (only Congress can designate wilderness areas).

In July 2004, Agriculture Secretary Ann M. Veneman proposed a new rule that responded to the lengthy litigation of the 2001 rule. The proposed rule would establish a process for governors to work with the Forest Service to develop locally supported rules for conserving roadless areas in their states. The proposed rule was published in the *Federal Register* on July 16, 2004, for a 60-day public comment period (69 FR 42636). Due to public requests for additional time, the comment period was extended by 62 days, for a total of 122 days. The Forest Service received approximately 1.8 million comments.

On May 5, 2005, Agriculture Secretary Mike Johanns announced the final state petitions rule, which replaced the 2001 roadless rule. Some of the key features of the rule include:

1. Governors have until November 13, 2006, to submit a petition to the secretary for state-specific rulemaking.
2. This process is voluntary. If a governor does not want to propose changes to the existing management requirements for inventoried roadless areas contained in currently approved land management plans, then no petition need be submitted.
3. The secretary is establishing a national advisory committee to assist with the implementation of this rule. Members of this committee will be representatives of national organizations interested in the conservation and management of inventoried roadless areas.
4. The advisory committee will have 90 days to review each petition submitted and provide the secretary with advice and recommendations. The secretary has 180 days to provide a response to the petitioner.

The secretary's response shall be to accept or decline the petition to initiate a state-specific rule making. If the secretary accepts the petition, the Forest Service will be directed to coordinate with the petitioner to initiate a state-specific rule making that addresses the proposed changes to the management requirements for inventoried roadless areas put forth in the petition. Agriculture Secretary Mike Johanns announced, on September 16, 2005, the selection of members to the roadless area conservation national advisory committee. The committee membership is geographically diverse, with members from 10 states and the District of Columbia. It is intended that the committee will provide advice and recommendations on implementing the state petitions for the inventoried roadless area management rule adopted by USDA in May of 2005. Members of the committee will review petitions submitted by states, seek consensus, identify issues, and provide the Secretary of Agriculture with various recommendations on implementing the state petitions rule.

WATERSHED RESTORATION

Large-Scale Watershed Restoration Projects

In the 1990s, the Forest Service increasingly embraced a fundamental truth formulated by Aldo Leopold, a one-time Forest Service employee who founded the science of wildlife management and pioneered the field of ecology in the 1930s. "Instead of learning more and more about less and less," Leopold noted, "we must learn more and more about the whole biotic landscape." Leopold understood that land health is impossible without a comprehensive, landscape-level approach to managing the land.

Beginning in 1997, the Forest Service emphasized a watershed approach to landscape-level land management. "Given the fundamental importance of water to all life," said Chief Dombeck, "healthy watersheds are the basic measure of our mission at the Forest Service to care for the land and serve people." In 1999, the Forest Service broke new ground by launching a series of collaborative large-scale watershed restoration projects. Around the country, 15 large watersheds, providing water for millions of people and habitat for numerous sensitive and threatened species, were chosen to become national prototypes for a more visionary management of ailing watersheds and ecosystems.

The Forest Service's large-scale watershed restoration projects covered parts of 23 states. In FY2000, the Forest Service invested $24 million in 12 watershed restoration projects across the country. The federal, state, tribal, and private partners put up about $22 million in matching funds. The projects ranged from the 3-million-acre Blue Mountain demonstration area, in Oregon, to the multistate Chesapeake Bay watershed partnership, in the mid-Atlantic region. A business plan for each large watershed project was required, together with on-the-ground projects designed to achieve stated objectives. Other requirements included annual progress reports and a plan for self-sufficiency after five years.

Short-term gains were immediately apparent. For example, project teams established more than 70 miles of riparian forest and 1,500 acres of native grass in critical watersheds. Partnerships were of every type, public and private, large and small; almost 13,000 individuals were involved. From the hardwood forests of the Mississippi Delta to the Green Mountains of Vermont, community development happened on many levels, attesting to the connection between ecological and economic health. From Pacific Northwest forests to New York's watershed, project partners pioneered new technologies, such as electronic ear tags to manage cattle grazing near streams and modified wood fibers that absorb pollutants from surface runoff.

Through the projects, the Forest Service leveraged scarce resources—people, dollars, and facilities—to accomplish shared objectives on a landscape level. The watershed partnership approach is based on a few key principles: a mutual long-term vision for the land; cooperative decision making across landownerships; shared costs and workloads; and a commitment to new ways of thinking and acting. Aside from specific project benefits, the large-scale watershed initiatives provided a vehicle for communicating to the public the importance of private and public forests for water quality. The projects helped to integrate program delivery, weaving together the urban, rural, and wildland landscapes and thereby connecting the forest to the faucet. On a landscape level, the large-scale watershed projects have helped strengthen the fabric, natural and social, of the lands and communities that together make up America.

Unified Federal Policy for Watershed Management

More than 800 million acres of the nation's land are managed by federal agencies for multiple uses, such as drinking water, irrigation, transportation, recreation, and wildlife habitat. The "clean water action plan" directs the Departments of Agriculture and the Interior to work with other federal agencies, states, tribes, and stakeholders to develop a unified federal policy (UFP) for watershed management on federal lands. The multiagency policy is designed to protect the health of aquatic ecosystems, protect public health, improve water quality, reduce polluted runoff, improve natural resources stewardship, and increase public involvement in watershed management on federal lands.

A working draft of the UFP was prepared by a federal interagency team with members from the Departments of Agriculture, Commerce, Defense, Energy, and the Interior; the Environmental Protection Agency; the Tennessee Valley Authority; and the U.S. Army Corps of Engineers. In June 1999, the draft was distributed for comment to the states and tribes, and 11 public meetings were held to solicit comments. No major conflicts were identified. The final policy, issued in October 2000, reflected input from 126 organizations and 122 individuals.

This UFP provides a basis for helping the federal government serve as a model for water quality stewardship. The primary UFP goals are to use a watershed approach to prevent and reduce pollution of surface and ground waters caused by federal land and resource management activities and to do so in a unified and cost-effective manner. The UFP calls on federal agencies to:

- Reach agreement on the use of a common science-based approach to watershed assessments of federal lands;
- Use a watershed management approach for protecting and restoring watersheds;
- Identify high-priority watersheds for focusing resources;
- Improve compliance with water quality requirements under the Clean Water Act; and
- Enhance collaboration with tribes, states, and interested stakeholders.

American Heritage Rivers

In his 1997 state of the union address, President Clinton announced the "American Heritage Rivers Initiative" to provide special recognition to outstanding stretches of America's rivers. This initiative is an innovative response to communities seeking federal assistance in revitalizing their economies, protecting natural resources, and preserving the history and culture of their rivers. Communities across America answered the president's call by nominating 126 rivers for designation as "American heritage rivers." An advisory committee reviewed the nominations and recommended 10 rivers to the president but encouraged him to make additional designations. The president chose to designate 14 rivers.

Without establishing new federal regulations on property owners, the American Heritage Rivers Initiative uses federal resources to cut red tape and lend a helping hand. The initiative relies on locally driven solutions; the federal role is to focus attention and resources on each designated river. For example, the government provides small business grants and loans; information and maps to help communities identify and evaluate historic, environmental, and economic resources; assistance in preparing a sound strategy and building a broad base of support; training in the use of soil and water quality information as a basis for decision making and program monitoring; research and interpretive assistance in compiling and communicating a river history; technical and financial assistance for river restoration and pollution prevention; and economic modeling to help communities assess benefits and costs of proposed projects.

The American Heritage Rivers Initiative was founded upon the belief that what is good for the environment is also good for the economy. The initiative brought citizens, businesses, and government together to clean up rivers, rejuvenate surrounding areas, and stimulate economic growth. The partnerships formed showed how active stakeholders working with local businesses and government agencies can make dramatic improvements.

MAJOR FIRE EVENTS AND POLICY MILESTONES

Three factors changed the face of wildland fire management in the 1990s: the impact of the 1994 South Canyon Fire; the rising number of large fires (1,000 acres burned or more); and the growing number of homes built by people from urban and suburban areas in fire-prone rural areas, the so-called wildland-urban interface.

The South Canyon Fire will long be remembered, along with such firefighting calamities as the 1910 Big Blowup and the 1949 Mann Gulch Fire, as a pivotal event in the annals of wildland firefighting. On July 6, 1994, on the outskirts of Glenwood Springs, Colorado, what was supposed to be a routine fire suppression effort on Storm King Mountain resulted in 14 firefighter fatalities. The tragedy riveted the attention of firefighters and the general public nationwide. Memorials to the fallen still serve as a focal point for wildland firefighters, much as the Vietnam Memorial serves as an emotional center for veterans.

The subsequent South Canyon Fire investigation report set in motion a series of reviews and an interagency effort to effect fundamental change, culminating in the 1995 federal wildland fire management policy and program review. The new interagency policy confirmed that firefighter and public safety is a universal responsibility and the first priority at the Forest Service. The policy also focused renewed attention on fire use for wildland health, on effective preparedness and suppression programs, on wildland-urban interface protection, and on coordinated program management.

The 1994 fire season was pivotal in another way, as well. In that year, more than 1.4 million acres burned on the national forests and grasslands. It was only the third time since 1919 that the national forest system had seen more than a million acres burn in a single fire season. The two previous severe fire seasons had come just a few years earlier, in 1987 and 1988. More than a million acres burned again in 1996, and then again in 2000. The trend was clear: The fires that had been postponed for 70 years through a policy of systematic fire exclusion would no longer wait. Large fires were returning to the interior West.

As Chief Dombeck put it, "Sooner or later, rivers will fill their flood plains and fire-adapted ecosystems will burn." For thousands of years, severe fires in the fire-adapted, higher elevation forests had etched patchwork patterns into the landscape every few decades or centuries. In a sense, Mother Nature was reclaiming her turf. But the worst fire problems had little to do with Mother Nature. Ironically, systematic fire exclusion had exacerbated the fire risk in many parts of the interior West. At lower elevations, western forest types historically had frequent low-intensity fires that kept the number of trees per acre low. For example, the density of ponderosa pines on Arizona's Kaibab National Forest has been estimated at only 56 per acre in 1881. Large, severe fires were rare in the open, park-like western forests.

Beginning in the 1930s, growing firefighting effectiveness excluded all fire from the forests, even surface fires. Small trees and brush, no longer kept out by fire, now built up in lower elevation western forests. Dense coniferous thickets commonly added 200 to 2,000 small trees per acre in old growth stands and 2,000 to 10,000 small trees per acre where the forest canopy had been removed through timber harvest. When fires now occur, the dense fuels can make the fires so severe that they destroy entire forest stands. In 2000, some 56 million acres of national forests in the interior West were at high or moderate risk of wildland fires that could compromise ecosystem integrity and human safety.

The heightened fire risk was exacerbated by the growing wildland-urban interface. A rising population density in many rural areas placed people and communities in forest ecosystems naturally prone to fire, increasing the threat to life and property. Wildland-urban interface fires, such as the 1991 Oakland Hills Fire, graphically illustrated the destructive power of wildland fire in an urban environment. Drought conditions in Florida in 1998 produced wildland fires that affected much of the state's population; entire counties were evacuated, and firefighting resources had to be brought in from across the country. In 2000, the Cerro Grande Fire burned parts of Los Alamos, New Mexico; and the Buffalo Creek, Hi Meadow, and Bobcat Fires threatened communities in Colorado. Wildland and rural fire managers were in a quandary. How could they meet traditional expectations for fire protection by a public that chose to live in fire-prone environments?

Such challenges, coupled with changing public attitudes toward natural resource use, contributed to a long-term revolution in federal wildland fire policy. A new fire management paradigm, inaugurated in the 1970s with the abandonment of fire exclusion, gained strength in the 1990s in tandem with the Forest Service's more holistic, ecosystem-based approach to natural resource management. The need for greater stakeholder involvement, the rising cost of fire protection, the growing number of large fires, and the increasing emphasis on safety all came together to produce a series of new policy initiatives. After decades of efforts directed at extinguishing every fire that burned on public lands, research has shown that our best intentions to stop all fires have disrupted the fire regimes that existed for thousands of years. Moreover, as more and more communities develop and grow in areas that are adjacent to fire-prone lands in what is known as the wildland/urban interface, wildland fires pose increasing threats to people and their property.

Following a landmark wildland fire season in 2000, on September 8, 2000, Secretary Glickman and Secretary of the Interior Babbitt delivered a national plan to President Clinton outlining steps that could be taken to better manage fire for the health of communities and environment. The report, "Managing the Impact of Wildfires on Communities and the Environment," recommended a fiscal year (FY) 2001 budget of $2.8 billion for the wildland fire programs of the Departments of Agriculture and the Interior. Congress appropriated funds to support the plan, including $1.1 billion for the Forest Service in FY2001.

The national fire plan 2000 called for increasing the national firefighting capabilities; rehabilitating and restoring lands and communities affected by fire; using techniques such as prescribed fire to reduce hazardous fuels; planning for fire preparedness; increasing cooperative programs in support of local communities; and funding to replenish and enhance the fire suppression accounts, which have been depleted by the year 2000 extraordinary fire costs, and to repay FY 2000 emergency transfers from other appropriations accounts.

The national fire plan has offered unprecedented opportunities for investing in the long-term health of the land while making the rural communities better places to live and work. Congress also provided the Forest Service with funding to hire 3,500 firefighters in 2001 to increase firefighting capability to the 100 percent most efficient level. The Forest Service and the Department of the Interior are working to successfully implement the key points outlined in the national fire plan by taking the following steps:

- Ensuring that necessary firefighting resources and personnel are available to respond to wildland fires that threaten lives and property;
- Conducting emergency stabilization and rehabilitation activities on landscapes and communities affected by wildland fire;
- Reducing hazardous fuels (dry brush and trees that have accumulated and that increase the likelihood of unusually large fires) in the country's forests and rangelands;
- Providing assistance to communities that have been or may be threatened by wildland fire; and
- Committing to the wildland fire leadership council, an interagency team created to set and maintain high standards for wildland fire management on public lands.

One of the most difficult issues with implementing the fire plan has been the need to reduce fuel buildup in the national forests and BLM lands. Many times the greatest need is immediately adjacent to communities and homes next to the federal forest areas. Reduction of the fuels, either through prescribed burning— fighting fire with fire—or by mechanical means, tends to annoy people who build homes and summer cabins specifically to be next to the trees. In addition, when prescribed fires are used, there is the issue of smoke and escaped fires.

COMMUNITY ASSISTANCE, TRIBAL AND CIVIL RIGHTS, AND URBAN ISSUES

Payments to States

Since 1908, states have received 25 percent of Forest Service revenues to help fund schools and roads. In addition, counties received 50 percent of BLM revenues from the revested Oregon and California Railroad and reconveyed Coos Bay Wagon Road grant lands. Payments were never stable, tied as they were to fluctuating and controversial timber sales. By 2000, with timber sales in decline since 1988, payments to states and counties had dropped by 36 percent.

In 1999, two bills were introduced in Congress to increase and stabilize payments to states by decoupling payments from federal receipts, but both were blocked by the congressional leadership. Two other bills were opposed by the administration for continuing to link payments to timber sales or other Forest Service funds. One of them passed the House in November 1999. Backed by the timber industry, many county commissioners and superintendents, and the National Education Association, it linked timber sales to payments for county schools and roads.

The administration responded by stating its willingness to work with Congress on the basis of five core principles: (1) providing a permanent, stable source of funding; (2) allowing flexibility at the local level; (3) promoting noncontroversial projects to build trust and collaboration; (4) promoting strong collaboration; and (5) establishing clear lines of authorities. After nearly 11 months of negotiation, a compromise was reached. The bill signed into law bases payments on the average of the state's three highest payments from FY86 to FY99. It also requires the counties that receive more than $100,000 to invest 15 to 20 percent in county projects and/or forest restoration, maintenance, or stewardship. Finally, it requires the Secretary of Agriculture to create citizen advisory committees representing environmental, commercial, and local interests.

On October 30, 2000, the president signed the Secure Rural Schools and Community Self-Determination Act, stabilizing payments to rural counties by providing about $1.1 billion above current payments over 5 years. Counties no longer have to depend on controversial timber sales to provide the funding for their local schools and roads. "For 92 years, the education of our rural school children was dependent on the harvest of trees," said Chief Dombeck. "This legislation reduces State dependence upon natural resource decisions to fund education."

In early 2006, the Bush administration proposed changes in the act. Specifically, and most controversial, it would sell off some 304,370 acres of national forest lands in 35 states. Funds from the sale of these often remote and hard-to-manage lands would be used to fund the act for the coming years. Apparently, the sale of these lands would replace the standard formula from the 2000 Act, and, after the sale of these properties, the Act and payments would disappear. The state with the largest amount of national forest land for sale is California, while Wisconsin has only 80 acres on the list. As the proposed action was announced, on February 28, 2006, opposition quickly mounted from all corners of the country. It is doubtful this ambitious proposal will pass Congress.

Healthy Investment in Rural Environments

"Healthy Investment in Rural Environments" was a legislative proposal in the FY2001 budget to decouple mandatory spending for on-the-ground forest restoration activities from timber receipts and to authorize mandatory spending on an expanded range of forest health and infrastructure projects utilizing local labor. For years, the Forest Service was criticized for using timber-related permanent and trust funds known as the "Knutson-Vandenberg" (K-V), "brush disposal," and the "salvage sale funds." Critics charged that the link to timber sale receipts biased the agency in favor of timber harvest and that the agency relied on the receipts to finance and maintain organizational capacity.

Beginning in 1998, Chief Dombeck emphasized financial accountability for the Forest Service, including trust fund reform and more public scrutiny and transparency for agency processes. He called for an administrative reform of the timber-related funds pending permanent legislative solutions. In its FY2000 budget justification, the Forest Service announced the preparation of a proposal to move the funds from the mandatory to the discretionary side of the budget. In June 1999, the agency listed options for replacing the funds with discretionary funding through the annual appropriations process. Included were 10 administrative actions approved for implementation by the chief.

Environmental Compliance and Protection Program

In the twentieth century, thousands of sites accumulated on the national forests and grasslands with hazardous wastes or sources of hazardous substances. Many such sites threatened public health and welfare, degraded water quality, destroyed fish and wildlife habitat, and diminished recreational opportunities. In the 1990s, through its environmental compliance and protection program, the Forest Service launched cleanup and restoration projects pursuant to the Comprehensive, Environmental Response, Compensation, and Liability Act (CERCLA) and the Resource Conservation and Recovery Act (RCRA). The Forest Service cleaned up most sites contaminated by its own past actions and established cleanup policies and direction for the agency. The Forest Service continues to work with other federal agencies, state enforcement agencies, Indian tribes, and interested parties to clean up sites and restore natural conditions.

Most cleanup sites were abandoned or inactive mines. The 1872 General Mining Act permits mining on public lands with few constraints. A 1998 inventory identified about 39,000 abandoned or inactive mines on national forest lands. Some 5,000 mine sites required cleanup, with about 1,700 sites qualifying for action under CERCLA. In addition, the national forests and grasslands harbored numerous landfills, dumps, and illegal drug laboratories, adding to the cleanup burden. Another 100 cleanup actions were required on lands used by or acquired from the U.S. Department of Defense to deal with hazardous substances and unexploded ordnance.

Under its "environmental initiative" and CERCLA authorities, the Forest Service encouraged the private parties responsible to clean up the sites they had contaminated. Since 1995, Forest Service actions under its authority resulted in more than $200 million worth of cleanup work performed or paid for by the responsible parties. Under CERCLA, the agency exercised a lead agency role at sites entirely on national forest lands and worked with the Environmental Protection Agency and state agencies on cleanups elsewhere.

The Forest Service incorporated its cleanup and restoration projects into its natural resource management programs, such as watershed restoration and minerals management. The cleanup program became part of the agency's overall mission strategy and was included in the regular Forest Service budget process to achieve goals targeted by the USDA hazardous materials management program. Sites were prioritized for cleanup based on the risk to human health and the threat to the environment, with a priority watershed approach playing a role.

Stewardship Contracting

In the 1990s, the Forest Service took steps to end the divisive debates surrounding timber harvest on the national forests by making watershed health and sustainable forest ecosystems agency priorities. Timber harvest continued, but at a fraction of the peak levels reached in the 1980s, down from more than 12 billion board feet per year to about 3 to 4 billion board feet per year. The primary purpose of timber harvest on the national forests became vegetation management, not furnishing wood fiber for the nation.

Traditionally, the Forest Service has relied not only on timber harvest but also on service contracts as vegetation management tools to reduce risks to forest health from disease, insects, and wildland fire. However, the early 1990s revealed the limitations of both tools. Public controversy continued to surround timber sales on the national forests. Furthermore, the declining commercial value of the vegetation that was needed to be removed rendered timber harvest increasingly infeasible.

In 1996, the Forest Service began to consider the alternative of stewardship contracting. Multi-year stewardship contracts are oriented toward achieving end results, promote collaboration with local community groups and other stakeholders, and exchange goods for services. By 1998, the Forest Service had identified 22 stewardship contracting pilot projects.

In FY99, Congress appropriated funds for up to 28 stewardship end-results demonstration contracts. The legislation included expanded authorities, such as retention of receipts, exchange of goods for services, and best-value award of contracts. In its progress report to Congress for FY2000, the Forest Service showed that its 28 stewardship pilot projects were widely distributed geographically, test all supplemental authorities, and address a broad array of ecologic as well as social and economic objectives. More than half the projects were completed before FY2003, with only one extending beyond FY2005.

Initial reactions to stewardship contracts were favorable. New coalitions emerged around the pilot projects, sometimes including groups typically opposed to Forest Service activities. Attention could focus on the desired condition of the land following treatment, not on resource-specific advocacy.

Since the 1970s, a divisive debate has debilitated national efforts to restore the public forest lands to health. By the 1990s, hopeful signs emerged of a new approach as former adversaries began to sit down together, putting aside what divided them to discuss what they had in common. The Quincy Library Group (QLG), in California's Sierra Nevada, was one such initiative. The group emerged in 1992 from a meeting between representatives of Friends of Plumas Wilderness, an environmental group, and Sierra Pacific Industries, a member of the timber industry.

The meeting was mediated by the supervisor of Plumas County, who chose Quincy Library as the venue to help keep the meeting civil.

That first meeting was followed by years of efforts by the QLG to change management of California's Lassen and Plumas National Forests and the Sierraville Ranger District of the Tahoe National Forest to promote forest health and ecological integrity while ensuring an adequate timber supply and local economic stability. The QLG proposed three strategies: (1) selecting trees, singly and in groups, for harvest throughout the forest to maintain a relatively continuous forest cover; (2) carrying out the fire and fuels management objectives; and (3) implementing a riparian management program, including wide protection zones and active restoration efforts. The QLG goal was a multi-age, multistoried, fire-resistant forest approximating presettlement conditions.

From FY95 through FY97, the Forest Service implemented a forest-health pilot project based on the activities advocated by the QLG. About 56,900 acres were treated through timber sales, but the QLG lobbied for a broader program. The group's efforts paid off when the Herger-Feinstein Quincy Library Group Forest Recovery Act was signed into law on October 21, 1998. The Act directed the Secretary of Agriculture, acting through the Forest Service, to conduct a pilot project along the lines advocated by the QLG. However, the Act did not appropriate specific funding for the project. The Forest Service estimated a cost of $31 million per year for full implementation of the pilot project QLG on about 50,000 to 70,000 acres per year.

In FY99, the Forest Service completed the required environmental impact statement, calling for a mitigation measure to protect California spotted owl habitat. The QLG strongly objected to the mitigation measure, maintaining that it would prevent full implementation of the project authorized by the Act. In 2000, with a project budget limited to $12.2 million, the Forest Service completed pilot project activities on about 20,500 acres.

Lands Legacy Initiative

The lands legacy initiative propelled the forest legacy program (FLP) from a small, underfunded effort to an important national program to protect private forests from development. Established by the 1990 Farm Bill, the FLP initially had limited support, reaching a funding low of $2 million in FY97. But there was the potential for using the FLP to protect private forests for the benefit of all Americans. Under pressure from development, many acres of private forestland are being converted and fragmented every day. Outright purchase to protect the remaining forests is not always a viable option; a voluntary approach is often preferable. Perpetual conservation easements can be a powerful tool for private forestland protection. The lands legacy initiative brought funding well above levels initially supported by Congress. From about $7 million in FY99, funding for the FLP jumped to almost $30 million in FY2000 and then to $60 million in FY2001.

Through the FLP, the Forest Service works with state foresters, local governments, land trusts, and interested landowners to conserve forest lands of regional and national significance from conversion to non-forest uses. Through conservation easements or fee-simple purchase, the partners cooperate with willing landowners to ensure that traditional uses and public values are protected on private forestland for future generations.

On February 14, 2000, $18.6 million in "forest legacy" grants for 29 projects encompassing nearly 250,000 acres in 19 states and territories were funded. The participating states submitted these projects to the Forest Service for funding. In addition to the projects, Congress earmarked $5 million for three other projects. By August, the program had protected 118,655 acres in 12 states. For example, a large land donation was made a short distance from rapidly developing areas of Salt Lake City, Utah. The land ranges from snow-covered peaks and alpine lakes to rich downstream meadows and pastureland; it remained in family ownership. By 2000, 22 states and territories were participating in the program, and another 9 states were developing or considering program plans.

Tribal Governments Relations Program

Since 1990, the Forest Service had maintained an active tribal government relations program to improve relations with American Indian and Alaska Native tribes, resulting in many government-to-government partnerships. In 1997, the Forest Service produced an American Indian/Alaska native resource book to help local managers work with and support local tribes. Subsequently, the chief created a task force to further strengthen relations with American Indian and Alaska native tribes.

Civil Rights

Since the Civil Rights Act of 1964, all administrations have sought to ensure that the federal workforce reflected the face of America and served all segments of the American public. The Forest Service has launched civil rights initiatives in several areas. One goal was to build a diverse workforce through multicultural recruitment initiatives. The Forest Service invested more than $2.3 million per year, in partnership with universities, on national recruitment initiatives. For example, the agency recruited more than 100 students per year through partnerships with historically black colleges and universities, institutions that serve Hispanics, tribal colleges, and the President's Committee on People with Disabilities to fill natural resource and other professional positions. At Tuskegee University, in Alabama, more than 400 students have participated in the forest resources program. Many are in the Forest Service today. At the University of California at Davis, Asian Americans, Pacific Islanders, and other minority students interested in natural resource careers were recruited. The Forest Service also shares career opportunities in the agency with colleges and universities that serve Latino Americans. The Forest Service tribal college initiative has 10 years of experience with capacity building in natural resources at 15 tribal colleges nationwide. The persons with disabilities initiative works through 146 colleges and universities to recruit persons with disabilities who are seeking careers in fields related to natural resources.

The Forest Service also developed a comprehensive planning process to build a diverse and highly skilled workforce. The agency is training future conservation leaders by helping schoolchildren learn about the environment in a multicultural setting. For example, the agency has provided hands-on learning opportunities to 800 schoolchildren at Bailey's Elementary School for the Arts and Sciences, in Bailey's Crossroads, Virginia. Through the central California consortium, the Forest Service is working with partners and local communities near Fresno to encourage schoolchildren—mostly minority—to enter fields related to natural resources.

Another goal was to create a supportive work environment for all employees. In 1997, the Forest Service tackled a backlog of 1,194 equal-employment opportunity (EEO) complaints that was undermining confidence in the agency's commitment to civil rights. Some 96 percent were resolved, with fewer complaints filed since. In January 1998, the Forest Service established a program for early dispute intervention and resolution, available to all employees, that serves as a USDA model. Two years later, the program enjoyed an 81 percent resolution rate. Other initiatives included a zero-tolerance policy for discrimination, retaliation, and all kinds of harassment; a complaint resolution model to help parties assess the ability to resolve complaints; a settlement justification procedure to monitor resolutions; a dispute resolution guide; a quick-response team to help resolve complex EEO cases; a survey-based program to improve the work environment; and civil rights training for all employees.

Beginning in 1997, the Forest Service sought to improve accountability by establishing civil rights directors and staffs in every region and research station. The agency commissioned an organizational effectiveness study and began implementing study recommendations for improving its civil rights organization. The Forest Service in the late 1990s developed a strategic outreach plan for underserved communities. The strategy was designed to help women, minorities, and people with disabilities understand and participate in all Forest Service programs and activities. In 1999, the senior, youth, and volunteer programs served more than 120,000 Americans, including about 40,000 women and 17,300 people from racial and ethnic minorities.

The Forest Service is also active in the USDA national commission on small farms. In 2000, the Forest Service worked with other USDA agencies to help more than 130 small farmers, many of them African American, to attend the second agricultural marketing outreach workshop, in Memphis, Tennessee. The Forest Service collaborates with Alaska Native corporations. For example, the agency helped 11 Alaska Native corporations complete forest stewardship planning. The new conservation education staff area is funding more than 70 projects nationwide, some focusing on underserved youth.

The Urban Resources Partnership

In 1993, through a USDA initiative, the administration launched the Urban Resources Partnership (URP). For seven years, federal agencies and partners collaborated with underserved communities to address environmental problems, based on a shared realization that a greener urban infrastructure will produce neighborhoods that are cleaner, healthier, more energy efficient, and, ultimately, more prosperous. The URP put government resources at the service of community-led projects through funding and onsite technical assistance. URP projects included restoring streambanks, establishing public trails, conducting antilittering/beautification campaigns, and enhancing water quality and urban wildlife habitat.

By 2000, the partnership included 13 designated areas nationwide—Atlanta, George; Boston, Massachusetts; Buffalo, New York; Chicago, Illinois; Denver, Colorado; East St. Louis, Illinois; Las Vegas, Nevada; Los Angeles, California; New York, New York; Philadelphia, Pennsylvania; San Francisco, California; Seattle, Washington; and south Florida. With the help of the local community, each participating locality established a steering committee that might include federal, state, and local agencies; nonprofit organizations; local businesses; and foundations. The steering committee established the local partnership's mission, investigated natural resource conditions and community needs, set priorities, and agreed to a grant application process. It then assembled a technical team to work on projects with community leaders.

The URP and its projects were partially funded through $300,000 grants by USDA to each of the 13 designated areas. Additional funds from USDA and other federal, state, and city agencies were used to hire a local program administrator. Communities matched each federal dollar with labor, in-kind donations, and funding from local sources. The URP helped recipients meet the matching requirement by facilitating activities, community groups, nonprofit organizations, foundations, and local government agencies. The URP initiative tapped the enormous power of community-based action through listening to local communities and helping them realize their dreams.

Millennium Green Initiative

In the 1990s, urban areas were rapidly expanding, often at the expense of neighboring farm- and forestland. Decades of development had left many of the urban areas with a tree canopy cover of less than 20 percent, adversely affecting streams and wetland buffer systems, water quality, storm water runoff, air quality, and a host of other factors related to human health and ecosystem sustainability. To help address the problem, the Clinton administration established a "White House Millennium Council to encourage, promote, and acknowledge the creation of healthier, more livable community environments in the new millennium. In July 1999, the council asked that USDA and the Forest Service take the lead in developing a "Millennium Green Initiative" as a part of the administration's millennium celebration.

One of the campaign's first initiatives was to establish millennium groves in the states, territories, and the District of Columbia. Millennium Green was officially launched in December 1999 with the dedication of the white oak in front of the USDA administration building by First Lady Hillary Rodham Clinton and

Secretary Glickman. Numerous celebrations followed, along with a number of related state initiatives and events in cities and communities across the country during the spring planting season. In honor of Millennium Green, a special Arbor Day celebration award was presented to USDA by the National Arbor Day Foundation in Nebraska City, Nebraska, in April 2000.

REINVENTING THE FOREST SERVICE

Forest Service Reinvention

In 1993, another initiative was put in place to "reinvent" government through more efficient, cost-effective, responsive ways of working on behalf of Americans. Among dozens of Forest Service reinvention actions, three achievements stand out: the "Enterprise Initiative"; "Service First"; and a recreation Web site.

The Forest Service's Enterprise Initiative was designed to integrate market mechanisms into everyday agency operations. Employees created their own small businesses serving internal customers, operating in a self-determined, self-motivated way to accomplish Forest Service work more effectively and efficiently. Successful implementation in one Forest Service region led to plans to expand the program into other regions in future years. The Enterprise Initiative put the best ideas from the world of private business to work to motivate and reward Forest Service employees for accomplishing high-quality work on time. "The Forest Service is growing its own small businesses," noted *Government Executive Magazine* (November 1999), "and possibly building the government of the future."

The Service First program was inspired by the reinvention initiative's focus on customer service and seamless government. The Service First initiative was authorized by Public Law 106–291, dated October 11, 2000:

> In fiscal years 2001 through 2005, the Secretaries of the Interior and Agriculture may pilot test agency-wide joint permitting and leasing programs, subject to annual review of Congress, and promulgate special rules as needed to test the feasibility of issuing unified permits, applications, and leases. The Secretaries of the Interior and Agriculture may make reciprocal delegations of their respective authorities, duties and responsibilities in support of the "Service First" initiative agency-wide to promote customer service and efficiency. Nothing herein shall alter, expand or limit the applicability of any public law or regulation to lands administered by the Bureau of Land Management or the Forest Service.

A partnership of the Forest Service and the BLM, Service First enabled the nation's two largest federal land managers to deliver one-stop customer service to users of public lands while improving their collective capability to care for the land. By pooling resources, the agencies could avoid duplication of effort; the two agencies co-located several offices, shared personnel, combined operations, harmonized processes and permits, and standardized public information.

To improve customer service, the Forest Service and its partners designed an Internet program, recreation.gov, that provides recreation information on all federal lands in the United States. The public lands are the greatest outdoor recreation resource in the nation. In the past, recreational users of those lands had to seek information through myriad sources and formats. Now, through a partnership of the Forest Service and six other federal agencies, users have a one-stop, 24-hour source of information on all federal lands.

Program and Financial Accountability

In the 1990s, longstanding controversies surrounding public land management policies, especially below-cost timber sales, brought the Forest Service's financial management and program structure under increased scrutiny. For more than 10 years, the agency was unable to produce auditable financial statements. Studies by the General Accounting Office and others found persistent financial management weaknesses, undermining the Forest Service's accountability to, and credibility with, both Congress and the American people.

Under Chief Dombeck, the Forest Service took decisive steps to put its house in order. In fiscal year 2000 (FY2000), after several years of careful preparation, the agency successfully implemented its foundation financial information system, a general ledger accounting system. It adopted off-the-shelf software used by 40 other agencies to meet federal accounting standards.

In the area of budget reform, the Forest Service developed an integrated set of land-health and service-to-people performance measures that link directly to mission-related outcomes and financial information. The budget structure was simplified to reflect the nature of the real work being done in the field, focusing on outputs and outcomes rather than budget line items and linking directly to the agency's draft strategic plan (2000 revision). The FY2001 budget presentation was reformatted using a performance-based approach, allowing Congress to appropriate funding on the basis of the agency's performance. A new budget formulation tool was planned for implementation during the FY2003 budget process. The new tool will permit preparation of forest-based budget requests that reflect both field needs and agency initiatives.

Other improvements toward a clean audit opinion included implementation of a comprehensive methodology for producing auditable financial statements. The agency also completed the first real property inventory in its history and adopted standard definitions for indirect costs. Lines of communication with the National Finance Center were improved to handle systems requests, resolve feeder system issues, and address cash reconciliation.

In 1998, the national leadership team was reorganized to create functional lines of accountability. An office of the chief financial officer was created and a field operations assessment initiated to address functional lines of financial accountability throughout the agency. A new platform was introduced to replace the agency's crumbling information-technology infrastructure, and the agency eliminated a backlog of more than 1,000 civil rights complaints.

The Forest Service's accountability initiatives helped restore the agency's credibility with Congress. In FY2001, the Forest Service worked with Congress to reengineer the budget structure for two major appropriations, those for the national forest system and for construction (including road management). The number of line items for these appropriations fell from 34 to 13, increasing the Forest Service's flexibility in the use of funds—a measure of confidence and trust.

The Millennium Bug (Y2K) Program

During FY2000, the Forest Service successfully executed a comprehensive program to prevent disruptions of business processes caused by Year 2000 (Y2K) failures. The agency also completed implementation of a new computer system and a new office automation suite. More than 32,000 personal computers were installed at more than 800 locations throughout the agency.

USDA Forest Service Strategic Plan (2000 Revision)

From the very beginnings of the national forest system, in 1905, the Forest Service based its natural resource management on the principle of sustainability—the very principle at the heart of the Forest Service's revision of the strategic plan. The "2000 revision" focused on outcomes—outcomes in managing the lands and resources of the national forest system, in collaboration with the American people; outcomes in delivering technical assistance through state and private forestry programs; outcomes in making use of scientific information from research programs; and outcomes in improving the management of, and accountability for, all Forest Service activities. The focus on outcomes such as the health of the land, the quality of water, and customer satisfaction represented an important change in focus for the Forest Service.

The four goals of the 2000 Revision were ecosystem health, multiple benefits for people, scientific and technical assistance, and effective public service. Associated with each goal were objectives, strategies to achieve the objectives, and measures of progress. Collectively, these components of the strategic plan provided purpose and context for future management actions and investments, setting milestones for evaluating progress toward the goals. Separate annual performance plans were designed to address specific management actions and investments needed to ensure progress toward the goals and objectives of the strategic plan.

Policy analysis (PA) published *Water and the Forest Service*, the first comprehensive survey of water quantity, quality, uses, and value on the national forest system. Over 25,000 electronic copies and 5,000 hard copies have been distributed. The report has been used by the chief, regional foresters, and others in speeches and testimony for congressional hearings. PA prepared a legislative proposal for grassbanking initiative for the 2002 Farm Bill.

Policy analysis has also developed strategic analysis of the agency's fire and fuels management direction; held briefings with Chief Dombeck; and redefined the underlying strategy for fire and fuels management, as embodied in the 30-day report to the president. The staff has negotiated a contract with the Pinchot Institute, funding the Institute's work on forest community partnerships and collaborative stewardship. The Forest Service has also maintained and expanded an effective working relationship with Institute staff and leadership.

The policy analysis group developed and coordinated the agency's plan for transition to the George W. Bush administration, in 2001. This effort included development of a strategic approach for transition, organization and development of briefing materials, the establishment of a "transition advisory board," and other activities. In 2005, several members of policy analysis were moved to be physically and philosophically closer to the chief, while others were transferred to a policy analysis section in the research and development staff.

Economic Recovery Grants

In June 2000, the Pacific Southwest Region announced grants through three programs totaling nearly $600,000. Just over $200,000 was shared among 11 Sierra Nevada counties through a number of economic recovery program grants. The grants helped support community planning and economic diversification. The rural economic assistance program of the Northwest Economic Adjustment Initiative provided 18 grants to be distributed among nine counties, for a total of $290,000. The Hale Halawai Ohana O'hanalei Community Center of Hanalei, Hawaii, was the recipient of a grant for $100,000 for watershed protection and enhancement planning in the Hanalei River watershed.

ROCKY MOUNTAIN FRONT ISSUES

Land Transfers and Acquisitions

Despite the lawsuits and numerous congressional hearings, the Forest Service was able incorporate through gifts and purchase several significant bodies of land, including the Land-between-the-Lakes and the Baca Ranch. The Baca Ranch addition added to the NFS a huge base of fundamentally intact ecosystem on the mountains of northern Arizona. The Land-between-the-Lakes came about through a transfer of land from the Tennessee Valley Authority to the Forest Service. These two large areas were significant in that the people and other agencies think highly of and have confidence in the Forest Service to administer these unique lands for the future.

Rocky Mountain Front Mineral Withdrawal

In 1805, when Meriwether Lewis and William Clark made their historic journey of discovery, they found vast western plains teeming with bison and elk, with wolves and grizzlies roaming the edges of huge ungulate herds. Some semblance of that pristine western landscape survives at the foot of the Rocky Mountains in Montana, an area known as the Rocky Mountain Front. Much of it is protected by the Helena National Forest and the Lewis and Clark National Forest.

Mining laws dating to 1872 allowed anyone to enter a national forest or grassland and stake a mining claim. The prospector was entitled to use the land's surface resources to develop the claim, with limitations imposed in 1955 to prevent the worst abuses. A discovery of hard-rock minerals could justify a patent on the claim for full mineral rights. Since 1909, the government had acted to constrain free access to minerals on public lands if such action conflicted with the public interest. In 1998, to protect the Rocky Mountain front, the government prohibited leasing in the area for oil and gas. During completion of the analysis for prohibition, 104 mining claims were staked in the area, eliciting a Forest Service decision to request a formal withdrawal from mining for hard-rock minerals. The Transfer Act of 1905 had left such withdrawals up to the Secretary of the Interior. Withdrawals of more than 5,000 acres were subject to congressional review.

In February 1999, Chief Dombeck petitioned the Secretary of the Interior to segregate 405,000 acres of the Rocky Mountain Front from mineral entry while a formal mineral withdrawal report was prepared. Working with BLM, the Forest Service completed the report, together with an environmental impact statement. In September 1999, after public hearings generated a mostly favorable response, Chief Dombeck asked the Secretary of the Interior to withdraw the Rocky Mountain Front from hard-rock mining for 20 years, with the option of subsequent 20-year withdrawals. Amended forest plans for the affected national forests reflected the withdrawal decision.

The withdrawal was needed to preserve the area for traditional and cultural activities by American Indians, to protect threatened and endangered species, and to conserve outstanding scenic values and roadless areas. The Front was home to nationally important wildlife populations, including the only remaining population of prairie-ranging grizzlies in the United States. Preservation of the area was intended to keep the ecosystem intact across the Bob Marshall wilderness complex and Glacier National Park, in accordance with the Forest Service's commitment to landscape-level, ecosystem-based natural resource management.

By the end of 2000, there were signs of growing public confidence in the agency. Favorable reports again outweighed negative stories in the media. Contentious debates had all but ceased in Congress over levels of timber harvest and appropriations for forest roads. For FY2001, in a striking vote of confidence, Congress raised the Forest Service's annual budget from $2.9 billion to $4.4 billion, a 47-percent increase and the largest in agency history.

FOUR THREATS

Dale Bosworth Appointed as Chief

Chief Mike Dombeck left the agency in early 2001, just after the George W. Bush administration came into office. The new administration wanted different policies and someone more in-touch with the agency regional foresters. Dale Bosworth was an ideal choice because he was highly regarded as the regional forester for the

Northern Region. Soon after his appointment as chief, in 2001, Dale Bosworth had to face a public that was wary of the Forest Service. Many people, especially in the new George W. Bush administration, believed that the Forest Service had gone too far—the reductions in timber harvest levels, its handling of the roadless issue, and the protection of T&E species especially rankled the administration. It felt that a change was needed at the top. Dale immediately changed the focus of the agency by proposing that the national forest system was itself endangered. The notion of four threats became a central focus. These threats included fire and fuels, invasive species, loss of open space, and unmanaged recreation.

Chief Bosworth described the first threat in 2004: "The underlying issue is that so many of our fire-dependent ecosystems have become overgrown and unhealthy. The answer is to reduce fuels before the big fires break out. Where fire-dependent forests are overgrown, we've got to do some thinning, then get fire back into the ecosystem when it's safe. And in shrubby systems such as chaparral in southern California, we've got to use more prescribed fire to take some of the heat out of those systems." Rehabilitation and restoration treatment priorities are highest where risks are greatest. Estimates are that high-priority treatment areas cover 397 million acres across all ownerships, public and private, an area three times the size of France.

The second threat, as outlined by Bosworth, is "the spread of invasive species. These are species that evolved in one place and wound up in another, where the ecological controls they evolved with are missing. They take advantage of their new surroundings to crowd out or kill off native species, destroying habitat for native wildlife. Where cheatgrass takes over, for example, the range loses forage value for deer and elk. We are losing our precious heritage—at a cost that is in the billions." Of 2,000 nonnative plants found in the United States, 400 are invasive species. The United States spends $13 billion per year to prevent and contain the spread of invasives. For all invasives combined, the price tag is $138 billion per year in total economic damages and associated control costs. In addition to nonnative plants, 70 million acres of forest in all ownerships (public and private land holdings) are at risk from 26 different insects and diseases (e.g., gypsy moth, hemlock woolly adelgid, dogwood anthracnose—the list goes on).

A strategic Forest Service response to invasive specifies is embodied in the national strategy and implementation plan for invasive species management that was launched in October 2004. The strategy is an aggressive program that harnesses the capabilities of the Forest Service as part of the healthy forests initiative.

Chief Bosworth describes the third threat as "loss of open space. Every day, America loses about 4,000 acres of open space to development. That's about 3 acres per minute, and the rate of conversion is getting faster all the time. In some places, we're losing large, relatively undisturbed forests that animals like marten, bear, and cougar need. In other places, we're losing rangeland that many plants and animals need. And where private open space is lost, recreational pressures on public lands tend to grow." More than 21.8 million acres of open space were lost to development between 1982 and 1997, about 4,000 acres per day, 3 acres a minute. Of this loss, close to 10.3 million acres are in forestland. The process continues today.

Finally, Bosworth explained the last threat: "unmanaged outdoor recreation. I'll use an example to explain what I mean. Off-highway vehicles, or OHVs, are a great way to experience the outdoors. But the number of OHV users has just gotten huge. It grew from about 5 million in 1972 to almost 36 million in 2000. Ninety-nine percent of the users are careful to protect the land. But with all those millions of users, even a tiny percentage of problem use becomes relatively huge. Each year, the national forests and grasslands get hundreds of miles of unauthorized roads and trails due to repeated cross-country use. We're seeing more erosion, water degradation, and habitat destruction. We're seeing more conflicts between users. We have got to improve our management so we get responsible recreational use based on sound outdoor ethics." Increasing use of the national forests for outdoor activities prompts the need to manage these forms of recreation, including the use of OHVs. OHV use grew to 51 million in 2004. OHV use is a legitimate use of NFS lands in the right places. However, depending on the site, unmanaged OHV use in the national forest can have serious impact on the land, among them (1) damage to wetlands and wetland species, (2) severe soil erosion, and (3) spread of invasive species.

PROCESS PREDICAMENT

Another effort, first sounded as early as 1995 by Chief Jack Ward Thomas and later reiterated by Chief Mike Dombeck, was what became called the "process predicament." Chief Dale Bosworth, in 2001, called a team to study the excessive "red tape" problem. By the following summer, the team presented a report called "The Process Predicament—How Statutory, Regulatory, and Administrative Factors Affect National Forest Management." The report, with suggested strategies to implement, addressed three problem areas:

1. Excessive analysis—leading to confusion, project delays, increased costs, and higher risks associated with the required consultations and studies. Much of this problem is caused by overlapping and sometimes conflicting laws.
2. Ineffective public involvement—procedural requirements that create disincentives to collaboration in national forest management, an almost unworkable appeals process, procedural delays, judicial review.
3. Management inefficiencies—poor planning and administration, a deteriorating skills base caused by the end of NFMA planning and retirements, and inflexible funding rules, compounded by the sheer volume of required paperwork and misinterpretations or misapplied planning procedures and requirements.

It was thought that by addressing these issues, the agency could save as much as $100 million annually. Although it was widely touted at the time, the effort largely failed because of agency inertia and the inability to get Congress to respond. Yet, in the aftermath of the huge fires in the summer and fall of 2002, the Forest Service was able to respond to the situation with the healthy forests initiative (HFI). This initiative was intended to reduce the risks that wildfires pose to people, structures, and the environment (see later discussion). The following year, Congress responded by passing the Healthy Forests Restoration Act of 2003, which was intended to enable the Secretary of Agriculture and the Secretary of the Interior to conduct better hazardous fuels-reduction projects (see later discussion). Much more work needs to be done on this issue. Another obstacle, not really considered by the report, is that special interest groups like the procedural nightmare, since it slows and often stops projects they oppose, especially timber sales.

FIRE AND HEALTHY FORESTS

An especially dangerous fire season in 2002 resulted from several years of severe drought in the Rocky Mountains, with fires starting in June and July. Especially destructive fires in Arizona, Colorado, and New Mexico set the stage for one of the most disastrous fire seasons in decades. The Hayman Fire, in Colorado, burned some 138,577 acres. The fire was set, unintentionally or not, by a Forest Service employee. The Rodeo-Chediski Fire, in Arizona, burned another 192,970 acres. Another big fire was the Missionary Ridge Fire, in Colorado, that burned 72,964 acres.

Then, on July 13, a fire started in southwest Oregon. It soon became Oregon's largest in recorded history. The fire, called the Biscuit Fire, blackened 499,965 acres. It was also the most expensive fire to fight. The Biscuit Fire encompassed most of the Kalmiopsis Wilderness. Yet the whole area was not intensively burned, as the fire burned in a mosaic pattern—approximately 20 percent of the area was only burned lightly, with less than 25 percent of the vegetation killed. Another 50 percent of the area burned very hot, with more than 75 percent of the vegetation killed. Many acres of critical habitat for wildlife and plant species burned, and the late-seral and old growth timber stands that remain are very precious.

The fire site was visited by President Bush, who announced a program to remove brush and ladder fuels from the national forests, as well as to restore and salvage log burned over areas. Called the healthy forests initiative (HFI), it was launched in August 2002 with the intent to reduce the risks severe wildfires pose to people, communities, and the environment. The HFI program is designed to protect forests, woodlands, shrublands, and grasslands from unnaturally intensive and destructive fires. Basically, the HFI program, much like the national fire plan of 2000, is designed to improve the condition of our public lands, increase firefighter safety, and conserve landscapes. The HFI speeds the process used to conduct timber sales on federal lands, which has led to much opposition from the environmental community. Supporters, including many western legislators, communities, and timber industry interests, believe that the expedited process would reduce the fire risk through the reintroduction of fire and careful logging/brush removal operations. But opponents, including many environmentalists and wildlife biologists, view the HFI as an attempt to use the fire issue to increase logging, much as the Timber Salvage Act of 1985 did.

The Healthy Forests Restoration Act of 2003 was written to enable the Secretary of Agriculture and the Secretary of the Interior to conduct hazardous fuels reduction projects on national forest system lands and Bureau of Land Management lands. The act was aimed at protecting communities, watersheds, and certain other at-risk lands from catastrophic wildfire and to enhance efforts to protect watersheds and address threats to forest and rangeland health, including catastrophic wildfire, across the landscape. President Bush, at the signing ceremony, said,

> For decades, government policies have allowed large amounts of underbrush and small trees to collect at the base of our forests.... The uncontrolled growth, left by years of neglect, chokes off nutrients from trees and provides a breeding ground for insects and disease. As we have seen this year and in other years, such policy creates the conditions for devastating wildfires. Today, about 190 million acres of forest and woodlands around the country are vulnerable to destruction. Overgrown brush and trees can serve as kindling, turning small fires into large, raging blazes that burn with such intensity that the trees literally explode.... The bill expedites the environmental review process so we can move forward more quickly on projects that restore forests to good health. We don't want our intentions bogged down by regulations. We want to get moving. When we see a problem, this government needs to be able to move. Congress wisely enabled a review process to go forward, but also wisely recognizes sometimes review process bogs us down and things just don't get done. The new law directs courts to consider the long-term risks that could result if thinning projects are delayed. And that's an important reform, and I want to thank you all for that. It places reasonable time limits on litigation after the public has had an opportunity to comment and a decision has been made. You see, no longer will essential forest health projects be delayed by lawsuits that drag on year after year after year.

However, not all of the special interest groups feel the same way about the Act, as it appears similar to the timber salvage bill of 1985 where relaxing the environmental law requirements led to "uncontrolled" logging in many fire-burned areas.

In the 2002 fire season, the Forest Service spent around $500 million on the four largest fires of the season. In all jurisdictions, the 2002 fires claimed the lives of 23 firefighters, destroyed more than 800 homes, scorched about 7 million acres, and cost $1.5 billion. Much of that money went to the fire aviation budget for aerial firefighting with the use of air tankers and helicopters. There also were 13 aviation accidents fighting wildfires, which resulted in six fatalities. The Forest Service grounded some of its large air tankers after several air accidents in which the tankers wings came off during critical fire fighting operations, but the grounding had lots of opposition from the western states and delegations that were faced with another bad fire season. Several of the larger tankers were approved for use in the 2003 fire season, but fire crews had to rely more on smaller air tankers, helicopters, and ground crews. In May 2004, the Forest Service and the Bureau of Land Management terminated the contracts for 33 heavy air tankers because of National Transportation Safety Board concerns about the airworthiness of the aircraft. In July 2004, the agencies determined the airworthiness of eight P3s and returned these planes to service. By 2005, the outlook for air tankers had improved, as forest firefighters had the following aerial resources at their disposal:

- At least 6 large helicopter tankers and helicopters and more than 700 helicopters total
- 28 single engine air tankers. as well as about 70 on standby
- 6 CL215 and CL415 air tankers

- 8 military C130 aircraft outfitted with modular airborne firefighting systems
- 7 P3 air tankers
- Up to 9 P2V air tankers

TERRORISM, *COLUMBIA*, AND HURRICANES

Terrorist Attacks and Disaster Relief

The Forest Service responded quickly when called to duty. Immediately after the September 11, 2001, terrorist attacks on New York City and on the Pentagon, in Virginia, just outside Washington, D.C., the Forest Service provided critical incident command teams to help in the turmoil and to provide necessary assistance to the survivors. When a disaster such as the events of September 11 occurs, the Forest Service is mobilized to manage and coordinate firefighting activities and to provide personnel, equipment, and supplies in support of state and local agencies.

The morning of September 11 found almost everyone across theUnited States glued to his or her TV or radio as the World Trade Center twin towers were destroyed by hijacked commercial airliners. Then the Pentagon was attacked in the same way, and a fourth plane went down in rural Pennsylvania. Several Forest Service incident management teams were called to assist in the aftermath. One such 39-person team, 22 of whom were Forest Service employees—California Interagency Incident Management Team 3 (CIIMT3)—came from all over California. After gaining special authorization to fly—since the FAA had grounded all flights in the United States, as well as those en route to this country—they left Mather Air Force Base in Sacramento to fly to Baltimore. Team members commented that it was quite eerie—no planes flying, airport terminals totally empty. As they were landing, an Air Force F-16 screamed by the plane, waiting for the code-word authorization. Without the code word, the airplane would have been shot down.

The team was assigned to the Anacostia Naval Station, on the Potomac, just east of the Pentagon, from which they could see black smoke rising from the west side of the huge building. The Team 3 assignment was to support four 80-person urban search-and-rescue teams assigned to duties directly involved in the recovery effort. It gathered information on the victims and the damaged building. During the team's two-week stay, many ranking political leaders visited the site, including Chief Dale Bosworth. The team assignment at the Pentagon ended when the last urban search-and-rescue team departed. The California team left on September 25 to return home. But, many of the team members didn't want to leave at the end of the assignment—it was a huge emotional high as well as a drain on the rescuers.

Teams from the Southwest and from Alaska were assigned to help at ground zero in New York City. An Oregon-based incident management team was also called for duty in the aftermath. One person assigned was Ellen Geis, a Grey Towers employee, who, for three and a half weeks, was in her "office" by 6:30 A.M. She worked straight through the day, usually until 8:30 P.M., when she fell, exhausted, into bed at her temporary home at Pier 90, along the waterfront in New York City. The job she had to do was to coordinate all Forest Service activities related to the September 11 terrorist attack on the World Trade Center with the Federal Emergency Management Agency (FEMA). She served as liaison with the critical interagency incident management teams and FEMA. The teams filled the vital role of doing the logistical planning with the New York Fire Department. They helped create an incident action plan to help the New York City Fire Department coordinate its efforts. Having an outside organization provide coordination was essential, especially because the fire department itself was so impacted by the disaster. "They [the FDNY] lost a lot of people," Ellen explained. This plan helped them organize and plan their "attack" on the fire and rescue efforts at ground zero.

In addition, the incident management teams provided places to live for the FEMA urban search-and-rescue teams at the Jacob Javits Convention Center and provided warehouse management of the many needed supplies coming into New York City for the efforts at ground zero. Ellen was at the FEMA disaster field office for two days before she went to ground zero, the site of the building collapse. "I was just in awe," she said of the devastation she saw there. "The destruction was just enormous, it was immense…. When the urban search and rescue teams started leaving, reality began to set in. The rescue effort was becoming a recovery effort. The urgency shifted into a healing phase," Ellen explained. "That was really sad for the families. They had been holding onto hope and reality was setting in. There was little chance even of finding the bodies."

In the aftermath of the national tragedy, the Forest Service was called upon by Congress to create the Living Memorials Project to honor and memorialize the losses that occurred on September 11, 2001. More than 50 living memorial projects have been supported in the Northeast. This project invoked the power of trees to bring people together and to create lasting, living memorials to the victims of terrorism, their families, their communities, and the nation.

Space Shuttle *Columbia*

Another disaster salvage operation took place from February 1 to April 30, 2003. This began after the space shuttle *Columbia* disintegrated on reentry and involved 15,000 firefighters and other personnel who volunteered to comb vast areas of the Southwest and Texas for pieces of the shuttle. The southern area incident command team red was called to organize the effort. The search focused on the Sabine and Angelina National Forests (Nacogdoches, San Augustine, and Sabine counties) in Texas. More than 100 federal, state, and local agencies and organizations were involved in the search effort, run out of the FEMA operations center in Lufkin, Texas.

Federal agency personnel were involved primarily with ground searching, recording debris sites, creating maps, recovering and escorting debris, and patrolling for theft of material by collectors. In addition to personnel, other resources provided by the federal agencies included helicopters (for searching areas that were too steep or inaccessible for ground crews and for picking up large pieces of debris), all-terrain vehicles, weather stations, satellite phones, videography equipment, GPS equipment, food caterers, and showers for the searchers. Volunteers were advised to bring the usual fire camp gear, including sleeping bags and tents, but were warned that they might encounter copperhead and cottonmouth snakes while working in the creek areas. The teams walked in grid patterns, looking for pieces of the spacecraft. Much of the area was so thick it was difficult to walk through. Workers were told to keep sight of the searchers next to them, but sometimes the groundcover was so thick—they could barely see two feet in any direction—that they had to stop and listen to make sure they were near the next person.

Hurricanes of 2005

The hurricanes of 2005, once again, provided opportunities for the Forest Service to assist in the complicated problems facing the recovery and cleanup following Hurricanes Katrina and Rita, which devastated large portions of coastal Louisiana and Mississippi in the fall. USDA, in coordination with FEMA, mobilized 1,800 Forest Service employees who are trained to respond to large-scale incidents. These teams had expertise in setting up logistics staging areas, distributing food products, and removing debris.

For Hurricane Rita, advance planning and contingency plans were put into effect, even before the hurricane made landfall. Forest Service incident command teams, in coordination with FEMA and the Texas Department of Emergency Management, in San Antonio helped evacuees who wished to evacuate the Texas coast. Inventories of food, water, and medical supplies within the state and in surrounding states were identified and positioned for distribution into affected areas.

USDA deployed more than 4,000 employees into the affected region, providing services to military, state, local, and federal agencies. A large proportion of those employees were from the Forest Service, which utilized its incident management abilities by managing evacuation centers and base camps, providing logistical support, clearing roadways, and operating mobilization centers and trailer staging areas. The Forest Service teams helped provide more than 600,000 people with commodities; 2.7 million meals were shipped, and 4 million gallons of water and 40 million pounds of ice were distributed to the affected communities.

FEATURING THE FOREST SERVICE: OLYMPICS AND CENTENNIAL

2002 Olympic Winter Games

The national forests were invited to serve as an Olympic venue for the 2002 Olympic Winter Games on the Wasatch-Cache National Forest in Utah. On February 8–24, the 2002 Winter Olympic Games provided for 78 events with almost 2,400 participants. The agency regarded the Olympic Games as a unique opportunity to showcase recreation on national forest lands while linking healthy ecosystems to quality of life. The Forest Service's main goal was to help ensure that

Olympic-related activities on the national forests were safe and environmentally sound. That required consulting on facilities development, avalanche forecasting, and educating the public about avalanche dangers. Other goals included working with local communities to help visitors to the games feel safe and welcome. In addition, the Forest Service worked to leave a legacy for future generations by upgrading and restoring out-of-date recreation areas and by helping to plant groves of Olympic trees at 1,600 schools and communities throughout Utah, with more than 7,000 trees to be planted over a four-year period.

Centennial of the Forest Service

Bosworth was able to oversee the events surrounding the centennial of the Forest Service in 2005. The New Century of Service program was a five-year effort focusing on public service as the Forest Service approached its 100-year anniversary. In the spring of 1905, the forest reserves (now national forests) were transferred from Department of the Interior management to USDA management. Then, on July 1, with the start of the new fiscal year, the USDA Bureau of Forestry was renamed the Forest Service. The New Century of Service program commemorated the Forest Service's rich history in land stewardship, its successes, and the lessons learned; it also looks forward to the next century, sharing and acknowledging excellence in the work, programs, and ideas of the agency. The New Century of Service program was responsible for many internal and external events before 2005 and during 2005; it ended in late 2005.

The lead-off for the centennial came in January 2005 with the Forest Service Centennial Forest Congress, held in Washington, D.C. The Centennial Congress began on January 3, exactly 100 years after the 1905 Forest Congress called by the American Forestry Association after Gifford Pinchot applied his political pressure through President Roosevelt.

The 2005 Forest Service Centennial Congress commemorated 100 years of conservation, assessed current challenges and opportunities, and initiated a dialogue for the twenty-first century to meet the needs of present and future generations. It brought together congressional leaders, representatives from agency partners and interests, leading academicians, select state and local government representatives, key governors, media leaders, and Forest Service leaders to honor the creation of the agency and to provide a contemporary focus for the future. Forest Service regions, research stations, and state and private areas convened centennial forums throughout the United States in advance of the Congress in order to provide various perspectives in framing challenges for the future. Congress provided money for the Forest Congress in the FY05 appropriations bill. In order to produce this Centennial Congress, the Forest Service worked closely with a variety of partners, including National Forest Foundation, the Nature Conservancy, the Boone and Crockett Club, the Society of American Foresters, and American Forests. A total of about 3,000 people participated in the event, including the 12 regional forums and the major event in Washington. At the Centennial Congress, the Secretaries of Agriculture and Interior, all the living chiefs of the agency, heads of other federal agencies, and interested parties participated, freely giving their comments on the past century and advice for the future.

Another major event was the participation by the Forest Service in the Smithsonian's thirty-ninth annual Folklife Festival, on the National Mall, on June 23–27 and June 30- July 4, 2005. The Folklife Festival is a living cultural exhibition that generally includes musical performances, craft demonstrations, illustrations of worklore, community heritage celebrations, discussions of traditional and grass-roots culture, and interviews and that often attracts more than a million visitors. The Secretary of the Smithsonian Institution invited the Forest Service to partici-pate "to produce a program on the occupational culture of forest management in the United States at the 39th annual Smithsonian Folklife Festival." The Folklife Festival coincided with the Forest Service's one-hundredth anniversary, on July 1, 2005. The Forest Service was only the third federal agency ever invited to partici-pate in the Festival (the White House and the Smithsonian were the first two).

Forest Service interviewers collected 420 video interviews during the selection process for the Folklife Festival. The theme of "Forest Service, Culture, and Com-munity" brought more than 100 participants to the National Mall, including tree pathologists, wildlife biologists, law enforcement officers, horticulturalists, bota-nists, bird banders, archaeologists, firefighters, smokejumpers, recreation special-ists, backcountry rangers, and camp cooks. An "interactive forest" featured two dozen live trees and provided an area for tree doctors, rangers, and interpreters to conduct hands-on tours for visitors. The "sounds of the forest" stage featured bluegrass, country-western, and folk music, much of it performed by Forest Service employees. Those selected by the Smithsonian to participate were chosen for their ability to showcase the many aspects of Forest Service occupational culture and the heritage of more than 30,000 employees.

REORGANIZING AND SAFETY

Albuquerque Service Center

The Albuquerque service center was established in 2005. In an effort to save money, the Forest Service began to centralize its human resources (HR) and bud-get and finance operations at a single location in Albuquerque, New Mexico, for an anticipated savings of $20 million a year. Forest Service Chief Dale Bosworth said that "this decision demonstrates the agency's commitment to becoming leaner, more efficient and more cost effective…. A single center, unifying all HR opera-tions, will provide the most consistent and cost effective service for our employees and managers. In addition, we will be more responsive to taxpayers."

The choice to centralize units resulted from a year-long agencywide review of HR performance prompted by the 2000 president's management agenda, which encouraged federal departments to become more efficient and cost effective. The study found, in comparing the agency's HR costs to those of other organizations in the public and private sectors, that the main reason for the high cost of administering an HR program in the Forest Service is that the agency is so decentralized. When the centralization is completed, there will be nearly 300 positions in Albuquerque, with another 130 distributed throughout the agency.

Labor Contracts and Safety

In early December 2005, Chief Dale Bosworth responded to a three-part *Sacramento Bee* report published November 13–15. The investigation uncovered a large number of injuries and hazardous working conditions among the 15,000 to 20,000 Latino workers or pineros who work in the woods doing planting and thinning for private contractors. The chief proposed that the Forest Service change the way it supervises labor contracts to better protect migrant Latino forest workers. He said, "My biggest frustration out of this is I want the Forest Service to have a culture of safety."

RESTORATION OF ECOSYSTEMS

Protection of resources and restoration of degraded areas were the primary reasons for the creation of the Forest Service and the establishment of the national forests and grasslands. The Organic Act, the Weeks Act, the Multiple-Use Sustained-Yield Act, the National Forest Management Act, and other statutes governing the management of the national forests and grasslands reinforce these fundamental purposes. Over the past century, the Forest Service has been quite successful in achieving these purposes while simultaneously meeting public demands for various uses of the national forest system. However, efforts are still required from all management levels in the agency to protect the forests and grasslands, which face serious threats to their long-term health, productivity, and diversity.

In the last part of 2005, the Forest Service initiated a new initiative called the restoration policy. Basically, the new policy is designed to develop "a strategic, integrated, science-based framework for restoring and maintaining forest and grassland ecological condition." Change to ecosystems are from nonnative invasive species, altered disturbance regimes, and climate change. These changes affect aquatic and terrestrial ecosystems in virtually every region of the country. Active management is often needed to reach reduce the threat posed by such changes. Yet the magnitude of ecosystem restoration needs greatly exceeds the organizational and financial capacity of the agency.

On many parts of the national forest system, ecological conditions and trends, combined with recent and projected climate trends, pose serious threats to the long-term health, productivity, and diversity of forest and grassland ecosystems. A few examples suffice to illustrate the threats:

- In the Great Basin, pinyon-juniper communities are replacing sagebrush-dominated plant communities as a result of fire suppression and overgrazing.
- In the East, oak-dominated systems are widely converting to maple, beech, and other shade-tolerant species due to alterations in natural and human disturbance regimes, a trend exacerbated by severe gypsy moth infestations.

- Native fish populations are declining and fragmenting because of manmade barriers to movement, altered flow regimes, and competition from nonnative fishes.
- Watersheds, riparian areas, and aquatic communities are degrading due to past management activities, fragmentation, overgrazing, and the impacts of nonnative invasive species such as purple loosestrife, salt-cedar, and zebra mussel.
- Nonnative invasive species such as emerald ash borer, hemlock woolly adelgid, white pine blister rust, and sudden oak death are causing widespread forest damage.
- Remnants of tallgrass prairie are suffering damage due to fire suppression and invasion by exotic species such as leafy spurge, Russian olive, and Kentucky bluegrass.
- In southern California, chaparral and coastal scrub communities are converting to weedy grassland due to extremely high numbers of human-caused fires.

The draft restoration framework offers four recommendations to improve the agency's ability to restore ecosystems:

- Adopting a national policy regarding ecosystem restoration, including defining ecosystem restoration as "the process of assisting the recovery of an ecosystem that has been degraded, damaged, or destroyed";
- Increasing the productivity of the agency's restoration efforts through improved integration of various programs;
- Effectively applying national forest and project planning to engage Forest Service resources, partners, and stakeholders in identifying and implementing restoration needs and priorities; and
- Using budget and performance incentives to increase accomplishment of ecosystem restoration objectives.

One recent example of ecosystem change occurred in northeastern Oregon. In 2005, the School Fire ravaged 52,000 acres of the Umatilla National Forest and adjacent grasslands held in state and private ownership. The fire produced an opportunity to replace the non-native grass species with native grasses, which are more resistant to fire and provide better grazing habitat for wildlife, cattle, and sheep. Helicopters were used to spread 21,000 pounds of grass seed across the blackened terrain. The project, as evaluated in early 2006, was highly successful in restoring and improving grassland and forest habitats.

☆ 3 ☆

Structure and Functions of the Forest Service

The Forest Service has several important divisions; the first manages 193 million acres of the national forest system, the second supports cooperation under state and private forestry functions, and the third conducts primary-research activities on ecosystems and their many components. Each one of these divisions is discussed in this chapter. In addition, several subtopics are presented to show the many varied activities of the agency, including work in international programs, roadless and wilderness programs, and forest fires and firefighting. Unfortunately, there are a host of other important functions, including engineering, landscape architecture, heritage, recreation, mining, geographic information systems (GIS), geography and geology, public affairs, fiscal, and human resources, that are not included for discussion.

MANAGING THE NATIONAL FOREST SYSTEM

As mentioned in Chapter 1, the current national forest system grew out of a late-nineteenth-century congressional act that gave the president authority to establish forest reserves on the public domain. This Creative or Forest Reserve Act of 1891 was supplemented by the Organic Act of 1897 and the Weeks Act of 1911. The forest reserves/national forests in the West were almost all set by 1900, while the national forests in the East began to take shape from 1916 through the late 1940s through purchase and land gifts. Few national forests have been established since that time; however, the names of the forests have in many cases changed and the land base for management has changed with the renaming. For example, the George Washington National Forest and the Jefferson National Forest are now managed together as the George Washington-Jefferson National Forests. The total area for the national forest system, as of September 2004, is 192.9 million acres.

The Forest Service is still purchasing small amounts of forestland to protect critical resources areas and provide increased public recreation opportunities. Eminent domain legal procedures are not used. There is also an active program of exchanging lands with private parties to achieve a desired national forest land-ownership pattern, which often translates to "blocking ownership"; that is, some private lands within a national forest official boundary are exchanged for national forestland along the edge of the forest or in a more remote section. Lands all under one ownership are easier to manage. In making these exchanges, there is a complicated system to determine the fair market value of lands purchased or exchanged, so that transaction is fair to the public and the landowner involved. The agency also responds to congressional requests to adjust boundaries. Occasionally, the agency accepts donations of land to protect archeological, historical, or other significant sites. At other times, Congress specifies transfer of land from one agency to another, such as a transfer of national forest system (NFS) land from the Forest Service to the National Park Service to create a new national park.

Since the beginning of the agency, in 1905, the Forest Service has been actively involved in surveying national forest boundaries to identify and protect private and public lands, as well as maintaining records of national forestland areas, land transactions, land status, permitted uses, and easements. The Forest Service also authorizes permitted uses on the NFS, such as power lines to provide electricity to communities, authorizing rights-of-way for roads to private in-holdings—such as mining claims—within the forest, ensuring that hydroelectric projects protect riparian areas on the national forest, and securing public road and trail access.

National forest watersheds provide about 14 percent of the surface water supply in the United States. There are approximately 6,000 watersheds on NFS lands that produce an average 190 million acre-feet of water annually. There are 3,336 municipalities, serving 60 million people, that get their tap water from NFS lands. A total of 173 trillion gallons of water are supplied by NFS municipal watersheds annually. The NFS also protects air quality through 88 Class I wildernesses totaling15 million acres. All of these areas are monitored for regional haze and are part of a nationwide multiagency network.

But management of the NFS has not been easy, especially in recent years. On average, the Forest Service has had more than 200 lawsuits pending at any given time that challenge resource management decisions. These land management decisions, filed under the National Environmental Policy Act of 1969, consist each year of some 10,000 decision memorandums, 5,000 environmental assessments, and 250 environmental impact statements. In the year 2001, more than 1,200 projects, plans, and permit decisions were appealed administratively.

Budget

The Forest Service budget is provided through the annual Department of the Interior bill, one of the 13 bills that fund the federal government. Funding for the Forest Service is included under Title II Related Agencies, Title IV Wildland Fire

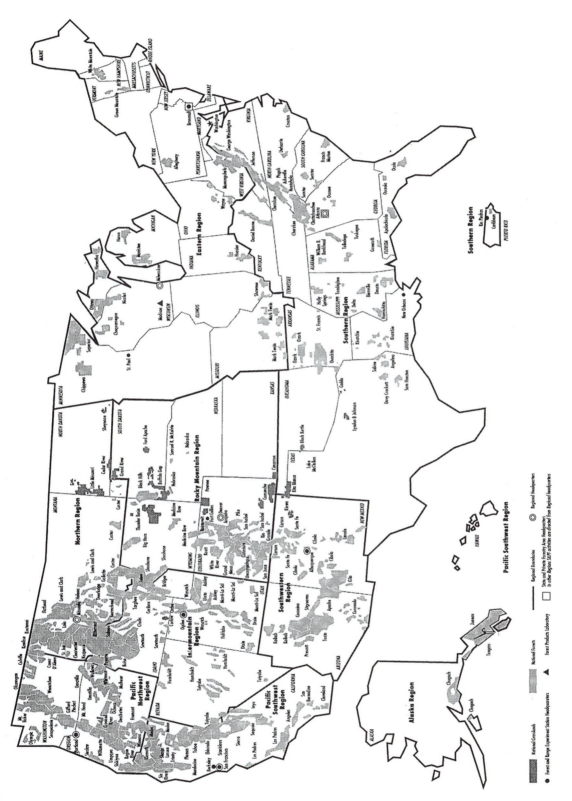

Map of the National forest system, showing regional boundaries. (USDA Forest Service)

Emergency Appropriations, Title V Emergency Supplemental Appropriations, and Title VIII Land Conservation, Preservation, and Infrastructure Improvement. The Interior bill funds the agencies of the Department of the Interior but also funds related agencies and/or other stand-alone agencies such as the Environmental Protection Agency, Health and Human Services, the Smithsonian Institution, the Forest Service, the Holocaust Museum, the Presidio Trust, the National Endowment for the Humanities, the Advisory Council on Historic Preservation, and the National Capital Planning Commission. The Forest Service is included in the Interior and Related Agency bill, but the Interior Department has no involvement in specific budget allocation or decisions. Originally, the budget was part of the Department of Agriculture annual budget. Chief Richard McArdle (1952–1962) explained that the Forest Service was funded under the annual Agriculture bill until FY 1956. In 1955, during hearings in the House of Representatives, McArdle was informed that the Forest Service budget was being transferred from the USDA to the USDI committee. This transfer had been ordered by Congressman Clarence Cannon of Missouri, chair of the House Appropriations Committee, who wanted to put all the public works appropriations under one subcommittee, which he would head. The reasons were purely political.

Employees

During the 20-year period from around 1985 to 2005, there has been roughly a 50 percent reduction agencywide in the number of staff foresters, engineering technicians, civil engineers, and contractors. At the same time, the Forest Service's workforce has continued to age and retire, and many of these lifelong employees are not being replaced because of budget concerns. The Forest Service's diversity profile does not match the general population but is getting better. The Forest Service continues to focus on hiring individuals from various ethnic groups and meeting its changing skill needs. The National Academy of Public Administration (NAPA) submitted a Forest Service workforce plan in November of 1999. In that plan, NAPA recommended developing a strategic recruitment plan that identifies "actions necessary to acquire and/or develop a workforce that meets changing mission priorities." Today, the agency has around 31,000 employees and a summer temporary workforce exceeding 14,000. (See Figure 3.1.)

Employment Programs

Congress has enacted a number of laws that authorize the federal government, and especially the Forest Service, to provide employment opportunities for seniors, youths, and volunteers. These programs provide job opportunities, training, and education for the unemployed, the underemployed, the elderly, the young, and others with special needs, while benefiting high-priority conservation work. In FY 2001, these programs included more than 108,700 participants and accomplished more than $115 million in conservation work on Forest Service lands.

FIGURE 3.1 Forest Service Employees 1891 to Present

Year	GLO[1] And FS[2] Employees	Full-Time Employees	Part-Time Employees[3]
1898–July 1	265	45	215
1899–Jan. 1	77	27	50
1899–June 1	191	44	157
1899–July 1	296	46	250
1899–July 15	350		
1899–Nov. 9	100	15	85
1899–Dec. 31	38		
1900–June 30	400		
1901–June 30	475		
1902–June 30	425		
1903–June 30	441		
1904–June 30	534		
1904–Dec. 31	734		
1905–June 30[4]	609		
1906–June 30	1,002		
1907–June 30	1,289		
1912–June 30	2,895	2,115	780
1938–June 30	4,280		
1955–June 30	18,430	9,116	9,314
1975–June 30	49,759	19,568	30,191
1980–June 30	61,279	21,421	39,858
1985–June 30	47,943	29,211	18,732
1990–Sept. 30	46,792	31,762	15,030
1995–Sept. 30	43,685	30,676	13,009
2000–Sept. 30	39,437	28,088	11,349
2003–Sept. 30	45,361	31,029	14,332

Notes: [1] USDI General Land Office employees. Includes GLO state superintendents and forest reserve supervisors; [2] Only those employed at the field level in national forest and inspection office levels in the organization are counted, as Washington office employees are counted separately; [3] Some rangers were carried over the winter, but most were released after the fall fire season; [4] Management of the Forest Reserves was transferred from the USDI General Land Office (Division R) to the USDA Bureau of Forestry on February 1, 1905. On July 1, 1905, the USDA Forest Service was established.

The Senior Community Service Employment Program (SCSEP) is designed to provide useful part-time employment, work experience, training, and transition to public and private unsubsidized employment for persons age 55 and over. The Forest Service is the only federal agency among 10 national sponsors. In 2001, 5,537 older workers participated in SCSEP, and 44 percent of these were women. The program operated with a $28.4 million budget, while accomplishing $39.4 million of useful work, thereby producing about $1.39 return on dollar invested. Approximately 29 percent of the enrollees (1,160 seniors) were placed in unsubsidized employment.

The Youth Conservation Corps (YCC) is a summer employment program designed for persons ages 15–18 to accomplish projects that further the development and conservation of natural resources. The Forest Service was directed to use not less than $2 million of agency appropriations for high-priority projects to be carried out by the YCC program. As of 2001, there were 891 YCC enrollees, 42 percent of whom were women. The YCC program had $2.2 million in operating costs, while accomplishing $2.6 million of work, producing $1.18 return on dollar invested.

The Volunteers in the National Forests program allows organizations and individuals to donate their talents and services to help manage the nation's natural resources. In 2001, 84,508 volunteers participated (including 80 international volunteers), accomplishing $38.6 million of work. Of the number of volunteers, 36 percent were women. More than 1.6 million volunteers have served since the 1972 enabling legislation.

The Forest Service has been operating Job Corps Centers since 1965. The Job Corps program is the only federal residential education/training program for the nation's disadvantaged youth. In the Job Corps program, as of 2001, there were 9,528 enrollees, ages 16–24, and the program had a $114.6 million budget. The enrollees accomplished around $18.3 million of work for the Forest Service. Enrollees, of whom 48 percent were minorities, were paid an $8.42 average starting hourly wage. By the end of the enrollment period, 91 percent of the students placed (based on participants enrolled) were able to find work in the private or public sector. Through an agreement with the U.S. Department of Labor, the Forest Service operates 18 coeducational Job Corps Civilian Conservation Centers on NFS lands:

Anaconda (MT)	Boxelder (SD)
Flatwoods (VA)	Jacobs Creek (TN)
Pine Knot (KY)	Timber Lake (OR)
Angell (OR)	Cass (AR)
Frenchburg (KY)	Lyndon B. Johnson (NC)
Pine Ridge (NE)	Trapper Creek (MT)
Blackwell (WI)	Curlew (WA)
Golconda (IL)	Ouachita (AR)
Schenck (NC)	Wolf Creek (OR)

Hosted programs provide conservation training and work opportunities on national forests or in conjunction with federal programs. Programs are administered through agreements with state and county agencies, colleges, universities, Indian tribes, and private and nonprofit organizations. In 2001, there were 8,333 participants who accomplished $16.3 million worth of work. Of the hosted-program enrollees, 23 percent were women and 29 percent were minorities.

Law Enforcement and Investigations

The Law Enforcement and Investigations (LEI) program is charged with the protection of people and natural resources on the national forest system lands, which are visited by hundreds of millions of people each year. The LEI program is composed of Forest Service law enforcement officers and agents who respond to around 200,000 incidents per year. These incidents encompass a wide range of criminal and noncriminal activity. As of 2005, Forest Service had approximately 380 uniformed officers patrolling NFS lands nationwide and 120 criminal investigators assigned to Forest Service offices throughout the country. In addition, law enforcement personnel made more than a million public contacts for a variety of reasons, such as providing general information, obtaining information on criminal matters, and assisting with visitors' problems.

LEI cooperates with federal, state, and local law enforcement agencies and other Forest Service programs to achieve these goals. The uniformed officers provide a high-visibility uniformed presence in the national forests. They also provide prompt responses to public and employee safety incidents, as well as violations of laws and regulations. They conduct criminal investigations. While the FS does not have immigration authority, the agency does have drug enforcement authorities and other responsibilities on the hundreds of miles of contiguous NFS lands along both the southwest and the northern borders. In addition, they reduce the production of domestic cannabis (marijuana) and other controlled substances and reduce smuggling of illegal drugs through NFS lands. Chief Dale Robertson said that "We calculated once that in the state of California the value of the marijuana grown on the national forests exceeded the value of the timber harvested in California that year. I mean, it was big business." The historian Harold Steen reported that the Forest Service increased law enforcement "by bringing in 'real professionals that were very serious about their job.' It did not always work well; the law enforcement officer reported to the forest supervisor who was used to making trade-offs. The 'law enforcement folk didn't relate to that at all.' When the public would enter a national forest, by their training, the law officers viewed the visitors with suspicion; after all, they might do something wrong. That was not the Forest Service way, and soon some officers were investigating their bosses, who apparently were not serious enough about crime prevention. But there in fact was some wrong-doing by a few forest supervisors themselves, and that news 'got to Congress.'" Chief Robertson found that the Forest Service annual appropriations contained a rider that law enforcement would be reorganized as a separate organization, in which officers reported to other officers instead of district rangers, forest supervisors, or regional foresters—a so-called stovepipe model. LEI authority now flows from top to bottom, instead of through the four administrative levels common to the

Law enforcement K-9 unit, Mt. Hood National Forest, Oregon, 2006. (Gerald Williams Personal Collection)

Forest Service. Robertson said, "My forest supervisors thought I sold them down the drain on that, but I didn't."

The National Forest System Drug Control Act of 1986, amended in 1988, placed primary responsibility on the Forest Service for federal drug enforcement on NFS lands, with authority over (1) marijuana cultivation, (2) metamphetamine production, and (3) smuggling across the U.S./Mexico and U.S./Canada borders. The LEO duties are problematic in cases involving hard drugs, especially meth labs abandoned or dumped on the forests because the perpetrators are long gone by the time the drug materials are found. These drug problems are becoming increasingly common in national forests located adjacent to large metropolitan areas. In some cases, dead bodies are also found dumped on the national forests, especially near large metropolitan areas—many related to drug and gang violence.

Law enforcement became a separate, independent organization with many law enforcement duties. The primary focus of law enforcement work is the protection of natural resources, protection of Forest Service employees (including protection of the chief on request or when threats against his life are made), and the protection of visitors. At times, accidental deaths and traffic accidents are reported and investigated in cooperation with local law enforcement agencies. Forest Service law enforcement officers (LEOs) are authorized to carry firearms and defensive equipment, make arrests, execute search warrants, complete reports, and testify in court. The LEOs enforce the 36 Code of Federal Regulations, parts 242–261. Part 242 refers specifically to subsistence hunting and fishing regulations and is applicable only to federal land in Alaska. Part 261 refers to regulations that apply to all NFS lands nationwide. A list of activities that LEOs perform routinely includes:

- Working closely with local, state, and other federal law enforcement officials
- Working cooperatively on search and rescue operations
- Providing emergency medical aid
- Investigating injuries and deaths on the NFS
- Assisting special agents with internal investigations of criminal activity
- Protecting archaeological/heritage resources
- Conducting informational and educational programs
- Investigating timber thefts
- Investigating forest fires
- Enforcing state motor vehicle laws on forest roads
- Investigating vehicle accidents
- Investigating vehicle break-ins and thefts
- Enforcing fish and wildlife regulations

- Investigating controlled substance distribution and manufacture (drug trafficking)
- Serving search and arrest warrants
- Investigating ecoterrorism

Timber Management

Approximately 73 percent of the 193 million acres of national forests is considered forested. Of the forested land, 29 percent is available for regularly scheduled timber harvest, while less than 1 percent is subject to some form of timber harvest treatment in any given year. The remaining 71 percent of the forested land is protected as wilderness or used for recreation or cannot be harvested due to environmental or economic conditions such as steep slopes, fragile soils, and lack of feasible access.

Timber Famine

The timber famine idea helped to start the late 1800s conservation movement. The phrase "timber famine" (also called "timber depletion") once raised the fears throughout the country in the late 1800s and early 1900s. It raised the specter of deforestation due to the encroachment of civilization on the forests and their resultant destruction, the conversion of the forests to agriculture, an increasing consumption of wood products, and destruction of the forests by wildfire. Probably the most disturbing notion of the timber famine idea was that the forests of America and the world would be cut down for profit and that nothing would remain for future generations. Much of the cut-over eastern and southern forests were converted to farm and grazing lands, and the wood was used for heating, building homes and other structures, and supplying the massive need for railroad ties. Eventually, however, the growing cities, railroads, and highways would accelerate replacement of both the forests and the farms.

Several early writers suggested that the loss of the forests would have catastrophic effects on the future, eventually causing the downfall of civilization. Reaction to the writers who brought such bad news and projections about the forthcoming timber famine was understandable, and the idea that the United States needed to save standing forests for the future won adherents. The idea of preventing such a catastrophe would take decades to mature. The basic question still is whether the notion of timber famine or depletion is a myth or reality. Was there really ever a crisis, or is it an interesting historical example of supply and demand? As early as 1864, George Perkins Marsh, in his book *Man and Nature; or, Physical Geography as Modified by Human Action*, warned that human actions were harming the land, especially the timber resource.

On August 21, 1873, Franklin B. Hough presented a paper titled "On the Duty of Governments in the Preservation of Forests" at the AAAS annual meeting, held in Portland, Maine. In the presentation, he proposed that the AAAS and Congress act to preserve and protect the remaining forests of the United States.

Hough became the first federal forester in the government in 1873. In the introduction to his book, *Report upon Forestry 1877,* Hough commented that the timber

> supplies have within a few years past been found scarce, and their prices have advanced to a degree that is sensibly felt by all classes of the population. ... But in these older and naturally well-timbered sections of the country, thoughtful persons have for years been watching the wasting of supplies and the complete exhaustion of one forest region after another with an anxiety natural with those who look forward to the probable conditions that must necessarily exist in another generation, and who feel the responsibilities of the present with regard to the future.... It has been observed in all countries and at all periods, that trees furnishing products demanded by commerce, or standing in the way of cultivation, become an object of inconsiderable waste.

President Theodore Roosevelt was convinced, probably by Gifford Pinchot, chief of the Bureau of Forestry, that timber depletion was a fact. In early 1905, the president addressed the issue of timber famine to the American forest congress:

> Our country, we have faith to believe, is only at the beginning of its growth. Unless the vast forests of the United States can be made ready to meet the vast demands which this growth will inevitably bring, commercial disaster, that means disaster for the whole country, is inevitable. The railroads must have ties.... The miner must have timber [for tunnel supports].... If the present rate of forest destruction is allowed to continue, with nothing to offset it, a timber famine in the future is inevitable.

In that sense, the application of scientific forestry principles (preservation/ protection of the forests and sustained yield) would bring salvation to the nation's timber famine. Even President Roosevelt, in a speech probably written by Pinchot, declared, at the White House conference on conservation that met May 13–18, 1908, that:

> We are on the verge of a timber famine in this country, and it is unpardonable for the Nation or the States to permit any further cutting of our timber save in accordance with a system which will provide that the next generation shall see the timber increased instead of diminished.

Many of the Progressive-era foresters believed that the only way to provide timber for the future, and thus to alleviate the timber famine, was to cut the forests slowly or conservatively. A few foresters believed that federal control of the timber industry would be the most effective way to prevent over harvesting. There were those, however, in the private forest industry who did not fully believe in the principles of conservation espoused by President Roosevelt, Pinchot, and the Forest Service. In any case, the prospect of slowing the harvest or government control was abhorrent to the industry.

Sustained Yield

The idea of sustained yield operations on the public and private forests was beginning to take hold in the 1910s and 1920s. For many it was the answer to holding off the coming timber famine. In 1911, Burt P. Kirkland, a Forest Service researcher, argued that national forests should be managed on a sustained yield basis so that the huge federal timber holdings could be used in the future when the private timber harvesting would be reduced because of overharvesting. David T. Mason, a former Forest Service employee, developed a comprehensive idea of sustained yield forestry practices that would hold the attention of both public and private foresters for the next several decades and would be applied by law, in 1937, to the Oregon and California Grants Lands, under GLO (now Bureau of Land Management) administration, and to the national forests, in 1944. However, the new term "sustained yield forestry" was essentially the same notion as that proposed by Pinchot, which he called "conservative lumbering." The notion of a timber famine is never far from discussions even today, although the terms have changed. Selective harvesting, sustained yield, nondeclining even-flow, forest depletion, community stability, old growth, regulation of/ best management forest practices, seedling replanting, plantation forestry, forest firefighting, insect and disease control, ecosystem management, and even the no-cut goals of several environmental organizations are grounded in the timber famine ideas of the early twentieth century.

Timber Harvesting

Timber harvesting has always been a goal of the national forest system. Beginning as early as the Organic Act of 1897, cutting trees for use has been a major activity of the agency. Although the Forest Reserve Act of 1891 established presidential authority to create forest reserves, there was no provision for their management. One of the underlying premises of the act was that the private timberlands were being cut at rates that could not be sustained, especially since reforestation was mostly a dream. The Organic Administration Act of 1897 was written, in part, to "furnish a continuous supply of timber for the use and necessities of citizens of the United States." However, the congressional debate and the 1897 Act's implementing regulations made it clear that timber cutting was always considered to be a permitted, not a required, part of forest management. The Organic Act also allowed the General Land Office (GLO) to manage the forest reserves. The first timber sale by the GLO (Case No. 1) was to the Homestake Mining Company for timber off the Black Hills Forest Reserve in 1898. Fifteen million board feet were purchased at a dollar per thousand board feet. The contract required that no trees smaller than eight inches in diameter be removed, and after harvest the brush left behind had to be "piled" and burned.

When the management of the forest reserves was moved from the Department of the Interior to the Department of Agriculture, in 1905, Chief Gifford Pinchot was concerned that the reserves (renamed national forests in 1907) should pay for themselves, that is, not be a drain on the U.S. Treasury. The most direct way for the Forest Service to show a profit was by charging for grazing and selling timber. By 1907, timber sold from the national forests amounted to just 950 million board feet, which was only 2 percent of the nation's 44 billion board feet cut that year. Pinchot finally gave up, stating that "the National Forests exist not for the sake of revenue to the Government, but for the sake of the welfare of the public."

Through the 1920s, there were few timber sales, and those that were made were usually quite large, involving entire drainages. These large timber sales, other than those for small operations, were designed for railroad logging operations that would harvest the drainages over decades. The timber sales program collapsed in the 1930s with the advent of the Great Depression.

A 1928 pamphlet titled "Deforested America," by Major George P. Ahern, warned of the risks of depending on private forests and the forest industry for future supplies of timber. Instead, Ahern argued, government control was required to ensure that sustained yield forestry would be practiced on commercial forestlands. The argument for federal regulation of private forestry was codified in Article X of the Lumber Code, which became effective on June 1, 1934. Although the code was ruled unconstitutional by the Supreme Court less than a year later, the timber industry was generally supportive of efforts at self-regulation to end widespread forest devastation, to increase cooperation between industry members, and to cooperate more closely with the Forest Service. Until 1940, almost 100 percent of the timber cut came from private holdings. The NFS supplied very little timber, in part because the private timber industry did not want the Forest Service to flood the market with cheap federal timber. The reality was that most of the national forest timber was inaccessible because of either a lack of roads or railroads, high elevation, or steep terrain.

Because of the defense needs that arose during World War II, timber sales increased in the early 1940s. The Forest Service began to think about the needs after the war, and Congress passed the Sustained Yield Management Act of 1944. This act allowed the agency to sign agreements with the timber industry and communities to establish either cooperative sustained yield units or federal units. Only one cooperative unit (Shelton, on the Washington's Olympic National Forest) and five federal units, in the states of Washington, Oregon, California, Arizona, and New Mexico, were ever established.

With the return of the veterans after the war, a baby boom took place (60 million births from 1946 to 1964) during a period of economic growth fueled by low interest rates and massive housing starts. Other federal agencies answered this call for goods, as well. The rapid depletion of old growth timber on private lands in the 1950s further reinforced the need for increased harvests on federal lands. During the 1950s, timber harvests on national forests almost tripled, from about 3 billion board feet in 1950 to almost 9 billion at the end of the decade. By this time, the timber cut on the NFS was approximately one-third of the nation's total. The impact was felt most in Pacific Northwest Region, the major producer of softwood timber in the national forest system (see Appendix 5). However, for those without a forestry background, the growing number of clearcuts resulted in something that closely resembled the devastated look of private lands. It was time to take action.

The Multiple-Use Act of 1960 set new priorities for the agency, essentially giving equal footing to the five major resources on the national forests: timber, wildlife, range, water, and outdoor recreation. By the late 1960s, the Forest Service faced increasing opposition because of major controversies on the Bitterroot National

Forest, in Montana, involving clearcutting and terracing and on the Monongahela National Forest in West Virginia, also about clearcutting. A lawsuit (*Izaak Walton v. Butz*) was filed on the Monongahela controversy by the Izaak Walton League. A court ruling in 1973 on the case went against the Forest Service practice of timber harvesting under the rules of the Organic Act of 1897. Congressional action was necessary to "fix" the law. Congress therefore passed sweeping legislation, called the National Forest Management Act of 1976, which pushed deep into the agency's traditional autonomy and imposed many new requirements and substantive restrictions, almost all of which revolved around timber harvesting.

Clearcutting

Clearcutting, that is the felling and removing all the trees from a specific area, has been a long-standing technique used extensively in the United States and in other countries. From the late to today, many people opposed to logging in general have focused on clearcutting. It has also been the focus of intensive discussion about the proper method for harvesting trees for their wood.

It was at George Vanderbilt's Biltmore forest estate (now part of the Pisgah National Forest) in the 1890s that Gifford Pinchot first harbored ideas about "new

Clearcutting patterns on Shelton Ranger District, Olympic National Forest, Washington, 1957. (USDA Forest Service)

forestry"—clearcutting versus selective logging while leaving young trees standing during harvesting, as recounted in Pinchot's 1947 autobiography, *Breaking New Ground*: "The old way of lumbering at Biltmore, and everywhere else, was to cut out all the young growth that would interfere with cheap and easy logging, and leave desolation and a firetrap behind…. We found that large trees surrounded by a dense growth of smaller trees could be logged with surprisingly little injury to the young growth, and that the added cost of taking care was small—out of proportion to the result. To establish this fact … was of immense importance to the success of Forestry in America." Thus, from the beginning of professional forestry in America, there was concern about logging methods that involved ecology and economics.

The first major controversy involving clearcutting erupted in the Adirondacks of New York State in 1900–1903. At the Cornell Demonstration Forest, Bernhard Fernow, chair of the Cornell School of Forestry, intended to convert the broadleaf forest into a conifer forest. The Adirondacks case came under public scrutiny, with Fernow eventually losing his position at Cornell as a result of the controversy; the school of forestry closed.

During the 1910s and 1920s, administrators of the national forests emphasized clearcutting as the most desired method of logging. Because most logging operations were then either railroad or river log drives, clearcutting was practical for the timber purchaser. At the time, huge blocks of national forest were sold to timber companies with the idea that extracting the standing timber in a watershed would take decades. But there were researchers, especially in the dry pine forests and elsewhere, who advocated selective logging.

In October 1934, after reviewing several research studies, Regional Forester C. J. Buck directed the national forests in eastern Oregon and eastern Washington to begin timber harvesting by selective logging, rather than by clearcutting in the dry Douglas-fir areas. Basically, there was a fundamental disagreement among Forest Service and academic researchers over clearcutting. Two University of Washington forestry professors, Burt P. Kirkland and Axel J. F. Brandstorm, argued that "selective timber management" was economically advantageous, because loggers did not have to take every tree, and that selective logging did not lay the landscape bare. Two Forest Service researchers, Leo Isaac and Thornton T. Munger, however, argued that selective logging was a short-term economic gimmick used during the Depression that would, in the long run, deplete the forests, since only the prime trees would be taken from a stand, leaving the less desirable species on site. They also argued that selective logging practices damaged the trees that remained on the site and that clearcutting was much better. The selective-logging method was used in the Pacific Northwest Region dry-site Douglas-fir area until the early 1940s, when C. J. Buck was forcibly transferred to the Washington office and the policy changed back to clearcutting.

Research continued in the Pacific Northwest, and by the early 1950s there was enough evidence to convince most professional foresters that clearcutting was the most desirable method of tree harvesting in the Douglas-fir region. These data were compelling from the economics standpoint and from the ecological standpoint, which argued that the seedlings required direct sunlight to grow. However, the research overlooked several important aspects and consequences of clearcutting: the visual disruption of the forest for at least a decade until the young trees grew tall and the aspect of having a monoculture of genetically similar trees. Even "hiding" clearcuts behind a row of standing tall trees and a public education effort to "educate" the public to clearcutting did not overcome the ill feelings toward this method of tree harvesting. Many people, then and now, believe that clearcutting is of economic advantage, rather than being necessary for tree regrowth or having ecological benefit.

In the late 1960s, Montana's Bitterroot National Forest, in a burst of timber harvesting in response to the national need for wood, began clearcutting, then terracing the cut-over slopes for better seedling regeneration. This caused a huge controversy. The Bitterroot's retired Forest Supervisor led protests, the *Missoulian* carried a series of news articles, and Senator Lee Metcalf commissioned a University of Montana study team to review the alleged mismanagement. The university team, led by Arnold Bolle, dean of the School of Forestry, was instrumental in bringing the Bitterroot's clearcutting to national attention.

Another clearcutting controversy, on West Virginia's Monongahela National Forest, contributed significantly to the management debate. Two coal miners who loved to turkey hunt on the Monongahela visited the area where they often hunted and instead found a massive clearcut. Angry, they talked with the local district ranger, the forest supervisor, and even Chief Ed Cliff. At all levels of the organization, they received essentially the same response—the Forest Service is composed of university-trained foresters hired by the government to care for the national forests, Congress wants timber cut from the forests, and clearcutting is the best way to accomplish the job. Cliff later noted that "I can admit . . . I didn't fully or quickly recognize the total potential of the strength of the opposition that was developing against such things as clearcutting. Clearcutting is a perfectly sound silvicultural management system if it's properly applied.... It soon got beyond the turkey hunting issue." The Izaak Walton League, an outdoor and fishing organization, filed a lawsuit on behalf of the turkey hunters on the premise that the 1897 Organic Act did not allow clearcutting, thereby challenging the legal basis for the customary timber management on the national forests. In 1973, the federal District Court for West Virginia ruled against the Forest Service (*Izaak Walton v. Butz*). After the Fourth Circuit Court of Appeals also ruled against the agency in August 1975 (*Izaak Walton v. Butz*), the Forest Service and Congress decided that something had to be done to change the old law on timber harvesting.

The Bitterroot and Monongahela battles resulted in a series of congressional hearings over clearcutting and forest management in general. Senator Frank Church, of Idaho, offered an analysis report on clearcutting that resulted in the "Church Guidelines" for limiting the size of clearcuts to 40 acres. The Forest Service voluntarily agreed to stay within these guidelines. The final result of the controversy was passage of the National Forest Management Act of 1976 (NFMA).

The problems with clearcutting persisted, despite NFMA and the Church guidelines. Chief Dale Robertson noted that "traditional forestry would no longer fly in the federal government . . . no matter how much we foresters thought it was good scientific forestry." He believed, with some strong evidence, that the results of clearcutting "looked like abuse of the land." Incremental backing away from clearcutting practices was not going to be enough for the public—it had to be a break with tradition. In 1992, Robertson proposed a policy, with seven criteria, that would eliminate clearcutting as a standard practice and reduce clearcutting by as much as 70 percent from the 1988 level. Backlash over clearcutting and this policy from environmental groups and the timber industry continue to make headlines. Especially strong were environmental comments that the Robertson proposal had loopholes as large as a logging truck. Clearcutting continued, but on a much smaller scale.

Ecosystem Management

Ecosystem management, the driving force behind current policy of the Forest Service, the USDI Bureau of Land Management, and other Interior agencies, combines philosophy, conservation, ecology, environmentalism, and politics. Although the term "ecology" has been around since the 1800s, management using an ecological framework is relatively recent. Aldo Leopold's book *A Sand County Almanac* (1949) and Rachel Carson's book *Silent Spring* (1962) influenced many people to look at the broader interaction between people and the environment. In 1970, Lynton Caldwell published an article that, perhaps for the first time, advocated using an ecosystem approach to public land management and policy. Then, in the late 1970s, Frank Craighead and John Craighead pioneered efforts to use broad ecosystems in the management of grizzly bears in the Yellowstone National Park and the surrounding national forests. By the late 1980s, many researchers and public land managers were convinced that an ecosystem approach to the management of public lands was the only logical way to proceed. The following five concepts define what ecosystem management should mean:

Define ecological boundaries—Ecosystems often have no visible boundaries. Need to analyze and manage across political and administrative jurisdictions. Keep all the pieces. Do not destroy whole or parts of ecosystems.

Utilize multiple levels of analysis and data collection—More research and better data are needed. Use many levels of analysis to understand ecological processes. Analyses should range from site-specific to broad watersheds, or even larger. Test models against reality.

Revise management actions—Be more adaptive, take more risks, try new methods and processes, increase experimentation, and remain flexible. Learn from mistakes. Monitor results of on-the-ground actions to see if expectations meet with desired outcomes. Revisit assumptions or hypotheses as needed.

Rethink organizational analysis—Internal change may be necessary. Undertake more training of employees and the public on basic ecosystem principles. Better cooperation between agencies; work at federal, state, and local levels, as well as with the private sector, to integrate and cooperate on data collection and management.

Consider people as part of ecosystems—People are fundamental to ecosystems, both affecting them and affected by them. Attitudes, beliefs, values, and customs that people hold can be significant in determining the future of ecosystems.

Old Growth and Ancient Forest Management

Old growth or ancient forest issues have been at the heart of many complaints, as well as research efforts, since the 1980s. The problems surrounding old growth involve the definition as well as the management of these areas. There are many definitions of old growth, some of which fall in the philosophical realm, others in the social/political arena, and still others in the technical forestry area. Each special interest group seems to have a slightly different definition of old growth. Beginning in 1991, several national environmental groups jointly decided to rename old growth " ancient forest." This was an organized effort to take the issue away from the federal management agencies and congressional representatives and senators in order to make it into a national issue. The environmental groups have been very successful in this effort. Every definition has different management consequences for the Forest Service, which holds the vast majority of standing old growth trees.

From the 1950s to the early 1980s, the Forest Service tended to view old growth as a timber resource that needed to be quickly harvested and replaced by new, fast-growing trees. Conversion of the old growth forest to a young, vigorous, fast-growing, second-growth forest was believed (especially by the timber industry) to yield a higher timber harvest than the standing "overmature" forests that were thought to be unproductive.

However, by the 1980s, the Forest Service position was gradually changing. Part of the reason for the shift was the continuing controversies regarding wilderness and other environmental matters, the hiring of numerous Forest Service specialists and their growing appreciation for ecological concerns, and an increasing amount of research on the role of old growth in the ecosystem. Whereas, a few years before, old growth was regarded as something that needed to be quickly replaced, it is now being regarded, to least to some degree, as a resource in its own right.

The discussions regarding old growth revolve around some basic elements: lack of clear definition, location, or inventory of the standing old growth, amount and location of allocated areas, and the type of management necessary for these areas, if any. Presently, the Forest Service and its sister agency, the Bureau of Land Management, as well as several universities, are making extensive studies of old growth. Their research concerns the old growth trees and what constitutes an old growth area or forest, the habitat it provides for a wide variety of plant and animal species, different methods of managing the old growth, ways in which the old growth forest sustains itself, and techniques to enhance the long-term production of second- and third-growth forests. Much remains to be done, since the vast majority of research is generally less than 20 years old.

The environmentalist position, depending on which group is involved, revolves around the idea that old growth is a resource in itself and is rapidly disappearing.

Many estimates of the proportion of old growth trees still growing range from about 5 percent from the Sierra Club and the Wilderness Society to more than 20 percent, according to the Forest Service. Much of the debate revolves around definitions or assumptions. Not only does old growth have an intrinsic value for people, which cannot be measured in dollars, but also it represents a very important habitat for certain species of animals and plants that need this environment for survival. While advocates of old growth realize that the old trees are important for jobs in the wood products sector, they argue that the philosophical and recreational benefits to people (such as rejuvenating the mind and refreshing the spirit, as well as offering recreational opportunities different from wilderness or pay campgrounds) outweigh the economic benefits of harvesting the knot-free, straight-grained, six- to eight-foot diameter trees to make two-by-fours.

Old growth conifer forest areas are highly valued by the timber industry for wood products. Timber producers are not really worried about the definitions of old growth, except as they might influence how much old growth might be "saved" in the national forests. The industry is very concerned about the allocation of old growth areas and acres for management other than timber harvest, as well as the long-term health of their companies.

Local communities are greatly concerned about timber harvesting, as it directly relates to the health and even survival of hundreds of small to medium-size cities. Probably the most important aspect of continued timber harvest in the hills and mountains around these timber-dependent communities is the availability of national forest timber. These often-large trees are purchased by local timber companies and processed in their local mills. Thus, for many communities, trees equal operating mills which equal jobs, a continuing tax base, and the survival of a way of life in these towns and cities.

The counties across the country that contain national forests or national grasslands receive 25 percent of the gross timber and other resource receipts (50 percent from the revested Oregon and California Railroad Grant land [O&C lands]) in lieu of property taxes. These varying receipts, which are to be spent only on roads and schools, add many millions of dollars to the annual budgets of these counties.

As the Forest Service presently sells and cuts much of its timber from mature and old growth tree stands, there is considerable pressure from the affected counties for the national forests to continue selling more trees. In the early 1980s, there was a timber industry depression (low demand and prices, but high bids for national forest timber), which caused a number of mill owners to sell out or declare bankruptcy; many towns were severely affected. Despite the occasional overreliance on timber and timber products, for many towns and cities there is "no other game in town."

Spotted Owls as Indicators of Old Growth

Besides the widely divergent opinions about the definition of old growth, there is one animal that has been the focus of a great deal of attention in the past 30 years. The Forest Service in the Pacific Northwest and California Regions chose the northern spotted owl (*Strix occidentalis caurina*) as an indicator of the general good health of an old growth ecosystem. This was in response to the NFMA regulations that require Forest Service land management plans to provide for diversity and viability of existing animal communities (36 CFR 219.19). Sometimes referred to as the "billion-dollar" bird by the timber industry, the spotted owl has come to symbolize the struggle for many of the remaining unharvested old growth lands.

Much like the arguments about old growth, there are also disagreements over the spotted owl. The central bone of contention is the habitat needs, and consequent need for protection from forest developments, for nesting pairs of spotted owls. At the beginning of the NFMA planning process, the direction from the Pacific Northwest Region was to manage 1,000 acres of land around known nesting spotted owl pairs. A 300-acre portion of the acreage immediately surrounding the nest was to be left intact, while partial harvesting of the "doughnut" surrounding the owl pair was permitted. However, research now indicates that each pair of owls needs to have 2,500 acres or more of old growth habitat for survival.

The research studies from which the habitat needs of the spotted owl were extrapolated are still being challenged by the timber industry as neither valid nor representative of all pairs. In addition, the industry believes that the studies have relied on too few spotted owl pairs to make intelligent management decisions that would unduly impact the timber industry and local communities. On the other hand, the environmentalists argued that not only is 2,500 acres not enough but that the proposals from the Forest Service in the early 1980s to protect only 40 percent of the known spotted owl pairs would lead to the eventual extinction of the species. They felt that extinction, or threat of extinction, would violate the Endangered Species Act of 1973. Thus, the battle lines were drawn around an owl species that is around a foot and a half tall.

In responding to appeals related to the 1984 Pacific Northwest NFMA regional guide, the Pacific Northwest Region agreed to address the issue of the spotted owls for the 19 national forests' planning process. A draft supplement EIS (SEIS) to the regional guide was sent out for public review in July 1986. More than 41,000 responses (almost 160,000 comments) were received on the SEIS. The only common ground in both camps was the agreement that the owls need additional study. In early August 1987, there was a decision at the chief's office in Washington, D.C., that publication of the final SEIS would be delayed until all the draft EISs for the 19 national forests in the Pacific Northwest Region were published and out for public review. In addition, the regional office and state BLM office put extra money and staffing into spotted owl research projects in several parts of the Pacific Northwest. The final SEIS was published, after many delays, in January 1992.

An action by an environmental group threw another curve at the spotted owl decision. In January 1987, GreenWorld, a Cambridge, Massachusetts–based group, petitioned the USDI Fish and Wildlife Service to study the northern spotted owl for possible listing as endangered under the Endangered Species Act of 1973. Such an action had been proposed a year earlier by the Sierra Club in California, but the

Oregon and Washington environmental groups effectively stopped the action because they felt it would disrupt the delicate balance between the timber industry and environmental groups. There was also a "worst-case scenario" fear that if the spotted owl were formally listed, then the political repercussions from the timber industry, affected cities, counties, and the states would be so severe that a complete review or revision of the Endangered Species Act would occur. A review of this Act under such conditions, which would make the snail darter controversy look like "small potatoes," was something that the environmental groups did not want. The USDI Fish and Wildlife Service study, which was formally announced on July 24, 1987, concluded that the Forest Service would have to fully protect not 40 percent but 100 percent of the known pairs. The timber industry and the Pacific Northwest Region believed that such a listing would severely reduce the timber harvest levels on the national forests in the region.

On August 3, the GreenWorld petition was supplemented by a petition from various Washington and Oregon chapters of the Audubon Society, the Natural Resources Defense Council, the Wilderness Society, the Defenders of Wildlife, the Oregon Natural Resources Council, and Headwaters, a southwest Oregon group. The legal counsel for this petition was the Sierra Club Legal Defense Fund, Northwest Office, in Seattle, Washington. The reason for the new petition was the feeling that the current logging of the old growth forest had already destroyed much of the habitat for the spotted owl. The petition recommended that the spotted owl be declared endangered in the Oregon Coast Range and Washington Olympics but only threatened in the Washington and Oregon Cascade Range.

The historian Harold Steen wrote that the BLM was especially reluctant to get involved with the Forest Service's problem with the spotted owl.

> Efforts to develop a joint plan "didn't get very far." Deputy Assistant Secretary of the Interior James Casons claimed that the Forest Service was "using a lot of poor information," and anyway, BLM lands "were different," and they had no need to "worry about this business." Casons appointed a team of biologists to study the spotted owl situation, to look especially "for information gaps where we might not know as much as we should." Not only did the team of biologists conclude that current BLM practices would place the owl in jeopardy, they recommended that the agency join the Forest Service in its efforts to produce an acceptable management plan. Casons was "enraged" by the conclusions and ordered "all the copies of the report turned in" for destruction or impoundment. He then "ordered the team to go back and change the report." Despite Cason's efforts to quash the report, a copy was made public.

An interagency agreement was signed in August 1988 by the heads of the affected federal agencies—the Bureau of Land Management, the Forest Service, the Fish and Wildlife Service, and the National Park Service. The agencies agreed to work toward a common goal of ensuring population viability for the spotted owl throughout its range. In late 1988, Chief Dale Robertson issued a record of decision on the supplemental spotted owl EIS for Oregon and Washington. The selected alternative directed the 13 national forests with spotted owls to establish a spotted owl habitat area (SOHA) network. Amounts of habitat to be provided in SOHAs varied from 1,000 acres in southern Oregon to 3,000 acres on the

Olympic Peninsula. The record of decision was soon appealed by the Washington Department of Wildlife and by timber and environmental groups, but the Assistant Secretary of Agriculture denied the appeals.

Interest groups obtained injunctions prohibiting the sale of old growth on BLM lands near spotted owl sites, and continuous litigation resulted in the "northwest compromise" (Hatfield-Adams Amendment) of 1989. This legislation applied to Washington and Oregon and was attached as a rider (Section 318) to the 1990 fiscal-year appropriations bill. It declared the FS's spotted owl SEIS and the BLM's spotted owl management plans adequate for preparing fiscal year 1990 timber sales. The compromise expanded the Forest Service's SOHA sizes by 12 to 25 percent and established 12 new agreement areas on BLM lands for a period of one year.

As a result of the uncertainty surrounding the status of the northern spotted owl, the FS recommended the formation of an interagency scientific committee to address the issue. This recommendation was agreed to by the heads of the affected agencies, and, in October 1989, the Interagency Spotted Owl Scientific Committee (ICS) was established. The charge to the committee was to "develop a scientifically credible conservation strategy for the northern spotted owl." Harold Steen, in his interview with Jack Ward Thomas, wrote that Thomas "believed that his initial assignment was flawed, in that the committee was to deal with only the spotted owl. They disagreed with this 'narrow mission.' The scientists could see that the question was not owls, it was 'the old-growth ecosystem.' To study only the owl would yield a single solution, instead of an array of alternatives. But the land management agencies were 'up against the wall,' and the Forest Service had 'lost its credibility' due to a political and legal gridlock. Thus, the request for a single answer." The answer came and went. The problem was expanded.

In June 1990, the Fish and Wildlife Service declared that the northern spotted owl was to be listed as a threatened species throughout its known range. This listing decision came on the heels of court rulings that the agency had been dragging its feet on listing the species because the listing was being affected by political factors, rather than being based strictly on biological criteria as stated in the Endangered Species Act of 1973.

On May 23, 1991, U.S. District Judge William Dwyer ordered the Forest Service to adopt a plan for the spotted owl in habitat areas of Washington, Oregon, and northern California. He issued an injunction that remained in place for three years against logging in national forests. Dwyer's decision, which stunned the Forest Service, was bitterly opposed by the lumber industry, counties, and local communities. This set up a situation that had to be resolved.

That same month, the House of Representatives chartered a group of experts known as the "scientific panel on late-successional forest ecosystems" (commonly called the "gang of four"). It was composed of Jerry Franklin, from the University of Washington; John Gordon, from Yale University; Norman Johnson, from Oregon State University; and Jack Ward Thomas, from the Forest Service. The timber industry, by this time getting quite agitated about the owl controversy, submitted to the Forest Service and the BLM its own "multiresource strategy," which was analyzed but not accepted because it did not provide enough protection for the owls. The study group's report later that year was rejected by the BLM, setting up a confrontation with the Fish and Wildlife Service.

Secretary Manual Lujan convened an endangered species committee (the so-called God squad), only the third time one had ever been called. In 1992, the committee held a number of hearings, which helped the BLM timber sales for that year, but the issue was still unresolved. On March 3, the final EIS and record of decision on spotted owls for the Forest Service were issued. The BLM did not agree, as it wanted its own solution. That same year, another committee, the "scientific analysis team" (SAT), was organized. The SAT recommendations, which kept on expanding the requirements for spotted owls and other old growth dependent species, led to the next phase, when the president of the United States became directly involved in the controversy.

FEMAT and ICBEMP

There are two large-scale ecosystem assessments that have affected Forest Service management greatly. The first came about on April 2, 1993, when President Clinton, Vice President Gore, and seven cabinet members met in Portland to engage the public in a discussion of issues relating to the spotted owl, old growth/ ancient forest, and jobs. A team of Forest Service and Bureau of Land Management scientists came together immediately after the conference to devise a plan for the management of western Washington, western Oregon, and northern California national forests and BLM westside Oregon land. The Forest Ecosystem Management Assessment Team (FEMAT) came up with a scientifically credible report within a 60-day time frame. After a 30-day extension, the FEMAT report and accompanying draft SEIS were sent to the printer. The final SEIS and record of decision, known as the President's Plan (now the Northwest Forest Plan), were published in early 1994.

At the same time, another large-scale assessment began for the interior portions of the Columbia Basin—eastern Washington, eastern Oregon, western Montana, and northern Idaho. Known as the Interior Columbia Basin Ecosystem Management Project (ICBEMP), the multivolume scientific assessment and thousands of pages of scientific reports cost around $35 million. In the summer of 1997, two draft EISs (one for eastern Oregon and Washington—the Eastside Project—and another for western Montana and northern Idaho—the Upper Columbia Basin Project) were produced. Huge unroaded areas in Idaho and Montana are still unresolved by Congress in terms of wilderness designation.

Grazing

Grazing was one of the first management issues on the forest reserves. NFS rangeland is managed to conserve the land and its vegetation while providing food for both livestock and wildlife. Under multiple use concepts, grazing areas also serve as watersheds, wildlife habitat, and recreation sites. Grazing privileges are granted on national forests and grasslands through paid permits; permittees cooperate with the Forest Service in range-improvement projects.

From the beginning of European settlement, raising of domestic livestock has been a prominent part of farming and grazing activities. For many decades, stock animals were free to roam over the unsettled, public domain areas along the edge of farm and grazing lands that were newly cleared from the forests. As the settlers moved westward, the size of the unsettled forest area was much reduced and public domain land occupied by homesteaders. Western ranchers were some of the strongest opponents of the creation of the forest reserves because they feared that grazing would be prohibited on them, perhaps rightly so. Concerned with erosion and other problems caused by overgrazing, the Secretary of the Interior banned grazing on federal forest reserves in 1894.

Although John Muir referred to sheep as "hoofed locusts," he acknowledged that regulated grazing was better than unregulated grazing. As early as 1896, Gifford Pinchot favored regulated sheep grazing on the forest reserves. Frederick V. Coville's independent study of sheep grazing in the Oregon Cascades during the summer of 1897 left no doubt that regulated grazing was less destructive to the forests than unregulated grazing—especially to young trees. Pinchot had similar investigations made in the Southwest. The official federal policy, developed in 1898, allowed restricted sheep grazing in the Oregon Cascades and extended eventually to all the other forest reserves. Cattle and horses were allowed to range freely. In 1900, the Department of the Interior established a free permit system to control the number of animals on the forest reserves and remaining public domain land.

Grazing policies continued unchanged after the transfer of the forest reserves to the Department of Agriculture and the new Forest Service in 1905. In 1906, the Forest Service announced that fees would be imposed: 25 to 35 cents per head for cattle and horses, with a lower rate for sheep and goats. Although free-ranging hogs were a problem in some areas, there were no fees announced for hog grazing. Forest rangers set up new grazing allotments and set dates for entering and leaving the forest reserves. The grazing revenues exceeded those from timber every year between 1906 and 1910, and periodically until 1920. In 1910, the Forest Service established an office of grazing studies, which began studying the effects of grazing on the national forests.

In 1917, with the United States entry into World War I, the number of grazed acres on the national forests increased dramatically. Studies of the increasing numbers of sheep and cattle grazed on national forests during the 1917–1919 period showed severe overgrazing. Range conditions were so poor that sheep permittees were unable to produce as much lamb meat as they expected.

The bulk of the research on range management took place at the Great Basin Experimental Station (Intermountain Research Station), on the Manti National Forest, outside Ephraim, Utah. The historian Thomas Alexander claimed that professional range management emerged in the Forest Service largely as the result of the Intermountain Station's grazing research staff. The typical district ranger was often concerned about the social and economic costs to local ranchers if they were forced to reduce stock numbers; while range researchers focused on the condition of the land. Over time, it was the condition of the land that determined policy, which was based on their research findings on carrying capacity. In the end, the numbers of animals on the national forests were reduced.

Controversy over grazing fees (which continues to this day) resulted in a 1924 Forest Service report on public and private fees. Stock owners immediately expressed objections to the study, leading to congressional hearings and passage of the McSweeney-McNary Act of 1928, which enhanced research activities on public and private forest and rangeland. During the Great Depression, grazing fees were lowered by 50 percent. The western drought in the early 1930s and the passage of the Taylor Grazing Act of 1934 tightened public land grazing regulations. An interagency rivalry over which agency could best administer and regulate grazing led to the creation of the U.S. Grazing Service in the Department of the Interior to counter Forest Service attempts to take over grazing management on all public lands. In 1946, the Grazing Service was combined with the General Land Office to create the Bureau of Land Management. In the late 1940s and early 1950s, there were additional rumblings from the grazing industry about having the national forests turned over to the states, but these proposals fell on deaf ears in Congress.

World War II saw another attempt to expand the number of animals grazing on the national forests. The Forest Service resisted this effort. The Forest Service reduced the number of animals allowed on the national forests in order to increase the quality of the grazing lands. This plan met strong opposition, and the controversy resulted in the Granger-Thye Act of 1950. In essence, Granger-Thye recognized the Forest Service's authority to collect fees for grazing privileges and endorsed grazing advisory boards, as long as representatives from the state game commissions were members, allowed cooperative range improvements, and allowed the issuance of 10-year grazing permits.

In the 1960s, controversy was again stirring over grazing fees. By the late 1970s, this resulted in the "Sagebrush Rebellion" in the western states. Supporters of the Sagebrush Rebellion wanted all Forest Service and Bureau of Land Management grazing lands transferred to the states. They assumed that, with the lands under state control, the ranchers would have more influence and thus get their own way over fees, allotments, and number of animals grazed. Because of local and national opposition, the Sagebrush Rebellion lost momentum, then stalled, and finally died by the mid-1980s, only to be revived in the 1990s. This movement today is called the " wise use," "county-supremacy," or "property-rights" movement.

Currently, NEPA decisions are being made on 8,783 Forest Service administered grazing allotments across the country in adherence to the Rescissions Act of 1995 (Public Law 104–19). Through 2001, 2,107 of the livestock grazing allotments were analyzed under NEPA standards. On the basis of these analyses, many improvements for better management have been undertaken on these allotments. In FY 2001, forage improvement took place on 33,667 acres of rangelands, while 1,357 structural improvements were constructed on NFS rangelands. Permitted livestock grazing totaled approximately 9.4 million animal head months (a head month is one-month occupancy by an adult animal). Monitoring of both implementation and effectiveness of the management actions will continue into the future.

One area, little known outside the agency and the grazing permittees, has been the noxious weed management program. Weeds, often nonnative or invasive species of grasses and plants, can directly affect the opportunities for grazing, as well as restoration of grazing lands on the national forests and grasslands. The Forest Service, in cooperation with the states, counties, and cities, works to prevent the spread of noxious weeds, treat existing infestations, and educate citizens about noxious weed problems. During FY 2001, some 143,938 acres were treated for weeds.

Mining

Mining is another allowed activity on the national forest system. There are approximately 5.3 million acres currently under lease for oil and gas, more than 150,000 mining claims, about 9,000 mineral material sales contracts and permits, more than 2,000 new operations proposed each year, and more than 15,000 operations to monitor and inspect. The largest coal mine in the United States is on NFS lands, and much of the nation's phosphate and lead production comes from NFS lands. The value of all energy and mineral production exceeds $2.1 billion per year. Annual revenues are about $170 million, 25–50 percent of which is returned to the states where production occurs. Minerals found on NFS lands provide more than $3.3 billion in private sector revenue. More than 95 percent of domestic platinum/palladium comes from the Custer and Gallatin National Forests. Mining on the NFS lands in FY 2000 contributed 575 million pounds (45%) of the U.S. production of lead, 178 million pounds of copper, and 529,000 ounces of gold. The Tongass National Forest, in Alaska, has one of the world's largest molybdenum deposits. During FY 2001, approximately 7.3 million barrels of oil, 93 billion cubic feet of gas, and 94 million tons of coal were produced on NFS lands. There are about 7,000 sand, gravel, and stone pits and quarries.

The Forest Service reviews approximately 2,000 new mining operations each year. There are about 7 million acres where there is a possibility for coal leasing (50 billion tons), while on another 45 million acres there is a possibility for oil and gas leasing, with 5.3 million acres are currently leased. There are more than 20,000 existing operations that require monitoring. In addition, an estimated 100,000 rock hounds, recreational mineral collectors, students, and geologic organizations use the national forests for education and recreational purposes. Recreational panning for gold is an activity that is rapidly increasing.

"Prosperous mining is impossible without prosperous forests," Forest Service Chief Gifford Pinchot told the mining industry in 1901 in his quest for support for forest conservation and federal forest reserves. The linkage between the fortunes of mining and forests in the United States grew following the discovery of the rich

Comstock silver lode at Virginia City, Nevada; large underground mines needed timbers to support the tunnels. Between 1860 and 1880, an estimated 600 million board feet of timber from Sierra Nevada forests were used in the Comstock. Many new sawmills were built around the country to supply mine timbers from local forests.

The federal government's regulation of mining was not a critical issue in Congress until the California Gold Rush of 1849 and later rushes in Colorado, Nevada, Idaho, and Montana. These "finds" resulted in claims being worked on public domain lands. After the Civil War, Congress passed a number of laws intended to establish some semblance of order in the mining industry. Two of these laws—the Lode Law of 1866 and the Placer Act of 1870—merely legalized what had been the unofficial law of the land. The General Mining Law of 1872 consolidated the earlier laws and confirmed the principle that minerals found on public domain land belonged to the person who found (located) them. The 1872 law also:

Set standards for making mineral claims on public land.
Set no royalty fees for production.
Set fees for transfer of the land from public to private ownership ($2.50 per acre).
Set the size of the claims.
Allowed a claimant to hold the land indefinitely as long as minimal work was completed ($100 value per year) on the claim.

A claim was set at 20 acres, with no limit on the number of claims that could be filed. A person could hold his claim by performing $100 worth of work each year or by obtaining permanent legal ownership of the minerals and land surface by paying a fee to "patent" the claim. Most important, the claimant was granted legal claim to the discovery of a valuable mineral deposit.

Richard Ballinger, appointed in 1907 to head the General Land Office and elevated to Secretary of the Interior in 1909, differed with Chief Gifford Pinchot over coal claims in Alaska. Ballinger wanted them patented, while Pinchot argued for federal leasing. Pinchot feared that a national coal famine would result if the private sector was allowed complete freedom to exploit coal fields without concern for future needs. The mining industry depicted Pinchot as out to curtail the citizen's right to engage in free enterprise—the "little man" was being crushed by government. By January 1910, the dispute between Pinchot and Ballinger reached the point that President William Howard Taft fired Pinchot.

In 1920, Congress passed the Mineral Leasing Act, which incorporated oil and natural gas, oil shale, phosphates, sulfates, carbonites, and other surface and sub-surface resources under a system of rental and royalty fees. The government still retained ownership of the land. The 1947 Materials Disposal Act set standards for the federal government to sell materials such as sand, gravel, building stone, clay, pumice, and cinders from federal lands. Competitive bidding was an integral part of the act.

In the early 1950s, the Forest Service and several conservation groups launched a campaign to expose abuses found under the various mining laws. The Forest

Service was not interested in the mining itself but rather in the staking of mineral claims on the NFS and the cutting of timber on the claims for commercial, not mining, purposes. The historian Harold Steen noted the problem derived, at least in part on several interrelated problems:

> During the postwar years, two loosely related activities caused the number of claims on national forests to spike: the uranium boom to feed the nuclear industry brought prospectors out in droves, and "unscrupulous developers" staked claims along lake shores and in similar areas where the market for summer homes was also booming. The endemic problem was now an epidemic; by 1955, new claims on national forests were being filed at a rate of five thousand per month.
>
> The Al Sarena Company was an Alabama firm that owned twenty-three heavily timbered, unpatented claims on the Rogue River National Forest in Oregon The company applied to take the claims to patent so that it could cut the timber, a process that included the requirement to prove "adequate mineralization." Another part of the process required that the Bureau of Land Management ask the Forest Service for comment, and agency mineral examiners protested that fifteen of the twenty-three claims had no minerals. The BLM accepted the Forest Service protest, and Sarena's appeals to the secretary of interior were rejected. Then in January 1953, the new Eisenhower administration decided to allow the Sarena Company itself provide new assays that showed valuable minerals on the fifteen claims. Within a year, the company had its patents, promptly selling two and one-half million board feet of timber, leaving according to the company's estimate another eighteen million. At no time was any mining undertaken.
>
> This "sordid" tale of political maneuverings, the unexplained loss and then the mysterious finding of assay samples, and "some pretty smoky undercover doings" kept Al Sarena on the nation's front page. There was "so much complaint to Congress" that appropriate House and Senate committees formed a joint committee and held hearings in Oregon and Washington, D.C. The mining industry was by now fully agreeable to certain revisions to the 1872 law, but feared there might be "further and more radical changes."

The resulting investigations found widespread problems: mining claims were being used as home and recreation-cabin sites, as excuses to cut the timber, to justify fishing and hunting camps in remote areas, for commercial businesses, and even as trash dumps. Congress responded by passing the Multiple-Use Mining Act of 1955. As a result, the Forest Service was able to reclaim thousands of "mineral" claims that were never used for their authorized and intended purpose, others that had no minerals, and even more that had not lived up to annual work requirements on the claim.

The Federal Land Policy and Management Act (FLPMA) of 1976 changed the procedures for filing mineral claims—the paperwork had to be filed with the Bureau of Land Management (rather than the local county courthouse), and all claims needed to be refiled by 1979. As a result of FLPMA, the federal government found that some 1.1 million mining claims were located on federal lands and also eliminated many fraudulent claims. Legislation to "fix" the General Mining Law of 1872 has been proposed many times over the years, but every effort has been successfully blocked by the mining industry and western congressional delegations.

The Forest Service manages fossil and geologic sites of interest as resources for present and future generations, scientific, education, interpretive, recreational, and aesthetic values. The most complete Champsosaurus skeleton in the world (55 million years old) came off Little Missouri National Grasslands. The agency has partnerships with communities, states, and universities for managing the paleontological resource.

Recreation

Recreation in the national forests is the "gold crown" of managing the national forests for the benefit and enjoyment of the public. Millions of acres of outdoor settings allow American and international visitors alike to enjoy a wide variety of premier recreation activities. From the Tongass National Forest, in Alaska, where glaciers and coniferous forests abound, through the wild and scenic rivers of Idaho, to the heritage sites of the Jemez Mountains, in New Mexico, and the tropical forest of the Caribbean National Forest, in Puerto Rico, outdoor fun is available on our national forests and grasslands.

By the late nineteenth century and the turn of the twentieth, many Americans were spending summers at camps, lodges, or boarding houses near mountain rivers and lakes. Often, these adventures would last a month or longer. At times, the man of the family would work during the week in the city, while the wife and children camped in the woods; on the weekends, the husband would rejoin the family. Many city dwellers built cabins for weekends and vacations in the forest and lakefront surroundings. Much of the pressure on the government for the establishment of forest reserves came from hiking and other outdoor recreation and conservation groups that loved the lure of the woods and felt strongly that forested areas should be placed under official government protection before they were transferred to private ownership.

Recreational activities on the NFS were not specifically included in the Forest Reserve Act of 1891, but they could reasonably be inferred to be included among the compatible uses of the forest reserves. The Organic Act of 1897 and implementing regulations allowed many activities on the forest reserves (renamed national forests in 1907), including camping and hunting. Most important was the potential for these visitors to start fires: "Large areas of the public forests are annually destroyed by fire, originating in many instances through the carelessness of prospectors, campers, hunters, sheep herders, and others, while in some cases the fires are started with malicious intent. So great is the importance of protecting forest from fire, that this Department will make special effort for the enforcement of the law against all persons guilty of starting or causing the spread of forest fires in the reservations in violation of the above provisions." Before the first forest rangers of the General Land Office (GLO) took to the woods, in the summer of 1898, picnickers, hikers, mountain climbers, campers, hunters, and anglers, individually and as families and other groups, were among the regular users of the forest reserves.

The first legislation to recognize recreation in the forest reserves was enacted February 28, 1899. The Mineral Springs Leasing Act permitted the building of sanitariums and hotels in connection with developing mineral and other springs for health and recreation. The act stated that regulations would be issued "for the convenience of people visiting such springs, with reference to spaces and locations, for the erection of tents or temporary dwelling houses to be erected or constructed for the use of those visiting such springs for health and pleasure" The revised GLO regulations set forth in the 1902 *Forest Reserve Manual* stipulated to the right of the public to travel on the forest reserves for pleasure and recreation. However, recreation was considered to be secondary to the need for forest management, especially grazing opportunities and, later, timber harvesting.

Recreational use of the forest reserves grew slowly at first, then more rapidly as automobiles became numerous and roads penetrated further into what had previously been remote and inaccessible areas. General prosperity and more leisure time increased the human flow into the national forests, a flow that eventually became a flood. Improvements were provided for forest visitors, starting with sanitary facilities to protect public health and fireplaces to prevent forest fires.

The low priority accorded recreation, along with budget limitations, precluded the federal government's getting into the recreation "business." Nevertheless, even without funds, beginnings were made by the early forest rangers, as this account shows:

> Forest rangers took time to clear inflammable material from around heavily used camp spots and to build crude rock fireplaces. They erected toilets and dug garbage pits whenever materials could be obtained. They developed and fenced sources of water supply for campers. They made and put up signs to guide people and caution them about care with fire. Congress made no appropriations for such special needs for many years but ingenious rangers fashioned camp stoves and fireplaces of rock, tin cans, and scrap iron; tables, toilets, and garbage pit covers were made from lumber scraps and wooden boxes, and crude signs were painted and displayed on rough-hewn shakes. Many of these earlier improvements were raw looking and some of them were clearly out of place in the forest environment, but they filled a real need.

As early as 1909, the North Pacific District reported 45,000 recreation visits and the Rocky Mountain District, 115,000 visits. Recreation was growing quickly, much of it because of the availability of automobiles and roads.

In the 1905 *Forest Service Use Book*, there were statements noting that the national forests served many purposes, some of which were related to early recreationists: "The following are the more usual rights and privileges ... (*a*) Trails and roads to be used by settlers living in or near forest reserves. (*b*) Schools and churches. (*c*) Hotels, stores, mills, stage stations, apiaries, miners' camps, stables, summer residences, sanitariums, dairies, trappers' cabins, and the like." The 1907 *The Use of the National Forests* (the public version of the *Use Book*) included such statements as this: "*Playgrounds*. Quite incidentally, also, the National Forests serve a good purpose as great playgrounds for the people. They are used more or less every year by campers, hunters, fishermen, and thousands of pleasure seekers from the near-by towns. They are great recreation grounds for a very large part of the people of the West, and their value in this respect is well worth considering."

By 1913, the annual Forest Service report raised the issue of the need for sanitary regulation to protect public health. The report also listed that 1.5 million "pleasure seekers" had visited the forests in the 1912–1913 fiscal year, of whom a little over 1 million were day visitors. Campers, including those who engaged in hunting, fishing, berry or nut picking, boating, bathing, and climbing, totaled 231,000, and guests at houses, hotels, and sanatoriums numbered 191,000.

The Forest Service undertook development of recreation facilities in the national forests as early as 1916. The first official campground was the Eagle Creek campground, east of Portland, in Oregon's Mt. Hood National Forest. The facility, then at the end of the now scenic Columbia River Highway, was a "fully modern" facility with tables, toilets, a check-in station, and a ranger station. The ranger in charge was Albert Wisendanger—reportedly the first "recreation ranger" in the Forest Service. In the summer of 1919, nearly 150,000 people enjoyed the Eagle Creek facilities.

At the same time, the Forest Service was opposed to the creation of a National Park Service to administer the national parks. At one time, the Forest Service proposed that it could manage all the national parks, but, obviously, this was not approved by Congress. When the USDI National Park Service was established in 1916, it was given a dual role—to preserve natural areas in perpetuity and to develop the parks as recreation sites.

Early in 1917, the Forest Service hired Frank A. Waugh, professor of landscape architecture at Massachusetts Agricultural College, Amherst (now the University of Massachusetts), to prepare the first national study of recreation uses on the national forests. "Recreation Uses in the National Forests," Waugh's 1918 report on the status of recreation, noted that some 3 million recreational visitors used the national forests each year. He summarized the types of facilities found in the forests—publicly owned developments, which consisted almost entirely of automobile camps and picnic grounds, and fraternal camps, sanatoria, and commercial summer resorts, provided by the public sector. In addition there were "several hundred" small colonies of individually owned summer cabins. With the first crude recreation use figures, collected during the summer of 1916, he figured a recreation return of $7,500,000 annually on the national forests. Waugh did not address winter sports, as they was just beginning on the national forests—as early as 1914, the Sierra Club was conducting cross-country ski outings on California's Tahoe National Forest.

The period from 1919 to 1932 was a time of slow progress in the development of recreation on the national forests. However, it was not an era without controversy and change. Responsive to the need for improved public service, the agency generally supported the idea of professional planning and design. To this end it hired a "recreation engineer," the landscape architect Arthur Carhart, in 1919, to begin recreational site planning. The year 1920 marked the completion of the first forest recreation plan for the San Isabel National Forest in Colorado. Carhart proposed that summer homes and other developments not be allowed at Trappers Lake, on the White River National Forest, in Colorado. In 1921, he surveyed the Quetico-Superior Lake region, in Minnesota's Superior National Forest, where he recommended only limited development. It eventually became the Boundary Waters Canoe Area Wilderness.

In 1921, while attending the first National Conference on State Parks, Carhart discussed national forest recreation uses. He was challenged by Park Service Director Stephen Mather, who stated that recreation was the work of the National Park Service, not the Forest Service. Differences of opinion over recreation have been a source of controversy between the agencies for decades. The National Conference on Outdoor Recreation, in 1924, criticized the two agencies for overdevelopment of their recreation programs. The conference went so far as to accuse the National Park Service of swapping the concept of preserving the nation's natural wonders for the concept of creating a "people's playground."

Arthur H. Carhart and Aldo Leopold believed that wilderness was a recreational experience unmatched by the drive to develop areas for heavy recreational use. The Gila Wilderness—the nation's first wilderness—was established on the New Mexico's Gila National Forest, in 1924. Carhart later wrote that "there is no higher service that the forests can supply to individual and community than the healing of mind and spirit which comes from the hours spent where there is great solitude."

Early in the decade, while ground was gained on the budgeting front, professional expertise in planning and design was lost. Arthur Carhart resigned because of what he perceived as a lack of support for recreation in the agency, and he was not replaced by a person trained in the landscape design disciplines. At the time, only three regions—Northern, Pacific Southwest (California), and Pacific Northwest—had personnel assigned to recreation duties. Other regions either had too little recreation activity to merit specialized personnel or were determined to develop their own forester-recreationists.

Throughout the decade of the 1920s, the Forest Service pursued a cautious conservative recreation site development policy. Generally, that policy held that the recreation role of the national forests was to provide *space* for recreation. Publicly financed recreation facilities remained limited in number and usually simple in nature. Yet, by 1925, there were some 1,500 campgrounds in the national forests. This policy of limited development of national forest recreation sites fit both the philosophical outlook of the forest managers and the budgetary goals of the Coolidge and Hoover administrations and of Congress.

"A National Plan for American Forestry" (the Copeland Report) was prepared by the Forest Service in March 1933, just before Franklin Roosevelt was sworn in as president. It was written to highlight the agency's many accomplishments and the need for the national forests. The report served as one of the bases for work to be done by the new Civilian Conservation Corps. The short section on recreation was written by Robert Marshall. Chief Silcox announced a reorganization plan in November 1935 that included a "division of recreation and lands" that was to be headed by Marshall. Recreation had finally arrived as a national priority of the Forest Service. Using mainly Civilian Conservation Corps labor, the Forest Service built recreation structures from coast to coast. Under Marshall's guidance, a tremendous variety of facilities were built, many of them elaborate, including bathhouses, shelters, amphitheaters, downhill ski areas, and playgrounds. Recreation was established as a national administrative priority of the Forest Service.

Following World War II, Americans aggressively sought an improved quality of life that included active participation in all forms of outdoor recreation. The socioeconomic influences of the postwar baby boom, increased affluence, increased leisure time, and improved transportation systems and population mobility led to unprecedented growth in demand for outdoor recreation. Visitors to the national forests were seeking hunting and fishing opportunities, developed campgrounds, downhill ski areas, picnic areas, wilderness experiences, water access, and hiking trails. The supply of recreation sites was soon overwhelmed by this demand.

In 1958, Congress created the Outdoor Recreation Resources Review Commission to review the overall outdoor recreation opportunities in the United States. When the final report was printed in 1961, the Commission made a number of recommendations that have affected forest recreation. The Commission recommended passage of a wilderness act—which was signed into law in 1964—and the creation of a Bureau of Outdoor Recreation in the Department of the Interior. Interior Secretary Stewart Udall appointed Edward Crafts, former Forest Service assistant chief, as the agency's first director.

At the start of the 1960s, there was another surge in the national interest in the "great outdoors." This ushered in an era of growing national recreation interests and the desire for preservation of lands and history. This was also an era when America looked to the federal government to solve the nation's problems and provide for social needs of the citizens. The Wilderness Act of 1964 created the national wilderness preservation system. Legislation to regulate national recreation and scenic areas, wild and scenic rivers, and national scenic trails followed during the next two decades.

In 1985, President Reagan established the President's Commission on America's Outdoors to review existing outdoor recreation resources, and to make recommendations to him that would ensure the future availability of outdoor recreation for the American people. The thrust of this commission's report was a move away from federal centralism and strongly toward public-private partnerships. The Forest Service response to socioeconomic changes of this period took the form of an exciting and imaginative national initiative, the "national recreation strategy." The preferred tool to meet this strategy was the development of partnerships between other public and private providers of outdoor recreation. This strategy is operational, and significant progress toward the objectives has been made.

The National Grasslands

The national grasslands are an unusual element of the national forest system, which is generally thought of as the management of national forests. The origin of the USDA Forest Service–administered national grasslands begins with the disposal of public lands in the early twentieth century. The Enlarged Homestead Act of 1909, for example, offered free land to those who would cultivate the Great Plains. Market demand for wheat during and after World War I further motivated "sodbusters" to settle previously bypassed grassland areas and plow them for cultivation.

The removal of the grass that held down the soil on these marginal farmlands contributed to the erosion of the "Dust Bowl" in the drought years of the 1930s. In that decade, an estimated 2.5 million people abandoned their small farms, mainly on the plains. Many of them migrated to the West Coast to work in the fields. The young author John Steinbeck was so affected by the sight of these families pouring into California to work the fruit harvests that he immortalized them in the novel *The Grapes of Wrath*. The economic and ecological plight of the nation spurred the government to action to address the effects of the Depression, especially in the "Dust Bowl" area of the Great Plains.

A national land utilization conference in 1931 called for a survey of these submarginal farmlands. Once these lands were identified, the government began to purchase them under the authorization of the National Industrial Recovery Act of 1933 and Emergency Relief Appropriations Act of 1935. The aim was to control erosion, produce more forage, and ensure economic stability for rural residents who had remained. Depleted cropland was planted with grass, and the grazing of cattle and sheep on the public rangelands changed from year-round grazing to grazing on a rotating basis. Various government programs undertook water and soil conservation projects.

The purchased lands were called land utilization (LU) projects after the title of the 1931 conference. The government obtained title to 11.3 million acres in 45 states for $47.5 million (about $4.40 an acre) by voluntary sales. After the LU lands were purchased, they were used for practical demonstrations of the best soil conservation techniques to set an example for adjacent private landholders. Between 1933 and 1946, 250 LU projects focused on grazing, forests, recreation, wildlife, and watershed protection. During the Depression years, relief agencies hired unemployed locals to work on LU soil conservation projects, enabling those who stayed on the land to survive. Specific projects of the Soil Conservation Service (SCS)—now the Natural Resources Conservation Service—included building stock water ponds and reservoirs, planting trees, seeding grasslands (with crested wheatgrass, a bunchgrass originally imported from Siberia), and controlling erosion and fire.

The LU lands were first administered by the U.S. Resettlement Administration, later called the Farm Security Administration. The Bankhead-Jones Farm Tenant Act of 1937 gave custody of the LU lands to the Secretary of Agriculture and authorized more extensive conservation efforts. In 1938, the SCS was given the task of managing the LU lands. The period after World War II was one of intense range rehabilitation by the SCS. About 5.8 million acres of these lands were sold or transferred to the USDI agencies, such as the National Park Service, the Bureau of Indian Affairs, the Fish and Wildlife Service, and the Bureau of Land Management.

By administrative order signed by the Secretary of Agriculture and dated December 24, 1953 (effective January 2, 1954), management of the remaining 5.5 million acres of LU lands was transferred from the SCS to the Forest Service. The original intent was that the Forest Service act as interim manager pending final disposal of these acquired lands. By 1958, about 1.5 million acres had been incorporated into adjacent national forests. Discussion over the future of these lands continued.

On June 20, 1960, some 3,804,000 acres were designated as the 19 national grasslands. The Forest Service was now responsible for their permanent retention and management. The 1960 order stated that the national grasslands were to be administered as part of the national forest system under the Bankhead-Jones Farm Tenant Act and that the Forest Service was to manage them for outdoor recreation, range, timber, watershed, and wildlife and fish. This new task created some internal confusion about the place of the national grasslands and their national function.

When the Forest Service took over management of the grasslands, existing SCS policies were not readily accepted by the Forest Service. The Forest Service had managed rangeland for 50 years, and many of its range staff felt that the grasslands should managed according to established agency practices. One area of difference was the need to work with grazing associations. In 1939, the SCS had entered into cooperative agreements with Great Plains states' grazing associations and districts. These associations had originated on the Great Plains as early as 1931, when stockmen organized to request that Congress withdraw public domain land from homesteading and permit it to be leased on a long-term basis.

Forest Service officials were reluctant to surrender to grazing associations control of activities such as issuing permits, collecting fees, and controlling trespass and fires. However, the mass transfer of SCS employees in Montana and the Dakotas to the Forest Service in this transition period led to the eventual acceptance of many of the SCS practices. The current policy is to rely on grazing associations where practical. This arrangement is most common in the larger LU rangelands in the northern Great Plains. By the 1970s, national grasslands in northern New Mexico, Oklahoma, and Texas had ceased to have grazing associations. Instead, the Forest Service issued individual grazing permits and fenced off grassland units to make separate pastures. The change was a logical adaptation to the region's ecology and land use patterns. (The LU lands purchased in New Mexico-Oklahoma-Texas area were smaller than those on the northern Great Plains. For example, the Black Kettle [Texas] allotments ranged from 30 to 1,500 acres.)

The national environmental focus on the national forests of the 1970s and 1980s spilled over to the national grasslands. District rangers on both national grasslands and forest districts found that local concerns over specific project impacts were transformed into national issues. On the grasslands this has meant the employment of more wildlife biologists and an increased stress on noncommodity resources.

In the late 1990s, management of the national grasslands in the Dakotas was given greater emphasis when they were given the same management treatment as the national forests, with one supervisor's office charged with managing several grasslands. Future management of the national grasslands will involve many more specialists, ecosystem management, collaborative stewardship, and cooperative efforts between all the special interest groups. It will not be an easy task. Currently, the Forest Service manages 20 national grasslands in four different regions of the country:

Buffalo Gap (SD)	Little Missouri (ND)
Comanche (CO)	Rita Blanca (NM)
Grand River (SD)	Cedar River (SD)
Ogala (NE)	Dakota Prairie (SD)
Black Kettle (OK)	Lyndon B. Johnson (TX)
Crooked River (OR)	Sheyenne (ND)
Kiowa (NM)	Cimarron (KS)
Pawnee (CO)	Fort Pierre (SD)
Caddo (TX)	McClellan (OK)
Curlew (ID)	Thunder Basin (WY)

In addition, the Forest Service manages the Midewin National Tallgrass Prairie. Located 40 miles southwest of Chicago, the prairie was part of the former Joliet Army Ammunition Plant and contains some relatively unaltered prairie sites. The National Defense Authorization Act of 1996 (P.L. 104–106) created the Midewin National Tallgrass Prairie. The act specified that 19,165 acres of land would potentially be transferred from the U.S. Army to the Forest Service. Before transfer to the Forest Service, Midewin remained closed to the public while the army cleaned up contamination from decades of manufacturing and packaging TNT and other high explosives; the arsenal had been the world's largest TNT factory. The Midewin National Tallgrass Prairie was established in 1996 and is the first national tallgrass prairie in the country. The Midewin National Tallgrass Prairie is administered in cooperation with the Illinois Department of Natural Resources. Requirements in the act stipulate that Midewin be managed to meet four primary objectives:

1. To manage the land and water resources of the MNP in a manner that will conserve and enhance the native populations and habitats of fish, wildlife, and plants.
2. To provide opportunities for scientific, environmental, and land use education and research.
3. To allow the continuation of agricultural uses of lands within the MNP consistent with section 2915(b).
4. To provide a variety of recreation opportunities that are not inconsistent with the preceding purposes.

The first land transfer from the Army to the Forest Service took place on March 10, 1997, and included 15,080 acres of land that was believed to be free from contamination. Subsequent land acquisitions place the current size of Midewin at 15,454 acres. The Midewin site has many parcels of private land intermixed with public land. A comprehensive land and resource management plan—the prairie plan—was completed in 2002. Beginning in 2004, 6,400 acres of Midewin were opened to the general public for nonmotorized recreation use. There may be other opportunities to enlarge the Midewin in the future.

The Shelterbelt Program

The shelterbelt program began in the 1930s during the great "Dust Bowl" years on the Great Plains, when millions of acres of farmland were literally being blown away. In the dry, rainless condition, soil was lost at a horrendous rate. Many farmers and farmers were forced from their land. Dust and dirt filled the air, and sands were drifting across fields, covering fences and houses and killing animals. By the early 1930s, one of many practices proposed by the Great Plains Agricultural Council to slow or halt the damage was the planting of trees to reduce wind- and drought-caused soil erosion.

Presidential candidate Franklin D. Roosevelt, in the summer of 1932, proposed that the federal government begin a program of planting trees in belts across the hardest-hit farmlands on the Great Plains. "Shelterbelts," as they became known, refers to the millions of trees planted on private property to reduce wind erosion and protect crops from wind damage. The eventual program, from1934 to1942, under Roosevelt's administration, both saved the soil and relieved chronic employment in the region.

The Forest Service was responsible for organizing the "prairie states forestry project," otherwise known as the shelterbelt program. This massive tree planting effort covered portions of North Dakota, South Dakota, Nebraska, Kansas, Oklahoma, and the northern part of Texas. The shelterbelt program was directed by Paul H. Roberts and headquartered in Lincoln, Nebraska.

The project used many different tree species, including oaks and even black walnut. Trees were usually planted in long strips at 1-mile intervals within a belt 100 miles thick. It was felt that shelterbelts at this spacing could intercept the prevailing winds and reduce soil and crop damage. Shelterbelts, with trees and shrubs of varying heights, could reduce wind velocities on their leeward sides for distances 15 times the height of the tallest trees. Reduced winds tended to create more favorable conditions for crop growth, reduce evaporation of water in the soil (and thus reduce the need for irrigation), reduce soil temperatures, stabilize soils, protect livestock, increase wildlife populations, and provide a more livable environment for farm families.

One of the project's first tasks was to obtain tree and shrub seeds and then to establish nurseries to grow the stock for replanting. Funding for the project almost ended in 1936, but Agriculture Secretary Henry Wallace pushed Congress for a continuation. On May 18, 1937, the Norris-Doxy Cooperative Farm Forestry Act expanded the shelterbelt project by requiring greater federal-state cooperation.

Although WPA and CCC workers planted the trees and shrubs, landowners were responsible for their long-term care and maintenance. During 1939, the peak year of the project, 13 nurseries produced more than 60 million seedlings. Over the project's duration, more than 200 million trees and shrubs were planted on 30,000 farms—a total length of 18,600 miles in all! The shelterbelts worked amazingly well, and the results can be seen even today, although many of the shelterbelt trees have been cut for their highly valued wood. Since 1942, tree planting to reduce soil losses and crop damage has been carried out by local soil conservation districts in cooperation with the USDA Soil Conservation Service (now the Natural Resources Conservation Service).

Wildlife Management

Wildlife management has been an integral part of managing the national forest system. The NFS includes 2.3 million acres of fishable lakes, ponds, and reservoirs and more than 197,000 miles of perennial streams. National forests and grasslands support habitats for more than 3,000 species of birds, mammals, reptiles, amphibians, and fish, as well as some 10,000 plant species. In 2000, more than 76,000 people engaged in eyes-on wildlife and migratory bird day events on national forests and grasslands. The national forests and grasslands also provide 80 percent of the elk, mountain goat, and bighorn sheep habitat in the lower 48 states, 28 million acres of wild turkey habitat, 5.4 million acres of wetland habitat, and habitat for 250 species of neotropical migratory birds and 2,800 species classified as sensitive,

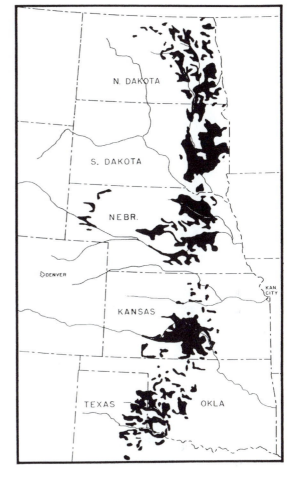

Major planting areas of the Shelterbelt Project 1933–1942. (USDA Forest Service)

threatened, or endangered plants, fish, or wildlife. Partnerships are of growing importance in the management of wildlife on the NFS. By 2001, $17.6 million in federal funds were matched by partners' $26.9 million, for a total of $44.5 million to accomplish partnership projects for wildlife, fish, and threatened, endangered, and sensitive species.

Wildlife, especially what we call big game (deer, elk, moose, bears), was an important part of the conservation movement of the late nineteenth century. Wildlife did not have the economic importance of other resources such as timber, forage, and water; however, it did capture the public's attention as much as efforts to preserve scenic vistas, waterfalls, and geysers. Conservationists such as George Bird Grinnell, founder of *Field and Stream* magazine, and Theodore Roosevelt, a cofounder of the Boone and Crockett Club, were alarmed by the huge decline of big game in the western states, especially as evidenced by the almost total elimination of the bison and the pronghorn antelope and the extirpation of the passenger pigeon. When Roosevelt sponsored Gifford Pinchot for membership in the club, Pinchot was able to expand the notion of forest conservation to embrace the cause of big game protection. Yet, when the federal forest reserves were transferred from the Department of the Interior to the Department of Agriculture, in 1905, the Forest Service apparently did not see much of a relationship between national forest administration and wildlife. Instead, the emphasis on timber and grazing resources set the future tone of the agency.

Moreover, the agency had to be cautious about regulating game animals and birds on the forest reserves for fear of trampling states' rights and giving its western critics reason to disband the reserves. The policy of the Forest Service was to "cooperate with the game wardens of the State or Territory in which they serve," according to the first book of directives issued by the agency in 1905 (the *Use Book*). Two years later, a provision in the Agricultural Appropriations Act of 1907 made it law that "hereafter officials of the Forest Service shall, in all ways that are practicable, aid in the enforcement of the laws of the States or Territories with regard to . . . the protection of fish and game." For a number of years, forest rangers often were deputized as state game wardens.

An unusual situation arose during the early 1900s when the Forest Service became interested in saving a small herd of bison/buffalo and long-horned cattle. On July 4, 1901, President William McKinley set aside the Wichita Forest Reserve in Oklahoma (32 Stat. 1973). The land came from part of the Apache-Comanche-Kiowa Indian Reservation. President Theodore Roosevelt renamed it the Wichita Forest and Game Preserve, on June 2, 1905. It was the first managed wildlife preserve or refuge in the United States.

Millions of bison or buffalo in the United States had been slaughtered for meat and sport during and after the extensive railroad building effort across the Great Plains. In October 1907, 15 bison were donated by the New York Zoological Society from their zoo to the Forest Service in Oklahoma. The Forest Service became, for the next 29 years, a manager of the almost vanished bison, managing the small herd much like cattle. The bison proliferated. This was the beginning of the restocking effort at the Wichita refuge. In 1910–1911, 11 pronghorn antelope from Yellowstone National Park were introduced, and they thrived, as well. A year later, 20 Rocky Mountain elk were relocated from Jackson Hole, Wyoming, to the Wichita refuge in an effort to reestablish elk to the prairie. In 1912, 6 wild turkeys were transplanted from Missouri, with 15 more added in 1945 from the Arkansas National Wildlife Refuge in Texas. Seven bighorn sheep were introduced in 1929 from Alberta, Canada, but they were unable to adjust to the climate and perished.

The Forest Service was instrumental in saving the almost vanished Texas longhorn cattle breed when 29 longhorns were brought from south Texas in 1927 to the Wichita National Forest. The longhorns, which have long been icons of the old West, especially the famous cattle drives of the middle 1800s, had been extensively interbred with other cattle species and were losing their distinctiveness. The *San Antonio Express News*, on August 7, 1927, commented on the longhorn cattle deal:

> The Longhorn is saved. Although he doesn't look in the least like a carrier pigeon, he was just about to go the same way that great bird went. Twenty-nine Longhorn cattle have been secured in south Texas and are on their way to the Wichita forest reserve, located 17 miles out from Lawton, Oklahoma, in the Wichita Mountains. Give thanks to Will C. Barnes of the forest service for this great accomplishment. . . . He played a leading role in the most colorful of all our national development movements. Barnes spent Friday in San Antonio, leaving early Saturday for Austin. . . . While here [in San Antonio], he was bubbling over with happiness at the success of his month's search in Texas for specimens of the old-time cattle. He and his assistant, John H. Hatton, actually looked over 50,000 cattle in their search. . . . Barnes was a practical cattleman for 26 years in New Mexico and Arizona, he had one of his most exciting moments of cattledom on Bob Sutton's ranch near Cotulla. On that ranch, Bob keeps a 15-year-old outlaw steer which bears the euphonious name of "Pizen Weed," and old Pizen Weed puts Barnes on a fence.
>
> More, Barnes lost his Panama hat as he ran for safety, and old Pizen Weed trampled it and gored it beautifully, finally getting it stuck on his horn where he wore it some little while. Barnes was wearing the hat as he left San Antonio. "Honestly," said the beleaguered representative of the forest service, "a good movie film of my flight and that wild outlaw charging around the Sutton corral with my Panama on his horn would have furnished a large laugh for any audience. Think, there must have been $1,000,000 worth of film actually lost." . . .
>
> [The cattle] will be assembled in Fort Worth . . . and after a final inspection and dipping [usually in an arsenic bath] for ticks, will go on to the reserve. These cattle have been bought in small bunches, here and there, where they could be found. No one man had enough of them, said Barnes. All were bought, paid for and a bill of sale taken. Most of them were from small owners to whom the price was of interest. The assembled herd will comprise 20 cows, three bulls, three steers and one bull yearling. "The bulls are a hard lot," said Mr. Barnes, explaining that they were extremely aged, and a bit off in flesh and general beauty. "One crop of calves from them and we will be safe," said Barnes. . . .
>
> The progenitors of these cattle were imported from Spain to America in 1522, according to researches made by Barnes. John B. Kendrick, once a Texas cowboy, now U.S. senator from Wyoming, is due thanks for saving the Longhorn, modestly asserts Barnes. . . . Kendrick, influential senator, is the man who persuaded Congress to appropriate the money that turned the trick, after repeated failures by Barnes . . . , "John B. Kendrick is the man who got the money out of Congress for saving the Longhorn, and I hope it is not forgotten," Barnes emphasizes.

The Wichita National Forest and Game Preserve was designated the Wichita Mountains Wildlife Refuge on June 4, 1936, then transferred to the USDI Fish and Wildlife Service, on November 27, 1936 (50 Stat. 1797 and 1 FR 2148). The refuge contains 59,020 acres. Today, herds of about 550 bison, 300 longhorn cattle, 380 elk, around 450 white-tailed deer, and more than 400 wild turkeys roam the refuge. Hunting is allowed for the deer, but not the turkeys. Excess bison, longhorn cattle, and elk are sold each fall.

The agency helped pioneer the field of wildlife management and stimulated many of the states to begin or improve their own programs. Hunters and anglers were the largest group of recreationists visiting the national forests, so it was natural for the Forest Service to focus its attention on fish and game animals. Federal game refuges created on national forests (see Appendix 1) to conserve wildlife were helpful in increasing populations of game animals, and these animals then could be hunted on adjacent lands. The growth of deer populations led to conflicts between hunters and ranchers. Recreational hunters wanted more game animals; ranchers, concerned with forage depletion wanted fewer.

In the 1920s, the Kaibab National Forest was in charge of the Grand Canyon National Game Preserve, located on the north rim of the Grand Canyon, which had been established in 1906. It was thought at the time that the preserve could protect between 3,000 and 4,000 mule deer. By the early 1920s, the deer population had swelled to roughly 100,000 animals. In 1923, some 20,000 mule deer starved to death. This was followed the next year by a drought. Conditions could not have been worse for the deer. Attempts were made to drive some of the deer across the canyon to the south rim, but the deer were uncooperative, and the effort failed. By the late fall of 1924, the Forest Service brought in rangers to shoot as many deer as they could. The state of Arizona, however, did not agree and arrested three of the rangers. The dispute went to the Supreme Court, where the Forest Service won a victory, in 1928, when the court found that Forest Service employees could hunt excess game to "prevent property damage," that is, to protect the forage resource from overgrazing by deer. By this time, the state had agreed to controlled hunting on the preserve. This agreement set forth the principles of game management, with the states managing the populations and the federal government managing the habitat.

It was in the Southwest that Aldo Leopold, a Forest Service employee from 1909 to 1928, developed his concept of wildlife management that led to the first textbook on the subject, *Game Management* (1933). Leopold favored the eradication of predators as a step in bringing back big game populations, but, after killing a mother wolf one day, his eyes were opened to the importance of predators in the natural balance of deer populations. However, the attempt at total extermination of wolves from the national forests would continue for decades. Forest rangers and hunters from the USDA Biological Survey killed as many predators as possible. The list of predators included grizzles, black bears, wolves, coyotes, foxes, badgers, eagles, and almost every other carnivore. Techniques included shooting, trapping, and the placement of poisons in areas where the animals would feed.

In 1929, the Forest Service hired its first wildlife biologist, Barry Locke, who was stationed in the Intermountain Region. He left two years later to serve as director of the Izaak Walton League. The economic depression of the 1930s at first halted wildlife programs for lack of funds. A few years later, the public works programs, especially the Civilian Conservation Corps, of the new Roosevelt administration provided employment that included work in natural resources conservation, including wildlife habitat improvement.

By 1936, the year Dr. Homer Shantz became first director of wildlife management, 61 people were assigned to wildlife work in the Forest Service. The national forests in the Southeast grew rapidly in number during the Depression through federal purchase of severely cut-over and eroded private lands. The management challenge for these lands was to make their recovering forests suitable places for wildlife. From this goal came the slogan "Good timber management is good wildlife management."

In the Pacific Northwest, the Forest Service found that public support for elk protection superseded demand for timber production. A lengthy battle ensued with the Park Service over the management of Mt. Olympus National Monument, which was established in 1909 to protect the Roosevelt elk (named after Teddy Roosevelt). Forest Service officials argued that the best use of the monument, then managed by the Forest Service, and surrounding national forests was to open the area to forest (timber) management, which would provide employment and recreation for the local population. The controversy came to a boil during the mid-1930s, when the Forest Service and the Bureau of Biological Survey recommended that the elk population in the monument be reduced by shooting to prevent overgrazing, disease, and starvation. Citizens were outraged, especially the editor of the *Seattle Post-Intelligencer,* whose wife was the daughter of President Franklin Roosevelt. When Roosevelt visited the area in 1937, he had already decided to include the monument and adjacent national forest system lands in a new Olympic National Park (established by Congress in 1939).

In the late 1940s, agency involvement in wildlife was reduced following the improvement of state fish and game programs and the rise of timber harvesting on national forests. Problem areas surfaced as squirrel hunters in the Southern Region, upset over loss of oak trees, exclaimed, in 1956: "You kill the hardwoods, we'll kill the pine." In the 1960s, turkey hunters on the Monongahela National Forest complained of clearcuts in their favorite hunting areas. The result was a lawsuit by the Izaak Walton League, congressional hearings, and passage of the National Forest Management Act of 1976. This law required the Forest Service to conduct its planning to ensure a diversity of plant and animal species and thus is responsible for the rapid increase in wildlife personnel in the late 1970s.

The Forest Service was not created to protect wildlife, but its rangers realized that if they did not manage these animal's habitats, nobody else would. Thus, the agency became an early leader in the field of wildlife management. One of the earliest attempts by the Forest Service to protect a species involved a bird—the California condor (*Gymnogyps californianus*). This vulture, with a wingspan of nine feet, was almost extirpated. The bird once ranged from British Columbia, Canada, to Baja California, Mexico, and through the Southwest to Florida and north to New York State. A large decline occurred when European settlers arrived on the West Coast and accelerated during the gold rush of 1849. Condors were shot and poisoned, while eggs and adult birds were collected for natural history museum collections. The last sightings of the condor in Arizona and New Mexico took place in the mid-1930s. In 1935, the Forest Service proposed constructing a new road through Sisquoc Canyon, on the Los Padres National Forest, in California. The road was to be built for better fire control in the area where condors have been known to nest. The National Audubon Society protested and contributed $270 to make field studies of the condor. By October 1936, because of the studies, the Forest Service decided not to build the road. However, it was unclear as to what the management should be. This was clarified when the controversial G-20 regulation was issued in 1936. The next year, regulation T-9-I was issued to replace the earlier regulation to protect the condors. Under the new regulation, 1,200 acres in Sisquoc Canyon were set aside as critical habitat for the condor. The effort was nearly too late as the number of condors continued to fall. By 1940, the species range was reduced to a horseshoe-shaped area in southern California.

A larger 35,000-condor sanctuary was established in 1947, but the bird's numbers were still declining. California condors nest in various types of rock formations in the Los Padres National Forest and in cavities in giant Sequoia trees. The last breeding pair of California condors was taken in 1987 from a nest in a giant sequoia tree on the Sequoia National Forest within an area now designated as part of the Giant Sequoia National Monument. Thanks to successful efforts in captive breeding and restoration of the magnificent bird to habitats in southern California and areas along the Grand Canyon, young birds raised in captivity have been reintroduced into the wild in western Monterey County, eastern San Luis Obispo County, and eastern Santa Barbara County in California, and near the Grand Canyon in Arizona.

In 1949, prior to the Endangered Species Act of 1973, the Puerto Rican parrot (*Amazona vittata*) was in serious trouble. The parrots were found only in the Sierra de Luquillo Mountains in eastern Puerto Rico, formerly a forest reserve of the Spanish Crown and currently managed as the Caribbean National Forest. This area contained the last forest habitat suitable for the unique and endangered parrots (listed as endangered by the Fish and Wildlife Service in 1967). The only parrot native to the United States once numbered as many as a million, but by 1949 there were only around 2,000 birds; this number was further reduced to 27 birds, then 13. The Forest Service tropical forest researcher Frank Wadsworth was successful in setting aside 3,200 acres for the parrot in 1949, and he was able to get limited recovery money from Puerto Rico, the Forest Service, the Fish and Wildlife Service, and World Wildlife. Hurricane Hugo, in 1989, killed about half of the remaining parrots in the wild. The wild population numbers around 50 parrots, with another 120 in two aviaries on the island.

Another bird species—the Kirkland's warbler—came close to extinction. The warbler (*Dendroica kertlandii*) is roughly sparrow-sized, standing around six inches tall and weighing in at roughly one-half ounce. It is one of the world's rarest birds. The only consistent breeding grounds for the Kirkland is in the dense jack pine forests in Michigan's Lower Peninsula in an area 100 miles long and 60 miles wide within the Au Sable River drainage area, a part of which is on the Huron-Manistee National Forest. Since 1995, a small population has been observed nesting on the nearby Hiawatha National Forest, on the Upper Peninsula. These birds are known as the "bird of fire" because intense heat is needed to create meadows, open the jack pine cone, and release the seeds for a new forest. Fire also removes plants that compete with the pines for forest space and creates a bed of ash that helps the new seeds to grow. Fires were more common before the twentieth century in the jack pine plains of Michigan and created large nesting areas for the Kirtland's warbler.

The USDI Fish and Wildlife Service, on March 11, 1967, listed the Kirtland's warbler as an endangered species. It is currently designated as endangered in the entire range. This species is known to occur in Michigan and Ontario, along their migratory corridor through parts of the Southeast, and in the Bahamas. The first steps to help the bird had been taken 10 years earlier, when the Michigan Audubon Society convinced the Michigan Department of Conservation (now the Department of Natural Resources) to set aside three 2,500-acre tracts to be managed for warbler habitat. The Forest Service on the Huron National Forest followed in 1960 with another 3,900-acre tract. As early as 1962, the Huron-Manistee National Forest developed a management plan for the Kirkland's warbler.

Restoration of their nesting habitat has been credited with increasing the bird's population. The Kirtland's warbler recovery team was established in 1975. This team, made up of representatives from the Fish and Wildlife Service, the Forest Service, the Michigan Department of Natural Resources, and the Michigan Audubon Society, monitors the recovery of the warblers and ensures that the objectives of the recovery plan are met. The recovery plan calls for managing jack pine habitat through harvest and/or burning on state (60%) and federal (40%) lands. In addition, the control of cowbird populations in the nesting areas has been highly successful. The goal is to have a minimum of 1,000 breeding males throughout the warbler's former range. The current number of Kirkland's warblers is relatively stable from spring to spring, reaching a high of 1,415 in 2005, with 458 found on the Huron-Manistee National Forest, on the Lower Peninsula, and in a small, newly established population of 18 on the Hiawatha National Forest, on the Upper Peninsula.

Passage of the Endangered Species Act of 1973 gave additional authority to land managers to protect individual species and habitats for threatened and endangered wildlife, fish, and plant species. The Forest Service caught up with this new reality with publication of *Wildlife Habitats in Managed Forests— The Blue Mountains of Oregon and Washington* (1979), edited by the future Chief Jack Ward Thomas. It was the first agency book to provide "concrete direction for the management of game and non-game species alike."

STATE AND PRIVATE FORESTRY

About 70 percent of America's forests are in state and private ownership, and 80 percent of the wood fiber potential comes from these lands. These lands are also critical to watershed conditions, fish and wildlife habitat, and the aesthetic quality of the nation's landscape; and they represent one of the best sources of carbon sequestration. Since these nonfederal forests represent most of the forests in our country, keeping these lands healthy, productive, and sustainable in the rural and urban areas on a cumulative basis is especially important to the nation.

With increasing fragmentation and development pressure, the unique federal role in maintaining the value and functions of these lands across ownership divisions has never been greater or more important. The state and private forestry (S&PF) programs in the Forest Service represent important tools for the protection, management, monitoring, and better use of America's forests. These programs connect forestry, without imposing regulations, to all land managers, whether small, urban woodlot owners, tribal foresters, or state or federal agencies. Through coordinated efforts, the programs of S&PF help facilitate sound forestry across ownerships on a landscape scale.

The Forest Service and its predecessors have been involved with cooperative assistance to forest landowners since 1876. Several forest reserves were created to protect the city water supply (such as the Bull Run Timberland Reserve, in 1892, Portland, Oregon's water supply). Since the early USDA Division of Forestry and later Bureau of Forestry did not directly manage the forest reserves, the main duty of USDA's forestry experts was to assist private landowners—including the writing of plans for millions of acres of private timberland. After 1905, when management of the forest reserves was transferred to the USDA and the new Forest Service, the department's foresters were quickly moved to field positions in the West. However, providing "practical forestry" assistance to private landowners remained one of the agency's most important missions.

In 1908, Gifford Pinchot recognized the obligation of the Forest Service to the private sector when he formally established the branch of state and private forestry (S&PF) in the Washington office. This was the second "leg" of the agency—the other being the national forest system. Cooperation was ongoing with the USDA Bureau of Entomology for pest control work and with the Bureau of Plant Industry on forest tree diseases. One of the new S&PF Division's first efforts was to aid states in the study of forest taxation. The agency published wholesale lumber price lists and supported lumber industry efforts to retain a tariff on lumber—with the understanding that those efforts were in the public interest. The lumber industry wanted the Forest Service to keep federal timber off the market. With the vast storehouse of national forest timber (much of it inaccessible), selling the trees before they were needed in the housing market would reduce private timber prices and generally weaken the lumber industry. Yet the Forest Service continued to sell small timber tracts to ensure that the national forests were used, not set aside as parks.

Interestingly, Gifford Pinchot wanted the Forest Service to control all forestlands, not just the national forests. He engaged the Society of American Foresters in a decades-long debate about the appropriate role of the federal government in forestry. Although he spoke with great passion, the decision by the Forest Service was that the states should control the timber industry outside the NFS. In the 1930s, Article X of the Forest Code called for the timber companies to voluntarily accept better management practices. When the U.S. Supreme Court said that the Forest Code was unconstitutional, many states turned to what today is called "best management practices" as a way to regulate timber harvest and reforestation.

Chief Henry Graves noted that cooperation fell into three categories: advising states in establishing forest policies, assisting them in surveying their forest resources (mainly timber), and helping forest owners with practical forestry problems. Section 2 of the Weeks Act of 1911 codified Chief Graves's ideas. It authorized the Forest Service to work together with its state counterparts to fight fire on federal, state, or private land. (Previously, if a fire started in private or state land, the Forest Service could not help until the fire entered the national forests.) With the Weeks Act in place, it did not matter where the fire started or ended; the main point was to put it out, and the money would be taken care of later. The Weeks Act also authorized $10,000 in matching funds for state fire protection agencies' local fire prevention programs.

The Clarke-McNary Act of 1924 greatly expanded the Weeks Act. The new Act used cooperation and incentives to improve private forestland conditions. Fire and taxes were the primary components of the Act, which allowed federal, state, and private interests to work together. Section 3 of the Clarke-McNary Act authorized the Forest Service to study tax laws and their effects on forestland management. Because of concerns over the nation's future wood supplies as they related to capital investments, logging activities, and even fire, the Forest Service assumed a responsibility in the tax matter. However, when Professor Fred R. Fairchild's 1935 report failed to find any relationship between taxes and management, the report quickly fell into obscurity.

On the basis of the Lea Act of 1940, which was designed to unify and coordinate efforts to control the white pine blister rust problem, irrespective of property boundaries, the Forest Pest Control Act of 1947 recognized a federal responsibility for forest insect and disease protection on all ownerships. This law also offered technical and financial assistance to state forestry agencies to control insects and disease outbreaks in forested areas.

Cooperative Efforts

The Cooperative Forest Management Act of 1950 expanded the Forest Service's cooperative efforts of the postwar decade, provided for technical assistance, and extended management assistance to all classes of forest ownership. The Forest Service gave priority to assisting small forest landowners. In 1952, the Forest Service initiated a major field inventory, the timber resources review (TRR), to analyze the condition of small forestland ownerships. Although drafts of the report were circulated within two years, the forest products industry protected its results so much that the final report was not published until 1958! The TRR report found that forest practices would need to be intensified to meet future demands and that small ownerships were in the greatest need of assistance. Although the Forest Service made efforts to institute such a program, it proved to be too controversial and expensive.

The Small Watershed Act (Public Law 566), in 1954, expanded the Forest Service authority to include flood prevention on farmland watersheds not exceeding 250,000 acres. The program covered flood prevention structures, upstream protection, and livestock control. The agency worked closely with the USDA Soil Conservation Service, the Agricultural Research Service, the U.S. Army Corps of Engineers, and the states to implement such projects.

The primary statutory authority for many of the current S&PF program activities is the Cooperative Forestry Assistance Act of 1978, as amended by the 1990 farm bill. In the past, the focus of the cooperative program has been timber production, wood utilization, fire protection, and insect and disease control, but the emphasis is changing. Cooperative forestry is now involved in urban forestry to maintain trees within urban areas, reach out to new constituencies, and build new partnerships in the inner cities. A new forest stewardship program seeks to help nonindustrial private forest owners, both technically and financially, to manage all the resources on their forestlands according to their own objectives. The rural development initiative is designed to help small communities diversify and strengthen their local economies. Regional foresters are responsible for the S&PF programs, with the exception of the Northeastern Area, which is located in Newtown Square, Pennsylvania. The Northeastern Area is a reflection of the large number of nonindustrial private woodland owners who reside in the Northeastern states.

There are several important programs that the Forest Service currently manages under state and private forestry. *Cooperative forestry* is an S&PF program that provides assistance to nonindustrial private forest landowners (NIPF), and community cooperative forestry supports the Forest Service mission in two important ways. First, it helps meet the needs of present and future generations by "connecting people to resources and ideas" and by assisting them to "sustain their communities." Second, it helps to sustain the health, diversity, and productivity of the forests and grasslands by helping people care for the land and its resources.

Economic action programs stimulate and assist natural resource dependent rural communities and natural resource based businesses to pursue self-sufficiency and sustainability. There is a special focus on helping build rural business infrastructures to aid such businesses in utilizing and marketing their products and services. The economic action programs as a whole and the funds from the national fire plan designated for rural communities are used to build local communities' capacity to address their own needs and to create opportunities.

Forest health protection is an important function of S&PF. The Forest Service provides technical and financial assistance to federal agencies, tribal governments, states, and (through state foresters) private landowners. The Forest Service and state foresters participate in a forest health-monitoring program. With USDA Animal and Plant Health Inspection Service, the Forest Service works to protect the nation's forests from exotic insects, diseases, and plants. The Forest Service provides technical assistance in the safe and effective use of pesticides, shares the cost of insect and disease prevention and suppression projects with states, and funds prevention and suppression projects on federal lands. The agency also evaluates and applies new, efficient, and environmentally sensitive technologies for forest health protection.

The forest legacy program is designed to effectively protect and conserve environmentally important forest areas that are threatened by conversion to nonforest uses. These lands can be protected through conservation easements and other mechanisms. This program is based on the concept of "willing seller and willing buyer." The program is nonregulatory in its approach. No eminent domain authority or adverse condemnation is authorized.

The forest products and conservation recycling program was founded to provide technical and financial assistance to businesses that employ 10 or less people, businesses that employ 11 to 99 people, and individual businesses that employ 100 or more people and to offer assistance to communities and nonprofit organizations seeking to better use small forest products and enhance recycling efforts at the community level.

Forest stewardship program promotes sustainable management of nonfederal forests by enabling 9.9 million NIPF landowners—who own 48 percent of the nation's forests—to better manage, protect, and use their natural resources. In cooperation with state resource management agencies, the program assists forest landowners with planning and implementation of riparian restoration, wildlife habitat enhancement, forest stand improvement, and other aspects of sustainable forest management. The program also assists NIPF landowners, on a voluntary, nonregulatory basis and in cooperation with states, by providing technical and inancial assistance to support development of long-term forest stewardship plans for the management of their forests and related sources.

The rural community assistance program is designed to provide technical or financial assistance to nearly rural communities and organizations. This total includes tribes/tribal organizations, minority communities/organizations, and underserved communities—usually black, Latino, and American Indian. Wildfire protection and prevention and hazardous fuels management were incorporated into rural-community strategic-action plans.

The wood in transportation program in FY2001 funded six projects that were completed and closed. Those projects designed and constructed timber bridges. These projects not only resulted in a wooden timber bridge but also assisted in providing technical assistance to engineers, highway officials, and others.

Forest Insect and Pest Problems

Forest insect and pest problems have been a major focus of the S&PF, along with the research branch, which help with identifying problems and assisting the states and private owners. Especially notable have been the chestnut blight, Dutch elm disease, and gypsy moth efforts.

The chestnut blight ravaged the American chestnut the East during the early twentieth century, almost totally eliminating one of the most important hardwood species from North America. The American Indians and early settlers of eastern North America looked upon the forests and saw an ecosystem that is considerably different from the one we know today. Formerly, the tallest trees in our eastern hardwood forests, chestnut trees, were towering, with many reaching 100 feet and some approaching 130 feet and 10 feet or more in diameter. The ability of the chestnut tree to reliably produce abundant nuts each fall supported large numbers of animals, including squirrels, turkeys, passenger pigeons, and many big game species.

The problem began with the planting of a few exotic chestnut trees (possibly the Japanese chestnut) in or near New York City shortly after the turn of the twentieth century. The ornamental trees brought with them a blight that would soon devastate the American chestnut. Blight was first detected on chestnut trees in the Bronx Zoo in 1904 and spread quickly through New England and the Middle Atlantic states to the Midwest and ultimately down the Appalachian chain to the Gulf states. By 1940, 3.5 billion of an estimated 4 billion trees had perished. The remaining half billion adult trees have been killed, and the record of devastation greatly surpasses that of the Dutch elm disease (discussed later). The Forest Service began to study the problem very early but could do little other than document the spread of the blight.

The loss of the American chestnut was sharply felt. Their nuts were an important food for both the people on the frontier and the animals that roamed the hardwood forests. The wood was somewhat like oak in appearance, though not as strong or dense, but its lightness, workability, and stability made it valuable for building and furniture. Its resistance to decay was especially valued in uses such as railroad ties and utility poles. Because it was readily available and easily split, the split-rail snake fences of the Appalachians, which are now common in showy restorations of frontier settlements, were made of chestnut. Because of the tannin in its bark and wood, chestnut was cut heavily to supply tanneries.

There are so few mature American chestnut trees left anywhere in the world today that the species is now threatened with extinction in the foreseeable future. Healthy specimens have effectively ceased to exist, and natural reproduction is essentially nil. Extinction would be imminent if it were not for the tree's remarkable capacity for sending up vigorous new shoots, albeit infected ones, from surviving root systems, which the blight ordinarily cannot destroy. Hence, the species survives in fair quantity, but almost entirely in the form of stunted understory shrubs that seldom are able to reach reproductive maturity before the blight gains its stronghold and girdles each sprout near its base, forcing the root system to send up new sets of shoots continually.

Even in the vast areas where all the American chestnuts have been killed decades ago, the blight fungus is still present. Forest Service research by the Northeastern Area, as well as by various universities, on the blight and resistant trees continues to this day. The American Chestnut Foundation (ACF), founded in 1983, is devoted "toward the restoration of an American classic." Research to improve understanding of the biology of the blight has been conducted at tax-supported research centers and. The goal of the ACF's plant-breeding program is to combine the natural blight resistance of the Chinese chestnut with the favorable tree and nut-producing characteristics of the American chestnut. The assumption is that a cross that is fifteen-sixteenths American chestnut will have characteristics very much like those of a pure American chestnut plus the resistance of the Chinese chestnut.

Dutch elm disease affects the American elm tree, which was noted as having a very widespread range across North America. The tree has a natural range from southern Newfoundland to the northern shores of Lake Superior, along the eastern slope of the Rocky Mountains, and through the Mississippi drainage to Florida. American elm is one of the largest, most impressive, and most abundant landscape trees in eastern cities. When fully mature, an American elm may reach an impressive 100 feet, with the broad arching branches that have often identified city streets with almost cathedral-like arches.

Dutch elm disease (DED) was first discovered in France in 1818. Dutch elm disease is the fungus (*Ophiostoma ulmi*), which is spread by bark beetles. These beetles feed in the upper branches of the tree and introduce the fungal spores to exposed tree, which can kill even a well-established 100-year-old elm in as little as two weeks. Within 10 years, the fungus was already widespread in the England. It was first reported in the United States in 1920, with the beetles believed to have arrived in a shipment of furniture. The disease spread slowly from New England westward and southward, reaching the Chicago area by 1960 and Minneapolis by 1970. Around 100 million American elms have succumbed to DED. Dead trees were everywhere, especially in the eastern and midwestern cities where the massive elms were dying in huge number. It was common for a city to lose 90 percent of its elm trees in as little as 10 years, leaving what one would think was an early winter—trees devoid of all leaves. But the trees never recovered—they were dead.

Research work on the mystery disease was carried out between 1919 and 1934 by several Dutch scientists, and the name of the disease was associated with this research. All species of elm (American, red or slippery, rock, and cedar elms) are highly susceptible to the disease. DED can remain active for years in the root system, and reinfections can occur. The disease can also spread from tree to tree along their common root system.

Although fungicides and insecticides have been used to control DED, the most effective control is what is referred to as sanitation. This refers to promptly removing dying elms to make sure that beetles cannot attack and spread DED. It also helps in reducing root-to-root transmission of the disease. University researchers have recently developed resistant hybrid elms, including the Prospector, Frontier, Urban, Homestead, Pioneer, American Liberty, Delaware #2, and Sapporo Autumn Gold. Some of these resistant species, however, do not look exactly like the American elm.

The Forest Service has also been an active participant in fighting *Gypsy moth* outbreaks and has tried to control other nonindigenous or invasive species. Gypsy moths, native to Europe and parts of Asia, in their larval/caterpillar stage tend to feed on deciduous trees, with such species as alder, apple, basswood, box elder, birch, oak, popular, and willow being favorites. Evergreen trees are usually not favorite foods of the European variety but are within the food appetite of the Asian variety. The moths can move across the landscape, given the proper food sources and wind conditions, covering as much as 13 miles per year. In addition, moth larvae and egg "nests" can travel across the country on cars, trucks, boats, and trains that can cause and have caused outbreaks of gypsy moths far removed from their northeastern area.

The gypsy moth was intentionally brought into the United States in 1869 by the French astronomer Etienne Leopold Trouvelot, who was living in Medford, Massachusetts, near Boston. He hoped to promote a disease-resistant silkworm for America and a new textile industry but succeeded only in making his neighbors mad. The first moth escaped into the environment the same year and soon was recognized as an invasive pest. The public perception of the gypsy moth as a problem came to a head two decades later when the gypsy moth population exploded.

Massachusetts's efforts to eradicate the gypsy moth in 1899 were considered so successful that the project was abandoned in 1900 while on the brink of success. The moths were then discovered in nearby Rhode Island, in 1901. In 1905, after the second irruption of the gypsy moth in Massachusetts and discoveries in New Hampshire, for a total area of some 2,224 square miles, the federal government stepped in to fight the pest in cooperation with the affected states. But, by then, the insect had spread too far into neighboring states to make eradication a success. That same year, a USDA researcher was sent to Europe to find and study the moths' native parasites. In 1906, the moth was found in Connecticut. Two years later, the USDA sent another researcher to Japan to search for additional parasites. By 1912, a population of the moths was found in Vermont. A federal quarantine was imposed on the gypsy moth. In 1913, the USDA Bureau of Entomology began a study of the female moths' pheromone. Gypsy moths spread throughout New England, and by 1914 the generally infested area included the southern half of New Hampshire, Rhode Island, eastern Connecticut, southern Vermont, and the eastern half of Massachusetts. By 1927, the area infested by gypsy moths exceeded 100,000 acres. The New England hurricane of September 21, 1938, spread the gypsy moths for hundreds of miles into new territory.

By the mid-1950s, the insect was detected in previously uninfested areas in New Jersey, New York, Pennsylvania, and Michigan. Attempts to eradicate the insect were quickly falling behind the area of infestation. In 1979, Maryland and Delaware reported heavy damage by the moths. By the following year, more than 5 million acres of forestlands had been defoliated. The defoliated area greatly expanded such that by 1981, some 12.8 million acres were infested and damaged. In 1994, the gypsy moth was a permanent resident in all or parts of 16 states and the District of Columbia.

Prior to 1966, the rate of spread of gypsy moths was relatively low, with a rate of about two to six miles per year. However, between 1966 and 1990, the rate of spread has averaged about 13 miles per year. If the Asian gypsy moth, common to eastern Russia, gains a foothold, the rate of spread could increase. The European gypsy moth caterpillar can eat the leaves more than 500 species of trees and shrubs. In North America, the preferred food source is the leaves on oak trees, as well as those on apple, basswood, poplar, willow, box elder, larch, and several species of alder, birches, and aspen. Maple and hickory are somewhat favored. Severely infested trees often become completely defoliated, or leafless. Three years of complete defoliation is usually enough to kill a tree; evergreen, young, or weak trees may succumb in just one year.

None of the natural insect parasites and predators from Europe and Asia were present in the United States to kill the larvae or moths. With no natural controls, people in the Northeast began using a variety of methods to kill the moths. Control methods in the late 1800s included using creosote or acid to destroy egg masses, burning infested trees and shrubs, banding trees to trap larvae, or spraying with insecticides. Paris green, the original gypsy moth insecticide that was used in 1890–1892, was replaced with lead arsenate in 1893. When biological controls did not do the eradication job, other methods were tried. Following World War I, the favored control method was chemical insecticides. They gave relief to homeowners in the cities and towns but did little in the heavily forested areas.

New chemical insecticide control methods were considered and experimented with both before and during World War II. Experiments that used airplanes to dispense insecticides were conducted as early as 1926 at Cape Cod. By the 1940s, airplanes and autogyros (early helicopters) to spray the insecticide were used successfully, and they have been used ever since. In the 1940s, cryolite, pyrethrum, and xanthone were used experimentally—in part because they were less toxic than lead arsenate—but they were considered ineffectual. The most promising new chemical was DDT. This highly effective, but also highly dangerous, insecticide was used experimentally in Pennsylvania, and the gypsy moth was considered eradicated in the state by 1948. However, undetected infestations led to further outbreaks and continued spread, and, by 1953, the pest had defoliated more than a million acres of forests. A major federal effort was initiated to eradicate the gypsy moth began in the late 1950s in New York, Pennsylvania, and Michigan, using DDT. During its use, DDT was applied to more than 12 million acres of forest in nine northeast states and Michigan for gypsy moth control. Questions concerning the nontarget effects of DDT led to its being replaced with carbaryl (Sevin) in 1958. The death knell for the use of DDT came after publication of Rachel Carson's book *Silent Spring* (1962). The use of DDT in the Forest Service Eastern Region ended in 1965. Seven years later, the Environmental Protection Agency (EPA) banned DDT for most uses, but, in 1973, the Forest Service requested that the EPA grant it an exception. The EPA rather reluctantly granted the agency the right to use aerial-applied DDT on a tussock moth outbreak in northeastern Oregon. It was the last application of DDT by aerial means.

Hope for total eradication was abandoned in the 1970s, and research efforts on effective means of gypsy moth control were initiated. Research projects included the use of *Borralinivirus reprimens,* called the nucleopolyhedrosis virus or NPV (registered under the trade name Gypchek), and *Bacillus thuringiensis (B.t.)* as biological control agents. The first widespread use of B.t. occurred in the Pacific Northwest in the early 1980s when outbreaks of the dreaded Asian gypsy moth were discovered in several cities and evergreen forest areas. The aerial spraying of B.t. in western Oregon proved to be as effective as the use of chemicals sprays. Yet, B.t., a natural control agent, has opponents who argue, often quite effectively, that the agent also kills related larvae of other species of moths and butterflies. Yet, so do applications of various chemicals.

Numerous spots of gypsy moth infestation have been identified across the country, and the numbers are growing. Usually, these spot infestations are tied to people—either on lawn and outdoor furniture and equipment, vehicles, and even railroad train cars. The reason is that the moths often lay large egg clusters on exposed surfaces that are easily transportable by people. The USDA Animal and Plant Health Inspection Service (APHIS) has the responsibility to check for moth egg masses on all movement of households from the Northeast to areas uninfected by the moths, but their resources are limited and their efforts only partially effective. APHIS has been an active partner with the Northeastern Area in investigating the moth biology, finding natural controls, monitoring areas, planting moth traps, and applying new methods to combat the infestations.

If the Asian gypsy moth gains a foothold in the western states, the rate of spread of the moths across the United States and Canada could increase. In areas of the East where forests have been ravaged by other exotic pests and diseases (e.g., Asian long-horned beetles, Dutch elm disease, and chestnut blight), the composition of the forests has changed dramatically over the past hundred years. Plant and animal species dependent on the original forests of the pioneers are now gone. If the gypsy moth continues on its rampage, the other large deciduous species will also be lost. The forests will never be the same again.

Yet there is a nagging question—how long does a nonnative species have to be in an area or country before it is considered native or at least ineradicable? How much money should the federal government and states pour onto eradication efforts before they finally realize that the effort is futile? The state of Massachusetts, where the moths escaped 130 years ago, has stopped all state funding of gypsy moth eradication, although counties, cities, and citizens continue to spray the trees in their areas. Perhaps other states will follow suit.

Conservation Education

"Through education, we connect people with the land so they take informed actions to sustain natural and cultural resources" is the mission statement of the Forest Service conservation education (CE) program. The agency is a leader in providing scientific knowledge through its research programs and offers outstanding opportunities for place-based learning about natural resources on more than 193 million acres of forests and grasslands within the NFS. It also provides an extensive delivery network for CE through more than 700 offices and 30,000 employees, as well as with partners such as state foresters. The Forest Service emphasizes delivery of CE to youth, urban populations, and forest visitors. Many conservation messages are spread through brochures, posters, seed packets, and scores of other highly successful methods.

Smokey Bear Campaign

The Smokey Bear anti-forest-fire campaign is overseen by the state and private forest branch of the Forest Service. During the early days of World War II, a Japanese submarine fired shells into an oil field near Santa Barbara, California. The threat posed by an enemy that was able to bombard the coast of the United States served as a warning that the forests were vulnerable to attack. The Forest Service wanted to somehow encourage the public to participate in forest fire prevention. Soon, a nationwide forest fire prevention campaign was launched. The Cooperative Forest Fire Prevention Campaign appealed for help from the newly formed Wartime Advertising Council. Initially, the 1942 and 1943 forest fire campaigns used propaganda slogans to spread the message, such as "Careless matches aid the Axis" and "Our carelessness, their secret weapon." For the 1944 campaign, the Walt Disney character Bambi was used.

During this time, Foote, Cone and Belding Communications, of Los Angeles, became the volunteer agency for the campaign. The campaign decided it wanted an illustration of a bear for the 1945 posters that would again illustrate a likable animal, as well as a firefighter. The new bear illustration was described by the director Richard Hammett as having a "nose short (Panda type), color black or brown; expression appealing, knowledgeable, quizzical; perhaps wearing a campaign (or Boy Scout) hat that typifies the outdoors and the woods." Blue jeans were added later. The bear was named "Smokey" after Joe "Smokey" Martin, who was a famous New York City Fire Department assistant chief. Albert Staehle, a nationally known artist, was asked to paint the first Smokey Bear. The 1945 Smokey poster showed him pouring water on a campfire. Smokey soon appeared in magazine and newspaper ads, and hundreds of radio stations donated valuable broadcasting time for his message.

It should be noted that the fire prevention animal is *not* Smokey the Bear. Officially, it is Smokey Bear, even though the 1950s song "Smokey the Bear" remains very popular and is loosely based on the Smokey story. Apparently, the middle word "the" was added because it made the song better for singing.

Rudolph "Rudy" Wendelin returned to the Forest Service in 1946 after serving in the navy and began working on Smokey Bear posters and continued to do so for the rest of his life. Rudy was the best-known Smokey Bear artist and soon became known as the "caretaker of the Smokey Bear image." After his retirement, in 1973, Rudy continued to paint Smokey and acted as a Smokey Bear program consultant. Harry Rossoll, another Forest Service artist, created four Smokey cartoons a month in the United States and Canada. Since that time, tens of millions of dollars have been contributed and donated to the Smokey campaign through radio, television, and print media.

On May 8, 1950, the 17,000-acre Capitan Gap fire was burning on the Lincoln National Forest, in New Mexico. A strong wind suddenly swept the fire toward a group of 25 firefighters, who nearly lost their lives. After the

Rudy Wendelin, Smokey Bear artist, Washington, D.C., c. 1960. (USDA Forest Service)

fire passed and the smoke cleared, the only living thing those firefighters saw was a badly burned bear cub clinging to a blackened tree. One of the fire fighters, Ray Bell, took the little bear to the ranger station to tend to the burns. The firefighters named him "Hotfoot Teddy," but the name was soon changed to Smokey. After the burns healed, the little bear was sent to the National Zoo in Washington, D.C., where he became the living symbol of Smokey and forest fire prevention, as well as the most visited attraction at the zoo. An orphaned bear was found in 1961 in the Magdelena Mountains of New Mexico. "Goldie," as she was named, was sent to the zoo to become Smokey's companion.

The Smokey Bear Act of May 23, 1952 (P.L 82–359) was written to protect Smokey's image from unauthorized use, since it was still in the public domain and the image could be used for any purpose. The act essentially copyrighted the act under the Secretary of Agriculture. It also had provisions for licensing appropriate use of the Smokey image. That same year, Ideal Toys manufactured the first Smokey Bear stuffed toy, which came with a postcard inviting the owner to become Smokey's "junior forest ranger." Children were quick to respond, and within three years there were more than half a million junior forest rangers. In 1965, Smokey Bear was given his own zip code—20252. By the 1970s, the Zoo received more than 1,000 letters a day addressed to Smokey, more than any person living in Washington, D.C., including the president, received.

In May 1975, the original Smokey Bear was retired from public duties; he died on November 8, 1976. After Smokey's death, his body was returned to near where he had been found some 26 years before. The Capitan (New Mexico) Women's Club came up with the idea for a park to honor Smokey as the symbol of fire prevention. The Smokey Bear Historical State Park was opened on May 15, 1979. He was buried under a huge rock that has the following bronze plaque:

SMOKEY BEAR. This is the final resting place for the first living Smokey Bear. In 1950 when Smokey was a tiny cub, wildfire burned his forest home in the nearby Capitan Mountains of the Lincoln National Forest. Firefighters found the badly burned cub clinging to a blackened tree and saved his life. In June 1950, the cub was flown to our Nation's Capital to become the living symbol of wildfire prevention and wildlife conservation. After 25 years he was replaced by another orphaned black bear from the Lincoln National Forest.

In the summer of 1990, Smokey II died. The Forest Service has decided not to replace the living symbol of Smokey at the National Zoo. Because of the Smokey Bear Program's growing popularity, Congress passed the Smokey Bear Act, in 1952, to protect the Smokey's image and the work of the Cooperative Forest Fire Prevention (CFFP) Council. The Act prohibits the use of Smokey Bear's name and costume without permission, permits licensing of the use of Smokey Bear, and allows the Forest Service to keep any Smokey Bear royalties and put them into a fund to be used only for forest fire prevention.

The Smokey campaign has been one of the most successful advertising campaigns in the history of the United States. The famous message "Only YOU Can Prevent Forest Fires" was created in 1947 and is still used today. Since the late 1950s, Smokey has been a float in the Tournament of Roses parade and the Macy's Thanksgiving Day parade. There is even a Smokey Bear hot-air balloon! The only authorized Smokey that can talk and move is the animatronic Smokey in the reception/information area in the national headquarters of the Forest Service in Washington, D.C. Smokey is the most recognized advertising character except for Santa.

In recent years, because of a growing concern over massive forest fires and the huge build-up of flammable forest "fuels" (dried grass, brush, and small trees, as well as diseased and bug-killed trees), Smokey's slogan was changed to "Help prevent wildland fires." The message change takes account of the fact that not every fire is bad, and in fact fire does have a useful place in the environment when carefully used.

Woodsy Owl Antipollution Campaign

Woodsy Owl is a mascot for the U.S. Forest Service created by Harold Bell in 1970, at the time of the first Earth Day. On September 15, 1971, Secretary of Agriculture Clifford Hardin introduced Woodsy Owl with the motto "Give a hoot! Don't pollute." The Woodsy Owl campaign was officially launched by the Forest Service as a "symbol for a public service campaign to promote wise use of the environment and programs that foster maintenance and improvement of environmental quality."

Woodsy is an anthropomorphic owl. He was created to raise awareness of the importance of protecting the environment. Woodsy was a short, plump character. There was a rule that the person inside the Woodsy costume could not be more than five feet four inches tall. Woodsy's target audience is children five to eight years old, but he is loved by all age groups. Woodsy is recognized by more than 80 percent of all American households and has become the leading symbol for environmental protection and improvement. His messages are carried to millions of children each year through a focused educational program sponsored by the Forest Service. The Forest Service manages the Woodsy program, as well as the related Smokey Bear program, through the conservation education staff in Washington, D.C. Woodsy, like Smokey Bear, never actually speaks in public appearances. The Woodsy Owl has received millions of dollars worth of donated television time and print media space for his public service message.

In 1974, Congress passed Public Law 93–318, the Woodsy Owl Act. This law serves to protect the image of Woodsy Owl, which was defined in the act this way: "The term Woodsy Owl means the name and representation of a fanciful owl, who wears slacks (forest green when colored), a belt (brown when colored), and a Robin Hood style hat (forest green when colored) with a feather (red when colored), and who furthers the slogan, Give a Hoot, Don't Pollute."

The Woodsy Owl Act of 1974 also established a licensing program. The purpose of the licensing program was to generate funds to promote education about the conservation of the environment and to fight pollution. The objectives of the licensing program were (1) to assist in carrying Woodsy Owl's conservation and antipollution message to the public; (2) to maintain the integrity of the Woodsy Owl image as America's icon for the conservation of the environment; and (3) to ensure that all products licensed to carry Woodsy Owl's name and message maintain standards of high quality and good taste. Licenses are granted for one-time use as well as for periods of up to five years. All licensees, unless specifically exempted by the Forest Service, are required to pay a fee or royalty for the use of the Woodsy Owl name and/or image and to carry the official logo.

Woodsy's appearance and message have recently been redesigned and revitalized. He is thinner and now sports a backpack, hiking shoes, and field pants. Forest Service Chief Jack Ward Thomas introduced the "new" Woodsy Owl character in 1997. Although Woodsy was a 25-year veteran, the agency recognized the need to revitalize his image and to broaden his role in conservation education. The Forest Service has expanded the message of Woodsy to "Lend a hand, care for the land," implying a broader message of conservation education rather than simple pollution or litter prevention. Today, Woodsy's messages include the four Rs: reduce, reuse, recycle, and rot (composting). An innovative program that creates "junior snow rangers" has been developed as part of the Woodsy program to promote conservation ethics and an understanding of winter ecology. The junior snow ranger program was piloted at the 2002 Winter Olympic Games, which was held on national forest system land in Utah.

RESEARCH AND DEVELOPMENT

The Forest Service Research and Development branch develops and maintains key databases for enhancing forest health, productivity, and conservation, including an extensive portfolio of long-term research databases, with many studies more than 60 years old. More than 500 permanent full-time scientists are working on the productivity, health, and diversity of the temperate, boreal, and tropical forests. Research scientists are held to high standards of scientific ethics, and many are recognized worldwide for the quality of their work. The prestigious Marcus Wallenberg Award (the forestry equivalent of the Nobel prize) has been awarded to four Forest Service research scientists.

Currently, the Research and Development branch manages 7 experimental stations scattered across the country, with 72 research work unit locations, 73 experimental forests and ranges, and 452 research natural areas. Research works with the NFS and university partners on a network of 62 long-term soil productivity sites across the United States and Canada with the goal of monitoring management effects on sustainability and productivity. It collaborates with research partners through hundreds of grants, agreements, and contracts worth more than $50 million. Scientific products include more than 5,000 publications, including patents, computer models, videos and books, that address the questions and needs of natural resource managers, scientists, and the public.

Gifford Pinchot found it necessary in his first year (1898) as chief of the division of forestry to establish a section of special investigations (research). By 1902, it was a division, with Raphael Zon as director and 55 employees, and it accounted for one-third of the agency's $185,000 budget. To decentralize research, Zon proposed creation of forest experiment stations. The first area experiment station was established in 1908 at Fort Valley, on the Arizona Territory's Coconino National Forest. These stations were Spartan local operations designed to serve the needs of the local forest. One exception, however, was the Wagon Wheel Gap Watershed Study, in Colorado, a cooperative project with the U.S. Weather Bureau to study the effect of timber removal on water yields. In 1909, forest researcher Carlos Bates, chose a remote site near the Rio Grande National Forest in Colorado for the nation's first controlled experiments on forest-streamflow relations. Little was known of the hydrology of mountain watersheds until Bates's innovative research on how water moves through soil to sustain streams in rainless periods.

Research's importance to forest management was formalized in 1915 with the creation of a branch of research in the Washington office, with the future chief Earle Clapp in charge. It was felt that research needed to operate out of a central office to ensure that project planning took place on a national scale. This move made research coequal to the administrative side of the agency. Forest Service research's original function was to gather dendrological or other data needed to manage the national forests. Independence from administrative duties allowed scientists to dedicate more time to research projects but required the agency to develop a staff of specialists to transfer research's technical information into field applications.

By the 1920s, the Forest Service had 12 regional research stations with branch field (experimental) stations. Congress passed the McSweeney-McNary Research Act on May 22, 1928, which legitimatized the experiment stations, authorized forest research on a broad scale, and provided appropriations. Although research funding declined in the 1930s, facilities expanded. Programs such as the Civilian Conservation Corps and the Works Progress Administration provided labor and materials to construct research facilities. By 1935, there were 48 experimental forests and ranges, and their physical plants were being further developed.

Research did not really expand until the postwar economic boom and the cold war generated funding increases. Employment of large numbers of professional scientists allowed the agency to fund projects in pure research, such as forest genetics and fire spread. In the late 1950s, the structure of Forest Service research changed from one of centers to one of projects. Under the new system, a senior scientist led a project and supervised its staff.

Grazing or Range Research

Grazing or range research began in the USDA Department of Botany (1868–1901) and later the Division of Agrostology. The USDA Division of Forestry became interested in range research, and, in the summer of 1897, Frederick Coville carried out the first range investigation on the impact of grazing on the forest reserves of the Oregon Cascade Range. This important study, the Coville report (Division of Forestry Bulletin No. 15), was published in 1898 and resulted in Oregon's forest reserves being reopened for grazing. In 1907, James Jardine and Arthur Sampson conducted studies to determine the grazing capacity of Oregon's Wallowa National Forest.

In 1910, the Forest Service established an office of grazing studies, which began studying the effects of grazing on the national forests. In 1917, with the United States entry into World War I, the number of animals grazed on the national forests increased dramatically. Grazing was allowed even in Glacier and Yosemite National Parks. Studies of the increasing numbers of sheep and cattle grazed on national forests during the 1917–1919 period showed that there had been severe overgrazing. The issue of the carrying capacity of the range was controversial because it determined how many animals a rancher could place on government land.

The bulk of the research on range management took place at the Great Basin Experimental Station (Intermountain Research Station), on the Manti National Forest, outside Ephraim, Utah. The historian Thomas Alexander claimed that professional range management emerged in the Forest Service largely as the result of the intermountain station's grazing research staff. The typical district ranger was often concerned about the social and economic costs to local ranchers if they were forced to reduce stock numbers, whereas range researchers focused on the condition of the land. Over time, it was the condition of the land that determined policy, which was based on research findings on carrying capacity. In the end, the numbers of animals on the national forests were reduced, except during World War II.

Controversy over grazing fees (which continues to this day) resulted in a 1924 Forest Service report on public and private fees. Stock owners immediately expressed objections to the study, leading to congressional hearings and passage of the McSweeney-McNary Act of 1928, which enhanced research activities on public and private forest and range land.

Fire Research

Fire research began in the Forest Service in the early part of the twentieth century and continues to this day. One impetus for forest fire research in the United States was the limited applicability of European models to the management of U.S. forests, especially in dealing with the threat that fire posed. European forests simply did not experience the fire danger that U.S. forests did. The Forest Service began its research program with Chief William Greeley writing that "firefighting is a matter of scientific management just as much as silviculture or range improvement." California District Forester Coert DuBois directed tests of light burning and fire planning and, in 1914, published his classic *Systematic Fire Protection in California*.

By 1921, the Forest Service dedicated the Missoula, Montana, headquarters of the Priest River Forest Experiment Station to fire research. Earle Clapp, the head of research, personally arranged for Harry Gisborne to be assigned to the station. Gisborne worked on fire research from then until his death during a fire inspection trip of the Mann Gulch fire in 1949. Fire research during the 1920s was subordinate to administration and focused on fire control rather than on fire itself. Under this pragmatic approach, fire researchers were expected to leave their field plots and statistical compilations for the fireline. Fire research in the southern United States focused on fire rather than on fire control, since "light burning" (human-set fires) was still an industrial practice. Thus, research on fire and wildlife management and long-leaf pine silviculture was carried on in the southern region.

When the Forest Service created a separate division of fire research in 1948, one objective was to have a national research agenda supervised by forester-engineers and forester-economists. The new division began operations with three laboratories. The next year, a new Fire Sciences Laboratory, in Missoula, Montana, and the Forest Fire Laboratory, in Riverside, California, both opened. Both were dedicated to developing and testing new firefighting equipment.

The Forest Service has a long and rich tradition of research in fire management from the prevention end. From the very beginning of the agency, in 1905, managers were interested in fires and their causes, especially human causation. Bill Bradshaw recounted that "the earliest fire prevention research I found was an economic analysis of fire prevention effectiveness published in 1927—'The Cape Cod Fire Prevention Experiment' conducted by the FS and the State of Massachusetts."

Fire research on the human causes of wildland fire got a boost in the Great Depression. In part, the impetus for this was the many reports of unemployed people intentionally setting fires so that they could in turn be hired by the Forest Service or states to put out the fires. Some of the biggest names in sociology in the 1930s were involved in research on southern woods burning. At the end of the decade, the Forest Service entered a formal contractual agreement with the American Academy for the Advancement of Science for further social and behavioral research on people who caused fires.

Other studies have focused on how well the fire prevention messages have been transmitted and understood. Lessons from this research area aided in designing effective fire prevention programs. Other studies have focused on how well the fire prevention messages have been transmitted and understood. Lessons from this research area aided in designing effective fire prevention programs.

Several researchers have played important roles in this research area, according to Bill Bradshaw: "Larry Doolittle at Starkville, Mississippi, was on the concluding end of sociology research for woods burning; Folkman received a USDA career service award for his pioneering behavioral research on fires caused by children playing with matches." Fire prevention research was conducted primarily by rural sociologists and sociologists in the Southern and the Pacific Southwest Stations.

Wood Products Research

Wood products research began in 1907, when McGarvey Cline, head of the Forest Service's wood use section, proposed that all wood product scientists be brought together under one roof. As a consequence, the University of Wisconsin constructed a special laboratory for its use in Madison, Wisconsin, and the Forest Products Laboratory (FPL) began operations on October 1, 1909, and was officially opened on June 4 of the following year.

Scientific research on wood and wood products began in earnest, with FPL scientists receiving a large number of patents over the years. Some of the first work at the FPL involved drying wood through a dry kiln process. Hundreds of species of wood were tested for their fiber strengths. A pulp and paper research unit was formed to study the mechanical and chemical processes in pulping. Research started on wood's chemical properties, distillation and extraction of chemicals from various woods, the manufacture of chemicals from trees, and the development of chemicals used to stabilize and moisture-proof wood products.

During World War I, the FPL was instrumental in efforts at producing light-weight but very strong airplanes. They tested the strengths of fuselages, wings, and propellers and developed effective ways to use wood, cloth, and paint (dope) to strengthen the new airplane airframes. During World War I, FPL's workforce rose from fewer than 100 to about 450. Paper was in short supply during World War I, so FPL scientists began research on tree species not commonly used for paper production.

In 1928, the McSweeney-McNary Act made special provisions for continuation of research at the FPL, and, by 1931, the FPL completed construction of a new laboratory building. In 1932, FPL gained notoriety as the place where the wooden ladder used in the famous kidnapping of Charles Lindbergh's child was analyzed. The advent of World War II caused the number of FPL employees to rise again, to around 700. They conducted research and development work on wartime needs such as airplanes, ships, buildings, containers, paper, and plywood. The FPL became the model for national laboratories around the world.

After the war, the FPL began to shift emphasis from old growth, high-quality wood, such as pine and Douglas-fir, to lesser-used species and to more efficient uses of existing timber supplies, including second- and even third-growth timber. The private sector became active after the war, funding small laboratories to conduct research on wood products, manufacturing techniques, and consumers. Many of these small private laboratories conducted their research on proprietary products with the research results not released to the public. FPLs research findings are in the public domain.

Today, FPL conducts basic research work on many wood-related topics, including wood-fiber recycling and better utilization of wood products, while continuing to test wood fibers and better ways of manufacturing wood products and training wood-technology researchers from all over the world.

Tropical Forestry Research

In 1928, the McSweeney-McNary Forest Research Act authorized the establishment of a forest experiment station in the "tropical possessions of the United States in the West Indies." That act and wording led to the 1939 establishment of the Tropical Forest Experiment Station, in Río Piedras, Puerto Rico, on the grounds

International Institute of Tropical Forestry, Puerto Rico, c. 1960. (USDA Forest Service)

of the Agricultural Experimental Station at the University of Puerto Rico. Today, the expanded International Institute of Tropical Forestry (IITF) has responsibility for programs in international forestry, state and private forestry, and research and development. The focus of the research program at the IITF is tropical American forests. The program is enhanced by laboratory facilities for chemical analysis of soils and water, the Luquillo Experimental Forest (LEF), and a network of the oldest tree plots in the western hemisphere. The research program develops and disseminates scientific research findings that contribute to the sustainable use of forest resources, the rehabilitation of degraded lands, and the management and conservation of tropical forests, wildlife, and watersheds. The Institute is dedicated to tropical forestry on an international level. Within the Forest Service's mission of caring for the land and serving people, the IITF mission is to develop and exchange knowledge critical to sustaining tropical ecosystem benefits for humankind.

The Luquillo Experimental Forest, composed of 11,231 hectares, has as its principle research focus on a long-term ecological (LUQ) program that is located in the Luquillo Mountains of eastern Puerto Rico. LUQ is part of a network of long-term ecological research (LTER) programs in the United States, funded in part by the National Science Foundation, that want basic research questions studied and answered. The main goal of LUQ studies is to understand the long-term dynamics of tropical forest ecosystems characterized by large-scale, infrequent disturbance (like hurricanes), the ways the forests change quickly (especially their recovery), and changes in wildlife habitat and species diversity over time.

The Forest Service, at the request of what was then Territory of Hawaii, founded the Institute of Pacific Islands Forestry (IPIF) in November 1957. The Institute is headquartered in Honolulu, Hawaii. This operation covers forest inventory, offers technical assistance, coordinates with the state Division of Forestry, and leads a program of research. Since 1963, the research and assistance work has expanded to include international tropical forestry issues in the Pacific region, including seven U.S.-affiliated political entities in the Pacific: the State of Hawaii, the Territory of Guam, the Territory of American Samoa, the Commonwealth of the Mariana Islands, the Republic of the Marshall Islands, the Federated States of Micronesia, and the Republic of Palau. This area of the Pacific Ocean comprises approximately 130 inhabited islands in a land/sea area that exceeds the land area of the coterminous United States.

The IPIF is a leading research institution that addresses many critical natural resource related issues in the Pacific. To address its broad mission, the Institute is organized into four interrelated teams: restoration, invasive species, wetlands, and forest management services. The primary goals of the first three teams are research and development and applications; the orientation of the forest management service team is delivery of technical assistance, particularly the delivery of applicable research findings to resource managers and the interested public of the Pacific. The research program located at the Institute of Pacific Islands Forestry conducts research in the broad areas of ecosystem processes, with emphasis on tropical ecosystems

Silvicultural and Forest Genetics Research

Silvicultural and forest genetics research received a boost in 1935 when James G. Eddy deeded the Eddy Tree Breeding Station to the government. Inspired by the work of Luther Burbank, Eddy, a lumberman, founded the station in 1925. It is now part of the Forest Service's Pacific Southwest Forest and Range Experiment Station, in California.

The Forest and Rangeland Renewable Resources Research Act of 1978, which supplanted the McSweeney-McNary Act, revised research's charter. Outside groups put increasing pressure on Forest Service research to develop baseline studies to guide management of national forest resources. Research became more complicated and, at times, isolated from local needs—a situation that is now changing with the new emphasis on ecosystem-based management and collaborative stewardship.

By the early 1980s, the findings of decades of important scientific forest research provided much-needed clues to the long-term health and productivity of the coniferous forests of the Northwest. Because of extensive research carried out on the H. J. Andrews Experimental Forest (part of the Willamette National Forest), Jerry Franklin and Chris Maser were able to make some preliminary conclusions that indicated that a new approach was needed. They led the Forest Service briefly into "new forestry" and then "new perspectives"—now called ecosystem management—in the search for alternative ways to manage the federal forests (see Chapter 2).

Recreation Research

Recreation research began in earnest during the 1920s, when many studies were undertaken on the need for recreational sites and structures to accommodate the rapidly increasing number of people visiting the national forests by auto. Many of these studies were carried out by newly hired recreational specialists at the regional offices. During the Great Depression of the 1930s, Civilian Conservation Corps workers were employed to improve and expand the use of recreation on the national forests and parks. Many of these sites are still used today by millions of visitors.

This situation existed until the early 1950s, when Samuel T. Dana was funded by the Forest Service to prepare an analysis of outdoor recreation. His report ("Problem Analysis: Research in Forest Recreation") was completed in 1957. Overall, the report "provided an excellent overview of problems in forest recreation, and which was quoted often during the development of the research program."

Dana's report recommended the creation of a division of forest recreation research within the agency, and soon after that such a division was established. Harry W. Camp was appointed as its first director in 1959. He believed that recreation as a research subject in its own right was being ignored and that there was a lack of qualified researchers and little support from national forest administrators and staff. Between 1963 and 1983, Forest Service recreation research became more clearly defined and gained in popularity and scientific significance.

It was not until 1960 that recreation research became a standard line item in the federal budget for the Forest Service. Formal research in the recreation area was just beginning in the 1960s, but it was not fully embraced by the national forest managers. By the mid-1960s, there were expanding opportunities for recreation research, many through affiliations with land-grant universities. Five cooperative forest recreation research units were established between 1962 and 1966. These cooperative units (and program leaders) were established at the following schools of forestry: Syracuse University (Elwood L. Shafer), Michigan State University (Hugh A. Davis), Utah State University (J. Alan Wagar), North Carolina State University (Stephen J. Maddock), and the University of Washington (J. Alan Wagar). Many of the graduate students at these schools eventually came to work for the agency.

Today, there are at least 20 cooperative agreements between the Forest Service and various universities involved in social science research. The list of cooperators includes Robert Lee (University of California and University of Washington); Perry Brown (Oregon State University); John Heywood (Ohio State University); Dave Simcox, Ron Hodgson, and Steve Dennis (California State University—Chico); Steve Hollenhorst (West Virginia University); Jim Gramann (Texas A&M); and Robert Sommer (University of California—Davis).

Research studies around visual or scenic resources have been many and varied, covering topics such as "seen areas," psychological and physiological responses to scenic views, attitudes, economics, esthetics of fire and timber harvesting, visual and scenic preferences, scenic-beauty mapping, and historic landscapes. The visual landscape system is used throughout the Forest Service at all levels of planning and management and has been used extensively by the Park Service, the Natural Resources Conservation Service, other federal and state agencies, and even many timber companies in the management of their lands. In 1996, the scenery management system (SMS) was expanded and replaced the visual-resource system as the preferred management scheme to document a "sense of place" for visitors to the national forests. In late 1996, a revised handbook for agency managers titled "Landscape Aesthetics: A Handbook for Scenery Management" was produced.

Probably the most significant change in recreation research came in the mid-1980s. A new Forest Service research work unit was established at Riverside, California, to study changing recreational uses, especially by "nontraditional" users. The Riverside research unit has worked extensively with the wildland-urban interface to research problems concerning how the urban culture interacts with the national forests in southern California. The research unit has been active in studying the way various user groups (especially Latino/Hispanic visitors) use the forests for recreation. Other studies and conferences have been important in the study of fire and rural residents.

Archaeological Research

Archaeological research began in the Forest Service during the 1970s with basic surveys and partial excavations on prehistoric sites. Although this was technically not research, thousands of sites and millions of acres of national forestland have been looked over (surveyed), prodded, "shovel tested," and excavated. Working cooperatively with the various universities and state historic preservation officers, the Service has generated thousands of reports and filed them with the states as part of compliance with the National Historic Preservation Act of 1966 and, often, the National Environmental Policy Act of 1969, for documentation of ground-disturbing projects. Most of the compliance surveys are carried out by Forest Service employees (archaeological technicians), while most of the excavation studies (research) are conducted by Forest Service archaeologists or by contracts with universities or professional contracting firms.

In 1989, Regional Forester Dave Jolly provided funding for two administrative studies in support of cultural resources research: a contract with the Museum of New Mexico for a chronological study of the Jemez Mountains and another study with a private firm to study pot hunting (illegal digging and collecting of Indian artifacts) at Perry Mesa, on the Tonto National Forest. A new cultural resources work unit was established in 1991 at Albuquerque, New Mexico. Albuquerque's unique cultural-heritage research work unit is focusing on "sustainable development, global change in history and prehistory, cultural conflicts in land use, and heritage resource management throughout the United States." The unit comprises archaeologists, anthropologists, and historians in an interdisciplinary effort to study and understand the characteristics of sustainable societies (how societies adapt to change), the cultural dimensions of ecosystem management (occurrence and causes of cultural conflict over land management), and the management and enhancement of heritage resources (focus on landscapes, land use, and the role of humans in ecosystems).

A growing area of concern is vandalism of archaeological and historical sites. Vandalism is a problem at precontact American Indian sites (common in the Southwest, where "pot hunters" hope to find old pottery), at locations with prehistoric rock art (both pictographs and petroglyphs), and at historic buildings (especially vulnerable are nonoccupied buildings). Vandalism of these remote sites is similar to problems that arise in urban areas. The first International Symposium on Vandalism in North America was held on April 20–22, 1986, under the auspices of the Forest Service, the Institute for Environmental Studies at the University of Washington, and Vandalism Alert. This symposium was held to "encourage and stimulate the exchange of ideas, solutions to problems, and descriptions of research needs."

Another research area of cultural anthropology has focused on American Indians' uses of the forests. Studies of subsistence gatherers/hunters are being carried out in the Alaska Region, originally by Robert Muth until he left the agency and then by Stewart Allen. Subsistence use areas in Alaska are being mapped using geographic information system technology to delineate where the historical and traditional hunting, fishing, and gathering areas are located. Continuing efforts to record American Indians' uses of cultural sites on the national forests have had varying success. A study on the Mt. Baker-Snoqualmie National Forest was successful in finding many traditional sites associated with vision quests, medicine plant gathering, vegetable gathering, salmon fishing, and big game hunting. Because of the confidential nature of the archaeological information, site data are not freely revealed to anyone outside the tribe or the state historic preservation office where the reports are filed. Thus, site specific information is withheld so that pot hunters, or even well-meaning individuals, will not vandalize sacred sites.

Social Science Research

Social science research began with the coming of ecosystem management in the Forest Service, when there was considerable discussion by Chief Jack Ward Thomas and others about what the physical, biological, and social components of ecosystems are and how they operate. This comes with the understanding that very few people, if any, can fully understand the complexity of ecosystems, much less manage them. Yet, as social science research in ecosystem management grows, it is obvious that the social/human aspects of ecosystems are just as complex as the physical and biological components.

With the arrival of the Forest Conference ("timber summit"), held in Portland, Oregon, on April 2, 1993, there has been a tremendous increase in research and writing on ecosystems and their management. The resultant massive 1993 report of FEMAT included a chapter on social assessment (chapter VII) and another on economic evaluation (chapter VI). The social assessment discussed the past and present political "climate," documented previous research, and conducted new research work on hundreds of communities in western Washington, Oregon, and northwestern California. The FEMAT assessment, which was started and finished within three months of the forest conference, has been used to illustrate one way to incorporate social science research into decision-making processes for the Forest Service and the Bureau of Land Management.

A large-scale assessment of the southern Appalachian area was completed in 1996. It included Report 4, which assessed the past and present social, cultural, and economic conditions of the southeastern states. A similar project was completed during 1996 in Region 5 (Pacific Southwest), which concerns ecosystem management of the Sierra Nevada, while an earlier study was conducted on the spotted owl in California. Thomas Keter has conducted extensive archaeological and historical research on the North Fork Eel River, in northern California, that incorporates many of these data on present ecosystems.

One part of the 1994 Northwest Forest Plan (which resulted from the FEMAT report) for the spotted owl region involved "adaptive management areas." These 10 areas were designed and designated to engage the public in setting management priorities and policies. These areas are a way to involve agency employees, research scientists, and local people, who have the greatest knowledge of and experience with the area and resources for the benefit of local communities. The Pacific Northwest Research Station, through the Seattle Forestry Sciences Laboratory research group, led by Roger Clark, provided assistance to teams of public and private members in their attempts to find equitable solutions to complex problems. Social "experiments" are encouraged to vary the intensity of management and output of resources. Yet, from a sociopolitical perspective, the adaptive management areas may face the same political consequences as the Sustained-Yield Management Act of 1944, which designated cooperative and federal sustained yield units.

Another arena is the recent emphasis (resulting from the 1990 Farm Bill) on increased funding and assistance to rural communities. The Forest Service has taken a lead in many rural development programs in states with national forests, especially in the West. A rural development research program in the Pacific Northwest Research Station was created in 1991. The research program is anchored in the *Forest Service Strategic Plan for the 90s: Working Together for Rural America* (1990) and *Enhancing Rural America: National Research Program* (1991). The program, according to Kent Connaughton (n.d.), includes agendas and working relationships with public and private individuals, groups, and agencies involved in rural and community development and that see natural resource conservation as an instrument of economic and social change. Members of the research team worked with the Forest Service, states, and other sources to compile relevant socioeconomic data for the Pacific Northwest. Having these data available at one location, rather than at scores of locations and agencies, should be beneficial to both social scientists and project planners. With the publication of the FEMAT (mentioned earlier) and subsequent environmental impact statements, this rural development research program is evaluating the effects of the implementation of both the Northwest Forest Plan and the efforts at community assistance provided for by Congress and the Clinton administration.

A number of university studies, underwritten by the Pacific Northwest Research Station, have tried to understand the role of social change in resource dependent communities. Their findings are shining considerable light on the internal and external factors that affect community change. Jo Ellen Force and Gary Machlis have studied the many relationships that tie local resource production, local historical events, and national economic and societal changes to community social change. They have concluded that social change in resource dependent communities (forestry, fishing, mining, and tourism) can be explained by the national and regional societal changes that are occurring and the local historical events that have shaped the community. They also found that the production or nonproduction of natural resources does not explain community stability or change.

Tourism is often touted as the savior of resource dependent communities ravaged by federal timber and fish policies. However, studies are lacking to prove such contentions. Like the 1980s efforts to have social scientists directly involved with national forest planning teams, the 1990s ecosystem management efforts were designed to involve social scientists, including Forest Service and academic researchers, in long-term planning and decision making. This, however, tends to blur the distinction between "pure" and "applied" research (and even raises the question whether this is research at all), as researchers in some cases are now part of interdisciplinary teams. For the social scientists, this means having to argue, even to battle, with team members who are physical and biological specialists and scientists. Social scientists have a role to fulfill in ecosystem management that requires much more than the traditional input to the process, which usually consisted of a written report that was put on the shelf to gather dust

INTERNATIONAL PROGRAMS

The Forest Service's International Programs promote sustainable forest management and biodiversity conservation internationally by linking the skills of the field-based staff of the Forest Service with partners overseas to address the most critical forestry issues and concerns. International programs regularly tap into the agency's wide range of expertise. Since international cooperation is necessary to sustain the ecological and commercial viability of global forest resources and to conserve biodiversity, most of the work is done in collaboration with other organizations. International collaboration on research and monitoring helps to reduce the impact of invasive pests such as the Asian gypsy moth and the hemlock woolly adelgid, which have severe impacts on timber resources.

The United States benefits from work done overseas. Innovative technologies are brought back to the country, cross-boundary environmental problems are addressed, and opportunities to hone Forest Service skills are increased. Last, strengthened international ties lead to mutual aid, as illustrated by assistance from Mexico, Canada, Australia, and Israel, which assisted with the devastating 2000 fire season in the western region of the United States.

International programs have three main staff units: technical cooperation, policy, and disaster assistance support program (DASP). Both technical cooperation and DASP work closely with USAID, although the latter coordinates primarily with that agency's Office of Foreign Disaster Assistance. Technical cooperation, specifically, develops and manages natural resource projects overseas on a wide range of topics (e.g., fire management and forest health). Finally, international programs' policy unit is actively involved in sustainability roundtables and international fora, which ensure that the U.S. position on global forest policies and agreements reflects the best interests of the country.

It may be said that Forest Service's involvement with foreign forestry began after the Spanish-American War of 1898. U.S. Army Captain George P. Ahern organized the Philippine Bureau of Forestry in 1900, and two years later he invited the USDA Bureau of Forestry chief forester, Gifford Pinchot, to visit and offer advice on the management of the forests in the tropical Philippines. Creation of the Luquillo (now Caribbean National Forest) forest reserve in Puerto Rico in 1903 further involved the agency in tropical forestry. The Forest Products Laboratory (in Madison, Wisconsin) began a program of tropical wood research shortly after its founding, in 1910, with Eloise Gerry writing the first of a series of research reports on South American forests and woods of commerce in 1918. It was the onset of World War II that set the basis for increased U.S. involvement in international forestry. During the war, government defense needs led the United States to sponsor studies of forest conditions in selected Latin America nations. Teams of foresters were dispatched to South America to locate sources of cinchona bark to meet the wartime need for quinine to treat malaria.

After World War II, foreign aid projects became the concern of international forestry in the Forest Service. During that period, two organizations involved U.S. foresters in forestry projects: the United Nations Food and Agriculture Organization (FAO) and the U.S. Agency for International Development (USAID). FAO was born in 1943, when President Franklin D. Roosevelt convened a conference to consider ways to organize international cooperation on agriculture. FAO's agenda excluded forestry until a group led by the Forest Service managed to get it added during the first FAO conference in 1945.

For years, foresters struggled to persuade developmental agencies that forestry was a critical element in land use planning. The basic problem was that most of these agencies were concerned primarily with agricultural production to feed the world's growing population. It was left to the Forest Service to promote forestry wherever its staff could find a forum. There were other forestry opportunities with the International Cooperation Administration (ICA), a semiautonomous agency within the U.S. Department of State. Early ICA forestry work was small-scale—one person assigned to a country. For example, in the early 1950s, a Forest Service employee, Eugene Reichard, served as forester in Colombia and Bolivia. Nonetheless, this agency was a primary conduit for Forest Service participation in international forestry.

In 1950, President Truman announced bilateral technical assistance to newly independent countries and to other developing nations. The Forest Service was called upon to provide two kinds of help: recruiting foresters and technical leaders for assignment overseas and receiving foreign nationals for academic studies or on-the-job training in forestry and related areas. Over the next two decades (1950–1970), the Forest Service furnished more than 150 professionals for long-term assignments or short-term details to technical-assistance programs overseas; in the same period, more than 2,500 foreign nationals went through Forest Service training programs.

In 1958, the unit became known as the Foreign Forestry Service in the Office of the Deputy Chief for Research, with A. C. Cline designated as its director in 1959. Two new sections were added in 1961: (1) technical support of foreign programs, and (2) training of foreign nationals. In 1987, the program filled more than 800 requests for technical consultation from 50 countries. The same year, 35 Forest Service employees served on one-year assignments in 20 foreign nations, with 8 others working on short-term projects and rendering technical assistance in such areas as recreational planning, range management, land use planning, forest industries, and nursery development.

Following publicity over the environmental impact of tropical deforestation, in the 1980s there was an increased public interest in international forestry. Chief Max Peterson in 1980 wrote of "our increasing need for involvement in forestry problems beyond our own domestic programs." The movement accelerated with a flurry of publications. USAID acted early with its forest resources management project in 1980, which led to the forestry support program (FSP) in the Forest Service and a joint USAID/Peace Corps Initiative.

Fire Management

The Forest Service cooperates with many countries on fire management issues to better understand the influence of fire on forest management and climate change and to incorporate fire mitigation strategies into forest management. Fire management assistance has been provided to Ghana, Indonesia, Brazil, Bolivia, Mexico, Bulgaria, Russia, Israel, Canada, Russia, Germany, and Holland.

Forest Monitoring, Remote Sensing, and GIS Assistance

The Forest Service and its partners integrate remote sensing and field technologies to monitor the health and status of forests and to apply these technologies to specific management issues. This service is based on existing cooperation with a number of countries, including Indonesia, Brazil, Mexico, and Russia. The objective is to develop more effective monitoring approaches, using integrated, cost-effective technologies applicable to a range of forest types, to address such issues as illegal logging, concessionaire performance, forest regeneration, carbon sequestration, fire impact, and indices of forest health. One project in Tanzania deals with monitoring in the Eastern Arc Mountains.

Forest Health and Invasive Species Assistance

Building on existing activities in Russia, China, South America, and elsewhere, the international programs part of the Forest Service focuses on methods to prevent, control, or mitigate the damage caused by existing and potential forest pests and pathogens. Emphasis is placed on control of invasive species through biological control and habitat management measures. Projects include work in China, Brazil, Mexico, and Russia.

Migratory Species and Habitat Management Assistance

The Forest Service applies its scientific and land management expertise to habitat management, ecosystem restoration, and biodiversity conservation, particularly for migratory species. Activities include the restoration of degraded forest systems, particularly riparian areas, development of conservation to maintain biodiversity, other environmental benefits in managed forests, and conservation education and training. Forest Service scientists also work to ensure that imperiled and endangered species are protected in multiple use ecosystems by determining habitat needs and population status and by assessing the impact of a wide range of management practices. Several projects operate in different parts of the globe, including Congo, Gabon, West Africa, Central Africa, Brazil, Caribbean, Mexico, and Russia.

Watershed Management

Watershed management has always been a key concern. Forest Service hydrologists have extensive experience in soil protection and water management under a wide array of forest conditions. Several projects are under way around the world, in Tanzania, Mexico, Albania, Russia, and Lebanon.

Protected Areas and Ecotourism

Protected areas and ecotourism are growing concerns around the world. The Forest Service manages a wide range of protected areas, from deserts in the Southwest to swamps in the Southeast to tundra in Alaska. The Forest Service has expertise in wilderness planning, including limits of acceptable change, monitoring, restoration of degraded sites, recreation/nature tourism, and wilderness education. Agency research emphasizes social issues related to wilderness, monitoring, restoration, and ecological processes in protected areas. By hosting several million visitors each year, the Forest Service has acquired extensive experience in the design and delivery of infrastructure and interpretive materials for visitors. With counterparts, agency specialists help to develop visitor guidelines and interpretive materials and visitor programs and environmental education programs for elementary and secondary schools, including curricula development and teacher training. Many worldwide projects have been undertaken, in Southern Africa, Mexico, Albania, Russia, and Jordan.

Forest Products

Forest products remain an important part of the Forest Service, both in the United States and in other parts of the world. As one of the nation's important players in forest products, the Forest Service conducts research and implements projects encompassing all aspects of sustainable forest products development. In partnership with other governments, nongovernmental organizations, and universities, the Agency works in the United States and overseas to develop more effective mechanisms, whether they be technical or institutional, for the sustainable development of forest products. Focal areas include the training of entrepreneurs working with nontimber forest products, reducing the environmental effects of pulp and paper mills, recycling, an increasing lumber yield per log.

The Forest Service participates and represents the United States on the United Nations Economic Commission for Europe (ECE) timber committee, which provides data, information, and policy input on timber industry issues in the European Union with the observation and participation of the United States. The Forest Service international program policy staff provides U.S. representation on a certification network for technical information. A scientist from the Forest Products Laboratory provides U.S. representation on timber trade and statistics reporting. The American Forest and Paper Association provides data on the wood products industry in the United States as well as on international efforts and issues important to the industry. The policy unit also provides information in other forest products areas such as certification and trade. Forest products assistance has been provided to Congo, Bolivia, and Albania.

Sustainable Forestry Practices

Sustainable forestry practices promote forest conservation through the development and dissemination of sustainable management policies and practices, with an emphasis on reduced-impact harvesting. Constructing roads can often be a source of ecological problems resulting from timber harvesting operations. These activities are responsible for a major part of the total soil erosion, often because of design or construction flaws or poor maintenance practices, and result in as much as 90 percent of sediments that pollute waterways, choke rivers, fill reservoirs, and devastate aquatic ecosystems. Yet, they are essential to access forest areas. The Forest Service works with many partners, including USAID Development

Missions (e.g., in Brazil and Indonesia), the Center for International Forestry Research, the Tropical Forest Foundation, and the UN Food and Agriculture Organization. Attention has been given to biodiversity conservation and carbon sequestration. The intended users include policymakers, concession managers, private landowners, community forestry groups, and forestry assessment programs. Technical assistance has been provided to the Congo, Madagascar, India, Brazil, Mexico, Russia, and Lebanon and to several Caribbean islands.

Policy Analysis and Development

Policy analysis and development plays an important role in both international and national discussions on how forests should be managed. This subject often sparks a lively debate in most countries of the world. The issues under discussion include sustainable forest management, international trade, economic growth, land tenure and land rights, biodiversity, land use, land conversion, and even national security. The many discussions reflect a wide range of perspectives concerning which of a forest's many values and benefits—commercial, spiritual, environmental, and recreational—should be protected. Usually there is a lot of talk but little agreement or consensus. The Forest Service has been actively involved with establishing legally binding agreements on forests, nonlegally binding approaches to sustainable forest management, issues related to key international programs, the Santiago Declaration, and reporting progress in meeting the agreements.

Disaster Assistance Support Program

The disaster assistance support program (DASP) of the Forest Service is a very important program for dealing with environment disasters around the world. With full program funding from the USAID's Office of U.S. Foreign Disaster Assistance (OFDA), the Forest Service provides disaster prevention, preparedness, and response expertise to the U.S. government. Because of its extensive emergency response capabilities and its experience in wildland and forest firefighting, the Forest Service is recognized as having unique skills and resources, in logistical support, aviation management, telecommunications, disaster preparedness and planning, and coordination and training, that are suited to respond to any type of disaster. DASP was formally established in 1985 with an interagency agreement between USAID and USDA. DASP assists with support personnel and humanitarian relief for international disasters—both natural and human-caused—including fires, floods, famine, earthquakes, and civil strife. DASP provides disaster prevention, preparedness, and response expertise to many U.S. relief efforts overseas. DASP trains and mobilizes personnel domestically to respond and mitigate foreign disasters, such as the floods in South Africa.

Disaster assistance response teams (DART) are deployed by the USAID office of foreign disaster assistance to assist in disaster prevention and preparedness and offer an emergency response to disasters in developing nations in Africa, Asia, Latin America, the Caribbean, and the Pacific regions. The DART concept is based on the incident command system that is used by domestic agencies to fight wildfires and to coordinate responses to disasters and emergencies. The objectives of the DART response teams, which are made up of volunteers, are consistent with the strategic plan for international cooperation signed by the Forest Service in 1995, the International Forestry Cooperation Act of 1990, and the Global Climate Change Act of 1990. Over the past 15 years, many relief teams have been sent to Africa (Angola, Namibia, Somalia, Rwanda, Sudan, Southern Africa, and other countries), as well as to Peru, Yugoslavia, and many other nations throughout the world. Partners in disaster relief include other government agencies, such as the USAID and the USDA Foreign Agriculture Service; the World Bank; and the United Nations Food and Agriculture Organization, as well as nongovernment organizations such as Ducks Unlimited and the Nature Conservancy and universities.

On December 26, 2004, a massive magnitude 9.0 underwater earthquake shook the coast of northern Sumatra, in Indonesia. The earthquake sent waves in every direction, triggering deadly tsunamis (so-called tidal waves) throughout South and Southeast Asia, as well as toward Somalia, Tanzania, and Kenya. The deadly waves, which struck mostly unannounced, killed more than 150,000 people and left millions of people without homes. The hardest hit were people living within a mile of the ocean, many of whom were the poorest people in the affected countries. Within hours of the disaster, the USAID office of foreign disaster assistance set up a DART for the hard-hit region. Two federal employees quickly arrived on the scene, a relief specialist from the Forest Service and another from the USDI Bureau of Land Management, both on assignment in Kenya. They were among the first relief specialists from the U.S. government to arrive on the scene. Four more employees from the USDA Forest Service and the Bureau of Land Management traveled to South Asia to support the disaster response. On January 10, 2005, the employees were personally thanked by President George W. Bush in an address to the USAID concerning the tsunami response.

ROADLESS AND WILDERNESS

At one time, all the land in what is now the United States could have been considered "wild," "virgin," and "primitive." Although these lands had been used and managed by fire for thousands of years by the American Indians, the early explorers felt that the land was undeveloped and underutilized as they understood the terms' meaning. As the white settlers moved from the East Coast to the interior, they began to greatly modify the environment by clearing the heavy forests, farming, diverting the rivers, and creating cities. By the middle of the nineteenth century, the westward movement was in full swing, with thousands of emigrants staking land claims in the famed Willamette Valley of Oregon, in the Puget Sound area of Washington, and in the central valley of California. Later, the Great Plains would be back-filled by farmers, especially after the development of the steel plow. Once the rich, prime flat lands were taken, the newer waves of settlers began to stake land claims in the heavily timbered foothills. They struggled to create farmland from the forest, cutting further into the dense evergreen forest. By the 1870s and 1880s, there was a national and regional stirring to preserve forested portions of the public domain land for future generations to enjoy, especially through by protecting the unique natural features of the West, such as Yellowstone National Park.

The history of wilderness cannot be separated from four very influential people who made is possible. The story begins in the 1920s with Arthur Carhart and Aldo Leopold, continues through the 1930s with the leadership of Robert Marshall, and finishes in the 1950s and 1960s with Howard Zahniser and passage of the Wilderness Act of 1964. The following documents the work of these master players in the political arena.

Arthur H. Carhart

Arthur H. Carhart was one of the landscape architects hired by the Forest Service. In 1919, he proposed that summer homes and other developments not be allowed at Trappers Lake, on the White River National Forest, in Colorado. He later surveyed the Superior National Forest in the Minnesota lake region and recommended only limited development. Secretary of Agriculture William H. Jardine signed a plan to protect the area in 1926, and it was dedicated as the Boundary Waters Canoe Area in 1964. Carhart resigned from the Forest Service in 1922, to practice landscape architecture and city planning in the private sector.

Chief William Greeley was willing to endorse the concept of wilderness areas and, in 1926, ordered an inventory of all undeveloped national forest areas larger than 230,400 acres (10 townships). Three years later, wilderness policy assumed national scope with the promulgation of the L-20 regulations. Commercial use of the areas (grazing, even logging) could continue, but campsites, meadows for pack stock forage, and special scenic spots would be protected.

Aldo Leopold

Aldo Leopold was an eastern intellectual who loved to hunt and explore the backcountry. In 1922, while working for the Forest Service, he recommended that roads and use permits be excluded on the Gila River headwaters, in the Gila National Forest. As a result, he was responsible for laying the groundwork in the early 1920s for a 500,000-acre wilderness area—the Gila Wilderness, established in 1924—the first administrative wilderness in the national forest system. Although his plan was approved in 1924, it was only local, not national, policy.

Leopold retired from the agency in 1928 to take the lead in establishing a new profession—that of game management, which he modeled on the profession of forestry. In 1935, Leopold and Bob Marshall were founders of the Wilderness Society. Although the main emphasis of his work was wildlife game management, he began to shift to a more ecological approach by the mid-1930s. Susan L. Flader, in a biography of Leopold, characterized this shift in philosophy: "Originally imbued like other early conservationists with the belief that man could rationally control his environment to produce desired commodities for his own benefit, Leopold slowly developed a philosophy of naturally self-regulating systems and an ecological concern with the land and a land ethic."

Robert Marshall

Robert Marshall as a young man worked for the Forest Service on the recreation portion of the *National Plan for American Forestry* (1933). In that report, Marshall foresaw the need to place 10 percent of all U.S. forestlands into recreational areas, from large parks to wilderness areas to roadside campsites. In the same year, he became the director of forestry for the Office of Indian Affairs, where he supported roadless areas on reservations. In 1937, Bob Marshall returned to the Forest Service as chief of a new division of recreation and lands in the Washington office. He drafted the "U Regulations," which replaced the "L-20 Regulations" for primitive areas and wildernesses. These regulations gave greater protection to wilderness areas by banning timbering, road construction, summer homes, and even motorboats and aircraft. Marshall had also checked plans for recreational development on national forests to see if they included access for lower-income groups, a real concern during the Depression years of the 1930s. He also thought that protection should be granted to large areas of more than 200,000 acres, with these areas being reclassified as primitive areas. In 1938, he and others made a trip through the western national forests to map and propose millions of acres of national forest lands for primitive or wilderness status.

First Roadless Inventory (1926)

The first roadless inventory began in 1926, under the L-20 regulations. An inventory of roadless lands larger than 230,400 acres (10 townships) was begun in 1926 under the direction of Leon F. Kneipp. The inventory found that, nationwide, there were 74 roadless tracts that totaled around 55 million acres, with the largest unit about 7 million acres. There was, however, no general Forest Service policy on wilderness designation, and each potential area would have to be judged on its own merit. Generally, the Forest Service felt that wilderness designation would be unfair to dependent communities that relied on the national forests for timber and range resources. In 1929, the Forest Service announced, under the L-20 regulations, two new administrative designations: research reserves and primitive areas. Research reserves would be preserved for scientific and educational purposes, while the primitive areas would keep those lands intact for the nature lover and the student of history. Forest Service Regulation L-20 (October 1930) states:

> The Forester shall determine, define, and permanently record a series of areas on national forest land to be known as [primitive areas]. . . . To prevent the unnecessary

elimination or impairment of unique natural values, and to conserve, so far as controlling economic considerations will permit, the opportunity to the public to observe the conditions which existed in the pioneer phases of the Nation's development, and to engage in the forms or outdoor recreation characteristic of that period; thus aiding to preserve national traditions, ideals, and characteristics, and promoting a truer understanding of historical phases or national progress. . . .

The establishment of a primitive area ordinarily will not operate to withdraw timber, forage, or water resources from industrial uses, since the utilization of such resources, if properly regulated, will not be incompatible with the purposes for which the area is designated.... Road or trail construction, other than that required for fire prevention, administration, or forest utilization, will be continued to the minimum. Occupancy under special use permits also will be held to the minimum. The exact nature of the special uses to be allowed within a given area will be specified in the plan of management, but as a general rule no hotels, resorts, permanent commercial camps, summer-home communities, individual summer homes, or commercial enterprises will be authorized within designated primitive areas. The objective of management of such areas will be to maintain primitive conditions of transportation, subsistence, habitation, and environment to the fullest degree compatible with their highest public use, and management plans should be shaped accordingly.

Second Roadless Inventory (1939)

For the next 10 years, the conservation management of the national forests basically amounted to custodial protection of the forest from fire. Very little timber harvest, road construction, or even recreation occurred. However, with the advent of the Great Depression, the Civilian Conservation Corps (1933–1942) built thousands of recreation sites, administrative structures, and access roads on the national forests. At this same time, Robert Marshall, John H. Sieker, and others were pushing for the designation of more primitive and wilderness areas. Under Marshall's direction, the U Regulations of 1939, in comparison to the L-20 regulations of a decade earlier, granted greatly increased protection:

A. Upon recommendation of the Chief, Forest Service, national forest lands in single tracts of not less than 100,000 acres may be designated by the Secretary as "wilderness areas," within which there shall be no roads or other provision for motorized transportation, no commercial timber cutting, and no occupancy under special use permit for hotels, stores, resorts, summer homes, organizational camps, hunting and fishing lodges, or similar uses: *Provided,* That roads over national forest lands reserved from the public domain and necessary for the exercise of a statutory right of ingress and egress shall be allowed under appropriate conditions determined by the Chief, and upon allowance of such roads the boundary of the wilderness area may be modified without prior notice or public hearing to exclude the portion affected by the roads.

B. Grazing of domestic livestock, development of water storage projects which do not involve road construction, and improvements necessary for the protection of the forest may be permitted subject to such restrictions as the Chief deems desirable. Within such designed wildernesses when the use is for other than administrative needs of the Forest Service and of other Federal agencies when authorized by the Chief and emergencies, the landing of aircraft and the use of motorboats are prohibited on national forest land or water unless such use by aircraft or motorboats has already become well established, the use of motor vehicles is prohibited and the use of other motorized equipment is prohibited except as authorized by the Chief. These restrictions are not intended as limitations on statutory rights of ingress and egress or of prospecting, locating and developing mineral resources.

C. Wilderness areas will not be modified or eliminated except by order of the Secretary. Except as provided in paragraph (a) of this section, notice of every proposed establishment, modification, or elimination will be published or publically [*sic*] posted by the Forest Service for a period of at least 90 days prior to the approval of the contemplated order and if there is any demand for a public hearing, the Regional Forester shall hold such hearing and make full report thereon to the Chief of the Forest Service, who will submit it with his recommendations to the Secretary.

Also included in the U Regulations was a new provision for "wild areas," which were to be smaller than wildernesses. Wild areas were to comprise fewer than 100,000 acres but more than 5,000 acres:

Suitable areas of national forest land in single tracts of less than 100,000 acres but not less than 5,000 acres may be designated by the Chief, Forest Service, as "wild areas," which shall be administered in the same manner as wilderness areas, with the same restrictions upon their use. The procedure for establishment, modification, or elimination of wild areas shall be as for wilderness areas, except that final action in each case will be by the Chief.

A third category, "roadless area," was set under the U-3(a) Roadless Areas (which could be any size). These were to be designated by the Secretary of Agriculture if they comprised more than 100,000 acres and by the chief if they contained fewer than 100,000 acres. Only three roadless areas were ever create, and all three were in Minnesota, where the Boundary Waters Canoe Area Wilderness is now located.

During and after World War II, little effort was undertaken to identify possible wilderness areas. However, with the opening of the national forests to road construction and timber harvest, many could see that roads were going to destroy potential wildernesses within a few decades. This set up the effort by the Wilderness Society and other groups to change the way that wildernesses were established.

Wilderness Act of 1964

Howard Zahniser became the leader of a movement to have Congress, rather than the agency, designate wilderness areas,. In 1949, Zahniser detailed his proposal for federal wilderness legislation according to which Congress would establish a national wilderness system, prohibit incompatible uses, identify appropriate areas, list potential new areas, and authorize a commission to recommend changes to the program. Nothing much happened with the proposal, but it did raise the awareness of the need to protect wildernesses and primitive areas from all forms of development.

In 1955, Zahniser began an effort to convince skeptics and Congress to support a bill to establish a national wilderness preservation system. Drafts of a bill were circulated the next year. By the late 1950s, it seemed that the wilderness bill would eventually become law, but there were many battles to be fought. At the same time, the Multiple-Use Sustained-Yield Act (MUSY) was also being pushed through Congress. Some have said that the MUSY was strongly supported by the Forest Service to counteract the wilderness legislation, and after passage of the Multiple Use Act of 1960 there were many who felt that there was no need to a separate wilderness bill since wilderness was one of the many multiple uses allowed in the act. Hubert H. Humphrey (D-MN) became a major supporter of the bill, but mining interests were very much opposed. The wilderness bill, which was stalled for several years in Congress, finally came out of committee with a compromise to allow mining in national forest wildernesses until 1984. Eight years after the bill was introduced, President Lyndon Johnson signed it into law, in September 1964. Ironically, Howard Zahniser, who had pushed so hard for the act, died a few months before the bill was made into law.

Roadless Area Review and Evaluation (RARE) Study

The Forest Service directed in 1967 that the regional offices were to undertake a review and evaluation study of all roadless areas of 5,000 acres or more or located adjacent to existing wildernesses or primitive areas that had wilderness potential. The reports, known as RARE, for Roadless Area Review and Evaluation, were to be made by 1969 (the date was later changed to 1972).

The Forest Service inventoried and studied 1,449 roadless areas comprising 55.9 million acres. All but two of these were in the western states. After the publication of the draft study, some 300 public meetings were held and almost 54,000 written and oral responses and 18,000 petition signatures were received concerning the study. The Forest Service nationally selected 274 roadless areas (12.3 million acres) as most desirable for possible wildernesses. Soon after the publication of the final RARE study, in October 1973, the Sierra Club sued the Forest Service in California (Region 5) over a roadless area that was not selected. As a result of the suit, the chief ordered that each roadless area in the nation have more comprehensive study before any development activity could occur. Many environmental and timber industry organizations strongly criticized the RARE study as being inadequate, especially in not balancing recreation and the need and demand for wood products.

At the same time, in the eastern United States, which had only one roadless area listed in the RARE study, a major wilderness bill was signed into law in 1975. This bill, sometimes referred to as the "Eastern Wilderness Act," provided for 15 wildernesses and 17 wilderness study areas. The act was also important in that the wilderness areas all contained at least some portions that had been previously logged or disturbed by roads or that contained private land.

French Pete and Willamette National Forest (NF)—An Important Test

Just as the RARE study was beginning, a controversy over the status of French Pete Creek drainage on the Willamette National Forest (NF), in Oregon, was beginning to heat up. When the Three Sisters Primitive Area, which had been established in 1937, was designated a wilderness, in 1957, by the Secretary of Agriculture, 53,000 acres on the western slopes were eliminated, including the French Pete Creek drainage. Basically, the Willamette NF officials believe this area to be more valuable for timber production than as wilderness. When the Three Sisters reduction occurred, a new wild area was established around nearby Mt. Washington, and there was talk of a "trade"—French Pete for Mt. Washington. Then, in 1964, with the passage of the Wilderness Act, the adjacent Three Sisters Wilderness was added to the national wilderness preservation system. When the RARE study began, in 1967, four roadless areas were considered within the French Pete area, but none was as large as the entire area eliminated.

In the spring of 1968, the forest supervisor announced a timber sale, with 11 cutting units in the French Pete area. The Save French Pete Committee was formed by local environmentalists to keep the area in its natural state. In the spring of 1969, after an ad hoc committee of 23 persons reviewed a new plan for the area, the forest supervisor decided to go ahead with a modified development plan. This time, however, many environmental groups appealed the decision, and, on July 7, representatives of the Save French Pete Committee met in Washington, D.C., with Thomas Cowden, an Assistant Secretary of Agriculture. In spite of these actions, the appeal was denied, and new timber sales were announced. However, after an appeal was made to the Oregon congressional delegation, the Secretary of Agriculture, Clifford M. Hardin, announced, on November 17, 1969, that the controversial timber sale would be delayed to allow more time for public discussion. The Willamette NF then undertook a study of the proposed development in French Pete. By the summer of 1971, more than 10,100 letters, cards, and telegrams had been received regarding the management of the area. Of these public responses, almost 8,500 were postcards sent primarily by lumber company employees, and another 1,100 were industry-spawned form letters against any preservation of the area. Fewer than 300 letters were received from individuals or environmental groups opposed to any new plan to develop the area.

National environmental leaders viewed French Pete as the most important issue in the Pacific Northwest and as a major test of strength of the region's powerful timber industry and the increasingly influential environmental groups, especially the Sierra Club. Demonstrations at the Willamette NF supervisor's office in 1968 were the first documented instance of demonstrators "marching" on a Forest Service office; letters were sent to the chief and to Congress, news releases given to the press, television coverage sought, articles in national magazines published, and comments in forestry journals submitted, all in an attempt by environmental and timber industry groups to influence the decision. Several Oregon senators and representatives introduced legislation to designate the area as a wilderness or a dispersed unroaded recreation area (which would allow recreation facilities and salvage logging of timber that was dead and down), but none passed Congress.

Finally, when RARE was more than five years old, 50,394 acres of French Pete were designated an addition to the Three Sisters Wilderness as part of the

Endangered Wilderness Act of 1978 (Public Law 95–237). This Act gave wilderness status to a number of areas nationally, including 17 that the Forest Service had not recommended for wilderness in RARE. The importance of French Pete was that the major environmental groups, especially the California-based Sierra Club, saw that the large and very influential timber industry and the Forest Service in the Pacific Northwest were not as all-powerful as they had once thought.

RARE II

Rupert Cutler was appointed by President Carter in April 1977 as Assistant Secretary of Agriculture to oversee the operations of the Forest Service. In this position, he directed the Forest Service to do a better job of inventorying the 274 wilderness study areas. There were concerns that some areas might have been overlooked and that RARE I did not adequately inventory the national grasslands or the eastern national forests. His idea was to quickly resolve the roadless area problems created by RARE and to recommend to Congress those areas that should be in wilderness and those that should be released for other types of management. The new study, quickly dubbed RARE II, was to be an in-depth study of all 2,919 roadless areas (62 million acres).

After the publication of the draft EIS in 1978, RARE II quickly became a household phrase among millions of Americans. Numerous public meetings and hearings were called, and the major opponents tried their best to gather support from their members and from individuals, governmental bodies, businesses, associations, and congressional leaders.

More than 264,000 comments were received regarding RARE II, which made for the largest public response to any proposed governmental action in history. The final EIS study, released in January 1979, recommended nationally 15 million acres (out of 62 million possible) for wilderness and 11 million acres for further planning. The nonwilderness lands would then be released for other forest uses. Although RARE II was now complete, it was unlikely that the wilderness issue would ever disappear so long as there was one group that wanted to log the valuable trees and another that wanted them kept intact.

There was a logjam of wilderness bills in Congress. In spite of the Forest Service's massive RARE II effort, which cost more than $6.6 million, Congress did not act on the proposal as offered by the Carter administration. Instead of enacting the recommendations of the RARE II proposal on a national basis, Congress, under the new Reagan administration, in 1980, began to attack the wilderness issue on a state-by-state basis. In Oregon, U.S. Senator Mark Hatfield, a former governor of the state, introduced a 600,000-acre wilderness bill, which became stalled in Congress because of opposition from Oregon representatives, one of whom wanted more wilderness while the other wanted less. The environmental groups were opposed to the language used to describe the lands that were not chosen for wilderness designation. The language included a call for a "hard" release, which basically meant that any roadless area that was not selected for wilderness classification was never to be reconsidered for wilderness designation.

The national environmental groups felt that an Oregon wilderness bill could not be passed in the immediate future, so they began to push for wilderness bills in Washington and California. However, Congressman Jim Weaver held a series of hearings in Oregon on a pro-wilderness bill that he proposed, after which the Sierra Club and the Oregon Wilderness Council selected 1.9 million acres of roadless areas for wilderness. They felt especially hopeful after the hearings that something might break loose because of the national timber depression and the failure of other states to agree on what was appropriate release language. Weaver's proposed legislation failed to pass.

In June 1979, the State of California initiated a lawsuit challenging the RARE II decision to designate certain inventoried roadless areas in the state as nonwilderness. Both the U.S. District Court and the Ninth Circuit Court of Appeals agreed that the RARE II Final Environmental Impact Statement (FEIS) did not comply with the requirements of the National Environmental Policy Act (NEPA). On October 22, 1982, the U.S. Court of Appeals for the Ninth Circuit, in San Francisco, upheld, in *California v. Block*, a lower-court decision from January 8, 1980 *(California v. Bergland)*, that the RARE II study was inadequate and violated NEPA . This created a difficult situation for the national forest system. The 1979 RARE II final EIS gave the Forest Service the authorization to harvest trees in roadless areas that were not proposed for wilderness designation. The court decision, which was not appealed, essentially placed the roadless areas in limbo. Following the court's decision, the wilderness planning regulations were revised in 1983 to require the evaluation of inventoried roadless areas for potential wilderness in NFMA forest planning.

New Roadless Area Study Ordered

USDA Deputy Assistant Secretary Douglas MacCleery directed, in the *Federal Register,* on September 7, 1983, that each national forest reevaluate the roadless areas in the forest planning process as potential wilderness. The planning effort, under way on each national forest in the country, started in the Pacific Northwest Region in 1979 and 1980 under the NFMA regulations. Regional Forester Jeff Sirmon, on October 17, 1983, also directed each of the national forests in the Pacific Northwest to reinventory and reevaluate, for the third time, every roadless area in its forest plans.

New inventories had to be made because many small changes to the roadless areas had been made during the "window of development" from 1979 to 1983. During that window, a number of roadless areas had been split by roads or reduced in size because of timber harvesting along their edges, and extensive "entries" were planned for the future. Yet, drastic changes to the areas did not happen, since the process for setting out timber sales and road construction projects often takes several years, and contractors are generally given several years' leeway to complete projects. Thus, the time from the planning stage to the completion stage may be five years or longer. However, thousands of development projects were planned for the released areas in order to relieve the forest areas that had already been heavily developed. Then, on December 13, 1983, a complaint was filed in the U.S. District Court for Oregon by the Oregon Natural Resources Council.

Further complicating the situation was the fact that, during the RARE (now referred to as RARE I) and RARE II studies, the Forest Service's Pacific Northwest Region did not allow the timber harvest for each national forest to be reduced, even though harvesting and other development activities were not allowed in the roadless areas during the study periods. Because the Forest Service thought the RARE I study would be completed quickly, the restriction on harvesting in the roadless areas was believed not to be a management problem, and it appeased the timber industry.

By the time the final EIS for the RARE II study was implemented, almost a decade had passed and the national forest lands that were available for development during the time period were being overcut. In addition, during the spring and summer of 1984, national forest officials in the region made an intense effort to encourage public involvement and to gather comments from the interested citizens. As a result, thousands of new concerns were voiced by the public about the latest revisions to the roadless areas proposals.

Because of the Ninth Circuit Court decision, the problems already mentioned, and the threat of a lawsuit by environmental groups, Regional Forester Jeff Sirmon announced, late in January 1984, that timber sales in the region would be reduced by 880 million board feet over the next two years. The reductions would come from planned timber sales from the released RARE II roadless areas that were in public contention or were likely to be very controversial.

Oregon and Washington Wilderness Bills

Oregon and Washington wilderness bills in 1984 helped break the logjam. For Oregon and Washington, the roadless areas of RARE I and RARE II were finally decided in June 1984 with the passage of the Oregon Wilderness bill. Shortly after the bill passed the Senate, the logjam of other bills, including the Washington bill, was broken, the bills passed and sent on to the White House. The Oregon Wilderness Act (PL 98–328) was signed into law by President Reagan on June 16, and the Washington Wilderness Act (PL 98–339) was signed on July 3. The problem with getting passage of the two bills through the Senate was the release language in the Oregon bill. The timber industry position, led by U.S. Senator James McClure, of Idaho, attempted to get hard release language that would make it impossible for these areas to be considered for wilderness designation again. The House, led by Morris Udall, of Arizona and John Seiberling, of Ohio, wanted soft release language, which would allow reevaluation of these areas in the future. After lengthy negotiations, Senator Hatfield carried the day with a compromise that basically allowed soft release language along with a few words to appease the timber industry. Essentially, the modified language allows reevaluation of those roadless areas that are still eligible for designation as wilderness over the *next* NFMA planning process (10–15 years). In spite of the valiant efforts of all involved to finally settle the roadless area question, these state wilderness acts, because of the release language, did not completely resolve the issue.

Current Status of the Wilderness Controversy

There are proposals by various environmental groups to create national parks in several national forests in different parts of the country. These far-reaching proposals, which stand little chance of passage by Congress, would take existing wildernesses, adjacent roadless areas, and nearby land to create several large national parks. However, the wilderness/roadless area issue has declined in intensity since the signing of the Wilderness Acts of 1984. At the national forest level, the wilderness/roadless area issue is basically in the hands of the interdisciplinary planning teams, which have been quite concerned about the release language, current management of the roadless areas, and their disposition in the planning process.

The release language that was so carefully worked out over several years reads as follows (from the Oregon Wilderness Act, Public Law 98–328, Section 7):

(2)   the Department of Agriculture shall not be required to review the wilderness option prior to the revision of the [Forest] plans, but shall review the wilderness option when the plans are revised, which revisions will ordinarily occur on a ten-year cycle, or at least every fifteen years....

(3)   areas in the State of Oregon reviewed in such final environmental statement ... and not designated as wilderness ... or remaining in further planning ... shall be managed for multiple use in accordance with land management plans [older unit plans, forest land use and timber plans, or the new NFMA plans]....

(4)   areas not recommended for wilderness designation, need not be managed for the purpose of protecting their suitability for wilderness designation prior to or during revision of such plans....

(5)   unless expressly authorized by Congress, the Department of Agriculture shall not conduct any further statewide roadless area review and evaluation of national forest system lands in the State of Oregon for the purpose of determining their suitability for inclusion in the National Wilderness Preservation System.

Although the language in the act seems clear, the Forest Service has found that, despite the language, which allows development of the nonchosen roadless areas, there is still significant controversy about some areas.

Roadless Area Management

As early as 1983, environmental groups were using nonviolent techniques to delay road construction in some controversial roadless areas. Since that time, there have been a number of protests concerning roadless areas, including rallies at the forest supervisor's offices, letters to the editor, spiking of standing trees, and tree-sitting in areas slated for harvesting. These activities have escalated in recent years and have been copied on other national forests across the country. Yet, in spite of the events, which are often staged for media attention, the legal appeals and lawsuits tend to take up the most time.

The roadless areas have been evaluated for their multiple resource potential. In most cases, the primary timber resource outweighs the other resources, but there are a number of instances where extracting that timber would be impractical from a timber management, engineering, economic, or social standpoint. As the roadless areas are modeled in FORPLAN, the complex linear computer model designed by Norm Johnson, the allocation and the timing of development activities depend on the structure of each forest model, as well as the socioeconomic management goals and resource objectives for each alternative under consideration. Also, just a slight tweaking of the objectives within an alternative, such as fixing the land allocations (sometimes called "preallocating") instead of letting the model choose or changing from maximizing present net value to maximizing timber, can lead to dramatic changes in the outputs and land allocations.

Roadless areas have been evaluated several times over the past 100 years for potential wilderness. In 2000, Chief Dombeck ordered the start of a new analysis process for roadless areas on all units of the national forest system. This decision was based on the assumption that roadless areas were a national issue and should be solved by a national task force on roadless areas. This decision by the national headquarters did not sit well with the regions and national forest officials who believed that these decisions should be made at lower levels of the agency. The roadless team held hundreds of meetings and elicited millions of comments before the new roadless area conservation rule was printed, on January 12, 2001. Under the 2001 rule, inventoried roadless areas were to be evaluated for potential recommendation as wilderness in the NFMA plan development and revision processes. On the basis of site-specific analysis and public involvement, management direction was to be developed for inventoried roadless areas during the planning process; these could include (1) protection of wilderness values pursuant to an administrative recommendation to Congress that the area be designated wilderness; (2) imposition of total or partial restrictions on certain uses and development activities, such as road construction or timber management; or (3) minimal restrictions on resource management and development actions and other allowable uses.

A decision by Chief Dombeck in late 1998 called for a moratorium on road building in roadless areas on the national forests. A task force of agency professionals was assigned to study the issue and make recommendations. A controversy erupted around an e-mail letter sent on January 19, 1999, to all Forest Service employees by Andy Stahl, head of the Association of Forest Service Employees for Environmental Ethics (AFSEEE). In the letter, Stahl requested that employees who agreed with the idea of saving the existing roadless areas send him their names to be attached to a letter sent to the president and other officials. Interestingly, the first signature on the letter was that of Jim Furnish, then forest supervisor of the Siuslaw NF, in western Oregon. Many employees who believed that signing the petition would end their careers were probably surprised that Furnish was elevated in the spring of 1999 to be the new deputy chief of resources, overseeing the operations of the national forest system in the Washington office.

On October 13, 1999, President Clinton announced that the remaining roadless areas on the national forests would again be reevaluated. The final EIS on roadless areas was published in January 2001. The rule covered inventoried roadless areas in 39 states, with only 12 of these states containing 97 percent of all the roadless areas—Alaska, Arizona, California, Colorado, Idaho, Montana, Nevada, New Mexico, Oregon, Utah, Washington, and Wyoming. President Clinton declared that any roadless area development would be put on hold indefinitely. The timber industry was outraged, while the environmental community was pleased.

However, the George W. Bush administration suspended the roadless rule and did not support the Clinton administration's decision in when the case went to court. In July 2003, the District Court for the District of Wyoming enjoined permanently the implementation of the 2001 rule. USDA Undersecretary Mark Rey wanted the states to have further input into the process of roadless area disposition. In mid-2004, a new *Federal Register* draft rule on roadless areas was posted that would turn certain responsibilities for recommending development (especially road construction) or conservation over to the governor of the affected state. Each of these states was given 18 months to finish a "petition process" regarding its recommendations for each roadless area. The Forest Service would then publish the rule making for each state, which would include the appropriate NEPA analysis and opportunities for public comment. The expected outrage from the environmental community was quick and loud. Later in 2004, the final roadless rule was published; it incorporated these changes to the 2001 rule.

FOREST FIRES AND FIREFIGHTING

The history of fire in the United States is long but rather straightforward. People in the United States and around the world have lived with fire, used fire for human benefits, and been frightened of the consequences of uncontrolled fire. In North America, fire has been both natural and human caused for many thousands of years. During the most recent major ice age, some 12,000 years ago (and perhaps even earlier), it is believed that people from Asia crossed the land bridge between Alaska and Siberia as the ocean level dropped. As the people in a new, uninhabited land, they used the resources available to make the land meet their survival needs. The use of fire was a very important tool that contributed greatly to their wide distribution across every ecological zone in North and South America by the time of European conquest in the 1500s.

When the Spanish and the Pilgrims arrived in North America, they found a vast continent inhabited by American Indian/First Nations people. Many areas resembled parks with tall trees, no underbrush, and scattered prairies full of wildlife. The new settlers took the forest and prairie lands and converted them to crop and grazing lands, as well as locations for homes and forts and, eventually, cities and roads. Forests and trees were considered to be a problem, so removing them became a priority. Not only were trees and forests not good for farming, they also sustained many wild animals (predators such as wolves, bears, cougars) that were considered to be dangerous to the settlers. For the next 300 years, the new settlers went farther and farther west, using the flaming torch to remove all the trees and forests to make the land more suitable for their purposes, much as the Indians had thousands of years before. But, this time, the changes were permanent. The Indians burned to create a mosaic of habitats, while the settlers burned to create monocultures for farms and grazing.

The forest and prairie ecosystems had adapted to Indians' use of fire for 12,000 to 30,000 years (as soon as the ice sheets receded). Now, with the new settlers, the Indians were removed and fires stopped, except for clearing the land (much like the slash-and-burn methods that are still used in many countries today). Ecosystems began to change. In the eastern parts of North America, Indians' use of fire ceased some 200 to 400 years ago, while in the West, Indians' use of fire persisted until around the 1850s. The forests have changed dramatically since. In addition, once the farms and farmers became established, fire became the enemy, since it could destroy people, houses, domesticated animals, and crops.

Historically, large fires raged in North America during the 1800s and early 1900s, after the Indians had been moved to reservations and could no longer burn the ecosystems. The public was becoming slowly aware of fires' potential for life-threatening danger. The eastern and lake states' forest areas were especially hard hit by several large and deadly fires—Maine and New Brunswick in 1825 and the Peshtigo fire of 1871, which covered more than a million acres and took more than 1,400 lives in Wisconsin. Fires at the same time were burning in Michigan, cindering about 2.5 million acres. Ten years later, these devastating fires were followed in Michigan by the destruction of another 1 million acres that went up in smoke, taking169 lives. In 1894, a large fire around Hinckley, Michigan, took the lives of 418 people. In 1903 and 1908, huge fires burned across parts of Maine and into upstate New York. In response, the first state fire organization in the East was established, in Maine. Millions of acres were burned, thousands of people lost their lives and homes, and entire towns were destroyed.

Of great importance to this cause were the devastating fires in the West. The first one was the 1902 Yacolt fire, in southwestern Washington, which burned more than a million acres in Washington and Oregon and cost the lives of 38 people. One result was the formation of the Western Forestry and Conservation Association, in 1909, led by Edward T. Allen. One year later, in the northern Rockies, some 3 million acres were burned in the "Big Blowup of 1910," and another 2 million acres burned in other areas. Fire became the enemy that must be stopped. Within a year, Congress passed the Weeks Act of 1911, which, in part, allowed the Forest Service to cooperate with the various states in fire protection and firefighting. The Forest Service also began a program of fire research, which continues to this day.

In 1891, the first protection of federal land for forestry purposes began with passage of the Forest Reserve Act of 1891. On-the-ground management would have to wait until the Organic Act of 1897 allowed forest rangers to be hired during the fire season (they were then laid off, sometimes before the fire season was over). However, these early rangers had perhaps one or two people to patrol a million acres. Firefighting was relegated to discovery of fires, educating campers, hunters, anglers, and hikers of the dangers of leaving campfires unattended, and alerting homesteaders and communities to any major fires heading their way.

Since those early days, there have been many federal and state statutes regarding the illegal setting of fires and punishments. The first federal law of record to deal specifically with fires on forest reserves—later called national forests—was signed into law on February 24, 1897 (29 Stat. 594). The law, entitled "An Act to Prevent Forest Fires on the Public Domain," prescribes that "any person who shall willfully or maliciously set on fire, or cause to be set on fire, any timber, underbrush, or grass upon the public domain, or shall carelessly or negligently leave or suffer fire to burn unattended [as in leaving a campfire burning] near any timber or other inflammable material, shall be deemed guilty of a misdemeanor and … shall be fined in a sum not more than five thousand dollars or be imprisoned for a term of not more than two years, or both." This law was reemphasized in the Organic Act of 1897 (30 Stat. 11, 34), which, in part, states that "The Secretary of the Interior [now Agriculture] shall make provisions for the protection against destruction by fire and depredations upon the public forests and forest reservations which may have been set aside or which may be hereafter set aside under said Act of March third, eighteen hundred and ninety-one, and which may be continued."

The Forest Service, since its inception, in 1905, has been very concerned about forest fires. The was reflected in the 1905 *Use Book*—and every subsequent *Use Book* and *Forest Service Manual*—and fire control has become a major responsibility of the agency. When the management of the forest reserves (now called national forests) was transferred to the new Forest Service, the new agency took on the responsibility to create professional standards for firefighting, which included having more rangers and hiring local people to help put out fires. The federal forest reserves/national forests today comprise around 193 million acres of Forest Service–administered land, along with another 250 million acres of mostly grazing lands administered by the USDI Bureau of Land Management. Millions more acres of public lands are controlled by various states, many in the West. The USDI National Park Service controls several million more acres with national park status.

The Weeks Act of 1911 (36 Stat. 961), with its modifications, established the notion that the federal government and the states could and should act together to prevent and fight fires. Cooperation between the levels of government has been the basis for fire management ever since. At the same time, many states began their own fire prevention associations, with many establishing departments of forestry and constructing lookout towers to monitor possible fire starts during hot, dry weather. The Forest Service began almost a century of cooperative efforts at fire control among the federal government, the states, communities, and tribes. The Weeks Act was followed by the Clarke-McNary Act of 1924 (43 Stat. 653) and others, which promulgated fire policies and made possible the implementation of cooperative national and state fire strategies.

By the mid-1950s, the Forest Service gradually assumed the primary responsibility for coordinating wildland and rural fire protection in the United States. During this time period, more than $200 million worth of World War II surplus equipment was passed to state and local cooperators. By 1956, air tankers, often military surplus B-17s filled with a borate mixture, and helicopters for transport were in use.

The Civilian Conservation Corps Firefighters

Until the 1930s, there were not enough firefighters to stop big fires. Forest rangers would simple "herd" the fires, keeping an eye on where they were burning and warning people ahead of the fire of the immediate danger. About the most the early rangers could do was to start a "backfire" or seek assistance from nearby communities. Rains or snows eventually put out the big fires.

With the advent of the Great Depression program in 1933 called the Civilian Conservation Corps (CCC), the Service had the manpower to start large-scale prevention efforts to clear brush, fight fires, and establish a modern forest lookout system atop most mountain ridges in the West and East. At almost a moment's notice, thousands of CCC men would be trucked from their camps and projects to help fight fires. Over the course of the nine-year CCC program, the enrollees worked millions of hours of firefighting duty. The CCCs successfully tested and used a 40-man (there were no women firefighters at this time) fire suppression crew. The CCC program also built and staffed thousands of lookout houses and towers across the country.

After World War II, the Forest Service and the BLM gained many thousands of new employees to take care of national priorities for increasing the timber harvest levels on the national forests and BLM-administered lands. New emphasis was placed on getting the fires out as soon as they were stopped. The policy of "hour control" was tested in the 1930s and 1940s with the goal of locating and stopping every fire within an hour of discovery.

The problems of fuel build-up or fuel-loading began more than 150 years ago. After the elimination of Indian fires in almost every ecosystem in North America, the brush and small trees began to grow. Without periodic "cleaning" by fire, they continued to grow and grow. What used to be small seedlings are now trees 100 years old or more. Brush and grasses now pile high in most forests. As the summer of 2000 showed, fire will be restored to the ecosystems, whether we want it or not. In the past, fire was carried by Indians, then by settlers. Now it is carried by lightning and the winds.

Control of forest fires has long been considered one of the most important aspects of forestry. Very-large-scale forest fires are primarily a North American phenomena, although many other countries face serious forest and brushfire conditions. Early European-trained foresters, under whose tutorage Pinchot and others learned the basics of forestry, had not dealt with large fires that had the potential to cover hundreds of thousands of acres in one fire. Forest fires in the United States were much more serious than those they had encountered.

Fire has long been used to clear land, to change plant and tree species, to sterilize land, for hunting, to maintain certain types of habitat, and for many other reasons. Indians are known to have used fire as a technique to maintain certain pieces of land or to improve habitats. Early settlers often used fire in the same way as the Indians, but major fires on public domain land were largely ignored and were often viewed as an opportunity to open forestland for grazing. Fires were fought, if at all, with shovels, brooms, rakes, fire lines, and backfires. When fires were near farms, settlers could use plows to make fire lines in crops near houses.

Lookout houses (many starting just as platforms atop trees) were used to locate fires from mountaintops during the fire season. The lookout houses varied from low ground houses to very tall towers, sometimes more than 100 feet tall. Just after World War I, the Forest Service contracted with the Army Air Service (Corps) to provide airplanes and pilots to spot fires from the air. This program worked successfully for more than 10 years until a comprehensive network of lookout houses and telephone systems was in place. Today, a computer network tracks every lightning strike, and aerial patrols monitor for active fire sites after lightning storms. The few remaining lookouts still operating are valuable for locating human-caused fires. The Clarke-McNary Act of 1924 allowed the Forest Service to administer grants-in-aid to equal the amounts contributed to firefighting by the states and to set standards for firefighting and equipment.

Smokejumpers

Near the end of the 1930s, another new tactic was employed—having firefighters jump from airplanes to remote locations to put out fires before they became too large to fight. Testing was carried out in 1939 on the Okanogan National Forest, in Washington state; the first smokejumping on a forest fire took place July 12, 1940, on the Martin Creek fire in the Nez Perce National Forest of Idaho. The two smokejumpers were Rufus Robinson and Earl Cooley.

On August 5, 1949, 13 smokejumpers lost their lives when a fire in Mann Gulch, on Montana's Helena National Forest, suddenly flared in high winds, leapt out of control, and enveloped the firefighters. This tragic event prompted the Forest Service to establish a new center in Montana and another in California dedicated to developing and testing new firefighting equipment.

The 10 A.M. Policy

In 1935, the Forest Service developed the "10 A.M." policy, which stipulated that a fire was to be contained and controlled by 10 A.M. the day after the fire was reported, or, failing that, by 10 A.M. the next day, and so on. Faced with the necessity of controlling a fire overnight, the Forest Service was compelled to call out massive numbers of firefighters to try to control these blazes in the initial attack.

The Forest Service in 1971, as a result of fire research, modified the 10 A.M. policy to accommodate natural (lightning) fires in those areas, providing they didn't exceed 10 acres in size. Thus, some fires were allowed to increase in size to 10 acres only if they did not destroy or threaten to destroy private property or endanger life or property adjacent to the wilderness. This policy was replaced seven years later with a policy of fire planning and prescribed fires.

Light Burning or "Let-Burn" Policy

The practice of annual burning of the forest litter (as the Indians and early settlers did) came under scrutiny in the early twentieth century. Studies in the 1910s and 1920s noted the dangers from so-called light burning or Paiute forestry. The practice was soundly criticized, but people, especially in the South, continued the practice for many years (later it would be found that the pine tree forests in the South greatly benefited from periodic fires). The arguments for and against the practice, which is similar to Indian-style burning, continue to this day. However, the term most commonly used now is "let-burn."

Another so-called let-burn policy came into being in the 1980s. This policy essentially allowed some fires, as in wilderness, to burn in the national forests, depending on conditions. The 1988 fires in the greater Yellowstone ecosystem were devastating to large areas in and around the national park. The fires led to great criticism of the Forest Service and the National Park Service by the media and Congress about the misuse of the let-burn policy, even though that policy was not used in these huge fires. This was a situation where the fuel load build-up was so severe that it was a time-bomb ready and waiting to happen. It did.

Park Service and Forest Service policy was debated. Increasing restrictions on let-burn fires became the norm, but, at least for the NFS, let-burn remains a viable option for natural (lightning-caused) fires in wildernesses if there is an approved fire plan for the area. Human-caused fires, unless undertaken by the agency, are to be put out. Also, any fire that threatens life or property will be attacked and put out as soon as possible. The Los Alamos fire in May of 2000—which burned almost 50,000 acres at the Los Alamos National Laboratory—once again evoked the anger of newspaper editors and members of Congress regarding fire policies—this time over the Service's lack of coordination with other agencies and the competence of the leadership and the fire crew itself.

The Current Fire Situation

The number of forest fires and the areas burned in the United States have fallen from the levels recorded a century ago. The peak in total acres destroyed by forest fires came in 1933, when 43.5 million acres burned, although the peak number of fires came in 1981, when 249,370 were recorded. Depending on weather and drought conditions, the severity of fires can vary greatly from year to year. In recent years, there has been an increase in large fires, with the year 2000 having more than 8.4 million acres burned with roughly half of these burned on the national forests; the 2001 fire season saw 3.6 million acres on fire, and this was followed by the widely publicized fire season of 2002, when huge fires, such as the Hayman and Biscuit, burned in the West, consuming about 7.2 million acres. A recent study by Ervin Schuster, at the Rocky Mountain Research Station, found that in the 1996–2000 period, fires larger than 300 acres amounted to only 2 percent of the total fires nationwide, but these same large fires consumed 95 percent of the acres burned and accounted for 86 percent of the costs of fighting all fires. Projections are for a continuing problem because of accumulated forest "fuels" (grasses, bushes, and small to medium-size "ladder" trees), ignitions from lightning and human sources, drier weather conditions, and warmer climate patterns, with increased risks for property and lives.

Because fires have been excluded from fire-dependent ecosystems for more than a century, fuels have built up to critical levels. There have been a variety of reports about the high fuel loads in the western forests, beginning after the disastrous 1988 Yellowstone fires. Congress established the national commission on wildfire disasters to report on the situation; a conference was held November 1993 to discuss the situation, and a report was printed. The following year, the Clinton administration developed the western forest health initiative, which reviewed federal fire policy. In December 1995, the federal agencies issued a report titled "Federal Wildland Fire Management Policy and Program Review: Final Report," which altered federal fire policy so that maximum protection was no longer given to private property; instead, equal protection would be extended to private property and federal resources. The policy is still that the protection of human life has the highest priority.

The General Accounting Office (GAO), in 1999, published a report on forest fuels and fire. The report, "Forest Service Efforts to Reduce Catastrophic Wildfire" (GAO/RCED-99–241), documented the crisis and previous efforts to stop the fires. The report observed: "To date, we have not seen the strong leadership or the marshaling of funds and resources within the agency that would indicate to us that the Forest Service feels a sense of urgency and assigns a high priority to reducing the threat of catastrophic wildfires." Another GAO report, "A Cohesive Strategy Is Needed to Reduce Catastrophic Wildfire Effects" (GOA/RCED-99–65), also printed in 1999, concluded that "the most extensive and serious problem related to the health of the forests in the interior West is the overwhelming accumulation of vegetation, which has caused an increasing number of large, intense, uncontrollable, and catastrophically destructive fires."

The Forest Service has been researching all aspects of forest fires for many years. Two agency labs are dedicated to fire research: the Riverside Fire Lab, in Riverside, California, and the Fire Sciences Lab, in Missoula, Montana. The agency has published more than 185 fire-related reports and books, as well as hundreds of articles, on various aspects of the fire problem. One example—there are many more—of fire research is FireMapper, which uses thermal imagery to accurately map and monitor major wildfires. It was tested in 2002 on fires in southern California. A study in 2002 used satellite imagery of forest fires nationwide. The information can be used for estimating smoke pollution caused by fires and smoke forecasting for prescribed burns under best conditions. Another research study deals with computer modeling, field experiments, and case studies to better understand fire behavior around homes. The findings suggest many ways to prevent residential wildfire disasters. A video, "Wildfire: Preventing Home Ignitions," was produced under the sponsorship of the FIREWISE Communities USA project and some 3,000 copies distributed.

In 2001, the Rocky Mountain Research Station Fire Lab, after an extensive review of the earlier models of fire conditions, developed a new system that proposed three fire regime condition classes (FRCC). Current estimates are that 51.1 million acres of the national forest system, or about 26 percent of the total, are considered to be at FRCC class 3— "significantly altered from the historical range," that is, at high risk for wildland fires. These areas should be given high priority with regard to fire danger and restoration efforts. An estimated 80.5 million acres of NFS, or about 41 percent of the total are at moderate risk from wildland fires—FRCC class 2—that is, "moderately altered from the historical range." Although these areas are believed to be at less risk from wildfires, there is concern that as the vegetation grows without fuel reduction treatments, they will likely move into the class 3 range.

The need to identify and prioritize the areas of the national forests that need fuel reduction treatment has been recognized several times. According to FS and BLM estimates, some 650 million acres of federal lands face serious risk or danger from wildland fires. This amounts to more than 85 percent of the total federal land base. In the summer of 2003, the General Accounting Office completed a report that was a critical assessment of the hazardous fuel situation on the national forests and USDI-BLM lands. The report found that the two agencies have identified three categories of land that need fuel reduction, but the report noted that "the agencies have not yet reliably estimated the amount or identified the location of these lands. Without identifying these lands there is no baseline against which to assess progress under the fuels reduction program." The report went on to suggest that the FS and BLM, at the national level, needs to use fuel ranking models and professional judgment to prioritize the millions of acres of federal lands for treatment. Without such prioritization, especially around the wildland-urban interface, land managers have a difficult time in assigning fuel reduction work. The GAO recommended that "the Forest Service and Interior (1) collect detailed nationwide data to identify and prioritize which federal lands need fuels reduction and (2) report acres treated to reduce wildfire risk, acres requiring multiyear treatments to reduce wildfire risk, and maintenance acres separately in annual performance reports."

In 2005, the GAO published another study of the fire situation in the United States. Among other recommendations, the report said that the federal agencies should prepare a master plan that takes into account the scale and magnitude of

Forest fire and elk in East Fork Bitterroot River, Montana, 2002. (USDI Bureau of Land Management)

known wildfire threats and the projected costs to fight these fires and to prevent additional fires. The report went on to say that the Department of the Interior and the USDA Forest Service have made great progress in fighting and preventing fires, but it also wanted the agencies to report to Congress and the people about the fire situation. "To date there have been no clear actions or a commitment by the agencies to explicitly identify and communicate to the Congress long-term options and the funding needed to pursue them."

Biophysical Impacts of Forest Fires

Fires in the forests, which once "crept" through the forests at ground level, have increasingly become high-risk crown- and total ecosystem replacement fires. Droughts and a gradual, warming world climate, especially in recent years, have become factors in fire frequency and intensity. Forest fire impacts on soil, water, vegetation, heritage sites, and wildlife have long been recognized in the scientific literature. Stress on the ecosystems, especially trees, also makes them more susceptible to insect (e.g., bark beetles) and disease threats; dead trees increase the fuel supply for future fires. For many decades, the Forest Service critically viewed fires as major ecological threats instead of looking fires as "natural" thinners of the forests that would continue to keep the forests relatively fire-free, reduce brush and competing vegetation, and slow or stop the spread of insects and disease. Even if fire were to be reintroduced on a large scale across ecosystems, the continuous growth of grasses, brush, and small trees would one day bring the fuel situation in the forests to critical levels. There is a need to continue the use of prescribed fires in the forests and grasslands.

As forest watersheds are burned, forestland erosion and increased sedimentation in the creeks, rivers, and reservoirs will result in increasing costs to municipal governments. Watersheds that burn have runoff different from the runoff generated when the burned area is in a forest; burned watersheds have more frequent runoff early in the year, with the threat of flooding, from burned-over areas, whereas forested areas tend to hold water longer in the year, allowing streams to flow year-round. Many species—some in T&E status—that are dependent on clean water face the threat of devastation after massive fires, especially bass, trout, bull trout, steelhead, salmon, and many smaller, nongame species. Almost all mammal, reptile, and amphibian species can be put in danger of population collapse or, at worst, extinction because of massive fires that damage or eliminate their native habitat.

However, some species, such as the lodgepole pine, require crown- and stand-replacement fires to reproduce and thrive. Some species need lower-level fires to survive and reproduce, especially the giant Sequoia, Kirtland's warbler, the red-cockaded woodpecker, among others

Community Impacts of Forest Fires

Areas of the ecosystem that are heavily overgrown with brush and small trees are threats to nearby communities. Houses in the wildland-urban interface (WUI) are especially vulnerable to wildland fire. Protection and clearing of burnable materials around homes and nearby forest areas are critical to the survival to structures. Creating a defendable space—a fuel break—around homes is critical to the survival of rural homes adjacent to forested federal lands, as well as those in fire-prone areas. The Forest Service, working with state and local zoning agencies, can recommend changes in building codes to encourage homebuilders and homeowners to take the utmost precautions in the urban-wildland interface (e.g., removing trees and brush within 10 feet of wood structures, cleaning needles and leaves from the roof, and using asphalt shingles, tiles, or steel roofs instead of cedar shakes).

Firefighting skill loss through retirements will increase over the next decade. Costs of fighting fires, especially the increasing reliance on very expensive, aging aircraft, will continue to escalate. Impacts to communities—including individuals and insurance companies—caused by wildfire will also rise (e.g., Los Alamos, Oakland, Hayman fire evacuations). Fighting crown- and stand-replacement fires is much more costly than using hand and mechanical thinning and prescribed fires to reduce the incidence of major fires. Potential and real loss of human life will become more of an issue as the population grows and dwellings are increasingly built in fire-prone areas. Additional public education efforts with new Smokey messages, public service announcements, and signs, will be needed.

The national fire plan 2000 emphasizes, in part, community assistance programs. The Forest Service leads these elements: state fire assistance; volunteer fire assistance; and economic action programs. The Department of the Interior has responsibilities for rural fire assistance and community and private-land assistance. The Forest Service has contributed millions of dollars to the communities since the first plan became effective, as well as making available firefighting equipment and training for firefighters.

In August 2001, the Secretaries of Agriculture and the Interior joined the Western Governors' Association, the National Association of State Foresters, the National Association of Counties, and the Intertribal Timber Council to develop and endorse a long-term national strategy to address the wildland fire and hazardous fuels situation and the needs for habitat restoration and rehabilitation. The strategy document, "A Collaborative Approach for Reducing Wildland Fire Risks to Communities and the Environment—Implementation Plan," published in May 2002, outlines a 10-year comprehensive strategy for managing wildland fires, hazardous fuels, and ecosystem restoration and rehabilitation of federal and adjacent state, tribal, and private forest and rangelands. The four goals of the collaborate process are (1) to improve prevention and suppression; (2) to reduce the quantity of hazardous fuels; (3) to restore fire-adapted ecosystems; and (4) to promote community assistance

In the research arena, for example, the Forest Service is actively involved with the fire wise program that focuses on America's fire-prone communities. Its goal is to encourage action that minimizes the loss of homes to wildfire. It teaches people to prepare for a fire before it occurs. Fire wise is a simple, three-legged template that works by (1) having wildland fire staff from federal, state, and local agencies provide communities with information about coexisting with wildfire and mitigation information relevant to specific areas; (2) encouraging community assessment of fire risk and networking among cooperating homeowners, agencies, and organizations; and (3) having the community itself identify and implement local solutions. The 11,376 communities at high risk of wildfire were identified in the *Federal Register* on Friday August 21, 2001.

Forest Health Restoration: What Can Be Done?

The forest health problem has been long in the making. Although most U.S. forests are in better condition than they were a century ago, many ecosystems, especially in the intermountain west, are widely thought to be in poor ecological health. Interest groups disagree over what constitutes a healthy forest, what has caused the problems, what the solutions are, and what methods to use.

On August 22, 2002, President George W. Bush announced the healthy forests initiative, designed to significantly step up efforts to prevent wildfire damage and reduce regulatory obstacles that hinder active forest management. The president proposed that Congress pass legislation to expedite procedures for forest thinning and restoration projects.

The most widely espoused strategy for forest health restoration is the use of pre-scribed fire and mechanical or hand thinning to removing brush and small diameter trees. Other methods that can be employed, depending on the site requirements, include precommercial thinning of medium-size trees, pruning branches near the ground, piling and burning the woody debris/slash, and selling the trees to help restore the health of ecosystems before wild fires begin. These efforts are specified in the National Fire Plan 2000 and almost every other fire-planning document. A Congressional Research Service report in 2000 summarized many of the methods: "Fuel treatments have been proposed to reduce the wildfire threats. Prescribed burning—setting fires under identified conditions—can reduce the fine fuels that spread wildfires, but can escape and become catastrophic wildfires, especially if fuel 'ladders' and wind spread the fire into the forest canopy. Commercial timber harvesting is often proposed, and can reduce heavy fuels and fuel ladders, but can increase the threat unless there is proper disposal of logging debris—tree tops, limbs, branches, needles/leaves (referred to as slash). Other mechanical treatments (e.g., precommercial thinning, pruning) can reduce fuel ladders, but also temporarily increase fuels on the ground. Treatments can often be more effective if combined (e.g., prescribed burning after thinning)."

Under the national fire plan, the hazardous-fuel treatment program has expanded significantly, with a greater focus on treatments intended to protect communities in the wildland-urban interface. Prescribed burning treatment for high fuel hazard situations on the national forests was done over 10.1 million acres between 1990 and 2002, with an average of 779,496 acres per year. Prescribed fire fuel treatments by other federal land management agencies for the 1995–2000 period were done over 2.8 million acres. During FY2001, 2.09 million acres of federal land were treated to reduce hazardous fuels, including 731,216 acres in wildland-urban-interface areas. In many cases, agencies contract with local businesses and hire local workers to meet expanded program needs. In FY2001, 549 projects in 19 states were selected for rehabilitation and restoration using national fire plan funds, and many of these are multiyear efforts. In FY2002, work continued on the multiyear projects begun in 2001 in response to the 2000 fire season. In FY2002, 2.5 million acres of federal land were scheduled for treatment.

An example of research into reducing fuel loads and thus reducing the possibilities for severe forest fires was conducted in the Baker City, Oregon, municipal watershed within the Wallowa-Whitman NF. The area was selected as a national pilot project for studying fuel treatment options, including thinning and prescribed fire. These data will be used to improve models such as CONSUME, the first-order fire-effects model (FOFEM), and the emission production model (EPM), as well as various smoke dispersion models such as CALPUFF and VSMOKE.

After a fire has occurred, forest and land restoration strive to restore quickly the burned areas to reduce erosion and renew the depleted ecosystem. Grass seeding (especially with native grasses), tree planting, and erosion control are common methods of restoration work.

The future of firefighting is tied to changing conditions that, for the most part, are beyond the control of the agencies assigned to fight the fires. Fire forecasters use historical data and future trends for each area, as well as current fire conditions—snow packs and spring rains, powerful Chinook and Santa Ana winds, dry lightning, and on-the-ground fuel conditions. Forests that have been damaged by disease and insects (e.g., the mountain pine beetle that threatens more than 21.7 million acres of forests) and those that are drought-stressed are weaker and more susceptible to fire. The advent of global warming is not favorable to the fire outlook for the coming decades.

Most forests today, as well as those in the foreseeable future, have unprecedented buildup levels of flammable materials, including needles, leaves, brush, and small trees. Whereas a century ago tree density was often low—sometimes as few as 25–40 trees per acre—today the same forest area may have more than 1,000 trees, which are smaller, weaker, and more susceptible to disease and insects. Throw in drought, global warming, and more people living in or near the forests, and the scene is set for an increasing risk of forest fires that will be increasingly expensive to fight, as well as endangering people and structures.

☆ ④ ☆

Challenges for the Twenty-first Century

Many challenges face the Forest Service and federal land management during the next hundred years. The most pressing is population gain. The latest population figures from the U.S. Census Bureau indicate that the population of the United States will grow from 298 million at the start of 2006 to 420 million by 2050. This is a massive increase—by midcentury, there will be almost half again as many people as today. The era of environmental awakening, started, many say, by Rachel Carson in her 1962 book, *Silent Spring,* has led to positive changes in the Forest Service. A related set of management issues includes (but is not limited to) ecosystem or ecology-based management, timber harvesting, closing of roads for wildlife protection, reduced budgets and personnel, and collaborative stewardship. The Sierra Club and other environmental organizations have called for eliminating the harvesting of any trees, not just old growth, on the national forests.

The future is unclear. There are powerful interest groups that want the Forest Service and the national forests to revert to an intensive management era to protect and preserve jobs and to use the trees and other natural resources to the fullest extent possible. At the other end are those who want the resources totally preserved, a "zero-cut" of the trees, and the exclusion of people from the national forests—a policy even more restrictive than those of the national parks. Other special interest groups want to increase their "share" of the resource uses available on the national forests, while a few call for the total elimination of all federal ownership of land. Most groups seem to believe that science and more data will "prove their case." But the reality is that decisions about the future management of the national forests, as well as the use of the natural resources, are essentially political in nature. Data and the scientific method can only give answers to questions, not set policy and practices.

Yet, without the foresight and dedication of a great number of people during the late nineteenth and early twentieth centuries, there would be nothing to debate today. The national forests would have long ago been carved into millions of private ownership plots and extensively logged and changed forever. The national forests are our legacy for future generations.

The following is a compilation of five challenges that present the USDA Forest Service with a host of issues and opportunities at the beginning of 2006. These are:

- Preventing fire in the forests.
- Watershed Protection/Restoration and Water Use.
- Regulating recreation on the national forests and grasslands.
- Preserving fish and wildlife.
- Involving the public in federal land and natural resource management decisions.

PREVENTING FIRE IN THE FORESTS

Historically, the vast majority of the acres burned each year have been on state and private lands and on lands managed by the U.S. Department of the Interior, not on national forest lands. In the 1990s, for example, less than 14 percent of the acres burned nationwide were on the national forests and grasslands. Severe fire seasons all but ceased on the national forests after the 1920s. From 1930 to 1986, the number of acres burned on the national forests never approached 1 million in any fire season, thanks to growing firefighting effectiveness. Then, in 1987, the large fires returned—with a vengeance.

The 1987 and 1988 fire seasons saw 1.2 and 1.5 million acres, respectively, burn on the national forests. During this time, the dramatic and devastating Yellowstone fires of 1988 caught the media attention, probably more so than the 1910 fires. These massive fires indicate the beginnings of a new pattern: large fires were returning to the interior West. More than a million acres burned on the national forestlands in 1994—only the third time this had happened since 1919. Many wildland firefighters in 1994 paid the ultimate price, with 134 entrapments and 35 fatalities, including 14 fallen firefighters on Storm King Mountain, Colorado. In response, the federal wildland fire community joined in a series of investigations and reports that culminated in the 1995 federal wildland fire management policy and program review. Drought conditions in Florida in 1998 produced wildland fires that affected much of the state's population; entire counties were evacuated, and firefighting resources had to be brought in from across the country.

The 2000 fire season was exceptionally destructive. The proportion of acres burned on the national forest system reached about 32 percent (2.3 million acres out of 7.3 million acres), mostly in the interior West. The last year more than 2 million acres burned on the national forests was 1919. The Cerro Grande Fire burned parts of the land around Los Alamos National Laboratory, in New Mexico. The major fires in 2002 were unprecedented, with huge fires burning in Arizona, Colorado, and Oregon. Then, in 2003, forest areas of southern California burned, exposing millions of residents to the danger of wildfires and smoke. The trend has been clear: The strategy that Smokey and the various federal and state agencies were implementing was not working. A hundred years of systematic fire exclusion was simply not enough to prevent major fires. Ironically, it seems that by excluding fire, officials simply postponed the destructive fires, allowing time for massive buildups of unburned fuels in the forests. Systematic fire exclusion had exacerbated the fire risk in many parts of the interior West.

Sooner or later, fire-adapted forests will burn. For thousands of years, severe fires in the fire-adapted, higher elevation forests had etched patchwork patterns into the landscape every few decades or centuries. But the worst fire problems had little to do with Mother Nature's naturally caused fire (e.g., those started by lightning). At lower elevations, frequent low-intensity Indian-set fires kept the number of trees burned per acre low. But the growing effectiveness of firefighting allowed small trees and brush to build up. Also, as some critics have noted, the firefighters have stopped most of the easy fires—small, low-intensity ones near roads and highways, leaving the more remote areas susceptible to larger fire. When fires now occur, the dense fuels can make the fires so severe that they destroy entire forest stands. In 2000, some 56 million acres of national forests in the interior West were at high or moderate risk of wildland fires that could compromise ecosystem integrity and human safety.

Congress commissioned an investigation of the fire crisis by the U.S. General Accounting Office. The resulting report was published in April 1999 under the title "Western National Forests: A Cohesive Strategy Is Needed to Address Catastrophic Wildfire Threats." Based on the GAO study, the Forest Service's fire and aviation management staff prepared a report published in October 2000 under the title "Protecting People and Sustaining Resources in Fire-Adapted Ecosystems: A Cohesive Strategy."

In accordance with the 1995 federal wildland fire management policy, the cohesive strategy "establishes a framework that restores and maintains ecosystem health in fire-adapted ecosystems for priority areas across the interior West." High-priority areas under the strategy are the wildland-urban interface, readily accessible municipal watersheds, threatened and endangered species habitat, and existing low-risk areas. The strategy has three elements:

1. Social (for example, increasing public awareness of fire's ecological role, collaborating with stakeholders in project implementation, and promoting local fire-safe practices).
2. Institutional (for example, establishing long-term policy objectives and assessment procedures).
3. Program management (for example, concentrating national programs on areas at risk, conducting regional assessments, adjusting local forest plans, expanding community FIREWISE programs, and strengthening fire-related research).

In the year 2000, a national fire plan was developed from reports prepared for President Clinton by the Secretaries of Agriculture and the Interior in response to the wildfires of 2000. The report's title is "Managing the Impact of Wildfires on Communities and the Environment." Implementation of the fire plan will, it is hoped, ensure sufficient firefighting resources for the future, restore ecosystems damaged by the recent fires, rebuild community economics, and reduce future fire risk through fuel reduction efforts. There are five key points to the national fire plan:

1. Firefighting—continue to fight fire and be adequately prepared for future fires.
2. Rehabilitation and restoration—restore landscapes and rebuild communities damaged by the wildfires.
3. Hazardous fuel reduction—invest in projects to reduce fire risk.
4. Community assistance—work directly with communities to ensure adequate protection.
5. Accountability—be accountable and establish adequate oversight coordination, program development, and monitoring for performance.

Two kinds of fires can be used on the national forests and grasslands to reduce flammable. "Prescribed fire" is set by managers; lightning fires or "naturally ignited fire" are used for management purposes. In both cases, an approved fire plan is necessary, especially in wildernesses, or else the fires will be extinguished before they have served their necessary function in the ecosystem. For both types, management goals include:

1. Site preparation (clearing away slash and exposing mineral soil for forest regeneration).
2. Fuels management (reducing fuels that might cause wildfires).
3. Habitat management (for example, mimicking American Indian fire use to recreate historical landscape mosaics for maximum biodiversity).

Fire exclusion proved so successful that historical conditions changed on millions of acres nationwide. Where frequent fire once kept much of the land under early-successional open forest, fire exclusion brought tremendous fuel buildups and allowed shade-tolerant species to become dominant. By the 1960s, land managers began to understand the adverse effects of fire exclusion. The Forest Service increasingly experimented with fire use in areas outside the South (where fire use had persisted on the coastal plain). In 1978, the agency formally abandoned the fire exclusion policy in favor of a flexible policy, including fire use based on local conditions. In 1995, the federal wildland fire management policy and program review embraced the growing need for fire use "to protect, maintain, and enhance resources." From 1994 to 2000, the Forest Service increased fuels treatments from 385,000 to 1,320,000 acres—mostly by the use of prescribed fire.

Smoke remains a problem with prescribed fire. Only the under the right conditions of wind and temperature can prescribed fire be used without inundating local areas in a blanket of smoke and heavy particulates. Management of health and air quality concerns is coordinated with state and local officials, but invariably some smoke goes the wrong direction or the winds suddenly shift. Of course, the smoke from a wildfire cannot be controlled, so at times there is a tradeoff between having fires and smoke in controlled situations and waiting for a big fire that can often "bury" communities under blankets of heavy smoke.

An increasing concern is the aftermath of fires. Clearly, during a fire, the destruction of trees and habitat for many species is of great concern. Logging the burned or scorched trees has become increasingly controversial since the 1985 Salvage Rider. In early 2006, there was a controversy involving the forestry school at Oregon State University. Dan Donato, a Ph.D. graduate student, published a study in the journal *Science* that found that logging in the aftermath of the Biscuit Fire, in southwest Oregon, had damaged or destroyed many of the seedlings that were naturally growing. This set off an intense debate among faculty members, the Forest Service, and the BLM over proper interpretation of the data, as well as about academic freedom at the university.

Wildland-urban interface fires helped change the face of wildland fire management in the 1990s. The wildland-urban interface (WUI) refers to urban areas (usually suburbs) that have spread into fire-prone rural areas through urban sprawl. WUI areas often have characteristics, such as heavy over- and understory vegetation, that can feed fires and endanger lives and property. The classic wildland-urban interface fire was the 1991 Oakland Hills fire, which burned a large suburban area in Oakland and Berkeley, California. The area abuts forested county parkland and itself has heavy, mostly nonnative vegetative cover on fire-prone slopes subject to prolonged drought. The fire burned 1,580 acres in several days, at times showing the extreme fire behavior associated with wildland fire blowups. It took 25 lives and destroyed some 2,700 homes and other structures, causing more than $1.68 billion in damages.

But this situation in California is not unique. Homes have mushroomed since the 1970s in fire-prone rural areas nationwide, built by people from urban and suburban areas who retire to them or use them for vacation homes. Many are clustered near national forest lands for the recreational opportunities and amenities they offer. In fact, many of the homes and home sites were sold because they abutted the national forest managed for forest values rather than favoring the building new homes. For many people, these homes were and remain an opportunity to get away from the cities and have large trees and wooden decks, while looking into the forest and seeing deer and squirrels play. Unbeknownst to many buyers of these new and often very expensive homes, they were living next to areas where forest and grass fires could threaten them. Thousands of vacation or summer homes on the national forests under special use permits have been built since the 1910s, and many are inhabited year-round. Additionally, many national forests surround parcels of private property with homes and structures. In some cases, privately owned property surrounded by national forest lands can prove hazardous. A number of these lands were old mining claims that were transferred from public ownership to private ownership under the mining laws. Most of these have long since been worthless for the extraction of minerals, but they are valuable as sites for summer homes and winter ski-season rentals.

The Forest Service and other federal and state agencies have been working on a number of strategies to lessen the forest fire impact on forests and people. One such program is FIREWISE. It is a unique program that works cooperatively with many federal and state agencies to prevent fire or reduce the possibilities of catastrophic fires with loss of life and property. As more people choose to build homes, operate businesses, and enjoy themselves in areas where forests border on suburban and urban areas, the threat from wildland fire increases. Private landowners need to take steps to protect their property by creating "defensible" or "survivable" spaces around structures can make the difference between having their home or finding a smoldering pile of ashes if a wildfire moves through the area. It should be recognized that neither wildland firefighting agencies or local fire departments can adequately protect people and the growing number of structures in WUI interface areas. Living next to the national forests can be dangerous for the people and devastating to personal property. As a rule, fire fighting is premised on saving lives first, property second. In most cases, lives have been saved but homes burned to the ground. There are many resources available to assist property owners, including a number of Web sites with information on fire-resistant building materials and safe practices, including replacement of wood shingles, awareness of the danger of storing wood next to homes and wooden decks, landscaping techniques that remove flammable trees and shrubs, and evacuation procedures to follow in case of an emergency. See the FIREWISE Web site, at www.firewise.org, for many ideas that have proven useful to homeowners.

WATERSHED PROTECTION/RESTORATION AND WATER USE

Consistent with the Organic Act of 1897, the first priority of the Forest Service is to maintain and restore the health of the nation's watersheds. Watersheds absorb rain and recharge underground aquifers. They provide wildlife and fish habitat and connect headwaters to downstream areas and wetlands and riparian areas to uplands. Healthy watersheds dissipate floods across flood plains, increase soil fertility, and help minimize damage to lives, property, and streams. They reduce drinking water treatment costs and increase reservoir storage life.

The Forest Service manages watersheds, and thus water, which are extremely important for the nation. The water on the national forest system contains roughly 50 percent of the cold water fishes and 50 percent of the anadromous spawning grounds on the West Coast. It should be noted that some 50 million Americans fish each year. In addition, the national forest system has more than 50 percent of the nation's wild and scenic rivers in the lower 48 states. Almost all the national forest watersheds are at extremely high elevations where snow and rainfall are the heaviest. Melting snow packs are often the only source of late-summer irrigation water in many areas of the West. The agency has the responsibility to protect these areas for the future.

Watersheds are the basis for ecological health, forest health, and sustainable resources uses. The Forest Service's obligation is to protect the nation's healthiest watersheds and to restore the ecological integrity of those where it has been disrupted. Healthy, properly functioning watersheds are resilient in the face of natural events such as floods, fire, and drought and are more capable of absorbing the effects of human-induced disturbances. How we manage forests and rangelands has a profound effect on the quality of watersheds and the water produced.

Most watersheds in the nation's forests and grasslands are healthy, supporting a variety of thriving ecosystems. In some areas, however, watersheds have deteriorated.

Dams, ditches, and levees fragment the water courses and alter streamflows. Overgrazing and fires can damage water courses, warming the water and increasing land erosion. Roads and logging can have adverse effects on watersheds if not carefully monitored. Symptoms of poor watershed health include declining water quality, increasing insect and disease outbreaks, and decreasing stocks of native fish and wildlife. Watershed health and restoration remain the oldest and highest calling of the Forest Service. Consistent with this notion, the Forest Service has committed to these programs:

1. Continue to make watershed health the overriding objective of national forest and grassland management.
2. Conduct watershed assessments to provide a better understanding of the effects of land management decisions on watershed conditions.
3. Use a watershed approach to prevent and reduce pollution of surface and ground waters from land and resource management activities.
4. Recognize the essential contribution of national forests and grasslands to public sources of drinking water, working with the states to identify and map each community that depends on national forests for its drinking water supply, and estimate how many people each system serves.
5. Assess each of the relevant forest plans to ensure they provide adequate protection to drinking water supplies. Work with federal, state, and local agencies, tribal governments, and interested stakeholders to identify priority watersheds to focus budgetary and other resources.
6. Continue to strengthen compliance with water quality requirements of the Clean Water Act and provide technical assistance to the states and tribes in their development of total maximum daily loads for national forest system lands.

Water-related issues are not only a national issue but also a world issue. It may be that from fighting over oil we next turn to fighting over water. Billions of people worldwide lack basic water, especially clean water, services and sources. Contamination of water supplies by human fecal matter, farming, and commercial use is common. Millions die annually from water-borne diseases. Groundwater supplies, such as the Ogallala Aquifer, in the United States, are being consumed or "sucked dry" faster than the water can be replaced naturally. Everywhere, agriculture has been enhanced by irrigation. With new strains of rice and wheat, helped along by fertilizers and weed-killers, the so-called green revolution has bumped food production manyfold over the past 50 years. But water remains the key ingredient. It is pumped from the lakes, rivers, and streams for farms, but it is also needed by people, fish, and animals. It will not be an easy issue to deal with, either in the United States or in other countries.

REGULATING RECREATION ON THE NATIONAL FORESTS AND GRASSLANDS

Outdoor recreation has many facets. People have viewed hunting and fishing as two of the oldest occupations that are necessary for life. Hiking and swimming are two of our oldest pleasures. Picnicking and camping date to the beginning of cities, when people have wanted to get away from the often dreadful city life that was in the throes of industrialization. But, much like today, the poorest people had little opportunity to enjoy the great outdoors. The Forest Service, since 1905, has had to cope with the continuing increase in the number of visitors to national forest lands and to help ensure a safe, enjoyable experience for visitors while working within the limits of the land.

Increasing populations, of course, means more forest visitors. People from different cultures want different amenities. Fire has been a constant companion of forest visitors since they started seeking recreation on the national forests. Activities today include wilderness use, driving for pleasure on the forest roads, camping, taking resort vacations, hunting, fishing, birding, photographing, swimming, walking, hiking, mountain climbing, spelunking, hang gliding, whitewater rafting and kayaking, off-road and all-terrain-vehicle riding, skiing both cross-country and downhill, and many other activities. Some activities fees are charged by the day or the year. Usually, guiding and outfitting on rivers or in the mountains are tightly regulated. Special-use permits are needed for commercial operations, such as ski areas and resorts.

The Forest Service held a national recreation summit, in October 1999, to devise a plan of action. Representatives of environmental groups, the recreation industry, individual recreation users, and the government were invited to review a draft recreation agenda and to suggest modifications. Then, 14 regional recreation summits were held across the country to solicit additional input from interested groups and individuals. A second national summit was held, in June 2000, with attendance mirroring that of the first national summit.

The national recreation and heritage program develops annual recreation action plans with clear objectives, specific projects, timelines, and proposed future budgets to address each of the emphasis areas. The plan is a "road map" to guide Forest Service recreation programs into the future. As appropriate, recreation fund increases will be requested during normal budget processes.

The greatest challenge to the future of national forest recreation is the perception that it rates far behind timber and grazing management as an agency priority. The reality is that recreation dollars drive the budget for the Forest Service. The importance of recreation will have to increase as the timber harvest remains low but the population increases greatly over the next century. Recreation on the national forests is a reality today and into the future.

PRESERVING FISH AND WILDLIFE—RESPONSIBLE HABITAT MANAGEMENT

Until the late nineteenth century, most Americans believed that the natural abundance of resources was inexhaustible. There was always more over the next hill. It was believed that wildlife species were incapable of being exterminated because there were vast numbers of them. Buffalo/bison and passenger pigeons, to mention a few, were found in the millions, even billions. Salmon numbered in the billions of fish. How could they ever be gone? But, by the early 1900s, they were nearly gone. Buffalo were relegated to a few areas like Yellowstone, while the last passenger pigeon died in a Cincinnati zoo in 1914. The number of salmon, especially in the Pacific Northwest, greatly declined. Overhunting and -fishing were the main causes of the rapid decline, but also responsible was the changing habitat—vast prairies became farms, grazing of cattle was encouraged, wholesale logging eliminated the forests, rivers and creeks were diverted and polluted, and towns and cities sprouted everywhere. Civilization had come to the West. The consequences for wildlife were not apparent, at least at first. The question on the minds of some was "Should the natural resources be used as quickly as possible, or should at least some be conserved or reserved for the future?" By the late 1800s, the answer came: reserve. Yet, even today, there are those in the United States who feel that the natural resources should be used now for the needs of today. Probably the best example of this thinking was Interior Secretary James Watt, in the 1980s.

Traditionally, the Forest Service has managed national forest habitat for wildlife and fish, leaving population management, including reintroductions, up to state and other federal agencies (such as FWS). The National Forest Management Act, and implementing regulations, calls for maintaining a diversity of plant and animal communities, not just the traditional huntable and fishable species. The Act specifies that the Forest Service must consider these factors in planning and management: viability, diversity, and indicator species of fish and wildlife. National forests must provide enough habitat to support a minimum number of reproductive individuals, and that habitat must be well distributed so that those individuals can interact with others in the planning area. The national forests must provide a diversity of habitats like that which would be expected in a natural forest, including tree species (36 CFR 219.19):

> [P]rovide for diversity of plant and animal communities based on the suitability and capability of the specific land area in order to meet overall multiple-use objectives, and within the multiple-use objectives of a land management plan adopted pursuant to this section, provide, where appropriate, to the degree practicable, for steps to be taken to preserve the diversity of tree species similar to that existing in the region controlled by the plan [which precludes planting of only those trees that have commercial value].

The viability requirement means that any management action must result in habitats that are capable of supporting viable plant, animal, and fish populations. In some national forest plans, as well as among the committee of scientists, there has been controversy over the type, amount, and distribution of habitat needed to meet this requirement. Last, the implementing regulations require that each forest plan shall set objectives for maintaining and improving habitat for the management indicator species selected by each regional forester for each particular forest. The regulations require that population trends of management indicator species be monitored. In the Forest Service manual, the intent is clear: to use management indicator species as a tool to understand how management actions affect wildlife and fish habitat.

A number of disputes have arisen between the Forest Service and other agencies over policies and procedures—particularly who was to be responsible for wildlife on the national forests. The agencies have, over many decades, signed agreements to work together to resolve differences. Working with the states has been a little more problematic, as each state has its own laws and regulations that usually apply as well to the national forests within the particular state. Management of animals, birds, fishes, and other species is handled by the states, except for threatened or endangered species, which the Fish and Wildlife Service or the National Marine Fisheries Service maintains through tight controls. Both the federal agencies and the states set limits on hunting and fishing. The Forest Service has little if any control over these regulations, except for placing certain lands off limits for hunting and fishing on the basis of habitat or other needs.

For salmon and other anadromous species, there is a potential train wreck ready to happen. The need for more water to sustain salmon habitat has come into conflict with the need to use the water for domestic drinking purposes, industrial needs, generation of electricity, or farming irrigation; in addition, road building, timber harvesting, and grazing practices cause siltation. Then add to the pot the major federal players—the Forest Service, the Bureau of Land Management, the Army Corps of Engineers, the National Marine Fisheries Service, the Fish and Wildlife Service, and even the Bonneville Power Administration. Then throw in the Indian treaties that promised historic quantities of salmon. The process works poorly at best. The salmon in many locations are slowly sliding toward extinction because these various government entities simply can't come to grips with the issue.

One of the little-known subissues involves hunting and fishing. By the early twenty-first century, the popularity of hunting and fishing was down. What was once a proud heritage passed down from one generation to the next has been interrupted, perhaps never to fully recover. People are not going to the great outdoors to hunt and fish as they once did. Federal tax money derived from the sale of hunting and fishing supplies has been decreasing. Also, state revenue generated by the sale of hunting and fishing licenses has been dropping. Most people in the United States see meat and fish as coming from the supermarket. There has been a disconnect between taking resources from the land and what is put on the table to eat. This is the same complaint that farmers have been making for decades: milk comes from the store in plastic or cardboard containers, not from the farm. There is little that the Forest Service or the other federal or state agencies can do to reverse the trend. The Forest Service has made successful annual efforts to encourage young anglers to fish the national forests, but there is no such effort under way for hunters.

But hunting and fishing are not the only subissues. The habitats of many species are managed by the Forest Service, including wolves, grizzly bears, wolves, pronghorn antelope, elk, deer, wolverines, bald and golden eagles, peregrine falcons, neotropical birds, spotted owls, marbled murrelets, pileated woodpeckers, red cockaded woodpeckers, condors, migratory birds such as ducks and geese, squirrels, and many other species. Each requires different management and, usually, separate nesting areas. So how can the Forest Service perform this complex wildlife management job and still allow other activities such as grazing and timber harvest? The answer is: carefully.

Interestingly, the national forests have, by default, become the areas where there is still the same relative diversity of species as was present during the millennia of management by the Indians. Most areas outside the national forests are relative "deserts" where the forests and prairies have been converted to farms and cities; exceptions are the national parks, refuges, and BLM lands. In the converted areas, the loss of habitat is severe, and the changes probably are permanent. Species once dependent on those lands for their existence are no longer able to survive. Many people continue to believe that if an area is converted for other uses, then the species will simply move to adjacent areas. However, these areas are already full. There is no place to go unless the larger species displace the smaller ones.

The national forests have become islands of mostly natural habitat surrounded by development. The forests are the last places left for many species. To keep the national forests in this vitally important role, it will be necessary to stop the continued fragmentation—through roads and clearcuts—of the forest habitats. It should be acknowledged that some species, such as deer, actually do better in disturbed areas where young ferns and brush provide summer food supplies, but most other species suffer or die from disturbances. Also, the more fragmentation, the less possibility there is for different populations to interact and breed, making inbreeding a real problem. Corridors and large undisturbed blocks of forest and prairie lands are essential for healthy wildlife and fish populations.

There are several subissues concerning the reintroduction of mammalian species onto to the national forest system—especially grizzly bears and wolves. Challenges for the Forest Service include sustaining habitat (for example, through prescribed fire to stimulate berry production for the bears); helping to manage encounters with humans and livestock; and helping to address deep-rooted, culturally ingrained public fears through educational programs. If the reintroduced species act aggressively toward humans or attack livestock, they will be relocated or destroyed.

The red wolf, native in the Southeast, has been reintroduced on national forests in eastern Tennessee and North Carolina; the gray wolf, native throughout most of the North and West, has been reintroduced onto national forests in the Southwest, the northern Rockies, and the Great Lakes region. There is potential for wolf recovery in some areas of the Northeast, where suitable habitat and prey species remain. A wildlife conservation foundation set up by Ted Turner, who owns more than a million acres of ranchland and other tracts nationwide, has proposed reintroducing wolves in the central Rockies to eventually help link wolf populations in the northern Rockies with those in the Southwest. The foundation has offered to play the traditional reintroduction role of the Fish and Wildlife Service, releasing the animals and managing the population, with the Forest Service and Bureau of Land Management furnishing most of the habitat.

Recovery depends on restoration of prey species such as deer, elk, and moose; science-based management; and habitat and legal protection. In Minnesota, successful wolf recovery has led to delisting; in the Southwest, released individuals have been shot, and program success is in doubt. The reintroduced wolves in the

Southwest and northern Rockies were designated as a nonessential, experimental population to allow management flexibility.

INVOLVING THE PUBLIC IN FEDERAL LAND AND NATURAL RESOURCE MANAGEMENT DECISIONS

Keeping the public informed and involved with federal land management decisions has evolved over the past 100 years. It began as simple efforts to convince the public of the value of conservation and the national forests—what they were about, how they were being managed, and how they could be used now and in the future. Initially, communication was one way—from the agency to the people. By the 1930s and 1940s, communication became less a matter of educating the public more a question of getting people involved. By the 1990s, ideas about communicating with the public changed once again, this time to enhancing collaboration, stewardship, and joint management, in some cases.

Interestingly, the National Forest Management Act of 1976 and the National Environmental Policy Act of 1969, as well as the Administrative Procedures Act of 1973, have set up procedures designed to inform the public about land management decision on the national forests. All projects have to undergo extensive and intensive internal preparation, sometimes taking several years, of reviews. Some of the projects call for an environmental impact statement to document the decision to proceed. Each step in the process involves at least some oversight from the public—at the earliest stages it is called "scoping"—although in reality few of the public are involved until a tentative decision is made to go ahead with the project. This process takes place for a thousand or more projects each year nationally. To the public, review of documents can be overwhelming. Many of the public simply turn off to the reviews, becoming overloaded with reading and trying to make substantial comments. However, local special interest groups and users of the national forests often take the time and expend the energy to try to understand the proposed projects.

The early practice of reaching out to the public was established by the Department of Agriculture. The USDA Division of Forestry began, as early as the mid-1880s, to take the growing interests in trees and forestry to the people. The Division printed thousands of pages of circulars, pamphlets, and articles about forestry, tree farming, and the uses of wood. In the summer of 1897, Gifford Pinchot, then hired as a special agent for the General Land Office, traveled to the West, met with newspaper editors, and was able to convince them that the forest reservation policy was good for the country and the states. It was his first experience at changing public opinion, and it continued to serve the Forest Service well for many years.

From the beginning, the Forest Service has relied heavily on publications of science and engineering to promote the best ways of managing the nation's forests, both public and private. Correspondence with the public was of paramount importance to Pinchot. The Forest Service's national headquarters staff, in Washington, through the strong efforts of Pinchot and Herbert A. Smith, editor for the agency, was wildly successful at contacting the public. By 1909, the Forest Service mailing list had about 750,000 names. Printed publications have always been, and remain today, an important part of communication with the public. Forest and recreation maps, which are printed for public distribution and sale, are often handled by the regional office and the national forest offices, while scientific reports are most often completed and published by the research stations.

Today, news releases, information sharing, and education are still the mainstays of Forest Service policy. Being responsive to public queries, media requests, chief and staff requirements, congressional exigencies, and field office needs is crucial to operating from the national and regional headquarters in an often highly charged political climate.

Photographs from days gone by and the current new century are always in high demand. The old black-and-white photos now stored at the National Archives are being digitized for use by any number of researchers and writers from across the country. The old 35-mm slide shows and acetate overheads are being supplanted by Power Point presentations. Many historical documents will soon be transformed to digital format for viewing by thousands of Internet users. With the advent of the twenty-first century, the type of work and workload for staff that works with the public is rapidly changing but is no less challenging.

CONCLUSION

The Forest Service has tended to be a lightning rod that has attracted considerable attention from all sectors. With battles to be fought appearing on the horizon, there is no doubt that the agency will continue to be in the forefront of the "war of words" over the proper management of the wilderness and roadless areas. As the Forest Service moves into the twenty-first century, it will have to respond in ways that are probably thought of as ill advised today.

There is, of course, the continuing concern about the relevance of the national forests, much less the Forest Service, as a needed part of American life. Those strongly in favor of the agency and the national public lands called national forests will strive to ever increase the lands for the future of the nation. Those who believe that the time has come for divesting the public lands to the waiting public will continue their efforts. Probably the best thing that can be said is that, because there are national forests today, we can argue about their future. If there were none, the point would be moot. Once the public forests are broken up or sold, there is no chance that they will return to the condition that we know today. Differing conceptions of what represents "the greatest good of the greatest number in the long run" (first stated for the Forest Service in 1905) will continue to direct the future management of the national forests.

---- ☆ **5** ☆ ----

Organization of Forest Service Management

FOUR ADMINISTRATIVE LEVELS

There are four levels of field units. The lowest level, where the majority of fieldwork gets accomplished, is at the ranger district. The headquarters of the district is called the ranger station. The second level is the national forest/forest supervisor's office (now often referred to as the forest headquarters), the third is the regional office/ headquarters, and the fourth is the Washington office/headquarters. Each of these units is discussed in this chapter.

Ranger Districts/Stations

The lowest level (sometimes referred to as the ground level) of the USDA Forest Service is the ranger district. It comprises one or more units of the national forest system under the overall administration of the forest supervisor's office (SO). From the records, it appears that the ranger district (RD) as a separate and smaller management unit came into existence around 1908, at about the same time that the regional offices (then called district offices) were first established. These early RDs were organized around grazing units, since grazing was the main administrative challenge for decades.

Many of these RDs had no permanent ranger station (RS), and the employees (often just one person) were living in the town where the SO was located. When the first RSs were built, they were usually located along main trails or adjacent to lakes and rivers, often near hydroelectric sites. Beginning around 1909, construction began on thousands of RSs, which at the time were nothing more than shelters without windows, some without doors or floors. The RS was considered a site where the ranger, on horseback, could get out of any inclement weather and keep warm and dry. This situation prevailed through the 1910s and part of the 1920s.

In the early 1920s, construction began on greatly improving the RSs, in part because of the greater need for field employees to work on the national forests in remote locations. Often the new RSs were located in the national forest at low elevations and supplied with telephones, radios, and road access. The older RSs were relegated to guard station status, with many being torn down or replaced by even cruder trail shelters. The Civilian Conservation Corps (1933–1942) constructed many thousands of new Forest Service buildings, including RSs, barns, garages, fire barracks, fences, lookouts, and bridges. Several thousand of these historic CCC buildings still exist on the national forests today. During the 1960s, many of the RSs were moved from remote locations to larger towns and cities. A number of the RSs and RDs were renamed to reflect the new location and town name (e.g., Layng Creek RS was changed to Cottage Grove RS, on the Umpqua National Forest).

Ranger districts were originally laid out to facilitate a grazing management organization, as timber harvesting was practically nonexistent. The first district rangers were appointed/assigned to RDs around 1912–1916. Many rangers had responsibility for more than one RD, which was often quite small in size so that one ranger could "range" the area quite easily in a day on horseback. The district rangers also were often the only employees employed year-round. During the winter months, many district rangers were assigned to the supervisor's office (SO) or regional office (RO), with duties including repairing tools, ordering equipment, carving signs, and making reports. It wasn't until the CCC era that the RSs were staffed year-round and district rangers spent most of their time on the RD.

By and large, this situation has not changed. What has changed, however, has been the shift in the number and size of the RDs. Until the mid-1920s, the RDs were small, usually less than 100,000 acres. Then, in the 1930s they became very large, with some containing as many as 500,000 acres. After World War II, when the national forests were opened for timber harvesting, new, smaller RDs began to be carved from the older, larger RDs to facilitate the new form of management: timber and road construction. Many national forests (NF) went through a process often referred to as "splitting" ("lumping" came later). This splitting was considered necessary because of the quickly increasing workload and the hundreds of new employees handling timber management, road construction, engineering, and firefighting. For example, the Willamette NF, in western Oregon, went from five RDs in the 1910–1940s to nine in the late 1950s, seven in the 1970s, and then only four in the late 1990s.

In the 2004 edition of the *Forest Service Organizational Directory* there are a total of 506 RDs, each led by a district ranger (there are, in addition, 10 managers of national grasslands). The RDs are located, by Forest Service region, are as follows:

Northern Region (R-1)	57 ranger districts
Rocky Mountain Region (R-2)	50 ranger districts
Southwestern Region (R-3)	52 ranger districts
Intermountain Region (R-4)	69 ranger districts
Pacific Southwest Region (R-5)	63 ranger districts
Pacific Northwest Region (R-6)	67 ranger districts
Southern Region (R-8)	84 ranger districts
Eastern Region (R-9)	52 ranger districts
Alaska Region (R-10)	12 ranger districts

FIGURE 5.1 National Forest System Lands as of September 30, 2004

Forest Service Region	Of NFS[1]	Acres of NF Lands	NFS Units[2]	Other NFS Unit Acres
Region 1: Northern	15	24,181,134	11	1,261,157
Region 2: Rocky Mountain	17	19,981,446	8	2,100,795
Region 3: Southwestern	12	20,353,490	12	454,259
Region 4: Intermountain	18	32,164,415	2	103,420
Region 5: Pacific Southwest	18	20,132,915	27	33,317
Region 6: Pacific Northwest	21	24,619,817	16	121,256
Region 8: Southern	35	12,881,841	32	412,366
Region 9: Eastern	17	11,907,106	34	175,532
Region 10: Alaska	2	21,973,662	0	0
Total	155	188,195,826	142	4,662,082

Total National Forest System (NFS) Lands	192,857,908 acres
Total Private Land Inside NF Boundaries	39,630,993 acres
Total Land Within NF Boundaries	232,488,901 acres

National Forest Lands in Special Categories (in acres)

Wilderness Areas	34,859,062
Primitive Areas	173,762
Scenic-Research Areas	6,637
National Scenic Areas	130,493
Wild, Scenic, and Recreation Rivers	950,906
National Recreation Areas	2,911,239
Game Refuge and Wildlife Preserves	1,198,099
National Monuments	3,659,974
National Volcanic Monuments	167,427
National Historic Areas	6,540
Protection Areas	27,600
Special Management Areas	91,265
National Botanical Areas	8,256
Recreation Management Areas	43,900
Total	44,235,160

Notes: [1] National Forests (NF) that are managed jointly are counted as separate forests; [2] National Forest System (NFS) Units, which are composed of 56 purchase units, 20 national grasslands, 6 land utilization projects, 20 research and experimental areas, and 35 small miscellaneous areas.

National Forests and Forest Supervisor's Office/Headquarters

National forests have been around since 1891, when the Yellowstone Park Timberland Reserve was established around the southern edge of Yellowstone National Park. These early national forests were known as "forest reserves" from 1891 until March 4, 1907, when they were given the present title. Each national forest has one or more official presidential proclamations or congressional actions. Other administrative units came along later, including wildernesses, research natural areas, national grasslands, national recreation areas, national monuments, and so on, some of which were established by Congress, others by the chief of the Forest Service. None of the other major units—RDs, regional offices, or the Washington office—has been established by the same process.

The early forest reserves (FR) were nothing more than lines drawn on a map, and the only people doing any "managing" were federal law enforcement officers—U.S. marshals—who were most concerned about sheep and timber trespass issues. Beginning in the summer of 1897, the first forest reserve superintendents were appointed (generally one superintendent for each state that had forest reserves) to administer the FRs. During the following year, the first forest rangers were employed by the USDI General Land Office (GLO) to administer the land. By the end of the GLO period (1897–1904), there were hundreds of politically appointed GLO rangers on the job throughout the West (there were no FRs in the East). T. S. Woolsey reported, in a 1916 *Forestry Quarterly* article, that the state forest reserve superintendents hired the GLO rangers as "the Congressman recommended … they had uniform pay with no office worth the term, and no clerical help. The ranger was ordinarily a temporary man, employed for a few months [during summer and fall fire season] … there were some good men, as well as very bad ones, but few were really competent." Also during this period, U.S. Geological Survey teams were sent to investigate and map the FRs, which they did in their USGS Reports, Part V—Forest Reserves, for 1898–1899, 1899–1900, and 1900–1901. Generally there was a forest supervisor appointed to each forest reserve (or major portion thereof). After 1902, the state superintendent position was dropped.

When the forest reserves were transferred from the Department of the Interior to the Department of Agriculture, in the spring of 1905, major shifts began to occur. The most visible was the change from politically appointed forest rangers to Civil Service personnel who had both writing and reading and practical forestry skills. After passing the Civil Service exams, the new rangers were assigned to one of the forest reserves/national forests.

Many national forest names and boundaries were changed in these early years, with many additional acres added but a few forests made smaller. Also, until 1911, many of the NFs were situated or bound by rivers, that is, the boundary between NFs was a river. Beginning in 1911, most of the boundaries were shifted to mountaintops or ridge lines so that management was within an entire river drainage.

FIGURE 5.2 National Forests, National Grasslands, Research, and Related Units in Each State

State/ Territory	Number of Units[1]	Acres of NF Lands	Percent of State
Alabama	6	667,314	2.0
Alaska	2	21,973,662	5.9
Arizona	7	11,262,527	15.4
Arkansas	6	2,593,028	7.4
California	48	20,769,716	20.4
Colorado	14	14,498,801	21.7
Connecticut	1	24	>0.1
Florida	7	1,156,827	3.1
Georgia	6	865,205	2.3
Hawaii	1	1	>0.1
Idaho	18	20,715,568	38.3
Illinois	5	293,101	0.8
Indiana	3	200,935	0.9
Kansas	1	108,175	0.2
Kentucky	4	811,042	3.1
Louisiana	2	604,373	2.0
Maine	3	53,040	0.3
Michigan	13	2,868,468	7.6
Minnesota	4	2,840,385	5.3
Mississippi	12	1,171,158	3.8
Missouri	3	1,489,327	3.3
Montana	14	16,923,859	18.0
Nebraska	4	352,252	0.7
Nevada	4	5,836,348	8.3
New Hampshire	2	732,413	12.3
New Mexico	16	9,419,498	12.1
New York	1	16,211	>0.1
North Carolina	8	1,254,876	2.0
North Dakota	6	1,105,997	2.4
Ohio	3	236,638	0.9
Oklahoma	3	400,172	0.9
Oregon	23	15,667,116	25.2
Pennsylvania	3	513,427	1.8
South Carolina	4	623,724	3.1

(continued)

FIGURE 5.2: *(Continued)*

State/ Territory	Number of Units[1]	Acres of NF Lands	Percent of State
South Dakota	5	2,014,005	4.1
Tennessee	3	700,974	2.6
Texas	9	755,389	0.4
Utah	10	8,193,568	15.1
Vermont	3	393,868	6.2
Virginia	4	1,664,071	6.4
Washington	17	9,276,203	21.2
West Virginia	8	1,041,094	6.6
Wisconsin	3	1,527,336	4.2
Wyoming	11	9,238,063	14.8
Puerto Rico	1	28,002	1.3
Virgin Islands	1	147	0.2
Total in United States[2]	295	192,511,012	8.3

Notes: [1] Units located in each state (counted twice if same unit located in two states); [2] The states of Delaware, Iowa, Maryland, Massachusetts, New Jersey, and Rhode Island have no national forest system lands within their boundaries, and neither does the District of Columbia.

The function of the forest supervisors office (SO) has changed over the years, especially after World War II. In order to meet the growing national demand for wood, the national forests pursued a course of opening the national forests to intensive and extensive timber management and road construction. New employees with new skills were needed for management. Most of the new employee specialists (e.g., landscape architects, silviculturists, engineers, and wildlife biologists) were hired to work at the SO so that they could be brought into RD level projects as needed. It was one way to expand operations at minimal cost to the RDs. It was only in the 1970s that many of these specialists were hired at the RD level.

In the 2004 edition of the *Forest Service Organizational Directory* there are a total of 110 national forest management units, each led by a forest supervisor. The total is less than the number of official national forests because quite a few national forests are combined for management purposes. In addition, several national forests in Region 8 are small enough to be led by a district ranger. The national forests are located, by region, as follows (with actual number of proclaimed NFs in parentheses):

Region 1 (Northern)	13 (15) national forests and prairie grassland
Region 2 (Rocky Mtn.)	9 (17) national forests

Region 3 (Southwestern)	11 (12) national forests
Region 4 (Intermountain)	13 (18) national forests
Region 5 (Pacific Southwest)	17 (18) national forests and Lake Tahoe Basin
Region 6 (Pacific Northwest)	16 (21) national forests
Region 8 (Southern)	14 (35) national forests
Region 9 (Eastern)	15 (17) national forests and national tallgrass prairie
Region 10 (Alaska)	2 (2) national forests (Tongass NF has three "areas")

Regional Offices/Headquarters

During the GLO era (1897–1905), forest reserve state superintendents were appointed from most of the states that contained reserves. Apparently, these superintendents were housed in their homes and operated from them. They had no staff, and, as reported by T. S. Woolsey, in 1916, "these superintendents acted as inspectors, and since they had no real administrative powers, papers had to be forwarded to Washington, thus causing much delay." After 1902, the state superintendent positions were abolished. With the coming of the USDA Forest Service, in 1905, big changes occurred. As early as 1907, Chief Gifford Pinchot established "inspection offices" in several locations in the West to oversee operations on the national forests. The main duties of the inspectors were fiscal oversight, personnel matters (especially dereliction of duty), timber sale inspections, and standardization of the operational details of everyday management of the national forests. In operation for a little over a year, the inspection offices were, as Woolsey reported, "not a success … because supervisors had too little authority and were inexperienced…. Another drawback was the chief inspectors taking all reports with [to] Washington and the fact that the office was saddled with June 11 [1906 Act allowing forest homesteads] field work which occupied at least half the time."

The situation changed in November 1908, when a new level of organization was founded: Six district (now regional) offices were located in Denver, Ogden, Missoula, Albuquerque, San Francisco, and Portland. In early November 1908, some 377 Forest Service employees from the national headquarters in Washington, D.C., were reassigned to the new district offices in the far West. Sometimes this movement of personnel from the national headquarters was referred to as the "great exodus." Prior to their leaving, the Washington office (WO) published a new *Manual of Procedure for the Forest Service in Washington and in District Offices*, which outlined in detail what the expected procedures and policies would be with this new field organization. Many of the technically trained foresters originally from the West were working in Washington, while many of the clerical types had never set foot out of the Washington, D.C., area. The goal of establishing the new district offices was to get decisions closer to the field operations (from a news release on November 27, 1908):

> The new field organization of the Forest Service will greatly facilitate the use of the National Forests by the people. It will mean that the National Forest business which formerly was transacted in Washington will be handled by officers on or near the ground. The establishment of the district headquarters [regional offices] is the

culmination of a plan towards which the Forest Service has been working steadily, since it took charge of the National Forests [in February 1905].

Each National Forest District will be in charge of a District Forester. The work at District headquarters will be distributed among four offices, Operation, Grazing, Silviculture, and Products, each equipped with me of special training for the work of their office....

From the District Foresters down, the personnel of the District offices is made up of men [and women] picked for their proved capacity, for their thorough training, and for their experience in the West. Most of them are men who not only have worked in the West after they entered in the Service, but who lived in the West before they took up the Government forest work. Many of them are men who formerly were employed on the National Forests and have been promoted to larger responsibilities as a result of their high efficiency.

Another 1908 Forest Service news release concerning the new field (district) offices states that:

When through [the reorganization], the change of administration to the six district headquarters will mean much in expediting and rendering the forest work more effective. The saving of time in getting action on matter[s] relating to administration will be one of the most important benefits. Now, it takes from four days to two weeks to get mail to Washington and receive reply at the various points in the fourteen National Forest states. With the mail going to six central cities in the West instead of to Washington, there will be a marked saving in time and getting action on matters relating to the administration of the forests and the benefit is sure to be felt by every forest user.

Yet another 1908 news release mentions the relative advantage that the new district organization would have in dealing with the public:

Each district will be in charge of an assistant forester who will deal directly with the Supervisors of the Forests of his district. Only questions of special importance will be submitted to the Washington office for action. In this way, the regular business of the forests will be much expedited, while the men who have charge of the business will be in constant touch with the users of the Forests.... One of the big problems of administration has been to get into close touch with the users of the National Forests, and this has already been partially solved by various expedients, such as delegating to local Forest officers the authority to transact a large part of the National Forest business. In this way the public and the Service have been constantly brought closer together. A second step in the same direction was the recent transfer of headquarters for supplies from Washington, D.C., to Ogden, Utah. A third step was the placing of a branch of the office of engineering, which has charge of permanent improvements on the forests, also at Ogden, which is centrally located.... The change will not affect the form of organization of the Forest Service at Washington. The office will be retained as at present, but with a smaller force. All of the investigative work done by the Service, except that directly connected with the administration of the National Forests, will continue to be directed from Washington.

In 1908, the following Forest Service districts (regions) covered most states in the West; there were only a handful of national forests in the East (Florida):

District 1—Montana and portions of Washington, Idaho, South Dakota, Michigan, Minnesota, and North Dakota

District 2—Colorado, Wyoming, South Dakota, Nebraska, and portions of Kansas
District 3—Arizona, Arkansas, Florida, New Mexico, and Oklahoma
District 4—Utah and portions of Idaho, Wyoming, Nevada, and Arizona
District 5—California and portions of Nevada
District 6—Oregon, Washington, and Arkansas

A seventh district office (Eastern District) was added in early 1914 to cover administration of the national forests in Arkansas and Florida. Later in the year, the district was expanded to cover the new and proposed national forests (under the Weeks Act of 1911) for Oklahoma (taken from District 3), North and South Carolina, Georgia, Tennessee, Virginia, West Virginia, and New Hampshire. In 1915, District 7 (D-7) added Puerto Rico. Passage of the Weeks Act of 1911 allowed the establishment (often through purchase) of national forest land in the Northeast and South. Although many purchase units were placed into national ownership, it was not until 1916 that the Pisgah NF, in North Carolina, was established. D-7 added the states of Alabama and Maine in 1917.

In 1921, Alaska was split from the North Pacific District to make its own District 8. Another slight reorganization occurred in 1924 when D-7 added Pennsylvania, then another in 1926, when the district added the states of Illinois, Kentucky, Maryland, New Jersey, and New York. In 1929, District 9 (Lake States or North Central District, now the Eastern Region) was created to cover the national forests in Michigan, Minnesota, and Wisconsin. All district offices were renamed regional offices (RO) on May 1, 1930. Region 9 was expanded in the same year to administer national forests in Illinois, Indiana, Iowa, Missouri, and Ohio. The Southern Region (R-8) was established in 1934, and the Alaska Region was renumbered Region 10.

During the spring of 1964, a team was organized to look into the Forest Service management and organization. Headed by Edwin Deckard (from the Bureau of the Budget), the "Deckard Report" looked into the national forest system administration at the levels of the ranger district, the supervisor's office, and the regional office. One outcome of this national review was a decision to divide Region 7 between Regions 8 and 9 during 1965 and 1966. The R-7 designation has not been used since.

In the 2004 edition of the *Forest Service Organizational Directory*, there are a total of nine regional offices (RO), each led by a regional forester:

Region 1	Northern Region (ID, MT, ND, SD), at Missoula, Montana
Region 2	Rocky Mountain Region (CO, KS, NE, SD, WY), at Lakewood, Colorado
Region 3	Southwestern Region (AZ, NM), at Albuquerque, New Mexico
Region 4	Intermountain Region (ID, NV, UT, WY), at Ogden, Utah
Region 5	Pacific Southwest Region (CA, HI, Guam, Pacific Trust Territories), at San Francisco, California (moved to Mare Island)

Region 6	Pacific Northwest Region (WA, OR), at Portland, Oregon
Region 8	Southern Region (AL, AK, FL, GA, KY, LA, MI, NC, OK, PR, SC, TN, TX, Virgin Islands, VA), at Atlanta, Georgia
Region 9	Eastern Region (CT, DE, IL, IN, IO, ME, MD, MA, MI, MN, MO, NH, NJ, NY, OH, PA, RI, VT, WV, WI), at Milwaukee, Wisconsin
Region 10	Alaska Region (AK), at Juneau, Alaska

Washington Office/National Headquarters

The first federal forestry employee was Franklin B. Hough. He was appointed on August 30, 1876, as forestry agent of the U.S. government through a last-minute amendment (19 Stat. 167) to the agricultural appropriations bill (19 Stat. 143), which put the agent under the jurisdiction of the Commissioner (later Secretary) of Agriculture. Congress provided a $2,000 appropriation, but Hough had no assistants, no clerical help, and no travel money. Yet his assigned task was great: "Ascertaining the annual amount of consumption, importation and export of timber and other forest products—and the measures that have been successfully applied in foreign countries, or that may be deemed applicable in this country, for the preservation and restoration or planting of forests." During the spring and summer of 1877, Hough traveled more than 8,000 miles, visiting logging and lumbering operations, wood industries, tree plantations, universities, and state governors and legislatures, and corresponded with other forestry leaders from around the world. He assembled a massive 650-page report, for which Congress authorized the printing of 25,000 copies. Volume I of the report was published in 1878, with volume II, a statistical study, printed in 1880. The following year, the Division of Forestry was established in the Department of Agriculture. Hough was named chief of the Division. Hough was replaced in 1883 by Nathaniel Egleston, who served uneventfully as chief until he was replaced by Bernhard Eduard Fernow, on March 15, 1886.

On June 30, 1886, Congress gave full recognition to the Division of Forestry with an appropriation of $10,000. Five years later, Fernow and several others were instrumental in getting Section 24 (often referred to as the Creative Act or Forest Reserve Act of 1891) added to a bill aimed at eliminating land fraud. On March 30, 1891, the first forest reserve was established by President Harrison around the southern edge of Yellowstone National Park. Within a year, some 15 forest reserves had been established, containing more than 13 million acres. President Cleveland added another 15 million acres in 1893, then stopped until an adequate means could be found to protect and manage the reserves. The waiting would last four years.

Meanwhile, the fledgling Division of Forestry grew slowly, with the forestry experts under the jurisdiction of the Department of Agriculture. Custodial management of the new forest reserves, however, was under the jurisdiction of the Department of Justice in cases relating to trespass (sheep and timber). On June 4, 1897, the Sundry

Civil Appropriations Act (often called the Organic Act of 1897) passed Congress (30 Stat. 34–36). This was the first time that Congress had authorized money to be spent to manage the forest reserves. The Organic Act called for the General Land Office to administer the forest reserves and for the U.S. Geological Survey to examine the reserves. The USDA Division of Forestry was not mentioned. In 1899, the USDA Division of Forestry was composed of four sections: working plans, economic tree planting, special investigations, and office work.

Meanwhile, in the USDI General Land Office, division "R" was established in 1901 to administer the forest reserves, and the USDA Bureau of Forestry took the place of the Division of Forestry. As early as December of 1901, the newly sworn-in president, Theodore Roosevelt, sent a message to Congress "stating that the forest reserves belonged [the management thereof] in the Department of Agriculture, and the 1901 Report of the Secretary of the Interior supported transferring the reserves to the Agriculture Department." However, it took another 4.5 years, and the overcoming of considerable opposition in Congress, to have the management of the forest reserves transferred to the USDA; this took place on March 1, 1905. During Pinchot's time as chief of the Bureau of Forestry (1898–1905), the size of the agency budgets had risen from $28,520 to $439,873. The *USDA Forest Service Briefing Book* shows the final 1993 budget for the USDA Forest Service as $2,346,796,000, with 55.7 percent of the total going to management of the national forest system; 16.0 percent for firefighting; 10.9 percent for construction; 7.8 percent to research; 6.6 percent to state and private forestry; 3.0 percent to land acquisition, range betterment, and so on. International forestry funding comes from different sources.

Nationally, Forest Service staffing grew from 11 employees in 1898 to more than 820 in 1905. In 1908, about a third of the WO work force was transferred to the new district offices in the far West. In 1992, according to the *USDA Forest Service Briefing Book,* the Forest Service employed slightly more than 35,000 permanent employees; in the summer, another 17,000 temporary employees are added. There are more than 200 different occupational job titles in the agency. The almost all-white, male Forest Service organization of the 1905 era has changed dramatically over the years. By 1992, 39.7 percent of employees were women, and 15.3 percent were minority members. The WO employees number around 900 people, and the nine ROs have about 2,000 employees; 78 research units and laboratories have some 2,000; 18 Job Corps Centers have almost 700 employees; numerous state and private forestry locations have about 200 employees; and the remaining 29,000 employees are found on the 122 national forests, 11 national grasslands, 4 national monuments, 16 national recreation areas, 5 national scenic areas, and 506 ranger districts.

The Washington office of the Forest Service was first located in the Atlantic Building (1901–1933). The WO was relocated to the Department of Agriculture's South Building in 1933, where it remained until the spring of 1990, when it moved to the refurbished Auditor's Building—since renamed the Sidney R. Yates Federal Building—where it remains today.

225

FIGURE 5.3 Forest Service Offices (as of March 2004)

511	Ranger District Offices
152	Research Project Labs, Sites, and Work Units
124	Forest Supervisor's Offices
20	National Grasslands
20	Research and Experimental Areas and Laboratories
18	Job Corps Centers
9	Regional Offices
6	Research and Experiment Station Offices
3	National Recreation Area
3	Tree Improvement and Genetics Centers
2	National Historic Landmark Buildings
2	National Volcanic Monuments
2	Smokejumper Bases
1	Forest Products Laboratory
1	Institute of Pacific Islands Forestry
1	International Institute of Tropical Forestry
1	National Tallgrass Prairie
1	State and Private Forestry Area
1	Washington (National) Office

Other Units That May or May Not Have Separate Offices

409	Wildernesses
141	National Wild, Scenic, and Recreation Rivers
55	Experimental Forests, Ranges, and Study Areas
55	Purchase Units
29	Other Areas (Fire Depots, etc.)
21	National Game Refuges and Preserves
20	National Recreation Areas
7	Nurseries and Seed Orchards
6	Land Utilization Projects
5	National Scenic Areas
3	National Monuments (plus manage one for the National Park Service and manage another with the BLM, state, and tribes)
1	National Historic Area
1	National Scenic-Research Area
1	Primitive Area

REORGANIZATION ATTEMPTS IN THE PAST: THE EXECUTIVE BRANCH

Gifford Pinchot's successful effort to take over the administration of the forest reserves from the USDI General Land Office culminated on February 1, 1905. Jerry O'Callaghan noted that the Forest Service, with its huge land base, has always been at the center of government reorganization efforts in the natural resources arena: "The anomaly of having the Forest Service with its 187 [193] million acres of federal lands in Agriculture, while Interior contains the Bureau of Land Management with 340 million acres, the National Park Service with 61 million acres, and the Fish and Wildlife Service with 96 million acres, frequently catches the attention of public administrators, management analysts, political scientists, and others called upon to study federal organizational terrain."

Theodore Roosevelt Administration

The first significant federal reorganization effort began in the Theodore Roosevelt administration with the Keep Commission of 1905–1909. On June 3, 1905, President Theodore Roosevelt appointed the "committee on department methods" to investigate the business methods and procedures of the federal government and to suggest improvements. The commission consisted of Charles H. Keep, Assistant Secretary of the Treasury, who was the chair, plus Gifford Pinchot and four other members. Politics being what they were, no funding was provided for the commission, although that allowed the members to have complete freedom in their investigations. The commission made many recommendations, most of which were embraced and implemented by Teddy Roosevelt's administration.

For the first time, thanks to the Keep Commission, reorganization came from the executive branch of government, rather than from Congress. This set the pattern for reorganization and reinvention efforts in the future. Fortunately, Pinchot's presence on the committee kept the Forest Service out of the reorganization spotlight. In fact, for years to follow, the Forest Service became widely acknowledged as the most progressive and innovative of the federal agencies.

Since that time, about every decade and/or presidential administration, there has been an attempt to reorganize the Forest Service, take away the national forests, combine the agency with the Department of the Interior, or make a new department. Some administrations have come very close to moving the Forest Service or the national forests to a different or new agency. Also, there have been a few attempts by the Forest Service to take on the responsibility of managing the lands of other agencies.

William Howard Taft Administration

President W. H. Taft, Teddy Roosevelt's handpicked successor, went against his predecessor in wanting to transfer the national forests from the Department of

Agriculture. In 1911, only six years after the transfer of the national forests to the USDA, there was an attempt to transfer the management of the national forests back to Interior. The unsuccessful effort, led by Interior Secretary Walter Fisher during the Taft administration, failed.

Woodrow Wilson Administration

In the 1910s, before the creation of the USDI National Park Service, in 1916, the Forest Service proposed to take over management of the national parks from the U.S. Army. One rationale was that the national parks were adjacent to national forests, with only a line on a paper map separating them, and that the FS had many national monuments and park-like lands already within national forest boundaries. Congress was not convinced. Bills were introduced in the 64th, 65th, and 66th Congresses (1916–1920) to transfer the national forests to Interior, but they failed to pass.

Near the end of the Wilson administration, a voluntary organization known as the "national budget committee of New York" proposed a reorganization plan for the federal government. The plan, reported in 1920, which gained widespread attention, suggested the establishment of a department of public works (after getting rid of the Department of the Interior). This new department would have all the functions of Interior, with the addition of the Forest Service, the Bureau of Public Roads, and several water development programs located in the War Department. The plan was not implemented.

Warren Harding Administration

The first strong executive branch effort to return the national forests to Interior came in 1921 when Secretary of the Interior Albert B. Fall proposed to transfer the national forests in Alaska. There were several attempts in Congress to make these proposed changes into law. Support for having the national forests stay at Agriculture—and thus opposition to any transfers—was requested in a December 1921 editorial in the Society of American Foresters, *Journal of Forestry*:

> There is every reason against, and none in favor of, the various bills now before Congress proposing to transfer the National Forests to the Interior Department. Two of these bills [S. 2382 and S. 2203]—the Cummins and the New bills—affect only the National Forests of Alaska. A third bill [S.2740], introduced by Senator King of Utah, proposes to transfer all the National Forests to that Department. The friends of forestry must be up and doing [fighting against these bills] lest quiescence should be mistaken for assent or lest public apathy be taken advantage of by interests unfriendly to conservation.
>
> It is possible that attempts will be made to ally public apprehension as to the real motives of these measure by representing them as a step in the reorganization of the government departments…. but there will be no patience with amateur or devious tampering. Forestry is one of the great branches of agriculture, as was properly and, let us hope, finally recognized in 1905, when the National Forests were transferred from the Interior Department, on its own confession of inability to handle them, to

the Department of Agriculture. To transfer them back again now would be not reorganization, but folly.

The *Washington Post* thought that the Forest Service was a good example of why reorganization was needed, pointing out that the agency was inefficient and did not cooperate with the Department of the Interior. However, the western livestock industry preferred the status quo over any untested new agency. At the national level, President Warren G. Harding was distracted greatly by the Teapot Dome scandal, as a result of which Interior Secretary Fall was convicted of accepting bribes. Just before Harding's untimely death, in 1923, he came to support the Forest Service:

There was also a plan conceived by the Brookings Institution in 1923 that looked at governmental reorganization. The Brookings report, much like the national budget plan three years previous, proposed a new department of public works and public domain, including the Forest Service and the Bureau of Public Roads.

Herbert Hoover Administration

In December 1932, near the end of the Herbert Hoover administration, there was a fleeting effort to reorganize all the resource agencies under one head. This proposal was for the Department of Agriculture to create a new division of land utilization, including the Forest Service, the General Land Office, the Bureau of Biological Survey, the Bureau of Chemistry and Soils, and other programs. The U.S. Army Corps of Engineers would have been moved to the Department of the Interior. After an ill-fated attempt to transfer the remaining public domain to the states was widely rejected, and after his failed reelection bid, President Hoover issued an executive order on December 9, 1932, to transfer the General Land Office to the Department of Agriculture. This attempt to reorganize federal lands management was disapproved January 19, 1933, by House Resolution 350. Pressing national problems resulting from the Great Depression ended any formal attempt by Hoover's lame-duck administration.

There were several congressional attempts to merge the Forest Service with the Department of the Interior in the mid-1930s. A proposal, in 1936, by a Senate committee (known as the Byrd Committee) presented a government reorganization plan. This new plan would have moved the General Land Office and the Geological Survey to the same department; grazing on public lands and in national forests would have been managed by the same agency; and the Oregon & California (O&C) railroad grant lands and national monuments within national forests would have been transferred to the Forest Service. This last was in response to the 1933 transfer of the national monuments managed by the Forest Service and War Department to Interior.

Franklin D. Roosevelt Administration

The Franklin D. Roosevelt (FDR) administration made a serious attempt to transfer the Forest Service into the Department of the Interior. The fight was led by Interior Secretary Harold S. Ickes and Agriculture Secretary Henry Wallace. An Executive Reorganization Order was promulgated in June 1933, which changed the name of the USDI National Park Service to the Office of National Parks, Buildings, and Reservations. The order also gave the Park Service administration of all the national monuments (16 of which were under Forest Service management), military parks, historic sites, and a number of cemeteries. Congress changed the name back to the National Park Service the following year.

In 1934, the Natural Resources Board, chaired by Secretary Ickes, recommended that new national park units be established from national forest land. By late 1934, Wallace, who would later be vice president under FDR, changed his mind and became an opponent of any Forest Service transfer.

At the same time, the Forest Service counterproposed that the new USDI Grazing Service (established in 1934) be taken into the agency. This proposal caused great concern at Interior, since control of grazing meant control over the vast public domain lands in the West (which in 1946 became the core land area of the new Bureau of Land Management). This grazing land proposal was not enacted, but it did create a very heated interdepartmental battle. Two years later, there was a proposal floated by the Forest Service that once again recommended that the agency take over administration of all public domain grazing lands managed by the BLM. The report was published as *The Western Range* as Senate Document 199, 74th Congress, 2nd Session (1936). Noting much happened in regard to action by the administration.

The President's Committee on Administrative Management (the Brownlow Committee) recommended, in 1937, that the Department of the Interior be renamed the Department of Conservation, without specifying what agencies would be in the department. The Forest Service, as well as ex-Chief Pinchot, bitterly opposed a move to include the Forest Service in a new department. Pinchot, in a speech to the annual meeting of the Agricultural History Society that was held at his home at Washington, D.C., noted his concern over the impending transfer that was recommended in the Brownlow Report:

> Many of its recommendations are excellent but certainly not the one which suggests that responsibility for forestry on private lands should remain in the Department of Agriculture, while responsibility for forestry on public lands should be transferred to the Department of the Interior, renamed the Department of Conservation. That would split the Government work relating to forestry in two.... It would tend to create in effect two Departments of Agriculture and two Departments of Conservation, which is ridiculous.

The agency officials would take a less strident, activist view for the next 30 years regarding Forest Service reorganization by the executive branch. However, many behind-the-scenes efforts were engaged in pushing such an effort and even encouraged each new proposal.

There was also a controversy, growing in late 1936 and early 1937, about, once again, the disposition and management of the O&C lands (O&C) and Coos Bay Wagon Road Grant Lands, in western Oregon. More than 2 million acres were under protective management by the General Land Office, and another million or so acres were within the boundaries of the national forests. Secretary Ickes and others proposed that the Interior Department manage the O&C lands for forestry purposes under the premise of sustained yield management. The congressional battles were intense, with the Forest Service opposing the change, as the historian Elmo Richardson pointed out:

> In the last days of the session, the Public Lands Committee sent the bill to the Senate floor by a unanimous vote and it passed…. The president signed it on August 28, 1937…. Ickes chortled: "This law gives us the power to set up a forestry division in Interior." Soon afterward, he instructed his department aides to plan such an agency as the center for ultimate assumption of all federal forestry jurisdictions. The jurisdictional debate involved in the creation of a new administration [the O&C Administration] for the O&C lands was no mere background matter. Ickes found in the legislation a striking means of demonstrating the sincerity of his proposal to reorganize Interior as a Department of Conservation in substance, if not in name.

By 1937–38, ex-Chief Pinchot joined the transfer battle and became very active in defeating the proposed transfer of the Forest Service to the Department of the Interior. Roosevelt disciplined the Forest Service for the lack of cooperation in the reorganization attempt. After the death of Chief Silcox, in 1939, Earle Clapp was selected to replace him. Yet, Clapp was never given the rank of chief, only "acting chief," because of his strident opposition to the reorganization, which earned him the displeasure of President Roosevelt. Forest Service leaders made a major effort to sidetrack or crush the impending transfer, almost defying Roosevelt—not a wise move. Ickes, on the other hand, was encouraged by the president.

Chief Earle Clapp noted that, in late 1939 and early 1940, the president had a draft executive order on his desk, prepared by the Bureau of the Budget, which included a provision to transfer the Forest Service to the Interior Department. After an unsuccessful attempt to keep the draft secret, it was leaked to Congress, where it met unexpected, forceful opposition. "The opposition became so overwhelming," Clapp reported, "that the President finally decided to eliminate the Forest Service transfer provision from the transfer Order." Apparently, the transfer order remained on FDR's desk waiting for a signature, but it was never signed.

Other portions of The Reorganization Act of 1939 that affected the USDA and USDI did get the president's signature: Reorganization Order #2 (May 9, 1940) removed the Bureau of Fisheries from the Department of Commerce and the Bureau of Biological Survey from USDA. Reorganization Order #3 (May 9, 1940) consolidated the two agencies in Order #2 into what became the new USDI Fish and Wildlife Service. Order #4 (April 11, 1940) transferred the USDA Soil Conservation Service programs on USDI lands to the Department of the Interior. By late 1940, energy was waning for a Forest Service transfer as the threat of impending war in Europe overcame any further reorganization efforts for the next decade.

Harry Truman Administration

President Truman launched another government reorganization effort in the late 1940s and early 1950s. In 1947, Congress established the Commission on

Organization of the Executive Branch of Government (PL 162 approved July 7, 1947), which was chaired by ex-President Hoover and was thus referred to as the "Hoover Commission." The 12-member commission created several committees to study the federal government functions. The Concluding Report was printed two years later. One of these committees—the Task Force on Natural Resources (Appendix L in the report)—recommended that the Department of the Interior be renamed the Department of Natural Resources and that the functions and operations of the various natural resource management agencies be transferred into either a Water Development Service or a consolidated Forest and Range Service (which would include the Forest Service and the BLM). Another of the task groups, this one called the Task Force on Agriculture (Appendix M of the report), recommended that the Department of Agriculture house the Forest Service, the Fish and Wildlife Service, O & C lands in western Oregon, and the grazing lands of the General Land Office.

The Commission itself could not come to agreement on a path to take regarding the Forest Service and the other land management agencies. In the end, the Hoover Commission simply renewed the ideas of the Hoover presidency—Corps of Engineers to Interior; the timber lands in western Oregon (referred to as the O&C railroad grant lands), as well as all grazing lands, to Agriculture; with the Forest Service and the Soil Conservation Service to remain at Agriculture. The new USDA agency would be called the Agricultural Resources Conservation Service. There were several minor proposals in 1951 and 1952 to transfer the BLM's O&C lands to the Forest Service (the Senator Harry Cain bill) and another by Interior Secretary Oscar Chapman to have the Forest Service placed in Interior, making a new "Public Lands Administration," by presidential order. Senate hearings on Senate Bill 1149 were held in 1952, but no changes were approved by Congress.

Dwight D. Eisenhower Administration

Early in the Eisenhower administration, the new Secretary of the Interior, Douglas McKay (a former governor of Oregon) was said to have been favorable to having the Forest Service and the BLM placed in a new Department of Natural Resources. The transfer was killed in 1954, because the western senators opposed the new department.

At the same time, a new study of the federal government was undertaken. The committee was titled the Advisory Committee on Government Organization. Called the second Hoover Commission because it was led by the former president, it met from 1953 to 1955. Unlike those of earlier efforts, the Commission's recommendations were quite simple. Recommendations included that the president, without separate legislation, combine forest and range management in the Department of Agriculture; that he appoint a committee to study the laws and federal departments that manage the land; that the natural resources agencies simply coordinate efforts rather than reorganize; and that there be a uniform policy for all agencies involved in the management of the rural lands. Congressional hearings were held in November 1955 and February 1956. One outcome was a report recommending consolidation of all federal forestry management into the Forest Service.

During 1958, the Department of the Interior and the Bureau of the Budget (now the Office of Management and Budget) opposed the consolidations. However, President Eisenhower proposed Reorganization Plan No. 1 of 1959 to transfer certain agency functions from the Department of the Interior to the Secretary of Agriculture. Upon further consideration, the president decided not to transmit the reorganization plan to Congress.

John F. Kennedy Administration

There were no reorganization plans put forward by either the president or Congress during the Kennedy administration. Yet there was still the lingering feeling among the agencies, especially the Forest Service, that Interior was ready and willing to grab more national forest land for national parks. To calm the simmering animosity, the Secretaries of Agriculture and Interior sent a letter to the president that outlined a "Treaty of the Potomac." The treaty proposed greater cooperation and an end to proposals to transfer lands and their management.

Lyndon B. Johnson Administration

Lyndon B. Johnson's administration looked at ways to improve management of the federal government. An Organizational Review Committee was organized under the leadership of Edwin Deckard, from the Bureau of the Budget, in the spring of 1964, to review the management and policies of the Forest Service. The team was composed of the Secretary of Agriculture, the director of the Bureau of the Budget, and the chairman of the Civil Service Commission. Ed Schultz was the representative to the committee from the Forest Service. The team spent five and a half weeks in the field visiting all the regional offices except Region 10, in Alaska. The Deckard team also looked into the appropriate size of ranger districts, national forests, and regional offices and recommended that these be standardized throughout the national forest system.

The Deckard report approved the basic principles of Forest Service management and even recommended strengthening the line and staff authority at all levels in the agency. The report noted a disparity in the number of ranger districts per forest, which range from 3 to 13, and in the size of the districts, from 211,200 to 3,118,900 acres. It recommended that an optimum ranger district have between 10 and 90 employees, manage 300,000–600,000 acres, and operate on a budget of $150,000–400,000 per year.

The Deckard report also looked into the regional office structure and asked whether the "historic Regional structure is valid at the present time in view of advances made through the years in transportation, communication, managerial methods, and administrative procedures." The report found that the Forest Service regional offices varied considerably in size and number of employees. For example, employment in Region 7 was 1,421 employees, while Region 6 had 7,414 employees. The acreage administered ranged from 4,252,722 acres in Region 7 to 30,800,215 acres in Region 4. Region 7 stood out in the analysis as a target for reorganization or elimination. The chief and staff decided to split Region 7 between Regions 8 and 9, which took place in late 1965 and early 1966.

The report also proposed top-level changes for the agency, including establishment of an associate chief, a deputy chief for the national forest system, and directors for the northeastern and southeastern state and private forestry areas. These changes were made and still survive to this day.

Richard M. Nixon Administration

During the Nixon administration, the Public Land Law Review Commission (PLLRC), which was established in 1964 by Congress to study and recommend changes or additions to the nation's land laws, published its findings. The PLLRC report, "One Third of the Nation's Land: A Report to the President and to the Congress," printed in June 1970, made 137 recommendations. One of the major conclusions of the study was that many federal lands eligible for disposition, including national forests, national monuments, and all Bureau of Land Management lands that had not been congressionally set aside, be reviewed by Congress for eventual disposal. In addition, the Commission was critical of the Forest Service for spending too much time and money on administering natural resources on the national forests. The Commission, with a strong commodity bias, recommended that "dominant use" replace multiple use as the "highest and best use of particular areas." One of the recommendations was to transfer the Forest Service to the Department of the Interior, which would be renamed the Department of Natural Resources. There was no specific legislation proposed to accomplish the PLLRC goal.

The Nixon administration also tried to reorganize the executive branch through the president's advisory council on executive organization, led by Roy L. Ash. The Ash Council, as it became known, was established on April 5, 1969. The Council embraced several of the PLLRC recommendations, as well as others proposed by the Brownlow committee of 1937 and the first Hoover commission, of 1949. The new Council proposed several alternatives. On April 29, it recommended the establishment of a separate Environmental Protection Agency (EPA), which came into being on December 2, 1970. Another major recommendation was made on May 12, 1970, when it proposed the creation of a new Department of Environment and Natural Resources (DENR) or a Department of Natural Resources (DNR). The DENR proposal was to be more inclusive and would have joined 44 federal agencies responsible for land management. The president released the "fallback" DNR recommendation in March 1971. This DNR proposal would have included the Forest Service, the Department of the Interior, various programs of the Bureau of Indian Affairs, the Soil Conservation Service, parts of the Army Corps of Engineers, and related land and water programs from other agencies, but these would not perform monitoring, conduct energy research, or set environmental, and enforcement programs, many of which are today handled by the Environmental Protection Agency.

Several members of Congress introduced or supported the administration position, although it was well known that for every agency and program there was probably one or more groups opposed to the transfer. Senator Frank E. Moss (Utah) introduced a bill in the 90th Congress to rename the Interior Department the Department of Natural Resources and Environment. After much discussion and several congressional hearings, the DNR proposal was stopped by the 92nd Congress. Defeat of the DNR was described in the book *Striking a Balance: Environment and Natural Resources Policy in the Nixon-Ford Years,* by John C. Whitaker, one of Nixon's deputy assistants. He believed the DNR proposal was killed by the so-called iron triangle of special interest groups, some members of Congress, and middle-level bureaucrats from the departments involved.

An internal government plan was proposed during the Nixon administration that called for reorganizing all the federal agencies into one of 10 "standard" regions based on the standard military regions. This reorganization would have changed several of the existing nine Forest Service regions. As soon as the idea was announced, it was dead.

In Nixon's second term, which began in 1973, he announced another reorganization plan. This time, however, he envisioned working through the problems via executive orders. One proposal sent to Congress on June 29, 1973, called for the creation of a new Department of Energy and Natural Resources (DENR). This was essentially a renamed DNR proposal from two years before, but without the energy research and development components of the old plan. However, this one too died in Congress. In 1976, after several years of debate over clearcutting and forest management practices, Congress moved to keep the Forest Service and the BLM separate. Two different but overlapping laws for the agencies were signed into law: the National Forest Management Act (NFMA) for the Forest Service and the Federal Land Policy Management Act (FLPMA) for the BLM.

Jimmy Carter Administration

Another attempt at reorganization came during the Jimmy Carter administration in the late 1970s. Carter made governmentwide reorganization an important plank in his platform during the 1976 presidential campaign. The following year, his first year in office, Carter formed a President's Reorganization Project (PRP).

On December 19, 1977, the PRP made public a proposal to create a new Department of Natural Resources, much like the Nixon administration proposal, which would merge all the Department of the Interior agencies and the Forest Service into one massive land management department. The document, when it was released to the public, requested comments, and, by the middle of February 1978, almost 18,000 letters had been received. Bob Wolf, a former congressional staffer, noted that initially the new administration wanted to reorganize the government land management agencies into a Department of Natural Resources: "I went to a meeting over in the Capitol and this fellow [William Marsh, the President's lead on the reorganization effort] called to explain to Hill staff types [the new plan].... I was sitting next to Bailey [Guard, the principle Republican staff leader], and this fellow [Marsh] was explaining how the government was going to be reorganized. And he was going at it quite earnestly. And at one point for reasons I don't understand he said, 'I didn't come to town and take this job to fail.' Well, at that Bailey Guard whispered to me, 'but he's gonna.' And that's what happened."

The most difficult portion of the proposal was to transfer the U.S. Army Corps of Engineers to the new department. This aspect was later dropped. The Department of the Interior was to be the leader for management of public lands.

Then, on March 1, 1979, President Carter announced a another federal agency reorganization plan under the authority of the Reorganization Act of 1946. This proposal was to create a Department of Natural Resources from the Department of the Interior, along with the Forest Service and the Department of Commerce's National Oceanic and Atmospheric Administration. Within that larger new department, the Forest Service, BLM, and the conservation division from the USDI Geological Survey would be combined into a new agency called the National Forest and Land Administration.

After extensive lobbying by many parties, the Carter reorganization attempt failed, in May 1979, just as the idea was submitted to Congress and a few hearing were held. Personal communications with former Associate Chief Rex Resler and Chief Max Peterson revealed that officials at the secretarial level in the USDA and in high levels of the Forest Service were taking strong efforts to block the reorganization plan. The officials, who did not fully inform Chief John McGuire, did so because they wanted him to be able to truthfully answer "no" if asked by Congress about Forest Service lobbying efforts to defeat the plan. President Carter, in the aftermath of the defeat, did order more extensive cooperation and coordination between the Forest Service and the Bureau of Land Management.

Ronald Reagan Administration

In the early and mid-1980s, after a rising tide of outrage among western landowners over land "mismanagement" by the BLM and the Forest Service , the new Ronald Reagan administration proposed selling these lands to the highest bidder as a way to placate the "Sagebrush Rebellion." While this effort was much ballyhooed across the country, the massive sale of millions of acres of federal lands never materialized. Should this selloff have occurred, there would have been no need for either agency in the future.

There was, however, an administration proposal, on January 30, 1985, that proposed an exchange of around 35 million acres of land between the Forest Service (some 10 million acres to the BLM) and the Bureau of Land Management (some 15 million acres to the Forest Service). The exchange was aimed at increasing efficiency of management by reducing costs and overlapping functions.

Hearings were held in the summer of 1985, but there was little support for the idea. The interchange proposal resulted in a legislative EIS published in early 1986. The most dramatic exchange of lands would have moved the BLM's Oregon and California Railroad Grant Lands (O&C) lands in western Oregon to the Forest Service, as well as transferring all the national forests in the State of Nevada to the BLM. Despite two efforts to make the proposal more palatable to the public, the effort was dead on arrival. Strong congressional opposition to the interchange, as well as opposition by local communities, counties, and states, essentially scuttled the program. Especially strong opposition came from the Association of O&C Counties in western Oregon, which saw that any such proposal in Congress might give lawmakers the opportunity to rework the lucrative O&C revenue sharing formula. From their viewpoint, the affected counties could have lost many millions of dollars annually. As far as Congress was concerned, the issue was dead on arrival. However, a number of smaller interchanges of forest and grazing lands occurred between individual national forests and BLM districts.

Randal O'Toole, in a 1988 book entitled *Reforming the Forest Service,* came up with a different way to reform the agency. His approach was to change the way Congress has prescribed, over the past 80 years, the way the Forest Service does business. Essentially, O'Toole suggested that the real need for change comes from inappropriate laws that were made decades ago and the creative ways in which the agency has carried out the intent of the law through regulatory means. In this case, reform would come from Congress, not the administration.

George H. W. Bush Administration

There were no significant proposals by the George H. W. Bush administration to transfer federal lands into one agency or move the Forest Service to Interior.

William J. Clinton Administration

The Clinton administration, early in 1993, proposed another reorganization of the Forest Service. According to newspaper accounts, the agency would be split along branch lines; research would go to the new USDI National Biological Survey, international forestry to USAID, and state and private forestry to USDA-SCS, while the national forest system would be transferred to the Department of the Interior. Nothing was formally proposed before Congress, although the new National Biological Survey (now Service) was established in 1993 in an effort to combine all the research functions and programs within the USDI into one agency.

The internal Forest Service "reinvention effort" resulted in a December 6, 1994, report, "Reinvention of the Forest Service: The Changes Begin," which outlined how the agency would accomplish its goals. The most controversial portion dealt with the elimination of several of the Forest Service regional offices by combining services in other locations. Region 10 (Alaska) and Region 1 (Northern) would be eliminated. Alaska NFs would go to the western portions of Washington and

Oregon, while the eastern parts of the two states would be combined with Region 4 (Intermountain). The Montana and North Dakota NFs would be transferred to Region 2 (Rocky Mountain, to be renamed as the Northern Plains). Other adjustments to the regional boundaries were proposed, based roughly on national, large ecosystems. In Congress and the various states, the proposal fell on deaf ears and was declared dead on arrival.

In the middle of 1996, the Senate Governmental Affairs Committee called for hearings to focus on combining the federal land management agencies into one agency. There was, apparently, a proposal to create a new "Hoover Commission" to study the workings of the federal government.

George W. Bush Administration

There is an active proposal in the George W. Bush administration to study the possibility of combining the various regional offices because of the need for greater cost efficiency. In late 2001, the Office of Management and Budget (OMB) requested that the Forest Service study proposals to reduce the number of regional offices around the country. Two scenarios were presented—the BLM regional office design or the Defense Department model. There were also efforts in FY 2002 and beyond to "outsource" many of the federal government jobs and work to the private sector, according to OMB's Circular A-76 rules. Discussion about which federal jobs are necessary led to a number of internal/external studies, and, in some cases, work formerly done by Forest Service employees went to private contractors (especially mechanical and maintenance work on fleet vehicles). In another major internal reorganization, functions relating to business operations, procurement, and information technology at all levels of the agency were consolidated in Albuquerque, New Mexico, in FY2005. Other major functions, such as human resources, are being evaluated for reorganization. These internal efforts, as well as outsourcing, are aimed at saving substantial dollars for the agency and the federal government, although the estimates of total dollars saved from personnel reductions seem far-fetched at best.

Future Administrations

As mentioned earlier, among the most popular proposals has been the recombining of the USDA Forest Service and the Department of the Interior or their merging into a new Department of Natural Resources. However, Marion Clawson put the agency reorganization question in the following light: "Does administrative reorganization of the federal resource agencies, if it could be accomplished, offer major possibilities for better public land and other resource management? Or is this a mirage, likely to divert and delude the unwary traveler? The present pattern of federal resource responsibility is a hodge-podge, explainable only by its history."

On the surface, merger of the USDA Forest Service with the other land management agencies in the Department of the Interior makes logical sense and would create administrative tidiness out of the administrative situation the land management agencies now face. Managing the federal lands under one set of rules and regulations, with one top administrator and one set of managers, is also logical and probably cost-effective. Such an overall federal land management agency would eliminate the overlap of top officials, research staffs, and experts, as well as duplication in what the people on the ground do, with fewer offices and lower administrative costs. However, there are also drawbacks, such as deciding which agency or agencies would take the lead, which rules would continue or be dropped, and which administrators would stay or go. Managers and staffs would have higher workloads with fewer personnel; consolidation would take time and money; special interest groups would likely oppose any change of agencies; local communities would feel that their interests in federal land management would not be taken into account in decisions; congressional support might be lacking. In addition, placing very different programs into one department will not eliminate policy conflicts and may not result in better decisions.

Ross Gorte and Betsy Cody, in their 1995 Congressional Research Service report, note that there are four policy implications in any merger proposal affecting the Forest Service and the BLM, (these points also apply to combining the Forest Service with other land management agencies): (1) federal fiscal impacts—that is, potential cost savings; (2) institutional effects—morale and ways of operating; (3) legal and political considerations—laws and legal authorities/regulations; and (4) effect on service to the public—the impact of having one agency, with one administrator and one set of laws and regulations, as well as centrally located offices. The authors note:

> Reducing costs by eliminating duplicative personnel and offices is one of the primary benefits cited in most merger proposals. The Carter administration had estimated the benefits of its DNR proposal at $100 million annually, but did not provide details about how these savings would be achieved. In 1984, the General Accounting Office reported that 64 locations had both BLM and Forest Service offices, and estimated that combining these offices could save $33.5 annually....
>
> Another benefit commonly cited by proponents is the creation of a more efficient and effective structure for managing the federal lands and resources, by merging duplicative efforts. The two agencies have nearly identical missions.... In areas with intermingled, adjoining, or neighboring lands, these functions arguably could be more effectively conducted by a larger single entity than by separate agencies.
>
> A merger could lead to some higher costs, as well, at least in the short-term. There would be implementation costs, associated with changing signs, logos, letterhead, etc. (Creating a new agency would have greater short-term implementation costs than moving one agency into the other.) There may be some personnel and planning costs from eliminating redundant positions and from transfers necessary to have the right people in the right locations. Buildings and other facilities and equipment might be redundant, and need to be sold (which would generate revenues, but might require expenditures to be prepared for sale.)

There are, of course, other considerations that are less tangible and much more difficult to measure, much less place a dollar amount on. Difficult decisions would have to be made, morale might suffer, many long-term employees would have to be moved or forced into retirement, agreements, leases, and contracts would be changed, and programs might be disrupted. In addition, the laws, regulations, structure, procedures, traditions, and history of each agency could make any new or combined agency difficult to create and administer, as illustrated by a Forest Service and BLM combination in which the Forest Service would dominate, since it has about three times as many employees as the BLM, as well as a strong re-search branch, state and private operations, and an active international program. However, any reorganization, especially if these functions were moved to different agencies, could fundamentally change the Forest Service in a negative way.

Any merger or consolidation of the Forest Service with the BLM, the National Park Service, the Fish and Wildlife Service, or the Natural Resources and Conservation Service, as well as a host of related agencies or functions, assumes that in the end the public will be better served by one agency rather than many. It is a simple and intuitive proposition, although such mergers could easily create a giant department that would be less responsive to the public and interest groups, as well as increase federal bureaucracy. It is also unclear that the public will be bet-ter served, money saved, or the number of laws and regulations reduced. To make such a megamerger happen, opposition from institutions, Congress, special interest groups, states, communities, and the general public would have to be overcome. Marion Clawson, more than 40 years ago, noted that: "Whatever one may think about the desirability of major reorganization of federal land management agen-cies, my judgment is that such reorganization *is highly unlikely*. There are simply too powerful forces against it, with no corresponding pressures for it. The federal land agencies concerned oppose major reorganization…. It is not only the agencies that are moved which resist change; those who might gain additional responsibility are cool, at least, and sometimes more than cool."

REORGANIZATION ATTEMPTS IN THE PAST: THE LEGISLATIVE BRANCH

Many proposals have been made regarding the possible reorganization in the Forest Service. In any of these attempts, Congress has been and will be a major player. Congress can change the agency by: (1) changing the laws under which the Forest Service operates, (2) approving a restructuring submitted by the executive branch, including approval of political appointees to leadership positions, and (3) writing legislation to accomplish a reorganization. Most often, Congress has been given the responsibility to review and change administration proposals for reor-ganization by establishing committees, holding hearings, writing bills, and voting on the results (as noted in the previous section). But the most influential method has been by passing legislation that has given new mandates to federal agencies, including the Forest Service.

Congress has passed several very important laws that changed the management of the national forest system. The Organic Act of 1897, the Multiple-Use Act of 1960, the Wilderness Act of 1964, and the National Forest Management Act of 1976 (see Appendix 6) are all examples. Over the years, literally hundreds of bills have been introduced in Congress to change the way the Forest Service and the other federal land management agencies operate. The Forest Service has been active for more than 100 years in providing testimony from top officials and providing background reports and analyses for committee hearings and members of Congress. Congressional committees and subcommittees often call for testimony from agency officials and concerned citizens. Many bills have been introduced to Congress for consideration. A few get out of subcommittee and reach the full committee for consideration. Fewer still reach the House or Senate floor for discussion and voting. The concerns of members of Congress should not be taken lightly. Inevitably, it is easier to do nothing than to uproot the agency, embroil the interested public, and impact local communities.

Marion Clawson noted that special interest groups are powerful influencers or catalysts in the congressional arena, especially if the group believes that any legislation will cause harm or be implemented at undue cost: "At the best, it is probably impossible to conceive of any federal agency reorganization which will have unanimous and enthusiastic support from the various groups interested in use of the federal lands…. In a word, the present rules of the game are known … and all prefer the known problems to the unknown ones."

There will certainly be further efforts in Congress and the executive branch to attempt a merger or consolidation of the major land management agencies. Past efforts have shown that such efforts usually fail, but perhaps a radically new perspective will change the nature of the debate that has been affecting the federal land management agencies for more than 100 years. Yet bills continue to be written and discussed in Congress that have had and will continue have important management implications for all federal agencies.

SEVERAL OPTIONS FOR INTERNAL REORGANIZATION

This section discusses several ways in which the four levels within the Forest Service could be changed without congress or presidential approval. I do not include research, state and private forestry, or international forestry in this analysis, partly because the lack of comprehensive knowledge and workload of these branches of the Forest Service. One option discussed is a proposal to form a national service center to provide information and assistance to Forest Service units around the country.

Often overlooked is the idea of changing the so-called deadwood in the highest levels of the agency. Long-term, highly experienced employees (often in regional offices and in Washington) are removed from their positions through forced retirements, generous retirement buyouts, or directed reassignments. In addition, the agency itself can change, and has changed, the way the organization operates thorough the implementation regulations (e.g., the National Forest Management Act, which implemented the regulations of 1979), law enforcement initiatives, civil rights procedures, ecosystem management, collaborative stewardship, and many other less obvious ways.

Ranger Districts

"Lumping" could and probably should be applied to the ranger district level, with perhaps two or three districts per national forest, rather than the usual four or more. As workloads under ecosystem management change (fewer timber and road projects, requiring fewer foresters and engineers), these specialists could be moved to the SOs. This would avoid duplication of specialists and would have the potential to greatly reduce some costs for the RDs. On the other hand, ecosystem management may require new specialists to implement ecosystem management at the RD level. Whether every RD will need a full complement of ecologists, biologists, soil scientists, watershed specialists, fire and fuels specialists, wildlife specialists, range conservationists, and so on remains to be seen.

One problem with lumping ranger districts (or having them operate out of the SOs, much like the BLM resource areas) is that this could limit contact with local communities or practically eliminate it. From the earliest days of the Forest Service, this person-to-person contact between at least the district ranger and local people has been much desired and very useful. Any loss of direct contact with community partners and leaders could easily reinforce the notion that big government really doesn't care about small towns. (Much of the loss of widespread support for the timber, grazing, and mining industries in the West came in the aftermath of decades of reorganizing by combining, centralizing, reducing costs, or eliminating the presence of the companies in the name of efficiency and cost reduction.)

Supervisor's Offices

T. S. Woolsey, as early as 1916, suggested that larger national forest units be established by combining smaller units so that an average forest would be around 3 million acres instead of as small as 1 million acres. An option might be for two or more supervisors' offices, especially those in the same state, to be combined, reducing costly overhead expenses. The lumping of SOs has happened many times in the past (e.g., Mt. Baker-Snoqualmie NF or the Grand Mesa, Uncompahgre, and Gunnison NFs) with good success.

However, there are still efforts to split some national forests, especially those that lie in different states (e.g., Wayne NF and Hoosier NF split in 1993). There are other opportunities to cooperate or even comanage adjacent units of different agencies (e.g., the forest supervisor of the Fremont NF, in Oregon, was for several years also district manager of the BLM Lakeview District).

Regional Offices

Internally, one of the most popular reorganization notions is to eliminate the field offices. Since the regional (RO) level is situated between the supervisor's office (SO) and the Washington office (WO), it seems like a good idea to reduce the size and complexity of the agency. As early as 1916, there were attempts to reorganize the new regional offices. T. S. Woolsey suggested that regional offices reduce their functions by either elevating some activities to the WO or lowering authority to the SOs.

Regional offices could be combined ("lumped") for greater efficiency. Fewer RO organizational subunits, with fewer deputy regional foresters and directors, would reduce overhead considerably. Each RO could streamline operations by reducing oversight of SOs and RDs, with the risk of long-range cost associated with an increased possibility of fiscal problems.

Washington, D.C., National Office

No one is seriously considering eliminating the national headquarters in Washington, D.C., although the number of people working there (or at any of the administrative units) and the function of the staff should be reviewed and evaluated. The most drastic reorganization would leave a skeleton organization at the WO level, probably only those staff that would be necessary to coordinate with the USDA, Congress, and other agencies in Washington.

Since many of the WO staff units exist to coordinate field-level activities within a national framework, transferring staff from the national headquarters could complicate coordination efforts, fragment efforts to speak with "one voice," and duplicate services (at the RO level). There would be a reduction of total costs and personnel at the WO level, but an increase at the RO or service-center level.

Service Centers

Over the past three decades, with the advent of forest-level NFMA planning, the agency hired a great number of natural resource ecologists, social science specialists, and experts at all levels of the agency. However, many of these specialists are now gone because the forest plans have been completed, the timber harvest reduced, the number of operating dollars and full-time positions cut, as well as because of changing national priorities. Today, the Forest Service is an agency that is returning to its roots of forestry, recreation, and wildlife management, while being gutted of many of the newer specialists and experts in many ecological and social-science fields. With relatively few highly talented specialists at the RO and WO levels to cover all aspects of forest management, there is the option of moving these remaining specialists and placing them at a "service center" organization. A model for this is the Department of the Interior's Denver service center, where experts can be called from any USDI unit to help with a problem.

Late in 2005, the Forest Service moved almost all oversight and management functions concerning business operations—including acquisition management, civil rights, competitive sourcing, and human resources management—to a new office in Albuquerque, New Mexico. In part this move was based on the assumption that one way to reduce costs was to consolidate operations formerly scattered across the country. In the past 100 years, the strength of the agency has always been in having operations removed from direct central authority with each region and station having a full complement of staff. This setup was based on the unproven assumption that better management could be provided at the regional and national forest levels rather at the remote national office in Washington, D.C. Today, the Forest Service is attempting to reduce staff and decrease costs, while increasing national oversight. The move has not been well liked by many employees, and the expected cost savings to the agency have yet to be realized.

Should a national service center be developed, a number of technical staff could be moved from the WO and various ROs to the service center to greatly enhance the expertise and capability of the staff. Such service center experts, for example, would include most if not all personnel attached to archaeology, history, social science, environmental education, cooperative forestry, engineering, pest management, land and minerals, the legal department, planning, and law enforcement. Aviation and fire management could be combined with interagency units in central locations, such as Boise or Missoula. However, at least one representative of these specialists would need to remain to coordinate with the service center and the SOs. Remaining at the ROs would be administrative services (much reduced), ecology, range, and watershed (increased), management systems, the inspector general, public affairs, recreation and wilderness, and timber management.

One problem with a service center organization is that travel costs, as well as relocation costs, would be considerable. Another problem is how this service center would fit into the existing Forest Service—would it have true line authority or just expert judgment? If it would have decision-making authority, then a fifth level of organization will be created. If just expert opinions were being given, then why would RO, SO, or RDs pay any attention to recommendations? Another related problem would be the question of who pays the salary and travel of the service center staff. Would it be like the Ft. Collins computer and ecosystem management groups, which are currently "detached" WO employees, or paid for using a different funding mechanism?

The upside would be that similar specialists would be centrally located, allowing for a synergy of ideas, sharing of solutions, and cooperation to do a better job. A downside might be the departure of a large number of people from the organization—those unwilling to move as well as those who felt that "this isn't the same Forest Service I came to work for." Much like the 1908 move to new district offices, this change could invigorate the agency, but at a potential great cost, since many employees would not want to move or would feel threatened by the radical change in organization and function of the Forest Service.

SEVERAL OPTIONS FOR REORGANIZATION OR ELIMINATION

With the dawning of twenty-first century, arguments have again surfaced about the role and importance of the national forests and the Forest Service as the managing agency. There are at least nine different proposals on the table to "solve" the current problems. The first is simply to keep everything as it is; the second is to do no active management, especially of timber harvesting and road building, to the national forests; the third is to change the laws and regulations that hamper good management of the national forests; the fourth is to transfer management of the national forests to another federal agency; the fifth, is to transfer the best lands to the National Park Service or private industry; the sixth is to set up long-term leases of public land; the seventh is establish land trusts; the eighth is to transfer the federal lands to the various states where the lands are located; and the ninth is to sell the public lands. Several of these options have subproposals worth considering. Each of the options is discussed in this section in varying degrees of detail.

Option 1: Keep Everything the Same

This option continues current management of the national forest system; it is what some might call the "no-change alternative." Here everything remains the same—the national forests remain in federal ownership, and the USDA Forest Service continues to manage the 192 million acres. There are incremental changes in the form of management priorities set by the chief, the president, the Secretary of Agriculture, and Congress. New terms are invented (such as ecosystem management) to describe the new priorities of the agency to both the employees and the public. John Fedkiw calls this notion the "pathway hypothesis," in which new knowledge is impressed on the national forests to make the forest management better. This involves a gradual shifting of management over time, taking into account new laws, changing emphasis by top agency leaders, and new scientific information. This is exactly what has happened to the agency over the past 100 years—incremental shifting of management because of new laws and changing society wants and needs.

Currently, after a century of relying heavily on the scientific model, the Forest Service seems to be gradually moving into the realm of collaboration with the public on management of the national forests and grasslands. Public relations and public involvement, both forms of collaboration, require better and additional efforts to work with the public to come to a common understanding of issues and concerns and to arrive at new ways for managing the federal forestlands. In the future, the Forest Service will need fewer specialists and more generalists.

Overall efficiency, in terms of economics (dollar return to the U.S. Treasury), remains low. The number of employees will probably be reduced over the years, but the workload will remain high. Profit to be derived from the lands remains a low priority. Public benefits, especially the need to meet increasing demands for recreational facilities, rules management.

Option 2: Return the Forests to No Management

As opposed to the no-change option, this could be called the "no-action alternative." In this scenario, active management means no management, as in the late 1880s. Letting natural processes evolve would be the major priority.

The national forests would become essentially national parks. The Forest Service would be done away with. Only fires that threaten lives or private property would be fought. Since there would be no priority for management other than wilderness, most multiple-use management would be forbidden. This option would be even more restrictive than national park status.

Centuries-old fire-dependent ecosystems would change, because of more deadly, catastrophic fires. Some animal and plant species would thrive, while others would have to adapt to the changing conditions or perish. Economic efficiency would be low, but expenditures for management would be very small. Profit would not be important, while some public benefits would be substantial. This option is strongly supported by a number of environmental organizations through "zero-cut" proposals.

Option 3: Change the Laws and Regulations That Affect Forest Service Management

Currently, the Forest Service is trying to get the agency back to operating, as it once did by identifying laws and regulations that impose unnecessary and burden-some rules on local decision makers. Recently, Jack Ward Thomas, former Chief of the Forest Service, noted the problems in the many laws that govern land management activities:

> consider that the various laws are applied by an array of departments and agencies … each with their own cadre of skilled and accomplished bureaucrats dedicated to the achievement of their mission…. If that were not bad enough, the situation is further exacerbated by the structure of committees and sub-committees in the Senate and House. The departments and agencies get their budgets through different committees who, likewise, fiercely guard "their" agencies and programs—for therein lies maximization of their individual and collective power…. This all adds up for a disaster waiting for a time and place to happen … significant land management actions on the federal estate are grinding to a halt. Some consider that outcome desirable and some object vehemently…. It seems likely that if the process [set into law, agency regulations, procedural guides, and differing interpretations of what is required] is everything and the outcome of little consequence you get "analysis paralysis" wherein there is furious and ongoing activity that leads to little or no management action. Again, some consider that outcome desirable and others object vehemently.

Randal O'Toole, in a 1988 book entitled *Reforming the Forest Service,* came up with a similar way to reform the agency. His approach was to change the way Congress has prescribed, over the past 80 years, the way the Forest Service does business. Essentially, O'Toole suggested that the real need for change comes from inappropriate laws that were made decades ago and the creative ways in which the agency has carried out the intent of the law through regulatory means. Reform would come from Congress, not the administration, but the process could be helped by an analysis of what really needs changing and why.

Congress has passed several very important laws that have changed the management of the national forest system, for example, the Organic Act of 1897, the Multiple-Use Sustained-Yield Act of 1960, the Wilderness Act of 1964, and the

National Forest Management Act of 1976. Congress has been actively involved with the agency through politically appointed chiefs (especially Jack Ward Thomas and Mike Dombeck, although every chief has been appointed or approved by the president, with the exception of Earle Clapp, who was only acting chief from 1939 through 1943), testimony from top officials, hearings on the many bills introduced in Congress each session, and reports and analyses.

As in every past effort, Congress is a very important player in any attempt at reconfiguring the laws under which the agencies manage the federal land, and the concerns of members of Congress should not be taken lightly. Congressional committees and subcommittees often call for testimony from agency officials, interest groups, and concerned citizens. Inevitably, it is easier to do nothing than to uproot the agency, embroil the interested public, and impact local communities. There are three important ways that Congress can change the agency: (1) it can change the laws under which the Forest Service operates; (2) it can approve a restructuring submitted by the executive branch, including approval of politically appointees to leadership; and (3) it can write legislation to accomplish a reorganization.

The Thoreau Institute, led by Randal O'Toole, drafted a bill in 1996 for consideration by Congress. There was little appetite in Congress for such an act. Jack Ward Thomas suggested several ways to achieve a reform of the laws:

> First, the idea of a Public Land Law Review Commission could be brought out and dusted off. The last effort, in 1969, was directed by a collection of big names that, basically, came up with nothing except that things were badly screwed up. And, that, I remind you, was before the onslaught of environmental legislation of the 1970s. But, now that things are even more seriously convoluted and dysfunctional, it may be time to try again. But, this time, the Commission should be composed of top level experienced natural resources professional and legal assistants with the mission of not "moaning and groaning" but of producing a legislative package to present to Congress.
>
> But, I don't think that Congress nor the Administration has the stomach for that. Why? I challenge you to examine the purpose of each of the laws in question. Who could disagree with the purpose of any one of the laws in question? I certainly can't. And, each of those laws has champions in the folks that know how to use those laws to achieve their objectives and in the Agencies that derive their powers and, even, reasons for their existence therefrom.
>
> However, the administration in power has the authority and ability to revise regulations. The administration could establish a "czar of regulations" related to public land management and task that person, and the heads of involved agencies, to simultaneously revise pertinent regulations with the aim of coordination, simplification, and efficiency. This could be ordered achieved within a time certain with only the czar would have authority to grant any extension of time lines.

There will certainly be further efforts by Congress and the executive branch to change the laws under which the major land management agencies operate. Past efforts have shown that such efforts are usually in vain, but perhaps a radically new perspective will change the nature of the debate that has been affecting the federal land management agencies for more than 100 years.

Option 4: Transfer Management to One Agency

Gifford Pinchot's successful effort to take over the administration of the forest reserves from the USDI General Land Office culminated on February 1, 1905. The Forest Service, with its huge land base, has always been near the center of government reorganization efforts in the natural resources arena. Almost every administration has at least put some thought and effort into putting the national forests into one large federal land management agency that includes the National Park Service, the Bureau of Land Management, the Fish and Wildlife Service, and the U.S. Army Corps of Engineers, along with programs of the Natural Resources Conservation Service. About once every decade or with each new presidential administration, there has been an attempt to reorganize the Forest Service, take away the national forests, combine the agency with the Department of the Interior, or make a new department. Some have come very close to moving the Forest Service or the national forests to a different or new agency. Also, there have been a few attempts by the Forest Service to take on the responsibility of managing the lands of other agencies.

However, there are also drawbacks. Any merger or consolidation of the Forest Service with the BLM, the National Park Service, the Fish and Wildlife Service, or the Natural Resources and Conservation Service, as well as related agencies or functions, assumes that in the end the public will be better served by one agency rather than many. It is a simple and intuitive proposition, although such a merger might create a larger, monolithic, more bureaucratic, and less responsive public agency. Some believe that such an all-powerful agency could stifle employee and management creativity and that public policy debates would become meaningless. It is also unclear that the public will be better served, money saved, or the number of laws and regulations reduced. To make such a merger happen, there are many barriers to be overcome.

Special interest groups are powerful influencers in the congressional arena, especially if the group believes that any legislation will cause harm or undue cost. These interest groups use the land and resources and are thus concerned about and opposed to any major changes to the management, especially by a new agency with new rules and new people in charge. It is probably impossible for all special interest or user groups to lend enthusiastic support for a new agency, as existing rules benefit some users while hurting others.

Option 5a: Transfer the Best Recreation Lands to the National Park Service

According to this proposal, the best recreation and scenic lands would be transferred to the National Park Service but the federal government would retain the most productive timberlands. In this case, the Forest Service would find itself out of the recreation business. Option 5a is similar to what happened to the New Zealand Forest Service in the 1980s, when the most pristine areas were made into national parks and the remaining forestlands sold to the highest bidder. In this option, all the wildernesses, scenic areas, wild and scenic rivers, national monuments, national volcanic monuments, geologic areas, national grasslands, national tallgrass prairie, and national recreation areas would be transferred to the Park Service. The Forest Service would retain the highly productive timberlands and probably the grazing lands.

It seems likely that most research, state and private forestry, and international forestry would be spun off to other federal agencies so that the remaining lands would be managed much like private or corporate tree farms. Under this alternative, only those functions necessary to implement a timber management program would be kept in the greatly downsized Forest Service. Remaining functions would include tree planting, genetic improvements, intensive management, thinning operations, vegetative management, and related activities. In all probability, the Forest Service would hire or contract with companies to cut and transport any trees to be harvested.

With this land management arrangement, the Forest Service would oversee and directly contract with private companies to cut, plant, and haul logs to sorting yards, where the agency would then sort and sell the logs to the highest bidders. The agency would have maximum control over the timing, location, and procedures in timber management operations. It would resemble a large timber corporation but have responsibility for public lands. Timber sales would occur only at the log sorting yards, which would be scattered around the country in strategic locations. The emphasis would be on getting top dollar for the logs, and the funds would then be either put back into replanting operations and/or returned to the U.S. Treasury.

Option 5b: Transfer the Best Timber Lands to Private Industry

The proposal to transfer or sell the most productive timberlands to private industry has been discussed by a number of forest economists over the years. Marion Clawson was a strong supporter of this option. Option 5b is similar to what happened to the New Zealand Forest Service in the 1980s.

One result would be that the federal government would be left (unless all the land was transferred or sold) with submarginal lands. The costs of management would be very high. Major restructuring of the nation's laws would be necessary.

Option 6: Long-Term Leases for Federal Land

Under a leasing arrangement, large watersheds would be leased to one corporation that would be given specific direction in the stewardship of the land, which would include recreation, road building, tree harvesting, planting, thinning, and second and third harvesting after decades of growth and management. This is what many would consider to be " hands-off" management of the national forests, yet the agency would retain a great deal of oversight of the process and procedures that the company would use to manage the forests. A long-term leasing operation would be the standard.

In the distant past, the Forest Service used this procedure for large timber sales. A number of watershed-scale timber sales were made in the 1920s that emphasized a decades-long management for sustained yield operations. Many of these sales, like the Westfir sale on the Willamette National Forest, were designed for railroad operations. Cutting would proceed initially at the lower elevations; then, as the timber was all cut, the railroad line would be slowly built up the drainage, with spur lines to smaller side drainages. Timber would then be cut, logs rolled or dragged to the rail line and transported to the mill. These sales were designed to take decades to finish, so, while the lower areas were harvested and replanted, the upper reaches of the watershed would be harvested. By the time the upper drainage was all cut, the lower elevations would have 30 to 50 years of new tree growth—ready for a new round of harvesting.

Canada uses a similar method of managing its rich timberlands. There are significant differences, however. The Canadian Forest Service does not have management of the crown forestlands; the provinces have direct control. Each province has its own provincial Forest Service, and each agency sets the rules for the long-term leases or contracts with corporations within the province. Public input to the process is limited, in part because of the different national laws for dealing with environmental procedures and processes.

Option 7: Establish Land Trusts

Land trusts are essentially large groups of interested groups and individuals who oversee the management of the national forests and other national lands. The most recent version of this was presented in the 2003 budget proposal by the George W. Bush administration that called for "charter forests." There is at least one proposal for an oversight committee (an advisory group) composed of interested citizens and interest groups to be formed to seek out issues and solutions, evaluate options/ alternatives, and propose management. This committee could exert considerable political pressure on the agency.

Option 8a: Transfer the Federal Lands to the Various States Where the Lands are Located

This option was argued long and hard for more than a century. The most recent arguments have centered on long-revered property rights. Initially, forest reserves created in the 1891–1893 era were noncontroversial, but in 1897 they became the center of a great western multistate outcry over the establishment of some 17 million acres of forest reserves, on February 22, 1897. The controversies were fueled by state legislatures, chambers of commerce, miners, timber barons, settlers, and sheep owners. Congress reacted by suspending most of the reserves but allowing the first management of them by the new forest rangers hired by the USDI General Land Office.

Other short-lived efforts to transfer federal land to the states or corporations followed. As early as the Taft administration (1908–1912), some officials favored the idea of massive federal land transfers. Various national timber industry groups favored national forest transfer to private interests after both world wars. Even the ranching industry led a "great land grab" movement in the late 1940s and early 1950s, seeking to have the public grazing lands transferred to those private interests that used the land for cattle and sheep grazing and thus had "vested interests."

The Public Land Law Review Commission of the late 1960s sparked another round of public-land-transfer ideas. Wayne Aspinall, chair of the commission, favored transferring most if not all of the public lands to the private and/or state sectors. He was reported to have said, "We must find the means to provide for the transfer of the public land into nonfederal ownership."

A quite different land-reform movement came about in the 1970s and 1980s with the "Sagebrush Rebellion." This effort was largely a landowner-inspired effort to take over or purchase, cheaply, federal grazing land (mostly Bureau of Land Management–administered land), which they were accustomed to using. This movement, which gained tremendous popularity in the mid- to late-1970s, was effectively taken over by the Reagan administration in the early 1980s. Reagan and Interior Secretary James Watt were sympathetic to the western-led effort, but it fizzled into political slogans and then an aborted " asset management" program to sell off unwanted portions of the public lands.

The "wise use" movement (an offshoot of the Sagebrush Rebellion) came into being after a Multiple-Use Strategy Conference, in August 1988. This national meeting was called by the people, organizations, and companies that utilize the many resources found on federal lands. It was intended to start an effort to counteract the highly successful efforts by environmental groups to enact tough environmental laws, enforce existing regulations, and stop or slow projects on federal land. At the conference, 21 goals were adopted, covering national parks, wilderness, grazing, mining, and timber harvesting.

The wise use movement members are almost all in the West, located in rural communities that are in some ways dependent on mining, forestry, and ranching. The wise use movement despises federal and even state ownership of land and the complexity of overlapping laws and regulations. Ideally, according to the wise use movement, federal ownership of lands would disappear, to be replaced by state or county ownership or even ownership by individuals and corporations. Today, these movements are referred to as the "property-rights," "home-rule," and "county-supremacy" movements.

There is no guarantee that the states would want to keep all the former national forests and grasslands, as well as BLM grazing lands, national wildlife refuges, and national parks. The cost of administering these lands would be horrendous. Disposal of the least desirable lands from the standpoint of economic efficiency would have a very strong appeal. Besides, from the various states' perspectives, selling the unwanted lands would give them more money to manage the more desirable lands. All of this is, of course, predicated on the notion that existing federal laws would not apply (e.g., the restrictions in the Endangered Species Act). If, however, Congress did not give any relief to the state from federal laws, then the states would face a huge management challenge. In addition, the states could face the "unfunded mandates" problem, which occurs when Congress directs the states to implement laws that are not funded by the federal budget.

Option 8b: Transfer the Federal Lands to the Regions Where the Lands are Located

This option, similar to Option 7a, would transfer management and oversight of the federal lands to a regional, multi-state entity. According to this idea, the current management is flawed because the agencies, including the Forest Service, often try to manage public lands from Washington, D.C., or from regional and state centers that have agency people making decisions. This option would keep the public lands under federal ownership but would transfer management decisions to a regional body that takes into account natural topographic and ecological features, as well as local citizens' wishes, in making decisions regarding these lands. This idea is similar to that proposed by John Wesley Powell, director of the USDI Geological Survey in the 1870s, after his monumental journey through the arid Southwest.

Option 9a: Sell the Public Lands

Selling the federal lands has always been a popular idea, at least in some circles. Behind this option is the assumption that all public land currently being held by the federal government should and must be transferred to the private sector. The notion is a very old one. Certainly, from the early 1800s, and especially by the late 1800s, there was always a desire for free or cheap land for the homesteader, miner, timber cutter, sheep and cattle grazer, and other people who would put the land to its best use. Many believe that land should have stayed in the public sector only temporarily, not permanently. In fact, under this assumption, one could view federal ownership of land as an anomaly in American history; the rights of the citizen should override those of the government except in times of national emergencies.

These issues have been raised for more than 100 years and were at the heart of the early forest reserve movement. In the 1940s, there was an attempt to take away or sell the public grazing lands to those ranchers that use the federal land. The effort failed. Another serious attempt to wrestle control of the grazing and timberlands came in the 1970s with the "Sagebrush Rebellion." Recently, these notions have been transformed—with the same rhetoric—into the " wise use," "county supremacy," and "property rights" movements. Despite the fact that proponents of these ideas have certainly enlivened the talk radio shows for the past several decades, all such proposals have failed.

Option 9b: Give Away the Public Lands

Another related option, which is never discussed, is that of giving the public lands to the citizens. In this scenario, the land would be equally divided into, perhaps, 40-acre plots. Deeds would be assigned (or through a lottery) to each person in the United States. The deed holders could then keep, lease, or sell their share of the public lands. In this option, there would be no "up-front" money required. Deeds would be mailed to the residents, and that would end the federal government ownership of the land. Conceivably, even the national parks and monuments could be included in the gifting. Developers could purchase from the citizens any number of "shares" of land. Restrictions, if any, would come from the states and counties through zoning or land use ordinances. There would be no federal land and no reason to have federal land management agencies.

CONCLUSION

The philosophical foundations of the movement to preserve and to use the natural resources on federal land have many deep roots that date to the nineteenth century. Since the decisions made by Congress in the 1890s, the national forest system has grown to more than 193 million acres. This land, owned by the people of the United States, has been managed by the USDA Forest Service since 1905. Forestry, as worked out by Gifford Pinchot, the first chief of the Forest Service, is synonymous with conservation of forests and other natural resources over the long term.

The future is unclear. There are powerful interest groups that want the Forest Service and the national forests to revert to an intensive management era to protect and preserve jobs and use the trees and other natural resources to the fullest extent possible. There are also those who want the resources totally preserved, a "zero-cut" of the trees, and exclusion of people from the national forests—a policy even more restrictive than those of the national parks. Other special interest groups want to increase their "share" of the resource uses available on the national forests. All groups seem to believe that science and more data will "prove their case." But the reality is that decisions about the future management of the national forests, as well as the use of the natural resources, are essentially political in nature. Data and the scientific method can give answers to questions, not set policy and practices.

Yet, without the foresight and dedication of a great number of people during the late nineteenth and early twentieth centuries, there would be nothing to debate today. The national forests would have long ago been carved into millions of private ownership plots and extensively logged and changed forever. The national forests are our legacy for future generations.

Selected Biographies of Persons Associated with the USDA Forest Service

GEORGE P. AHERN

George Ahern was born in New York in 1859. He received an appointment to West Point, where he graduated in 1882 at the bottom of his class. His first assignment was as secretary to Sitting Bull, then a prisoner at Ft. Randall in South Dakota. In 1888 to 1891, Lt. Ahern led a series of expeditions in the northern Rockies. He explored what became Glacier National Park and named a lake after his wife, but it was later renamed. He enrolled in the senior class of the Yale Law School, completing a thesis titled "The Necessity for Forestry Legislation" before returning to his regiment, in Ft. Missoula, Montana, where he used whatever spare time he could muster to spread the new ideas of forestry and conservation. Although still in the army, Ahern made lecture tours through Montana and helped create the Montana Fish, Game, and Forestry Commission. With his friend Gifford Pinchot, he explored the Bitterroot and Clearwater area in 1895, which later became forest reserves. In the summer of 1897, he guided Pinchot and his associate Henry Graves—Pinchot was secretary of the National Academy of Science's forest reserve commission—to examine possible forest reserves in western Montana. In 1897, he taught military science and forestry at the College of Agriculture (now Montana State University) in Bozeman, Montana.

At the outbreak of the Spanish-American War in 1898, Captain Ahern was called back to regular army service. In 1898, Ahern landed troops under fire at Tayabacao, Cuba. Transferred to the Philippines, he was appointed in 1900—at Pinchot's request—as director of the Philippine Bureau of Forestry, a post he held for 14 years. When Pinchot made a world tour in 1902, he met Ahern in Manila, where they set out on a cruise of 2,000 miles among the islands to make a study of forests, then extended their cruise to Nagasaki and Yokohama, Japan. Although the Philippine Bureau of Forestry was not a part of the U.S. Forest Service, Ahern sought advice from Gifford Pinchot, Henry Graves, Carl Schenck, and Filibert Roth. The Bureau developed a modified system derived from the United States, as well as from the older Spanish forest management system (which had started in 1863). On the Bataan Peninsula, he established the Philippine Forest School, in 1910. That same year, he visited China, which modeled the new Chinese forestry regulations after the examples set in the Philippines. He retired in 1914, but his influence lasted through the start of World War II.

WILLIAM WILLARD ASHE (1905–1932)

On June 4, 1872, William Ashe was born in Asheville, North Carolina. At 15, he entered the University of North Carolina as a sophomore. He obtained the degree of B.Litt. in 1891 from the University of North Carolina and earned an M.S. in 1892 from Cornell University. He was forester of the North Carolina Geological Survey from 1892 to 1905, when he joined the Forest Service, with which he was subsequently connected until his death. He was a close friend of Gifford Pinchot, and they coauthored the *North Carolina Geological Survey Bulletin 6*, "Timber Trees and Forests of North Carolina" (1897), a work that attracted wide attention. He wrote extensively on the management of southern forest types, especially chestnut, popular, white oaks, and loblolly, longleaf, and shortleaf pines. Ashe was secretary of the national forest reservation commission that examined millions of acres of eastern forestland, much of which had been severely cut over and damaged, as possible locations for new national forests under the authority of the Weeks Act of 1911. Ashe served as the editor of commission reports from 1918 to 1924. Ashe planted one of the first commercial stands of longleaf pine in North Carolina. He devised a new cupping system to extract more pitch from the southern pines for the naval stores industry in the South. Ashe is memorialized in the W.W. Ashe Forest Nursery on the De Soto National Forest. Also, there are 12 species and varieties of woody plants that bear his name.

RICHARD A. BALLINGER

On July 9, 1858, Richard Ballinger was born in Boonesboro (now Boone), Iowa. He graduated from Williams College, in Massachusetts, in 1884. Ballinger studied law for two years and was admitted to the Massachusetts bar. After practicing law for a short time, he moved west to settle in Port Townsend, Washington. He then moved to Seattle, where he opened a successful law practice. He became an expert in laws dealing with public land settlement and mining. Ballinger was elected mayor of Seattle and served from 1904 to 1906. President Taft asked him to serve as Secretary of the Interior. Ballinger, upon taking the secretarial post, announced that he would be changing from the stewardship or conservation policy of the Roosevelt administration to a policy that would not impede the development of the West.

In 1909–10, Ballinger was personally involved with several coal mining matters in Alaska. The resulting controversy would result in President Taft firing Gifford Pinchot, in January 1910, for insubordination. In the end, Ballinger's troubles with the Roosevelt-era conservationists and the battles over the firing of GLO special agent Louis Glavis in 1909, as well as of Gifford Pinchot and Overton Price in 1910, destroyed him and his tenure. Ballinger left office on March 13, 1911, a broken man. In 1912, the Republicans split the party into the regular Republicans, led by Taft, and the Progressive Party (or Bull Moose Party), led by former President Roosevelt. The Progressives were angered with Taft and the way the Ballinger-Pinchot affair was handled. The disarray in the Republican Party paved the way for the election of the Democrat nominee, Woodrow Wilson, in the fall of 1912. Ballinger was never able to fully recover from the damage done to his reputation by the controversy with Pinchot. Ballinger returned to Seattle, where he practiced law until his death, in 1922.

WILL C. BARNES (1907–1928)

Barnes was born in San Francisco, California, on June 21, 1858, but he lived in Nevada, Indiana, Minnesota, then again Indiana. He served in the U.S. Army from 1879 to 1883, when he was awarded the Congressional Medal of Honor for extraordinary bravery in action against the Apache Indians. He went on to work in the livestock business in Arizona and New Mexico, where he gained important experience in grazing operations. Barnes served in the territorial legislatures of both Arizona and New Mexico. He also served as the chair of the Arizona Live Stock Board, where he learned of the many issues dealing with grazing on public lands. Barnes entered the Forest Service in 1907 as an inspector of grazing in Washington, D.C. From 1915 to 1928, he was assistant forester in charge of grazing. In 1929, he became secretary of the U.S. Geographic Names Board, a position in which he continued for the next two years. Barnes helped with an unusual grazing issue—in 1927, he and several others traveled to Texas to select the best longhorn cattle to breed on the Wichita National Forest in Oklahoma. The longhorns, which have long been icons of the old West, especially the famous cattle drives of the middle 1800s, had been extensively interbred with other cattle species and were losing their distinctiveness. The effort, one of two federal attempts at saving this unique breed of cattle, was highly successful. Barnes devoted the rest of his life to writing. He is credited with authoring many articles and several books, including *Western Grazing Grounds and Forest Ranges* (1913), *The Story of the Range* (1925), and *Apaches and Longhorns* (1941). In 1938, two years after his death, a prominent sandstone butte at the eastern edge of Phoenix was named Barnes Butte.

ANN M. BARTUSKA (1989–PRESENT)

Ann Bartuska holds a B.S. in biology from Wilkes College, Wilkes Barre, Pennsylvania, an M.S. in botany from Ohio University, and a Ph.D. in biology from West Virginia University. Her research work focused on ecosystem processes in landscapes disturbed by coal mining. From 1982 to 1989, she managed the North Carolina State University research, development, and assessment programs associated with the effects of acid rain and air pollution under the national acid precipitation assessment program. She was named assistant station director for continuing research at the Southeastern Forest Experiment Station in 1989, where she was responsible for research in Georgia and Florida. She relocated to the Washington office in the forest environment research staff in 1991 as wetlands specialist, with specific responsibilities to develop a national wetlands research program. She became the first director of ecosystem management when that staff was created in 1992. Bartuska spent 1993 as Forest Service liaison to the National Biological Survey of the Department of the Interior. She then returned to the Forest Service as director of forest health protection in October 1994. In January 1999, she became the first woman and the first ecologist to be named director of forest management. In 2000, she also became responsible for the range management program and began integrating forest and rangelands into an all-vegetation focus. She left the agency in 2001 to direct the invasive species initiative at the Nature Conservancy. Bartuska was selected in 2003 to serve as Forest Service's deputy chief for research and development. She was on the board of the Council of Scientific Society Presidents and served as vice president for public affairs from 1996 to 1999. She was president of the Ecological Society of America in 2002–2003.

CARLOS G. BATES (1907–1949)

Carlos Bates was born in Topeka, Kansas, on October 14, 1855. He graduated from the University of Nebraska in 1907. That same year, he joined the Forest Service in Colorado. Bates suggested to Chief Pinchot that the Forest Service needed to establish forest research facilities across the country. He moved to Minnesota to work at the Lakes States Forest Experiment Station in 1928, where he remained the rest of his distinguished career as the first authority on forests and streamflows. He was one of the dedicated pioneer researchers devoted to the cause of scientific forestry. Bates worked on many successful projects, including the reforestation work in Nebraska's sand hills, which would eventually become the Nebraska National Forest; the earliest streamflow studies at Wagon Wheel Gap, which began in 1910 and lasted for the next 16 years; reforestation studies in the Lake States; and the great shelterbelt project for erosion control during the 1930s in the Great Plains.

DALE N. BOSWORTH (1966–PRESENT)

Dale Bosworth became the fifteenth chief of the Forest Service on April 12, 2001. Bosworth was born in Altadena, California. He holds a B.S. degree in forestry from the University of Idaho. His father, Irwin Bosworth, served as supervisor of the Lassen National Forest. Bosworth began his career in the Northern Region as a forester on the St. Joe National Forest (now a part of the Idaho Panhandle National Forest), in Idaho, and later served on the Kaniksu, Colville, and Lolo

National Forests. He was later promoted to district ranger on the Clearwater National Forest. Bosworth next moved to the Flathead National Forest as the planning staff officer before becoming the deputy forest supervisor there. He then moved to Missoula as the assistant director for land management planning for the Northern Region, where he was involved with the development of forest plans.

In 1986, Bosworth was named forest supervisor of the Wasatch-Cache National Forest, in Utah, in the Intermountain Region. From there, in 1990, he became deputy director of forest management in the Forest Service national headquarters in Washington, D.C., where he served until 1992, when he became deputy regional forester for the Pacific Southwest Region, headquartered in San Francisco, California. From that position, Bosworth was promoted to regional forester for the Intermountain Region in 1994. In August 1997, he was selected to be the regional forester for the Northern Region, headquartered in Missoula, Montana. Bosworth held this position until he was chosen to be chief of the Forest Service in the spring of 2001, a position he continues to hold.

During his time as chief of the Forest Service, Dale has brought a new dimension to the agency. Bosworth was very interested in addressing the issue of "analysis paralysis," that is, the internal and external overuse of laws and regulations that were essentially tying the agency in knots—projects took years to design, analyze, and review and were seemingly only occasionally implemented. Along with this was the great increase in administrative appeals and lawsuits by special interest groups. Probably his most memorable effort was to alert the public to what he called the four threats: fire and fuels, invasive species, loss of open space, and unmanaged recreation. Since 2002, Chief Bosworth has been actively involved with President George W. Bush's healthy forests initiative, as well as a new emphasis on restoration of damaged ecosystems.

SIR DIETRICH BRANDIS

Sir Dietrich Brandis was born in Bonn, Germany, on April 1, 1824, and, after studying botany at the Universities of Copenhagen, Goettingen, and Bonn, he accepted, in 1856, a position as forester in Burma. At the time, no systematic forestry program had been introduced to the British Empire. After Brandis had his first successes in the application of the principles of forestry, the demand for his services throughout India became pressing. In 1864, he was appointed the first inspector general of forests. From 1881 to 1883, when he retired, Brandis organized professional forest work in Burma, Bengal, Bombay, Madras, and other British possessions.

His influence on Gifford Pinchot and other early Forest Service foresters was profound, since he often personally directed the European-style forestry training. Brandis saw the need for educated and trained foresters, and, as early as 1886, he selected young Englishmen and put them in forestry training at the French and German forest schools, and especially at Nancy, France. This was the same method used to train Pinchot in forestry matters. Brandis also saw the value of having local men trained for work at the lower levels of the government forestry organization. He believed that this action would help win the hearts of the local people in the management of government forests.

ARTHUR H. CARHART (1919–1922)

Art Carhart was born in Mapleton, Iowa, in 1892. Carhart received his B.S. degree from Iowa State University in 1916. He became a national leader of the early-twentieth-century conservation movement, especially regarding wilderness. In 1919, he joined the Forest Service as its first landscape architect—he was called a "recreational engineer"—to begin recreational site planning. Carhart, in December 1919, completed a working draft of a recreation plan for the San Isabel National Forest, in Colorado. The following year, the plan was revised and called the "Recreation Plan San Isabel National Forest"—the first such plan in the Forest Service. Arthur Carhart visited the Superior National Forest in 1921 and began working to develop the Superior as primarily a recreation forest, especially the area called the Boundary Waters. The following year, he authored "Recreation Plans: Superior National Forest." The plan was approved in November, setting early recreation standards for the agency. However, Carhart resigned from the Forest Service in 1922 because of what he perceived as a lack of support for recreation in the agency. He went on to practice landscape architecture and city planning in the private sector in Denver. He worked for the rest of his life in the private sector as a landscape architect and, after 1931, as a freelance writer.

Arthur Carhart published his first book, *The Ordeal of Brad Ogden: A Romance of the Forest Rangers*, in 1929. For the next eight years, he wrote and sold novels, short stories, and articles of all description. He then worked as the regional information executive for the U.S. Office of Price Administration. Returning to his writing, he wrote his next book, *The Outdoorsman's Cookbook* (1944). Over his lifetime, Carhart wrote more than 4,000 articles, many for the *American Forests*, the publication of the American Forestry Association. He also wrote 24 books, ranging from western novels to books on hunting, fishing, and conservation. He left his personal papers and copies of his many books to the Denver Public Library. He died in 1978.

RACHEL CARSON

Rachel Carson was born in Springfield, Pennsylvania, on May 27, 1907. She started her studies at the Pennsylvania College for Women as an English major but switched to biology and graduated in 1929. Carson worked during the summer at the U.S. Marine Laboratory in Woods Hole, Massachusetts. With a scholarship, she went on to Johns Hopkins University for a graduate degree in biology in 1932. The year before graduating from Johns Hopkins, she accepted an appointment as staff biologist at the University of Maryland. In 1935, she was hired as an aquatic biologist by the federal government in the Bureau of Fisheries (now part of the

USDI Fish and Wildlife Service). In 1936, Carson was appointed a junior aquatic biologist with the Bureau of Fisheries and became one of only two women then employed with the Bureau at a professional level. Carson's first book, *Under the Sea-Wind* (1941), highlighted her unique ability to present deeply intricate scientific material in clear poetic language that could captivate her readers and pique their interest in the natural world. In 1943, Carson was promoted to the position of aquatic biologist in the newly created U.S. Fish and Wildlife Service, where she authored many bulletins directed at the American public. She became the editor-in-chief in 1949, but she resigned three years later to devote all her time to writing. Carson's second book, *The Sea Around Us* (1951), was published and eventually translated into 32 languages. It was on the *New York Times* best-seller list for 81 weeks. It was the success of her second book that prompted Carson to resign her position at the Fish and Wildlife Service in 1952 to devote her time to writing. Her third book, *The Edge of the Sea* (1956), opened a new, ecological perspective to the public and scientists around the world. But it was Carson's fourth book that aroused the most comment.

Carson had become interested in the danger of pesticides while still associated with the Fish and Wildlife Service. Her concern was accelerated with the introduction of DDT in 1945. Her marine studies had provided her with early documentation on the effects of DDT on marine life and led her to conclude that the overuse of pesticides, herbicides, and fungicides was causing undue harm to the wildlife bird and other species in the Chesapeake Basin. Although she generally supported the people, including foresters in the public and private sectors, who applied the chemicals, she was especially hard on the government in allowing the overuse of what she considered harmful chemicals. The publication of her book *Silent Spring* (1962) unleashed a torrent of criticism of her research and personal attacks on her professional integrity. Even before the book was in print, the chemical industry mounted a massive campaign to discredit Carson. However, many of the research findings had already been published by others, so the criticisms were for naught. Yet, she did not urge the complete banning of pesticides but rather proposed research to ensure that pesticides were used safely and an effort to find alternatives to dangerous chemicals. The federal government ordered a complete review of its pesticide policies. As a direct result of the government review, DDT was banned. The book had the effect of invigorating the conservation movement into a new environmental movement and awakening concerns among the public about the environment. Carson died from cancer, in 1964, at the age of 57. To honor the memory of this extraordinary woman, the USDI Fish and Wildlife Service named one of its refuges near Carson's summer home on the coast of Maine the Rachel Carson National Wildlife Refuge in 1969.

CHARLES CARTWRIGHT (1967–1997)

Charles "Chip" Cartwright is a native of Petersburg, Virginia. He received a B.S. degree in forestry and wildlife management from Virginia Polytechnic Institute and

State University, in Blacksburg, Virginia. He was one of the first USDA graduates of the U.S. Army War College and received special commendations from the War College commandant. Chip began his forestry career in 1967 as a temporary fireman/lookout on the St. Joe National Forest (now the Idaho Panhandle), in Idaho. After that, he served in a variety of positions throughout New Hampshire, Florida, Montana, Virginia, Oregon, Washington, and Utah. Throughout his career, Chip was a leader in pursuing affirmative action and diversification of the workforce. He forged new working relationships with several American Indian tribes and developed new approaches to the recruitment of black Americans. He helped develop a new mentoring program for forest supervisors. In 1979, Chip became the first black district ranger, serving on the Conconully Ranger District of the Okanogan National Forest in Washington. In 1988, he was named supervisor of the Jefferson (now the George Washington-Jefferson) National Forest, in Virginia, the first black forest supervisor in the history of the Forest Service. He served as acting deputy regional forester in the Rocky Mountain Region with leadership responsibilities for four states and served as the acting deputy regional forester in the Intermountain Region where he was responsible for all natural resource programs that are administered throughout six states. Chip Cartwright was the assistant director for ecosystem management in the national headquarters for the Forest Service from 1992 to 1994. He was appointed as the first black regional forester for the Southwestern Region in 1994, serving until 1997.

AUSTIN CARY (1910–1935)

Austin Cary was born in East Machias, Maine, in 1865. He was granted an A.B. in 1887 and an A.M. degree in 1890. In addition, he studied biology at Johns Hopkins and Princeton Universities. Cary was employed briefly by the Bureau of Forestry in Washington, D.C. As a surveyor and investigator, he was sent to Maine, Michigan, and Wisconsin to gather data about the growth of pines. In 1898, Cary went to work for the Berlin Mills Company, a large lumber business in Maine. He was the first professional forester employed by a forest products company in America. While working for the company, he was invited to survey, map, and cruise timber on some 120,000 acres of George Vanderbilt's Pisgah Forest, in North Carolina. Much of this land would become part of the Pisgah National Forest in 1916. This is the same area that Gifford Pinchot worked as Vanderbilt's professional forester.

In 1910, Cary came back to the Forest Service, where he was appointed as logging engineer in Washington, D.C. He had been a pioneer working on the private forestry, but then his influence broadened into every public forest region of the United States. He traveled extensively in his new position, where he talked with lumbermen, students, and private-forestland owners. Cary first visited the South in the fall of 1917. He recognized the potential of the South to become a major timber-growing region, which it eventually did. He also came to understand the necessity of communicating forestry practices and principles to the people. Cary contacted timber owners, learned southern-style practical forestry, spoke at many meetings, and wrote about issues and ways to solve them. When he retired from the Forest Service, in 1935, he became a consultant to several southern timber companies.

EARLE HART CLAPP (1905–1943)

Earle Clapp was born in North Rush, New York, on October 15, 1877. Clapp attended Cornell University, then transferred to the University of Michigan, where he received his B.A. in forestry in 1905. He first started to work for the Forest Service on the Medicine Bow Forest Reserve as a timber surveyor. In 1906, he worked on several forest reserves (now national forests) to develop techniques for determining minimum prices for timber. The following year, Clapp was appointed as chief of timber sales in the Washington, D.C., office. In 1909, he worked in the national forests in the Southwest; then, in 1915, he was made the chief of the new Forest Service branch of research. He was appointed associate chief in 1935, then acting chief in 1939 after Chief Silcox died. Clapp was never officially chief of the agency, apparently because President Roosevelt did not want to approve the appointment. Clapp served in an acting capacity until 1943, when Lyle Watts was appointed chief, although the agency considers him to be the sixth chief of the Forest Service.

During Clapp's time as chief, he was faced with the continuation of the Civilian Conservation Corps projects on the national forests, meeting the need for forest experts to help in the aftermath of the disastrous New England hurricane of 1938, opposing transfer of the Forest Service from Agriculture to Interior, and mobilizing the nation's forest resources behind the effort to meet the nation's timber needs during World War II. Cutting of national forest timber was stepped up; special studies and tests of wood and wood products were made for the armed forces by the Forest Products Laboratory; and forest lookout stations were staffed along both the East and West Coasts in 1942–1943 to detect enemy aircraft as part of the Aircraft Warning Service. Clapp was persistent, but mostly unsuccessful, in supporting federal regulation of timber cutting on private forestland, urging the addition of 150 million acres of mostly cutover land in the East and South to the national forests and alleviating poverty in depressed communities by means of reforestation projects. During his last two years in the job, Clapp was given a major responsibility—preparing a new appraisal of the nation's forest situation.

EDWARD PARLEY CLIFF (1931–1972)

Ed Cliff was born in the tiny community of Heber City, Utah, on September 3, 1909. He attended Utah State College, graduating with a degree in forestry in 1931. He started with the Forest Service the same year on the Wenatchee National Forest, in Washington. He stayed in the Pacific Northwest until 1944, when he went to the Washington, D.C., office of the Forest Service. Two years later, he was put in charge of range and wildlife in the Intermountain Region, then became regional forester for the Rocky Mountain Region in 1950. Two years later, he returned to Washington, D.C., as assistant chief of the Forest Service. He was then appointed the ninth chief, in 1962.

Serving as chief of the Forest Service from 1962 until 1972, Cliff experienced a decade of rapid change in the agency and in the country. Earth Day and a number of new environmental laws, including NEPA and the establishment of the Environmental Protection Agency, would soon become major challenges to the Forest Service, but the agency was unprepared. He devoted much time to promoting a better understanding of public-forest-management problems among grazing interests and the timber industry, and especially the general public. He helped the agency develop a long-range forest research program. Public interest in the management of the national forests, as well as demands for numerous forest resources, expanded quickly during this era. During the late 1960s, controversy erupted over clearcutting on the Monongahela National Forest, in West Virginia, and clearcutting and terracing on the Bitterroot National Forest, in Montana. These controversies would lead to congressional hearings on clearcutting in 1972 and, four years after Chief Cliff retired, the National Forest Management Act of 1976.

Important for the national forest recreationists was Cliff's vision in moving the Forest Service more into recreational improvements and programs. This was necessary because of the explosion in outdoor recreation, as interest in hiking, camping, wilderness travel, mountain climbing, and many other national forest outdoor activities rapidly increased. The Wilderness Act of 1964 gave congressional blessing to a new national wilderness preservation system and established more than 9 million acres that had previously been designated "wild" or "wilderness" as the core. The Forest Service also became involved in the new Job Corps program in the mid-1960s by operating nearly 50 camps on the national forests; it also participated in the nationwide natural beauty campaign, rural-areas development, and the war on poverty. After his retirement, Cliff remained active in forestry matters. He served on the National Materials Policy Commission and worked for the United Nations, traveling to 21 countries.

SALLY COLLINS (1983–PRESENT)

Sally Collins was born in Ames, Iowa. She received a B.S. in recreation from the University of Colorado, then an M.P.A. from the University of Wyoming. Sally worked for the Forest Service as a temporary employee during the summer when she was in college. She then took a job with the BLM in Colorado state office first as a wilderness specialist, then as a National Environmental Policy Act coordinator, and later as a mineral leasing specialist. Collins joined the Forest Service on the Siuslaw National Forest as forest planner and coordinated mineral leasing work for the Pacific Northwest Region. From there she went to a staff officer position on the Deschutes NF, then became the deputy forest supervisor for three years. She was appointed the Deschutes NF forest supervisor, a job that she enjoyed for the next seven years. Collins entered the senior executive development program and within a month of finishing and being certified for senior executive service was moved, in 2000, into the associate deputy chief position for the national forest system at the national headquarters in Washington, D.C. Collins was made associate chief in August 2001, the second woman to ever hold this position and the highest-ranking woman in the agency.

WILLIAM ADAMS DAYTON (1910–1955)

William Dayton was born in New York City on December 14, 1885. He obtained his B.A. in 1905 and an M.A. in 1908 from Williams College. In 1910, he was appointed a plant ecologist in the Forest Service. During the first few years with the Service, he spent about half his time doing range ecology work in Arizona, California, and Oregon. These studies provided data for the deferred and rotation system of grazing that is in general use in the national forests. Dayton was made chief of the division of dendrology and range forage investigations. Dayton was responsible for building the Forest Service herbarium of more than 100,000 specimens, recognized as the largest and most complete collection of annotated range plants in the country. He probably worked harder than any other person to standardize the nomenclature of native range plants. His interest in plant names evolved from his early work on range plants and his contact with thousands of plant specimens. His range work has also resulted in the preparation of two books: *Important Western Browse Plants* (1931) and *Range Plant Handbook* (1937).

HILDA DIAZ-SOLTERO (1999–2002)

Hilda Diaz-Soltero was born in Puerto Rico in 1949, part of a third generation of professionals dedicated to public service. Diaz-Soltero earned degrees in geology and astronomy at Vassar College. Later, she earned a master's degree in wildlife from the University of Puerto Rico. She served as deputy secretary, then secretary of natural resources for Puerto Rico. In 1986, she worked for the Nature Conservancy as director of its conservation programs in Ecuador, Paraguay, and the Caribbean. A year later, she joined the USDI Fish and Wildlife Service as field supervisor of its Caribbean field office. In 1994, Diaz-Soltero began working for the National Marine Fisheries Service as the director for the Southwest region.

She joined the Forest Service in July 1999 as the associate chief, in which position she oversaw the national forest system, research and development, and state and private forestry. Diaz-Soltero was the first woman, the first Hispanic, and the first person to have been brought from outside the agency to occupy this position. The agency was facing changing and challenging times, with the need to better incorporate new scientific information into management. In addition, the agency was reexamining its relationships with communities and private landowners and creating opportunities for new partnerships to promote an ecosystem approach.

Diaz-Soltero left the national headquarters in 2001 to take on the directorship of the Pacific Southwest Research Station in California. She retired from government service in 2003.

MICHAEL P. DOMBECK (1978–2002)

Mike Dombeck became the fourteenth chief of the Forest Service on January 6, 1997. He was born on September 21, 1948, in Stevens Point, Wisconsin. It was there, in northern Wisconsin's lake country, that his appreciation for natural resources was cultivated. Dombeck worked as a fishing guide in the region for 11 summers, from 1966 to 1977. He earned undergraduate and graduate degrees in biological sciences and education from the University of Wisconsin-Stevens Point and the University of Minnesota. He earned his doctorate in fisheries biology from Iowa State University and is noted for research contributions on muskies and lake habitat management. In addition, Dombeck has authored numerous scholarly publications and made frequent national and international scientific presentations.

He spent 12 years with the Forest Service. From 1978 to 1985, he was a fisheries biologist in Michigan and Wisconsin. During 1985–1987, Dombeck was the regional fisheries program manager, Pacific Southwest Region. In his last Forest Service post, as national fisheries program manager in Washington, D.C., 1987–1989, he was recognized for outstanding leadership in developing and implementing fisheries programs and forging partnerships. He also spent a year as a legislative fellow working in the U.S. Senate with responsibility for natural resource and Interior appropriations issues.

Dombeck served from 1989 to1992 as a science adviser and special assistant to director, Bureau of Land Management, Washington, D.C. Then, in 1993, he became the acting deputy assistant secretary for the USDI Land and Minerals Management Service. He also served in 1993–1994 as the chief of staff to assistant secretary for Land and Minerals Management, Department of Interior. Dr. Dombeck was named acting director of the Bureau of Land Management (BLM) in February 1994. He focused on two major objectives: creating a long-term BLM vision to improve the health of the land and reinventing the agency to reduce red tape, streamline functions, and improve customer service. As new chief of the Forest Service in 1997, his primary emphasis for management was to repair relations with external organizations. In doing so, he introduced a new phrase into the Forest Service lexicon: collaborative stewardship. During his tenure, he placed a moratorium on building new roads in areas that were officially recognized as roadless. This set off a firestorm of criticism from many members of the public and Congress, and there was even a strong internal backlash. This increased when Dombeck decided that the final disposition of roadless areas should be a national decision rather than a local one. He believed that this would take the heat off national forests and regions. Instead, it provoked widespread criticism, especially internally. Dombeck resigned shortly after the George W. Bush administration came into office. He is now the Professor of Global Environmental Management at the University of Wisconsin-Stevens Point. He continues to publish books and give lectures on natural resource issues.

BOV B. EAV (1985–PRESENT)

A native of Cambodia, Bov Eav earned a degree in forestry in 1970 from the Université des Sciences Agronomique in Chumkar Daung, Cambodia. Moving to the United States in 1972 as a Fulbright Fellow, he completed a master's in forest biometrics in 1974 and a Ph.D. in forest biometrics and remote sensing in 1977, both degrees from the State University of New York's College of Environmental Science and Forestry, in Syracuse. He was hired by Lockheed Engineering and Management Services, where he managed scientific payloads for the NASA space shuttle program and developed very-high-altitude imagery to detect forest areas under attack by forest pests and diseases. In 1985, he joined the Forest Service in Ft. Collins, Colorado, as an operations research analyst, then served as an associate director. Nine years later, Eav was the director of the national center for health management in Morgantown, West Virginia, but he returned to Ft. Collins as an enterprise team director dealing with forest health. In 1997, he was appointed director of the Northeastern Research Station in Newtown Square, Pennsylvania. Four years later, Eav became the associate deputy chief for research and development in the national headquarters in Washington, D.C. In 2006, we became the director of the Pacific Northwest Research Station in Portland, Oregon. He has been actively involved in international efforts, including the UN Development Program and the International Development Research Centre in Canada. In addition, he headed cooperative geographic information systems (GIS) and remote sensing projects for the Academy of Forestry of the People's Republic of China and the New Zealand Forest Research Institute.

NATHANIEL HILLYER EGLESTON (1883–1898)

Nathaniel Egleston was born into an old New England family in Hartford, Connecticut, on May 7, 1822. A graduate of Yale in 1840, he continued on to be awarded the D.D. degree from the Yale Divinity School four years later. He became a prominent Congregational minister and was one of the founders of the Chicago Theological Seminar. He became quite interested in conserving forests and wrote many articles about the need for forestry, contributing stories to magazines and journals. Because of his great interests, he was sent as a delegate to the first American Forestry Congress, held in Cincinnati, Ohio, in April 1882. The following year, USDA Commissioner Loring appointed Egleston as the second chief of the USDA Division of Forestry. This action was seen by many as an act of favoritism in the corrupt spoils system. (Loring demoted the energetic and prolific Franklin G. Hough, whom he disliked.) Egleston, however, proved to be a weak administrator.

Conscientious and sincere in promoting forestry, Egleston wrote a number of popular pamphlets and articles on the subject for such magazines as *Popular Science Monthly, Harper's, Atlantic,* and the *New Englander.* In his first annual report, he wrote that action should be taken to ensure that the extensive public domain forestlands owned by the federal government were properly cared for and were used for the general welfare. He also recommended that the federal government establish forestry schools and experiment stations.

President Cleveland appointed Bernhard E. Fernow the chief of the USDA Division of Forestry on March 15, 1886. Egleston appears to have been relieved rather than upset when he was replaced by the more qualified Fernow three years later. Fernow was not pleased that Egleston still hung on, but he did not fire him, and he remained with the division until 1898, working on annual reports for the Division of Forestry.

ELIZABETH ESTILL (1988–PRESENT)

Elizabeth Estill was born in Knoxville, Tennessee. She graduated from the University of Tennessee with B.S. and M.S degrees in ecology. She went on to Harvard University as a Loeb Fellow in Advanced Environmental Studies. At Harvard, she focused on public administration, while teaching at the Harvard Graduate School of Design. For 14 years, she worked her way through the ranks of the Tennessee Valley Authority, becoming the director of the Land between the Lakes, a national recreation demonstration area in western Kentucky and Tennessee. She joined the Forest Service in 1988 as assistant director of recreation, cultural resources, and wilderness in the national headquarters. She was appointed director of the same unit, then associate deputy chief of the national forest system. In 1992, Estill was named regional forester for the Rocky Mountain Region of the Forest Service. She was the first woman regional forester in agency history. She held this position for four years, then was transferred to the Southern Region as regional forester, in which position she oversaw management of forests and grasslands in 13 states and Puerto Rico covering more than 12.6 million acres. In 2001, she was transferred to the Washington office to become the deputy chief for programs, legislation, and communications. Estill was placed in special assignment in 2005 to be the liaison with multiple state and federal agencies concerning management of the Mississippi River delta area.

ROBIE MASON EVANS (1910–1949)

Robie Evans was born August 7, 1884, in Fryeburg, Maine. He was educated at Dartmouth College, from which he graduated in 1906. He attended Kimball Union Academy in Meriden, N.H., then completed his studies at the Yale School of Forestry with a M.F. degree in 1910. He joined the Forest Service, then headed west. By 1916, he was supervisor of the Wallowa-Whitman National Forest, at Baker, Oregon. Six years later, he was transferred to the Washington office to assist in the organization of the growing eastern national forests under the Weeks Act of 1911. He served as assistant district forester for 12 years in the old eastern Region 7. Eastern national forest acreage increased during the Great Depression, and there was increasing cooperation between the federal government and the states. Evans was then chosen as regional forester of the Eastern Region.

During his tenure as regional forester, more than 500 CCC camps in the Eastern Region needed to be organized and the Forest Service had to provide and guide work projects for the enrollees. The New England hurricane of September 1938 killed 682 people and left more than 3 billion board feet of timber blown down on private land. Evans helped set up the northeastern timber salvage administration. World War II brought on new tasks, including organizing the Aircraft Warning Service (AWS) to watch for enemy airplanes that never came. The AWS sites were usually located at lookout towers scattered around the national forests. The war also intensified forest fire protection that was extended to military and manufacturing installations in the Northeast. In addition, the timber production war project was organized to enhance the production of wood products for the war effort. Through depression, recovery, war, and postwar activities, Evans steered a skillful and safe course with a steady hand.

BERNHARD EDUARD FERNOW (1886–1898)

Bernhard Fernow was born January 7, 1851, at Inowrazlaw, a province of Posen, Prussia. He was the first professional forester to practice in North America. Fernow is often regarded as the father of American forestry. Beginning in 1869, Fernow received training and experience at the famous Prussian Forest Academy at Munden, where he studied for two and a half years. Fernow served in the Prussian army during the Franco-Prussian War. After military service, he spent a year studying law at the University of Kronigsberg, then returned to forestry work. Fernow worked in the forests of Prussia for several years. He immigrated to the United States in 1876 following a visit to the Philadelphia Centennial Exposition. Two years later, he became the manager for Cooper Hewitt and Company's 15,000 acres of woodlands in Pennsylvania. The trees were used for making charcoal.

The first American Forestry Congress met in Cincinnati, Ohio, in 1882. Fernow was the only professionally trained forester to attend the monumental meeting. As a result, he served as a leader at the international congress and served as its secretary, chair of the editorial committee, and other positions from1883 to 1895. Fernow was appointed by President Grover Cleveland in 1886 as the third chief of the Division of Forestry in the USDA. Fernow reorganized the staff of the Division of Forestry. He was able to start programs of research in silviculture, forest pathology, wood technology, forest products, and tree planting. All of these programs were oriented toward the practical rewards for managing woodlands. He and his staff over the next 12 years produced more than 200 articles, monographs, circulars, and bulletins. He traveled widely, giving hundreds of public addresses, speeches, and informal talks to the public, students, and even scientists.

Fernow was perhaps the first to emphasize that management of woodlands and forests was important to the future generations. Sustained yield or conservative use of all natural resources, especially wood, was the key to his understanding of practical forestry. He believed that the federal and state governments should manage their forestlands by example, serving as a guide to how the private sector should or could manage its lands. He resigned from the division in 1898 and was replaced by Gifford Pinchot.

From 1898 to 1903, Fernow served as director of the New York State College of Forestry at Cornell University. This was the first forestry school in North America. After controversies about the proper management of the school lands in the Adirondacks, especially the use of clearcutting, the State Legislature of New York cut the funding for the forestry school. From 1903 to 1907, Fernow was a consulting forester in the United States, Cuba, and Mexico. In 1907, he taught briefly at Pennsylvania State College. He then immigrated to Canada and became dean of the faculty of forestry in the University of Toronto, the first forestry school in Canada. He retained this position until his retirement in 1919.

ELOISE GERRY (1910–1954)

Eloise Gerry was born in Boston in 1885. She held both bachelor's and master's degrees from Harvard University's Radcliffe College for women, where she had specialized in the anatomy of wood and trees and their physiological responses. In 1921, she earned a Ph.D. from the University of Wisconsin. Gerry was the first woman appointed to the professional staff of the Forest Products Laboratory and one of the first women in the United States to specialize in forest products research. She arrived a few days after the laboratory's formal opening and dedication. In the summer of 1910, FPL had neither a microscope nor a microtome. The botany department of the University of Wisconsin provided quarters in Science Hall for Gerry, as well as the use of a microscope.

About 1915, she pioneered microscopical investigations of the turpentine pines of the South. Her job was to find out what could be done to maintain the industry as the virgin forests disappeared and to increase the oleo resin yields from the small trees that made up the young stands. At a time when women scientists were a rarity and their venturing into the southern forests was practically unheard of, she packed her microscope and headed for the pine forests of Mississippi and Louisiana. The results of her work were later summarized in the *Naval Stores Handbook* (1935). In her travels through the South, Gerry came to believe that children had a need to understand the nearby forests and the products coming from the forests. She published a series of children's short stories in *American Forests and Forest Life* under the title "Pine-Burr Stories." World War I interrupted the naval stores project, and Gerry turned to developing better methods of selecting wood for use in aircraft, including airframes and propellers, and to teaching the fundamentals of wood structure. Her ability to write about her important work is reflected in more than 120 publications in technical and trade journals, in Forest Products Laboratory publications, and in publications of the Forest Service and the U.S. Department of Agriculture. Eloise Gerry retired after more than 44 years of government service.

JAMES WALTER GIRARD (1907–1945)

Jim Girard was born May 4, 1879, at Pleasant View, Tennessee. In the winter of 1907–1908, he joined the Forest Service as a temporary employee to mark standing timber and scale cut logs. He was then employed as forest guard on the Lewis and Clark NF, rapidly advancing to become a forestry expert and then forest ranger. In 1921, Jim rewrote the *National Forest Stumpage Appraisal Manual.* His knowledge of and experience in both private industry and the Forest Service enabled him to clearly understand log production, including cutting trees down, skidding, disposing of slash, and many other forestry operations in the national forests.

From 1923 to 1929, Girard served as general manager of the Herrick Lumber Company, in Burns, Oregon. He returned to the Forest Service in 1929 as senior logging engineer in Washington, D.C. Since 1934, as assistant director of the nationwide forest survey, he was responsible for the development of the general field procedure used in the national survey. On the basis of studies of species, taper, and tree form, he prepared volume tables for a large number of tree species in all parts of the country. He was coauthor of *Timber Cruising* (1939), which was for its time the best and most practical book on standing timber measurements. He wrote a short 35-page autobiography with the title *The Man Who Knew Trees: The Autobiography of James W. Girard* (1949).

HENRY SOLON GRAVES (1897–1900, 1910–1920)

Henry "Harry" Graves was born in Marietta, Ohio, on May 3, 1871. He graduated from Yale in 1892, then received his master's degree in 1900. Graves, once second in command under Pinchot in the Division of Forestry, was the dean of forestry at Yale. He was a close friend of Pinchot's and one of the original seven members of the Society of American Foresters, which was formed at Pinchot's home in November 1900. Graves was an eminent professional forester, serving as the first professor and director of the newly founded Yale Forest School.

He was selected the second chief of the Forest Service to take over the reigns of the five-year-old agency in January of 1910, soon after the firing of Gifford Pinchot by President Taft. Graves was described as strongly puritanical and no-nonsense (he frowned on smoking in the office and forbade whistling), yet he commanded respect and even affection from his staff. Graves felt the burden of trying to rebuild the morale that was shattered by Pinchot's firing. Initially, Graves had to restore relations with the Department of the Interior, then work to bring about a strong Forest Service. He also had to fight to keep control of the national forests, as there were a number of state and private interests that wanted the forests returned to state or local control. He and his staff showed that the Forest Service was the best-qualified agency to manage the national forests.

Soon after the declaration of war in the spring of 1917, Graves was commissioned a major in the Corps of Engineers and sent to France to make advance preparations for the 10th Engineers (Forestry), and later the 20th Engineers. He returned to America in the spring of 1918 as a lieutenant colonel and soon after inaugurated a movement looking toward developing a national forest policy for the United States.

His 10-year stint as chief of the Forest Service was characterized by a stabilization of the national forests, the purchase of new national forests in the East, and a strengthening of the foundations of forestry by putting it on a more scientific basis. But his great contribution was the successful launching of a national forest policy for the United States, a permanent and far-reaching achievement. During his tenure as chief, the Forest Products Laboratory was established at Madison, Wisconsin; the Weeks Law was enacted in 1911, allowing federal purchase of forest lands (mostly in the East); and the research branch of the Forest Service was organized.

WILLIAM BUCKHOUT GREELEY (1904–1928)

William Greeley was born in Oswego, New York, on September 6, 1879. He graduated from the University of California in 1901 and from the Yale Forest School three years later. Forestry school dean Henry Graves wrote: "Greeley had the highest mark of any recent graduates. He is a special star and I recommend him for almost any work which may come along." After starting with the Bureau of Forestry in 1904, he quickly was promoted through a variety of Forest Service positions to the Washington office as assistant chief in charge of silviculture. During the Great War, after Chief Graves returned from France, in 1918, Greeley took his place overseas with the 20th Engineers (Forestry), ending the war as a lieutenant colonel (after the war he preferred to be addressed by his military title, "Colonel Greeley"). He was appointed chief after Graves resigned, making Greeley the third chief of the Forest Service.

Greeley was able to put into actual practice the national forest policy that was inaugurated by Henry Graves. After Greeley was appointed chief, he faced a number of challenges, including the acquisition of new national forests east of the Mississippi River; making cooperation with private, state, and other federal agencies a standard feature of Forest Service management; fighting renewed efforts to place the Forest Service back into the Department of the Interior; and "blocking up" the national forests (exchanging or purchasing lands inside or near the forest boundaries to simplify management). During his administration, the Clarke-McNary Act of 1924 became law, extending federal authority to purchase forestlands and to enter into agreements with various states to help protect state and private forests from wildfire. This was also the time, during the Roaring Twenties, when prosperity brought about tremendous growth in recreation on the national forests—which led to the need to develop and improve roads for automobile use, campgrounds for forest visitors, and summer home sites for part-time residents.

WILLIAM L. HALL (1899–1919)

Bill Hall was born in Johnson County, Missouri, on May 28, 1873. He graduated from the State Agricultural College at Manhattan with a B.S. degree. Hall worked as a student on a cooperative tree planting with the Kansas Experimental Station through the USDA Division of Forestry. This planting project started his forestry career. He got a full-time appointment in 1899 with the division and was put in charge of Forest Extension. While in this work, he organized the Dismal River tree nursery—later called the Bessey nursery—which was probably the first, and for many years the only, nursery in the United States devoted to reforestation. A million or more hardwood and pines seedling were planted by the Forest Service in the sandhill region of western Nebraska on what is now the Nebraska National Forest.

From 1905 to 1910, Hall was in charge of the branch of forest products. He organized a staff for managing the thousands of "June 11" claims (claims under the Forest Homestead Act of June 11, 1906), which was an important, laborious, and costly project that lasted for years and that was tainted by land fraud. During this period, he also made a survey of the White Mountains in New England and of the southern Appalachians to determine the possibilities of land purchases for national forests. Initially, this proposal encountered hostile and determined opposition. However the effort culminated in 1911 with the passage of the Weeks Act that authorized the purchase from willing sellers of often-devastated forestland for national forests. Hall then headed the section in charge of selecting and buying the land. He resigned in 1919 to work as a consulting forester and timberland owner in the South.

BENJAMIN FRANKLIN HOUGH (1873–1885)

Franklin Hough was born on July 22, 1822, in Martinsburg, New York. Franklin received his M.D. in 1848 from Western Reserve College. He began a long correspondence with Louis Agassiz, of Harvard, John S. Newberry, of Columbia, and Spencer F. Baird, of the Smithsonian. Hough's growing reputation for scientific thoroughness led to his appointment in 1854 to direct the New York state census. His fondness for statistics also led him to assist with the 1870 U.S. census. He found during the decades of the 1850s and 1860s that there had been a steady decline in lumber production in New England. He came to believe that, should the trend continue, the timber resources of the Northeast and possibly the country would soon become exhausted.

Hough was concerned enough about the timber decline that he presented a paper at the August 1873 meeting, held in Portland, Maine, of the American Association for the Advancement of Science (AAAS). His paper, titled "On the Duty of Governments in the Preservation of Forests," presented the case that the Mediterranean countries had overused their resources—especially trees—and caused untold harm to the environment. Former forest areas and even cultivated lands had become virtual wastelands. He argued that actions were necessary so that the same problems would not happen in the United States. He suggested that "in this great work of popular education, agricultural societies and kindred associations may do much" to inform and educate landowners and the public about the need to preserve forests. He also proposed the establishment of forestry schools and even outlined seven laws that would protect and regulate the use of U.S. forests. In addition, Hough argued that the AAAS should "take measures for bringing to the notice of our several State Governments, and Congress with respect to the territories, the subject of protection to forests, and their cultivation [use], regulation, and encouragement; and that it appoint a special committee to memorialize these several legislative bodies upon this subject, and to urge its importance."

The speech was an instant success. The following day, the AAAS appointed a committee of nine prominent men to pursue the matter with the president and Congress. The committee wrote a memorial (petition) to Congress telling of the need for forest protection and urging Congress to create a federal commission on forestry matters, including someone to investigate present forestry conditions. Several members of the AAAS committee, including Hough and the Harvard botanist George Emerson, went to Washington the following February. They met with President Ulysses Grant and several representatives and senators but had little success. Finally, in August 1876—at the end of the session—Congress passed an agricultural free-seed bill with a rider attached that provided $2,000 for the appointment of a special forestry agent (19 Stat. 143, 167). The position was placed in the Department of Agriculture. Agriculture Commissioner Frederick Watts appointed Hough to that new position on August 30, 1876. He became the first federal expert on forestry and the first chief of what became the Division of Forestry.

Hough had been gathering data on forestry matters for at least five years as he wrote letters to foreign government requesting information, and he traveled some 8,000 miles across the country in the spring and summer of 1877 revising his information and gathering more data. The result was a 650-page volume, "Report on Forestry 1877." Congress was so impressed with the research that it ordered 25,000 copies to be printed and distributed in 1878. A statistical volume for the same report was printed two years later. This volume contained Hough's recommendations for a national policy for the reservation and management of federal timberlands, which were then mostly in the public domain. He also recommended that timber harvesting on these be controlled by long-term leases, similar to those in Canada; that forest experiment stations for tree planting be established; and that a campaign to educate the public about the need for forest protection and appropriate uses of the forests in the future be undertaken.

The forestry expert position that Hough held was elevated to division status in 1881. Hough spent the summer of 1882 in Europe gathering more information about forestry practices. During the same year, the third forestry volume was published, but it was only about half the length of the previous volumes. Among several recommendations in the report, Hough suggested "that the principal bodies of timber land still remaining the property of the government ... be withdrawn from sale or grant." Despite repeated attempts to do just what Hough had recommended, nothing would happen in Congress for another nine years, until passage of the Forest Reserve or Creative Act of March 3, 1891. Meanwhile, Hough's relationship with USDA Secretary George B. Loring deteriorated. In 1883, Loring demoted Hough from chief of the Division of Forestry to special agent, the same title given to the two agents that Loring had personally hired. Hough was replaced in 1883 by Nathaniel Egleston, a political appointee with little forestry knowledge. Hough stayed in the division, although his despair deepened.

DOUGLAS CAMERON INGRAM (1909–1929)

Douglas Ingram was born in Scotland into an old and respected family. Ingram had one year of college in England before coming to America in 1901. He took the five-month-long University of Washington forestry short course. Ingram started his Forest Service career in the summer of 1909 on the Ochoco Ranger Station, on the Ochoco National Forest, in central Oregon. From 1909 to 1917, he worked on several districts and had jobs as a forest guard, an assistant forest ranger, a forest ranger, and a grazing assistant at the Ochoco supervisor's office. Ingram was promoted to the regional office in 1918 as a grazing examiner. In 1921, he was given charge of all grazing studies for the Pacific Northwest Region. For years, he collected plant specimens on almost every national forest in the Pacific Northwest Region. He traveled from forest to forest doing range analyses for grazing and plant collecting. Ingram was also an accomplished photographer, and many of his photographs showed range conditions and forest flora. He felt that, in his grazing position, it was incumbent on him to identify the flora in the forests and grazing lands. Ingram was a prolific collector and organizer of specimens.

Starting in 1920, with his move to the regional office, he ranged from forest to forest, east to west, in Washington and Oregon, collecting, photographing, and analyzing range conditions. Ingram was promoted to assistant chief for range management in 1929. Later that year, he and Ernanie St. Luise, a summer employee from the University of Washington, died on the Camas Creek Fire in eastern Washington. The ridge where they died was renamed Douglas Ingram Ridge, and a stream close by was renamed St. Luise Creek.

EVAN W. KELLEY (1906–1944)

Evan Kelly was born in Sierra City, California, on October 19, 1882. He grew up in nearby Downieville, worked in the mines; then, in 1906, he was a forest guard on the Tahoe National Forest. Four years later, he became supervisor of the Eldorado National Forest. Soon his ability at organization attracted the attention of the regional office, and from 1915 to 1917 he advanced to making regionwide inspections in the division of operations. In World War I, Kelley was a captain and later major in the 10th Forestry Engineers in France. After the war, he became fire control inspector for the Washington office. He wrote the first Forest Service minor roads manual, as well as the first fire-control equipment manual. His was appointed as regional forester for the Eastern Region 7 in 1925. He was transferred to the Northern Region at Missoula, Montana, in 1929. During World War II, he was put in charge of the gigantic Guayule Emergency Rubber Project in California.

EDWARD SOBIN KOTOK (1942–1976)

Born on September 13, 1919, in Palo Alto, California, Kotok earned a bachelor's degree in forestry from the University of California in 1941. He served in the Army from 1941 to 1945, achieving the rank of major at age 24. He was responsible for establishing and directing antiaircraft batteries on the West Coast and the invasion of the Japanese-held island of Attu, in the Aleutians. In 1946, he received an M.F. degree from the University of Michigan. His career took him to assignments in Oregon, Arizona, Colorado, Utah, Montana, and Washington, D.C., where he was chief of structural and forest systems and engineering research. He retired in 1976 after working for the Forest Service for 34 years as a research forester and administrator.

WILLIAM KREUTZER (1898–1939)

William Kreutzer became America's first ranger in the USDI General Land Office in the summer of 1898. His first instructions were to "go back to the Plum Creek Reserve, ride as far and as fast as the Almighty will let you, and put out those forest fires." During his first 20 years of service, living mostly in the woods and off the backs of two or three horses, he managed to complete correspondence courses in law, business, and accounting, as well as pursuing his ongoing studies of all things relating to the forests. This love of education, combined with his passion, patience, and persistence, served him and the Forest Service well over the decades. He was promoted to forest inspector and moved to the Colorado Front Range, to what was then called the Colorado National Forest. Bill Kreutzer died on January 2, 1956.

ALDO LEOPOLD (1909–1928)

Aldo Leopold was born on January 11, 1887, in Burlington, Iowa. He attended the Sheffield Scientific School at Yale and, in 1906, began his forestry course work at the Yale School of Forestry. Leopold received his B.S. degree in 1908 from the Sheffield School, then graduated in 1909 with a master's in forestry. Soon after graduation, he joined the Forest Service. By 1911, Leopold had been promoted to deputy forest supervisor and a year later to supervisor of the Carson National Forest, in the New Mexico Territory. In 1914, after an acute illness, Leopold was assigned to the office of grazing in the Forest Service Southwestern District Office (D-3), in Albuquerque, New Mexico. He began his life's work on wildlife management issues, including game refuges, law enforcement, and predator control, as well as founding a number of big game protective associations in New Mexico and Arizona.

Concerned with the rapid pace of road expansion after World War I, Leopold recommended, in 1922, that roads and use permits be excluded on the Gila River headwaters on the Gila National Forest. This notion, two years later, evolved into the 500,000-acre Gila Wilderness, established in 1924—the first administrative wilderness in the national forest system. Although his plan was approved, it was only a local policy, not a national one. Leopold left the Southwest in 1924 to serve as the assistant, then the associate director of the Forest Products Laboratory in Madison, Wisconsin. He was unhappy at the Laboratory and resigned from the Forest Service in 1928 to take the lead in establishing a new profession of game management.

Leopold was hired to undertake a game survey of nine Midwestern states, which was summarized in "Report on a Game Survey of the North Central States" (1931). Leopold's book *Game Management* (1933), based in part on his game survey work, helped define a new field of managing and restoring wildlife populations. He accepted an appointment to a new chair in the Department of Agricultural Economics at the University of Wisconsin. Leopold spent the next several decades dealing with wildlife management issues, but his interests also expanded to the field of ecology. He was one of the founding members of the Wilderness Society in 1935.

In 1939, the University of Wisconsin created a new Department of Wildlife Management, with Leopold as its first chair. He held this position until his death. The new science and profession of wildlife management wove together the related fields of forestry, agriculture, ecology, biology, zoology, and education. He believed that people, who often destroyed landscapes, could use the same tools to help rebuild the land. Leopold began working on a manuscript of ecological essays that he titled *Great Possessions*. While fighting a fire near his cabin, he died of a heart attack on April 21, 1948. His ecological essays book was retitled and published as *A Sand County Almanac* (1949), and it remains in print today. Leopold is an iconic figure in the ecology movement.

PAUL HOWARD LOGAN (1927–c1965)

Paul Logan was born around 1899 in Tuskegee, Alabama. Much of his family and work background is murky at best. Logan attended either Howard University in Washington, D.C., or Lincoln College, located about 60 miles outside Philadelphia, Pennsylvania, in the 1910s. It is not known if he graduated, or what he studied; however, Forest Service records indicate that he had a B.S.F. (bachelor of science degree in forestry). He joined the U.S. Army in World War I. He most likely began to "pass" in white society at that point. Around 1922 or 1923, he enrolled at Cornell University, in its forestry program. In the summer of 1924, he worked as a fire patrolman on the Bitterroot National Forest, in Montana. Logan was, apparently, the first recorded black person to work as a professional in the Forest Service.

In 1926, he graduated from Cornell University with a B.S in forest management, and he worked for about five months for private lumber companies in Washington before beginning his lengthy career with the Forest Service.

He began his Forest Service career as a junior forester (or "technical assistant") on the Olympic National Forest, in the Pacific Northwest Region, in 1927, where he was a ranger working on timber sales. By 1935, Logan was chief lumberman on the Olympic; he then transferred to the Snoqualmie National Forest. In 1939, he joined the timber management staff in the regional office in Portland, Oregon. With the exception of six months spent on war emergency work in Alaska, in 1942, Logan served in Portland for the next five years. He left Portland for the regional office in Missoula, where he worked from 1947 to 1950. At some point, he moved to regional office in San Francisco as chief check scaler and timber sale inspector. He then did a two-year tour to East Pakistan (now called Bangladesh) for the Foreign Operations Administration to help mechanize timber harvest methods. After leaving East Pakistan, Logan went back to the California Region, doing timber sale preparation and valuation work. By 1964, Logan was heading up sale administration and timber trespass.

ARIEL LUGO (1979–PRESENT)

Ariel Lugo, a native of Mayaguez, Puerto Rico, received his B.S. and M.S. from the University of Puerto Rico and a Ph.D. in ecology from the University North Carolina at Chapel Hill. He worked in Puerto Rico for the Department of Natural Resources doing planning, resource analysis, and basic research. He then went to the University of Puerto Rico to head the center for energy and environmental research, then became acting director of the University of Florida's center for wetlands. Lugo was also appointed a staff member of the federal Council on Environmental Quality. Since 1986, he has served as director of the International Institute of Tropical Forestry, in Puerto Rico. This institute is viewed in the Forest Service as the gateway to cooperation, technology transfer, and information exchange among scientists, government officials, resource managers, and the public in the Caribbean and Latin America area.

Ariel Lugo has published more than 250 professional articles and reports on such subjects as subtropical wet forests, mangrove forests, hardwood forests, and even freshwater prairies. His most recent studies, which he has led, are focused on tropical forests and climate change, remote sensing, the carbon cycle, tropical wetlands, tree plantations and natural forests, wildlife and neotropical migratory birds, and soil and water quality. His international work has resulted in assignments with UNESCO, the World Bank, and the Organization of American States. He is an adviser to many international organizations but finds time to offer lectures and short courses at a variety of academic settings in the United States, Latin America, and even Spain. He has received grants and awards for his many research projects from national and international organizations including the National Science Foundation, the EPA, the Department of Energy, and the Man and the Biosphere programs.

MARGARET MARCH-MOUNT (c1923–1943)

Margaret March-Mount began work on the Bighorn National Forest around 1923 and soon after moved to the Shoshone National Forest, where, in addition to her regular job, she did publicity for the Cody Club, a private society to revive the history of Buffalo Bill. She later worked on Marquette (now Hiawatha) National Forest and then moved to Milwaukee, Wisconsin, in 1929, to work with the Lakes States (now Eastern) Regional Office to coordinate conservation activities, especially that of tree planting, with women's clubs. To promote tree planting efforts, she went on speaking tours before women's garden clubs, schoolchildren, and many civic groups. Before the time of Smokey Bear, she established the "squirrel club" for children to promote fire prevention. March-Mount started the wildly successful "penny pines" project to get student donations to fund the planting of pines on national forests. This program was designed so that the Forest Service would plant 1,000 seedlings for every four dollars received. She moved to the Forest Service national headquarters in the 1930s to continue the tree planting effort nationwide. March-Mount is credited with motivating the national Daughters of the American Revolution (DAR) to promote the planting of 5 million seedlings in 36 states and the District of Columbia. She retired from the Forest Service in 1943 and moved to Hollywood, California. March-Mount, who was awarded an honorary degree in 1950 from the Biltmore Forest School, in North Carolina, was perhaps the most famous Forest Service conservation educator of the early twentieth century.

GEORGE PERKINS MARSH

George Perkins Marsh was born on March 15, 1801, in Woodstock, Vermont. He attended Dartmouth, where he studied European languages. After graduation, he taught at a nearby military academy. He prepared for the law, setting up a law office in Burlington, Vermont, in 1825. He gave up legal practice in 1842. He was elected as a Whig to Congress in 1843 and served four terms. In 1848, because of his strong support for Zachary Taylor, he was appointed U.S. minister to Turkey. He returned home in 1854 and became a lecturer. During the Lincoln administration, Marsh was sent to be the minister plenipotentiary (ambassador) to the new Kingdom of Turkey, after which he served in Turin, Florence, and Rome from 1861 until his death in 1882.

One fact about this remarkable man was that he was a keen observer of nature. Even before he left Vermont, he observed that nature and the forests near his home were disappearing to the axe. The slopes, visible from his home (which is now a National Park Service site), were evidence of the rush to control nature by removing every trace, cutting or burning every tree, bush, and shrub, damming every stream. The result was, according to Marsh, devastation. His travels and observations in parts of Europe and the Middle East convinced him that deforestation and uncontrolled grazing were devastating the land. Marsh was convinced that people had to change their indiscriminate use of nature; otherwise, the earth was doomed to deserts, fire, drought, and every other possible ravage. In 1864, Marsh published his masterful volume *Man and Nature; or, Physical Geography as Modified by Human Action*, which outlined his many observations and called upon people to change their ways. The book was an immediate success (and is still in print today). It was widely read and, as many would say, started the conservation movement in America. As his biographer, David Lowenthal, noted, this book was the first to distinguish between what God had preordained and what people had imposed with or without God's divine wisdom; Marsh believed that people could choose a better way to treat the earth. Marsh slightly revised the book in 1885 and changed the title to *The Earth as Modified by Human Action; a Last Revision of "Man and Nature."*

ROBERT MARSHALL (1925–1933,1937–1939)

Bob Marshall was born on January 2, 1901. He graduated in 1923 from the New York College of Forestry at Syracuse University, then took graduate work at the Harvard Forest (part of Harvard University), and in 1930 received a Ph.D. in plant physiology from Johns Hopkins University. Marshall entered the Forest Service in 1925 as junior forester at the Northern Rocky Mountain Experiment Station. He was promoted to assistant silviculturist two years later. In 1933, he resigned from the Forest Service to become director of forestry for the U.S. Indian Service, in Washington, D.C. While in the Indian Service, Marshall was able to work with the tribes to increase their management of reservation forests, including the establishment of roadless areas on a number of Native American reservations.

He returned to the Forest Service in 1937 as chief of the division of recreation and lands in Washington, D.C. As the first director of recreation, he provided crucial leadership in developing Forest Service recreation policies. Marshall's concern for lower-income people, as evidenced by his book *The People's Forests* (1933), led to the development of a dozen organizational camps. He was also instrumental in the preservation of wilderness areas on national forest lands, as well as establishing a process for identifying large roadless areas that appropriate for designation as wildernesses. He was a walker of renown and considered a 40-mile hike over rough mountain trails a day's pleasure. He once walked 70 miles in a little over 24 hours. He spent over a year in the area near Wiseman, Alaska, where he wrote *Arctic Village* (1933), a description of Eskimo life in a very remote village just north of the Arctic Circle. In 1938 and 1939, he returned to Alaska for his vacations. He died unexpectedly on a train while traveling from Washington, D.C., to New York City in November 1939.

RICHARD EDWIN MCARDLE (1924–1962)

Richard McArdle was born on February 25, 1899, in Lexington, Kentucky. He received his B.S. and M.S. degrees in forestry at the University of Michigan in 1923 and 1924. Just after graduating, he began working for the Forest Service as a silviculturist for the Pacific Northwest Forest and Range Experiment Station, in Portland, Oregon. McArdle took three years off, beginning in 1927, to complete his Ph.D., returning to Portland to the research station. He left the Forest Service in 1934 to become the dean of the University of Idaho's School of Forestry. He then returned to the Forest Service to serve as director of a new forest and range experiment station at Fort Collins, Colorado, then as director of the Appalachian (now Southern Research) Station, in Asheville, North Carolina. He moved to the Washington, D.C., office in 1944, then served as the eighth chief of the Forest Service, serving from July 1952 to March 1962.

McArdle, the first chief to hold a Ph.D. and to have been a researcher, felt the need for a balanced management of the national forests. He also pushed for long-range plans on the national forests and in the research branch. During McArdle's term as chief, the *Timber Resource Review* was published, which, for the first time, evaluated the total timber resources in the United States. Management of the national forests came under public scrutiny, especially for the emphasis placed by the Forest Service on timber management to meet the increasing demand for the post–World War II housing boom. The result of this public concern was passage of the landmark Multiple-Use Sustained-Yield Act of 1960, which established broad policy for the development and administration of the national forests in the public interest.

McArdle was successful in increasing intensive management of the national forests, as well as providing for reforestation of logged and other lands, curbing mining and grazing abuses, and accelerating various recreation projects. During his tenure, the Forest Service was assigned the management of 4 million acres of western plains lands, which it organized as national grasslands. McArdle was also instrumental in upgrading Forest Service personnel, hiring new specialists to bring about intensive management, and increasing the professionalism of employees. He improved relations with the timber industry by backing away from earlier proposals to regulate timber harvesting practices on private lands. After his retirement, McArdle served on the boards of various forestry organizations, served as the executive director of the National Institute of Public Affairs, and gave lectures at various colleges and universities.

WILLIAM JOHN MCGEE

WJ (he used no periods between his initials—and was sometimes referred to as "no stop McGee") McGee was born on April 17, 1853, near Farley, Iowa. He studied Latin, German, mathematics, law, astronomy, and surveying at home. Later, he focused his studies on archeology and geology. Largely self-taught, he corresponded with established scholars, especially in the area of his greatest interest—geology. This was at a time when there was little university training available in most of the areas that WJ was most interested in. Between 1871 and 1881, he conducted geologic and topographic surveys of northeastern Iowa. By virtue of his studies on glaciation in the upper Mississippi Valley, he went to work for the U.S. Geological

Survey in 1883, then headed by Major John Wesley Powell. Ten years later, he was hired as an ethnologist at the Bureau of American Ethnology (BAE) but quickly set himself up as "ethnologist in charge" and heir apparent to Powell, who was rapidly declining in health.

McGee's direct involvement in the forestry and conservation movement probably began in 1901, when he accompanied Secretary of Agriculture James Wilson, Gifford Pinchot, Frederick Newell, and Joseph Holmes on a 10-day trip to the southern Appalachian mountain areas. They were there to investigate forested areas for a proposed Appalachian Forest Reserve. After his resignation from the BAE in 1903, McGee's personal life declined; he was now jobless and plagued by cancer and separated permanently from his wife. On March 14, 1907, President Theodore Roosevelt created the Inland Waterways Commission, and McGee was elected vice chairman and secretary, posts he held until his death. The opportunity enabled him to make two lasting contributions to the conservation movement: The first was his scientific view of a river and its watershed as an ecosystem that tied together forestry, soil, and water conservation in an ecological fabric. The second was his perspective that conservation was more than wise use—it was government management of resources for the common good, which fit perfectly into the model of conservation espoused by Gifford Pinchot and President Roosevelt. McGee died in 1912.

JOHN RICHARD MCGUIRE (1941–1979)

John McGuire was born on April 20, 1916, in Milwaukee, Wisconsin. He graduated with a degree in forestry from the University of Minnesota. He briefly went to work for the Forest Service, then decided to go back to school to be a research forester. He earned his M.F. degree from Yale University in 1941 and worked at the Forest Service research facility on campus. When World War II broke out, he entered the army, moving up to the rank of major with the Corps of Engineers in the Pacific Theater. After the war, he returned to the Forest Service in a research position at the Northeastern Forest Experiment Station, in New Haven, Connecticut. He moved in 1950 to a research station at Upper Darby, Pennsylvania, while completing his M.A. in economics at the University of Pennsylvania. In 1962, McGuire became director of the Pacific Southwest Forest and Range Experiment Station in Berkeley, California. He moved to the national headquarters in Washington in 1967, then was chosen as the tenth chief in 1972, during a time of increasing environmental awareness by the public. He served as chief until 1979.

While serving as chief, McGuire made changes to strengthen the roles of the branches of state and private forestry and that of research to help implement the Forest and Rangeland Renewable Resources Planning Act (RPA) of 1974 and the National Forest Management Act of 1976. McGuire faced increasing opposition to forestry practices being carried out on the national forests. Most notable were the congressional hearings over clearcutting on the national forests. The hearings came about after a report by a committee headed by Arnold Bolle, dean of the

University of Montana School of Forestry, on clearcutting on the Bitterroot National Forest, in Montana, and a lawsuit over clearcutting on the Monongahela National Forest, in West Virginia. McGuire was instrumental in having the Forest Service review, then change its forest management practices and modify and integrate its methods of land management. Major issues facing the chief were the roadless area review and evaluation (RARE and RARE II), the mounting controversy over the management of national forests, and the new direction from Congress that mandated planning at the national forest, regional, and national levels through the Resources Planning Act of 1974 and the National Forest Management Act of 1976. The 1973 Endangered Species Act was passed not long after he became chief—and the controversy about implementation of this act reverberates to the present. The 1975 Eastern Wilderness Act was signed into law, establishing several million acres of new wilderness, many in the eastern states. Additional legislation passed late in McGuire's tenure as chief included the Cooperative Forestry Assistance Act of 1978, the Renewable Resources Extension Act of 1978, and the Forest and Rangeland Renewable Resources Research Act of 1978. These three laws provided an updated authority for forestry research and forestry programs not related to public lands.

EDITH MOSHER (1905–1920)

Edith R. Mosher was born in 1872 on a farm near Centreville, in southern Michigan. She studied both literature and science and graduated from Ypsilanti State Normal School (later to become Eastern Michigan University) in 1892. She began teaching kindergarten in Grand Rapids, Michigan, and at the New York University summer school. In 1900, at the age of 26, she bought a round-trip ticket to attend the National Teachers' Association meeting in Washington, sold the ticket on arriving, and took a Civil Service examination. She was employed by the Bureau of the Census from 1900 to 1902. From 1902 to 1905, she worked for the USDI General Land Office. On March 1, 1905, she went to work for the Forest Service, performing miscellaneous clerical duties. She was promoted to the position of clerk, effective April 2, 1910. In May 1911, Mosher was promoted again and put in charge of boundary records. She resigned from the Forest Service in 1920.

She is considered the founder of environmental education in the Forest Service. In her writings, she used her initials, "E.R.," for fear that an article by a woman would not be published. Mosher saw the lack of teaching aids in conservation, so she wrote a 76-page booklet, "Forest Study in the Primary Grades," that proved to be very popular. This set the stage for environmental education and working with schoolchildren for years to come.

JOHN MUIR

John Muir was born in Scotland in 1849. He moved to Wisconsin, where he attended the University of Wisconsin. After recovering from a serious accident to his eyes, he felt compelled to undertake a five-month, 1,000-mile walk from Indiana to the tip of Florida. The following year, Muir voyaged to California, living at times in the wondrous Yosemite Valley, where he studied botany and the geology of the new state park. He settled in Martinez, California, where he became a successful farmer. Returning to his work as an advocate for wilderness and forest preservation, he wrote many articles about the need to transfer Yosemite State Park (the core area of Yosemite National Park) back to the federal government and rename it a national park. The effort was partially successful in 1890 when the "donut" area of national forest land around the state park was made into Yosemite National Park (the state park area was returned to the federal government and added to the national park in 1906). Two years later, he helped to organize and become the first president of the Sierra Club.

Muir was an eloquent spokesperson for the preservation movement in the late 1800s and early 1900s. Even today his name evokes a deeply felt admiration and resolve. He wrote many articles for national publication, as well as several books. His writings addressed many controversial issues, including the notion that the Earth and its resources had been made to people to use and to use up for the benefit of society. Muir argued that all living things are equally important parts of the land and that animals and plants have as much right to live and survive as people. Unlike many of the nature writers of his time, Muir tended to write about the environment as he had experienced it. In an 1897 article for the *Atlantic Monthly*, Muir wrote, "Any fool can destroy trees. They cannot run away; and if they could, they would still be destroyed,—chased and hunted down as long as fun or a dollar could be got out of their bark hides…. God has cared for these trees, saved them … but he cannot save them from fools,—only Uncle Sam can do that."

Muir and Gifford Pinchot were part of the 1896 national forest commission that traveled through the West looking at existing and potential forest reserves. Despite their differences over sheep grazing and, eventually, the construction of Hetch Hetchy Dam, in Yosemite National Park, they remained friends and often wrote to each other about their wonderful experiences together in the western mountains. Muir lost his last major battle, which concerned Hetch Hetchy Dam. The battle was ignited by the authorization by Congress, in 1913, of the creation of the Hetch Hetchy dam and reservoir in the picturesque valley just north of Yosemite Valley but still within the park boundaries. Political leaders in San Francisco, especially after the 1906 earthquake, were successful in winning support for a dam to create the reservoir, which would supply clean water and power to the city. Muir died in 1914, some two years before the dam was constructed in the scenic valley. There are many features on national forests and national parks named for Muir, including Muir Glacier in Alaska and Muir Woods National Monument in California.

EDWARD NORFOLK MUNNS (1912–c1951)

Ed Munns was born in St. Louis, Missouri, on January 13, 1889. He graduated from the Bradley Polytechnic Institute in Illinois, then earned his master's degree in forestry from the University of Michigan. He joined the Forest Service in 1912, where his first assignment was as forest assistant on the Angeles National Forest. This area was composed of the headwaters of critical watersheds in southern California. His observations on California's watershed conditions and problems, brought together in his comprehensive report to the California State Legislature in 1923 during a temporary assignment as assistant state forester, laid the groundwork for many of the state conservation policies and programs.

During World War I, while detached to Washington, he took advantage of his extensive travels to observe and record and to question everyone on forest and streamflow conditions. In addition, his avid reading on many aspects of land use gave him a keen insight into the close ties between forestry and industrial, agricultural, and water problems, and their social aspects. This extensive knowledge led to his selection as chief of the division of forest influences when it was established in 1937 to meet the serious need for a systematic nationwide attack on the causes of floods and erosion and the development of effective methods to overcome them. Prior to that time, he had served as chief of the office of experiment stations (1925–1928) and, subsequently, as chief of the office (later the division) of silvics. He wrote extensively and is probably best known for his two-volume bibliography *A Selected Bibliography of North American Forestry* (1940), the first comprehensive listing of books, articles, and research publications to that time.

FREDERICK ERSKINE OLMSTED (1900–1911)

Fritz Olmsted was born in Hartford, Connecticut, on November 8, 1872. He graduated from the Sheffield Scientific School of Yale University in 1894 and joined the U.S. Geological Survey. Olmstead went abroad, where he studied under Sir Dietrich Brandis in India and Germany. Olmsted received a forestry diploma from the University of Munich in 1899. Gifford Pinchot appointed Olmsted an agent in the Division of Forestry on July 1, 1900. In 1898–1902, he developed working plans for a number of large timberland owners in New York, Tennessee, Georgia, Arkansas, and North Carolina. Olmsted was made assistant forester in 1903. This was without any doubt the most important single line of work undertaken by the government forest service because it laid the foundation for the present national forest system. Olmsted had a genius for getting the best out of the men working under his direction, being chary of orders, guiding his subordinates rather than instructing them, and making every man feel and accept full responsibility.

Olmsted was in a position to be one of the leaders in the Washington office when the Transfer Act of 1905 placed the national forests under the newly created Forest Service. His first work was to organize and build up an effective inspection system. In 1906, he became the chief inspector of the Forest Service. The following year, Olmsted became inspector of the California District, headquartered in San Francisco. He resigned from the Forest Service in June 1911, then went East and joined with Fisher and Bryant in Boston in a firm of consulting foresters. He worked in eastern hardwoods for three years, then moved to California as a consulting forester. He organized the Tamalpias Fire Protective Association and was its directing head and was employed as forester by the Diamond Match Company to introduce and supervise conservative cutting on the company's California holdings.

R. MAX PETERSON (1949–1987)

Max Peterson was born near Doniphan, Missouri, on July 25, 1927. During World War II, he served with naval aviation. In 1949, Peterson received a bachelor's degree in civil engineering from the University of Missouri. He went to work as an engineer in the Plumas National Forest, in California, then worked on several other national forests in California. In 1958, Peterson was awarded a Rockefeller Foundation fellowship to Harvard University, where he earned a master's degree in public administration in 1959. He returned to work at the Northern Region in Missoula, Montana. Two years later, he was moved to the national headquarters, where he remained until 1966, when he was transferred back to California to serve as regional engineer. He was made regional forester for the Southern Region in 1972, then returned to Washington, D.C., two years later. Peterson was appointed the eleventh chief of the Forest Service on June 27, 1979, and served in this capacity until 1987.

Max Peterson was the first nonforester (and the first engineer) named to head the Forest Service. He served during a time of increasing turmoil and criticism of the Forest Service. In the face of severely reduced budgets, he had to reduce the Forest Service workforce by 25 percent—a daunting challenge under the best of conditions. There were also a mounting number of discrimination complaints, lawsuits, and litigation against the agency. Major accomplishments during his era were the establishment of regulations for implementing the National Forest Management Act of 1976; his handling of the aftermath of the RARE II decision and of the "timber depression" and housing slump of the early 1980s; his concerns about the use of herbicides and pesticides on the national forests; his influence on various wilderness bills before Congress; his handling of the growing concerns about old growth logging, below-cost sales (especially in Alaska), timber relief or "bail-out," and the needs of threatened and endangered species; and, last but not least, his response to an erupting volcano. Public trust in the Forest Service's ability to effectively manage the national forests was declining because of these multiple and sometime intractable issues, but Peterson was able to oversee the changing management of the national forests in these trying times. After his retirement, he was very active, becoming the executive director of the International Association of Fish and Wildlife Agencies and serving on the national boards of several natural resource organizations.

GIFFORD PINCHOT (1898–1910)

Gifford Pinchot, was born on August 11, 1865, in Simsbury, Connecticut. His New York City–based family was composed of well-to-do upper-class merchants, politicians, and landowners. Pinchot, as a young boy, took advantage of several opportunities to visit foreign countries, as well as gain a good education at some of the best eastern schools. When he entered Yale, in 1885, his father asked, "How would you like to be a forester?" At this time, not a single American had made forestry a profession. Gifford stated, "I had no more conception of what it meant to be a forester than the man in the moon…. But at least a forester worked in the woods and with the woods—and I loved the woods and everything about them…. My Father's suggestion settled the question [of a career] in favor of forestry."

Neither Yale nor any other university offered a degree or even a course in forestry, so Pinchot, after graduation, decided to study the subject in Nancy, France. After a year of forestry school, he returned to the United States to prepare for his lifelong work and interest. He worked for three years as a resident forester for George Vanderbilt's Biltmore Forest Estate at Asheville, North Carolina. In 1895–1897, he became involved with the national forest commission created by the National Academy of Sciences to travel through the West to investigate forest public land for possible forest reserves. He was named the fourth chief of the Division of Forestry in 1898.

The management of the forest reserves was transferred from the Department of the Interior to Agriculture and the new Forest Service in 1905. The first chief, or forester, of the new Forest Service was Gifford Pinchot. Pinchot, with President Theodore Roosevelt's willing approval, restructured and professionalized the management of the national forests, as well as greatly increased their area and number. He had a strong hand in guiding the fledgling organization toward the utilitarian philosophy of the "greatest good for the greatest number." Pinchot added the phrase "in the long run" to emphasize that forest management consists of long-term decisions. During his period in office, the Forest Service and the national forests grew spectacularly. In 1905, the forest reserves numbered 60 units covering 56 million acres; in 1910, there were 150 national forests covering 172 million acres. The pattern of effective organization and management was set during Pinchot's administration, and "conservation" (an idea he popularized) of natural resources in the broad sense of wise use became a widely known concept and an accepted national goal.

Gifford Pinchot is generally regarded as the "father" of American conservation because of his great and unrelenting concern for the protection of the American forests. He was the primary founder of the Society of American Foresters, which first met at his home in Washington in November 1900. He served as chief with great distinction, motivating and providing leadership in the management of natural resources and protection of the national forests. He continued as forester until 1910, when he was fired by President Taft in a controversy over coal claims in Alaska. He was replaced by Henry "Harry" S. Graves.

ALBERT FRANKLIN POTTER (1901–1920)

Albert Potter was born on November 14, 1859, in the Sierra foothills of California; because of health problems, he moved to eastern Arizona when he was 24. He started in the cattle business near Holbrook in 1880 but by 1896 had switched to sheep raising and was soon a down-to-earth leader among sheep owners, probably the best-organized livestock interest in the West in the 1890s and early 1900s. In 1898, Potter spent some time in Washington conferring with USDI General Land Office and USDA Bureau of Forestry officials. The Bureau of Forestry leaders, especially Pinchot, were so impressed by Potter that they asked him to return to Washington and assist in administering the new forest reserves in the West. Three years later, Potter disposed of his grazing interests, then returned to Washington in October 1901 to become the "grazing expert" in the USDA Bureau of Forestry that was under Pinchot's leadership. Potter was the first cattle owner and westerner to hold a high post in the Bureau of Forestry. He organized the Forest Service grazing policies and remained in charge of this vital work for 19 years.

Potter became an assistant forester early in 1907 and an associate forester—the second highest post in the agency—in early 1910 after Gifford Pinchot and Overton W. Price were fired by President Taft. Potter served briefly as acting chief forester. He might have been the chief forester except for Pinchot's successful effort to put Henry S. Graves in that position. Potter again became acting chief forester during World War I, from June 1917 to February 1918, when Graves was with the U.S. Army in France as head of the 20th Engineers (Forestry). One of Potter's most important contributions to the Forest Service was his fight to establish the power of government to maintain its rules and regulations. By the spring of 1920 when Graves resigned, Potter concluded that his mission had been accomplished and others should take over his duties. He retired on April 15 to southern California, where he enjoyed many years of deep-sea fishing. He died on January 1, 1944.

OVERTON WESTFELDT PRICE (1899–1910)

Born on January 27, 1873, in Liverpool, England, Overton Price began work at Biltmore Estate near Asheville, North Carolina, under the direction of Gifford Pinchot, the Estate's forest planner. One year later, Price went to Germany to obtain technical forestry training. Two years at the University of Munich were supplemented by a year of practical experience in various European forests. This work abroad was largely guided by Sir Dietrich Brandis. On his return to America, Price engaged in practical work at Biltmore, then under the direction of Carl A. Schenck, and in the north woods.

In June 1899, he entered the USDA Division of Forestry as a forestry agent, and a year later he was promoted to the position of superintendent of working plans. He was one of the founders of the Society of American Foresters, in 1900. A year later, Price became assistant chief in the new USDA Bureau of Forestry. In January 1910, his connection with the Forest Service was terminated along with that of Gifford Pinchot by President Taft over the controversy about coal lands in Alaska. Shortly afterward, he became treasurer, and, subsequently, vice president, of the National Conservation Association, which had been founded by Pinchot.

At the time of his death by suicide, in 1914, he was a consulting forester to the government of British Columbia, Canada, and a forestry adviser to the estate of the late George W. Vanderbilt. Much of the Biltmore Estate forestlands were donated to the Forest Service in 1914, and they became part of the new Pisgah National Forest in 1916. As a technical forester, Price made substantial contributions to the development of the national forest system by directing the work of others and by the influence he exerted on the organization of the work of the federal forestry.

SAMUEL J. RECORD (1904–1911)

Born in Crawfordsville, Indiana, on March 10, 1881, Record received his B.A. and M.A. degrees from Wabash College in 1903 and 1906. From July 1, 1904, to April 30, 1907, Record served as assistant forest range in the Forest Service. In 1907, he was made chief of the section of reconnaissance, then supervisor of the national forests in Arkansas. He was again appointed forest assistant July 20, 1910, which position he held until March 31, 1911.

In 1910–1911, Record was instructor in forestry at the Yale Forest School. He received his appointment as assistant professor of forest products at Yale during 1911, earning a full professorship in 1917. In charge of tropical forestry since 1923, he was named as dean of the school of forestry in 1939, which position he held at the time of his death, though his retirement from the deanship had been announced. In 1921, he became a senior member of the Society of American Foresters and was elected a fellow in 1940. He served on the editorial board of *Forestry Quarterly* from 1912 until it became the *Journal of Forestry* in 1917.

MARK E. REY

Mark Rey is a native of Canton, Ohio. He holds a B.S. in wildlife management, a B.S. degree in forestry, and a M.S. in natural resources policy and administration, all from the University of Michigan in Ann Arbor. In 1974–1975 he worked as a staff assistant for the USDI Bureau of Land Management in Billings, Montana, and Washington, D.C. From 1976 to 1984, he served in several positions with the American Paper Institute/National Forest Products Association, a consortium of national trade associations. He served as vice president for public forestry programs for the National Forest Products Association from 1984 to 1989. In 1989–1992, he served as executive director of the American Forest Resource Alliance. From 1992 until 1994, Rey served as vice president for forest resources for the American Forest and Paper Association.

Beginning in January 1995, Rey served as a staff member with the U.S. Senate Committee on Energy and Natural Resources. He was the lead staff person for the committee's work on national forest policy and Forest Service administration. He has been directly involved in virtually all of the forestry and conservation legislation considered during the past several sessions of Congress, with principal responsibility for a number of public lands bills. On October 2, 2001, he was sworn in as the USDA Under Secretary for Natural Resources and Environment by Agriculture Secretary Ann M. Veneman. In that position, he oversees the USDA Forest Service and USDA Natural Resources Conservation Service.

AUDREY RICHARDS (1917–1951)

Audrey Richards began her career as a schoolteacher in her home town of St. Marys, Ohio, but left after three years to study botany at Miami University in Ohio. She received her bachelor's degree in 1912, a master's in 1914 from that institution, and then a doctorate from the University of Wisconsin in 1922. For more than 30 years, Richards served as one of the foremost wood products pathologists. She began this career in 1917, when she was appointed an assistant in forest pathology. For seven years, she was the only woman in the Forest Products Lab; as branch chief she held the highest position ever achieved by a woman. In World War I, she was primarily concerned with the pulp and pulpwood industry and conducted research in Canadian, New York, and Wisconsin mills. Richards was placed in charge of the pathology unit at the Laboratory in 1928, a position she held until retirement.

Among the many projects that she was involved in were efforts to determine the effect of fungi on the wood decking of an aircraft carrier; how to protect wood from decay in the tropics; how to prevent stains; how to differentiate discolorations in wood; why the floor of the library rotted away two years after it was built; why fence posts decay; and why wood pulp, veneer, and magazines get moldy. Much of the work begun at the Lab was basic and resulted in fundamental knowledge for future research. Richards was author or coauthor of publications covering such subjects as the relation between durability and chemical composition of wood, the effect of decay on the chemical composition of wood, and the comparative resistance of wood-destroying fungi to various preservatives. She worked with Dr. Catherine Duncan to establish a standardized method of evaluating wood preservatives. More than 30,000 test specimens were examined in the course of this work. She was a frequent contributor to meetings of the American Wood-Preservers' Association and for years was the only woman member.

ARTHUR CUMING RINGLAND (1900–1917)

Arthur Ringland was born September 29, 1982, in Brooklyn, New York. He signed on in 1900 as a student assistant in the Division of Forestry under Gifford Pinchot. He entered Yale Forest School in 1903. He received the Master of Forestry degree in 1905 and entered the USDA Forest Service. First assigned to the Lincoln Forest Reserve, in New Mexico, he surveyed and posted its boundaries. He was transferred to the section of forest boundaries in Washington, D.C., during 1906, and became chief of the section in 1907. In 1908, when the Forest Service established six regional districts in the West, he became the first district forester of District 3, in Albuquerque, New Mexico.

His Forest Service career was interrupted in 1917 by assignment as captain in the 10th Engineer Regiment (Forestry) of World War I. After the war, he was chosen by Herbert Hoover, head of the American Relief Administration Mission, to supervise the agency's efforts in Czechoslovakia. During 1925–1929, he was executive secretary of the National Conference on Outdoor Recreation. In 1931, he became the European forestry representative of the USDA, in effect the first agricultural attaché; he was assigned to the U.S. embassy in London. In this capacity he traveled widely in Europe, representing the United States in forestry matters. Upon creation of the Civilian Conservation Corps, in 1933, he was appointed conservation liaison officer of the 4th Corps Army Area, at Fort McPherson, Georgia. During 1937–1940, he served as chairman of the Watershed Control and Flood Coordinating Committee of the USDA. After retiring, he was active in a number of public agencies. He served as a trustee of the American Freedom from Hunger Foundation and as an adviser to President Kennedy's American Food for Peace Council and was active with the Citizens Committee on Natural Resources.

PAUL H. ROBERTS (1915–c1951)

Roberts was born August 6, 1891, on his parents' ranch in Maxwell, Nebraska. He graduated in 1915 from the University of Nebraska with a B.S. in forestry with range specialization. Roberts's first job in the Forest Service was at Magdalena, New Mexico, in 1915, doing range work. By 1916, he was given the task of writing a range management plan for the Sitgreaves Forest, in Arizona. After World War I, he returned as inspector of grazing. He became supervisor of the Sitgreaves National Forest in 1922. In 1931, he was transferred to Washington, D.C., to become the first administrative officer for the branch of research.

In the fall of 1934, the Roberts was directed to devise a plan to grow trees on the wind-blown prairies in North and South Dakota, Nebraska, Kansas, Oklahoma, and Texas. The Great Plains Shelterbelt Project, also known as the Prairies States Forestry Project, was under way. Before it was completed, some 223 million trees would be planted in 18,599 miles of shelterbelts on 30,000 farms. Up to 10,000 Works Progress Administration enrollees (mostly farmers in the affected areas) and Civilian Conservation Corps enrollees were employed during the planting season. Paul was associate director, later director, of the project from the beginning until its transfer to the Soil Conservation Service, in 1942.

In 1942, the Forest Service was assigned the war emergency project of producing natural rubber from the bushy plant, guayule (*Parthenium argentatum*). Roberts led the project as associate director at Salinas, California. Roberts become director of the project two years later. By the end of the war, the guayule project had produced about 3 million pounds of natural rubber. He was transferred to regional office at Missoula, Montana, in 1946. There he worked on the efforts to control outbreaks of the Douglas-fir tussock moth in northern Idaho through a massive aerial spraying program. Then, in 1950, he was in charge of a spruce beetle project in Colorado. Beetles were attacking Englemann spruce that had been blown down in 1939 on the White River Plateau. In this huge project, workers using hand pumps sprayed orthodichlorobenzine on some 784,000 individual trees.

F. DALE ROBERTSON (1961–1993)

Dale Robertson was born in Denmark, Arkansas, on July 17, 1940. He joined the Forest Service in 1961 after receiving a degree in forestry from the University of Arkansas. His early assignments were in the South. After moving to the Washington office, he completed a master's degree in public administration from the American University in Washington, D.C., in 1970. Shortly afterward, he was reassigned to the Pacific Northwest, returning in 1980 to the Washington office. After the retirement of Max Peterson, in January 1987, Dale Robertson was appointed the twelfth chief of the Forest Service.

Soon after his appointment as chief, Robertson had to face a public wary of anything the Forest Service had to say or proposed to do. Especially troubling was growing controversy about the harvest of old growth (ancient forest) trees in the Pacific Northwest and the protection of several species of animals and plants that fell under the protection of the Endangered Species Act of 1973. He appointed several task forces to consider all options, but when the decisions were made they did not satisfy everyone. Several new resource programs were developed under Robertson's leadership, including the highly successful "Rise to the Future," a program designed to enhance the production of fish on the national forests.

Realizing that traditional forestry had "hit the wall," Robertson led efforts by the Forest Service to find new and creative ways to manage the national forests, especially by emphasizing noncommodity (nontimber) resources and "new forestry," "new perspectives," and ecosystem management. Under his direction, the Forest Service led the way into the reduction and even elimination of clearcutting and the establishment of an ecologically based management system for the national forests. The new Clinton administration believed that Robertson was not advancing changes fast enough in the Forest Service. As Jack Ward Thomas said, Robertson was caught on the edge of a paradigm shift in the agency. "He was trying to take us there. Unfortunately, his string ran out before he quite got the agency there." Robertson and Associate Chief George Leonard were reassigned (many say fired) in November 1993 and transferred to the Department of Agriculture.

FILIBERT ROTH

Filibert Roth was born in Wurttemberg, Germany, on April 20, 1858. His parents settled first in Michigan but soon moved to Wisconsin. In 1882, he entered the University of Michigan, where he graduated with a bachelor's degree in 1890. Roth was hired by the USDA Division of Forestry in Washington, D.C. There he studied forestry by reading the German masters. When the Cornell School of Forestry was founded, in 1898, with Fernow as the head, Roth went there as assistant professor. After controversy about a plan to clearcut state forest land in the

Adirondacks, the forestry school was closed by the New York State legislature in 1901. Returning to government service, Roth was appointed superintendent of the national forest reserves, in the USDI General Land Office (GLO). He was able to create a professional organization called Division R (for forest reserves) and, with the help of the Forest Service, produced the first manual for management of the reserves. The 98-page book was called the *Forest Reserve Manual* (1902). It set the basis for management of the forest reserves until they were transferred to the new USDA Forest Service in 1905.

But the lure of teaching was strong, and two years he later quit the GLO to teach at the new department of forestry at the University of Michigan. As the leading technical forester in the state, he took an active interest Michigan forestry matters. He was made state forest warden, in charge of the Au Sable and Houghton State Forests, and outlined the fundamental ways and means of rebuilding the clearcut and largely destroyed pine forests. In 1908, a Commission of Inquiry was ordered by the Michigan legislature. Using the findings and recommendations of this Commission, the legislature established an entirely new scheme for handling the bankrupt forest lands of the state; the damaged lands were deeded to the state, replanted, and used for public forestry purposes—and soon there were some 50 state forests.

CHARLES SPRAGUE SARGENT

Charles S. Sargent was born April 24, 1841. He graduated in 1862 from Harvard near the bottom of his class. He served as an officer in the Union Army, after which he spent three years traveling around Europe. His horticultural and agricultural interests were piqued after his return to Boston. In 1873, he was appointed the first director of the Arnold Arboretum, in Jamaica Plain, Massachusetts. He served for the next 55 years as director of the Arboretum. Sargent built up an elaborate network of botanists with whom he corresponded and whom he occasionally employed as collectors and taxonomists. Sargent's knowledge of forest trees and shrubs laid the foundation of dendrology, without which there would be no science of forestry.

In 1880, he prepared the section on American forests that would appear in the Tenth U.S. Census. Sargent's study, titled the *Report on the Forests of North America* (1884), presented some of the first information on the distribution, habits, and taxonomy of 412 species of trees. The *Report* became a standard reference work. In this volume, Sargent warned that, if timber management policies were not changed from devastating clearcutting followed by massive fires and erosion, the nation would experience what would become known as a timber famine. From 1887 until 1897, he edited *Garden and Forest,* a weekly magazine that discussed many issues related to forestry, trees, national parks, and the need for national forests for the general public. Sargent supervised the publication of *Silva of North America* (14 volumes printed between 1891 and 1902). Sargent also wrote the shorter *Manual of the Trees of North America* (1905).

In 1895, Sargent agreed to chair a National Academy of Sciences commission to examine the government timberland/forest reserve policy. The commission recommended to the Department of the Interior and President Cleveland the establishment of 13 additional or expanded forest reserves. When the president proclaimed these reserves, on February 22, 1897, the action aroused a huge outcry in the West. This, in turn, led to the Organic Act of 1897, which suspended the new reserves for nine months but also allowed their management. The final commission report, published later in 1897, called for conservation and the establishment of wise forest harvesting policies. One of the members of the 1896 national forest commission was Gifford Pinchot, who served as the commission secretary and with whom Sargent had many disagreements. Sargent was the leading spirit in saving the redwood forests of northern California and in establishing Glacier National Park, in Montana.

CARL ALWIN SCHENCK

Carl Schenk was born on March 26, 1868, in Darmstadt, Germany. He received degrees from the Institute of Technology in Darmstadt and the University of Tubingen and earned a Ph.D. at the University of Giessen. He was a forestry assistant to Sir Dietrich Brandis and Sir William Schlich. Gifford Pinchot and Sir Dietrich Brandis recommended Schenck to fill the role of chief forester for George Vanderbilt at his 120,000-acre Biltmore Forest property, near Asheville, North Carolina. George Vanderbilt hired Schenck in 1895. The Biltmore Forest was the first large tract of forestland in the United States to come under professional forest management (the Biltmore Forest today is part of the Pisgah National Forest). On September 1, 1898, he opened the first forest school in the United States, only a month before the Cornell School of Forestry opened. Within 15 years, the school would graduate more than 400 trained foresters who introduced scientific forestry methods throughout North America. The Biltmore Forest School emphasized the practical side of forestry, rather than the theoretical. Students were required to devote an entire year to field operations and were required to intern on the Biltmore estate or in the timber industry. Forestry schools soon opened at the University of Minnesota, Pennsylvania State University, Yale (founded in 1900 by a grant from James Pinchot, Gifford Pinchot's father), and many other universities.

Schenck was fired in 1909 after an argument with the Biltmore Estate staff, and in the face of Vanderbilt's anger over a hunting and fishing lease that Schenck signed. Schenck continued to operate the Biltmore Forest School for another five years but closed it in 1913 for lack of enrollment. He then returned to Germany, became an officer in the Germany Army during World War I, and worked as a consulting forester and teacher after the war. After World War II, he was hired by the American occupation forces as chief forester for the Greater Hesse area.

EDWARD A. SHERMAN (1905–1940)

Edward Sherman was born in 1871 in Humboldt County, Iowa. He graduated from Iowa State College of Agriculture and Mechanic Arts at Ames, with a B.A. degree in 1896, and was awarded a M.S. degree in forestry in 1927. Except for service in the U.S. Army during the Spanish-American War, in 1898, he was in newspaper work from 1896 until 1903, when he entered government forest work as supervisor in the General Land Office. In 1905, he became a member of the Forest Service when it was established in the Department of Agriculture. During the succeeding 10 years, he was in charge of various western national forests, chief inspector of the Northern Rocky Mountain Region, and regional forester of the Intermountain Region, with headquarters in Ogden, Utah.

Transferred to the Washington office in 1915, he was placed temporarily in charge of the division of lands and was promoted a few weeks later to the position of assistant forester in charge of the division. In 1920, he was made associate forester, and he became assistant chief and adviser in 1935. In this important position, Sherman personally inspected every one of the 161 national forests in the country and gained personal knowledge of land exchange and acquisition matters, to which he devoted years of work. He also worked on most of the special national projects in the Forest Service program, including the classification of national forest lands and establishment of national forest boundaries.

FERDINAND AUGUSTUS SILCOX (1905–1917, 1933–1939)

Ferdinand Silcox was born on Christmas Day in 1882, at Columbus, Georgia. He graduated from the College of Charleston, South Carolina, in 1903, with honors in chemistry and sociology. He went on to take a master's degree in forestry at the Yale Forest School in 1905. He served with the Forest Service in the northern Rockies after graduation. Silcox entered the Engineer (Forestry) branch of the U.S. Army in 1917 as a captain and left as a major. He was selected to handle labor problems at the shipyards in the Puget Sound and Columbia River districts during much of World War I. After the war, Silcox worked in the private sector for 11 years as a director of industrial printing relations in Chicago and New York before being appointed as chief. The Great Depression was in full swing when Silcox took over as the fifth chief of the Forest Service; he led the agency during some of its most difficult times. He was able to effectively help millions of unemployed workers deal with the Depression through the Civilian Conservation Corps (CCC) and Works Projects Administration (WPA) projects in the national forests. The Forest Service provided space for the 200-man CCC camps, thousands of work projects, and experienced project leaders. More than 2 million unemployed young men enrolled in the CCC during the nine years of its existence.

Extensive cooperation with the U.S. Army, the Department of Labor, and other federal and state land management agencies was needed to get these programs to work effectively. His previous work for the army and in the private sector proved to be invaluable for getting the job done. An able administrator, Silcox treated his associates and subordinates with great consideration and kindness. He had an enduring humanitarian viewpoint, which resulted in his doing his best to help the "have-nots" in society. His ideas of forest conservation and advocacy in favor of public regulation of timber cutting all brought strong opposition as well as loyal support.

Silcox's contributions to the forest conservation movement were many, but especially significant was his success in focusing public attention on the conservation problems of private forestland ownership. The Forest Service also made a study of western range use and surveyed forested watersheds for flood control. Under the Shelterbelt or Prairie States Forestry Project, 217 million acres were planted by 33,000 plains farmers under the auspices of the Works Progress Administration and the Civilian Conservation Corps.

JEFF M. SIRMON (1958–1994)

Jeff Sirmon was born on October 14, 1935, in Franklin, Alabama. He graduated with an engineering degree from Auburn University in 1958, at the same time serving as project engineer for the National Forests in Alabama. In 1961, he became assistant forest engineer for the National Forests of South Carolina. After a short term in the U.S. Army, in 1962, he became engineer in roads and highways for the Southern Region. In 1963, he transferred to the Lassen NF as forest engineer, moving in 1967 to the Pacific Southwest Region as engineering development officer. He went to the Washington office in 1969, serving as branch chief in the engineering division. Three years later, he was named assistant regional forester for engineering in the Northern Region. In 1974, he became deputy regional forester for the Intermountain Region, and he was promoted to regional forester in 1980.

Sirmon was appointed regional forester for the Pacific Northwest Region in 1982. He was a major influence in the restoration and recovery of the Mount St. Helens area. There he oversaw the worst part of the "timber depression" that occurred in the early 1980s, when the timber industry was expecting that the record inflation would continue at the same time that the NFMA forest planning effort and the RARE II controversy would reduce the available supply of timber. After the "timber depression" during which the industry overbid on sales before the housing market fell, Congress came through with timber contract relief in 1984. Questions about the adequacy of NFMA plans plus the *California v. Block* court decision on RARE II caused Sirmon to restructure the planning process in favor of more balanced multiple use to position the agency to fight the expected legal challenges.

He was transferred to the Washington office in the fall of 1985 as the deputy chief for programs and legislation. In 1991, he was named the first deputy chief of international forestry. He oversaw the U.S. involvement in the forestry part of the 1992 Earth Summit, held in Rio de Janeiro. Sirmon also developed formal agreements between the Forest Service and the governments of Brazil and Indonesia. He helped set a new agenda for international forestry programs for the Forest Service, including the agency's participation in programs in Puerto Rico, Hawaii, and even the Solomon Islands. Sirmon was a delegate to the U.S. Forestry Congress at Mexico City in 1985 and the U.S.-Japan natural resources forestry panel at Tokyo in 1988; was an adviser to the World Bank on a three-week mission to Brazil in 1989; and received the Presidential Rank Award for Meritorious Executive Service in 1986.

HERBERT A. SMITH (1901–1936)

Born in Southampton, Massachusetts, December 6, 1866, Dr. Herbert "Dol" Smith prepared for college at Phillips Exeter Academy. In 1889, he received his B.A. from Yale, receiving special honors in English. In 1897, he received the Ph.D., also from Yale. He entered the Bureau of Forestry in 1901 at the request of Gifford Pinchot. He was in charge of editorial and public education work for the bureau, where he worked for the next 36 years. Dol Smith was a pioneer in the broad field of public relations; he also did much to introduce the study of forest conservation into public schools.

As editor of all Forest Service publications, he improved the quality of service publications, established a trend in having free research publications that were well written and easy to understand, and promoted the direction of the agency in all matters related to forestry and conservation. After retirement, Smith worked with Gifford Pinchot to polish his history of the early years of forest conservation in the United States. This book was published in 1947 as *Breaking New Ground*.

HELEN E. STOCKBRIDGE (1901–1932)

Helen Stockbridge, an early Forest Service employee, was born on November 1, 1871, in Gardiner, Maine. She entered the Forest Service in 1901 as a library assistant, and three years later she was made the librarian of the agency. She was in charge of the library for 31 years, where she filled every request, no matter how vague or even ridiculous. She kept and maintained a current list of agency literature and contributed greatly to Edward Munns's two-volume work *A Selected Bibliography of North American Forestry* (1940). Many authors, researchers, and students used her skills at finding the right book, article, or report. She prepared dozens of bibliographies and authored several papers on the literature of forestry. In addition to her regular work in the national headquarters, she was the secretary and treasurer of the Society of American Foresters (SAF), where she helped in editing, printing, and distribution of such publications as *The Proceedings* (of the SAF), *Forestry Quarterly*, and the *Journal of Forestry*.

ROBERT Y. STUART (1906–1933)

Robert Stuart was born in the South Middleton Township, Cumberland County, Pennsylvania, on February 13, 1883. He graduated with a B.A. from Dickinson

College in 1903, worked for a year in business, then entered Yale Forest School, receiving a master of forestry degree in 1906. He entered the Forest Service the same year, working as a technical assistant. He was attached to the Northern District (Region) as a forest assistant, an inspector, an assistant chief of operation, silviculture, and an assistant district forester. He came to the Washington office in 1912 as inspector in the office of management. In the fall of 1917, Stuart was commissioned as a captain, then major in the 20th Engineers (Forestry) in France; he returned to the Washington office in 1919. After returning briefly to the Forest Service, he resigned in 1920 to work with forestry for the State of Pennsylvania under Commissioner of Forestry (later Governor) Gifford Pinchot. He began a program to buy state forestland, established statewide system of forest fire lookouts, and started a forest nursery system. He returned to the Forest Service in February 1927 as chief of public relations and was appointed the fourth chief on May 1, 1928, after the resignation of Chief Greeley.

Stuart was instrumental in getting the Forest Service prepared to deal with the crisis caused by the crash of the stock market in the fall of 1929. With the beginnings of the Great Depression, Stuart led the Forest Service in creating job opportunities for the unemployed on the national forests, especially in connection with the road system. During his term, the McSweeney-McNary Act of 1928 promoted forest research, while the Knutson-Vandenberg Act of 1930 was designed to expand tree planting on the national forests. Stuart was chief when the system of wilderness, primitive, and natural areas under the L-20 regulations of 1929 came into place (replaced by the U Regulations in 1939). A revision of grazing fees to reflect livestock prices also was instituted during his tenure as chief.

Before President Roosevelt's inauguration, Stuart had the Forest Service complete a 1,677-page report (called the "Copeland Report"), which outlined projects in the national forests that had not been completed. When Roosevelt created the Civilian Conservation Corps (CCC) in the spring of 1933 as part of his "new deal" to relieve the severe economic stress among young unemployed men, the Forest Service was ready with a long list of projects. When the first CCC camps were established, in July, the Forest Service provided space for the 200-man camps, thousands of work projects, and experienced project leaders. Many new national forests were established during his term of office, especially through the South and Midwest. Stuart died tragically following a fall from his seventh-floor office on October 23, 1933, which many attributed to overwork.

GEORGE B. SUDWORTH (1886–1927)

George Sudworth was born in 1864 in Kingston, Wisconsin. He obtained a B.A. from the University of Michigan in 1885. He taught briefly at the Michigan Agricultural College (Michigan State), then came into the USDA Division of Forestry in 1886. In 1904, Sudworth was appointed chief of dendrology in the USDA Bureau of Forestry. He became the nation's most distinguished authority on American trees. He authored a large number of publications about American trees, dendrology, and other aspects of forestry. He discovered and named a large number of new species and varieties of trees, many of which he personally collected. Probably his most known writings were *Check List of the Forest Trees of the United States* (1898, 1927) and *Forest Trees of the Pacific Slope* (1908). In addition, he wrote about cypress, juniper, spruce, balsam firs, and pine trees in the Rocky Mountain Region. At the time of his death, in 1927, he was the oldest member of the Forest Service, having worked there for nearly 41 years.

LLOYD WESLEY SWIFT (1928–1963)

Lloyd Swift was born on September 4, 1904, on the Swift Ranch, near Ione, California. He attended the UC-Davis and UC-Berkeley, where he earned a master's in range science. Upon graduation, Swift joined the Forest Service, working in range and wildlife management in the California and Rocky Mountain Regions. In 1942, he moved to the Washington office, where he served as the assistant and then the director of wildlife management. He was instrumental in establishing a multiresource management program to promote the health of water, fisheries, wildlife, vegetation, and soil. He collaborated with state fish and game agencies to achieve integrated federal and state natural resource management programs. Upon retirement from the Forest Service, Swift served as a consulting biologist for USAID, FAO, UNESCO, and the UN Special Fund in the United States, Africa, and the Middle East. He was the first executive director of the World Wildlife Fund, president of the Cosmos Club, president of the Washington Biologist Field Club, and a member of the Boone and Crockett and Explorers Clubs and professional organizations in the wildlife field.

JACK WARD THOMAS (1966–1993)

Jack Ward Thomas was born in Fort Worth, Texas, on September 7, 1934. Thomas received a B.S. degree in wildlife management from Texas A&M University in 1957, then his M.S. in wildlife ecology from West Virginia University, in 1969, and a Ph.D. in forestry (natural resources planning) from the University of Massachusetts, in 1972. Thomas began his long career as a wildlife researcher with the Texas Game and Fish Commission in 1957, moving in 1966 to the Forest Service in Morgantown, West Virginia, as a research wildlife biologist, then in 1969 to the Urban Forestry and Wildlife Research Unit, at Amherst, Massachusetts. In 1974, he became the chief research wildlife biologist and project leader at the Blue Mountains Research Lab, in La Grande, Oregon. In the late 1980s and early 1990s, Thomas participated in several studies of the northern spotted owl and old growth habitat in the Pacific Northwest. In the spring of 1993, in the wake of the President Clinton's Forest Conference, in Portland, Oregon, he was named to head the Forest Ecosystem Management Assessment Team (FEMAT) to present a resolution, based on the best scientific evidence, to resolve the spotted owl crises in the Pacific Northwest and in northern California. It was partially as a result of his work on this project that Thomas was chosen to be the thirteenth chief of the Forest Service.

Amid controversy about how new chiefs should be appointed, Thomas was given the job on December 1, 1993, as a political appointee with the assurance that he would be converted to a career appointment through the Senior Executive Service (through which Chiefs Peterson and Robertson were appointed). Thomas moved quickly to address a demoralized agency, with the public opposed to practically anything that the Forest Service proposed to do. The controversy about the Northwest Forest Plan for the spotted owl region was especially troubling. Another challenge that he faced was implementation of the so-called salvage rider, passed by the 104th Congress to address timber salvage on forests that had extensive fire-killed trees. Vocal opponents, although small in number, increasingly directed violence at the agency and its employees. An additional problem was the USDA Assistant Secretary Jim Lyons's intervention in local decisions on the national forests. It was a practice that exacerbated a politically charged climate in Washington and sometimes left the national office trying to play "catch-up" with the department.

Jack Ward Thomas has published approximately 250 books, chapters, and articles, primarily on elk, deer, and turkey biology, wildlife disease, wildlife habitat, songbird ecology, northern spotted owl management, and land-use planning. He has published several books, including *The Elk of North America—Ecology and Management, Wildlife Habitats in Managed Forests—The Blue Mountains of Oregon and Washington,* and *Wildlife Habitats in Managed Rangelands—The Great Basin of Southeastern Oregon.* Thomas served on the editorial board of the *Journal of Forestry,* was an associate editor of the *Western Journal of Forestry,* and served as associate editor of *Landscape and Urban Planning.* He received a number of awards, including the USDA Distinguished Service and Superior Service Awards; was an Elected Fellow of the Society of American Foresters; won the National Wildlife Federation's Conservation Achievement Award for Science; received the Aldo Leopold Medal of The Wildlife Society; was given the General Chuck Yeager Award by the National Fish and Wildlife Foundation; and received the USDA-FS Chief's Award for Excellence in Technology Transfer. In addition, Thomas served as president of The Wildlife Society in 1976–1977.

ELEANOR S. TOWNS (1978–2002)

Eleanor Towns is a native of Rockford, Illinois. Towns holds a B.S. degree from the University of Illinois, an M.S. degree from the University of New Mexico, and a J.D. (juris doctor) degree from the University of Denver's College of Law. Towns joined the Forest Service in 1978. She was director of lands, soils, water, and minerals for the Rocky Mountain Region, headquartered in Denver, Colorado, then became the director of lands for the Forest Service in the Washington office. She came to the Forest Service from the Bureau of Land Management.

Towns was the first black woman to serve as a regional forester. Her work in the Southwestern Region of the Forest Service entailed managing a budget of more than $300 million, a workforce of more than 2,000 employees, and a land base of more than 22 million acres in the states of Arizona and New Mexico. She is highly regarded for her cordial working relationships with members of Congress and her collaborative efforts with cattlemen, environmental groups, industry representatives, and state, local, and tribal and pueblo governments. President Bill Clinton granted Towns meritorious presidential rank for sustained superior accomplishment in the management of programs for the federal government. The award recognized her for her handling of the escaped prescribed fire on the grounds of the Los Alamos National Laboratory; her work on restoration issues in the Southwestern Region; her tackling of grazing clashes between ranchers and environmentalists; her work in diversifying the workforce; and her testimony before congressional committees on behalf of the chief of the Forest Service.

FRANK H. WADSWORTH (1938–2002)

Frank Wadsworth was born in Chicago on November 26, 1915. He spent two years in a junior college, then went on to a forestry program at the University of Michigan, from which he received, in 1937, both a B.F. and M.F. in ecology. He began work at the Southwestern Forest and Range Experiment Station in 1938. Four years later, near the start of World War II, he took a research position at the Tropical Forest Experiment Station, in Puerto Rico. By 1956, he had become the station director, as well as the supervisor of the Caribbean National Forest. In 1949, prior to the passage of the Endangered Species Act of 1973, Wadsworth became involved with the Puerto Rican parrot recovery. He was successful in setting aside 3,200 acres for the parrot in 1949—which once numbered in the millions but which had been reduced to a population of around 2,000 birds, which was further reduced to 27 birds, then 13. Wadsworth was able to get limited recovery money from the Puerto Rico, the Forest Service, the Fish and Wildlife Service, and the World Wildlife Fund. Currently, there are some 120 parrots living. In 1950, Wadsworth earned a Ph.D. in tropical forestry from Michigan. For 24 years, he edited the *Caribbean Forester*. He has traveled around the world to consult with many nations and organizations about tropical forestry, including the International Tropical Timber Organization, USAID, the UN Food and Agriculture Organization, and the International Union of Forestry Research Organizations. By 1997, Wadsworth had written almost 100 publications. During his many years at the tropical station, he produced an amazing number of research papers, reports, books, and presentations, and in the process became recognized as perhaps the most knowledgeable tropical forestry expert in the world.

LYLE FORD WATTS (1913–1952)

Lyle Watts was born in Cerro Gordo County, Iowa, in 1890. He was a graduate of the Iowa State College school of forestry, earning both the B.S. in forestry in 1913 and the master of forestry degree in 1928. He entered the Forest Service in 1913 in the Rockies. In 1928, he left the Forest Service to serve for a year to organize the school of forestry at Utah State Agricultural College (Utah State University). After reentering the Forest Service, in 1929, he served again in the Rockies, then became regional forester first in Milwaukee, Wisconsin, and later in Portland, Oregon. In 1943, he was appointed the seventh chief of the Forest Service.

Watts served as chief during much of the turbulent war period. Yet, with the obvious progress being made in the war effort, his attention turned to planning what the national forests and the Forest Service would be like after the war. He and his staff quickly realized that the national forests should be opened up to development that was scientific and orderly. In the aftermath of the war, many of the GIs went back to college, many in the fields of professional forestry and engineering. Watts encouraged the Forest Service to hire these new graduates to assist in the development of forest road systems and intensively managed, sustained yield forests.

Watts oversaw the expansion of the federal role of cooperator with the various states and private industry in the fields of forest fire protection, pest control, tree planting, woodland management and harvesting, wood-product marketing and processing, grazing, and so on. Watts was a member of the technical committee on forestry and primary forest products for the United Nations Interim Commission on Food and Agriculture in 1944 and 1945.

RUDY WENDELIN (1933–1973)

Rudy Wendelin was born February 10, 1910, in Herndon, Kansas, but grew up in nearby Luden. He graduated from the University of Kansas with a degree in architecture, then attended art school in Milwaukee, Wisconsin. In 1933, he started his career with the Forest Service as a draftsman and illustrator. With the creation of the Cooperative Forest Fire Prevention Program, in 1942, the Forest Service wanted the general public involved in the new fire prevention campaign. Disney's character *Bambi* was used first as the animal model for the program and tested well. But, in August 1944, a bear named Smokey was introduced as the new symbol of fire prevention. Albert Staehle was the first artist to draw Smokey. Not long thereafter, Rudy, back from his navy experience in World War II, came on board the Smokey fire prevention program; it was the beginning of a relationship that lasted more than 40 years. Rudy drew hundreds of images of Smokey, which appeared on posters, plaques, banners, and many associated fire prevention products. Wendelin retired in 1973, but his drawing of the internationally famous bear continued in use for decades, and he remained strongly committed to the Smokey fire prevention message. The Smokey image has been used for fire prevention in many nations around the world. The only nonhuman figure that is better known in the United States than Smokey is Santa Claus. Rudy designed the commemorative postage stamp for Smokey, the only stamp in the Post Office history to feature a single animal. Because of Smokey's immense popularity, mail delivered to him at the National Zoo was given a special zip code—20252.

Wendelin has received many awards for his Smokey work. He was presented with the Medal of Honor by the Daughters of the American Revolution for his wonderful and colorful artwork work in popularizing Smokey Bear and the fire prevention message. He also received the Horace Hart Award from the graphic arts industry and both the Silver and Gold Smokey Bear Awards from the USDA. Rudy died at age 90 on August 31, 2000, after a car accident.

HOWARD CLINTON ZAHNISER

Howard Zahniser was born on February 25, 1906, in Franklin, Pennsylvania. He attended Greenville College, in Illinois, and received a degree in humanities. In 1930, Zahniser was employed by the USDA Biological Survey (which would several years later become the core agency of the new USDI Fish and Wildlife Service). He worked for 12 years for the Fish and Wildlife Service in the information division, where he honed his interests in nature. In 1942, Zahniser found work in the USDA Bureau of Plant Industry, Soils, and Agricultural Engineering. He worked as the director of the Bureau's information and editorial division. He served as book editor of *Nature* magazine, as well as editor of The Wilderness Society's magazine *The Living Wilderness*.

After Robert Marshall's untimely death, in 1939, Zahniser stepped forward to lead the wilderness battle in the public arena and Congress. Zahniser became the primary leader in the move to have Congress, rather than the federal agencies, designate wilderness areas. As early as 1949, Zahniser detailed a proposal for federal wilderness legislation under the terms of which Congress would establish a national wilderness system. Nothing happened to the proposal, but it did raise the awareness for the need to protect wildernesses and primitive areas from all forms of development. Six years later, he began an effort to convince skeptics and Congress to support a bill to establish a national wilderness-preservation system. Hubert H. Humphrey (D-MN) became a major supporter of the bill. Ironically, Zahniser, who pushed so hard for the act, died on May 5, 1964, just few months before the bill became the law of the land. President Lyndon Johnson signed the Wilderness Act into law on September 3, 1964. The act designed 9.1 million acres of wilderness in the new National Wilderness Preservation System, most of these coming from the national forests. Because of Zahniser's relentless efforts, he has often been called the "Father of the Wilderness Act."

RAPHAEL ZON (1901–1949)

Raphael Zon was born in the Russian town of Simbirsk on December 1, 1874. He graduated from the Simbirsk Classical Gymnasium. Zone then entered the Imperial University in Kazan, where he specialized in natural sciences in comparative embryology. While at the university he helped to organize the first trade union in Russia and for that was arrested, thrown into jail, and sentenced to 10 years in exile in the province of Northern Archangel. Raphael was released on bail and seized that chance to escape from Russia. He reached the United States in 1897 with only 19 cents in his pocket. He went back to school and earned a degree in forest engineering in 1901 from Cornell University.

On July 1, 1901, Raphael Zon entered the Forest Service in Washington, D.C., as student assistant, at a salary of $25 per month. He became a forest assistant in 1904. As head of the office of silvics from 1907 to 1914 and of the office of forest investigations from 1914 to 1923, Zon called for freeing research investigation from administrative snarls. He played a leading role in the establishment of a system of forest experiment stations beginning in 1908 at Fort Valley, on the Coconino National Forest in Arizona. The research stations provided much needed information on tree growth, the disposal of slash, and the relationship between forests and streamflows. He was also a prime mover in the creation of the Forest Products Laboratory, in Madison, Wisconsin, in 1911. During World War I, President Wilson appointed him to the National Research Council. In 1923, he became the director of the newly established Lake States Forest Experiment Station, in St. Paul, Minnesota. In this position, he supervised a staff of researchers that contributed greatly to the progress of forest conservation in the Great Lake states of Michigan, Wisconsin, and Minnesota.

Zon shared, and maybe developed, the idea of tree planting in the Great Plains to reduce major soil erosion from the winds and rain, especially on farms and grazing lands. The Great Plains shelterbelt program to plant millions of trees started in 1934. An enthusiast about shelterbelts, he helped plan the project and was in charge of the technical phases of its development. Shelterbelts were planted from the Canadian border to northern Texas roughly along the ninety-ninth meridian.

His published works total some 200 titles. A pioneer in the study of the relation among forests, flood control, and streamflow, Zon set forth his findings in a bulletin, *Forests and Water in the Light of Scientific Investigation* (1927). At first violently attacked, his theories are now widely accepted. Probably his most lasting book, coauthored with William N. Sparhawk, was *The Forest Resources of the World* (1923). It was the first attempt to make a systematic and accurate inventory of the Earth's forests. After his retirement from the Forest Service, in 1944, Zon pursued a number of writing projects in connection with the UN Relief and Rehabilitation Administration and the journal *Unasylva*. Zon died on October 27, 1956.

☆ **7** ☆

Relationships with Other Federal Agencies

USDI GENERAL LAND OFFICE

The General Land Office (GLO) was created in 1812 to dispose of the vast public domain lands in the Midwest and the West. During its existence, more than 1 billion acres of land were transferred from federal to state and private ownership. In the late 1890s, the General Land Office (GLO), in the Department of the Interior, initially had management of the forest reserves. From the time of the passage of the Forest Reserve Act of 1891 until the passage of the Organic Act of 1897, management of the reserves was in the hands of the U.S. marshals. Their main concern was trespass on the reserves by timber cutters and sheep owners. Mining was permitted, but usually the miners complied with the General Mining Act of 1872. This all changed in 1897 with the Organic Act. For the first time, management of the public domain forest reserves was undertaken by the GLO. Prior to 1897, the main function of the GLO had been to supervise the selling or granting of the public domain to homesteaders and railroads. The Organic Act of 1897 split management of the reserves between the GLO and the Geological Survey.

The GLO was not prepared for this task but was quick to establish management of the forest reserves. Initially, the GLO hired state supervisors for each state that had reserves. These men were hired beginning in the summer of 1897and were kept on until 1902. During the summers, beginning in 1898, the state supervisors hired forest supervisors and rangers, who worked only during the summer fire season—usually July 1 to October 1. The forest rangers and supervisors were, for the most part, not rehired by the new Forest Service in 1905. The GLO employees at all levels were political appointees; no experience was necessary. They were appointed by their U.S. senators—who at the time were also appointed by their state legislatures—or by the GLO national headquarters, in Washington, D.C. Although some of the early forest rangers were woodsmen, most were not.

One ranger appointed in 1898 in western Oregon was Smith Bartrum. He wrote that, at that time:

> To qualify for the requirements at this time [1899 for a GLO Forest Ranger position] was; That a Ranger was to equip himself with one saddle horse, one pack horse, with riding and pack saddles, saddle bags for pack-horse, one axe, one shovel, provisions for at least six weeks or two months, adequate cooking utensils, all at his own expense, his salary was $60.00 per month.
>
> The Forest Ranger at that time must be prepared to range alone in the mountains in any and all kinds of weather, to know the general compass directions, legal sub-divisions of surveyed lands. To be able to find himself and go anywhere without loosing [sic] your direction; To be able to spot a fire and go to it at the earliest possible moment, night or day, and suppress it, never leaving a fire until safe. Estimate the acreage of the burned over area. Make an estimate of the amount in board feet, of merchantable timber destroyed, and its value. To be familiar with the names of the different species of timber, to be able to operate a compass, to know the strip and circle method of cruising timber, and to have had experience in logging operations.
>
> After these qualifications was [sic] proved satisfactory to the Washington D.C. Office, you were then instructed to report in writing to your Forest Supervisor. You might see him once in a season, often not at all. You would receive simple written instructions [of] what you were to do.

More typical, however, was the GLO ranger who was appointed because he knew the right people (usually the senator) or someone already hired would recommend him to the supervisor. One such ranger was described this way: "In 1899, 1900 and 1901 Capt. C.V. Dodd, a Civil War Veteran. … His equipment consisted of two horses, a pistol with four shells, a large badge and a full beard." A number of the GLO rangers had no experience in the great outdoors. The way many of the GLO rangers operated was to sit in a comfortable cabin and wait for someone to report a fire. If it was a large fire, then the ranger would not fight the fire, since he did not have anyone to help him. The fire would go out on its own, or the fall rains would extinguish the flames. No action was needed other than keeping an account of the acres burned. Several GLO rangers were fired when they were found to be derelict in their duties. More than one ranger was found working on his farm rather than patrolling the reserves. Others were just incompetent.

Yet a few were men experienced in forestry or mining, and these men actually took well to the rigors of ranging the forest on horseback for three months each summer. Some thought it was, as we would call it today, a great paid vacation. Some rangers took their wives and kids along to camp in the forest. Generally, their work was seen as unsatisfactory. Gifford Pinchot, perhaps the first person hired by the GLO in 1897, did an inspection trip to the forest reserves that summer. He, to his dying day, remained solidly against GLO management because of his personal observation of fraud, graft, incompetence, and greed. Several of his comments touched on his dislike for the GLO; he called the GLO an organization marked by "political stupidity, and wrong-headed points of view," as well as an office that was full of "crookedness and incompetence." Of course, there were no forestry schools at the time, and scientific forestry was a European idea thought not to be practical in the United States.

By the early 1900s, land fraud involving the forest reserves and the GLO management came to a head. Binger Hermann, who had been a U.S. representative from Oregon, was the General Land Office Commissioner (equivalent today to the director of the Bureau of Land Management). He was indicted in the land fraud deals and tried twice but acquitted each time. (He was again elected to Congress in 1903.) His partners, however, were not quite so lucky. In another land fraud case, John Mitchell, U.S. senator from Oregon, was tried and convicted. While he was appealing his conviction, he died, in 1905, from complications of a tooth extraction. Before the trials ended, 33 persons were convicted, including U.S. representatives, members of the Oregon legislature, and other important persons in the state.

Competence in the GLO was boosted in 1901 when Filibert Roth was appointed as head of a new Division R (for the forest reserves). Roth, who began work with the USDA Division of Forestry in 1892 and later taught at the Cornell school of forestry, was in constant communication with Gifford Pinchot and his professional forestry staff. Roth was able to publish his *Forest Reserve Manual* in 1902, which for the first time laid out duties and procedures for the forest reserves. The book was, at the time, seen as the best example of how to manage the reserves. Many of the procedures, some from the USDA Bureau of Forestry, were used to help form the Forest Service *Use Book* in 1905. Roth resigned in 1903 to move to the new University of Michigan school of forestry.

Management of the forest reserves was transferred from the GLO to the USDA Forest Service on February 1, 1905, with the passage of the Transfer Act of 1905. Almost all the GLO rangers were not rehired by the new agency, but a few very competent men stayed on for at least the next several years until a complete transition was accomplished. This, for all practical purposes, ended the direct relationships between the GLO and the Forest Service. Yet, the Department of the Interior would, over the next decades, attempt unsuccessfully to pull the reserves/national forests back into Interior.

USDI GEOLOGICAL SURVEY

As noted earlier, the Geological Survey was called upon by Congress to help with the management of the forest reserves. This cooperative effort began in 1897 and lasted until 1905, when the Forest Service took over all management functions of the forest reserves. The main duty of the Geological Survey was to map the existing forest reserves, as well as to evaluate human activities in and near the reserves and any potential uses of the reserves, especially the mineral potential. During the nine-year period, and for years afterward, the Geological Survey sent teams of men to the western reserves (there were none in the East). The teams, often in association with the GLO rangers and Bureau of Forestry experts, rode in wagons and on horseback to look at every piece of ground in the reserves. They also took the first photographs—now at the National Archives—of these forest reserves. Over the next 10 years, the Geological Survey published many significant reports of their early findings.

FIGURE 7.1 U.S. Geological Survey Reports on Forest Reserves, 1897–1905

No. 4	"The Forests of Oregon" by Henry Gannett. 57th Congress, 2nd Session, Document No. 212. Series H, Forestry, 1. Washington, DC: USGPO. 1902.
No. 5	"The Forests of Washington" by Henry Gannett. 57th Congress, 2nd Session, Document No. 213. Series H, Forestry, 2. Washington, DC: USGPO. 1902.
No. 6	"Forestry Conditions in the Cascade Range, Washington, Between the Washington and Mount Rainier Forest Reserves" by Fred G. Plummer. Series H, Forestry, 3. Washington, DC: USGPO. 1902. Now part of the Mt. Baker-Snoqualmie NF.
No. 7	"Forestry Conditions in the Olympic Forest Reserve, Washington" by Arthur Dodwell and Theodore F. Rixon. Series H, Forestry, 4. Washington, DC: USGPO. 1902. Now part of the Olympic NF and Olympic NP.
No. 8	"Forestry Conditions in the Northern Sierra Nevada, California" by John B. Leiberg. Series H, Forestry, 5. Washington, DC: USGPO. 1902. Now part of several NFs.
No. 9	"Forestry Conditions in the Cascade Range Forest Reserve, Oregon" by Harold Douglas Langille, Fred G. Plummer, Arthur Dodwell, Theodore F. Rixon, and John B. Leiberg. Series H, Forestry, 6. Washington, DC: USGPO. 1903. Now part of the Willamette, Umpqua, Rogue River, Winema, and Deschutes NFs.
No. 22	"Forestry Conditions in the San Francisco Mountains Forest Reserve, Arizona" by John B. Leiberg, Theodore F. Rixon, and Arthur Dodwell. Series H, Forestry, 7. Washington, DC: USGPO. 1904. Now the Coconino NF.
No. 23	"Forestry Conditions in the Black Mesa Forest Reserve, Arizona" by Fred G. Plummer with notes by Theodore F. Rixon and Arthur Dodwell. Series H, Forestry, 8. Washington, DC: USGPO. 1904. Now part of the Sitgreaves, Tonto, Apache, and Coconino NFs.
No. 29	"Forestry Conditions in the Absaroka Division of the Yellowstone Forest Reserve, Montana and the Livingston and Big Timber Quadrangles" by John B. Leiberg. Series H, Forestry, 9. Washington, DC: USGPO. 1904. Now part of the Gallatin and Lewis & Clark NFs.
No. 30	"Forestry Conditions in the Little Belt Mountains Forest Reserve, Montana, and the Little Belt Mountains Quadrangle" by John B. Leiberg. Series H, Forestry, 10. Washington, DC: USGPO. 1904. Now part of the Lewis & Clark NF.
No. 33	"Forestry Conditions in the Lincoln Forest Reserve, New Mexico" by Fred G. Plummer and M.G. Gowsell. Series H, Forestry, 11. 1904. Washington, DC: USGPO. Now Lincoln NF.
No. 37	"The Southern Appalachian Forests" by H.B. Ayres and W.W. Ashe. Series H, Forestry, 12. Washington, DC: USGPO. 1904. Part of several NFs.
No. 39	"Forestry Conditions in the Gila River Forest Reserve, New Mexico" by Theodore F. Rixon. Series H, Forestry, 13. Washington, DC: USGPO. 1904. Now the Gila NF.

19th Annual Report (1897–1898), with separate map volume. Forest Reserve (FR) reports for:

"Black Hills FR (South Dakota and Wyoming)" by Henry S. Graves, "Bighorn FR (Wyoming)" by F.E. Town.

(continued)

FIGURE 7.1 U.S. Geological Survey Reports on Forest Reserves, 1897–1905

"Teton FR" from notes by T.S. Brandegee.

"Yellowstone Park FR (Southern Part)" by T.S. Brandegee.

"Priest River FR" by John B. Leiberg.

"Bitterroot FR" by John B. Leiberg.

"Washington FR" by H.B. Ayres.

"Eastern Part of Washington FR" by Martin W. Gorman.

"San Jacinto FR (Preliminary Report)" by John B. Leiberg.

"San Bernardino FR" by John B. Leiberg.

"San Gabriel FR" by John B. Leiberg.

"Forest Conditions of Northern Idaho" by John B. Leiberg.

"Pine Ridge Timber, Nebraska" by N.H. Darton.

20th Annual Report (1898–1899), with separate map volume. Forest Reserve (FR) reports for:

"Pikes Peak, Plum Creek, and South Platte Reserves" by John G. Jack.

"White River Plateau Timber Land Reserve" by George B. Sudworth.

"Battlement Mesa FR" by George B. Sudworth.

"Flathead FR" by H.B. Ayres.

"Bitterroot FR" by John B. Leiberg.

"The San Gabriel FR" by John B. Leiberg.

"The San Bernardino FR" by John B. Leiberg.

"The San Jacinto FR" by John B. Leiberg.

21st Annual Report (1899–1900), with separate map volume. Forest Reserve (FR) reports for:

"Lewis and Clarke [sic] FR, Montana" by H.B. Ayres.

"Mt. Rainier FR, Washington" by Fred G. Plummer.

"Olympic FR, Washington" by Arthur Dodwell and Theodore F. Rixon.

"Cascade Range FR…Together with the Ashland FR and Forest Regions … " by John B. Leiberg

"Stanislaus and Lake Tahoe FRs, California, and Adjacent Territory" by George B. Sudworth.

"Classification of Lands" by Henry Gannett (ed.), Descriptions of timber in U.S.G.S. Quadrangles in CA; in OR; in WA; ID; AK; and WY.

"Woodland of Indian Territory [OK]" by C.H. Fitch.

"Timber Conditions of the Pine Region of Minnesota" by H.B. Ayres.

Relations between the USDI Geological Survey and the Forest Service were always cordial. The Forest Service and the Geological Survey continue to be partners in mapping the reserves/national forests to this very day. Forest Service maps use the latest USGS topographic maps for management and provide base-line geographic information that is used in the popular recreation maps. The Forest Service and the Geological Survey have for more than 100 years worked together on naming geographic features. These names are those that are attached to places on maps such as towns, rivers, creeks, and mountains. They are essential to know in the management of the national forests. Many of the features, such as mountains, rivers, and creeks, within the national forests were named by or for Forest Service employees.

USDI NATIONAL PARK SERVICE

Relations with the USDI National Park Service over the past 100 years have been testy at best. Interestingly, the Forest Service under Chief Foresters Gifford Pinchot and Henry Graves opposed the creation of a new agency to administer the national parks and most of the national monuments (NM) that were authorized by the Antiquities Act of 1906. As early as 1904, Pinchot wanted to have jurisdiction of the national parks passed from the U.S. Army, which was then managing the parks, to the Forest Service, since the lands were so similar. This attempt at control of the national parks failed to gather many supporters and subsequently failed. If Pinchot had not been fired by Taft in 1910, the Forest Service would probably have succeeded in taking over management of the national parks. Of course, Pinchot's support for the damming of Hetch Hetchy Valley in the northern part of Yosemite National Park was fuel to the fire of the opponents.

After years of trying, the Park Service bill passed both houses of Congress, but in slightly different forms, during the summer of 1916. The House version allowed grazing in the parks and monuments, while the Senate version did not. The conference committee kept the grazing provision for all national parks except Yellowstone. The National Park Service was established in 1916 in the Department of the Interior. The proponents of the new agency, including John Muir and the Sierra Club, became outspoken critics of the Forest Service, primarily because of its opposition to the creation of the Park Service and its support for the Hetch Hetchy project.

Late in 1915, just before the National Park Service was created, Stephen Mather, soon to be the Park Service head, invited the chief of the Forest Service to discuss the future management for the national monuments inside the national forests. Part of the discussion involved the expansion of Sequoia National Park by taking land from the Sierra National Forest. The Forest Service was not opposed, but only if the Park Service did not take in too much national forestland. Mather also desired to expand the Grand Canyon National Monument into the neighboring national forests. The Forest Service disagreed, but the expansions went ahead. Chief Forester Henry Graves believed that "there seems to be continuous trouble over the National Parks." There were continuous efforts by the Park Service, Congress, and citizen groups to have many of the national monuments made into national parks. Over the years, a number of national parks and monuments were carved out of national forest land, as well as by donations of private land. This situation created a lingering suspicion that the Park Service was trying to grab the best national forest areas for national parks.

At the same time, America became involved with the World War in Europe. In April 1917, the United States declared war on the Axis powers (Germany and its allies). Efforts on the home front were focused on providing wood, wool, and meat from the national forests. On the Mt. Olympus National Monument in Washington, a U.S. Army Spruce Production Division railroad logging operation was allowed along the northern flank of the monument to access the much-needed Sitka spruce and Douglas-fir trees. The spruce lumber was highly desired for aircraft fuselage and wing parts, while the fir was valued for ship building. The Park Service made a comparable effort to help the war effort providing meat, such as elk and bison, for the troops, as well as by allowing grazing on the parks, as was being done on the national forests. After the war, the arguments and counterarguments between the Park Service and the Forest Service continued to fly for decades. In essence, there was a fundamental disagreement over management of the national forests and the national parks and monuments. Horace Albright, later the director of the Park Service, noted that the Park Service had few places to acquire land unless it dipped into the national forests, and argued that the Park Service would protect these lands, rather than allow the many uses permitted by the Forest Service.

Proposals to expand the Yellowstone National Park south and west into the Jackson Hole and Grand Teton areas led to renewed conflict between the agencies. As early as 1916, Horace Albright visited the area and envisioned it as a new national park. However, not all was well between the Forest Service and the Park Service, and the feud became bitter. In 1924–1925, a presidential committee of five was established to survey and make recommendations regarding park expansions. In hearings, the Forest Service was strongly opposed to expansion of Yellowstone National Park southward into the Jackson Hole country, believing that the land was more valuable for timber, minerals, and grazing than for national park purposes. In the end, the Forest Service had local support and won the contest, at least for the next decade or so, but the Park Service continued the campaign in the area and eventually succeeded in creating the Grand Teton National Park. In the mid-1920s, Alaska lands became the battleground in the struggle over national monuments and parks. Katmai NM was established in 1918, and Glacier Bay NM was added in 1925 from the Tongass National Forest. The latter caused an outcry of opposition from Alaskan newspapers (in 1980, both these monuments were reestablished as national parks).

On March 3, 1933, President Herbert C. Hoover, on his last day in office, approved legislation authorizing the president to reorganize the executive branch and administrative agencies of the government. The job fell to the new president, Franklin D. Roosevelt, who on June 10 issued an executive order for reorganization, to take effect 61 days later. Executive Orders 6166 and 6228 transferred all the national monuments from the Forest Service to the National Park Service.

The Forest Service opposed the transfer of the national monuments to the National Park Service, but it was a presidential decision that it would go along with.

The fate of several national forests was, for the most part, decided in battles over the creation of new national parks rather than national monuments. Four of the national monuments managed by the Forest Service (see Table 7.1) had been transferred previously to the National Park Service: Bandelier NM, in 1932; Grand Canyon NM, in 1919; and the Cinder Cone and Lassen Peak NMs, in 1916. The remaining 15 national monuments under Forest Service management were transferred in 1933 by Executive Order 6166. These Forest Service NMs contained more than 451,000 acres:

TABLE 7.1: National Monuments Managed by the USDA Forest Service 1906–1933

Monument Name	Forest	Location	Acres
Bandelier[1]	Santa Fe	New Mexico	22,075
Chiricahua	Coronado	Arizona	4,480
Cinder Cone[2]	Lassen	California	4,800
Devils Postpile	Sierra	California	800
Gila Cliff Dwellings	Gila	New Mexico	160
Grand Canyon[3]	Grand Canyon	Arizona	818,560
Holy Cross	Holy Cross	Colorado	1,392
Jewel Cave	Harney	South Dakota	1,280
Lava Beds	Modoc	California	45,967
Lassen Peak[2]	Lassen	California	1,280
Lehman Caves	Nevada	Nevada	593
Mount Olympus	Olympic	Washington	298,730
Old Kasaan	Tongass	Alaska	38
Oregon Caves	Siskiyou	Oregon	480
Saguaro	Coronado	Arizona	81,958
Sunset Crater	Coconino	Arizona	3,040
Timpanogos Cave	Wasatch	Utah	250
Tonto	Tonto	Arizona	640
Walnut Canyon	Coconino	Arizona	960
Wheeler	Cochetopa and Rio Grande	Colorado	300
Total Acres			1,279,223

Notes: [1] Transferred to NPS on February 25, 1932.

[2] Transferred to NPS on August 9, 1916.

[3] Transferred to NPS on August 15, 1919.

The transfer of management of these national monuments from the USDA Forest Service to the USDI National Park Service did not sit well with the Forest Service. Relations between the Forest Service and the Park Service had for several years been strained, even unfriendly at times. The antagonism felt by the Forest Service toward the Park Service came to a head several times over the next decades—over the creation of the Olympic National Park, in Washington, in the late 1930s; in the 1940s with the creation of the Grand Teton National Park, in Wyoming; during the 1960s over the North Cascades National Park, in Washington; and, in the 1970s, over the addition of the Mineral King area, on the Sequoia National Forest, to the Sequoia-Kings Canyon National Park.

Following the Alaska Native Claims Settlement Act of 1971, Forest Service Region 10 (Alaska) proposed in 1973 that seven new national forests containing 39.2 million acres be created in southern and central parts of the state. The idea floated around the region and Congress, waiting for a solution to the long-running debates over disposal of the huge Bureau of Land Management (BLM) holdings in Alaska. President Jimmy Carter, on December 1, 1978, during the congressional fights over the disposition of the BLM-administered lands in Alaska, established 17 new national monuments—totaling 55,975,000 acres—and 38,930,000 acres of national wildlife refuges. The Forest Service, for the first time since 1933, when all the national monuments were transferred to the Park Service, gained one new national monument on Admiralty Island and another at Misty Fiords, both on the Tongass National Forest, while the BLM gained the Gates of the Arctic, Kenai Fjords, Kobuk Valley, Lake Clark, and Wrangall-St. Elias National Monuments. (Note: It is unclear why the Park Service spells the word "Fjord" the Norwegian way, while the Forest Service prefers "Fiord.") Needless to say, the proclamations greatly upset many people in the state of Alaska, especially the Alaskan congressional delegation.

Between 1978 and 1980, when the final decisions over the Alaska "D-2 lands" passed Congress, there were many debates over the Park Service and the Forest Service proposals to vastly increase the holdings of the two agencies. With the passage of the Alaska National Interest Lands Conservation Act (ANILCA), on December 2, 1980, the huge expansion of the national forest system in Alaska failed to materialize. Instead of many new national forests in the state, ANILCA made small additions to the Chugach and Tongass National Forests and transferred the old Afognak Forest and Fish Culture Reserve (established in 1902), then part of the Chugach National Forest, to the Alaska Native corporations. The National Park Service, on the other hand, gained as national parks and/or national preserves all the 1978 national monuments, as well as gaining new national park status for Aniakchak and Cape Krusenstern, as well as national park recognition for two older national monuments at Glacier Bay and Katmai.

It is evident that the almost 193 million acres of national forest system lands, which contain many of the tallest, scenic mountain ranges in the West, hold great potential for creating national parks. To a lesser degree, so too do the lands administered by the BLM in the western states. There has been at least one informal "treaty" between the Forest Service and the Park Service according to which the "parkies" would hold off carving out national forest land to create national parks. However, just as with the designation of wilderness lands on the national forests, there will always be battles and hard feelings about the transfer of federal land between the Forest Service and the Park Service.

USDI BUREAU OF LAND MANAGEMENT

The Bureau of Land Management (BLM) was created in 1946 by the joining together of the older General Land Office with the newer U.S. Grazing Service. The Grazing Service came into existence as a direct result of the Taylor Grazing Act of 1934. The USDI created a Division of Grazing to administer grazing districts on suitable public rangeland, which was a major policy shift from disposing to managing these unique federal lands. The division was given bureau standing in 1939.

The main responsibility of the BLM has been the management of the remaining public domain and railroad/wagon road grant lands that have been returned to the government in western Oregon. The BLM also has the primary responsibility for the management oversight of the mineral domain that underlies the public lands. Like its sister agencies, the BLM is heavily involved in forest and rangeland planning, as well as keeping the official land-status records of all public federal lands. Following the lead of the Forest Service, the BLM has adopted the multiple-use and now the ecosystem-management philosophy. In many cases, other public lands, especially the national forests, are adjacent to and sometimes intermingled with BLM holdings in the western states.

Since the 1960s, both the BLM and the Forest Service have sought closer cooperation and coordination of their policies, especially in the western portion of Oregon. It is here that the BLM has large holding of timberland, millions of acres which were taken back—the term used is "revested"—from the Southern Pacific Railroad, which was determined by the Supreme Court to have violated the terms of its railroad land grant. Known as the Oregon & California Railroad Grant Lands (or simply O&C), these low-elevation forestlands are in sharp contrast to almost all of the other BLM lands across the West. In 1937, the O&C Administration, which oversaw the management of the western Oregon O&C lands, was affected by a law titled the Sustained Yield Act of 1937 that was intended to provide remedies for stabilizing timber supplies, sawmills, and employment in communities. The Act was designed to allow the Secretary of the Interior to establish sustained yield units on the O&C lands, but none were established, as the timber industry strongly opposed the establishment of these units (the Forest Service equivalent came in 1944 with the Sustained Yield Forest Management Act). The BLM essentially operated under these acts until congressional discussion over forest management in the Forest Service came to a head in the passage of the Federal Land Policy and Management Act of 1976 (FLPMA)—the National Forest Management Act of 1976 (NFMA) is the equivalent for the Forest Service—which gave the BLM its "organic act." Fortunately, FLPMA was not hotly debated in Congress and the press, as was NFMA. FLPMA aimed to bring clarity to a long line of executive branch decisions.

For the Forest Service, the BLM has operated as a sister agency, with similar concerns over similar problems. The laws, regulations, and leadership were, and remain, slightly different. Basically, the BLM tends toward greater central control by its national headquarters than does the Forest Service. Sometimes the slight differences between BLM rules or interpretations of rules and those of other federal agencies are used by the various interest groups to gain a slight advantage in playing one agency against another. Yet there are many similarities. During the 1990s, several BLM districts and Forest Service ranger districts were comanaged by one person. One such example was the Lakeview BLM district, which was managed for several years cooperatively with the Fremont National Forest. Another example, also from Oregon, is the BLM Oregon state office staff, which is located in the same downtown building in Portland as the Forest Service regional office. Some of the functions, such as fire management and archaeology, are joint, but most are separate.

During the mid-1980s, there was an active discussion about the possibility of moving management of the western Oregon O&C lands to the Forest Service. The Reagan administration proposed that the two agencies interchange certain lands in the West for ease of management. Both agencies worked feverishly for months to analyze the effects of such a merger. By 1986, a draft analysis—"Legislative Environmental Impact Statement for the Bureau of Land Management-Forest Service Interchange"—was to cover the anticipated impacts. This proposal aroused a great public outcry, especially from the affected counties, which derived much of their annual operating budgets from money supplied by law from the two agencies. Even after a major revision, the proposal was tabled by Congress. However, some less formal interchanges that did take place. It remains to be seen if close cooperation will continue in the future.

In 1990, the BLM and the Forest Service became both entangled in the management of old growth forests in the Pacific Northwest. Federal Judge Dwyer issued an injunction against the agencies that required them to stop all logging of old growth trees that were the habitat for the northern spotted owl. (This was discussed in Chapter 3.) President Clinton gave the two agencies 60 days to come up with a scientifically credible plan to manage for the spotted owl and other old growth dependent species. The BLM and the Forest Service called together agency experts, as well as those from various universities, to develop such a plan. Within 90 days—after a 30-day extension—the forest ecosystem management assessment team (FEMAT) produced a draft plan. At the same time, another overlapping team produced a supplemental environmental impact statement (SEIS) to discuss the implications for management. After the draft was circulated, the SEIS team was given until the following year to deliver a final SEIS. Then the northwest forest plan was written and signed by the two agencies, as well as by cooperating federal agencies such as the Fish and Wildlife Service and the National Marine Fisheries Service. Cooperation between the BLM and the Forest Service was never more thorough and productive. Yet, within a few years, cracks again developed over interpretations of the plan, court decisions, and national headquarters decisions.

At the same time, a less visible, but no less important, interior Columbia basin ecosystem assessment project (ICBEMP) team was assembled to assess the interior Columbia River basin. The goal was to address issues such as forest fires, noxious weeds, habitat restoration, and the socioeconomic conditions of the huge geographic area. The analysis included all ownerships—federal, state, and private. Part of the project—referred to as the westside team—was stationed at Walla Walla, Washington. This team was composed primarily of Forest Service employees. The westside team was concerned with the ecosystems of central and eastern Washington and Oregon within the Columbia basin drainage. An upper or eastside team of mostly BLM employees was headquartered in Boise, Idaho. Its work concerned the ecosystems of the easternmost reaches of the Columbia basin in Idaho, Montana, and slivers of other states.

Two draft environmental impact statements—one for the westside and the other for the eastside—were published in 1997. The teams were combined the following year to publish consistent assessments of the complete area. In response to public comments, new scientific information, agency review, and direction from the Secretaries of Agriculture and Interior, a supplemental draft EIS (SDEIS) was released in March 2000. The project released a final EIS and proposed decision in December 2000. In January 2003, the regional executives for the Forest Service, Forest Service research, the Bureau of Land Management, the Fish and Wildlife Service, the National Marine Fisheries Service, and the Environmental Protection Agency signed a memorandum of understanding (MOU) completing the project. The regional federal managers decided that instead of a formal decision on management of the basin, they would adopt a strategy of incorporating the science learned from the decade-old assessment into ongoing land use planning efforts. Unlike in the FEMAT process, the decision makers believed that this decision would lead to greater flexibility in the management of federal, state, and private lands in the basin. The agencies signing the MOU agreed to cooperatively implement the interior Columbia basin strategy. The agencies developed an aquatic/riparian habitat framework in July 2004 to clarify the interior Columbia basin strategy in relation to the aquatic and riparian habitat components.

USDI FISH AND WILDLIFE SERVICE

The origins of the USDI Fish and Wildlife Service began in 1871, when Congress established the Bureau of Fisheries, which was concerned primarily with commercial fishing. During 1940, the bureau was combined with the USDA Bureau of Biological Survey and renamed as the Fish and Wildlife Service (USF&WS). The new agency was divided into two bureaus in 1956—the Commercial Fisheries and the Sport Fisheries and Wildlife. Commercial Fisheries was shifted into the Department of Commerce in 1970, where it became the National Marine Fisheries Service. The remaining bureau was combined with the Fish and Wildlife Service in 1974.

Alaska's Afognak Forest and Fish Culture Reserve (later part of the Tongass National Forest) was established in 1892 to protect and preserve "salmon and other fish and sea animals, and other animals and birds." The first national wildlife refuge was established in 1902 by President Theodore Roosevelt when he set aside Pelican Island, off Florida, as a sanctuary for egrets, terns, and pelicans. Bureaucratic struggles resulted in the transfer of the bureau to USDI in 1939, and it was combined with the USDI Bureau of Fisheries to form the Fish and Wildlife Service.

Controversy has never been far behind regarding issues such as predator control programs (especially the use of poisons and traps), use of pesticides (inspired by Rachel Carson's 1962 book *Silent Spring*), propagation of trout and salmon through hatcheries (restocking of lakes and rivers), uncontrolled deer populations (as on the Kaibab National Forest), federal limits on waterfowl hunting and possession limits, and the management of national wildlife refuges. In recent years, enforcing provisions of the Endangered Species Conservation Act of 1969 and the Endangered Species Act of 1973 has become a bureaucratic nightmare that often pits scientists against developers and even other agencies. The most celebrated case involving the Endangered Species Act (ESA) was the 1976 case *Hill v. TVA*, over the status of Tellico Dam and the snail darter, an endangered fish. Recently, significant controversies involving the ESA have erupted over the northern spotted owl, the pileated woodpecker, and the reintroduction of the grey wolf into Yellowstone National Park, as well as the red wolf in the Southeast, the Mt. Graham red squirrel, grizzly bears, the California condor, Kirtland's warbler, the red-cockaded woodpecker, and several species of salmon in the Columbia River system.

In many cases, the animal, plant, or fish species find its home habitat on the national forests, and, in some instances, its only nesting, migratory, summer, or winter habitats can be found on the forests. The USF&WS has worked closely with the Forest Service, as well as the states, to ensure that habitats and, in some cases, the animals or fish themselves are protected for the future. In one instance, however, politics seems to have played an important role in what should have been a scientific investigation and management plan. The northern spotted owl in the Pacific Northwest by the late 1980s had become a political football. Political appointees (from multiple administrations) in charge of the USF&WS delayed for years a decision on whether to place the spotted owl on the threatened and endangered species list, knowing that placing the owl on the list would involve a reduction in the timber harvest on the federal and state lands where the owls nest. After more research had been done on the owl than on any other species, there was increasing agitation from the timber industry, affected communities, and people on all sides of the issue. After a successful lawsuit, the owl was listed in June 1990 as a threatened species. There were incredible amounts of news coverage, political cartoons, and hand wringing over the decision. As expected, there was a drastic reduction in timber harvest activities on the BLM and Forest Service. The controversy resulted in President Clinton's becoming directly involved with the Northwest forest plan to save the birds from extinction. Although the USF&WS was not one of the two agencies preparing the plan, it had oversight and presented opinions about the plan and its anticipated consequences for the owl and for related species, such as the marbled murrelet.

USDC NATIONAL MARINE FISHERIES SERVICE

The USDC National Marine Fisheries Service (NMFS) is a relative newcomer to resource management. National Marine Fisheries Service, which is part of the National Oceanic and Atmospheric Administration (NOAA), established in 1970, is the federal agency responsible for the stewardship of the nation's marine resources and their habitat. The public trust responsibility is derived from numerous laws, primary of which are the Magnuson-Stevens Fishery Conservation and Management Act, the Marine Mammal Protection Act, and the Endangered Species Act. Marine resources (generally in waters from 3 to 200 miles offshore) provide an important source of food and recreation for the nation, as well as thousands of jobs and a traditional way of life for many coastal communities. NMFS scientists and resource managers work to ensure the long-term sustainable use of the marine resources and their habitats for future generations.

The Magnuson-Stevens Act of 1996 provides a wide array of protections, requiring very conservative management targets, tight time frames for rebuilding stocks, consideration of habitat impacts, reducing bycatch (e.g., dolphins in tuna nets), and assessment of economic impacts on fishing-dependent communities. Under the Endangered Species Act of 1988, NMFS handles the listing, protection, and recovery of threatened and endangered marine, estuarine, and anadromous species. The Act requires federal agencies to use all reasonable methods available to conserve endangered and threatened species, to facilitate an increase in their populations, and to improve the quality of their habitats. NMFS develops and implements conservation and recovery plans, and works to prevent species from becoming threatened or endangered. The NMFS has been involved with anadromous fish stocks on both the Atlantic (salmon and striped bass) and the Pacific coasts (salmon issues).

NMFS has been an active agency since the 1990s in overseeing the management and recovery of certain salmon and steelhead fish stocks that are native to the Columbia River basin, as well as Alaska and California rivers—especially the Klamath and the Sacramento Rivers—which flow into the Pacific Ocean. Plans produced by the Forest Service and the BLM are routinely evaluated for the management of these important natural resources. In the late 1990s, NMFS evaluated the Tongass National Forest in Alaska timber harvesting plans and concluded that continued harvesting could lead to further declines in habitat needed for spawning and rearing and could contribute to the loss of salmon stocks. Since 1990, nine stocks of salmon and steelhead have been listed as threatened or endangered in these drainages. It is hoped that recent attempts to include hatchery fish in the counts of native fish that return from the ocean to spawn will be resolved in favor of keeping the two stocks split. Addressing the growing concerns over the fate of native fish species will continue to drive the agency and public opinion well into the future. The NMFS cooperates in managing terrestrial habitats with not only the Forest

Service but also with the BLM, the National Park Service, the Bonneville Power Administration, the Corps of Engineers, the Environmental Protection Agency, the Bureau of Reclamation, Indian tribes, states, cities, boroughs, municipal water districts, agricultural water districts, timber companies, and private landowners.

USDA NATURAL RESOURCES CONSERVATION SERVICE

The Soil Erosion Service was established in 1933. Its name was changed to the Soil Conservation Service (SCS) on April 27, 1935. This agency was the predecessor of the Natural Resources Conservation Service (NRCS). The Soil Erosion Service was created during the depths of the Great Depression, which was accompanied by devastating Dust Bowl conditions, where rich farmlands in the Great Plains were literally blowing in the wind. The SCS was concerned that soil erosion was a menace to the national welfare. The USDA Bureau of Soils, as early as 1899, begun making soil surveys to assist farmers. The resulting soil survey maps and descriptions of the soil were intended to make farmers aware of the soil conditions where they were farming so that they could make better decisions about avoiding unnecessary damage to the soils and could produce better crop yields. The SCS worked directly with farmers in cooperation with conservation districts.

As part of the Department of Agriculture Reorganization Act of 1994, the SCS's name was changed to the Natural Resources Conservation Service. The NRCS has had to adapt and tailor its services to changing agricultural conditions (especially drought and decreasing water supplies), congressional acts (including the various farm bills), and public concerns. In addition to working with individuals, the NRCS and the districts work with government agencies at all levels.

The Forest Service is one of many cooperating partners in many efforts through the state and private forestry program. A very early concern of Gifford Pinchot and all of the chiefs of the Forest Service since has been to help rural people and communities plant trees to cut erosion, help keep water clean, and provide shade and habitat for fish and other aquatic species. Many times, the Forest Service has provided tree seedlings to the NRCS to be distributed, often free of charge, to farmers and citizens. In one program, the Forest Service worked with the SCS from 1947 to 1985 on the Yazoo-Little Tallahatchie flood prevention project to control massive land erosion. The area, which was under treatment for almost 40 years, covered 19 counties of Mississippi—around 5.7 million acres. The western portion of the Yazoo River watershed project area, about 1.5 million acres, was a level, alluvial plain that was part of the Mississippi Delta. The remaining acres were rolling uplands. Both areas had been heavily impacted by exploitative farming and logging practices. In 1966, another 720,000 acres were added to the recovery project. The U.S. Army Corps of Engineers managed about 282,000 acres within the project area, while the Holly Springs National Forest made up another 142,000 acres. Funding was provided by Congress to the SCS, which then allocated funds for forest replanting in the area. Both agencies supplied technical assistance to landowners, and the SCS also prepared conservation plans for each farm in the affected counties.

☆ 8 ☆

Chronology of Key Events and People

Many chronologies of conservation have been developed over the years for many different purposes. The following chronology selects important events and people associated with conservation, forestry, and the Forest Service. Probably the most often visited chronology is The Library of Congress Web site "Documented Chronology of Selected Events in the Development of the American Conservation Movement, 1847–1920." Other chronologies include Samuel Trask Dana, *Forest and Range Policy: Its Development in the United States* (1956); Samuel Trask Dana and Sally K. Fairfax's *Forest and Range Policy: Its Development in the United States* (1980), the second edition of Dana's 1956 classic; Richard C. Davis (ed.), *Encyclopedia of American Forest and Conservation History* (1983), two volumes; Bernhard E. Fernow's *Report Upon the Forestry Investigations ... 1877–1898* (1899); Chris McGrory Klyza's "Land Protection in the United States, 1864–1997" (*Wild Earth*, Vol. 8, no. 2 [Summer 1998]: 35–42); Harold K. Steen, *The U.S. Forest Service: A History* (1976); and USDA Forest Service's "Highlights in the History of Forest Conservation" (1976).

1799

The Federal Timber Purchasers Act of February 25 (1 Stat. 622) appropriates $200,000 to buy timber and timberland for naval purposes. Blackbeard and Grover Islands, off the Georgia coast, are purchased. These are the first federal purchases of timbered land for government use.

1807

An Act of March 3 (2 Stat. 445) forbids anyone to settle on or occupy the public lands until authorized by law. U.S. marshals are authorized to remove trespassers and to use measures to ensure compliance with the law.

1812

The General Land Office is established in the Treasury Department on April 25 (2 Stat. 716). The major work of the new agency is to sell or grant the huge public domain land to settlers, miners, railroad corporations, wagon road companies, and similar entities.

1817

An Act of March 1 (3 Stat. 347), renews the 1799 Act, directs the president to reserve live oak or cedar timbered public lands that may have use for the U.S. Navy. Under this Act, 19,000 acres are reserved on Commissioners, Cypress, and Six Islands, in Louisiana. The live oak lands are administered by the Navy Department.

1822

Congress passes an act for "the preservation of timber of the United States in Florida," which is intended to prevent the theft and destruction of government-owned timber.

1825

Following extensive logging and land clearing for farms, two huge forest fires, known as the Miramichi and Piscataquis fires, burn perhaps 3 million acres in Maine and New Brunswick. Late in the century, many gigantic fires will burn in the Lake States.

1827

The Federal Timber Reservation Act of March 3 (4 Stat. 242) establishes the Santa Rosa live oak timber reserve near Pensacola, Florida, for the exclusive use by the navy. This is the first federal timberland reservation that is used for forestry purposes. Thirty thousand acres of the Santa Rosa peninsula (which extends into the Bay of Pensacola) is intended to be the first forest experiment station with planting live oaks, clearing brush, creating firebreaks, and keeping trespassers out, but the idea becomes a political issue and is dropped by 1832.

1828

The Naval Appropriations Act approves spending not more than $100,000 to purchase land necessary for the continuous supply of live oak and other timber for the Navy. This is spent on the Santa Rosa Naval Timber Reserve and Experiment Station. Henry M. Brackenridge, in a letter to Secretary Samuel Southard, of the Navy Department, discusses the culturing of live oak. This is one of the first American papers on silviculture.

1830

State of Missouri petitions Congress to grant the state a township of land to experiment with planting and growing of trees. The petition is turned down, but the idea is kept alive.

1831

The Timber Trespass Act of March 2 (4 Stat. 472), relating to the live oak and other timber reservations, becomes the basis for present-day laws for the prevention of timber trespass on federal land. Fines for timber trespass will be not less than three times the value of the timber cut.

1832

D. J. Browne publishes *The Sylva Americana*. This is the first compilation of the description of forest trees in the United States. This book influences Americans' understanding of trees and forest in the years to come.

1841

The Preemption Act of September 4 (5 Stat. 453) allows settlers to purchase public domain land before auctions. Also, citizens more than 21 years of age can settle on 160 acres of public domain land subject to certain restrictions. The land can be purchased for $1.25 per acre.

1843

Reservations of live oak lands in Louisiana are opened for settlement. The disposal of live oak reservations continues until 1923.

1847

George Perkins Marsh, a U.S. congressman from Vermont, delivers a seminal speech to the Agricultural Society of Rutland County, Vermont, calling attention to the destructive impact of human activity on the land, especially through deforestation, and advocating a conservationist approach to the management of forested lands. Marsh's speech is published the following year as an "Address Delivered before the Agricultural Society of Rutland County, Sept. 30, 1847."

1849

The Department of the Interior is established on March 3 (9 Stat. 395–397) with responsibility for the public lands. This new department incorporates the

General Land Office (Department of the Treasury), the Indian Affairs Office (War Department), the Patent Office (Department of State), and the military pension offices (War and Navy Departments).

1850

The first federal timber agents are appointed by the Secretary of the Interior to protect public timberlands. The agents are discontinued five years later when their duties are transferred to the district land registers and receivers in the General Land Office.

Citing the observations of Alexander von Humboldt and others on the effects of deforestation, Thomas Ewbank, the Commissioner of Patents, warns in his two-volume *Report of the Commissioner of Patents, for the Year 1849* (House of Representatives Executive Document No. 20) that "the waste of valuable timber in the United States, to say nothing of firewood, will hardly begin to be appreciated until our population reaches fifty million. Then the folly and shortsightedness of this age will meet with a degree of censure and reproach not pleasant to contemplate." Articles on the long-term harm produced by forest destruction appear in the reports of the commissioners of patents and of agriculture in this decade and during the 1860s, 1870s, and 1880s.

1851

Henry David Thoreau delivers an address to the Concord (Massachusetts) Lyceum and declares that "in Wildness is the preservation of the World." In 1863, this address is published posthumously as the essay "Walking" in Thoreau's *Excursions*.

1854

Henry David Thoreau publishes *Walden; or, Life in the Woods*. The book is an account of his retreat to the New England countryside and his growing disillusion with the growing industrialization and urbanization in America. This volume, still in print 150 years later, has given inspiration to millions of conservationists and environmentalists.

1857

James Russell Lowell publishes an article in *The Crayon* calling for the establishment of a society to protect American trees such as the recently "discovered" California redwoods.

1858

The Georgia state legislature petitions Congress to appoint a federal commission to inquire into the extent and duration of the southern pine belt.

1860

Henry David Thoreau delivers an address to the Middlesex (Massachusetts) Agricultural Society, titled "The Succession of Forest Trees," in which he analyzes aspects of what later came to be understood as forest ecology and urges farmers to plant trees in natural patterns.

In an early example of the government-sponsored scientific and ethnographic survey reports on the West, Congress publishes the 13-volume *Reports of Explorations and Surveys, to Ascertain the Most Practicable and Economical Route for a Railroad from the Mississippi River to the Pacific Ocean* (sometimes referred to as the Pacific Railroad Surveys 1854–1855). These reports, and other similar railroad survey expeditions through the West, include accounts of surveying and mapping that greatly increase knowledge of and interest in the Western landscape.

1862

The Department of Agriculture is established on May 15 (12 Stat. 387).

The Homestead Act of May 20 (12 Stat. 392) allows those willing to head West to acquire—for almost free—160 acres of land by paying a filing fee and then living on the land for five years. Nearly 550 million acres of public domain land pass into private ownership because of this law.

With the Civil War raging across much of the South and East, Congress passes authorizes a number of huge land grants that are given to railroads, canal companies, and even military wagon road companies (Oregon only) to encourage westward expansion. The largest recipients of the land grants are the Northern Pacific, Central Pacific, Union Pacific, and Oregon and California Railroads. Nearly 200 million acres of public land are transferred to the railroads in the second half of the nineteenth century. These huge railroad land grants are intended to allow the railroads to sell grant land adjacent to the railroads to homesteaders in order to offset the building costs of the rail line.

1864

George Perkins Marsh publishes *Man and Nature; or, Physical Geography as Modified by Human Action* (revised 1874 as *The Earth as Modified by Human Action*), the first systematic analysis of humanity's destructive impact on the environment, especially in his personal observations in the Mediterranean area. This important book becomes (in Lewis Mumford's words) "the fountain-head of the conservation movement."

In precedent-setting legislation, Congress passes a bill on June 30 (13 Stat. 325) granting Yosemite Valley to the State of California as a public park. The Yosemite Valley and Mariposa Big Tree Grove are granted to the state of California to hold these lands forever "for public use, resort, and recreation." These lands are incorporated into Yosemite National Park in 1906 (34 Stat. 831) after California discovers that it cannot manage the land effectively.

Henry David Thoreau's *The Maine Woods*, in which Thoreau calls for the establishment of "national preserves" of virgin forest, "not for idle sport or food, but for inspiration and our own true re-creation," is published posthumously.

1866

Congress, on July 25, grants the Oregon & California Railroad Company alternate, odd-numbered sections of nonmineral land within 20 miles on either side of the railroad line in western Oregon and northern California. Remnants of the western Oregon grant are to be returned to the federal government in 1916. These lands will become the basis for the Bureau of Land Management lands in western Oregon.

1870

The ninth U.S. census, for the first time, includes a survey of forest resources under the direction of F.W. Brewer.

1871

Congress passes an act authorizing the expenditure of $5,000 for the "protection of timberlands." This is intended to be used for protection of the naval timber (live oak) reservations. This is the first appropriation for the protection of publicly owned timber. The next year, the amount is doubled and applies to all public lands.

The Peshtigo Fire in the fall near Green Bay, Wisconsin, kills 1,500 people and blackens 1.28 million acres. This fire is burning at the same time as the Great Chicago Fire. Other fires in nearby Michigan burn another 2.5 million acres. Numerous homes, towns, and settlements are swept away by the flames. Other major fires in the Lake States later include the fire in the Thumb region of Michigan, in 1881 (1 million acres burned and 169 lives lost) and the Hinckley fire in Wisconsin, in 1894 (several million acres and 418 lives lost).

Henry George publishes *Our Land and Land Policy, National and State*, an influential critique deploring the squandering of the public domain and its natural resources.

1872

Congress passes "An Act to set apart a certain Tract of Land lying near the Head-waters of the Yellowstone River as a public Park," thus establishing Yellowstone National Park, Wyoming, the first in the history of the nation and of the world; the *Report of the Superintendent of the Yellowstone National Park for the Year 1872*, published the following year, provides a portrait of the new park at its birth. The park is established as a "public park or pleasuring-ground for the benefit and enjoyment of the people."

At the initiative of J. Sterling Morton, of the State Board of Agriculture, Nebraska observes "Tree-Planting Day" on April 10, inaugurating the tradition that soon becomes known as Arbor Day. By 1907, Arbor Day is observed annually in every state in the Union, most importantly in the nation's schools, where (as revealed in works such as the 1893 booklet *Arbor Day Leaves*) it provides several generations of young Americans with their most significant training in conservation principles and practice.

The General Mining Act of May 10 (17 Stat. 91) allows almost unrestricted access to public domain lands to search for and patent-transfer from public ownership to private ownership mineral-bearing lands for a minimal fee of $2.50 per acre.

1873

The Timber Culture Act of March 3 (17 Stat. 605–606) expands portions of the Homestead Act of 1862 by allowing settlers to plant trees as a substitute for the provision requiring that settlers live on the land. Settlers are granted a patent (private ownership) to as much as 160 acres in the Great Plains if at least one-fourth of the land is planted with trees and kept growing in a healthy condition for 10 years. Great land frauds come about because of this law, with almost 11 million acres of public domain being disposed of before the law is repealed in 1891 (see the Forest Reserve Act of 1891 listing).

Under the influence of Marsh's *Man and Nature; or, Physical Geography as Modified by Human Action*, Dr. Franklin Benjamin Hough, on August 21, reads a paper at the annual meeting of the American Association for the Advancement of Science (AAAS), in Portland, Maine, titled "On the Duty of Governments in the Preservation of Forests"; this inspires the AAAS, on the following day, to prepare and submit a memorial (petition) to Congress "on the importance of promoting the cultivation of timber and the preservation of forests," which spurs congressional interest in forest protection. Hough is a physician, statistician, and naturalist living in Lowville, New York.

Initial publication of *Forest and Stream* magazine, which—especially under the leadership of George Bird Grinnell, senior editor and publisher from 1880 to 1911—becomes the major American sportsmen's magazine by the turn of the century and a forum for conservation advocacy.

Lectures on forestry begin at Yale University. The following year, Cornell adds forestry instruction, and Michigan follows in 1881. By 1887, instruction or course work in forestry are offered at the New Hampshire, Massachusetts, Michigan, Missouri, and Iowa agricultural colleges, as well as the universities of Pennsylvania and North Carolina and at Cornell and Yale.

1874

In February, Hough and a cowriter, George B. Emerson, present the AAAS memorial to President Ulysses S. Grant, who then passes it to Congress as a special message and transmits a draft of proposed forestry legislation.

Secretary of the Interior Columbus Delano writes, in the annual department report, that he has concerns about "the rapid destruction of timber," on both private and public lands. He believes that some type of protective legislation is "absolutely necessary" to protect the public interest.

1875

American Forestry Association (AFA) is founded, in Chicago, on September 10, by John A. Warder and a number of concerned botanists and horticulturists; Franklin B. Hough is prominent at the organization meeting; before 1900, the AFA emphasizes appreciation and protection of trees rather than forestry as an economic problem.

Congress passes "An act to protect ornamental and other trees on Government reservations and on lands purchased by the United States, and for other purposes," forbidding the unauthorized cutting or injury of trees on government property.

1876

John Muir publishes "God's First Temples: How Shall We Preserve Our Forests?," one of his earliest pieces of published writing, in the *Sacramento Record-Union*; in this article he suggests the necessity for government protection of forests.

After Congress allocates $2,000 in a Department of Agriculture appropriations bill on August 15 (19 Stat. 143, 167) for "some man of approved attainments" to report to Congress on forestry matters, Franklin B. Hough is appointed first federal forestry agent by Commissioner of Agriculture Frederick Watts. Hough's task is to gather statistics about the state of the nation's forests, including the supply and demand for timber and other forest products, efforts in other countries to manage their forests, and the means used in the United States to preserve and renew the forests, and to investigate the links between forests and climate.

1877

Carl Schurz begins a four-year term as Secretary of the Interior; under his leadership, the Department of the Interior takes an active interest in conservation issues for the first time, and Schurz himself advocates far-sighted conservation policies, such as the creation of forest reserves and a federal forest service. J. A. Williamson, a militant advocate of public forest control, is appointed as the Commissioner of the USDI General Land Office (GLO). Responsibilities for federal timber protection are taken from the GLO land registers and receivers and placed with a special force of timber agents. A drive is started against timber thieves and depredations, especially unlawful use and fire.

J. A. Williamson, Commissioner of the General Land Office, summarizes abuses inflicted upon public timberland in the *Annual Report of the Commissioner of the*

General Land Office for the Fiscal Year 1877. The timber depredations report, on pages 16–26, is intended to arouse Congress to action, but little response is forthcoming.

1878

The Free Timber Act of June 3 (20 Stat. 88–89) give miners the right to cut timber on public domain mineral claims for both mining and domestic purposes in the states of Colorado, Nevada, New Mexico, Arizona, Utah, Wyoming, Idaho, and Montana, as well as in the Dakota Territory. The Timber and Stone Act of June 3 (20 Stat. 89–91) authorizes the sale of nontillable public timberland for personal use. The minimum price is to be $2.50 per acre, with a maximum of 160 acres per person in the states of Washington, Oregon, California, and Nevada. More land frauds result.

John Wesley Powell, the geologist in charge of the U.S. Geographical and Geological Survey of the Rocky Mountain Region, publishes *Report on the Lands of the Arid Region of the United States,* a pioneering work recognizing the West's unique environmental character, advocating irrigation and conservation efforts in it, and calling for the distribution of western lands to settlers on a democratic and environmentally realistic basis. Franklin B. Hough issues the landmark 650-page *Report upon Forestry* to Congress, the first fruit of the federal government's forestry activities and a wide-ranging survey of information and issues pertinent to the management of the nation's forests, as well as the international situation with regard to forestry matters. Congress orders that 25,000 copies of the report be printed.

A bill is introduced in Congress to protect public domain timberland from sale or disposal, with the commercially valuable timberlands to be held by the government to prevent destruction by fire and waste, ensure the restoration and reproduction of the forests, and regulate sale of trees for timber. An office of forester is to be set up in the Interior Department, with employment of foresters to manage the public forests. The bill fails to pass, but the ideas are kept alive for another 20 years.

1879

The annual Sundry Civil Appropriations Act on March 3 (20 Stat. 377) officially establishes the U.S. Geological Survey as a bureau of the Interior Department, with responsibility for "the classification of the public lands." The Act also authorizes the appointment of a Public Lands Commission (20 Stat. 394–95) to review federal public land policy; members include John Wesley Powell, Clarence Dutton, and Clarence King. The Commission spends several months traveling in the West, surveying land use. The Commission's report to Congress expresses differing views among the Commissioners on how to rationalize land policy, including the need for a law to correct abuses of existing homestead and timber use laws; it advises that public lands covered with timber be withdrawn from settlement that portions of these forestlands be set aside as forest reserves. However, all the recommendations are ignored by Congress.

1880s

The American Forestry Association and the American Association for the Advancement of Science advocate designation of western timberlands as permanent public reservations.

1880

The tenth U.S. census includes, for the second time, a survey of forest resources, under the direction of Charles S. Sargent.

1881

The Division of Forestry is provisionally established in the Department of Agriculture, with Franklin B. Hough as its first chief; its role is largely confined to dispensing information and technical forestry advice to private landowners. The remaining volumes of the *Report upon Forestry* are issued until 1884 under Hough and his successor, Nathaniel H. Egleston.

1882

The American Forestry Congress meets in Cincinnati in April and Montreal in August. Dr. Bernhard E. Fernow is the secretary of the Forestry Congress.

George Perkins Marsh dies in Italy, where he has been serving as U.S. minister since 1861. At the time of his death, he is working on additional revisions to the latest edition of *Man and Nature* (which he has retitled *The Earth as Modified by Human Action*).

1883

Thomas Donaldson documents the many types of fraudulent land entries on public domain land in his book *The Public Domain*, published by the U.S. Government Printing Office.

1884

Charles Sprague Sargent, the visionary director of Harvard University's Arnold Arboretum, publishes a "Report on the Forests of North America (Exclusive of Mexico)" as part of the tenth census; in addition to containing important scientific information, this influential work warns of the need to reform destructive timber management policies.

1885

Six bills are introduced in Congress for the creation of public forest reserves. None pass.

1886

In an appropriations bill for the Department of Agriculture, the Division of Forestry is granted permanent status within the Department (24 Stat. 100, 103); Bernhard E. Fernow is named the Division of Forestry chief.

1887

In December, Theodore Roosevelt invites a number of influential sportsman friends to dinner in Manhattan to discuss the creation of a hunting and conservation organization. He and George Bird Grinnell, editor of the highly regarded *Forest and Stream Weekly*, devise the idea. The following month (January 1888), the Boone and Crockett Club is founded, with Roosevelt elected the club's first president. This organization plays a major role in associating big game hunters with the conservation movement; the Club eventually publishes several volumes of writings on hunting and conservation, including *American Big Game in Its Haunts: The Book of the Boone and Crockett Club*, in 1904.

Charles Sprague Sargent founds and directs *Garden and Forest*, a literate, thoughtful, and informative weekly that does much to foster awareness of and interest in American forests, trees, horticulture, landscape design, and scenic preservation during the 10 years of its publication. His editorials from 1888 to 1897 help stimulate public opinion in favor of federal forest and park conservation.

The Division of Forestry releases a "Report on the Relation of Railroads for Forest Supplies and Forestry." The report warns about the huge need among the railroads for wooden ties and wood to fire the steam engines. It will be years before the practice of soaking railroad ties with creosote dramatically reduces the need for replacement wood ties cut from the private forests.

1888

The American Forestry Association presents a bill to Congress, written by Bernhard E. Fernow, chief of the Division of Forestry. The unsuccessful bill, which provides for the withdrawal from homesteading or sale of all public timberlands, is resubmitted over the next three years, until it becomes the basis for the Forest Reserve Act of 1891.

1889

The American Forestry Association presents a report of timber trespass and timber thievery on the public lands to President Benjamin Harrison. The report notes that between 1881 and 1887, more than $36 million worth of timber has been taken unlawfully, with only about $475,000 worth recovered by the government.

Editorials by Robert Underwood Johnson in *Century* magazine in the 1889–1891 period help turn public opinion in favor of federal forest conservation.

1890

Congress authorizes (26 Stat. 146) the Secretary of the Interior to employ Indians to cut of 20 million board feet of green timber on the Menominee Indian Reservation, in Wisconsin. This is the first law regulating the cutting of timber on government-managed lands.

1891

The General Revision Act of 1891, otherwise known as the Payson Act and the Forest Reserve or Creative Act of March 3 (26 Stat. 1095, 1103) "to repeal timber-culture laws, and for other purposes" becomes law. This Act is a rider—section 24—to a broader bill to repeal the Timber Culture Act of 1873, the Preemption Act of 1841, and other homestead acts. Section 24 empowers the president to create "forest reserves" (later known as national forests) by withdrawing forest covered land from the public domain; this creates the legislative foundation for what became the national forest system.

President Benjamin Harrison issues Presidential Proclamation 17 on March 30 (26 Stat. 1565), setting aside the Yellowstone Park Timber Land Reserve a 1,239,040-acre tract of land on the southern edge of Yellowstone National Park in Wyoming as the nation's first forest reservation, the first unit in what eventually becomes the national forest system. Today, the reserve is called the Shoshone National Forest. Before President Harrison's term of office expires, he establishes some 13 million acres of forest reserves from public domain forestland in the West.

1891–1902

Charles Sprague Sargent publishes his 14-volume *The Silva of North America; A Description of the Trees Which Grow Naturally in North America Exclusive of Mexico*, the seminal work on American dendrology.

1892

Gifford Pinchot is hired as the first American professional forester on the Biltmore Estate of George W. Vanderbilt near Asheville, North Carolina. This forest area is later donated to the Forest Service to be part of the national forest system, and it later becomes part of the Pisgah National Forest.

President Benjamin Harrison issues a proclamation setting aside a tract of land in Alaska as a forest and fish culture reservation (known as the Afognak Forest and Fish-Culture Reserve), thus creating what is in effect, if not in name, the first national wildlife refuge.

1896

The National Academy of Sciences establishes a committee on the forest reserves, chaired by Charles Sprague Sargent, with Gifford Pinchot as its youngest member. The committee tours the existing and potentially new forest reserves in the West in the summer of 1896. It proposes to greatly increase the area of the forest reserves by creating or enlarging 13 reserves covering more than 21 million acres (the president establishes the reserves on February 22, 1897, leading to the Organic Act of 1897) and to establish two national parks—Mt. Rainier (created from the Mt. Rainier Forest Reserve, in 1899) and Grand Canyon (created from the Grand Canyon Forest Reserve, in 1903, and Grand Canyon National Monument, in 1919).

1897

As part of an appropriations bill, Congress, after heated discussion, passes what is known as the Forest Management Act, or Organic Act, on June 4 (30 Stat. 11, 34), delaying for nine months the establishment of the forest reserves approved on February 22, except for those in California. The Act makes explicit the purposes of forest reserves (later national forests): to protect the forest, provide water, and allow timber harvest, as well as to use resources for recreation, lumbering, mining, and grazing. It provides the blueprint for the forests' management until the 1960s. This Act also places federal forest administration under the jurisdiction of the USDI General Land Office. There is a requirement that forest survey and mapping work be completed by the USDI Geological Survey, which establishes a Division of Geography and Forestry. Another provision of the Act allows "in lieu" trading of public land inside the forest reserve boundaries for other public lands outside the boundaries. Great land frauds ensue. Pinchot is hired by the GLO as a "confidential forestry agent" to investigate the management of the forest reserves. GLO forest reserve superintendents are hired to oversee the management of the reserves on one or more states in the West.

This year and the next, John Muir publishes two articles in the *Atlantic Monthly*, "The American Forests" (1897) and "The Wild Parks and Forest Reservations of the West" (1898), which reveal the shift in his thought from compromise to absolute opposition on the question of "use" of protected resources; these articles are later republished in his book *Our National Parks*, in 1901.

1898

Gifford Pinchot is appointed chief of the USDA Division of Forestry on July 1 (30 Stat. 597, 618) and requests that his title be "the forester" (this new title will remain until 1935 when the title "chief" is reestablished); he begins crusade to convert the public and the forest industry to support for scientific forest management. The USDI-GLO hires the first forest rangers to work on the forest reserves during the summer fire season. The forest ranger jobs are to stop fires, build trails, look for timber thieves and grazing trespass, and try to find out more about the huge forest reserves and their resources.

The first four-year curriculum in forestry in the United States starts at Cornell University, in New York. In this same year, the Biltmore Forest School is also established. Other schools of forestry soon follow.

1899

The Act of February 28 provides for recreational use of the forest reserves. This is the first law to recognize the value of forests for recreational use.

1900

Congress appropriates $5,000 for the investigation of forest conditions in the Appalachians with the notion that some land could be purchased for forest reserves.

The Society of American Foresters is established on November 19 in the office of Gifford Pinchot, in the old Department of Agriculture building in Washington, D.C; Pinchot, Henry Graves, Overton Price, E. T. Allen, William Hall, Ralph Hosmer, and Thomas Sherrard are the founding members; the meetings will later be held in Pinchot's home.

1901

The USDA Division of Forestry becomes the Bureau of Forestry on March 2 (31 Stat. 922, 929). A Forestry Division is created on November 15 in the USDI General Land Office, with Filibert Roth at its head. The first timber sale on the forest reserves is from the Black Hills Forest Reserve, in South Dakota. In the annual report of the Interior Secretary Ethan Allen Hitchcock, Roth recommends that the forest reserves be placed in the USDA Bureau of Forestry. This does not happen until 1905.

Theodore Roosevelt becomes president of the United States upon the death of President McKinley on September 14, and conservation becomes a cornerstone of his domestic policy. In his first annual message, Roosevelt outlines his goals of forest conservation and preservation (including the use of forest reserves as wildlife preserves), and the need for government-sponsored irrigation projects in the arid West.

1902

Bernhard E. Fernow publishes *The Economics of Forestry: A Reference Book for Students of Political Economy and Professional and Lay Students of Forestry*, a

comprehensive overview of forestry principles and their contemporary and historical relationship to public policy, written at a time when forestry practices are in the
vanguard of conservationism.

1903

Concern about the administration of public lands in the West, particularly the
question of grazing leases for cattlemen, prompts the Roosevelt administration to
appoint a Public Lands Commission to study and report on public lands issues;
the Commission's members are W. A. Richards, Frederick H. Newell, and Gifford
Pinchot.

1905

Acting under the influence of Gifford Pinchot, the American Forestry Association sponsors the American Forest Congress in Washington, D.C.; attended by
leaders of lumbering, mining, grazing, and irrigation industries and by leaders in
education and government, the Congress underscores the great need for natural
resource management as important to the national economic well-being.

Gifford Pinchot succeeds in having the oversight of national forest reserves
transferred from the General Land Office to the Bureau of Forestry. This is accomplished by "An Act Providing for the Transfer of Forest Reserves from the
Department of Interior to the Department of Agriculture," known as the Transfer
Act of February 1 (33 Stat. 628). This change also symbolizes a shift of emphasis
from preservation to scientific forestry and cements Pinchot's dominance in public
conservation policy.

The name of the Bureau of Forestry is changed, on March 3 (33 Stat. 861, 872–
873), to the Forest Service. The USDA Division of Biological Survey becomes the
Bureau of Biological Survey, also on March 3 (33 Stat. 861, 877). Another March
3 (33 Stat. 1264) act repeals the forest lieu provision of the Organic Act of 1897
that is the source of many land frauds.

The president is authorized to set aside areas in the Wichita Forest Reserve
as a game refuge. That portion of the reserve is transferred to the USDI Fish and
Wildlife Service in 1936.

1906

The Forest Service begins charging for grazing cattle and sheep on the forest
reserves on January 1.

The American Antiquities Act of June 8 (34 Stat. 225) forbids persons without
proper authority to appropriate, excavate, injure, or destroy an historic or prehistoric
ruin or monument of antiquity on land owned or controlled by the government. It
also authorizes the president to establish national monuments for the preservation
of features of historic, prehistoric, and scientific interest.

The Forest Homestead Act of June 11 (34 Stat. 233) allows settlers to homestead within forest reserves if the land is more valuable for farming than for timbering. Great land frauds develop.

An act is passed by Congress, becoming law on June 30 (34 Stat. 669, 684), that gives 10 percent of the revenues from the national forests to the states or territories where the forest reserves (national forests) are located. The money is earmarked for public roads and schools.

President Roosevelt issues a presidential proclamation on September 24 establishing Devil's Tower National Monument, Wyoming, as the nation's first national monument

This year and the following, Gifford Pinchot prepares several bills for Congress to place the national parks under the Forest Service management so that they may be open for resource development; these measures are successfully opposed by Rep. John F. Lacey, chairman of the House Public Lands Committee and a congressional spokesman for the preservationist approach to conservation; Pinchot's effort ultimately backfires by sparking the preservationists' campaign to establish a permanent separate bureau to administer the national parks.

1907

Through provisions embedded in the Forest Service subsection of an Agriculture appropriations act, Congress renames forest reserves "national forests" and forbids their further creation or enlargement in six Western states (Oregon, Washington, Idaho, Montana, Colorado, and Wyoming), except by act of Congress (34 Stat. 1256, 1269); when the bill passes Congress on February 25, Pinchot and his staff work feverishly to identify 16 million acres of forest in these six states to be designated national forests by President Roosevelt before he signs the bill into law, on March 4. Since then, these have often been referred to as the "midnight reserves." California is not included in the ban but is added in 1912 (37 Stat. 497).

The president establishes two additional national monuments later in the year—the Gila Cliff Dwellings, in New Mexico (November 16) and the Tonto, in Arizona (December 19). Both these monuments are on national forest land.

In his seventh annual message, President Roosevelt makes an especially forceful case for utilitarian conservationism, asserting that "the conservation of our natural resources and their proper use constitute the fundamental problem which underlies almost every other problem of our National life" and that his administration has been trying "to substitute a planned and orderly development of our resources in place of a haphazard striving for immediate profit."

John Muir publishes "The Tuolumne Yosemite in Danger" in *Outlook*, the opening salvo in his campaign to save Hetch Hetchy Valley, in the northern part of Yosemite National Park, from damming. The Tuolumne River will be used as a reservoir to provide drinking water for San Francisco. The campaign preservation becomes a national issue for a decade. This issue signals the ideological split of the conservation movement between advocates of preservationist conservationism (those who seek to retain natural areas in their "natural" state), as advocated by Muir, and advocates of utilitarian conservationism (those who seek to manage the sustainable harvesting of natural resources for human benefit), as pronounced by Pinchot.

1908

The first Governors' Conference on the Conservation of Natural Resources is called by President Roosevelt and organized by Gifford Pinchot and his associate WJ McGee, whom Pinchot calls "the scientific brains of the new [conservation] movement." The conference is largely financed by Pinchot. The conference is held May 13–15 at the White House, propelling conservation issues into the forefront of public consciousness and stimulating a large number of private and state-level conservation initiatives. The Conference's *Proceedings* are published in 1909. A second Conference is held at the end of the year to receive the recommendations of the National Conservation Commission.

The first forest reserve created by Congress, rather than by presidential proclamation, is established on May 23 (PL 137-35 Stat. 268) as the Minnesota Forest Reserve. The name is changed to the Chippewa National Forest in 1928.

The Agricultural Appropriations Act of May 23 (35 Stat. 251, 260) increases payments to the states for schools and roads to 25 percent of the national forest receipts.

The Forest Service reorganizes the field offices to include district offices (now regional offices) to create a buffer between the national office and the national forest offices. Six new offices are created (Portland, San Francisco, Albuquerque, Denver, Ogden, and Missoula). Several others are later established, in Philadelphia, Atlanta, Milwaukee, and Juneau.

The first Forest Service forest experiment station (the Coconino Forest Experiment Station) is established at Fort Valley, on the Coconino Plateau, in Arizona. In 1911; it later is renamed the Fort Valley Forest Experiment Station and then, in 1924, the Southwestern Forest Experiment Station. More experiment stations follow in other locations in the West.

The National Conservation Commission, appointed in June by President Roosevelt and composed of representatives of Congress and several executive agencies—Gifford Pinchot is chair—compiles an inventory of natural resources in the United States. The three-volume report submitted to Congress on January 22, 1909, presents Pinchot's concepts of scientific resource management as a policy recommendation. The *Proceedings* underscore the importance of private conservation activity, including that of women's groups.

1909

The Calaveras Bigtree National Forest is created in California by Congress on February 8 (PL 237, 35 Stat. 626). Part of the forest is transferred to the state of

California in 1990 to become the Calaveras State Park. The 1909 Act authorizes the acquisition of lands in California to protect stands of giant Sequoia (*Sequoia washingtoniana*).

President Roosevelt convenes the North American Conservation Conference, held in Washington, on February 18 and attended by representatives of Canada, Newfoundland, Mexico, and the United States. Statements of principles of conservation for North America are adopted.

President Roosevelt, on March 2—just before he leaves office—issues a proclamation establishing Mount Olympus National Monument, Washington. The 630,000-acre monument is carved from the center of the Olympic National Forest. This monument will affect Forest Service policies in the 1930s.

1910

Having publicly leveled charges of official impropriety against Secretary of the Interior Richard A. Ballinger, Gifford Pinchot is dismissed from government service by President Taft on January 7. Pinchot then turns to pressing for implementation of his policies through the National Conservation Association, which he founded the previous year. Pinchot serves as the association's president from 1910 until it dissolves in the 1920s.

Henry Graves, a close friend of Pinchot, is appointed chief of the Forest Service. Graves had been in charge of the Yale School of Forestry from its founding in 1900.

Pinchot publishes *The Fight for Conservation*, a summary of his beliefs about the nature and importance of the conservation movement. "Conservation means the greatest good to the greatest number for the longest time," Pinchot writes (p. 48); "it demands the complete and orderly development of all our resources for the benefit of all the people, instead of the partial exploitation of them for the benefit of a few. It recognizes fully the right of the present generation to use what it needs and all it needs of the natural resources now available, but it recognizes equally our obligation so to use what we need that our descendants shall not be deprived of what they need" (p. 80).

Between January and April, following a joint congressional resolution, a joint committee of the Senate and the House holds hearings on the Ballinger-Pinchot controversy, investigating the activities of both the Department of Interior and the Forest Service; though dominated by politics, these investigations—transcripts of which eventually fill some 13 printed volumes—are also, in the historian Samuel Hays's words, "a gold mine of information about resource affairs" in this era.

The USDA Forest Service's Forest Products Laboratory is dedicated in June at Madison, Wisconsin, in cooperation with the University of Wisconsin. The laboratory quickly becomes the world's most authoritative institution for the scientific study of wood and its uses.

Huge forest fires burn in Idaho and Montana and adjacent states, blackening more than 3 million acres at the cost of 85 lives; 74 of the dead are firefighters.

This deadly fire helps to prod Congress to act and results in the incorporation of federal-state firefighting cooperation clauses in the Weeks Act of 1911.

1911

The Weeks Act of March 1 (36 Stat. 961) authorizes interstate compacts for water and forest conservation and federal acquisition of land for the purpose of protecting watersheds; it also places large amounts of eastern forestland under federal jurisdiction for the first time since they were purchased and provides financial aid for efforts to protect from fire timberlands at the heads of navigable streams.

In an important Supreme Court case, *United States v. Grimaud,* the court rules that Congress has the constitutional right to reserve lands for national forests, to delegate authority to the Secretary of Agriculture to make rules and regulations, and to prescribe penalties for violations of the regulations. The court also confirms the right to charge fees for grazing permits.

1912

An act of Congress (37 Stat. 269, 288) provides that 10 percent of all forest receipts will be used for roads and trails within the national forests in the states from where the receipts came. This provision is made permanent the following year (37 Stat. 828, 843).

1913

Debate over the fate of Hetch Hetchy continues in the national press throughout the year. Intensive campaigning by the Sierra Club and the Appalachian Mountain Club, as well as by concerned individuals throughout the country, fails to turn Congress. The Raker Act, granting San Francisco permission to build a dam in the Hetch Hetchy Valley, is signed into law by President Woodrow Wilson on December 19 (38 Stat. 242).

A new National Forest Reservation Commission is authorized to acquire lands subject to rights of way, easements, and reservations for possible national forest purposes in the East.

1915

The Special Use Permit Act of March 4 (38 Stat. 1086, 1101), part of the annual Agricultural Appropriations Act, authorizes the Secretary of Agriculture to grant permits for summer homes and other recreational structures on the national forests.

The chief of the Forest Service establishes a new branch of research under the leadership of Earle H. Clapp.

The U.S. Supreme Court orders the Oregon and California Railroad (O&C) grant lands in western Oregon to be returned to the government because of failure by the company—now the Southern Pacific Railroad—to live up to the provisions of the land grant. Many of these lands eventually become the Bureau of Land Management's highly productive O&C lands.

1916

The Chamberlain-Ferris Act of June 9 (39 Stat. 218) returns, or revests, 2.8 million acres of unsold Oregon & California (O&C) Railroad grant lands in western Oregon to federal ownership. Today, just over 2 million acres of the O&C lands are managed by the Bureau of Land Management, and almost 500,000 acres are managed by the Forest Service.

With the strong support of Interior Secretary Franklin K. Lane, the National Park Service Act (39 Stat. 535), on August 25, creates a National Park Service within the Department of the Interior; Stephen T. Mather is the first director.

The first national forest established in the East under the Weeks Act of 1911 is the Pisgah National Forest, on October 17 (Proclamation 1349, 39 Stat. 1811). Portions of the forest were managed by Gifford Pinchot for George Vanderbilt before Pinchot came to the Forest Service, in 1898.

1918

Several new national forests (NF) are proclaimed in the East under the Weeks Act of 1911: the Shenandoah NF (later called the George Washington NF), in Virginia (PL 1448 and 40 Stat. 1779); the Natural Bridge NF (later called the Thomas Jefferson NF), in Virginia (PL 1450 and 40 Stat. 1780); and the White Mountain NF, in New Hampshire (PL 1449 and 40 Stat. 1779). All three NFs were established on May 16. In addition, the Alabama NF (now the William B. Bankhead NF) is proclaimed, on January 15, from public domain land in Alabama (Proclamation 1423 and 40 Stat. 1740).

1919

Arthur Carhart, a Forest Service landscape architect, proposes that the Trappers Lake area in the White River National Forest be protected from further development. The proposal is accepted. He then works in Minnesota, where he proposes that the Quetico-Superior area be protected, as well. Later, this area will become the Boundary Waters Canoe Area Wilderness.

1920

The Capper Report (*Timber Depletion, Lumber Exports, and Concentration of Timber Ownership*) is sent to the Senate on June 1. The report, called for by Senate Resolution 311, gives Congress needed information on timber depletion, lumber prices, lumber exports, and timber ownership. It contains the most complete nationwide data on forest ownership available at the time.

The War Department and the Forest Service agree to airplane forest fire patrols over the national forests in California and other western states. This effort continues through the 1930s.

1921

Aldo Leopold recommends the creation of a large wilderness in the Gila National Forest, in Arizona. Three years later, the same area becomes the first designated wilderness in the world.

1922

The Secretary of Agriculture is authorized, on March 20 (42 Stat. 465), to exchange land in the national forests for private land of equal value within the national forest boundaries.

In the annual Agricultural Appropriations Act, on May 11, Congress appropriates $10,000 for the improvement of public campgrounds on the national forests. This is the first money used for improvement of recreational facilities in the national forests.

1924

The Clarke-McNary Act of June 7 (43 Stat. 653) expands or modifies many aspects of the Weeks Act of 1911. The Act authorizes appropriations for cooperation with state agencies for fire control and eliminates the provision that national forest lands can be purchased in the headwaters of watersheds on navigable streams only for watershed purposes and for the production of timber.

The Gila Wilderness, at nearly 575,000 acres in size, is officially established by the Forest Service on June 3 on the Gila National Forest in NM. This is the first wilderness declared administratively in the United States.

1926

The Act of June 15 (44 Stat. 745) forbids the further creation of or additions to the national forests in Arizona and New Mexico, except by act of Congress.

An Oregon & California Railroad Land Act on July 13 (44 Stat. 915) provides for payments to western Oregon counties of an amount equal to the taxes that would have been paid if the O&C land were held by private owners.

The National Program of Forest Research is prepared under the supervision of Forest Service research director Earle Clapp. This report leads to new legislation two years later in the form of the McSweeney-McNary Act of 1928.

1927

A cooperative federal group, known as the Forest Protection Board, is established. Members of the board include representatives of the Park Service, the Forest Service, the GLO, the Bureau of Indian Affairs, the Bureau of Biological Survey, and the Weather Bureau. The idea is to enhance cooperation among agencies in the prevention and suppression of forest fires.

1928

The McNary-Woodruff Act of April 30 (45 Stat. 468) authorizes $8 million over the next three years to purchase land under the Weeks Act of 1911 and the Clarke-McNary Act of 1924 for national forest purposes.

The McSweeney-McNary Act of May 22 (45 Stat. 699) authorizes a broad, 10-year program of Forest Service forest and range management research, including a nationwide survey of forest resources. A total of $3,625,000 can be spent over this period.

1929

The Forest Service adopts its first set of wilderness regulations—Regulation L-20—for the designation and management of primitive areas. Although 75 primitive areas are protected (over 14 million acres), road building and timber harvesting are allowed. This is the first agencywide wilderness program.

The beginning of the Great Depression arrives with the stock market crash on October 29, often called "Black Tuesday." (In earlier days, depressions were referred to as "panics," while more recently they are said to be "recessions.") The Great Depression, is the worst economic turndown in modern times, with around 33 percent of the workforce unemployed by 1932. Initial federal responses are slow and largely ineffectual, since they rely on the private sector to get the country through the crisis. But the depression only deepens.

1930

The Knutson-Vandenberg (K-V) Act of June 9 (45 Stat. 527) authorizes funds for reforestation on the national forests and the creation of a revolving fund for reforestation or timber stand improvements on national forests.

The Shipstead-Nolan Act of July 10 (46 Stat. 1020) withdraws from entry all public land north of Township 60 in northern Minnesota. The Act directs the Forest Service to manage the Boundary Waters area for its scenic beauty and recreation and to maintain natural water levels. This law is the first congressional action to protect land as wilderness, although it will take decades more for wilderness protection to be designed for the area.

1933

The Forest Service submits *The National Plan for American Forestry* (the Copeland Report) to Congress on March 27. Bob Marshall is the writer of the recreation portion. It sets the standard for operating during the Great Depression.

On March 31 (48 Stat. 22), Congress authorizes funds to relieve the huge unemployment problem among the youth of America and to expend these funds on the promotion of natural resources. Using this Emergency Conservation Act authority, President Roosevelt issues an executive order on April 5 establishing an Office of Emergency Conservation (commonly known as the Civilian Conservation Corps). By July, some 250,000 young men are employed in the nation's forests and parks doing conservation-type work. The first CCC camp, appropriately named Camp Roosevelt, is located on the George Washington NF, near Luray, VA. By the end of the CCC era, some 2 million young men, locally employed men (LEMs), veterans of World War I, "territorials," and American Indians are employed.

President Roosevelt issues an executive order on June 10 placing all national monuments within the Department of the Interior. Many of the monuments had been under Forest Service and War Department management.

1934

The Civil Works Emergency Relief Act of February 15 (48 Stat. 351) authorizes the creation of the Works Projects Administration (WPA) and the Resettlement Administration, both designed to give a much-needed assist to the huge unemployed workforce created by the Great Depression by providing jobs.

The Fish and Game Sanctuary Act of March 19 (48 Stat. 400) authorizes the president to establish game refuges on the national forests.

In May, a devastating windstorm sweeps across the Great Plains and blows away some 350 million tons of topsoil, some of the dust landing on ships 300 miles out in the Atlantic Ocean. The Prairie States Forestry Project (commonly called the Shelterbelt Project) starts with emergency funds administered by the Forest Service. Millions of trees are planted by CCC and WPA workers on private lands to reduce wind erosion in the Great Plains in an area stretching from the border with Canada almost to the Gulf of Mexico.

The Taylor Grazing Act of June 28 (48 Stat. 1269) establishes a federal grazing program on land administered by the Forest Service and the General Land Office. President Franklin D. Roosevelt moves to implement the Act by withdrawing all land in 12 western states from homestead entry. This provision is extended to all the lower 48 states the following year. Thus, the Act marks the end of the official federal policy of disposing of unappropriated public domain lands. The U.S. Grazing Service is created to administer the General Land Office lands. In 1946, the Grazing Service and the General Land Office will form the basis for the new Bureau of Land Management.

1935

The Resettlement Administration—authorized the previous year—is created by executive order on April 30 to assist farmers and other subsistence and poor rural residents during the Depression. The Forest Service is given the task of helping small forest communities near national forests. The program is transferred to the USDA in 1936, then moves to the Farm Security Administration the following year.

The Prairies States Forestry Project (Shelterbelt Program) begins near Mangum, Oklahoma. The massive tree planting effort on land stretching from the Canadian border almost to Mexico culminates seven years later with some 217 million trees planted. The grand idea, which proves very successful, is to plant strips of trees at right angles to the prevailing winds to reduce duststorms and soil erosion, protect crops and livestock, lessen drought conditions, and provide useful employment for farmers.

1936

The Forest Service transmits its report *The Western Range* to the Senate on April 28. This report is in response to Senate Resolution 199 requesting the best information about the status and conditions of the western range lands and is highly critical of Department of the Interior management.

The Wichita National Forest in Oklahoma is abolished on November 27 (Proclamation 2211 and 50 Stat. 1797), while the Wichita Mountains Wildlife Refuge is placed by the USDA Bureau of Biological Survey (a few years later to be renamed the USDI Fish and Wildlife Service).

1937

The Civilian Conservation Corps name officially replaces the Emergency Conservation Work name on June 28 (50 Stat. 319).

The Bankhead-Jones Farm Tenant Act of July 22 (50 Stat. 522) provides for the "retirement" of submarginal agricultural lands. Many of these lands revert to the federal government to be incorporated into national forests and national grasslands.

O&C Act authorizes the Secretary of the Interior, on August 28, (50 Stat. 874) to establish sustained yield units on the almost 2.7 million acres of revested Oregon and California Railroad and Coos Bay Wagon Road grant lands in western Oregon. The Act also establishes the O&C Administration to manage these highly productive forestlands.

1938

After years of controversy, and the personal involvement of President Franklin Roosevelt, the 648,000-acre Olympic National Park, in the state of Washington, is established (PL 778, 52 Stat. 1241), on June 29, from the older Mt. Olympus National Monument and the Olympic National Forest.

The New England hurricane in September blows down millions of trees. The Northeastern Timber Salvage Administration (1938–1942) is set up under the supervision of the Forest Service to salvage as much as possible of the blown-down timber before it became a huge fire and insect hazard. The project to implement a timber salvage program in the area hard hit by the 1938 New England Hurricane receives funds from the Federal Disaster Act of 1937. Within two years, some 700 million board feet of timber are salvaged by around 10,000 Civilian Conservation Corps and some 15,000 WPA workers.

1939

The Forest Service adopts the U-Regulations to replace the L-20 Regulations for the management of wildlands (wilderness and primitive areas) in the national forest system. The new U-Regulations address the establishment of new wilderness areas (more than 100,000 acres), wild areas (5,000–100,000 acres), and roadless areas. Primitive areas under the older regulations are to be reclassified into the new categories. Bob Marshall and other Forest Service national office staff travel to the West to view possible roadless areas for wilderness status.

The Tropical Forest Experiment Station is started at Rio Piedras, in Puerto Rico. It is renamed the Tropical Forest Research Center in 1955 and is now called the International Institute of Tropical Forestry.

1940

The Lea Act provides for federal cooperation in the protection of forestlands from white pine blister rust, regardless of ownership, as long as funds expended are matched by state or local authorities or by individuals or organizations.

1942

The Aircraft Warning Service (AWS) is created to spot enemy aircraft flying over the East and West Coasts. Many of these AWS sites are located in Forest Service fire lookout towers and houses, which are staffed 24 hours a day. The program ends in late 1943 with the advent of large coastal radar facilities.

The Civilian Conservation Corps ends on June 30.

1944

The Sustained-Yield Forest Management Act of March 29th (58 Stat. 132) authorizes the Forest Service and the BLM to establish cooperative sustained yield units to manage federal forestland with private forest landowners and federal units consisting of only federal land tied to one community. One cooperative unit (Shelton, Washington) is signed up, as well as five federal units, before the program is essentially abandoned by 1950.

1946

President Truman's Reorganization Plan No. 3 creates the USDI Bureau of Land Management by merging the USDI General Land Office and the U.S. Grazing Service on May 16 (60 Stat. 1097, 1099). The Grazing Service budget is cut by 80 percent, resulting in the firing of most of the Grazing Service personnel. Marion Clawson serves as the first director of the BLM.

1947

The Federal Pest Control Act of June 25 (61 Stat. 177) makes the protection of all forest lands against destructive insects and disease a federal priority.

1948

The Thye-Blatnick Act of June 22 (64 Stat. 568) authorizes the Forest Service to purchase land within the Quetico-Superior wilderness (which later becomes the Boundary Waters Canoe Area). It also directs special payments to the affected counties of Cook, Lake, and St. Louis in Minnesota.

1949

The Anderson-Mansfield Reforestation and Revegetation Act authorizes appropriations for the reforestation and revegetation of the national forests. The Act states that "it is the declared policy of the Congress to accelerate and provide a continuing basis for the needed reforestation and revegetation of national forestlands and other lands under administration or control of the Forest Service."

Aldo Leopold's *A Sand County Almanac* is published, just after his death. The book and thus the author—a forester and conservationist—become known for starting a new era of concern about how people view the land and resources. This book, along with others, becomes the backbone of the environmental movement in the 1960s and 1970s. Even today, his writings are used to promote the concepts of ecosystem management and environmental ethics.

1950

The Granger-Thye Act of April 24 (64 Stat. 82) broadens the authority of the Secretary of Agriculture to accept contributions for administration, protection, improvement, reforestation, and related work on nonfederal lands within or near national forests and adjusts the range regulations.

The Cooperative Forest Management Act of August 25 (64 Stat. 473) authorizes the Secretary of Agriculture to cooperate with state foresters in assisting private landowners.

1952

The Smokey Bear Act of May 23 (66 Stat. 92) protects the Smokey symbol from unauthorized use.

1953

The Forest Service is assigned the management of some 7 million acres of "land utilization" (LU) lands that were acquired (usually by purchase) during the Great Depression under the provisions of the Bankhead-Jones Farm Tenant Act of 1937. The lands were previously managed by the Soil Conservation Service. Many of these acres become the national grasslands in the 1960s.

Research in forest insects and diseases is transferred to the Forest Service from two other USDA bureaus. Forest Service range research is transferred to the USDA Agricultural Research Service.

1954

Controverted O&C lands—those O&C lands inside the national forest boundaries—have been the subject of a dispute between the Departments of Agriculture and the Department of the Interior; they are to be managed under the Act of June 24 as national forest lands (68 Stat. 270), although the proceeds will be distributed to the counties using the same formula as that used for the USDI-BLM O&C lands.

The Willamette National Forest in Oregon announces plans to designate 200,000 acres of the Three Sisters Primitive Area as wilderness. The remaining 53,000 acres in the French Pete drainage are to be in general forest. The plan creates a tremendous uproar among conservationists, who want the remaining acres added to the wilderness. Politicians become involved, but it is settled almost 25 years later when the land is added to the Three Sisters Wilderness. The Sierra Club begins its involvement in national environmental issues, especially those involving wildernesses.

1955

The Multiple-Use Mining Act of July 23 (69 Stat. 367, 375) returns surface rights from mining claims on federal land to the United States, unless the claim is proven valid.

An Act of August 1 (69 Stat. 434) repeals provisions of the Timber and Stone Act of 1878, as amended, which provided for the sale of public lands that were found to be valuable chiefly for timber or stone production.

1956

The Al Sarena mining claim case becomes a partisan political scandal related to alleged Department of the Interior improprieties in issuing questionable mining patents on valuable timberlands.

1957

Congress approves Operation Outdoors, a five-year Forest Service program that is designed to expand and improve recreation facilities in the national forests.

1958

The Forest Service publishes a report called "Timber Resources for America's Future." The report notes that future demands for timber will have to be met by a significant increase in activities on the nation's forests. Suggestions for improvements include more restocking of trees, better planting stock, more complete tree utilization, and expanded control of forest insects, diseases, and fires. The following year, the Secretary of Agriculture proposes "A Program for the National Forests" that is based on the report.

The National Outdoor Recreation Resources Review Act is signed into law on June 28 (72 Stat. 238). The Act establishes the Outdoor Recreation Resources Review Commission (ORRRC) to determine the outdoor recreation requirements of the American people and the resources needed to meet these demands in 1958, 1976, and 2000. The final reports of the Commission are released three years later.

1960

The Multiple-Use Sustained-Yield Act of June 12 (74 Stat. 215) directs the Forest Service to manage the national forests for multiple uses and to give each natural resource—identified as outdoor recreation, range, timber, water, and wildlife and fish—equal consideration.

The national grasslands designation is established in the Forest Service on June 20. Nearly 4 million acres of land utilization (LU) land are transferred to the new category, which now contains 22 national grasslands.

California's Tahoe National Forest hosts the 1960 Winter Olympic Games. This is the first time the Olympic Games are held on national forest system lands.

1962

Rachel Carson publishes *Silent Spring*, which documents the use, overuse, and misuse of pesticides, herbicides, and fungicides in the United States and the crippling and deadly unintended effects they are having on plants and animals, including humans. Opposition to the findings in her book is immediate and strident, but the research and conclusions are proved to be fundamentally sound. Carson's book, along with Aldo Leopold's *A Sand County Almanac* (1949), marks the beginning of what many call the modern environmental movement.

1963

On May 28, the Outdoor Recreation Cooperation Act (77 Stat. 49) becomes law. This Act, which amends the Recreation Study Act of 1936, promotes the coordination and development of programs related to outdoor recreation, which are scattered among 18 federal agencies. The Act gives technical assistance to the states, authorizes recreation research, and gives new duties to the Bureau of Outdoor Recreation. Congress authorizes the Secretary of the Interior to prepare a national plan for outdoor recreation and to provide technical assistance for the promotion of regional and interagency cooperation.

The Pinchot Institute for Conservation Studies is dedicated on September 24 by President John F. Kennedy when he visits Grey Towers, Pinchot's family home, in Milford, Pennsylvania.

The Clear Air Act of December 17 (77 Stat. 392) amends the 1955 Clean Air Act to provide encouragement for uniform laws among the states and local governments regarding research, enforcement, and cooperation among the federal agencies to control air pollution from federal facilities.

1964

The president signs the Wilderness Act into law on September 3 (78 Stat. 890). The Act designates 54 areas (9 million acres) of national forest land as the National Wilderness Preservation System, drawn from lands previously designated administratively as wilderness, wild, or canoe areas. The Act also directs the Forest Service to inventory the remaining 5.5 million acres of primitive areas and other roadless areas for wilderness potential. The National Park Service and the Fish and Wildlife Service are given similar directions for the lands they manage.

Congress establishes the Land and Water Conservation Fund—originally funded by recreation user fees and motorboat fuel taxes—on September 3 (78 Stat. 897, 900) to aid in the purchase of private lands for conservation and related purposes. The funds are used by the federal government, as well as given as grants to state and local governments.

The Public Land Law Review Commission is established on September 19 (78 Stat. 982).

Congress creates the Job Corps, modeled on the Great Depression's Civilian Conservation Corps. Within a year, there are 6,500 Corpsmen in 47 camps throughout the national forests. The program expands to other agencies and even to the private sector.

1966

The National Historic Preservation Act of October 15 (80 Stat. 915) declares that it is national policy that "the historical and cultural foundations of the nation should be preserved as a living part of our community life and development in order to give a sense of orientation to the American people." The Act establishes a national program for the preservation of historic properties, including a national register of historic sites and structures; a grants-in-aid program to the states; and a matching-fund program to aid the National Trust for Historic Preservation.

The Endangered Species Preservation Act of October 15 (80 Stat. 926) authorizes the Secretary of the Interior to carry out a program of conserving, protecting, restoring, and propagating selected species of native fish and wildlife. Federal funds from the Land and Water Conservation Fund can be used to acquire habitat for endangered species.

1968

The Wild and Scenic Rivers Act of October 2 (82 Stat. 906) creates three tiers of classification of rivers: wild, scenic, and recreational. This Act is motivated by Congress's desire to protect the country's dwindling stretches of free-flowing rivers.

The National Trails System Act of October 2 (82 Stat. 919) establishes a system of national scenic, national recreational, and state and metropolitan trails. The Appalachian Trail and the Pacific Crest Trail are designed as national scenic trails in this Act, with 14 other trails identified for possible inclusion in the system.

1970

The National Environmental Policy Act of 1969 (83 Stat. 852), signed on January 1, 1970, requires, among other things, that an environmental impact statement (EIS) be printed and available for decision makers and the public in connection with any "major federal actions significantly affecting the quality of the human environment." The Act also establishes the Council on Environmental Quality.

The first "Earth Day" is celebrated, on April 22. The idea was conceived by Senator Gaylord Nelson from Wisconsin.

Two new federal agencies are established: the Environmental Protection Agency (EPA) and the National Oceanic and Atmospheric Administration (NOAA), created by executive branch reorganization (Plans Nos. 3 and 4) on December 2 (84 Stat. 2086). The EPA is directed to enforce environmental standards, monitor environmental conditions, and conduct research. NOAA is placed in the Department of Commerce to oversee existing federal programs in marine fishing resources. The National Marine Fisheries Service manages the NOAA program, including that for anadromous fish.

The Bitterroot National Forest controversy over clearcutting and terracing comes to a head. The Forest Service's Northern Region studies the problem, and a University of Montana team, led by Arnold Bolle, also studies and reports on the situation. The report, "A University Looks at the Forest Service," or the Bolle Report, as it becomes known, brings the clearcutting controversy to the halls of Congress.

1971

The Alaska Native Claims Settlement Act of December 18 (ANCSA) (PL 92–203, 85 Stat. 688) transfers up to 44 million acres of BLM-administered land to Alaska native people or corporations. A year later, the Secretary of the Interior withdraws 80 million acres of the BLM lands from consideration by the state of Alaska or by Native people. Many of these withdrawn lands are recommended to Congress for inclusion as national forests, national parks, national wildlife refuges, or wild river systems. Congress has five years to act, although it takes until 1980 to it to actually transfer the land.

The Wild and Free Roaming Horse and Burro Act directs the Secretary of the Interior to manage and protect such animals from "capture, branding, harassment, or death" and to maintain them on specific sanctuaries on the public lands. Both the BLM and the Forest Service are required to protect any feral populations (domesticated animals that have reverted to a wild state) on public lands.

The Forest Service undertakes the first Roadless Area Review and Evaluation (RARE), later called RARE I, under the direction of the Wilderness Act of 1964. After extensive study, the agency recommends to Congress 12 million acres of new wilderness. Interest groups contend the acreage is too small and assert that the Forest Service did not complete an EIS on the project. The agency settles a lawsuit out of court by agreeing to start a new evaluation (pegged RARE II).

The "Church Guidelines" for clearcutting on the national forests are published after the Senate Subcommittee on Public Lands investigates timber harvest practices on the Bitterroot, Monongahela, and other national forests. The guidelines generally restrict clearcuts to not more than 40 acres.

1972

The Supreme Court rules in *Sierra Club v. Morton*, otherwise known as the "Mineral King" case, a dispute between the Forest Service and the developers of a proposed ski area in the Sierras. The court decision is that litigants have standing to initiate lawsuits to protect the environment. Justice William O. Douglas's dissenting opinion is frequently cited for raising the question of a tree's right to sue on its own behalf (or "should trees have standing?").

1973

The Endangered Species Act of December 28 (87 Stat. 884) establishes a process for listing species as endangered or threatened, protecting their critical habitats, and developing recovery plans. The Act also establishes the distinction between endangered species and threatened species and the concept of critical habit needs. Federal agencies are required to make sure their actions do not harm endangered species.

In *Izaak Walton League v. Butz*, the U.S. District Court for the Northern District of West Virginia decides that commercial timber cutting on the Monongahela National Forest, in West Virginia, violates the Organic Act of 1897. Great public concern over clearcutting paves the way for congressional hearings and the eventual passage of the National Forest Management Act of 1976.

1974

The Forest and Rangeland Renewable Resource Planning Act (RPA) of August 17 (88 Stat. 476) directs the Secretary of Agriculture to undertake long-range planning to ensure an adequate timber supply and the maintenance of environmental quality. The Forest Service is required to assess all lands and to prepare a program every 10 years.

1975

The Eastern Wilderness Act of January 3 (PL 93–622 and 88 Stat. 2096) designates 16 new wildernesses in the East. The Act also requires the Forest Service to consider other eastern national forest lands east of the 100th meridian for possible wilderness designation.

The Fourth Circuit Court of Appeals, on August 17, upholds the 1973 *Izaak Walton v. Butz* case, which results in a ban on clearcutting on the national forests in West Virginia and other states subject to the District Court. The Forest Service does not appeal to the Supreme Court and applies the decision to the rest of the agency.

1976

The Payment in Lieu of Taxes Act of October 20 (90 Stat. 2662) directs the Secretary of Agriculture to pay local governments an annual fee based on a formula for the public lands within their boundaries. This applies to national forests and grasslands.

The National Forest Management Act (NFMA) of October 22 (90 Stat. 2949) replaces much of the language of the 1897 Organic Act as a result of the ruling against the Forest Service in *Izaak Walton v. Butz*, in 1973. The Act establishes the national forest planning process and requires, among other things, that the forests be managed to maintain species diversity. The Act is an amendment to the Resources Planning Act of 1974.

1977

The Forest Service begins the RARE II process. Results are announced in 1979, with the Forest Service proposing to add 15 million acres of new wilderness and an additional 11 million acres of wilderness study areas. The decision by the agency does not sit well with environmental groups. However, the Forest Service is not the final authority for designation—Congress is. Following RARE II, wilderness decisions tend to made by Congress on a state-by-state basis.

1978

The Endangered American Wilderness Act of February 24 (92 Stat. 40) adds 1.3 million acres of wilderness in 10 western states. The Act also adds the French Pete area to the Three Sisters Wilderness after years of political wrangling.

The Forest and Rangeland Renewable Resources Research Act of June 30 (92 Stat. 353) authorizes a comprehensive research program on and a survey of the nation's renewable resources.

The Cooperative Forestry Assistance Act of July 1 (92 Stat. 365) brings together all cooperative forestry programs under one statutory authority and provides grants to the states for management and planning of forestry-related programs.

Because Congress cannot agree on Alaska national interest lands legislation, Interior Secretary Cecil Andrus withdraws 100 million acres of land in Alaska from consideration for selection, and, on Dec. 1, 1980, President Carter temporarily designates 56 million of these acres as 15 new national monuments under the authority of the Antiquities Act of 1906.

1980

The Alaska National Interest Lands Conservation Act (ANILCA) of December 2 (95 Stat. 2371) protects 105 million acres, of which 56 million acres become wilderness. More than 43 million acres are added to the National Park System, with 10 new national parks, monuments, and preserves created. The Act, also known as the D-2 Lands Act, adds more than 55 million acres to the national wildlife refuge system, expanding existing refuges and creating 10 new refuges. Three million acres of additional national forest land are created, as well as more than a million acres of wild- and scenic-river corridors. The Admiralty Island and Misty Fiords National Monuments are established under Forest Service control. These are the first Forest Service–administered national monuments created since 1933.

1982

A series of RARE II wilderness bills passes Congress covering the states of Alabama, Indiana, Missouri, and West Virginia. These bills designate approximately 83,000 acres of new wilderness. The Georgia National Seashore is also established.

1988

The Wise Use movement gets a start as a backlash to the many new environmental regulations, as well as federal government intervention and even federal land ownership. This new movement, a revision of the 1970s Sagebrush Rebellion, takes on a decades-old problem of federal land management in the West and wrestles with the issues surrounding federal and state management. The movement, by the late 1990s, becomes known as the property-rights or county-supremacy movement.

1990

The first Global ReLeaf Forest is established in Au Sable, Michigan. Some 23,000 jack pines are planted to provide forest cover for the endangered Kirtland's warbler.

1992

The "Earth Summit" or "Rio Conference" is held in Rio de Janeiro, Brazil. Most nations attend the conference, and many agreements are signed. The forestry component is led by the Forest Service. Unexpected opposition arises from several developing nations that do not want the larger, more developed countries to tell the developing countries how to manage their resources.

Congress requests that a large-scale ecosystem assessment begin in the Forest Service, to cover the Sierra in California and Nevada (the final report is published in 1996).

1993

President Clinton calls for and attends the Forest Conference in Portland, Oregon, in April. He gives the USDA Forest Service and the USDI Bureau of Land Management, in cooperation with the USDI Fish and Wildlife Service, 60 days to come up with a scientifically sound plan for managing the spotted owl habitat in western Washington, western Oregon, and northwestern California. Researchers from the Pacific Northwest Research Station lead the massive undertaking. After a 30-day extension, the Forest Ecosystem Management Assessment Team (FEMAT) prepares an extensive report and an accompanying EIS and have the draft environmental impact statement documents "on the street" by July. The head of the project is Jack Ward Thomas, a long-time Forest Service wildlife researcher who becomes chief of the agency.

The Upper or Eastside Columbia River Basin team begins a project to assess the federal portions (mostly lands controlled by the Forest Service and the BLM) of the interior Columbia River Basin for future management. The project assessment area covers central and eastern Washington and Oregon, Idaho, and western Montana. The Upper Columbia Basin Team joins with the Eastside Team (now called the Interior Columbia Basin Ecosystem Management Project, or ICBEMP) to produce the draft documents for review by 1997. The science-based project incorporates an extensive number of researchers and specialists from the Forest Service and the Department of the Interior, as well as university experts and researchers from across the country.

The Forest Service and other federal agencies join to work with the public through a series of very successful programs, including the "Bring Back the Natives" (to conserve native fish species), "Every Species Counts" (to manage, protect, and conserve plant communities and aquatic species), "Rise to the Future!" (to form partnerships to improve aquatic habitats and increase opportunities for the public to fish), and "Get Wild!" (to cooperatively manage and improve healthy ecosystems and high-quality wildlife habitat).

1994

The Northwest Forest Plan (NWFP) EIS is finalized and implemented after the comment period and responses are closed. Ten "Adaptive Management Areas" (AMA) are established by the NWFP, and three of these (Cispus AMA, in Washington; Applegate AMA, in Oregon; and Hayfork AMA, in California) are later included as United Nations International Model Forests. In addition, 147 communities affected by the NWFP are provided with economic adjustment assistance.

Chief Jack Ward Thomas initiates "Course to the Future," a hands-on, comprehensive strategy for implementing ecosystem management. This new program contains elements to (1) protect ecosystems, (2) restore deteriorated ecosystems, (3) provide multiple benefits for people within the capabilities of ecosystems, and (4) ensure organizational effectiveness.

In December, the Forest Service releases a comprehensive plan for reinventing the agency—including changes in organization, culture, and work. The plan is the culmination of 14 months of intensive consultation and input from interested parties across the country, including employees and permittees. It is dead on delivery to Congress because of strong opposition from affected congressional members, states, and counties.

1995

The Forest Service continues to apply ecosystem management as the key natural resource management policy for the national forests and grasslands. Proposed planning regulations (36 CFR) that incorporate the principles of ecosystem management are released for public comment.

The Forest Service develops the "western forest health initiative," composed of 300 projects in the West, to make forests less susceptible to drought, insects, diseases, and wildfire and to restore forests destroyed by 1994 wildfires.

The 1995 Rescissions Act authorizes the Forest Service's emergency timber salvage sale program to remove diseased or insect-infested trees and dead, damaged, or downed trees affected by fire or insect attack. The inclusion of associated trees that may be alive (so-called green trees) in the timber salvage areas ignites widespread opposition to the program.

1996

On February 10, President Clinton signs legislation into law that transfers some 19,080 acres from the Army's Joliet TNT Arsenal to the Forest Service. The transferred area is renamed the Midewin National Tallgrass Prairie, the first such area in the United States. The area is located southwest of Chicago.

A large-scale assessment of the southern Appalachian area is completed by the Forest Service. The assessment assembles and analyzes broad-scale biological, physical, social, and economic data to facilitate better, more ecologically based forest-level resource analysis and management. A similar project is also completed in Region 5 (Pacific Southwest) concerning ecosystem management of the Sierra Nevada. This congressionally requested assessment, called the Sierra Nevada Ecosystem Project (SNEP), assesses the historical, physical, biological, ecological, social, and institutional conditions, as well as projected future trends under different management strategies. An earlier study on the spotted owl is conducted and reported on, igniting an immediate controversy.

The Ocoee Ranger District on Tennessee's Cherokee National Forest hosts the whitewater events of the 1996 summer Olympics. A unique partnership formed to restore the polluted river and to provide long-term benefits to the community results in a stretch of world-class whitewater river. Recreation visitor use is very high during the Olympic Games.

1997

The Interior Columbia Basin Ecosystem Management Project (ICBEMP) team produces two draft EIS documents covering the federal portions (managed primarily by the Forest Service and the BLM) of the interior Columbia River Basin. The EISs come under immediate fire from all sides.

The Forest Service provides leadership for USDA in the Federal Non-Native Invasive Species Task Force, established by Vice President Al Gore. The purpose of the task force is to develop the administration's strategy for eradicating, controlling, and monitoring nonnative species of insects, diseases, invasive plants, and aquatic pests.

1998

The Forest Service calls for a moratorium on road building in roadless areas on the national forests. Hailed by some, condemned by others, the moratorium is the first of several efforts by the agency to curb road building in roadless areas and to reduce the impact of roads and road construction on watersheds.

Chief Mike Dombeck initiates the "natural resource agenda," consisting of sustainable ecosystems, recreation, roads, and water. The Forest Service's highest priority is to restore and protect the health of America's forests.

The Land and Water Conservation Fund purchases 30 areas of forested lands. One of the purchases is a 550-acre parcel along the Big Sur coastline in California that provides habitat for 12 wildlife species identified on federal or state threatened or endangered species lists.

The H. J. Andrews Experimental Forest, in the Willamette National Forest, in Oregon, celebrates its 50th year. Research over its half-century of existence focused on understanding old growth and regenerated forest conditions (microbial species, plants, fish, and animals, including the spotted owl), logging operations, road construction, and hydrologic processes. The many collaborative efforts on the "Andrews" have involved researchers from the Pacific Northwest Research Station, the USDI Bureau of Land Management, and Oregon State University. The data, information, evaluation, and interpretation of the research work have led to new ideas about the functions and functioning of ecosystems. These prominent forest researchers have introduced the concepts of "new forestry," "new perspectives," and "ecosystem management" to the land management and regulatory agencies, as well as to the rest of the world.

1999

In June 1999, the Department of Agriculture, the Secretaria De Medio Ambiente, Recursos Naturales y Pesca (SEMARNAP), and the Department of the Interior sign the wildfire protection agreement. The purpose of the agreement is to enable wildfire protection resources from the territory of one country to cross the United States-Mexico border in order to suppress wildland fires on the other side of the border. The meeting also focuses on the Fire Training Matrix, an agreement among the Forest Service, the Department of the Interior, the Agency for International Development (USAID), and SEMARNAP.

The second committee of scientists recommends changes to the National Forest Management Act regulations. Draft regulations are published in the *Federal Register*. In October 1999, the Forest Service begins holding 23 town-hall meetings to discuss the proposed planning regulations, which are designed to assist the agency in managing national forests and grasslands. At meetings nationwide, participants are briefed on the major themes of the proposed regulations and given an opportunity to work in small groups to address specific questions presented by the facilitator of the meeting. The information gathered is used to develop the final regulations, which were expected in the summer of 2000.

On October 13, 1999, President Clinton directs the Forest Service to begin a public dialogue about the future of inventoried roadless areas throughout the National Forest System. This proposal places the Forest Service at the forefront of one of the most significant conservation efforts in United States history. The public is notified of the intent to prepare an environmental impact statement to examine alternative methods to meet the goals established by the president. The proposal also establishes a process for identifying the social and ecological values that make roadless areas of all sizes important and unique. The final rule is expected in late 2000.

The Forest Service and the Department of the Interior lead an interagency effort to develop the working draft of the unified federal policy for the clean water action plan. The Forest Service distributes copies of the working draft to governors, tribal leaders, members of Congress, and stakeholder groups in response to the president's direction to federal agencies to adopt a comprehensive strategy to better safeguard rivers and other bodies of water on federal lands.

A court rules that "survey and manage species," that is, those not listed under the Threatened and Endangered Species Act but that are sensitive and/or indicators of how well an ecosystem is functioning, should be extensively studied by the Forest Service.

2000

On February 16, the president announces that he is asking Secretary of Agriculture Dan Glickman to lead a study regarding the possibility of establishing a new national monument to protect the remaining 38 Sequoia groves and surrounding areas on the Sequoia National Forest. A Forest Service team is given 60 days to recommend or reject national monument status for the area of more than 400,000 acres. On April 15, on a visit to California, President Clinton proclaims a 328,000-acre Giant Sequoia National Monument on the Sequoia National Forest. The new monument is in two sections that protect about half of the remaining Sequoia groves.

The national fire plan, "Managing the Impact of Wildfires on Communities and the Environment," released September 8, 2000, is developed from the report by the Secretaries of Agriculture and the Interior to the president in response to the wildfires of 2000. The plan is designed to provide sufficient firefighting resources for the future, restore ecosystems damaged by the fires, rebuild community economics, and reduce future fire risk through fuel reduction efforts. Key points of the plan are (1) firefighting—to continue to fight fire for the remainder of the 2000 season and to prepare adequately for next year; (2) rehabilitation and restoration—to restore landscapes and rebuild communities damaged by the wildfires of 2000; (3) hazardous fuel reduction—to invest in projects to reduce fire risk; (4) community assistance—to work directly with communities to ensure adequate protection; and (5) accountability—to be accountable and to establish adequate oversight coordination, program development, and monitoring for performance.

2001

In the aftermath of the September 11 attack on New York City and the Pentagon, near Washington, D.C., several Forest Service incident management teams are called to assist. One such 39-person team, 22 of whose members are Forest Service employees, is from all parts of California. After gaining special authorization to fly—since the FAA had grounded all flights in the United States—they fly across the country. The team is assigned to assist in recovery efforts at the Pentagon. Meanwhile, teams from the Southwest and from Alaska are assigned to help at ground zero in New York City. The teams fill the vital role of doing logistical planning for the FDNY.

2002

On February 8–24, Utah's Wasatch-Cache National Forest and Intermountain Region (R-4) host the 2002 Winter Olympic Games. The winter games are composed of 78 events with almost 2,400 participants.

An especially dangerous fire season results from several years of severe drought in the Rocky Mountains, with fires starting in June and July. The Biscuit Fire, in southwestern Oregon, is the largest—almost 500,000 acres—and the most expensive fire to fight; it is finally brought under control. The fire site is visited by President Bush, who announces a program to remove brush and ladder fuels from the national forests, as well as to restore and salvage log burned-over areas.

2003

The Healthy Forests Restoration Act of 2003 enables the Secretary of Agriculture and the Secretary of the Interior to conduct hazardous fuels reduction projects on national forest system lands and Bureau of Land Management lands. The Act is aimed at protecting communities, watersheds, and certain other at-risk lands from catastrophic wildfire

The space shuttle *Columbia* breaks apart over the skies of the Southwest and Texas. From February 1 to April 30, 15,000 firefighters and other personnel volunteer to comb the Texas countryside looking for pieces of the shuttle. The search focuses on the Sabine and Angelina National Forests, in Texas. More than 100 federal, state, and local agencies and organizations are involved in the search effort.

2005

In early January, the 2005 Forest Service Centennial Congress commemorates 100 years of Forest Service conservation, assesses current challenges and opportunities, and initiates a dialogue for the twenty-first century to meet the needs of present and future generations. Around 3,000 people participate in the event, including the 12 regional forums and the major event in Washington, D.C.

Another centennial event is the 39th annual Smithsonian Folklife Festival, on the National Mall, on June 23–27 and June 30–July 4. The Secretary of the Smithsonian Institution invites the Forest Service to participate "to produce a program on the occupational culture of forest management in the United States." The

Folklife Festival coincides with the Forest Service's 100th anniversary, on July 1, 2005. The Forest Service is only the third federal agency ever invited to participate in the festival (the White House and the Smithsonian were the first two).

Hurricanes Katrina and Rita once again provide opportunities for the Forest Service to assist in recovery and cleanup; the two storms devastate large portions of coastal Louisiana and Mississippi in the fall. Some 1,800 Forest Service employees with expertise in setting up logistics staging areas, distributing food products, and removing debris are sent to respond.

APPENDIX 1

National Forests by Name, State, and Acres (2004)

Allegheny NF (PA)	513,184
Angeles NF (CA)	655,439
Angelina NF (TX)	153,180
Apache-Sitgreaves NF (AZ, NM)	2,632,018
Apalachicola NF (FL)	565,585
Arapaho and Roosevelt NF (CO)	1,534,809
Ashley NF (UT, WY)	1,382,347
Beaverhead-Deerlodge NF (MT)	3,354,545
Bienville NF (MS)	178,542
Bighorn NF (WY)	1,107,670
Bitterroot NF (MT, ID)	1,581,164
Black Hills NF (SD, WY)	1,247,991
Black Kettle NGL (OK, TX)	31,286
Boise NF (ID)	2,903,791
Bridger-Teton NF (WY)	3,400,208
Buffalo Gap NGL (SD)	596,693
Butte Valley NGL (CA)	18,425
Caddo NGL (TX)	17,873
Caribbean NF (PR)	28,002
Caribou-Targhee NF (ID, UT, WY)	2,630,666

Carson NF (NM)	1,391,674
Cedar River NGL (ND)	6,717
Chattahoochee and Oconee NF (GA)	864,424
Chequamegon-Nicolet NF (WI)	1,527,297
Cherokee NF (TN, NC)	637,124
Chippewa NF (MN)	666,542
Choctawhatchee NF (FL)	1,152
Chugach NF (AK)	5,396,529
Cibola NF (NM)	1,631,266
Cimarron NGL (KS)	108,175
Clearwater NF (ID)	1,679,739
Cleveland NF (CA)	434,369
Coconino NF (AZ)	1,855,679
Coeur D'Alene NF (ID)	726,362
Colville NF (WA)	954,406
Comanche NGL (CO)	443,081
Conecuh NF (AL)	83,858
Coronado NF (AZ, NM)	1,786,587
Croatan NF (NC)	159,885
Crooked River NGL (OR)	112,357
Curlew NGL (ID)	47,790
Custer NF (MT, SD)	1,186,557
Daniel Boone NF (KY)	557,789
Davy Crockett NF (TX)	160,657
Delta NF (MS)	60,215
De Soto NF (MS)	517,939
Deschutes NF (OR)	1,598,059
Dixie NF (UT)	1,888,507
Eldorado NF (CA, NV)	681,023
Fishlake NF (UT)	1,461,228
Flathead NF (MT)	2,358,784
Fort Pierre NGL (SD)	115,923
Francis Marion and Sumter NF (SC)	623,709
Fremont NF (OR)	1,207,039

Gallatin NF (MT)	1,808,259
George Washington-Jefferson NF (VA, WV, KY)	1,788,504
Gifford Pinchot NF (WA)	1,319,409
Gila NF (NM)	2,708,836
Grand Mesa, Uncompaghre, and Gunnison NF (CO)	2,967,476
Grand River NGL (SD)	154,783
Green Mountain and Finger Lakes NF (VT, NY)	407,769
Helena NF (MT)	975,761
Hiawatha NF (MI)	894,654
Holly Springs NF (MS)	155,661
Homochitto NF (MS)	191,585
Hoosier NF (IN)	200,703
Humboldt-Toiyabe NF (NV, CA)	5,715,553
Huron Manistee NF (MI)	977,212
Inyo NF (CA, NV)	1,902,035
Kaibab NF (AZ)	1,559,200
Kaniksu NF (ID, MT, WA)	1,627,788
Kiowa NGL (NM)	136,417
Kisatchie NF (LA)	603,393
Klamath NF (CA, OR)	1,737,694
Kootenai NF (MT, ID)	1,812,396
Lassen NF (CA)	1,070,344
Lewis & Clark NF (MT)	1,862,289
Lincoln NF (NM)	1,103,748
Little Missouri NGL (ND)	1,028,071
Lolo NF (MT)	2,113,994
Los Padres NF (CA)	1,761,278
Lyndon B. Johnson NGL (TX)	20,309
Malheur NF (OR)	1,465,293
Manti-La Sal NF (UT, CO)	1,270,699
Mark Twain NF (MO)	1,488,378
McClelland Creek NGL (TX)	1,449
Medicine Bow-Routt NF (WY)	2,220,943
Mendocino NF (CA)	911,653

Midewin NTGP (IL)	15,277
Modoc NF (CA)	1,663,401
Monongahela NF (WV)	898,292
Mt. Baker-Snoqualmie NF (WA)	2,557,132
Mt. Hood NF (OR)	1,068,859
Natahala NF (NC)	531,055
Nebraska NF (NE)	141,549
Nez Perce NF (ID)	2,224,230
Ocala NF (FL)	383,595
Ochoco NF (OR)	851,095
Oglala NGL (NE)	94,480
Okanogan NF (WA)	1,499,171
Olympic NF (WA)	627,701
Osceola NF (FL)	162,157
Ottawa NF (MI)	987,318
Ouachita NF (AR, OK)	1,777,477
Ozark-St. Francis NF (AR)	1,159,286
Pawnee NGL (CO)	193,060
Payette NF (ID)	2,326,793
Pike and San Isabel NF (CO)	2,229,033
Pisgah NF (NC)	512,671
Plumas (CA)	1,175,998
Prescott NF (AZ)	1,239,246
Rita Blanca NGL (TX, OK)	92,989
Rogue River-Siskiyou NF (OR, CA)	1,723,173
Sabine NF (TX)	160,881
St. Joe NF (ID)	869,266
Salmon-Challis NF (ID)	4,235,977
Sam Houston NF (TX)	163,051
Samuel R. Mckelvie NF (NE)	116,079
San Bernardino NF (CA)	671,686
San Juan-Rio Grande NF (CO)	3,699,606
Santa Fe NF (NM)	1,572,301
Sawtooth NF (ID, UT)	1,804,089

Sequoia NF (CA)	1,143,562
Shasta-Trinity NF (CA)	2,209,826
Shawnee NF (IL)	268,111
Sheyene NGL (ND)	70,446
Shoshone NF (WY)	2,437,218
Sierra NF (CA)	1,311,913
Siuslaw NF (OR)	633,955
Six Rivers NF (CA)	989,038
Stanislaus NF (CA)	898,121
Superior NF (MN)	2,094,778
Tahoe NF (CA)	870,190
Talladega NF (AL)	391,131
Thunder Basin NGL (WY)	549,219
Tombigbee NF (MS)	66,874
Tongass NF (AK)	16,577,133
Tonto NF (AZ)	2,872,935
Tuskegge NF (AL)	11,252
Uinta NF (UT)	880,691
Umatilla NF (OR, WA)	1,406,985
Umpqua NF (OR)	983,128
Uwharrie NF (NC)	50,174
Wallowa-Whitman NF (OR, ID)	2,263,921
Wasatch-Cache NF (UT, ID, WY)	2,289,329
Wayne NF (OH)	235,427
Wenatchee NF (WA)	1,731,485
White Mountain NF (NH, ME)	747,441
White River NF (CO)	2,279,062
Willamette NF (OR)	1,677,995
William B. Bankhead NF (AL)	181,033
Winema NF (OR)	1,045,551

The following statewide supervisors' offices manage the national forests in their respective states, including all the smaller national forests, except for the Idaho Panhandle NFs, which manage only the Kaniksu, Coeur d'Alene, and St. Joe NFs in the northern Idaho area.

Idaho Panhandle NFS (ID, WA)
National Forests in Alabama (AL)
National Forests in Florida (FL)
National Forests in Mississippi (MI)
National Forests in North Carolina (NC)
National Forests in Texas (TX)

APPENDIX 2

American Forest Congresses

For 125 years, national meetings of forestry leaders, conservationists, and policy-makers have been convened to discuss critical forest issues of the day. The first was the American forestry congress, which also held concurrent meetings in Canada. Six of the subsequent forest congresses were organized and convened by the American Forestry Association, while the 2005 centennial forest congress was sponsored by the USDA Forest Service. Each of the congresses will be examined in more detail, but in summary they were:

American Forestry Congress, Cincinnati, Ohio, April 1882
American Forest Congress, Washington, D.C., January 1905
American Forest Congress, Washington, D.C., October 1946
Fourth American Forest Congress, Washington, D.C., October 1953
Fifth American Forest Congress, Washington, D.C., October 1963
Sixth American Forest Congress, Washington, D.C., October 1975
Seventh American Forest Congress, Washington, D.C., February 1996
Centennial Forest Congress, Washington, D.C., January 2005

1882 AMERICAN FORESTRY CONGRESS

The public policy of the United States during much of the nineteenth century was to dispose of the public domain just as fast as possible to settlers, ranchers, railroads, and industries. This was a time when there was no federal income tax, so selling the public domain and taxing imported goods (tariffs) were the only ways to raise money to fund the government. Forests were being cleared for farm crops, animal grazing, and town development at an ever-increasing rate. But a few voices were being raised about forest losses and the potential for a timber famine in the future. In 1873, Dr. Franklin B. Hough delivered a paper, "On the Duty of Governments in the Preservation of Forests," at the American Association for the Advancement of

Science (AAAS) meeting in Portland, Maine. The AAAS, taking Hough's recommendations to heart, memorialized (petitioned) Congress, calling for the protection of forest resources. (Three years later, Hough was appointed the first federal expert on forestry in the USDA. He published his "Report upon Forestry" in 1878, with a second report in 1880 and a third in 1882.)

The first forest congress, in 1882, was organized by a few local politicians and a newspaperman in Cincinnati, but they quickly enlisted the aid of Dr. John Warder, a founder of the American Forestry Association, in 1875. Cincinnati residents were delighted at the ceremonial tree planting in Eden Park. Several trees were planted to honor past presidents—catalpa for Harrison, southern oak for Washington, red oak for Lincoln, and hickory for Jackson. Other plantings were held throughout the week at other parks in the city. The forest congress helped to energize the forestry movement in the United States. When the forest congress met in Montreal later in the year, it did the same for Canadian forestry. Secretary of the Interior Carl Schurz tried to reform the antiquated land laws, but he was looked upon by most western representatives in Congress as someone who did not understand the needs of a growing nation. Despite the public celebrations surrounding the forest congress, it remained the policy of the federal government to sell or transfer public lands to private ownership. Congress and the administration showed no interest in changing this policy.

1905 AMERICAN FOREST CONGRESS

By 1905, 23 years after the first congress, the climate had changed radically. The nation was shocked at the widespread land frauds related to disposal of federal land. Federal investigations resulted in convictions and prison sentences for many public officials. U.S. Senator John Mitchell, of Oregon, was convicted and sentenced to jail. He died while his prison sentence was under appeal. S.A.D. Puter's 1908 book, *Looters of the Public Domain,* written in the Multnomah County jail in Portland, Oregon, became a bestseller. The profession of forestry came of age, with many of the top colleges in the country offering courses in forestry. In 1900, the Society of American Foresters was founded by Gifford Pinchot. Millions of acres of western lands had been withdrawn from entry and declared forest reserves, and there was a federal Bureau of Forestry in the Department of Agriculture.

The second forest congress, although not so designated, was the American Forest Congress (AFC), held under the auspices of the American Forestry Association January 2–6, 1905, in Washington, D.C. Invitations went out to almost 400 executives from timber, railroad, grazing, irrigation, and mining companies, as well as to educators, government officials and members of Congress, and foresters from across the country. Overall, some 2,000 people attended one or more sessions of the AFC. The average attendance at the eight sessions was 1,000. Secretary of Agriculture James Wilson was designated the president of the congress, President Theodore Roosevelt the honorary president, and James Pinchot the first vice president. A reception was held for the delegates at the White House, where they were greeted by President Roosevelt.

The goals of the AFC were "to establish a broader understanding of the forest in its relation to the great industries depending upon it; to advance the conservative use of forest resources for both the present and future need of these industries; to stimulate and unite all efforts to perpetuate the forest as a permanent resource of the nation." Pinchot, on the other hand, in his autobiography *Breaking New Ground* (1947), had a more practical goal for the AFC—"the meeting was planned, organized, and conducted for the specific purpose of the transfer [of the forest reserves] by the Bureau of Forestry [from the General Land Office]." It was most certainly the most important meeting devoted to forestry ever held up to that time. Nelson McGeary, author of the biography *Gifford Pinchot: Forester-Politician* (1960), noted that "the meeting, packed with persons favorable to forest conservation, was primarily a propaganda device for demonstrating to Congress and the country the sizeable amount of support that had been built up for practical forestry [as espoused by Pinchot and the Bureau of Forestry]." Many of the speakers praised Pinchot and the Bureau of Forestry for their strong leadership in forestry and conservation.

Roosevelt gave his keynote address to the AFC at the National Theater on January 5. The speech, probably written by Pinchot, got the attention of the participants when, in his opening remarks, the president said,

> For the first time the great business and forest interests of the nation have joined together … to consider their individual and common interests in the forest…. You all know, and especially those of you from the West, the individual whose idea of developing the country is to cut every stick of timber off it and then leave a barren desert for the homemaker who comes in after him. That man is a curse and not a blessing to the country. The prop of the country must be the businessman who intends so to run his business that it will be profitable for his children after him…. Your coming is a very great step toward the solution of the forest problem–a problem which cannot be settled until it is settled right…
>
> If the present rate of forest destruction is allowed to continue, with nothing to offset it, a timber famine in the future is inevitable. Fire, wasteful and destructive forms of lumbering, and the legitimate use, taken together, are destroying our forest resources far more rapidly that they are being replaced…. Fortunately, the remedy is a simple one, and your presence here today is a most encouraging sign that there will be such forethought [and action]….
>
> I ask, with all the intensity that I am capable, that the men of the West will remember the sharp distinction I have just drawn between the man who skins the land and the man who develops the country. I am going to work with, and only with, the man who develops the country. I am against the land skinner every time.

Roosevelt also made it clear that he wanted the have all government forest work consolidated in one department. In his welcoming address, he said, "I would like to add one word as to the creation of a national forest service which I have recommended repeatedly in messages to Congress, and especially in my last. I wish to see all the forest work of the Government concentrated in the Department of Agriculture. It is folly to scatter such work, as I have said over and over again."

Pinchot was adamant about having widespread agreement on the necessity of federal forests and forestry. He said, in a speech titled "A Federal Forest Service," at the American Forest Congress:

The administration of the forest reserves [named changed to national forests in 1907] is based upon the general principle repeatedly by President Roosevelt as the policy of his administration, that the reserves are for use…. Timber, water, grass, minerals are all to be open to the conservative and continued use of the people. They must be used, but they must not be destroyed … The forests now under government control should remain under government control so far as they are needed for public uses. We must have forest reserves, and we shall have to extend their area later on, not merely by presidential proclamation, but by purchase, both East and West. Forest lands … are absolutely essential to the welfare of all of us.

F. E. Weyerhaeuser attended the AFC, where he spoke on behalf of the Weyerhaeuser Lumber Company. In his presentation, titled "Interest of Lumbermen in Conservative Forestry," he said, "Practical forestry ought to be of more interest and importance to lumbermen than to any other class of men…. At present lumbermen are ready to consider seriously any proposition which may be made by those who have the conservative use of forests at heart." Almost all the industry representatives at the meeting echoed this same theme. However, Weyerhaeuser was dismayed at Roosevelt's accusation that the timber industry demonstrated indifference to the future of the forests by its destructive cutting practices. Weyerhaeuser believed that cooperation between the industry and the Forest Service was set back for a decade or more; he said that the industry was "licking its wounds" after the AFC. The AFC was, in reality, a conference of users of the forests, and as such they had vested interests in the protection of forests.

The weeklong session ended with the approval of 18 resolutions. Among them was a plea to all state authorities for the enactment and enforcement of laws for the protection of forests from fire and for reducing the burden of taxation on lands held for forest reproduction. Attendees called for the repeal of the Timber and Stone Act of 1873 and the reform of the lieu land selection process included in the Organic Act of 1897. Also called for was the unification of all governmental forest agencies, including the administration of the forest reserves, within a single agency. Another resolution called for the establishment of eastern forest reserves. Within months, the Forest Service, with Gifford Pinchot as chief, had been established. The lieu land laws and Timber and Stone Act were repealed, and many western states passed fire laws. Six years later, the Weeks Act of 1911 allowed the establishment of national forests in the East and encouraged fire cooperation with the states and the federal government. Since almost all the public domain forestland had by then been transferred to private ownership, the act authorized the purchase of lands that had often been devastated by previous logging. This Act was expanded by the Clarke-McNary Act of 1924. As a result, today, there are 25 million acres of new national forests in the East. These have been added to the national forests in the western states, and the total area of the national forest system is now almost 193 million acres.

1946 AMERICAN FOREST CONGRESS

World War II ended in the summer of 1945. What lay ahead was the great need to rebuild a devastated Europe and great parts of Asia. In America, 11 million

1905 Forest Congress in Washington, D.C. (USDA National Agricultural Library)

young men and women were returning from military life to civilian life and were eager to find housing and start families. Many went to college under the G.I. Bill of Rights. This was the year that marked the death of Gifford Pinchot, and the loss was mentioned by many of the speakers at the third American Forest Conference, convened by the American Forestry Association in Washington in October 1946. The goals of the Congress were to dramatize to the American people the condition of their forest resources after four years of war; to bring together representatives of government, industry, agriculture, labor, and the public for joint consideration of the forest situation; and to enlist the aid and support of all citizens interested in the preservation and use of forests in formulating a national program of forestry. More than 400 delegates met in the headquarters of the United States Chamber of Commerce.

The Congress had been preceded by an AFA-sponsored appraisal of forest resources. The two-year study, directed by John B. Woods, examined the forest situation state by state. Forest Service Chief Lyle Watts complained that the appraisal unfairly criticized of the management of the national forests and did not properly distinguish between national forests and those under private management. "Let me be frank," Watts said. "I do not believe that most conservationists and those among us who give first concern to the interests of the whole people of America are going to find certain of the proposals and arguments not viable. I for one vigorously reject some of them." Watts was not the only person to closely evaluate the forest resource appraisal; it was also examined by a 19-member committee appointed by the directors of AFA. The committee met at Higgins Lake, Michigan, to come up with a series of proposals, based on the appraisal, that would serve as the basis for the discussions at the Forest Congress. Samuel Trask Dana, then dean of the University of Michigan's forestry school and an AFA director, was the moderator at the Higgins Lake meetings. The Higgins Lake proposals, as they were known, were grouped around four main subjects: protection of the forest resources, timber management and utilization, forest management for multiple use, and promotion of southern forestry.

There were labor representatives at the congress—Anthony Wayne Smith, of the Congress of Industrial Organizations (CIO), and Ellery Foster, of the International Woodworkers of America (IWA). They argued against many of the proposals, as did Howard Zahniser, of the Wilderness Society. Because of the divided nature of the Congress, it did not accomplish much other than to highlight the differences on how to promote forestry on public and private lands. Federal regulation of private forestry was still a burning issue for many at the Congress.

Several months after the Forest Congress, President Harry Truman, in an Arbor Day speech, on April 10, 1947, noted that

> Only recently, in Washington, a great Forest Congress convened, the third such meeting in our history, bringing together representatives of agriculture, labor, industry, and government to consider the problems of our forests. And we have today, without question, a very real forest problem. Once, when the Nation's vast forests seemed inexhaustible, we could afford to be lavish, even careless, with this great natural resource. Today, we are coming to think of trees as a crop which, with care and protection, can produce endless harvests of essential timber. The forests of the future will consist of trees we purposefully grow, rather than the trees we found here. The products of the forests contributed mightily to building this Nation. They will be needed for our continued progress and prosperity. If this country is to be sure of an adequate supply of forest products, it must stop destructive cutting and unwise depletion, and build up timber growth.

1953 AMERICAN FOREST CONGRESS

The 1950s were heady times. The Second World War was over, and so was the Great Depression. Things were getting back to a normal, but life was fundamentally different from the normal of the 1930s and 1940s. There was a new national feeling of pride, independence, and freedom. The United States could do anything it put its mind to do. Housing starts were soaring, Forest Service and BLM timber sales were setting new highs almost every year, and industrial forestry was beginning to gain respect. Forestry schools were pouring out graduates, with the Forest Service and the BLM hiring many of these new college-educated foresters and silviculturists. Others headed South to work on the expanding industrial forests of the pulp and paper industry. The Eisenhower administration took over the White House, and Republicans took over Congress for the first time in 20 years; the New Deal had ended. The new chief of the Forest Service was Richard McArdle. He was the first chief in many years who did not have federal regulation of private forestlands on his agenda.

The fourth American Forest Congress met at the Statler Hotel, in Washington, on October 29, 1953. There were 400 delegates, and the meetings were open to outsiders. The purpose of the Congress was to review the progress made in the past seven years and to take advantage of the experience provided by the varied groups that were becoming interested in forest conservation. This Congress had on the program the president of the United States, his chief of staff, the Secretary of Agriculture, and the Secretary of the Interior. The Forest Congress also had two women on the program—one a representative of the Garden Club of America and another from the General Federation of Women's Clubs. (The first woman who was invited and presented at any forest congress was Mrs. L. P. Williams, of the General Federation of Women's Clubs, in 1905. Her comments were printed in the 1905 *Proceedings of the American Forest Congress.*)

The AFC program for American forestry had three important goals: to meet the essentials of forest protection from fire, insects, and disease; to improve the national timber crop in volume and quality to a degree sufficient to wipe out all deficits and build up a reserve by utilizing more fully the productive capacity of our public and private lands; and to obtain the maximum economic and social benefit from our forests by realistic application of the principle of multiple use in their management. Beginning with President Dwight Eisenhower's speech and continuing throughout the meeting, the theme was cooperation. Chief McArdle promised that if he could get enough money for roads, the national forests would get their timber cut up to sustained yield levels.

Dr. Detlev Bronk, president of the National Academy of Sciences, was the keynote speaker. His talk was titled "Forestry in the World Resource Picture." He stressed the role of research and science in conservation and forestry and said that we could protect and develop natural resources by the discovery of new knowledge rather than by developing new lands. However, Anthony Wayne Smith, from the labor side, accused the timber industry of liquidating the timber stands in the Pacific Northwest, which would put an end to big-log forestry and substitute "matchstick forestry." He believed, correctly, as it turned out, that this liquidation would mean low wages, ghost company and timber-dependent towns, and increases in human misery. He was the only speaker who called for returning to Pinchot's idea for direct federal regulation of private timber harvesting. Sherman Adams, Eisenhower's chief of staff, said: "Let us look critically at the role of the federal government. To appraise our strength is to know our weaknesses, the things we haven't got. We have as yet no recognized public land use policy. We have no well-defined water policy. We have no very clear and generally accepted national forest policy. Here, stop a moment, and consider if in these particular fields there is not enough work for men and women of conservation to do for the next generation." The fourth Forest Congress did not result in any policy changes by the Forest Service or Congress. It did, however, result in improving the relationship between the Forest Service and the private sector.

1963 AMERICAN FOREST CONGRESS

The 1960s saw the beginnings of the environmental movement, which culminated in the signing, on January 1, 1970, of the National Environmental Policy Act of 1969. In 1962, Rachel Carson's book *Silent Spring* was published; it told of the dangers of overuse of various pesticides and herbicides, especially DDT. Many believe that her book awakened the nation and spurred what we now call the modern environmental movement, which represented a fundamental shift from the earlier conservation/forestry movement of Pinchot. Because the national forests were being managed mostly for timber production, Congress passed the Multiple Use Sustained Yield Act of 1960, which was intended to equalize all the resources. Forest research was enhanced when the McIntire-Stennis Act of 1962 was signed into law. There were many bills in Congress about preserving wild and scenic rivers, trails, and wilderness. It is notable that the fifth American Forest Congress was the first to devote any attention to forest products other than timber.

Like the two preceding congresses, the fifth Congress had a committee that prepared what was called "a conservation platform for American forestry." The committee, which met in Atlanta, was composed of 41 leaders from many parts of the conservation movement. Background material for the committee, prepared by Charles Randall, included a review of American forestry since the preceding Forest Congress, seven years before. The committee noted the increasing demands on the forests caused by a quickly expanding population and a growing economy. They concluded that the goal of national policy must continue to be the maximum sustained contributions—think timber—from all forest ownerships to the economy and provision for the health and spiritual—think recreation—wellbeing of all citizens.

Samuel Trask Dana was the keynote speaker, and he recognized the growing demands on the forest to meet both tangible (timber and grazing) and intangible (recreation and wilderness) needs. As for multiple use, he said, "Virtually universal recognition of this fact is now accompanied by the rather general and reassuring belief that the practice of multiple use and sustained yield will automatically provide ample supplies both of wood and other desired products.... There are bound to be special situations where the private and public interest do not coincide ... when this is the case does government do nothing, does it acquire key areas, or does it offer private owners subsidies of the kind and amount necessary to safeguard the values at stake?"

A luncheon was held during the Congress that was billed as an "AFA Salute to the Department of the Interior." Secretary of the Interior Stuart Udall addressed the luncheon by referring to President John F. Kennedy's recent conservation trip through the West and Midwest. On that trip, Kennedy called for a third wave of the conservation movement to tackle the unsolved problems of the 1960s. Udall noted that there were many obsolete and conflicting land laws that the Interior Department had to follow in managing the mineral, water, grazing, and timber resources on public lands. He called on the Forest Congress to help push for a review of public land laws and policy. The secretary concluded by saying, "Through this Fifth American Forest Congress the knowledge of qualified people will be brought to bear and the will of the general public will further come to light. It is for us who have positions of executive or legislative responsibility to heed and take notice. To the fulfillment of these obligations let us all commit our imagination, skills, and talent." The final product of the fifth Forest Congress was what was called "the conservation program for American forestry." The program was submitted to the AFA membership and was approved by an overwhelming majority. Shortly after the Congress, the Public Land Law Review Commission was established by the U.S. Congress. One year later, the Wilderness Act of 1964 fundamentally changed the way that public lands would be managed in the future.

1975 AMERICAN FOREST CONGRESS

The 1970s brought a flood of environmental legislation from the U.S. Congress. Earth Day, on April 22, 1970, was a national event. It represented a new environmentalism, the counterculture, the rise of "alternative lifestyles," and the questioning of the establishment by much of the country's youth. These notions ran head-on into what had been accepted forest management practices for more than a half-century. The first of the Forest Service roadless area reviews (RARE) was printed, then rejected by the courts as being inadequate. The Endangered Species Act of 1973 gave a huge lift to wildlife, fish, and plant management on all lands in the United States. The decade of the 1970s began by turning the forestry world upside down and ended with forestry under attack in the courtrooms and in the press.

The sixth American Forest Congress was called to mark the 100th anniversary of the American Forestry Association. Like the first Congress, in 1882, the sixth was held in Washington, D.C., opposite the old AFA headquarters at 919 17th Street, N.W. Several committees developed the program and issues to be addressed. There were discussions about the environmental requirements of the new laws, world forestry, and forest protection, management, research, and education. However, there was no discussion, at least in the formal meeting, of the new environmental issues that were making the headlines. Senator Mark Hatfield, of Oregon, was the keynote speaker.

Keith Arnold, associate dean of the Lyndon B. Johnson School of Public Affairs at the University of Texas, in his summary of the Congress, said, "The accelerating momentum of change belies our ability to even describe the world as we know it today. We must invent something beyond periodic policy assessments. In the past, they have been sufficient. In the present, they are clearly inadequate and in the future, they will be worthless. Policy formulation is a continuing, complex, and comprehensive task which has been accomplished on an ad hoc basis up to now. At the close of this Sixth American Forest Congress, it is obvious to me and I believe to you, that we need something new." Indirectly, two new laws addressed many of the concerns expressed by Arnold and others at the Forest Congress—the

National Forest Management Act of 1976, for the Forest Service, and the Federal Land Policy and Management Act of 1976, for the BLM.

1996 AMERICAN FOREST CONGRESS

A little over 20 years later, another forest congress was called—the seventh. The 1996 Congress was billed as a "citizens' congress" with no delegates, no invitations, and no cap on the number of attendees. It was intended to open constructive dialogue about our nation's forests with a broad cross-section of the American public. Attendees represented many environmental organizations; state and federal forestry and natural resource agencies; forest products industries; recreational groups; and special interest and community groups, students, and ordinary citizens. Discussion centered on a variety of forest-related issues that were discussed by forest policy leaders at the Yale Forest Forum from 1993 to 1995. The seventh Congress was the result of three years of planning and public roundtables. Between June 1995 and February 1996, 51 local roundtables and 43 collaborative meetings were held to discuss common ground shared by Americans about forests. Each local roundtable brought together a mix of people who were concerned with local and national forest policy issues. Nearly all the roundtables produced a common vision and a set of principles to achieve that vision. Seven draft elements of a vision based on the work of the roundtables were presented to the Forest Congress.

The Forest Congress met in Washington, D.C., for three and a half days in February 1996. Attended by 1,519 people, the Congress brought together a wide variety of participants, volunteers, support team members, and observers. About 1,100 attendees participated in table discussions throughout the process. Each table represented people who held a wide diversity of views (often diametrically opposed ones) and allegiances and mixed people of different ethnic backgrounds, gender, and places of residence. The two key questions posed were "What is our common vision?" and "What principles do we agree on to guide us toward our vision?" The groups in Washington expanded the 7 draft elements to 13. After continued discussion, 6 more draft principles were added. Working groups took the 19 elements and reworked them into 21 principles, of which 15 were accepted by at least 50 percent of the conferees. Thirty-nine additional draft principles emerged during a "missing principles" session, 14 of which were accepted by 50 percent of the group. Unfortunately, the Congress yielded little in the way of accomplishments. It did result in greater involvement in international efforts by the Forest Service and other agencies.

2005 FOREST CONGRESS

In early January 2005, the Forest Service Centennial Congress met in Washington, D.C. It was the first event of the centennial celebration of the agency. It was also 100 years to the day after the 1905 Forest Congress was convened. The Centennial Congress had the theme "A collective commitment to conservation."

It opened on January 4 and closed on January 6. Like the seventh Congress, the Centennial Congress used regional forums in the summer and fall of 2004. Although the forums were originally designed to follow various themes, they ended with discussions about all aspects of Forest Service management. The Centennial Congress did not focus forestry in other agencies or in the private sector. The U.S. Congress provided needed appropriations for the Centennial Congress, as well as supplemental funding by the Forest Service. USDA Under Secretary Mark Rey, who ultimately approved the Centennial Congress, did not want the meeting to approve any binding resolutions to be presented to the administration. More than 600 people registered for the Congress.

The first day, January 4, opened with remarks by Agriculture Secretary Ann Veneman and Interior Secretary Gale Norton. A panel of retired chiefs of the agency followed, with candid remarks by Max Peterson, Dale Robertson, Jack Ward Thomas, and Mike Dombeck. That evening's highlight was the premier showing of the two-hour, high-definition video *The Greatest Good,* which documents the 100 years of the Forest Service. The video production was highly regarded and has since been shown at hundreds of venues across the country. In 2006, a slightly modified version was broadcast on PBS stations in the larger metropolitan markets.

The next day focused on reports from the 12 centennial regional forums, which were presented as three-minute videos of key findings and recommendations to the full group of participants. On the last day, January 6, a panel of USDA assistant and under secretaries talked about what they experienced during their tenures in the Forest Service oversight role. Former Assistant Secretaries Rupert Cutler, John Crowell, and George Dunlop and former Under Secretary Jim Lyons gave insightful talks about their roles in trying to manage the unmanageable—the Forest Service. Each speaker, it became evident, still is strongly committed to the same actions he promoted when he was in office.

Chief Dale Bosworth, with Associate Chief Sally Collins, summarized what they had heard from the many speakers and the regional forums. Although no formal resolutions were adopted to present to the U.S. Congress regarding possible changes in the direction of the agency, there were many suggestions about what could be done in the future. In the month that followed, the national headquarters pulled together 11 key themes coming out of the Centennial Congress and addressed the scope of each theme.

1a: Partnerships

Partnerships are a means by which citizens, organizations, institutions, businesses, and federal, state, and local agencies can become involved in the care of national forest system lands, participate in forest and rangeland research, or take part in state and private forestry programs. Partnerships have been used by the Forest Service to accomplish needed and beneficial work. The resulting relationships build connections to the national forest system and promote broader understanding of conservation issues. Centennial Congress and forum participants endorsed the need to continue to expand and build capacity for partnership work with the agency.

Budget trends and agency and legislative initiatives also indicate that the Forest Service will need to build more capacity for working in partnership. Agency projections are for flat or declining budgets in terms of real purchasing power at the same time that demands for agency programs, forest and rangeland research, and use of the national forests and national grasslands are predicted to grow. Implementing programs and projects in partnership will be one way of meeting these increasing demands. More important, communities and organizations want to participate in Forest Service management activities. Communities and organizations bring an understanding and level of expertise that expands the capacity of the agency, which in turn expands the community's capacity. To meet the stewardship challenges of today and the future, the Forest Service needs to expand the use of partnerships and build relationships with current and future constituents.

1b: Collaboration

Collaboration is a process through which parties that see different aspects of a problem can constructively explore their differences and search for solutions that go beyond what any one group could envision alone. Recently, legislation such as the Healthy Forests Restoration Act (HFRA) of 2003 and "Payments to States" encourages the use of collaboration as a strategic process to bring together a variety of interests to agree on and design viable projects. The Forest Service currently has resources available on collaboration (including the national partnership office); however, collaboration has yet to be institutionalized as a way of conducting business and accomplishing high-priority projects. Delegates to the Centennial Congress stressed that collaboration must become the dominant paradigm in project planning and that Forest Service employees must become more comfortable in these collaborative efforts. The Forest Service also needs to bring constituencies into the decision process early; be clear in defining the decision space in each collaborative effort; and be inclusive and welcoming of diverse interests. Additionally, the Forest Service should proactively address cross-boundary concerns in planning and implementation.

2: Education/Communications

Delegates to the regional forums and the Centennial Congress challenged the Forest Service to expand its communication and environmental educational efforts, reach a wider, more culturally diverse audience, and provide the opportunity for lifetime learning. As the demographics of the United States change, increased focus on education and communication will allow the Forest Service to reach new and currently underserved audiences in its second century.

Delegates to the Centennial Congress repeatedly stressed the need for conservation education to be incorporated into the core curriculum starting in the early grades and continuing through high school and college. Increasing this focus would also allow the Forest Service to improve its communication of forestry research and natural resource information. Delegates also discussed the need to tell stories that appeal to a wide variety of audiences while highlighting the importance of national forests for providing drinking water, offering recreation, improving public health, and dealing with climate change. Additionally, delegates at both the Centennial Congress and the regional forums challenged the Forest Service to widen its education goals to include improving environmental literacy, increasing knowledge of different ecosystems, and exploring the global impacts of local decisions involving forest products.

3: Cross-Boundary Challenges

To meet the agency's mission of sustaining the health, diversity, and productivity of the nation's forests and grasslands for present and future generations, the Forest Service must work across jurisdictional and ownership boundaries to manage landscape-level ecosystem processes that maintain these systems. It is necessary to match the scales at which dominant natural disturbances and other processes occur with the scale of management planning and implementation. Since national forest system lands rarely make up a complete landscape, working on a larger scale would require coordination with other private and public landowners to integrate management goals and on-the-ground actions. Landscape-level ecosystem conservation and management are of particular importance in addressing resource issues such as managing wildlife population, controlling fire and fuels, dealing with invasive species, reducing losses of open space, and maintaining water sources.

4: Demographic Changes

The demographics of the United States are changing at extremely rapid rates. An estimated 80 percent of the nation's population currently lives within a large urban area or will do so in the near future. These populations are ethnically, economically, and educationally diverse. This level of diversity is placing unprecedented demands on different services and products from our nation's forests and our forestland managers. In order to meet these demands, the Forest Service will have to adopt faster and more effective ways of addressing the increasing demands of these changing populations. As the Forest Service embarks on its next 100-year journey, land management success in its many definitions will likely require identifying new constituencies, understanding what drives demographic changes, and working more effectively to better connect with these new constituencies. Since a large segment of our society resides in urban areas, it will serve the Forest Service well to explore the benefits of our urban forests and to use these benefits to help connect the urban populations to our wildland forests and demonstrate the value our wildland forests add to their lives.

5: Increasing Accountability/ New Business Models
(Fostering an Innovative, Flexible, and Accountable Organization)

Delegates at the regional forums and the Centennial Congress urged the Forest Service to build on its many successes and to meet its numerous challenges. Arguably, for the agency to succeed in all of these areas it will have to be more innovative and flexible, yet remain accountable. Some of the delegates referred to this as a new business model. Though this is not a new concept for the Forest Service, the forums brought it into focus.

Agency flexibility and innovation includes, for example, financing new schemes and technologies and forming a "skunk works" team to help the agency predict challenges and opportunities. It also includes a continued emphasis on coordination with other land management agencies, rewarding the sharing of knowledge, and promoting entrepreneurship and risk taking. Innovation and accountability focuses, for example, on the streamlining of various systems and procedures, such as fee and permit systems, and improving the way the agency handles financial management. To meet all of these challenges, the agency needs to continue to build capacity inside and outside the organization. An important aspect of this is the agency's ability to recruit capable staff at all levels of the organization.

6: Science and Technology Integration

Conflicting demands by society and individuals regarding land use change, open spaces, recreational opportunities, and water usage the need to protect threatened and endangered species and other natural resources, while complex in nature, may be better understood through applied science. As political agendas influence management decisions, as individuals and communities continue to put more demands on the agency for natural resources goods and services, as demographics continue to change and increasing global populations create resource scarcity, the agency will have to find better ways to integrate science into management decisions and technology developed by the Forest Service and its collaborators and university partners.

With increasing emphasis on social, political, and economic sciences, agency researchers, university partners, and collaborators will help the agency make better, more durable decisions. Integration of knowledge through technology transfer will help educate decision makers and inform the public that it serves. As it embraces its legacy as a consummate land management agency, it must also embrace science as a cornerstone of its management strategy and use the available technology to effectively communicate and provide information to the public on what it does and the value it adds to their lives and to those of future generations.

7: Strategic Approaches to Conservation Issues

Overarching trends, such as resource consumption, urbanization, the spread of invasive species, population growth, and global climate change, can substantially influence the ability of the Forest Service's to carry out its mission goals. It is important that the agency develop the capacity to evaluate the implications of these large-scale trends and to put into place effective strategies to respond to them. Centennial Congress participants identified a variety of large-scale trends that they felt should be systematically taken into account by the Forest Service. The example most often mentioned was the export of the environmental effects of U.S. resource consumption and the need to develop strategies to address both the consumption and the production sides of the conservation equation. Chief Bosworth also mentioned this issue in his opening address. The other trends raised by participants were population growth, the spread of invasive species, rapid urbanization, and global climate change. Some of these issues are already encompassed by the Chief's four threats and/or by other efforts to develop strategic approaches to sustainability.

8: Recreation Challenges

Outdoor recreation is an important force in America and provides mental, physical, economic, and social benefits to individuals, families, and communities. The Forest Service and its partners host about 214 million visitors annually. The number of visitors is expected to grow as the U.S. population grows. The Forest Service is under constant pressure to expand its capacity to meet public recreation needs. With this demand comes the increasing complexity of managing these activities for optimum enjoyment while minimizing social and environmental conflicts.

Reaching out to new constituencies and developing environmental literacy, especially among urban cultures and youth, is an increasing responsibility the agency decision makers must accept. In this age of limited resources, institutionalizing the role of volunteers and partners is critical to increasing the agency's service capacities and ensuring long-term sustainability of enjoyable recreation experiences and healthy forests. Managers must also put more emphasis on nurturing existing relationships with permittees, local communities, and industries. The recreation program provides most visitors with site and trip information, site interpretation, and safety messages. Thus, communication with visitors can assist the Forest Service in effectively managing the complexities of its recreation program and ensuring that recreational use is responsible and compatible with sustaining healthy landscapes now and in future generations.

9: Restoration (Biomass Utilization and Fuels)

Delegates to the regional forums and the Centennial Congress challenged the Forest Service to expand its policy on biomass utilization. There is a strong desire to see the Forest Service take an integrated approach, with all deputy-chief areas represented. There is a perception that the agency is unwilling to change targets and allow a reliable and sustained supply of biomass to be utilized prior to piling and burning. There is an increased need to seek creative solutions and new markets for biomass. Many of the rural communities and small businesses are dependent upon a reliable and sustainable supply of biomass.

Delegates at the Centennial Congress argued that the Forest Service should be a leader in biomass utilization today and in the future. Biomass utilization should cross boundaries in a cooperative manner dedicated to advancing a comprehensive, science-based approach to the harvesting and utilization of woody biomass from hazardous fuels reduction projects in and around at-risk communities adjacent to national forest system lands, tribal lands, private lands, and other ownerships. The Forest Service should develop a strategic plan that incorporates a business plan for the future.

10: Volunteers

Centennial forum and Congress participants endorsed the expansion of a skilled and trained volunteer cadre to assist in the conservation of natural resources. The Forest Service has had great success reaching out and recruiting citizens and groups interested in giving back some of their time, talent, and resources in an effort to achieve an outcome on the ground. Many volunteers are looking for a way to give back, a way to learn and understand the outdoor environment, a way to spend time with family and friends, and, most important, to have a relationship with other people in the agency.

11: Ecosystem (Environmental) Services

Ecosystem services include those services and functions traditionally viewed as free "public goods," such as clean air, clean water, wildlife, and scenic landscapes. Lacking a formal market, these natural assets are not recognized or accounted for

2005 Forest Service Centennial Congress in Washington, D.C. (USDA Forest Service)

in economic decisions that drive change in natural areas and affect the quality of air and water. The public's inability to connect benefits vital to human health and livelihoods with healthy forest ecosystems leaves the nation's forests undervalued and susceptible to increasing development pressures and conversion. Discussions that took place at the forums and the Centennial Congress suggested that the Forest Service should address this issue.

APPENDIX 3

Forest Service Badges, Patches, and Chinaware

Gifford Pinchot, as chief of the Bureau of Forestry, began thinking about the need for a unique badge of authority for his agency employees even before the forest reserves were transferred from the Department of the Interior to Agriculture. When the shift finally took place, early in 1905, and the bureau was named the Forest Service in the summer of the same year, Pinchot set about at once to create a new official badge for the forest rangers (the earlier General Land Office used a nickel-plated, round badge).

The Washington office staff agreed that the vast responsibilities of the new Forest Service required such a symbol (badge) to help ensure public recognition of the agency and respect for its officers and their authority, both in Washington and in the field. A reliable symbol was especially needed for those employees in the field who were charged with applying and enforcing federal laws and regulations, many of them new, in the face of an often suspicious and hostile local populace.

For creation of the badge, Pinchot announced a contest among Washington office employees. A highly varied collection of tree-related designs resulted, including scrolls, leaves, and maple seeds. The judges appreciated their artistic merits but were dissatisfied because none included generally recognized symbols of authority.

Edward T. Allen, one of the judges, strongly believed that a conventional shield was the best authority symbol. As it turned out, he and an associate, William C. Hodge, Jr. (who, like Allen, worked both in the Washington office and in California between 1904 and 1906), came up with the design that became the official badge. The two men were together in the spring of 1905, perhaps in Allen's office or at a railroad depot in Salt Lake City (the meeting place is unclear).

Allen, who was attracted by the type of shield used by the Union Pacific Railroad, began tracing an outline of the shield (from a Union Pacific timetable) on a sheet of paper. He inserted the large letters U and S halfway from the top to the bottom of the shield, leaving a space between them. Hodge, looking on, was inspired to sketch a fir tree on a sheet of "roll-your-own" cigarette paper he took from his pocket. He then laid this between the U and the S. The two men then quickly wrote "FOREST SERVICE" across the top and "DEPARTMENT OF AGRICULTURE" across the bottom. The placement of the two names was probably dictated by available spaces. Whether this design had any influence on the soon-to-develop and still widely used but unofficial expression "U.S. Forest Service" is debatable. In any case, Pinchot and his assistant, Overton Price, were pleased with the design and called off a planned second contest.

FOREST SERVICE BRONZE BADGES

The large bronze badge—about two and a quarter inches in diameter, slightly convex with raised letters and tree—was issued to all field officers by July 1, 1905. Less than two years later, Pinchot issued an order on the wearing of the badge: "Here-after the badge will be worn only by officers of the Washington office when on inspection or administrative duty on the National Forests, by Inspectors, and by Supervisors, Rangers, and Guards and other officers assigned to administrative duty under the Supervisors." The present bronze badge, first issued in 1915, is smaller (one and five-eighths inches across) than the original.

Badges for fire guards were nickel-plated bronze with the words "FOREST GUARD" across the top, "U.S." on the left of the tree, "F.S." on the right, and "DEPARTMENT OF AGRICULTURE" on the bottom. Another forest-guard badge type was made with "FOREST GUARD" across the top, "U.S." to the left of the tree, "D.A." on the right, and "FOREST SERVICE" at the bottom. Neither of these Forest Guard badges had a raised edge around the border of the badge. The words were stamped into the surface, and the tree was highly symmetrical. Another badge was issued, probably to forest guards or lookouts, that was the same as the regular Forest Service bronze badge, only nickel-plated. Finally, a flat bronze badge has been recently issued. Beginning around 1922, a smaller seven-eighths-inch bronze badge was authorized for uniform wear. This badge was the same as the larger badge, except smaller. It was used on dress uniforms until around 1972. The smaller badge was often issued and worn by women employees on their jackets and vests; the women's uniform was designed in the 1960s. This smaller badge was sometimes, incorrectly, referred to as the "women's badge."

Other than three size variations and three forest-guard variations, two other minor image changes were made. One was made in 1920, when the large letters U and S were lengthened, but the tree remained the same; the other change was made in 1938, when Chief F. A. Silcox approved a revision of the standard Forest Service shield in which the tree image in the middle became longer than in the original 1905 version. Also, the tree and root shapes on the shield changed slightly, with the tree becoming more symmetrical and the roots becoming slightly shorter. These changes were evident on both the badges and the Forest Service shields everywhere. Since the late 1930s, there have been no additional changes to the image on the official badge.

Forest Service badges were attached to the official uniforms in three different ways. The most common type is a single pin-back style, vertical pin (called a "finding") with one side attached by solder to the back of the badge. Another variation, found thus far on only one badge worn by Forest Service Chief Richard McArdle, has two vertical pin-back clasps soldered on the back of the badge. Also, there is an uncommon attachment with two vertical posts soldered on the back of the badge that attach to a uniform with pinch clips. The smaller one-inch badge has three methods of attachment—pin-back style, pinch clip, and military-style post and screw. The Forest Service manual (FSM) specifies the uses and wearing of the badge in FSM 6159.49a and b.

Forest Service law enforcement, however, has a different official badge. This unusual shield stylistically resembles the regular FS patch in shape, but it has several variations: an additional point at the top of the badge, an eagle with wings outspread and head facing to the left sitting on the top, and a slightly "fatter" main body. The badge was designed by agent Bill Dixon from R-8 in the 1970s. It is similar to other law-enforcement badges of different agencies. The badge is silver with the top containing the words "FOREST" and "SERVICE" on two lines. These are separated by a bar across the narrow part of the badge from the remaining words. In the middle is a round symbol of the USDA in the center and a larger

Forest Service Badges over time. (Gerald Williams Personal Collection)

circle with the words "UNITED STATES DEPARTMENT OF AGRICULTURE" circling the upper three-quarters of the circle. On each side of the round symbol are the highly stylized letters "U" on the left and "S" on the right. Immediately above these letters, between the letters and the word "SERVICE," are two five-pointed stars—one on each side. At the bottom of the patch are the words "LAW ENFORCEMENT" on one line and the "& INVESTIGATIONS" on the second line, both inside a raised banner.

SHOULDER PATCHES

In the 1950 and 1960s, several of the national forests in different parts of the country authorized—at least informally—the wearing of special cloth shoulder patches for their forest. National forests in California, as examples, had their own patches that were shaped like the badge but had words sewn along the top indicating the national forest of the wearer.

In the early 1960s, a cloth shoulder patch was authorized for wear on the left shoulder of official uniform shirts and jackets. The first authorized patch, issued in 1962, was flat on the bottom and sides but rounded on the top. A curved overhead bar was added to designate which national forest or other office the wearer was from. All of this was part of an effort—beginning in 1961—to present a new image of the employees to the public. During this time, there were newly redesigned hats, shoulder patches, forest unit bars ("rockers"), and name tags. The current the Forest Service shield patch was authorized in 1974 and introduced to the agency on March 20, 1975. The new patch, in the same shape as the badge, has the shield outlined in yellow, with the words and tree also in yellow against a green background.

There are two variations: (1) an older, smaller two-inch Forest Service flat-bottom patch, sometimes called the women's patch, which is identical to the larger four-inch patch, and (2) the newer, smaller two-inch Forest Service shield patch, also referred to as the women's uniform patch, which is identical to the larger four-inch patch except that the word "DEPARTMENT" is abbreviated "DEPT." and the word "AGRICULTURE" is abbreviated "AGRIC."

There were also two shoulder patches that are distinctly different from the other patches: (1) a color variation—that of the Forest Service patch for winter snow-ranger uniforms—orange border with black letters and tree on a white background and (2) another snow-ranger patch with a slightly smaller, black-bordered shield with a larger orange shield outline. Apparently, the snow-ranger patches were worn from 1939 to 1967. There were several reasons for this unusual patch. The patch was worn on both shoulder sleeves of heavy winter coats (the bronze badge would be underneath on a shirt, if it was worn). It was highly visible against a dark green jacket, and, when the ranger fell in the snow, the bronze badge would not be lost or cause injury to the ranger. These patches were often worn above the left breast pocket on snow parkas.

Another special patch is that of Forest Service law enforcement. This resembles the regular FS patch in shape, size, and color with the following variations: at the top of the patch the words, in yellow thread, "FOREST" and "SERVICE" are on two lines. In the middle is a round symbol of the USDA in the center (outlined in yellow) and a larger circle with the words (in green) "DEPT. OF AGRICULTURE" circling the upper two-thirds of the yellow circle. On each side of the round symbol are the letters "U" on the left and "S" on the right. Immediately above these letters, between the letters and the top word "SERVICE," are two five-pointed stars—one on each side. At the bottom of the patch is the word "ENFORCEMENT" (in green) inside a yellow thread ribbon.

A very different shoulder patch has been authorized in recent years for Forest Service volunteers. This off-white patch is somewhat like the older

New Forest Service patches. (Gerald Williams Personal Collection)

Forest Service uniform patches; it is about three and a quarter inches tall and two and a quarter inches wide, with a flat bottom and rounded top. The patch is outlined in an olive-green thread. The off-white background has sewn with olive-green thread the words "FOREST SERVICE," with the word "VOLUNTEER" underneath. Above the words is a shallow "V" in a pea-green color that has two olive-green evergreen trees (without needles) having three branches on each side of the main stem. The trees overlie a pea-green sun.

CHINAWARE

Forest Service tableware (or chinaware) was produced for the USDA Forest Service from the 1920s to the 1940s. The various dinner and serving pieces were hardy "everyday" versions of restaurant-type tableware. The dishes were used for many years in Forest Service administrative sites (including cabins and lookouts) and also, apparently, in the Civilian Conservation Corps camps in the 1930s and early 1940s. There are many stories about the disposal of the dishes into dumps or outhouses when sites were moved or abandoned. Many pieces have remained in the hands of the agency, while some were brought home by employees, and others can be found in the collections of chinaware collectors.

Generally, the tableware is off-white in color with one or two (usually two) medium to dark green stripes or bands on the inside of plates and saucers and on the outside rims of cups and bowls. Each item also has a three-quarters- to one-inch-tall Forest Service shield, in the same green color as the stripes, near the top rim or edge of the piece. However, a cereal bowl, coffee cup, and creamer have been found with a dark green Forest Service shield but no stripes.

The following is a list of the Forest Service tableware makers and the types of chinaware pieces associated with each manufacturer. The name of the chinaware maker can be found on the bottom of each piece. In recent years, reproduction chinaware under the Buffalo and Jackson names has been available.

Known makers of Forest Service chinaware included:

Buffalo China, Buffalo, NY
Carr China Co., Grafton, NY
Jackson Custom China, Falls Creek, PA
McNicol China, Clarksburg, WV
O.P.CO., Syracuse, NY (O.P.CO. was a brand name of the Onondaga Pottery Company, which became Syracuse China.)
PA-CE-CO China, El Cerrito, CA (PA-CE-CO China was a brand name of Tepco.
Shenango China, New Castle, PA.)
Sterling, East Liverpool, OH
Tepco, El Cerrito, CA (The name derives from the Technical Porcelain and Chinaware Company.)
Wallace China, Los Angeles, CA

APPENDIX 4

Game Refuges on National Forests

The Forest Service became involved with national game refuges and preserves as early as 1892, in Alaska, with the Afognak Forest and Fish Culture Reserve. The Act of August 11, 1916 (39 Stat. 446, 476) authorized the president to establish game refuges for the protection of game animals, birds, and fish on any lands purchased under the Weeks Act of 1911. These lands were almost all in the East. The National Forest Refuge Act of March 10, 1934 (48 Stat. 400) authorized the president, upon the recommendations of the Secretaries of Agriculture and Commerce and with the approval of the legislatures of the states affected, to establish fish and game refuges or preserves within the national forests. Many national and state refuges were established and managed on the national forests until the 1940s, when they were abolished. Wildlife refuges are currently managed by the USDI Fish and Wildlife Service. None are located on the national forests.

FIGURE A4.1 National Game Refuges and Wildlife Preserves on the National Forest System

Name	State	National Forest	Date	Acres
Afognak Forest and Fish Culture Reserve	Alaska	Chugach	1892	512,000
Apache Migratory Waterfowl Refuge	Arizona	Apache	1937	2,680
Big Levels Game Refuge	Virginia	George Washington-Jefferson	1933	31,725
Black Hills Game Refuge (Meade RD)	South Dakota	Black Hills	1925	5,548

(continued)

FIGURE A4.1 *(Continued)*

Name	State	National Forest	Date	Acres
Catahoula Wildlife Preserve	Louisiana	Kisatchie		36,177
Cherokee National Game Refuge #1	Tennessee	Cherokee	1924	30,000
Cherokee National Game Refuge #2	Tennessee	Cherokee	1924	14,000
Cibola Game Refuge (Zuni RD)	New Mexico	Cibola	1925	45,515
Clear Lake Bird Refuge	California	Modoc	1912	33,640
Custer State Park Game Sanctuary	South Dakota	Harney	1925	44,360
Francis Marion Preserve	South Carolina	Francis Marion	1947	50,600
Grand Canyon Natl. Game Preserve	Arizona	Kaibab	1906	886,208
Kirtland's Warbler Management Area	Michigan	Huron-Manistee	1963	
Marquette Game Reserve (Brady RD)	Michigan	Marquette	1925	2,948
Medicine Bow Game Refuge (Pole Mtn RD)	Wyoming	Medicine Bow	1925	
Mineral King	California	Sequoia	1920	15,770
Mount Olympus National Monument	Washington	Olympic	1909	299,370
Norbeck Wildlife Preserve	South Dakota	Black Hills	1920	33,656
Noontootly Game Preserve	Georgia	Chattahoochee	1938	24,670
Ocala National Game Refuge	Florida	Ocala	1930	79,735
Ouachita #1 (Pigeon Creek)	Arizona	Ouachita	1933	8,440
Ouachita #2 (Oak Mountain)	Arkansas	Ouachita	1933	8,500
Ouachita #4 (Caney Creek)	Arkansas	Ouachita	1933	8,300
Ouachita Wildlife Preserve	Arkansas	Ouachita	1933	78,000
Ozark #1 (Livingston)	Arkansas	Ozark	1926	9,122

FIGURE A4.1 *(Continued)*

Name	State	National Forest	Date	Acres
Ozark #2 (Barkshead)	Arkansas	Ozark	1926	5,927
Ozark #3 (Moccasin)	Arkansas	Ozark	1926	3,932
Ozark #4 (Haw Creek)	Arkansas	Ozark	1926	4,108
Ozark #5 (Black Mountain)	Arkansas	Ozark	1926	19,074
Pisgah National Game Refuge	North Carolina	Pisgah	1916	98,513
Pryor Mountains Game Preserve	Montana	Custer	1968?	
Red Dirt Wildlife Preserve	Louisiana	Kisatchie		36,117
Salt Creek Game Refuge	Oregon	Willamette	1926	38,000
Sequoia National Game Refuge	California	Sequoia	1926	15,770
Sheep Mountain Game Refuge	Wyoming	Medicine Bow	1924	28,318
Sun River Game Preserve (State)	Montana	Lewis and Clark	1913	
Tahquitz Game Preserve	California	San Bernardino	1926	27,573
Three Sisters Game Refuge	Oregon	Willamette	1926?	
Wichita National Game Preserve	Oklahoma	Wichita (now a USF and WS refuge)	1905	60,800

FIGURE A4.2 Game Refuges on National Forests, December 31, 1929

State	State Game Refuges		Federal Game Preserves		Other FS Game Areas	
	Number	Acres In NFS	Number	Acres In NFS	Number	Acres In NFS
AL	1	16,000				
AK			1	140,681		
AR	23	1,102,601	2	793,377		
AZ			5	21,500		
CA	31	2,034,853	3	48,343	2	19,800

(continued)

FIGURE A4.2 *(Continued)*

State	State Game Refuges		Federal Game Preserves		Other FS Game Areas	
	Number	Acres In NFS	Number	Acres In NFS	Number	Acres In NFS
CO	18	2,666,484			24	202,607
FL	1	60,000				
GA			1	14,000		
ID	20	3,033,578			8	644,818
MT	19	1,213,831			42	573,030
NE	1	206,026				
NV	10	1,155,282				
NH	3	7,960				
NM	55	1,134,127	1	45,515		
NC	2	31,101	1	98,381		
OK			1	60,800		
OR	11	735,226			2	166,600
PA	2	17,860				
SD	2	26,060	2	49,908		
TN			1	30,000		
UT	10	1,157,526			1	5,000
VA	5	7,200				
WA	24	2,284,058			1	13,517
WV	2	23,000				
WY	18	2,739,898	2	84,450	7	114,900
Total	258	19,652,580	20	1,386,955	87	1,740,272

FIGURE A4.3: Game Refuges on National Forest System Lands, CY 1936

State Game Refuges		Federal Game Preserves		Other FS Game Areas	
Number	Acres In NFS	Number	Acres In NFS	Number	Acres IJ391 NFS
349	21,277,964	31	4,080,600	120	4,139,818

APPENDIX 5

Forest Service Timber Sales and Harvest Levels

Fiscal Year[1]	Number of Sales	Timber Sold[2]	Timber Harvested[2]
1905			.068
1906			.139
1907		.950	.195
1908			.393
1909			.352
1910			.380
1911	5,144	.830	.375
1912	5,179	.799	.432
1913	5,696	2.137	.496
1914			.626
1915			.566
1916			.595
1917			.736
1918			.730
1919			.705
1920	7,182	1.327	.805
1921	6,448	1.170	.801
1922	6,820	1.277	.723
1923	6,873	1.879	.995

(continued)

FIGURE A5 *(Continued)*

Fiscal Year[1]	Number of Sales	Timber Sold[2]	Timber Harvested[2]
1924 (calender)	7,525	1.333	1.144
1925 (calender)	7,265	1.772	1.022
1926 (calender)	7,528	1.489	1.193
1927 (calender)	7,462	.643	1.360
1928 (calender)	7,934	2.690	1.272
1929 (calender)	8,350	1.050	1.497
1930 (calender)	9,451	3.370	1.653
1931 (calender)		.605	1.222
1932 (calender)			.612
1933		.357	.474
1934	16,433	.462	.675
1935	17,520	.670	.752
1936	18,389	.988	1.021
1937	19,126	1.491	1.291
1938	21,916	1.075	1.288
1939	22,717	1.842	1.291
1940	25,037	1.779	1.740
1941	25,553	1.465	2.067
1942		2.839	2.205
1943		3.693	2.360
1944		2.859	3.333
1945		2.392	3.145
1946		2.687	2.730
1947		3.786	3.834
1948		3.742	3.759
1949		2.615	3.741
1950	24,248	3.434	3.502
1951	22,399	4.913	4.688
1952	21,148	4.731	4.806
1953	22,020	4.714	5.360
1954	21,044	6.432	5.854
1955	23,402	10.068	6.578
1956	21,842	6.837	6.898
1957	21,687	6.533	6.998

FIGURE A5 *(Continued)*

Fiscal Year[1]	Number of Sales	Timber Sold[2]	Timber Harvested[2]
1958	22,495	13.293	6.421
1959	24,277	9.359	8.341
1960	23,852	12.167	9.367
1961	24,779	8.857	8.381
1962	23,030	10.326	9.032
1963	27,020	12.175	10.026
1964	29,976	11.682	10.954
1965	25,706	11.510	11.244
1966	23,923	11.294	12.138
1967	23,266	11.640	10.759
1968	22,479	11.684	12.128
1969	23,418	19.483	11.865
1970	26,610	13.382	11.527
1971	23,243	10.636	10.341
1972	25,419	10.340	11.700
1973	28,851	10.199	12.357
1974	34,429	10.241	10.958
1975	35,977	10.824	9.174
1976 (new FY)	43,012	11.823	13.007
1977	44,466	9.920	10.482
1978	54,373	10.996	10.080
1979	64,135	11.330	10.377
1980	89,337	11.290	9.178
1981	92,041	11.457	8.036
1982	143,723	10.030	6.747
1983	235,585	11.061	9.244
1984	343,006	10.662	10.549
1985	366,874	10.819	10.941
1986	349,977	10.967	11.787
1987	289,043	11.319	12.712
1988	251,557	10.968	12.596
1989	275,895	8.415	11.951
1990	262,781	9.230	10.500
1991	271,963	5.786	6.559

FIGURE A5 *(Continued)*

Fiscal Year[1]	Number of Sales	Timber Sold[2]	Timber Harvested[2]
1992	250,852	4.459	7.289
1993	255,825	4.515	5.917
1994	215,268	3.056	4.815
1995	216,272	2.885	3.866
1996	190,123	3.385	3.725
1997	198,110	3.688	3.285
1998	165,697	2.955	3.298
1999	155,888	2.200	2.939
2000	114,351	1.745	2.542
2001	133,919	1.534	1.938
2002	130,248	1.619	1.726
2003			
2004			

Notes: [1] The original government fiscal year was July 1 to June 30. In 1976, Congress changed the FY starting and ending dates to October 1 and September 30. For the period 1924–1932, the dates were compiled for the calendar year; [2] Measured in billions of board feet.

APPENDIX 6

Major Laws Affecting the USDA Forest Service

In this appendix, we present a short list of major laws that specifically affect the management of the USDA Forest Service. There are literally hundreds of laws that, in one way or another, affect the everyday management of the agency. Please consult the 1,184-page volume *The Principal Laws Relating to Forest Service Activities* (1993), with additional supplements, for the most recent wording of applicable laws. Also, the laws may be found on the Web sites of a variety of legal service and universities. Each law also has implementing regulations that were developed by the various agencies. The Forest Service regulations, manuals, and handbooks can be located in their electronic forms by searching the FS's Web site www.fs.fed.us/publications. These directives, as they are called, at least triple or quadruple the number of pages devoted to just the wording of the laws. Of course, there are many laws that could be discussed, but the following list of the 13 most significant laws is intended to show the breadth and depth of the laws affecting management of the national forests and grasslands:

- Forest Reserve Act of 1891
- Organic Act of 1897
- Transfer Act of 1905
- Forest Service Name Change Act of 1905
- Weeks Act of 1911
- Clarke-McNary Act of 1924
- McSweeney-McNary Act of 1928
- Multiple-Use Sustained-Yield Act of 1960
- Wilderness Act of 1964
- Wild and Scenic Rivers Act of 1968
- National Environmental Policy Act of 1969
- Endangered Species Act of 1973
- National Forest Management Act of 1976

FOREST RESERVE (CREATIVE) ACT
OF MARCH 3, 1891 (26 STAT. 1095)

Prior to 1891, there were efforts by individuals and groups to preserve the remaining public domain forestland in the United States for future generations. The new conservation effort derived from the philosophical writings of Emerson, Thoreau, Muir, and others and was supported by a few associations, such as the American Forestry Association, and a few influential magazine and journal editors, such as Robert Underwood Johnson (*The Century Magazine*) and Charles Sprague Sargent (*Garden and Forest*). Several state and local efforts were successful in creating park and forest preserves in the East and in establishing Yellowstone National Park, in 1872, in the West. Direct linkage to the 1891 Act can be traced through a paper read by Dr. Franklin Benjamin Hough at the annual meeting of the American Association for the Advancement of Science (AAAS), in Portland, Maine, on August 21, 1873. His paper, titled "On the Duty of Governments in the Preservation of Forests," contains the first major attempt to make the scientists and the public aware of a forest problem. In part, Hough's address stated:

> The presence of stately ruins in solitary deserts, is conclusive proof that great climatic changes have taken place within the period of human history in many eastern countries, once highly cultivated and densely peopled, but now arid wastes. … We cannot account for the changes that have occurred since these [Middle East] sunburnt and sterile plains, where these traces of man's first civilization are found, were clothed with a luxuriant vegetation, except by ascribing them to the improvident acts of man, in destroying the trees and plants which once clothed the surface, and sheltered it from the sun and the winds. As this shelter was removed the desert approached, gaining new power as its area increased, until it crept over vast regions once populous and fertile, and left only the ruins of former magnificence.
>
> In more temperate climates the effect is less striking, yet it is sufficiently apparent everywhere and throughout our whole country, but especially in the hilly and once wooded regions of the Eastern and Northern states. In these portions of our Union the failure of springs and wells, the drying up of brooks which once supplied ample hydraulic power through the summer, and the increasing difficulties of procuring water to supply canals for navigation, and wholesome water for cities, are becoming every day something more than a subject of casual remark. It is destined to become a theme of careful scientific and practical inquiry, to ascertain how these growing evils may be checked, and whether the lost advantages may be regained.…
>
> I would venture to suggest that this association might properly take measures for bringing to the notice of our several State governments, and Congress with respect to the Territories, the subject of protection to forests, and their cultivation, regulation, and encouragement; and that it appoint a special committee to memorialize these several legislative bodies upon this subject, and to urge its importance. A measure of public utility thus commended to their notice by this association would doubtless receive respectful attention. Its reasons would be brought up for discussion, and the probabilities of the future, drawn the history of the past, might be presented before the public in their true light. Such a memorial should embrace the draught of a bill, as the form of a law, which should be carefully considered in its various aspects of public interests and private rights, and as best adapted to secure the benefits desired.

The day after Hough's speech, the association passed a resolution to memorialize (petition) Congress on the necessity of the federal government to fund a federal agent to report to Congress on the state of the nation's forests. The AAAS appointed a nine-member committee, which was headed by Hough. Hough and his friend George B. Emerson roughed out the petition. In February 1874, they arrived in Washington to gather additional support and to personally discuss the memorial with President Ulysses S. Grant, who in turn sent it to Congress. In part, the memorial maintained that forest preservation and growth were of "great practical importance" to the nation, that timber shortages were inevitable in the near future, and that Congress should pass a law to create "a commission of forestry," appointed by the president and the Senate, to study and report on the state of the nation's forests. More than two years later, on August 15, 1876, Congress appropriated $2,000 to be used to "appoint a man of approved attainments" to study and report on forest supplies, harvesting, imports and exports, uses, and growing conditions, as well as conditions in other countries. Hough was appointed the first federal forestry agent, and his position was assigned to the Commissioner of Agriculture. Within a year, he compiled a 650-page book titled *Report upon Forestry 1877*. Congress was so impressed with this massive work that 25,000 copies were ordered printed in 1878. Hough remained at this work, producing two more reports, until 1883, when he was replaced by Nathaniel H. Egleston.

Over the next decades, a variety of efforts were under way to persuade the president and Congress to allow for the creation of forest reservations from public domain land (that is, land that was not under private ownership). In 1889, members of the American Forestry Association met with President Benjamin Harrison and presented a petition that advocated the adoption of a national forest policy. The president took no action. The American Forestry Association then memorialized Congress to establish forest reservations and to create a commission to administer them.

Action by Congress on the first issue, the creation of national forests, came two years later. The second issue, management or administration of any such reservations, would have to wait another eight years. The year 1891 became pivotal in the fight for the protection of federal forestlands. Early in the year, Congress was debating and revising a series of older land laws that allowed the government to give away or sell large portions of the public domain. The western states contained the only remaining large blocks of public land still under federal ownership, and many people became concerned that the land and forests were being transferred to the private sector in a reckless manner. The various Homestead Acts and Timber-Culture Act were felt to be especially generous. In addition, more than a few settlers and "land grabbers" were making a mockery of the legislation by undertaking illegal schemes to take more land than they were allowed and by not following the intent of the laws.

In the spring of 1891, while Congress was debating the repeal or modification of these liberal homesteading laws, a rider (amendment) was attached to the legislation that would allow the president to establish forest reserves. This important amendment (section 24) to the Act of March 3, 1891 (26 Stat. 1095), afterward referred to as the Creative Act or Forest Reserve Act, was a long, wordy sentence that read:

> Sec. 24. The President of the United States may, from time to time, set apart and reserve, in any State or Territory having public land bearing forests, in any part of the public lands wholly or in part covered with timber or undergrowth, whether of commercial value or not, as public reservations, and the President shall, by public proclamation, declare the establishment of such reservations and the limits thereof.

The first forest reserve established under this act was the Yellowstone Park Timber Land Reserve, on March 30, 1891. This forest reserve in Wyoming bordered the southern edge of Yellowstone National Park. The second forest reserve was the White River Plateau Timber Land Reserve, in Colorado, established on October 16, 1891. The next year saw an additional eight forest reserves established, while in 1893 another seven reserves came into being. None of these reserves came with any method or means to manage these lands. The Pacific Northwest played a pivotal role in the forest management debate in Congress, much as it still does today. In the fall of 1893, the small (18,560 acres) Ashland Forest Reserve was created, on September 28, in southern Oregon, to protect the city of Ashland's watershed, much as the earlier Bull Run Reserve (of 1892) was established to protect the water supply for the city of Portland. President Cleveland established another reserve on the same day—the Cascade Range Forest Reserve. It would have been established earlier except that land fraud was suspected in certain areas. Whereas the other two reserves were small in size, the Cascade Range Forest Reserve encompassed 4,492,800 acres and was 235 miles in length, making it the largest forest reserve in the nation. By the end of September 1893, some 17 million acres of federal forest reserves had been established nationwide. The president then stopped creating any additional forest reserves until Congress could come up with a means to manage the lands. The stoppage would last for almost four years.

During the 1895–1896 period, protest petitions against the creation of the reserves, which had been almost nonexistent for the earlier forest reserves, began to come into the USDI General Land Office (GLO) office in Washington, D.C. Most protests came from sheep owners who used the alpine meadows for sheep grazing, a few homesteaders in or near the reserves, and miners with existing mines or mineral claims. However, these protests were largely ineffectual. In the winter of 1895–1896, the entire Oregon delegation in Congress was ready to eliminate or severely reduce the Cascade Range Forest Reserve. This situation was averted only by the actions undertaken by William G. Steel, who was the strongest advocate of forest reserves in Oregon. He traveled to Washington, D.C., and spending several months convincing the president and USDI bureaucrats to keep the reserve intact. Ironically, some people engaged in partly successful schemes to profit illegally from the creation of this and other forest reserves in Oregon.

ORGANIC ACT OF 1897 (30 STAT. 11, 34)

National Forest Commission of 1896

There were efforts in Congress to change the procedures for establishing federal forests. Probably the most vocal advocate of change was Gifford Pinchot. He was a strong leader in trying to establish a commission, as early as 1894, to report on the public timberlands. R. U. Johnson, as editor of the widely read *Century Magazine*, proposed several times in 1895 the formation of a committee to investigate the forest reserves and to make recommendations about their needs and management. Even the *Report of the Secretary of the Interior, 1895* recommended a national forestry commission to study the wooded lands of the United States. At the behest of many supporters, the Secretary of the Interior requested, on February 15, 1896, that Wolcott Gibbs, president of the National Academy of Sciences, convene a group of forestry experts to study the forest reserve situation. The following people were selected as members of the commission:

> Charles S. Sargent—chair of the commission; head of the Arnold Arboretum at Harvard University; author of *The Sylva of the United States*; editor of the influential *Garden and Forest*.
>
> General Henry L. Abbot—retired from the U.S. Army Corps of Engineers; spent time in the mid-1850s as a lieutenant in the U.S. Pacific Railroad surveys in the West.
>
> Alexander Agassiz—curator of the Harvard Museum of Comparative Zoology; son of Louis Agassiz.
>
> William H. Brewer—Yale University who served on the Geological Survey of California and was the official botanist of the State of California.
>
> Arnold Hague—geologist with the U.S. Geological Survey.
>
> Gifford Pinchot—secretary of the commission and consulting forester.
>
> Wolcott Gibbs—member ex officio; president of the National Academy of Sciences.

Gibbs wrote to the forestry committee experts, posing the following questions to be answered by November 1, 1896, before Congress was out of session:

- What entity should retain ultimate ownership of the forests that now belonged to the government; that is, what portions of the forest on the public domain should be allowed to pass, either in part or entirely, from government control into private hands?
- How should the government forests be administered so that the inhabitants of adjacent regions might draw their necessary forest supplies from them without affecting their permanency?
- What provision was possible and necessary to secure for the government a continuous, intelligent, and honest management of the forests of the public domain, including those reservations already made or that may be made in the future?

On June 1, 1896, Pinchot and his friend Harry Graves (who became the second chief of the Forest Service, in 1910) left early so that they could personally investigate several forest areas in the northern Rockies. Graves was paid for these investigations by Pinchot, as the commission was not given the authority to hire any employees. On June 11, 1896, the Congress authorized $25,000 to cover expenses of the forest commission; the members served without compensation. The rest of the commission, minus Gibbs and Agassiz, assembled in Chicago near the end of June. The main party, along with John Muir, arrived in Montana on July 16. They spent several weeks traveling through the Black Hills, Yellowstone National Park, forest reserves in the northern Rockies, and the forest areas along the Great Northern (the old Northern Pacific railroad grant land) line. They visited the upper Flathead River country, went down the Kootenai River, then went on to Spokane, Washington. The commission met in Missoula, Montana, traveling to examine the forest areas in western Montana, then headed west past the headwaters of the Columbia River and on to Lake Chelan and the forest areas in the Cascades of Washington. They next visited Oregon, with a portion of the party going to western Washington and the Olympic Mountains and the other going to southern Oregon. The party then went on to northwestern California, the Sierras in California, and afterwards to southern California, Yosemite, and Arizona, with its Grand Canyon, then on to New Mexico, Colorado, ending up, in early September, in Brookline, Massachusetts, where Sargent made his home.

The Forestry Commission disagreed much of the time, but the members did agree on the need for a Mt. Rainier National Park in Washington State (established from the Mt. Rainier [Gifford Pinchot] National Forest in 1899) and a Grand Canyon National Park on the border of Arizona (established from the Kaibab and Tusayan [Prescott] National Forest in 1919). The commission also proposed the creation of new or expanded forest reserves containing a total of 21,279,840 acres. On the basis of a draft report, Interior Secretary David R. Francis wrote a letter, on February 6, 1897, to President Grover Cleveland, recommending that 13 forest reserves be established. He suggested the proclamations should be on George Washington's birthday, February 22. On that date, President Cleveland issued proclamations to establish these reserves, which were afterward known as the "Washington's Birthday Reserves."

The following forest reserves were established on February 22, 1897:

San Jacinto, California	737,280 acres
Stanislaus, California	691,200 acres
Washington, Washington	3,594,240 acres
Mt. Rainier, Washington	1,267,200 acres
Olympic, Washington	2,188,800 acres
Priest River, Idaho and Washington	645,120 acres
Bitterroot, Idaho and Montana	4,147,200 acres
Lewis & Clark, Montana	2,926,080 acres
Flathead, Montana	1,382,400 acres
Big Horn, Wyoming	1,198,080 acres
Teton, Wyoming	829,440 acres

| Uinta, Utah | 705,120 acres |
| Black Hills, South Dakota | 967,680 acres |

The final Forestry Commission report was finished by commission secretary Gifford Pinchot on May 1, 1897. It was printed by the Congress and the National Academy of Sciences soon thereafter.

Washington's Birthday Reserves

The 21 million acres of new forest reserves were added to an existing 13 million acres already set aside, creating a forest reserve area as large as the state of Illinois. However, opponents of the forest reserve system were getting ready to strike. There was an immediate outcry from the western states to have the new reserves canceled. Many were favorable to the forest reserves, but they were barely heard over the opponents' outcries.

Arguments against the new forest reserves were almost identical to those made by the earlier protestors in Oregon and elsewhere. Some wanted all the reserves eliminated, while others wanted the reserves to be reduced in size. As before, much of the opposition was led by western stockowners. The furor caused by those opposed to these forest reserves was unprecedented. Many in Congress from the western states pressured the new president, William McKinley, to rescind the orders of the outgoing president, but McKinley chose not do so. Congressional delegations from Washington, Idaho, Oregon, California, Montana, Wyoming, and Colorado began working hard to defeat the Washington Birthday Reserves.

The anti–forest reserve protesters howled because of their perception that their basic rights had been denied, much as property rights advocates protest today. The basic elements under discussion revolved around various philosophic, social, and economic implications of government control of the West. Many of the opponents of the forest reserves saw that their economic advantage derived from free grazing on federal lands and unfettered timber use was coming to an end. Although the long tradition of unregulated use in the West actually went back no more than 10 or 20 years, the idea that the federal government could permanently close off the public domain was unthinkable to many. Pressures were soon being applied by the users of the public domain to state and congressional delegations to convince them to restrict or eliminate the federal government, rather than to expand its powers. The Washington's Birthday Reserves created a situation in which the very foundations of the Western movement and the concept of free land were in question—and many did not like the answers.

Organic Act of 1897

The loud, persistent outcry against the new reserves resulted in the passage by Congress within weeks of the Sundry Civil Appropriations Bill for 1898, which would, in part, restore the entire Washington's Birthday Reserves to the public domain. The outgoing President Cleveland pocket-vetoed the bill on his last day in office. This created a situation in which the government had no money to operate. The new president, McKinley, quickly called Congress into extra session on March 15. The tide was starting to swing in favor of the forest reserves, and the initial wording that would have restored all the forest reserves to possible patent by homesteaders, available under other Timber and Stone Acts and various mining acts, was dropped.

The extra session of Congress added a number of new provisions to the Sundry Bill that would have a profound impact on the way the forest reserves would be managed for the next 100 years. The revised bill (also known as the Pettigrew Amendment) contained amendments to the Sundry Civil Appropriations Act of June 4, 1897, which suspended the Washington's Birthday Reserves for nine months, until March 1, 1898, in all the affected states except California. During that suspension, many thousands of acres of heavily forested land were transferred from public domain status to private ownership. The portion of the Sundry Civil Appropriations Act that dealt with the forest reserves (since referred to as the "Organic Act of 1897") had other provisions that would affect the national forests for many years. One of the clauses provided that approval of any new reserves would be contingent on whether the reserve met three criteria: protection and improvement of the forests, watershed protection, and timber production.

Hiring of Forest Rangers

The Organic Act of 1897 allowed for organization and management of the reserves by forest rangers under the direction of the Secretary of the Interior, a change from the earlier practice of having essentially no management at all, which had been the case since 1891. During the summer of 1897, the USDI General Land Office appointed superintendents for each state that had forest reserves, and by the following year supervisors for each forest reserve and forest rangers had been appointed to patrol the reserves. Employment for the positions of forest superintendents, supervisors, and rangers was based on political favoritism, not on qualifications. Later, Gifford Pinchot rather bitterly noted that "unfortunately the Interior Department, with its tradition of political toad eating and executive incompetence, was incapable of employing the powers the act gave it."

These and other frustrations set the stage for the transfer, on February 1, 1905, of the forest reserve management to the Department of Agriculture under the inspired leadership of Pinchot. At the time, there were around 730 GLO employees (see Figure 1.1), a number that decreased to about 600 by June 30, 1905, but then increased to more than 1,000 a year later. Many of the employees did not apply to work for the Bureau, but a few GLO rangers were actively sought for their knowledge and experience. The number of Forest Service employees who administer the 155 national forests and 193 million acres of today is 31,029.

Embedded in the Organic Act was the provision that land survey work be accomplished not by the General Land Office but instead by the USDI Geological

Survey. A special unit, the Division of Geography and Forestry, was established in the Geological Survey. The work, assigned by the Secretary of the Interior, was to inventory forest species by type and condition, as well as to map the forest reserves. Three survey reports were published: in 1897–1898 (covering 13 forest reserves), in 1898–1899 (10 forest reserves), and in 1899–1900 (covering 6 forest reserves with 3 additional timber reports). The Geological Survey produced 13 professional reports between 1902 and 1904. The Geological Survey work was taken over by the new USDA Forest Service in 1905.

There are a number of provisions in the Organic Act, or the implementing regulations, that have implications for management. Several deal with legitimate uses of the forest reserves, such as grazing, which directly ties to the controversies that led to the Act itself. Both the Act and the regulations affected the future management of the forest reserves (now called national forests). The Organic Act of 1897 allowed usage of the forest reserves for legitimate purposes:

> The Secretary of the Interior may permit, under regulations to be prescribed by him, the use of timber and stone found upon such reservations, free of charge, by bona fide settlers, miners, residents, and prospectors for minerals, for firewood, fencing, buildings, mining, prospecting, and other domestic purposes, as may be needed by such persons for such purposes; such timber to be used within the State or Territory, respectively, where such reservations may be located.

In addition, the Act specified the reasons for the establishment and use of the forest reserves:

> No public forest reservation shall be established, except to improve and protect the forest within the reservation, or for the purpose of securing favorable conditions of water flows, and to furnish a continuous supply of timber for the use and necessities of citizens of the United States; but it is not the purpose or intent of these provisions, or of the Act providing for such reservations, to authorize the inclusion therein of lands more valuable for the mineral therein, or for agricultural purposes, than for forest purposes.

These provisions in the Act, as well as the implementing regulations of June 30, 1897, permitted extensive use of the forest reserves. The Act also gave the Secretary authority "to regulate their occupancy and use." The implementing regulations under Section 12 states that "the Secretary of the Interior is authorized to grant such licenses and privileges, from time to time, as may seem to him proper and not inconsistent with the objects of the reservations nor incompatible with the public interests." This has been interpreted over the years as allowing or authorizing, for the first time, the imposition of various licenses and fees on users of the national forests.

Since the beginning of the forest reserve system, in 1891, sheep grazing has been the major problem. John Muir referred to sheep as "maggots" and was very opposed in the deliberations of the Forestry Commission of 1896 to allowing sheep to graze on the reserves. Pinchot, however, believed that sheep grazing was damaging to the young trees but that, by careful regulation, any damage could be controlled. The Organic Act regulations contain the following statements about livestock grazing on the forest reserves:

13. The pasturing of live stock on the public lands in forest reservations will not be interfered with, so long as it appears that injury is not being done to the forest growth, and the rights are not thereby jeopardized. The pasturing of sheep is, however, prohibited in all forest reservations, except those in the States of Oregon and Washington, for the reason that sheep-grazing has been found injurious to the forest cover, and therefore of serious consequence in regions where the rainfall is limited. The exception in favor of the States of Oregon and Washington is made because the continuous moisture and abundant rain-fall of the Cascade and Pacific Coast ranges make rapid renewal of herbage and undergrowth possible.

After the Act was passed, investigations of the grazing situation on other forest reserves in the West were undertaken. After extensive surveys of damage caused by sheep grazing on the reserves, officials allowed many operations to continue but imposed restrictions on the amount of stock permitted and the timing of entry and exit from the reserves so as to lessen possible damage. This opening of the reserves to grazing, after scientific study, essentially eliminated the sheep- and cattle owners' opposition to the reserves.

Timber was highlighted in both the Act and the regulations. Money obtained from the sale of timber, which "is optional," according to Section 22 of the regulations, was to go to the U.S. Treasury. A number of people, especially from the timber industry, have argued unsuccessfully that the Organic Act "required" timber harvesting. But a close examination of the law and regulations reveals that timber harvesting was always intended to be optional at the discretion of the agency in charge, not required. One key provision—that of making timber sales by marking each tree—in the Organic Act was eventually replaced in 1976 with the passage of the National Forest Management Act. This was the direct result of problems in the timber harvesting provisions of the Organic Act that were highlighted in the lawsuit *Izaak Walton v. Butz* (1973) over clearcutting on the Monongahela National Forest, in West Virginia.

Forest Lieu Clause

Another provision in the Organic Act was the "Forest Lieu" clause, which allowed homesteaders and owners within the proclaimed forest reserve boundary to select public domain land outside the boundary in lieu of (in exchange for) their claims. The Organic Act stated:

> the settler or owner thereof may, if he desires to do so, relinquish the tract to the Government, and may select in lieu thereof a tract of vacant lands open to settlement not exceeding the area the tract covered by his claim or patent; and no charge shall be made in such cases for making the entry of record or issuing the patent to cover the tract selected…

This provision, although intended for the isolated homesteader, soon led to massive land frauds (see next section) in the West. The problem came about, mostly, because of the two words "or owner" in the Act. This set up a situation in which legal owners of the land claims (e.g., timber and railroad companies) could in essence exchange land within the reserve boundary (even though they were not living on the land) for even richer land outside the boundary at no cost. The Organic Act of 1897 was followed by land fraud on a gigantic scale. The nine-month delay provision of the Organic Act of 1897 and the lieu land provision created situations in which railroad, land, and timber thieves took advantage of the law to fatten their bank accounts at the expense of the taxpayers.

Land frauds in connection with the establishment of new forest reserves became even more common after the passage of the Organic Act of 1897. As new lands were being evaluated for possible inclusion in the forest reserve system, numerous land grabbers were paying people by the hundreds to file fraudulent land claims and then quickly "sell" their "legal" claims to the men who had paid them to file for the land. The speculators would then hold the claims, and, when a forest reserve was proclaimed by the president, hurry to the General Land Office and request that the government trade the claimed land inside the forest reserve boundary for land of equal value outside the boundary. Because the forest reserves were usually in the high mountains, the speculators would trade their less valuable mountain claims for more valuable land at lower elevations. Then the speculators would often sell their newly acquired land at high prices to big timber companies, remove the standing timber and then sell the high-priced "agricultural" land to homesteaders, or simply cut the timber and let the land revert to the state or county without paying taxes. No matter how they were done, the frauds amounted to millions of dollars lost by the federal government.

Employees of the General Land Office, local townspeople, surveyors, and even elected officials were often bribed to give advance information of the establishment of new forest reserves. Thousands of dollars were paid to surveyors, land office receivers and recorders, inspectors, prospectors, attorneys general, congressmen, and even U.S. senators. Thus, the withdrawal and establishment of forest reserves quickly became a very lucrative business for everyone except the federal government.

As early as July 21, 1901, the Portland *Oregonian* newspaper published an article, titled "Big Timber Graft," about the proposed Coquille Forest Reserve, in southwest Oregon. The article stated that "there are many ways in which the Government may lose and private corporations and individuals may make illegitimate gain from such reservations as is now proposed for Southern Oregon." Within five days, GLO Commissioner Binger Hermann, himself a politician from southern Oregon who was later indicted in Oregon land frauds, suspended all timber and stone claims in the area under consideration as a forest reserve. There was a strong possibility that his relatives and friends had made illegal land claims within the proposed reserve.

Stephen A. Douglas Puter, self-proclaimed "king of the Oregon land fraud ring," related that at least several of the forest reserves in Oregon, Washington, and elsewhere had actually been established at the suggestion and encouragement of the speculators, including himself. The first of the land fraud indictments in Oregon was returned against Puter and several associates on October 27, 1903. A jury convicted the defendants, including Puter, on December 6, 1904. The guilty parties were not sentenced at that time in order to allow them to testify in subsequent trials. The convicted ring members disappeared and scattered around the country, but within two or three years, they were all back in custody. While serving time in the Multnomah County (Oregon) jail for land fraud, Puter, in collaboration with Horace Stevens, wrote a book titled *Looters of the Public Domain.* This insider account of the defrauding of the U.S. government gave names, dates, and dollar amounts in the coordinated actions of many speculators in California and the Pacific Northwest, especially Oregon. Puter, in turning state's evidence, testified against his one-time friends, including Binger Hermann and Senator John H. Mitchell, of Oregon.

Senator Mitchell was indicted, then convicted, on July 5, 1905, of receiving fees for expediting fraudulent land claims through the General Land Office. He was sentenced to six months in jail. Mitchell died of complications following a tooth extraction on December 8, 1905, while his conviction was under appeal. Hermann was forced to resign as head of the GLO by President Roosevelt. Hermann went to trial in January 1910 but was not convicted because the prosecution had difficulty proving his direct involvement in the case. This was the last of the big land fraud trials in Oregon, which put scores of federal, state, and local officials under indictment and sent many to jail. Puter was later elected to the U.S. House of Representatives as a representative from Oregon.

On January 7, 1907, President Theodore Roosevelt proclaimed thousands of acres of timberland as a new forest reserve in Whatcom County, Washington, near the Canadian border. As a howl of protest was heard around the state, including from the newspaper *Seattle Times*, Senator Samuel H. Piles threatened federal legislation to repeal the withdrawal. Gifford Pinchot and the president yielded to intense lobbying and restored the land to the public domain, claiming that the set-aside had been a "clerical error." Soon thereafter, Senator Charles W. Fulton, of Oregon, who had been implicated in the land frauds in the state, introduced an amendment to the annual agricultural appropriations bill. The legislation took away the president's power to establish national forests in the six western states of Washington, Oregon, Idaho, Montana, Wyoming, and Colorado. Note that California was again excluded from the list of states, as it was in 1897. After 1907, Congress alone was able to establish national forests. With less than a month remaining for the Act to be signed into law, Gifford Pinchot, chief forester of the two-year-old Forest Service, and his able assistants drew new forest reserve boundaries on maps of the United States. Information about the forestlands that were within the boundaries came from several years of USDI Geological Survey reports and the practical experience and knowledge of the forest rangers and supervisors, as well as from communities and special interest groups. As soon as the maps were finished and a proclamation written, Pinchot took everything to the president, who signed the paper to establish another new forest reserve. In a matter of a few days, Roosevelt proclaimed more than 16 million acres of new forest reserves, since referred to as the "midnight reserves." The Fulton amendment, at the suggestion of Gifford Pinchot, also changed the name of the forest reserves to national forests in order to make it clear that the forests were to be used, not preserved. By the end of June 1907, the national forest system contained 146 national forests covering 147,820,000 acres.

The Legacy

The Organic Act of 1897, although modified many times by the Congress, set the standards for the management of the national forests for a century. The Organic Act of 1897 is still on the books; it has not been replaced, only amended and greatly reduced in length. The Act that guided the Forest Service for almost all of the twentieth century is today mostly a faint memory. But it was responsible for setting up the first management of the national forests, as well as creating almost a century of controversy and turmoil over federal management, land fraud, timber management, land uses, grazing, mining, and scores of related issues. The positions taken by the anti–forest reserve movement in the late 1890s and early 1900s closely resemble the arguments and sentiments tied to the Sagebrush Rebellion, wise use, and property rights movement that began in the 1970s and are still active.

Provisions of the Organic Act regarding timber cutting became the center of attention in the early 1970s when a dispute arose about clearcutting on the Monongahela and Bitterroot National Forests. After congressional hearings and a loss in a key lawsuit over clearcutting on the Monongahela National Forest, the National Forest Management Act of 1976 (NFMA) was devised by Congress and the Forest Service to replace or greatly supplement key provisions of the Organic Act. However, even though the NFMA and implementing regulations (requiring an extensive and costly planning process) provided more "clarifying" words and phrases, controversy still exists; in fact, it may have been exacerbated by the NFMA.

The names and boundaries of many of the national forests have been changed over the past 100 years, but the land areas have remained essentially intact (see the Appendix on National Forest Names). In the East, national forests came into existence through another law: the Weeks Act of 1911 (see later discussion), which allowed the purchase of private lands, along with donated lands, to create national forests in the Appalachian Mountains and in the Midwest and the north-central states. Presently, the national forest system consists of 155 national forests, 61 purchase units, 20 national grasslands, six land-utilization projects, 20 research and experimental areas, and 35 other areas (including national monuments, national volcanic areas, national recreation areas).

The vast national forest lands that were set aside to protect them from overexploitation by timber companies, homesteaders, and livestock interests are still is existence today. Controversy about the management of these forestlands abounds, much as it did a century ago. The national forests are still under attack; management is being pressured to change; special interest groups are highly polarized. Still, the fact that there are national forests and national parks speaks well for a young country with vast natural resources that chose to save millions of acres for the people. The fact remains that without these precious national forestlands, still in public ownership after more than 100 years, there would be one less thing to argue about.

TRANSFER ACT OF 1905 (33 STAT. 628)

As early as 1897, Pinchot became convinced that the forest reserves should be transferred from control and management by the USDI General Land Office to the USDA Bureau of Forestry. After President McKinley was assassinated, in 1901, Theodore Roosevelt was suddenly elevated to the office of president. This was totally unexpected but completely satisfactory to Pinchot. Roosevelt was a friend of the Pinchot family, and Gifford and the new president were close friends, having many of the same interests and both being passionate about the outdoors. Pinchot was able, with very little convincing, to consider Roosevelt a strong supporter of scientific forestry and conservation. One of the first messages to Congress by the new president was revealing; it proposed the transfer of the reserves to the USDA. The transfer, in fact, would have to wait four years. Of course, during this time Pinchot was actively pushing for it. Every instance of GLO fraud and graft was used to press the point. Pinchot then saw his opportunity when he convinced the American Forestry Association to hold an American Forest Congress in January 1905. The main reason for this meeting, from Pinchot's viewpoint, was to have the delegates pressure Congress to allow the transfer. Within a few weeks after the meeting, the transfer was passed by Congress and the reserves transferred to the USDA Bureau of Forestry (several months later, the name was changed to the USDA Forest Service—see discussion later in this appendix).

Agriculture Secretary James Wilson signed a letter—written by Pinchot—directing Pinchot to take charge of the forest reserves. The letter contains the classic utilitarian phrase "the greatest good, for the greatest number, in the long run." Apparently, Pinchot added "in the long run" to emphasize that trees take decades to grow, and thus the "greatest good" may change over time:

> By this Act the administration of the Federal forest reserves is transferred to this Department. Its provisions will be carried out through the Forest Service, under your immediate supervision.... All officers of the forest reserve service transferred will be subject to your instructions and will report directly to you. You will at once issue to them the necessary notice to this effect. In order to facilitate the prompt transaction of business upon the forest reserves and to give effect to the general policy outlined below, you are instructed to recommend at the earliest practicable date whatever changes may be necessary in the rules and regulations governing the reserves, so that I may, in accordance with the provisions of the above Act, delegate to you and to forest reserve officers in the field, so much of my authority as may be essential to the prompt transaction of business, and to the administration of the reserves in accordance with local needs.
>
> In the administration of the forest reserves it must be clearly borne in mind that all land is to be devoted to its most productive use for the permanent good of the whole people; and not for the temporary benefit of individuals or companies. All the resources of forest reserves are for *use*, and this use must be brought about in a thoroughly prompt and businesslike manner, under such restrictions only as will insure the permanence of these resources. The vital importance of forest reserves to the great industries of the western states will be largely increased in the near future by the continued steady advance in settlement and development. The permanence of the resources of the reserves is therefore indispensable to continued prosperity, and

the policy of this Department for their protection and use will invariably be guided by this fact, always bearing in mind that the *conservative use* of these resources in no way conflicts with their permanent value. You will see to it that the water, wood, and forage of the reserves are conserved and wisely used for the benefit of the home-builder first of all; upon whom depends the best permanent use of lands and resources alike.

The continued prosperity of the agricultural, lumbering, mining, and live-stock interests is directly dependent upon a permanent and accessible supply of water, wood, and forage, as well as upon the present and future use of these resources under businesslike regulations, enforced with promptness, effectiveness, and common sense. In the management of each reserve local questions will be decided upon local grounds; the dominant industry will be considered first, but with as little restriction to minor industries as may be possible; sudden changes in industrial conditions will be avoided by gradual adjustment after due notice; and where conflicting interests must be reconciled the question will always be decided from the standpoint of the greatest good of the greatest number in the long run.

FOREST SERVICE NAME CHANGE
ACT OF 1905 (33 STAT. 861, 872–873)

As noted, Gifford Pinchot, then the Forester for the USDA Bureau of Forestry, was successful in getting management of the forest reserves transferred from the Department of the Interior to the Department of Agriculture. There was only one slight problem. Pinchot did not like the name Bureau of Forestry, as he thought that forestry was a service to the people rather than just another Washington bureau. Through pressure on Congress, he was able to insert language into the annual agriculture appropriations bill that changed the name to the Forest Service. It was a small item, but the name is still around 100 years later. The Act was passed and signed into law on March 3, 1905, but was not effective until July 1, the start of the fiscal year at that time. Pinchot, in his 1947 autobiography, wrote, "One more change gave me great personal satisfaction. I never liked the name 'Bureau.' … So when 'Bureau of Forestry' disappeared from the Agricultural Appropriation Bill and 'Forest Service' took its place, no one was more pleased than I." At this point, both the Transfer Act and the Name Change Act completed the FS's transition from the USDI to the USDA, where it remains to this day.

WEEKS ACT OF 1911, PUBLIC LAW 435 (36 STAT. 961)

Floods, fires, and foresters all contributed to the passage of the Weeks Act of 1911, which marked the shift in federal policy from disposal of public land to expansion of the public land base by purchase. It was the origin of the eastern and most southern national forests. The importance of forests in watershed protection, for example, was an early subject of concern among those who argued for forest reserves. The role of forests in moderating stream flow was unclear in the early stages of the forest conservation movement, but the idea gained enough credence that "securing favorable conditions of water flows" was defined as a primary function of the newly formed federal forest reserves in the Forest Management (Organic) Act of 1897.

It may have been the memory of the disastrous Johnstown, Pennsylvania, flood, on May 31, 1889, in which more than 2,000 people died, that helped dramatize the consequences of watershed deforestation to people in the East. Foresters, largely based in the USDA Forest Service, recognized the importance of forests in flood protection, whereas the U.S. Army Corps of Engineers did not. The Corps' idea of flood control was dams and levees. Forest Service Chief Gifford Pinchot felt that the Corps of Engineers' position undermined one of the key arguments for creating additional forest reserves. The issue of flood control became important in gaining political support for purchase of lands for national forests in the East. Because of major floods and soil erosion in 1907 along the Monongahela and Ohio Rivers caused by the massive clearcut areas in the mountains, the West Virginia legislature authorized the government to purchase lands in the state for conservation purposes. This action predated the Weeks Act by two years.

Rain was also important to irrigators in the arid West, and urban residents wanted pure drinking water, so these two groups supported watershed protection through creation of forest reserves. It was recreationists in the East, however, who sought the creation of additional federal forests. They were supporters of the proposed White Mountain reserve in Maine and New Hampshire (now the White Mountain National Forest, established in 1918). In the South, the Appalachian National Park Association was formed in 1899 to petition Congress for a large park in the southern Appalachians. Support in Congress was, however, only lukewarm. Horace B. Ayres and William W. Ashe produced a formal report, *The Southern Appalachian Forests* (USGS Professional Paper No. 37 [1905]). (An earlier version of the study was printed in the Agriculture Secretary James Wilson's report in 1901; Roosevelt used portions of it in his 1901 speech to Congress quoted earlier.) Agriculture Secretary James Wilson, in the letter of transmittal to President McKinley, wrote that:

> The rapid consumption of our timber supplies, the exhaustive destruction of four forests by fire, and the resulting increase in the irregularity of the flow of water in important streams have served to develop among the people of this country an interest in forest problems which is one of the marked features of the close of the [nineteenth] century. In response to this growing interest the government set aside in the western forest reserves an area of more than 70,000 square miles. There is not a single forest reserve in the East.

In 1905, the American Forestry Association endorsed the proposal to establish eastern national forests through federal purchase, and Congress's defeat of the bill led them and other advocates of forest reserves to shift their argument from nature preservation to utilitarian concerns over flood protection. Congressman John W. Weeks, of Massachusetts, was enlisted in the effort and, in 1906, made a motion in Congress to authorize federal purchase of private lands to be used as forest reserves. The notion of spending public money on recreation sites did not appeal to the powerful Speaker of the House, Joe Cannon, who declared "not one cent for scenery" in the debate against the proposal. There were other obstacles to be overcome, including the question whether it was constitutionally legal for the federal government to purchase lands. That issue was put to rest early in the debate.

In the meantime, a need for fire control offered a second reason for the shift of ownership of forestlands to the federal government. The lack of fire protection efforts on the part of the private sector and even the states made such protection a national priority for the new Forest Service. When scientific forestry began in North America, its practitioners regarded fire protection as a fundamental mission of the forestry profession. Public opinion, however, gradually moved toward the forester's view that wildfire control was useful for forested lands.

Congress was finally convinced of the necessity of forest cover in the South by a demonstration. As the Weeks bill was slowly grinding through Congress, Gifford Pinchot, chief of the Forest Service, came up with a novel way to demonstrate the principle of the relationship among trees, soil, and water. At one of the hearings, Pinchot showed the committee member a photograph of a denuded area. Pinchot held the photo at an angle, then poured water on the image—the committee could quickly see how the water ran off the photograph. Pinchot then poured water on a sloping ink blotter. He drew attention to how the water was absorbed by the ink blotter and how little water was left to drain off the bottom of the blotter. Pinchot told the congressional committee that the same principle worked on the forested areas.. In short, forests prevent floods.

Purchase of Forestlands in the East

After years of debate, the Weeks Act of March 1, 1911, was passed. It allowed the government to purchase important private watershed land on the headwaters of navigable streams for the purpose of "conserving the navigability of navigable rivers." Many of these lands had been cut over, burned over, or farmed out. As a result, this Act directly supported the creation, though land purchases, of new national forests in the eastern United States, where there was little public domain land left. As noted, the lands were to be purchased, not taken by condemnation of the land (or the right of eminent domain). The Act, in section 4, called for the creation of a National Forest Reservation Commission (NFRC), consisting of the Secretary of War, the Secretary of the Interior, the Secretary of Agriculture, two members of the Senate, and two members of the House of Representatives. The NFRC was authorized to "consider and pass upon such lands as may be recommended for purchase … and to fix the price or prices at which such lands may be purchased." The first chair of the NFRC was Secretary of War Henry L. Stimson, who was elected on March 7, 1911, at the first meeting of the commission. For the next 65 years, until the commission was eliminated by the National Forest Management Act of 1976, the commission was chaired by various Secretaries of War and, later, the Army.

Section 11 of the Act required that the acquired lands "shall be permanently reserved, held, and administered as national forest lands…. And the Secretary of Agriculture may from time to time divide the lands acquired under this Act into such specific national forests and so designate the same as he may deem best for administrative purposes." Millions of acres of land in the South and the Northeast would eventually pass from private ownership into public ownership as national forests.

Under the terms of the Weeks Act, all of the states had to pass some type of enabling legislation that would allow the federal government to purchase lands in the state for national forest purposes. Several of the southern states, including North Carolina, South Carolina, Tennessee, Georgia, Alabama, and West Virginia, passed enabling legislation before the passage of the Act. One form of inducement or appeasement to the states, which would lose revenue from the taxation of private land once it was transferred to the federal government, was to return part of any revenues generated by timber sales on the new national forests. Congress tacked section 13 to the Weeks Act, providing that 5 percent, later increased to 25 percent, "of all moneys received during any fiscal year from each national forest ... shall be paid ... to the State in which such national forest is situated ... for the benefit of the public schools and public roads." This was similar to the arrangement states in the West enjoyed.

During the first year of operation, the NFRC approved seven purchase units—that is, lands identified as having areas within a specified boundary worthy of purchase—in the southern states. Four more were approved in fiscal year 1912, another in FY1914, and two more in FY1918. In the 1920s, 10 more were approved, while during the 1930s, another 32 units were approved; only one new purchase unit was approved in 1941. After the NFRC picked land within a purchase unit, with the survey work being conducted by the Forest Service, negotiations would commence between the owner and the federal government. Only after the owners, the affected counties, and the states agreed could the land pass into federal ownership and await designation as a national forest.

The NFRC was busiest for the two years after the Weeks Act was passed. Prices paid for the land varied considerably. Lands that had extensive standing old growth timber were much more valuable than cutover or burned areas. Some lands were greatly desired by the NFRC but were not purchased for a variety of reasons, the most common of which was disagreement over the purchase price. The people living in the mountains of the South were very suspicious of the federal government, having been often "taken" by the industrial buyers who bought cheap timberland and made millions of dollars. Yet, for the most part, the Forest Service was welcome. The Pisgah National Forest, the first national forest made up almost entirely of purchased private land, was established on October 17, 1916. The new forest's core portion came from the privately owned Biltmore Forest, once managed by Gifford Pinchot. Land purchases for the Pisgah began in 1911, soon after the passage of the Weeks Act. The work involved in establishing national forests was far from over. Forest Service Chief Henry S. Graves commented in 1919:

> The very magnitude of the national forest enterprise has created in the minds of many people the impression that the problem in this country is already on the way to definite solution. In point of fact, only certain initial steps have been taken.... It is my hope that we may secure sufficient public support to enable us to accelerate the

acquisition by the Government of the important remaining areas [in the East] before it is too late.... Forests on critical watersheds should be owned by the public for their protective value. Public forests serve, also, as centers of co-operation with private owners and as demonstration areas for the practice of forestry as well as furnishing their direct benefits in producing wood materials, as recreation grounds, etc.

By 1920, around 2 million acres had been added to the national forest system, mostly in the South, through purchases made under the authority of the Weeks Act. The total amount of once-forested land recommended and purchased through the commission recommendations topped out at 22 million acres. In 1976, the duties of the NFRC were transferred to the Secretary of Agriculture by the National Forest Management Act of 1976.

Restoring the Weeks Act Forests

Massive efforts began in the 1920s to restore and replant the new national forests. Nurseries were built and millions of trees planted. The Civilian Conservation Corps (1933–1942) was the biggest boon to the effort. Not only did the CCC plan seedlings, but it also often assisted with erosion control. It planted huge quantities of one plant from China that was a wonder in stopping soil erosion—kudzu. It was only years later that kudzu became a major problem in the South. The CCC provided thousands of men to stop forest fires on the national forests. The CCC was also involved with state projects during the 1930s. Its workers built and improved hundreds of state parks and campgrounds, many of which are still around today.

Tree planting in the South on national forests has grown like a weed. The program has been steadily helped by pioneering forestry research at the Southern and Appalachian/Southeastern Forest Experiment Stations. In 1925, approximately 2,000 acres were planted or seeded; by 1930, fewer than 1,000 acres were planted or seeded. The planting greatly increased during the CCC's existence, with around 400,000 acres planted from 1934 to 1941. During the Second World War, fewer than 29,000 acres were planted; the number then slowly rose to around 16,000 acres by 1950, 57,000 acres by 1960, 80,000 acres by 1970, and 103,000 acres by 1980—which was the highest level of planting and seeding. The highest point in tree replanting came in 1987, when 2.7million seedlings were planted. Currently, more trees are planted in the South than in any other region of the United States. The change from the mostly denuded national forestlands of the 1920s and 1930s to the healthy, tree covered slopes and mountains of today has been remarkable, with around 2.9 million acres planted and seeded from 1925 to 1985. It is a stunning testament to the tenacity of the Forest Service in its drive to restore and protect the forestlands in the Weeks Act forests.

THE CLARKE-MCNARY ACT OF JUNE 7, 1924 (43 STAT. 653)

The Clarke-McNary Act of 1924 greatly expanded the Weeks Act. The new Act eliminated the provision that national forestlands could be purchased only in the headwaters of watersheds on navigable streams for watershed purposes and for the production of timber. It also emphasized the need for cooperation and incentives to improve private forestland conditions. Fire and taxes were the primary components of the Act, allowing federal, state, and private interests to work together. Most states formed fire protection associations and state forestry departments that are still active today. The Act also provided for federal-state cooperation in the growing and distribution of tree seedlings for reforestation work and for cooperative work in farm extension, and it authorized money to study the serious forest taxation issue. As a result, owners of hundreds of millions of acres of state and private forestland are working together in organized protection programs, while technical assistance is provided through the Forest Service state and private forestry program. Most states also have extension foresters at work and provide assistance through the USDA Natural Resources Conservation Service. Four years later after the original bill, the McNary-Woodruff Act of 1928 authorized the expenditure of an additional $8 million to purchase land under the Weeks Act.

MCSWEENEY-MCNARY ACT OF 1928 (45 STAT. 699)

The McSweeney-McNary Act of 1928 was amended several times and finally repealed by the Forest and Rangelands Renewable Resources Research Act of 1978. However, the 1928 Act had several important elements that relate to Forest Service research. The Forest Service set up the first experiment station, in 1908, in Arizona. Then, two years later, the Forest Products laboratory was established in Madison, Wisconsin. This was the first government facility devoted to pure research in wood technology and utilization. In 1921, the first forest experiment station was established, in Asheville, North Carolina. However, there was little in the way of a coordinated research program in the agency. The McSweeney-McNary Forest Research Act of 1928 authorized such a program. Passage of the McSweeney-McNary Act of 1928 gave research a recognized separation from national forest administration, and this remains the pattern today.

This Act also made specific authorizations for research work over a 10-year period and authorized such additional sums as might thereafter be necessary. The Act authorized the establishment of some 14 regional experiment stations within the continental United States, and one each in Alaska, Hawaii, and the West Indies dependencies that would be the backbone of Forest Service research. Research funding, however, was dampened by the stock market crash of 1929 and the Great Depression that followed. Funding increased during the war years and after, but, by the 1950s, reduced budgets were resulting in a declining research program, especially at the smaller western facilities.

In 1953, to help meet changing needs, USDA announced a series of significant reorganizations, including the mergers of the Northern and Intermountain Stations (headquartered in Ogden, Utah) and the Southwestern and Rocky Mountain Stations (headquartered in Fort Collins, Colorado). Over the next five decades, the research stations formed and reformed their research programs to meet the ever-evolving needs of natural resource management. Population growth, coupled with the public's increasing interest in land management activities, intensified the need to help resource managers and planners balance economic and environmental demands for forest and rangeland resources. Other combinations have occurred since then. In addition, the forest and range experiment stations have been renamed and are now known simply as research stations. Much of the work authorized by the Act was taken over by the Forest and Rangelands Renewable Resources Research Act of 1978, which directed the Secretary of Agriculture to collect, analyze, and periodically report information about forest and range renewable resources on all ownerships.

MULTIPLE-USE SUSTAINED-YIELD ACT OF 1960, PUBLIC LAW 86-517 (74 STAT. 215)

The Multiple-Use Sustained-Yield Act (MUSY) of June 12, 1960, was the congressional embodiment of 55 years of Forest Service management and policy. The Organic Act of 1897 guided the agency for decades, gearing management to protection of the forests and water and the production of timber. For the most part, federal forest management was not controversial during this period, but major changes were on the horizon. Part of the reason behind the Act was a realization that people could not get everything they wanted or needed from the national forests' finite resources. It was also not possible to perform a balancing act in allocating the available natural resources. By the mid-1950s, the first inkling of a shift in management philosophy came with the congressional debates about multiple use bills. The Forest Service assigned Assistant Chief Ed Crafts to draft the language for a multiple-resource bill. The first bill was introduced in 1956 by Senator Hubert H. Humphrey, of Minnesota. There was a growing concern that in the decade of rapid development of the national forests since the end of World War II, the Forest Service was leaning so much toward management of timber that other resources, especially recreation, were getting short shrift. Another problem was that there was no specific statutory language in any of the previous laws that specifically addressed the Forest Service programs that had evolved by the 1950s, including wildlife and recreation. The Forest Service was opposed or neutral to a multiple use bill as it was changed in committee, but Crafts was able to make the bill acceptable to the agency and won its strong support.

The Forest Service was beginning to feel the heat from growing opposition to its policies about logging in or near recreation sites. One focus of this contention was California's Deadman Creek area. The 3,000-acre site contained a stand of old growth Jeffrey pine. When the Forest Service announced plans to do "sanitation salvage" in the area, reaction was swift and allegations were made that recreation and scientific values were being ignored in favor of the timber value. Similar conflicts arose in many parts of the West.

By the late 1950s, the conservation groups generally supported the Humphrey bill, with the exception of the Sierra Club, which felt that support of the multiple use bill would jeopardize the Club's efforts to pass a wilderness bill. During the spring of 1960, agreements were made with various groups to clarify wording of the Act so that timber would not dominate, recreation would be given equal standing with other resource uses on the national forests, and the Organic Act of 1897 would be supplemented, not replaced. After the Act was signed, in 1960, the Forest Service was active in managing the national forests so that all resources (timber, wildlife, range, water, and outdoor recreation) were treated equally. Many rangers did their utmost to embody the principles of multiple use in their management. For some, however, the Act simply redefined what the Forest Service had been doing for decades: timber harvesting and road construction. Many people outside the agency saw that forests were not managed any differently under MUSY—that they were still just a road leading to an ugly clearcut. This example of redefining the old ways rather than managing differently on the ground had implications for the forest management controversies of the 1970s, 1980s, and 1990s.

Also in 1960, the Fifth World Forestry Congress, met in Seattle, Washington, with delegates from 55 nations. The theme of the Congress was multiple use, providing an opportunity for the Forest Service to highlight its new authority under MUSY. McArdle, in his presidential address, explained to that "multiple use is a familiar term to foresters of the United States." He stated that "the five basic renewable resources shall be utilized in the combination that will best serve the people. Emphasis is on utilization, not preservation." The historian Harold Steen noted that "McArdle listed the multiple uses, but in reverse order, making recreation last instead of first. An inadvertent slight or not, it fit well with a series of advocacy skirmishes at the fringes of activity. Sierra Club representatives with no official spot on the program talked of 'Multiple Abuse.' Four decades later the flap seems rather tame, but this sort of 'ungentlemanly' and even 'shocking' behavior only hinted at what was to come, as the Forest Service lost more and more of its long-held support from the Sierra Club and other environmental groups. For example, since the 1920s the Club had routinely elected Forest Service chiefs as its honorary vice-president, which ended early in the 1950s."

The passage of the Wilderness Act of 1964, opposed by the Forest Service as being authorized by MUSY, set the stage for strident antagonism from the old conservation organizations and new environmental groups that reverberates with the Forest Service to this day. One important aspect of the MUSY was the creation of multiple use planning, which brought a number of new specialists, such as soil scientists and wildlife biologists, into daily land management decisions.

WILDERNESS ACT OF 1964, PUBLIC LAW 88-577 (78 STAT. 890)

Much of the history of the Wilderness Act has been discussed in the previous chapters. But a short recap of the story will help elucidate the issues involved the in roadless and wilderness debates since the 1920s. Two names appear in discussion of early history of roadless areas, wilderness, and the national forests: Aldo Leopold and Arthur W. Carhart. Aldo Leopold, then a young forest supervisor on the Carson National Forest (NF), and one of his rangers discussed the idea of setting aside wilderness areas as early as 1913. In the summer of 1919, Art Carhart, a Forest Service landscape architect, surveyed a summer home site area on the White River NF, in Colorado. After talking with several wealthy hunters, he became convinced that the Trappers Lake area should remain wild and pristine, with no homes or roads allowed. He designed a recreation plan to preserve the pristine conditions of the area and was able to convince his superiors to halt plans for development. It was a watershed event in the Forest Service. Carhart and Leopold talked together in the Rocky Mountain District Office, and both came to the conclusion that saving or preserving some of the wildest, most natural areas of national forest lands should be a priority of the agency.

One year later, Francis B. Summer urged the newly formed Ecological Society of America to back an effort to set aside untouched forest areas. Leopold, in 1921, wrote an article in the *Journal of Forestry* suggesting that a wilderness of at least 500,000 acres be established in each of the 11 western states. Leopold, by then the assistant district forester in Albuquerque, New Mexico, made an inspection trip to the headwaters of the Gila River, in New Mexico, in the spring of 1922. He wrote a wilderness plan for the area that excluded roads and additional special use permits, except for grazing. Trails and telephone lines for fighting forest fires were to be permitted. The plan was not universally embraced by the staff in the Forest Service, who tended to believe that development should come before preservation. Battle lines were thus drawn that influenced the wilderness discussions and battles for the remainder of the twentieth century. The 500,000-acre Gila Wilderness, the first administrative wilderness, was established by District Forester Frank Pooler on June 3, 1924, on the Gila NF, in New Mexico.

On September 26, 1926, an area of the Superior NF, in Minnesota, which had been surveyed by Arthur Carhart in the early 1920s, became protected for recreation use by an order signed by the Secretary of Agriculture. In 1964, the area became the Boundary Waters Canoe Area (since October 21, 1978, the Boundary Waters Canoe Area Wilderness). In 1926, the first wilderness/roadless area review was carried out by the Forest Service. Roadless areas had to be larger than 10 townships (230,400 acres) to be considered for wilderness status. This inventory identified 74 tracts of undeveloped land totaling 55 million acres. However, each wilderness had to be approved on its own merit. At the national level, there was a series of policy decisions (L-20 Regulations in 1929 and U-Regulations in 1939) that made wilderness and primitive area designation relatively easy. In 1938, Robert Marshall, the director of the Forest Service recreation and lands section and the person who drafted the U-Regulations, came to the West to evaluate forest areas over 100,000 acres for wilderness, wild areas (5,000–100,000 acres), or roadless areas (any size). Many recommendations were made, and a number of new wild areas and wildernesses were established. Between 1924 and 1964, the Forest Service set aside 9 million acres of administrative wilderness across the nation.

Just after the end of World War II, Howard C. Zahniser, of the Wilderness Society (founded in 1935 by Bob Marshall, Aldo Leopold, and others) became the leader in a movement to have Congress, rather than the agency, designate wilderness. In 1949, Zahniser detailed his proposal for federal wilderness legislation. Nothing happened to the proposal, but it did raise the awareness for the need to protect wildernesses and primitive areas from all forms of development. In the early 1960s, Senator Hubert H. Humphrey (D-MN) became a major supporter for a national wilderness act, which finally came out of committee after being stalled for years in Congress. The Forest Service, as well as the National Park Service, opposed the bill. It took four years for the two agencies and the advocacy groups to agree on language in the bill.

The historian Harold Steen noted that "'the strongest, longest continued and most effective opposition to wilderness legislation came from the forest industries.' Other industries—mining, livestock, and highway construction—were also opposed. McArdle thought that the highway industry mounted 'exceedingly effective opposition.' Users of public lands such as sportsmen joined with the American Forestry Association to defeat wilderness legislation. The Society of American Foresters, by mail ballot, favored the continuation of wilderness creation by executive order, instead of congressional involvement. When John Kennedy entered the White House, the political balance shifted. Both agriculture secretary Orville Freeman and interior secretary Stewart Udall 'enthusiastically endorsed legislation to preserve wilderness.' McArdle thought that the 'big change was in Interior,' because Agriculture had 'been doing what we could to further the legislation.'" On September 3, 1964, less than 10 months after the Kennedy assassination, President Lyndon Johnson signed the wilderness bill into law.

Overnight, the existing Forest Service administrative wildernesses became part of the national wilderness preservation system (NWPS). The Wilderness Act also set up procedures for the Forest Service and the Department of the Interior to evaluate existing primitive and roadless areas for possible inclusion into the NWPS. The Forest Service directed the regions to undertake a roadless area review and evaluation (RARE) in 1967 on roadless areas larger than 5,000 acres. The Forest Service conducted 300 hearings, which were attended by more than 25,000 people, and gathered more than 50,000 oral and written comments. The 1972 report identified 1,449 roadless areas comprising 55.9 million acres, with 12.3 million acres proposed for wilderness. Chief John McGuire ordered another, more intensive study of roadless areas soon afterward. Dubbed RARE II, the 1979 report recommended 15 million acres for wilderness and 11 million acres for further study.

The highly contentious question of whether Congress would establish additional wilderness areas was solved by passage of the Oregon and Washington Wilderness Acts, in 1984, which included "soft release language" (that is, they allowed normal activities—including logging—during the current forest planning period of 10–15 years in roadless areas not chosen for wilderness, after which time the areas could be reevaluated), rather than "hard release language" (specifying that areas not chosen would be open and available for any activity—especially logging—and could never be reevaluated for wilderness). Since that time, many millions of acres of wilderness have been added to the NWPS, mostly on a state-by-state process. As of September 30, 2004 (the most current figures), the Forest Service administers 34,859,062 acres of wilderness, with wilderness areas located in 38 states. California has the largest number of national forest wildernesses (54), with some areas located in adjacent states; Alaska has the largest land area in wilderness (5,753,448 acres), while Mississippi has the smallest (6,046 acres).

WILD AND SCENIC RIVERS ACT OF 1968, PUBLIC LAW 90-542 (82 STAT. 906)

For more than 100 years, the federal government passed laws that allowed for the construction of dams, reservoirs, and canals, almost all of which either blocked existing rivers or took valuable water from them. For the most part, water was a *quantity* issue, not a *quality* issue. Then the Federal Water Pollution Control Act of 1948 focused on funding water treatment plants, identifying polluted bodies of water, and locating the polluters for legal action. However, federal legislation to protect water quality had to wait almost two decades.

Rachel Carson's 1962 bestseller *Silent Spring* provided the impetus for the nation's first water quality legislation. It became abundantly clear that national policies and attitudes toward rivers were creating a crisis. Industrial pollution was rampant, pesticides were pouring in virtually unchecked, municipal raw sewage was dumped into the rivers that were also being used for city water supplies. Rivers were being dammed, dredged, diked, diverted and degraded at an alarming rate. People were using the polluted rivers for recreation, including fishing. Aquatic species were disappearing or had high levels of heavy metals, making them unfit for human consumption. Special interest groups and organizations, such as the National Wildlife Federation, the Izaak Walton League, and the National Audubon Society, began campaigning for strong federal water quality bills. One result was the 1965 Water Quality Act, which established the Water Pollution Control Administration within the Department of the Interior. Water quality was for the first time treated as an environmental concern, rather than simply a quantity or public health concern. The 1965 law was followed by the 1966 Clean Water Act, which provided construction grants for wastewater treatment facilities.

At the same time, support grew for the idea that the development of our nation's rivers needed to be balanced by some means for protecting rivers that possessed outstanding qualities. These sentiments culminated in the enactment of the Wild and Scenic Rivers Act of 1968. Rivers may be designated by Congress or, in some instances, be nominated by a governor and approved by the Secretary of the Interior, the agency that manages the program. Designation for inclusion in the national wild and scenic rivers system (NWSRS) provides certain protections from development and from the adverse effects of water resources projects. The Act establishes three categories of rivers: wild, scenic, and recreational. A river is included in one of these categories depending on its characteristics, values, and the desired level of protection.

The Act provides protection for a designated river or segment by limiting the licensing of dams, reservoirs, and other water project works that either are on or adversely affect protected segments. The Act provides for the acquisition of lands by the federal government in the river corridor. Another source of constitutional authority for the Wild and Scenic Rivers Act is the "property clause" (art. IV, §3, cl. 2), which authorizes Congress to make "needful rules and regulations" regarding federal property. But designation as a wild and scenic river does not "lock it up," as some critics have claimed. The idea of the NWSRS is not to stop use of a river; instead, the goal is to preserve the character of a river for today and into the future. Each river designation is unique, with different historical uses allowed in or adjacent to the river.

Rivers or river segments in the NWSRS are managed by various federal agencies, including the U.S. Army Corps of Engineers, the BLM, the National Park Service, the Forest Service, and the Fish and Wildlife Service. Several states, such as California and Oregon, have established a state system that supplements the federal NWSRS. Plans have to be developed, with public input, for each river or segment. Included in each plan are the NWSRS boundaries, with maps; historic uses; current usage; animal, fish, and plant surveys; economic dependence, and other data. Each wild and scenic river plan is basically a NEPA document (see the discussion of the National Environmental Policy Act of 1969 later in this appendix).

As of September 30, 2004, the Forest Service manages 950,906 acres of wild and scenic rivers. National forests in Oregon have the most designated rivers, with 318,902 acres; Idaho is next, with roughly half that amount, or 159,586 acres, while New Hampshire has the least, with only 282 acres.

NATIONAL ENVIRONMENTAL POLICY ACT OF 1969, PUBLIC LAW 91-190, (83 STAT. 852)

On January 1, 1970, President Richard M. Nixon signed the National Environmental Policy Act of 1969 (NEPA), the culmination of years of struggle by special interest groups and the authors of the act, Senator Henry M. Jackson and Congressman John D. Dingle. The Act required that an environmental impact statement (EIS) be prepared when any federal agency proposed a "major federal action significantly affecting the quality of human environment." The bill had not provoked any major controversy in Congress, and it received only cursory comment from legal journals and the public. But it was to have profound implications for every federal land management agency.

The National Environmental Policy Act of 1969 (NEPA) mandates that all federal agencies or departments protect the environment. Section 101 (b) of the Act states: "it is the continuing responsibility of the federal government to use all practicable means, consistent with other essential considerations of national policy" to avoid environmental degradation, preserve historic, cultural, and natural resources, and "promote the widest range of beneficial uses of the environment without undesirable and unintentional consequences." NEPA requires analysis and a detailed statement of the environmental impact of any proposed federal action that significantly affects the quality of the human environment. Each agency designates a "responsible official" who must ensure that NEPA issues are addressed as part of the agency's actions. All agencies must use a systematic interdisciplinary approach to environmental planning and evaluation of projects that may have an effect on the environment.

The driving force of NEPA is the EIS process. An EIS is a document written to aid in decision making by the federal land manager and by the public. An EIS presents alternatives to a proposed action and the environmental consequences of those actions. NEPA sought to put environmental concerns on an equal basis with economic motivations and technological feasibility in decision making. Every EIS must include at least the expected environmental impacts of the proposed action; unavoidable adverse environmental impacts; alternatives, including no action; the relationship between short-term uses of the environment and maintenance of long-term ecological productivity; irreversible and irretrievable commitments of resources; and secondary/cumulative effects of implementing the proposed action. Provisions of the Act, as well as its implementing regulations, require public involvement, opportunities for the public to comment, and an agency response to these comments in the EIS. Agencies must also include an environmental review process early in the planning for proposed actions.

Because different federal actions may not have similar or significant effects on the physical and human environment, there are differing levels of review under NEPA. There are two types of actions that do not require extensive NEPA environmental documentation: categorical exclusions and statutory exclusions:

> *Statutory Exclusions*—Certain types of actions—primarily emergency actions and actions which restore facilities to predisaster conditions—are exempt from NEPA requirements altogether, pursuant to the Stafford Act. This exemption is called a statutory exclusion. NEPA documentation is not required if a project is statutorily excluded. However, the exemption from NEPA does not apply to other environmental laws or executive orders which could have their own review and documentation requirements.
>
> *Categorical Exclusions*—NEPA provides for each agency to develop a list at 44 CFR 10.8 of categories of actions that are determined through agency experience to typically have no significant environmental impact and thus may generally be excluded from detailed documentation (EA or EIS).

Review and documentation for actions that qualify for one or more of these categories is generally minimal but should address any extraordinary circumstances and the requirements of other environmental laws or executive orders. Though detailed NEPA documentation is not necessary, requirements of other laws must be documented as appropriate.

There are two levels of NEPA analysis. The first level, usually conducted at the project site, is called the *environmental assessment (EA)*. For those projects that are not excluded because they fit into the exempt categories, an EA is required in order to determine if significant impacts exist. An EA is defined as a concise public document that serves to provide sufficient evidence and analysis regarding the significance of the environmental impacts of the proposed federally funded action and alternatives to that proposal to aid in decision making. An EA must be thorough and well documented and must provide the public an opportunity to participate in accordance with the law. The EA concludes with a one of two decision documents, either a finding of no significant impact (FONSI) or a notice of intent to prepare an *environmental impact statement (EIS)*. A notice of intent to prepare an EIS eventually results in the creation of an environmental impact statement. An EIS is a critical examination of any potential impacts from the proposed project and proposed alternatives. The EIS concludes with a record of decision (ROD), a document that explains the reasons for selecting a certain action or alternative.

While NEPA provides a process for federal agencies to follow when their proposed actions may affect the environment, there are additional laws that provide specific restrictions and protections to the environment and that may affect the nature of the action that can be taken. Completion of requirements under NEPA may not satisfy requirements of other environmental and historic-preservation laws and executive orders.

NEPA established a three-member Council on Environmental Quality (CEQ) as a part of the Executive Office of the President. The CEQ is required to assess the nation's environmental quality annually and review all federal programs for compliance with NEPA. The CEQ issued regulations (40 CFR 1500–1508) in 1978 implementing NEPA. The regulations include procedures to be used by federal agencies for the environmental review process. In 1981, the CEQ issued a pamphlet titled "Forty Most Asked Questions" to assist government agencies and to efficiently respond to public inquiries about the NEPA regulations.

After more than 35 years of NEPA, federal agencies have published thousands of EISs, running from a few pages to many volumes, on proposed projects. While some have criticized the NEPA process as long and costly, its call for public involvement and participation has resulted in more informed decisions, and agencies now employ new natural resource specialists to help the agency and the public understand the implications of its decisions on the natural and human environments. Court challenges to federal decisions have caused an increase in litigation. From the standpoint of special interest groups, NEPA has been both a burden and a godsend: a burden in terms of cost and time for project analysis, documentation, and public involvement, and a godsend because it has led to better decisions based on expected consequences and impacts. NEPA has opened a whole new avenue for citizen involvement in federal land management planning and decision making. The NEPA process has been so successful that processes patterned after it are being used in other countries, such as Australia and the Philippines.

ENDANGERED SPECIES ACT OF 1973, PUBLIC LAW 93-205 (16 USC 1531–1544)

The Endangered Species Act (ESA) passed the Senate by voice vote and the House of Representatives by a vote of 355 to 4. The bill was signed into law on

December 28, 1973, by President Richard M. Nixon. The Act has been amended many times. "Nothing is more priceless and more worthy of preservation than the rich array of animal life with which our country has been blessed," President Nixon said. "It is a many-faceted treasure, of value to scholars, scientists, and nature lovers alike, and it forms a vital part of the heritage we all share as Americans." Decades after he signed the landmark law, President Nixon's words still ring true. The ESA replaced the Endangered Species Conservation Act of December 5, 1969 (P.L. 91-135, 83 Stat. 275), which itself had amended the Endangered Species Preservation Act of October 15, 1966 (P.L. 89-669, 80 Stat. 926).

Efforts to protect and recover animal species began long before the ESA was signed into law. For example, the Bald Eagle Protection Act of 1940, which made it illegal to hunt the eagle, increased public awareness of the majestic national symbol. Then, in the 1970s, a ban on the poison pesticide DDT helped to stabilize and increase the population of eagles in most areas of the country. So successful was the program of recovery that the bald eagle was slated by the late 1990s for delisting from the endangered species list.

Soon after the passage of the current ESA, Congress became embroiled over a controversy involving the Tellico Dam. A three-inch fish called the snail darter was stopping completion of the dam. During the congressional debates, many in Congress made the argument that when they voted for ESA, they had intended that the law would protect only animals such as the bald eagle and the grey wolf—sometimes called "charismatic megafauna" (large, attractive animals)—and that they certainly would have never voted to protect such an insignificant species as the snail darter.

However, since the snail darter controversy, Congress has had multiple opportunities to limit the coverage of the Act but has not done so. In fact, when Congress amended the law in 1988, it went in the other direction, directing that priorities for recovery plans be based on need and "without regard to taxonomic classification." Although the ESA's overall framework has remained basically unchanged, significant amendments were adopted during 1978, 1982, and 1988. In 1978, the definition of species was modified to limit the listing to vertebrates, and, in 1982, listing decisions were required to be based solely on biological and trade information without considering economic or other effects and provision was made for the designation of "experimental" populations that could be subject to lessened protection. Public notice and reporting requirements were added in the 1988 amendments. The ESA, like many laws, contained a provision requiring reauthorization every five years. Although the ESA was due for reauthorization in 1993, no legislation has yet been enacted; nonetheless, the ESA remains in full effect.

Listing

As with most other federal regulations, a species is proposed for addition to the lists in the *Federal Register*. The public is offered an opportunity to comment, and the rule is finalized or withdrawn. Species are selected by the Fish and Wildlife Service

(F&WS) from a list of candidates. To determine which species should become candidates, the F&WS and the National Marine Fisheries Service (NFMS) rely largely upon citizen petitions, federal agency surveys, and other field studies. The Act provides very specific procedures on how species are to be placed on the list (e.g., listing criteria, public comment periods, hearings, notifications, time limit for final action). Selection from the list of candidates for a proposed rule is based on a priority system. Four basic provisions in the Act define the most important elements of the ESA.

Recovery

The ultimate purpose of the Act is to save species from extinction. The goal of F&WS and NMFS is to recover listed species and remove them from the list. This is accomplished through a variety of tools, including recovery planning, consultation, and scientific and incidental take permits. Depending on the species, plans are either prepared by a panel of recognized experts under the direction of F&WS or NMFS employees or contracted to consultants on the species. Regional directors are responsible for approving recovery plans for listed species in their region. Within 60 days of listing, the responsible region must prepare a one-page outline of the major recovery actions needed for the species.

Consultation

All federal agencies must consult with F&WS or NMFS when any activity permitted, funded, or conducted by that agency may affect a listed species or designated critical habitat or is likely to jeopardize proposed species or adversely modify proposed critical habitat. F&WS and NMFS conduct several types of consultations on federal activities, including informal, formal, early, and emergency consultations for listed species or designated critical habitats, as well as informal and formal conferences for proposed species or proposed critical habitats.

Takings

The ESA prohibits any person subject to the jurisdiction of the United States to take any endangered species of fish or wildlife, but not plants, within the United States. The term "take" means "to harass, harm, pursue, hunt, shoot, wound, kill, trap, capture, or collect, or attempt to engage in any such conduct."

For the Forest Service, many provisions and listings under the ESA and its predecessors have affected management of the national forests. Since many of the forests have habitat for eagles, the Bald Eagle Protection Act of 1940 covered many timber and related activities on the national forests. The expanded Bald and Golden Eagle Protection Act of 1962 included protection for golden eagles and added even more management considerations, such as where the eagles were found nesting and roosting. As a result, development plans were often changed and roads rerouted because of the presence of an eagle's nest.

Congress, in 1966, passed the Endangered Species Preservation Act. The Act authorizes the Secretary of the Interior to make a list of endangered domestic fish and wildlife. It also directed federal land agencies—the Departments of Interior, Agriculture, and Defense—to preserve endangered species habitat on their lands "insofar as is practicable and consistent with their primary purpose." The Puerto Rican parrot and the Kirkland's warbler are only two of the covered species.

The California condor, found in the national forests of southern California, was added to the ESA list on March 11, 1967. It is currently designated as endangered, except where listed as an experimental population. On October 16, 1996, the California condor was designated as an experimental population, nonessential in portions of Arizona, Nevada, and Utah. This allowed researchers to reintroduce adults into their traditional ranges without fear that the ESA rules would inhibit the process. A number of efforts to raise condor young in zoos have been successful enough to release a dozen or so condors back into the wild. The Los Padres National Forest, in southern California, has played an important role in the reintroduction of the condor to the wild.

The Endangered Species Act of 1973 distinguishes between threatened and endangered species, and these designations have different management implications. The Act allows the listing of a species that is in danger in just part of its range, allows listing of plants and invertebrates, authorizes unlimited funds for species protection, and makes it illegal to kill, harm, or otherwise "take" a listed species. In order to protect species that are in danger in part of their range, the federal agencies has had to take on management of species that otherwise would have not been considered, like the marbled murrelet in the Pacific Northwest. The small bird is found in relative abundance along the coast of Alaska and British Columbia but is rare in Washington and Oregon. The ESA makes it clear that special management—especially a ban on logging old growth trees within flying distance of the Pacific Ocean—is required for this species. The ESA, according to Chief Dale Robertson, "really knocked the timber program in the head."

The Supreme Court ruled, in 1978, that the ESA required that construction of the Tellico Dam be halted. The arguments that $78 million had already been spent on the dam and that the endangered snail darter was only a tiny fish did not impress the court. The "plain intent" of the law, said six of the nine members, is to save all species "whatever the cost." Congress responded to the court ruling by creating the "god squad" in the ESA (section 7): a cabinet-level committee that could exempt selected species from protection. The following year, the god squad decided, with the Supreme Court concurring, that the snail darter should take precedence over construction of the Tellico Dam. The Tennessee congressional delegation responded by slipping a rider into an appropriations bill exempting the Dam from the ESA. The rider narrowly passed. The Tennessee Valley Authority completed the dam, presumably rendering the snail darter extinct. However, in 1980, more snail darters were found in the river below the dam, and the species turned out not to be in such danger, after all.

The ESA has been credited (or blamed) for a precipitous decline in national forest timber sales. Environmentalists responded by deluging the Department of the Interior with petitions for more species listings. In 199X, Congress placed a moratorium on further listings of species. This effectively denied protection for unlisted species that meet the legal definitions of "threatened" or "endangered" species. The NMFS list the wild salmon runs in the Columbia Basin (see Chapter 2 and Chapter 6).

The impact of the ESA on the Forest Service has been profound. Prior to the ESA, management of species was limited to the sprinkling of wildlife biologists, sometimes only in the regional offices. From the point of view of the Forest Service, as well as of other federal land management agencies, the ESA, according to Chief Dale Robertson, "really backed us into the corner.... The Endangered Species Act drove an arrow through the heart of multiple use." For any given species, the law was clear—either it was a T&E species or it was not. If it was not, then any form of management could take place, but when a T&E species was involved, then management was very restricted, with no tradeoffs. In the late 1970s and early 1980s, the agency responded by hiring many new specialists in wildlife and fish management.

Research geared up with an increasing amount of money and personnel assigned to wildlife and ecosystem projects. Interestingly, the spotted owl issue was first raised in the mid-1970s by Eric Foresman, a researcher with the Forest Service. At the insistence of the Forest Service regional office, people were hired to call spotted owls, surveys were made to identify habitats, and management actions, such as the creation of protection areas around spotted owl nests, were initiated on the national forests. Research efforts increased not only on the spotted owl but also on other old growth dependent species. Ironically, increased research on the spotted owl over the past two decades has shown that the species is declining in many areas. One reason for this is habitat changes. In addition, another owl—the barred owl—is replacing the spotted owls in their traditional habitat in many areas. It remains to be seen if the spotted owl will be around by the end of the twenty-first century.

Without the ESA, it is unlikely that the FS would have spent as much time and money as it did on wildlife and fish projects—after all, the management goal for decades had been to increase the timber harvest, not to protect species. Wildlife and fish biologists, who traditionally focused on big game and fishable species, were now burdened with new laws, regulations, handbooks, and a national order to take all species into account in the management of the national forests and grasslands. In some cases, it could be argued, the national forests and parks have the only remaining habitats for forest species that were here when the Europeans arrived. The vast majority of private lands have been converted to tree farms, rangelands, croplands, roads and highways, and cities. The national forests and parks are islands surround by a sea of development.

NATIONAL FOREST MANAGEMENT ACT OF 1976, PUBLIC LAW 94-588 (90 STAT. 2949)

In the early 1970s, congressional hearings began on the clearcutting controversies involving the Bitterroot and Monongahela National Forests, as well as a federal court decision on the Organic Act of 1897 (see Chapter 1). The Forest Service and the timber industry turned to Congress to either throw out the Organic Act of 1897 or modify its language. The debate centered around two bills. One was introduced by Senator Hubert Humphrey, of Minnesota, and was more favorable to the timber industry, whereas the other, introduced by Senator Jennings Randolph, of West Virginia, was supported by environmentalists. After much debate, the National Forest Management Act of 1976 was passed. It was based primarily on the Humphrey bill but included modifications to placate the environmental community.

Arguments in Congress about how to fix the Organic Act were like those around the wording of any new law—they focused on whether the language should be general or specific. Some members wanted broad statements that gave broad discretionary authority to the land managers and that would cover any possibility; others wanted language to mandate specific actions on the ground. In 1989, former Chief R. Max Peterson said: "It became obvious to most that neither Congress nor anyone else could possibly write management prescriptions that would fit the many physical situations on National Forests…. This led to a recognition that the legislation would have to set forth a process rather than specify answers."

NFMA was signed into law on October 22, 1976. The Act amended the Resources Planning Act of 1974 (RPA) and provided a comprehensive blueprint for managing the national forests. NFMA required the Secretary of Agriculture to appoint a committee of scientists—not officers or employees of the Forest Service— to provide scientific advice and counsel on how to implement the new law. It took almost three years for these implementing regulations to become final. The regulations required the beginning of a long-range planning process for each national forest. Since that time, the Forest Service has spent many millions of dollars devising forest plans for each national forest. The first plans were completed by 1980, and the last dribbled in by the late 1980s. One unintended consequence of the massive forest planning effort was the hiring of many new "ologists," that is, professional employees in fields other than forestry and range conservation. Several thousand employees were employed during, and sometimes after, the planning period, including ecologists, fishery biologists, wildlife biologists, computer experts, GIS coordinators, economists, sociologists, and anthropologists. Other NFMA requirements mandated public involvement in the planning process revised definitions of sustained and nondeclining yield and clearcutting (which the Act defines as an acceptable practice). Another requirement was that the government "preserve and enhance the diversity of plant and animal communities … so that it is at least as great as that which would be expected in a natural forest." One provision in the NFMA gave the national forests official status in law; many of the original national forests created between 1891 and 1907 were established by a series of presidential proclamations.

An act similar to NFMA but applicable to the BLM was also passed and signed into law. This 1976 act is called the Federal Land Policy and Management Act (FLPMA) and has similar requirements for long-range planning on BLM-administered lands.

In 1998, a second committee of scientists was formed to rewrite the NFMA regulations, which were felt by many to be outdated. The committee recommended many changes to the regulations. Draft regulations were announced in the summer of 1999, along with a public review period. The final regulations were printed in 2000.

Bibliography

REFERENCES CONCERNING THE USDA FOREST SERVICE

Any number of sources discuss the beginnings and the current operations of the USDA Forest Service. The listing can run to thousands of entries and hundreds of pages. But, first, one should consider contacting the national or chief historian, the Forest History Society in Durham, North Carolina, or Grey Towers National Historic Landmark, in Milford, Pennsylvania.

- The Forest Service national historian is located in the national headquarters in Washington, D.C., in the office of recreation and heritage resources. A contractor has placed many documents and photographs on a Web site at http://demo.jorge.com.
- Forest History Society, 701 Vickers Ave., Durham, NC 27701, phone 919-682-9319; e-mail coakes@duke.edu; Web site www.lib.duke.edu/forest/index.html.
- Grey Towers National Historic Landmark, 151 Grey Towers Drive, Milford, PA 18337; phone 570-296-9634; e-mail lmckean@fs.fed.us.

Oral Histories

Transcriptions of oral histories provided by former chiefs McArdle, Cliff, McGuire, Peterson, Robertson, Thomas, and Dombeck as well as by many deputy and associate chiefs and regional foresters are available through the Forest History Society. Also, oral histories about individual national forests and experiment stations are available.

Books (some out of print)

Clary, David. 1986. *Timber and the Forest Service*. Lawrence: University Press of Kansas.
Fedkiw, John. 1999. *Managing Multiple Uses on National Forests: 1905–1995*. FS-628. Washington, DC: USDA Forest Service.

Hays, Samuel. 1959. *Conservation and the Gospel of Efficiency: The Progressive Conservation Movement 1890–1920*. Cambridge, MA: Harvard University Press.

Kaufman, Herbert. 1960. *The Forest Ranger: A Study in Administrative Behavior*. Baltimore, MD: Johns Hopkins Press for the Resources for the Future.

LeMaster, Dennis. 1984. *Decade of Change: The Remaking of Forest Service Statutory Authority during the 1970s*. Westport, CT: Greenwood Press.

Lewis, James. 2005. *The Forest Service and the Greatest Good: A Centennial History*. Durham, NC: Forest History Society.

MacCleery, Douglas. 1992. "American Forests: A History of Resiliency and Recovery." Pamphlet. Durham, NC: Forest History Society.

Miller, Char. 2001. *Gifford Pinchot and the Making of Modern Environmentalism*. Washington, DC: Island Press.

Miller, Char, ed. 1997. *American Forests: Nature, Culture, and Politics*. Lawrence: University Press of Kansas.

Miller, Char, and Rebecca Staebler. 2004. *The Greatest Good: 100 Years of Forestry in America*. 2nd ed. Washington, DC: Society of American Foresters.

Pinchot, Gifford. 1947. *Breaking New Ground*. New York: Harcourt, Brace and Company. Reprint ed., 1998 with a new introduction. Washington, DC: Island Press.

Pyne, Stephen. 1982. *Fire in America: A Cultural History of Wildland and Rural Fire*. Princeton, NJ: Princeton University Press.

Pyne, Stephen. 1997. "America's Fires: Management on Wildlands and Forests." Pamphlet. Durham, NC: Forest History Society.

Robbins, William. 1985. *American Forestry: A History of National, State, and Private Cooperation*. Lincoln: University of Nebraska Press.

Roth, Dennis. 1995. *The Wilderness Movement and the National Forests*. College Station, TX: Intaglio Press.

Rowley, William. 1985. *U.S. Forest Service Grazing and Rangelands: A History*. College Station: Texas A&M University Press.

Shands, William, and Robert Healy. 1977. *The Lands Nobody Wanted [Policy for National Forests in the Eastern United States]*. Washington, DC: The Conservation Foundation.

Steen, Harold. 1994. *View from the Top: Forest Service Research*. Durham, NC: Forest History Society.

Steen, Harold. 1998. *Forest Service Research: Finding Answers to Conservation's Questions*. Durham, NC: Forest History Society.

Steen, Harold. 1999. *Forest and Wildlife Science in America: A History*. Durham, NC: Forest History Society.

Steen, Harold. [1976] 2004. *The U.S. Forest Service: A History*. Seattle: University of Washington Press.

Steen, Harold, ed. 1992. *The Origins of the National Forests: A Centennial Symposium*. Durham, NC: Forest History Society.

Steen, Harold, ed. 2004. *The Chiefs Remember: The Forest Service, 1952–2001*. Durham, NC: The Forest History Society.

Steen, Harold, ed. 2004. *Jack Ward Thomas: The Journals of a Forest Service Chief*. Durham, NC: The Forest History Society.

Williams, Gerald. [2000] 2005. *The USDA Forest Service–The First Century*. Washington, DC: USDA Forest Service.

GENERAL BIBLIOGRAPHIC REFERENCES

The following is a listof references concerning Forest Service policy and changes to the agency over time. The Forest History Society, in Durham, NC, has a constantly updated electronic bibliography that is available for searching subjects and authors. In addition, there are several bibliographic sources on North American forestry, five specifically oriented to the Forest Service. General bibliographic references to the Forest Service, forestry, conservation, and environmental sources can be found in the following books:

Davis, Richard C. 1977. *North American Forest History: A Guide to Archives and Manuscripts in the United States and Canada*. Santa Barbara, CA: ABC-Clio Press and The Forest History Society.

Davis, Richard C., ed. 1983. *Encyclopedia of American Forest and Conservation History*. 2 vols. New York: Macmillan.

Dodds, Gordon B. 1971. "Conservation and Reclamation in the Trans-Mississippi West: A Critical Bibliography." *Arizona and the West* 13 (Summer): 143–171.

Etulain, Richard W., ed. 1994. *The American West in the Twentieth Century: A Bibliography*. Norman: University of Oklahoma Press.

Fahl, Ronald J. 1977. *North American Forest and Conservation History: A Bibliography*. Santa Barbara, CA: Forest History Society and the ABC-Clio Press.

Jaehn, Thomas, compiler. 1990. "The Environment in the Twentieth-Century American West: A Bibliography." Occasional Papers #2. Albuquerque: University of New Mexico, Center for the American West.

Munns, Edward N. 1940. *A Selected Bibliography of North American Forestry*. 2 vols. USDA Miscellaneous Publication No. 364. Washington, DC: USGPO.

Neiderheiser, Clodaugh M. 1956. *Forest History Sources of the United States and Canada: A Compilation of the Manuscript Sources of Forestry, Forest Industry, and Conservation History*. Saint Paul, MN: Forest History Foundation.

Ogden, Gerald R. 1976. *The United States Forest Service: A Historical Bibliography, 1876–1972*. Davis: University of California, Agricultural History Center.

Steen, Judith A. 1973. *A Guide to Unpublished Sources for a History of the United States Forest Service*. Santa Cruz, CA: Forest History Society.

West, Terry, and Dana E. Supernowicz. 1993. "Forest Service Centennial Bibliography, 1891–1991." Pamphlet. Washington, DC: USDA Forest Service, History Unit.

Williams, Gerald W. 1995. *Selected References Concerning the USDA Forest Service: Social, Political, and Historical Sources of Information*. R6-SP-UP-04-95. Portland, OR: USDA Forest Service, Pacific Northwest Region.

GENERAL FOREST SERVICE REFERENCES

The references listed here include historical and contemporary sources that have particular relevance to Forest Service policy past, present, and future. The list was selected by the compiler and reflects his concern for general Forest Service (FS) policy, social and political issues that face the agency, and federal forestry work programs. Particular emphasis is given to historical sources to give the reader the opportunity to delve into the background of controversies and solutions that still face the agency today.

This appendix is contains materials on the Forest Service at the national level, as well as some regional materials. It is concerned with the overall purposes of the national forests, as well as with policy, perspectives, history, reorganization attempts, agency transfer proposals, differences with other federal land-management agencies, and leadership, especially that of Gifford Pinchot. Included are sources on diverse topics, such as the World War I Forestry Regiments, aerial forest-fire detection patrols after World War I, fires and lookouts, smokejumpers, range and grazing, forest homesteads, land frauds, recreation use, public involvement, sociology and economics, community stability, women and minorities employees at the agency, clearcutting, below-cost timber sales, sustained-yield forestry, wilderness/RARE & RARE II, the spotted owl controversy, "new forestry," "new perspectives," and ecosystem management.

USDA Forest Service Bibliographic Sources

Abbasi, Susan R. 1979. *Proposed Department of Natural Resources: A Summary and Analysis.* CRS Report 79-79. Washington, DC: U.S. Library of Congress, Congressional Research Service.

Abrahamson, Lawrence, and Carolyn Klass. 1982. "Gypsy Moth." Cornell Cooperative Extension Information Bulletin 188. Ithaca, NY: Cornell University.

Ahern, George P. 1928. *Deforested America.* Washington, DC: Privately printed. Reprinted in 1929 by the U.S. Senate as Document 216, 70th Congress, 2nd Session.

Albright, Horace M. 1960. "Highest Use vs. Multiple Use." *Sierra Club Bulletin* 45 (April/May): 3–7.

Allen, Durward L. 1987. "Leopold: The Founder." *American Forests* 93 (September): 26–29, 69–70.

Allen-Diaz, Barbara. 1991. "Interview." *Women in Natural Resources* 12 (3) (March): 32–36.

Alexander, Thomas G. 1987. *The Rise of Multiple-Use Management in the Intermountain West: A History of Region 4 of the Forest Service.* FS-399. Washington, DC: USDA Forest Service.

Allin, Craig Willard. 1982. *The Politics of Wilderness Preservation.* Westport, CT: Greenwood Press.

Allison, Rachel. 1993. "Administration Policies and Old-Growth: An Interview with Assistant Secretary of Agriculture James R. Lyons." *Journal of Forestry* 91 (12) (December): 20–23.

Alston, Richard M. 1983. *The Individual vs. the Public Interest: Political Ideology and National Forest Policy.* Boulder, CO: Westview Press.

Anderson, H. Michael, and Charles F. Wilkinson. 1984. "Meeting the Criteria: The Law, Decisionmaking … and the Fate of the Forest Plan." *Forest Planning* 5 (9) (December): 14–20.

Apple, Daina Dravnieks. 1995. "Changing Social and Legal Forces Affecting the Management of National Forests." *Women in Natural Resources* 18 (1) (Fall): 4–10.

Backiel, Adela. 1995. "Adela Backiel [USDA Deputy Under Secretary Over the Forest Service]: An Interview by Daina Dravnieks Apple." *Women in Natural Resources* 16 (3) (March): 24–29.

Backiel, Adela, and Ross W. Gorte. 1992. "Clearcutting in the National Forests." Report 92-607 ENR. Washington, DC: Library of Congress, Congressional Research Service.

Baker, Richard A. 1985. *Conservation Politics: The Senate Career of Clinton P. Anderson.* Albuquerque: University of New Mexico Press.

Baker, Robert D., Robert S. Maxwell, Victor H. Treat, and Henry C. Dethloff. 1988. *Timeless Heritage: A History of the Forest Service in the Southwest.* FS-409. Report by Intaglio, Inc., College Station, TX. Washington, DC: USDA Forest Service, History Section.

Baker, Robert D., Larry Burt, Robert S. Maxwell, Victor H. Treat, and Henry C. Dethloff. 1993. *The National Forests of the Northern Region: Living Legacy.* FS-500. Report by Intaglio, Inc., College Station, TX. Washington, DC: USDA Forest Service.

Baldwin, Donald Nicholas. 1972. *The Quiet Revolution: Grass Roots of Today's Wilderness Preservation Movement*. Boulder, CO: Pruett.

Baltic, Tony J., John G. Hof, and Brian M. Kent. 1989. *Review of Critiques of the USDA Forest Service Land Management Planning Process*. General Technical Report RM-170. Fort Collins, CO: USDA Forest Service, Rocky Mountain Forest and Range Experiment Station.

Barnes, Will Croft. 1913. *Western Grazing Grounds and Forest Ranges*. Chicago: The Breeder's Gazette.

Barnes, Will Croft. 1926. *The Story of the Range*. Washington, DC: USDA Forest Service.

Barnes, Will Croft. 1941. *Apaches and Longhorns: The Reminiscences of Will C. Barnes*, ed. Frank C. Lockwood. Los Angeles: Ward Ritchie Press.

Barney, Daniel R. 1972. *The Last Stand: The Nader Study Group Report on the U.S. Forest Service*. Washington, DC: Center for the Study of Responsive Law.

Bassman, Robert. 1974. "The 1897 Organic Act: A Historical Perspective." *Natural Resources Lawyer* 7 (3) (Summer): 503–520.

Beasley, Lamar. 1995. "A Conversation with Lamar Beasley [Retired Deputy Chief for Administration]." *Inner Voice* 7 (1) (January/February): 11–12.

Benedict, Warren V. 1981. *History of White Pine Blister Rust Control—A Personal Account*. Publication FS-355. Washington, DC: USDA Forest Service.

Bergoffen, Gene S. 1962. "The Multiple Use-Sustained Yield Law: A Case Study of Administrative Initiative in the Legislation Policy-Forming Process." M.S. thesis. Syracuse: Syracuse University, College of Forestry.

Bergoffen, William W. 1976. *100 Years of Federal Forestry*. USDA Forest Service, Agriculture Information Bulletin 402. Washington, DC: USGPO.

Beuter, John H. 1985. *Federal Timber Sales*. CRS-LM 423. Washington, DC: Library of Congress, Congressional Research Service.

Blaisdell, James P., and Lee A. Sharp. 1979. "History of Rangeland Use and Administration in the Western United States." In *Rangeland Ecosystem Evaluation and Management*, ed. K. M. W. Howes, 1–24. Perth, Australia: Australian Rangeland Society.

Boerker, Richard H. Douai. 1919. *Our National Forests: A Short Popular Account of the Work of the United States Forest*. New York: Macmillan.

Bowers, E. A., Bernhard E. Fernow, Frederick L. Olmsted, J. T. Rothrock, V. Colvin, Theodore Roosevelt, and Gifford Pinchot. 1895. "A Plan to Save the Forests: Forest Preservation by Military Control." *The Century Magazine* 49 (4) (February): 626–634.

Browning, James A., John C. Hendee, and Joe W. Roggenbuck. 1988. *103 Wilderness Laws: Milestones and Management Direction in Wilderness Legislation, 1964–1987*. Bulletin Number 51. Moscow: University of Idaho, Idaho Forest and Range Experiment Station.

Burns, John E. 1980. "Invalids Need Not Apply: The Forest Service Ranger Exam." *Persimmon Hill* 10 (2) (Spring): 56–63. Publication of the National Cowboy Hall of Fame and Western Center, Oklahoma City, OK.

Butler, Ovid McOuat, ed. 1934. *Rangers of the Shield: A Collection of Stories Written by Men of the National Forests of the West*. Washington, DC: American Forestry Association.

Cameron, Jenks. [1928] 1972. *The Development of Governmental Forest Control in the United States*. New York: Da Capo Press.

Carhart, Arthur Hawthorne. 1955. *Timber in Your Life [The Full Story of the Uses and Misuses of One of Our Most Crucial Natural Resources]*. Philadelphia: J. B. Lippincott.

Carhart, Arthur Hawthorne. 1959. *The National Forests*. New York: Knopf.

Carson, Rachel. 1962. *Silent Spring*. Boston: Houghton Mifflin.

Catton, Theodore, and Lisa Mighetto. 1998. *The Fish and Wildlife Job on the National Forests: A Century of Game and Fish Conservation, Habitat Protection, and Ecosystem Management*. Washington, DC: USDA Forest Service.

Cermak, Robert W. 2005. *Fire in the Forest: A History of Forest Fire Control on the National Forests in California, 1898–1956.* R5-FRR-003. Valley, CA: USDA Forest Service, Pacific Southwest Region.

Chapman, Herman Haupt. 1937. "Reorganization and the Forest Service." *Journal of Forestry* 35 (5) (May): 427–434.

Clary, David A. 1986. *Timber and the Forest Service.* Lawrence: University Press of Kansas.

Clawson, Marion. 1951. *Uncle Sam's Acres.* New York: Dodd, Mead.

Clawson, Marion. 1975. *Forests for Whom and for What?* Washington, DC: Resources for the Future.

Cliff, Edward P. 1981. *Half a Century in Forest Conservation: A Biography and Oral History of Edward P. Cliff.* Washington, DC: USDA Forest Service.

Cohen, Stan. 1982. *A Pictorial History of Smokejumping.* Missoula, MT: Pictorial Histories Publishing Company.

Cohen, Stan. 1980. *The Tree Army: A Pictorial History of the Civilian Conservation Corps, 1933–1942.* Missoula, MT: Pictorial Histories Publishing Company.

Cole, Olen, Jr. 1999. *The African-American Experience in the Civilian Conservation Corps.* Gainesville: University Press of Florida.

Comanor, Joan. 1995. "Joan Comanor [Forest Service Deputy Chief for State & Private Forestry]: An Interview by Daina Dravnieks Apple." *Women in Natural Resources* 17 (2) (December): 22–27.

Commission on Organization of the Executive Branch of Government. 1949. "Reorganization of Department of [the] Interior: A Report to Congress by Commission on Organization of the Executive Branch of Government, March 1949." Washington, DC: USGPO.

Congressional Research Service. 1993. *Multiple Use and Sustained Yield: Changing Philosophies for Federal Land Management? The Proceedings and Summary of a Workshop Convened on March 5 and 6, 1992, Washington, DC.* 102nd Congress, 2nd Session, Committee Print No. 11. Washington, DC: USGPO.

Conrad, David E. 1997. *The Land We Cared for … A History of the Forest Service's Eastern Region,* ed. Jay H. Cravens. Milwaukee, WI: USDA Forest Service, Region 9.

Cooley, Earl. 1984. *Trimotor and Trail [Smokejumping].* Missoula, MT: Mountain Press.

Coville, Frederick V. 1898. *Forest Growth and Sheep Grazing in the Cascade Mountains of Oregon.* Bulletin No. 15. Washington, DC: USDA Division of Forestry.

Crafts, Edward C. 1970. "Saga of a Law [Multiple-Use Sustained-Yield Act of 1960].… This Saga Is the Story of one of the Most Important Forest Conservation Bills of Modern Times … " *American Forests* 76 (6) (June): 12–19, 52–54.

Crafts, Edward C. 1972. *Forest Service Researcher and Congressional Liaison in the Forest Service: An Eye to Multiple Use.* Santa Cruz, CA: Forest History Society.

Crafts, Edward C. 1975. *Congress and the Forest Service, 1950–1962.* Berkeley: University of California, Bancroft Library, Regional Oral History Office.

Cravens, Jay H. 1994. *A Well Worn Path [FS forester in 1940s–1970s].* Huntington, WV: University Editions.

Culhane, Paul J. 1981. *Public Lands Politics: Interest Group Influence on the Forest Service and the Bureau of Land Management.* Baltimore: Johns Hopkins University Press for Resources for the Future.

Dana, Samuel Trask, and Sally K. Fairfax. [1956] 1980. *Forest and Range Policy: Its Development in the United States.* New York: McGraw-Hill.

Dana, Samuel Trask. 1929. "Where Does the Forest Service Belong?" *Journal of Forestry* 27: 901–903.

Dana, Samuel Trask. 1956. *Forest and Range Policy—Its Development in the United States.* New York: McGraw-Hill.

Dana, Samuel Trask. 1967. *The Development of Forestry in Government and Education*. Berkeley: University of California, Bancroft Library, Regional Oral History Office.

Davies, Gilbert W., and Florice M. Frank, eds. 1995. *Memorable Forest Fires [1910–1988]: 200 Stories by U.S. Forest Service Retirees*. Hat Creek, CA: History ink Books.

Davies, Gilbert W., and Florice M. Frank, eds. 1996. *Forest Service Humor: [More Than 300] True Stories, Yarns, Anecdotes, Letters, Memos, Poems and Cartoons*. Hat Creek, CA: History Ink Books.

Davies, Gilbert W., and Florice M. Frank, eds. 1997. *Forest Service Memories: Past Lives and Times in the United States Forest Service [More Than 300 Stories]*. Hat Creek, CA: History Ink Books.

Davies, Gilbert W., and Florice M. Frank, eds. 1998. *Forest Service Animal Tales: More Than 200 Stories about Animals in Our National Forests*. Hat Creek, CA: History Ink Books.

Davis, Norah Deakin. 1991. "International Forestry: The Forest Service's Fourth Leg." *American Forests* 97 (7/8) (July/August): 17–20.

Davis, Richard C., ed. 1983. *Encyclopedia of American Forest and Conservation History*. 2 vols. New York: Macmillan.

Doig, Ivan. 1975–1976. "The Murky Annals of Clearcutting: A 40-Year-Old Dispute." *Pacific Search* 10 (December/January): 12–14.

Doig, Ivan. 1976. "Early Forestry Research: A History of the Pacific Northwest Forest and Range Experiment Station, 1925–1975." Portland, OR: USDA Forest Service, PNW Forest and Range Experiment Station.

Donoghue, Linda. 1985. "Linda Donoghue, Fire Prevention Researcher: The First Editor of This Journal Talks about Her Work, Her Interest in Seeing a Diversified Workforce, and Her Life." *Women in Natural Resources* 10 (4): 26–30.

Dorman, Robert L. 1998. *A Word for Nature: Four Pioneering Environmental Advocates, 1845–1913*. Chapel Hill: University of North Carolina Press.

Drake, George L. 1955. "U.S. Forest Service, 1905–1955: An Industry Viewpoint." *Journal of Forestry* 53 (2) (February): 116–120.

Droze, Wilmon H. 1977. *Trees, Prairies, and People: A History of Tree Planting in the Plains States*. Denton: Texas Woman's University.

Durham, Leslie Aileen. 1995. "The National Grasslands: Past, Present and Future Land Management Issues." *Rangelands* 17 (April): 36–42.

Egleston, Nathaniel H. 1884. *Report on Forestry*. Vol. 4. Washington, DC: USGPO.

Ellefson, Paul V., Antony S. Chong, and Robert J. Moulton. 1995. *Regulation of Private Forestry Practices by State Governments*. Station Bulletin 605–1995. St. Paul: University of Minnesota, Minnesota Agricultural Experiment Station.

Enarson, Elaine Pitt. 1984. *Woods-Working Women: Sexual Integration in the U.S. Forest Service*. Tuscaloosa: University of Alabama Press.

Engle, Ed. 1989. *Seasonal [FS Employee]: A Life Outside*. Boulder, CO: Pruett.

Fedkiw, John. 1999. *Managing Multiple Uses on National Forests, 1905–1995: A 90-Year Learning Experience and It Isn't Finished Yet*. Washington, DC: USDA Forest Service.

Fedkiw, John, Douglas W. MacCleery, and V. Alaric Sample. 2004. "Pathway to Sustainability: Defining the Bounds on Forest Management." Durham, NC: Forest History Society.

Fernow, Bernhard Eduard. 1899. *Forestry in the U.S. Department of Agriculture during the Period 1877–1898*. Washington, DC: USGPO.

Fernow, Bernhard Eduard. 1899. *Report upon the Forestry Investigations of the United States Department of Agriculture, 1877–1898*. U.S. House of Representatives, 55th Congress, 3rd Session, House Document 181. Washington, DC: USGPO.

Flader, Susan L. 1974. *Thinking Like a Mountain: Aldo Leopold and the Evolution of an Ecological Attitude toward Deer, Wolves, and Forests.* Columbia: University of Missouri Press.

Floyd, Donald W., ed. 1999. *Forest of Discord: Options for Governing Our National Forests and Federal Public Lands.* Bethesda, MD: Society of American Foresters.

Forest Service Wives. 1980. *Sampler of the Early Years [Forest Service Women Stories].* Washington, DC: Foresters' Wives Club of Washington, DC.

Forest Service Wives. 2000. *What Did We Get Ourselves Into? Stories by Forest Service Wives.* Missoula, MT: Northern Rocky Mountain Retirees Association.

Forestry and Irrigation. 1905. "Forest Reserve Management Transferred: Control of the Reserves Passes from the Department of the Interior to the Department of Agriculture." *Forestry and Irrigation* 11 (2) (February): 60–61.

Fox, Stephen. 1981. *John Muir and His Legacy: The American Conservation Movement.* Boston: Little Brown.

Frank, Bernard. 1955. *Our National Forests.* Norman: University of Oklahoma Press.

Fritz, Edward C. 1983. *The Case against Clearcutting: Sterile Forest.* Austin, TX: Eakin Press.

Fritz, Edward C. 1989. *Clearcutting: A Crime against Nature.* Austin, TX: Eakin Press.

Frome, Michael. 1962. *Whose Woods These Are: The Story of the National Forests.* Garden City, NY: Doubleday.

Frome, Michael. 1971. *The Forest Service.* New York: Praeger.

Frome, Michael. [1974] 1997. *Battle for the Wilderness.* Salt Lake City: University of Utah Press. Frome, Michael. 1998. "Some Recollections of the Wilderness Wars." *Wild Earth* 8 (2) (Summer): 67–69.

Gable, John Allen. 1986. "Adventures in Reform: Gifford Pinchot, Amos Pinchot, Theodore Roosevelt and the Progressive Party." Grey Towers Lecture No. 1. Milford, PA: Grey Towers Press.

Gamache, Adrien E., ed. 1984. *Selling the Federal Forests.* Institute of Forest Resources Contribution No. 50. Seattle: University of Washington, College of Forest Resources.

Geier, Max G. 1998. *Forest Science Research and Scientific Communities in Alaska: A History of the Origins and Evolution of USDA Forest Service Research in Juneau, Fairbanks, and Anchorage.* PNW-GTR-426. Portland, OR: USDA Forest Service, Pacific Northwest Research Station.

Geraci, Victor, compiler. 2005. *The Lure of the Forest: Oral Histories from the National Forests in California.* R5-FR-005. Vallejo, CA: USDA Forest Service, Pacific Southwest Region.

Gillam, Bertha. 1997. "Bertha Gillam [Forest Service Director of Range Management]: An Interview by Daina Dravnieks Apple." *Women in Natural Resources* 18 (3) (Spring): 25–32.

Glover, James M. 1986. *A Wilderness Original: The Life of Bob Marshall.* Seattle, WA: The Mountaineers.

Godfrey, Anthony. 2005. *The Ever-Changing View: A Histories of the National Forests in California.* R5-FR-004. Vallejo, CA: USDA Forest Service, Pacific Southwest Region.

Gorte, Ross W. 1992. *Forest Service Planning: Accommodating Uses, Producing Outputs, and Sustaining Ecosystems.* OTA-F-505. Washington, DC: U.S. Congress, Office of Technology Assessment.

Gorte, Ross W., and Betsy A. Cody. 1995. "The Forest Service and Bureau of Land Management: History and Analysis of Merger Proposals." Report 95–117 ENR. Washington, DC: Library of Congress, Congressional Research Service.

Granger, Christopher M. 1949. "The People's Property [the National Forests]." In *Yearbook of Agriculture 1949,* ed. USDA, 299–304. Washington, DC: USGPO.

Granger, Christopher M. 1965. *Forest Management in the United States Forest Service.* Berkeley: University of California, Bancroft Library, Regional Oral History Office.

Graves, Henry Solon. 1912. "Shall the States Own the Forests?" *Outlook* 102 (December 28): 935–944.

Gray, Gary Craven. 1982. *Radio for the Fireline: A History of Electronic Communication in the Forest Service, 1905–1975.* Publication FS-369. Washington, DC: USDA Forest Service.

Greeley, William Buckhout. 1926. "A Quarter Century's Achievement [of Raphael Zon]." *Journal of Forestry* 24 (8) (December): 847–849.

Grosvenor, John R. 1999. *A History of the Architecture of the USDA Forest Service.* EM-7310–8. Washington, DC: USDA Forest Service, Engineering Staff.

Grover, Frederick W. 1972. *Multiple Use in U.S. Forest Service Land Planning.* Santa Cruz, CA: Forest History Society.

Guck, Dorothy Gray. 1955. "Occupation—Ranger's Wife." *American Forests* 61 (3) (March): 32, 65–66.

Gulick, Luther Halsey. 1951. *American Forest Policy: A Study of Government Administration and Economic Control.* New York: Duell, Sloan and Pearce.

Hanson, Chad. 1999. "End Logging on National Forests: The Facts." *Earth Island Journal* (Summer Insert): 1–16.

Hardy, Charles E. 1983. *The Gisborne Era of Forest Fire Research: Legacy of a Pioneer.* Publication FS 367. Washington, DC: USGPO.

Harmon, Frank J. 1977. "Remembering Franklin B. Hough." *American Forests* 86 (1) (January): 34–37, 52–53.

Harper, Verne L. 1972. *A Forest Service Research Scientist and Administrator Views Multiple Use.* Oral history. Santa Cruz, CA: Forest History Society.

Hays, Samuel P. 1959. *Conservation and the Gospel of Efficiency: The Progressive Conservation Movement, 1890–1920.* Harvard Historical Monographs, No. 40. Cambridge, MA: Harvard University Press.

Heiken, Doug. 1994. "FACA [Federal Advisory Committee Act]—Pillar of Open Government or Pariah of Public Participation?" *Inner Voice* 6 (3) (May/June): 14–15.

Hendee, John C., George H. Stankey, and Robert C. Lucas. 1978. *Wilderness Management.* Miscellaneous Publication 1365. Washington, DC: USDA Forest Service.

Herrett, Wendy. 1989. "Wendy Herrett: Team Player for the Forest Service." Interview. *Women in Natural Resources* 10 (1) (March): 6–10, 38.

Hessel, J. N. 1991. *Diamond Hitch Days: Tales of the Early Forest Service in Montana & Idaho.* Caldwell, ID: Caxton Printers.

Hirt, Paul W. 1994. *A Conspiracy of Optimism: Management of the National Forests Since World War Two.* Lincoln: University of Nebraska Press.

Hough, Franklin Benjamin. 1873. "On the Duty of Governments in the Preservation of Forests." Salem, MA: Salem Press. Reprinted from the *Proceedings of the American Association for the Advancement of Science 1873.* Reprinted (1971) in part in *Conservation in the United States: A Documentary History. Land and Water 1492–1900,* ed. Frank E. Smith, 686–694. New York: Chelsea House.

Hough, Franklin Benjamin. 1878–1882. *Report upon Forestry.* Vols. I (1878), II (1880), III (1882). Washington, DC: USGPO.

Howitz, Eleanor C. J., ed. 1974. *Clearcutting: A View from the Top.* Washington, DC: Acropolis Press.

Ickes, Harold L. 1940. *Not Guilty: An Official Inquiry into the Charges by Glavis and Pinchot against Richard A. Ballinger, Secretary of the Interior, 1909–1911.* Washington, DC: USGPO.

Ise, John. [1920] 1972. *The United States Forest Policy.* New York: Arno Press.

Kaufman, Herbert. 1960. *The Forest Ranger: A Study in Administrative Behavior.* Baltimore: Resources for the Future, Inc. and the Johns Hopkins University Press.

Kneipp, Leon F. 1976. *Land Planning and Acquisition, U.S. Forest Service. Interviews in 1964 and 1965 by Amelia R. Fry; Edith Mezirow; and Fern Ingersoll.* Berkeley: University of California, Bancroft Library, Regional Oral History Office.

Kotok, Edward I. 1975. *The U.S. Forest Service: Research, State Forestry, and FAO.* Berkeley: University of California, Bancroft Library, Regional Oral History Office.

Kresek, Ray. 1985. *Fire Lookouts of Oregon and Washington.* Fairfield, WA: Ye Galleon Press.

Kresek, Ray. [1984] 1998. *Fire Lookouts of the Northwest.* 3rd ed. Fairfield, WA: Ye Galleon Press.

Larson, Charlotte. 1989. "Interview—Charlotte Larson: Being a Pilot in the Forest Service Is an Elitist Job, Yes, but Varied and Demanding, Too, Especially during the Fire Season." *Women in Natural Resources* 11 (1) (September): 22–25.

Larson, Geraldine. 1985. "The Surprising Career of Geraldine 'Geri' Larson: The First and Highest Ranking Line Officer in the Forest Service." *Women in Forestry* 7 (2) (Summer): 12–16.

Lawter, William Clifford, Jr. 1994. *Smokey Bear 20252 [zip code]: A Biography.* Alexandria, VA: Lindsay Smith.

LeMaster, Dennis C. 1984. *Decade of Change: The Remaking of Forest Service Statutory Authority during the 1970s.* Westport, CT: Greenwood Press.

LeMaster, Dennis C., and Luke Popovich. 1977. *Crisis in Federal Forest Land Management: Proceedings of a Symposium.* Washington, DC: Society of American Foresters.

LeMaster, Dennis C., and John H. Beuter, eds. 1989. *Community Stability in Forest-Based Economies: Proceedings of a Conference in Portland, Oregon, November 16–18, 1987.* Portland, OR: Timber Press.

LeMaster, Dennis C., David M. Baumgartner, and David Adams, eds. 1982. *Sustained Yield: Proceedings of a Symposium Held April 27 and 28, 1982, Spokane, WA.* Pullman: Washington State University, Conference Office.

LeMaster, Dennis C., Barry R. Flamm, and John C. Hendee, eds. 1987. *Below-Cost Sales: A Conference on the Economics of National Forest Timber Sales. Proceedings of a Conference Sponsored by the Wilderness Society, February 17–19, 1987, Spokane, Washington.* Washington, DC: Wilderness Society.

Levitan, Sar, and Benjamin Johnson. 1975. *The Job Corps: A Social Experiment That Works.* Baltimore: Johns Hopkins University Press.

Lewis, James G. 2005. *The Forest Service and the Greatest Good: A Centennial History.* Durham, NC: Forest History Society.

Lockmann, Ronald F. 1981. *Guarding the Forests of Southern California: Evolving Attitudes toward Conservation of Watershed, Woodlands, and Wilderness.* Glendale, CA: Arthur H. Clark Company.

Loehr, Rodney C., ed. 1952. *Forests for the Future: The Story of Sustained Yield as Told in the Diaries and Papers of David T. Mason, 1907–1950.* St. Paul, MN: Forest Products History Foundation.

Lund, Walter H. 1967. *Timber Management in the Pacific Northwest, 1927–1965.* Oral history. Berkeley: University of California, Bancroft Library, Regional Oral History Office.

Marshall, Robert. 1930. *The Social Management of American Forests.* New York: League for Industrial Democracy.

Marshall, Robert. 1933. *The People's Forests.* New York: Harrison Smith and Robert Haas.

Mason, Alpheus Thomas. 1941. *Bureaucracy Convicts Itself: The Ballinger-Pinchot Controversy, 1910, and Its Meaning for Today.* New York: Viking Press.

Mason, David Townsend, and Donald Bruce. 1931. *Sustained Yield Forest Management as a Solution to American Forest Conservation Problems*. Portland, OR: Mason, Stevens, and Bruce.

Mastran, Shelley Smith, and Nan Lowerre. 1983. *Mountaineers and Rangers: A History of Federal Forest Management in the Southern Appalachians, 1900–81*. FS-380. Washington, DC: USGPO.

Mattey, Joe P. 1990. *The Timber Bubble That Burst: Government Policy and the Bailout of 1984*. New York: Oxford University Press.

Maunder, Elwood R. 1978. *Early Forest Service Research Administrators*. Santa Cruz, CA: Forest History Society.

McArdle, Richard E. 1975. *Dr. Richard E. McArdle: An Interview with the Former Chief, U.S. Forest Service, 1952–1962*. Santa Cruz, CA: Forest History Society.

McCarthy, G. Michael. 1977. *Hour of Trial: The Conservation Conflict in Colorado and the West 1891–1907*. Norman: University of Oklahoma Press.

McCloskey, J. Michael. 1966. "The Wilderness Act of 1964: Its Background and Meaning." *Oregon Law Review* 45 (4) (June): 288–321.

McCloskey, J. Michael. 2005. *In the Thick of It: My Life in the Sierra Club [1961–1999]*. Washington, DC: Island Press.

McGeary, Martin Nelson. 1960. *Gifford Pinchot: Forester-Politician*. Princeton: Princeton University Press.

McGuire, John R. 1982. "The National Forests: An Experiment in Land Management." *Journal of Forest History* 26 (2) (April): 84–91.

McGuire, John. 1988. *An Interview with John R. McGuire: Forest Service Chief 1972–79*. Durham, NC: Forest History Society and the USDA Forest Service.

Meine, Curt. 1988. *Aldo Leopold: His Life and Work*. Madison: University of Wisconsin Press.

Merz, Robert W. 1981. *A History of the Central States Forest Experiment Station, 1927–1965*. St. Paul, MN: USDA Forest Service, North Central Forest Experiment Station.

Miller, Char. 1992. *Gifford Pinchot: The Evolution of an American Conservationist*. Pinchot Lecture Series. Milford, PA: Grey Towers Press.

Miller, Char, ed. 1997. *American [National] Forests: Nature, Culture, and Politics*. Lawrence: University Press of Kansas.

Minden, Anne E. 1990. "Special Agent, USDAFS: Women Are Slowly Making Their Way to the Top Spots in Natural Resources Law Enforcement Management." *Women in Natural Resources* 12 (1) (September): 27–29.

Miner, Cynthia. 1984. "Opened Doors: Women Foresters and the U.S. Forest Service." *Women in Forestry* 6 (3) (Fall): 4–5.

Morgan, George Thomas, Jr. 1961. *William B. Greeley: A Practical Forester*. St. Paul, MN: Forest History Society.

Morrison, Ellen Earnhardt. [1976] 1989. *Guardian of the Forest: A History of the Smokey Bear Program*. Alexandria, VA: Morielle Press.

Nash, Roderick. 1966. "The Strenuous Life of Bob Marshall." *Forest History* 10 (3) (October): 18–25.

Nash, Roderick. 1968. *Wilderness and the American Mind*. New Haven: Yale University Press.

National Academy of Sciences. 1897. "Report of the Committee … Upon the Inauguration of a Forest Policy for the Forested Lands of the United States, to the Secretary of the Interior, May 1, 1897." Washington, DC: USGPO.

Nelson, Charles A. 1971. *History of the U.S. Forest Products Laboratory, 1910–1963*. Madison, WI: USDA Forest Service, Forest Products Laboratory.

Nelson, De Witt. 1976. *Management of Natural Resources in California, 1925–1966.* Oral history. Berkeley: University of California, Bancroft Library, Regional Oral History Office.

Nelson, Robert E. 1989. *The USDA Forest Service in Hawaii: The First Twenty Years (1957-1977).* GTR-PSW-111. Berkeley: USDA Forest Service, Pacific Southwest Forest and Range Experiment Station.

Olson, Sherry H. 1971. *The Depletion Myth: A History of Railroad Use of Timber.* Cambridge, MA: Harvard University Press.

Otis, Alison T., William D. Honey, Thomas C. Hogg, and Kimberly K. Lakin. 1986. *The Forest Service and the Civilian Conservation Corps: 1933–42.* FS-395 (August). Washington, DC: USGPO.

O'Toole, Randal. 1984. "A Reputation to Consider: Recent Events Cast Doubt on Whether the Forest Service Could Still Be Considered One of the Nation's Most Successful Organizations." *Forest Planning* 5 (3) (June): 11–15.

O'Toole, Randal. 1988. *Reforming the Forest Service.* Covelo, CA: Island Press.

Peffer, E. Louise. 1951. *The Closing of the Public Domain: Disposal and Reservation Policies, 1900–1950.* Stanford University Food Research Institute Misc. Publication 10. Stanford, CA: Stanford University Press.

Peirce, Earl S., with Susan R. Schrepfer. 1972. *Multiple Use and the U.S. Forest Service, 1910–1950.* Santa Cruz, CA: Forest History Society.

Peirce, Earl S., and William J. Stahl, compilers. 1964. *Cooperative Forest Fire Control: A History of its Origin and Development under the Weeks and Clarke-McNary Acts.* Washington, DC: USDA Forest Service.

Peterson, R. Max. 1988. "Land Management Planning on the National Forests: In Retrospect and Prospect." *Forest Lands of the Northwest: Selecting Among Alternative Uses—The 1888 Starker Lectures*, pp. 27–34. Corvallis: Oregon State University, College of Forestry.

Peterson, R. Max. 1991–1992. "An Interview with R. Max Peterson [Forest Service Chief 1979–1987]." Oral history. Durham, NC: Forest History Society.

Pinchot, Gifford. [1899] 1903. *A Primer of Forestry. Part I—The Forest.* 2nd ed. USDA Division of Forestry Bulletin 24. Washington, DC: USGPO.

Pinchot, Gifford. 1905. *A Primer of Forestry. Part II—Practical Forestry.* USDA Division of Forestry Bulletin 24. Washington, DC: USGPO.

Pinchot, Gifford. 1914. *The Training of a Forester.* Philadelphia, PA: J.B. Lippincott Company.

Pinchot, Gifford. [1910] 1967. *The Fight for Conservation.* With a new introduction by Gerald D. Nash. Seattle: University of Washington Press.

Pinchot, Gifford. [1947] 1972. *Breaking New Ground.* Seattle: University of Washington Press,. Reprint, 1987, Island Press, Washington, DC, with an introduction by George T. Frampton; 1998, Island Press, Washington, DC, with an introduction by Char Miller and V. Alaric Sample.

Pinkett, Harold T. 1970. *Gifford Pinchot: Private and Public Forester.* Urbana, IL: University of Illinois Press.

Ponder, Stephen Edward. 1986. "Federal News Management in the Progressive Era: Gifford Pinchot and the Conservation Crusade." *Journalism History* 13 (2) (Summer): 42-48.

Price, Raymond. 1976. *History of Forest Service Research in the Central and Southern Rocky Mountain Regions, 1908–1975.* GTR-RM-27. Fort Collins, CO: USDA Forest Service, Rocky Mountain Forest and Range Experiment Station.

Pyles, Hamilton K. 1972. *Multiple Use of the National Forests.* Oral history. Santa Cruz, CA: Forest History Society.

Public Land Law Review Commission. 1970. *One Third of the Nation's Land: A Report to the President and to the Congress.* Washington, DC: USGPO.

Puter, Stephen A. Douglas, and Horace Stevens, collaborator. 1908. *Looters of the Public Domain*. Portland, OR: Portland Printing House.

Pyne, Stephen J. 1982. *Fire in America: A Cultural History of Wildland and Rural Fire*. Princeton: Princeton University Press.

Rakestraw, Lawrence. [1955] 1979. "A History of Forest Conservation in the Pacific Northwest, 1891–1913." New York: Arno Press.

Rakestraw, Lawrence. 1981. *History of the United States Forest Service in Alaska*. Anchorage: Alaska Historical Commission and USDA Forest Service.

Resler, Rexford A. 1984. "The Future of Federal Forest Lands: Why the Public Will Retain Ownership of the Federal Forest and Rangelands." In *Selling the Federal Lands*, ed. Adrien E. Gamache, pp. 47–62. Seattle: University of Washington, College of Forest Resources.

Richardson, Elmo R. 1962. *The Politics of Conservation: Crusades and Controversies, 1897-1913*. Berkeley: University of California Press.

Richardson, Elmo. 1983. *David T. Mason: Forestry Advocate [His Role in the Application of Sustained Yield Management to Private and Public Forest Lands]*. Santa Cruz, CA: Forest History Society.

Ringland, Arthur Cuming. 1970. *Conserving Human and Natural Resources*. Oral history. Berkeley: University of California, Bancroft Library, Regional Oral History Office.

Robbins, William G. 1985. *American Forestry: A History of National, State, and Private Cooperation*. Lincoln: University of Nebraska Press.

Roberts, Paul H. 1963. *Hoof Prints on Forest Ranges: The Early Years of National Forest Range Administration*. San Antonio, TX: Naylor.

Roberts, Paul H. 1965. *Them Were the Days*. San Antonio, TX: Naylor.

Roberts, Paul H., Evan W. Kelley, and John Weiman Keller. 1974. *Forest Service Issues*. Oral history. Berkeley: University of California, Bancroft Library, Regional Oral History Office.

Robinson, Glen O. 1975. *The Forest Service: A Study in Public Land Management*. Baltimore: Resources for the Future, Inc. and the Johns Hopkins University Press.

Rodgers, Andrew Denny, III. [1951] 1991. *Bernhard Eduard Fernow: A Story of North American Forestry*. Durham, NC: Forest History Society.

Roth, Dennis M. 1980. "Public Lands, States' Rights, and the National Forests." *The Forest Service History Line* (Fall): 2–3, 8–11.

Roth, Dennis M. 1986. *Timber Management in the Pacific Northwest: Oral History of Five Region 6 Employees: Al Wiener, Walt Lund, John [Jack] Usher, and Glen Jorgensen*. 3 vols. Washington, DC: USDA Forest Service, History Unit.

Roth, Dennis M. [1988] 1995. *The Wilderness Movement and the National Forests*. Reprints of FS-391 and FS-410 with photographs. College Station, TX: Intaglio Press.

Roth, Dennis M., and Frank Harmon. 1995. "The Forest Service in the Environmental Era." FS-574. Washington, DC: USDA Forest Service.

Rothman, Hal K. 1989. "'A Regular Ding-Dong Fight': Agency Culture and Evolution in the NPS-USFS Dispute, 1916–1937." *Western Historical Quarterly* 20 (2) (May): 141–161. Reprinted in Char Miller, ed. 1997. *American Forests: Nature, Culture, and Politics*. Lawrence: University Press of Kansas.

Rothman, Hal K. 1994. *"I'll Never Fight Fire with My Bare Hands Again": Recollections of the First Forest Rangers of the Inland Northwest*. Lawrence: University Press of Kansas

Rowley, William D. 1985. *U.S. Forest Service Grazing and Rangelands: A History*. College Station: Texas A&M University Press.

Runte, Alfred. 1991. *Public Lands, Public Heritage: The National Forest Idea*. Niwot, CO: Roberts Rinehart Publishers in cooperation with the Buffalo Bill Historical Center.

Salmond, John A. 1967. *The Civilian Conservation Corps, 1933–1942: A New Deal Case Study*. Durham, NC: Duke University Press.

Sample, V. Alaric, Jr.. 1984. *Below-Cost Timber Sales on the National Forests*. Washington, DC: Wilderness Society, Economic Policy Department.

Sample, V. Alaric, Jr. 1991. *Land Stewardship in the Next Era of Conservation*. Milford, PA: Grey Towers Press.

Scheips, Paul J. 1981. *Will Croft Barnes: A Westerner of Parts*. Great Western Series No. 15. Washington, DC: Potomac Corral, The Westerners.

Schenck, Carl Alwin. 1955. *The Biltmore Story: Recollections of the Beginnings of Forestry in the United States*. St. Paul, MN: American Forest History Foundation–Minnesota Historical Foundation.

Schenck, Carl Alwin. 1974. *The Birth of Forestry in America: Cradle of Forestry in America: The Biltmore Forest School, 1898–1913*. Santa Cruz, CA: Forest History Society; Reprint, 1998, Forest History Society: Durham, NC.

Schiff, Ashley L. 1962. *Fire and Water: Scientific Heresy in the Forest Service*. Cambridge, MA: Harvard University Press.

Scott, Doug. 2004. *The Enduring Wilderness: Protecting Our National Heritage through the Wilderness Act*. Golden, CO: Fulcrum.

Sea, Susan. 1990. "Overview of Forest Service Law Enforcement: The Number of Women Is Increasing Proportionally to the Increase in Numbers of Law Enforcement Officers and Special Agents in the Agency." *Women in Natural Resources* 12 (1) (September): 9–10.

Shands, William E., and Robert G. Healy. 1977. *Policy for National Forests in the Eastern United States: The Lands Nobody Wanted*. Washington, DC: Conservation Foundation.

Shoemaker, Leonard C. 1958. *Saga of a Forest Ranger: A Biography of William R. Kreutzer, Forest Ranger No. 1, and a Historical Account of the U.S. Forest Service in Colorado*. Boulder: University of Colorado Press.

Sieker, John H., and Lloyd W. Swift. 1968. *Forest Service Recreation and Wildlife*. Oral history. Berkeley: University of California, Bancroft Library, Regional Oral History Office.

Sirmon, Jeff M. 1994. "Interview with Jeff M. Sirmon, Deputy Chief for International Forestry." Pamphlet. Washington, DC: USDA Forest Service.

Smith, Darrell Hevenor. [1930] 1974. *The Forest Service: Its History, Activities and Organization*. New York: AMS Press.

Smith, Frank E. 1966. *The Politics of Conservation*. New York: Pantheon Books.

Steen, Harold K. 1976. *The U.S. Forest Service: A History*. Seattle: University of Washington Press.

Steen, Harold K. 1991. "The Beginning of the National Forest System." FS-488. Washington, DC: USDA Forest Service, History Unit.

Steen, Harold K., ed. 1992. *The Origins of the National Forests: A Centennial Symposium*. Proceedings of the symposium "One Hundred Years of National Forests: National Forest History and Interpretation," held in Missoula, MT, June 20–22, 1991. Durham, NC: Forest History Society.

Steen, Harold K., ed. 1994. *View From the Top: Forest Service Research [Oral Histories] by R. Keith Arnold, M. B. Dickerman, Robert E. Buckman*. Durham, NC: Forest History Society.

Steen, Harold K., ed. 1998. *Forest Service Research: Finding Answers to Conservation's Questions*. Durham, NC: Forest History Society.

Steen, Harold K., ed. 1999. *Forest and Wildlife Science in America: A History*. Durham, NC: Forest History Society.

Steen, Harold K., ed. 2004. *The Chiefs Remember: The Forest Service, 1952–2001*. Durham, NC: Forest History Society.

Sutton, S. B. 1970. *Charles Sprague Sargent and the Arnold Arboretum*. Cambridge, MA: Harvard University Press.

Swain, Donald C. 1963. *Federal Conservation Policy, 1921–1933*. Berkeley: University of California Press.

Tanner, Thomas, ed. 1987. *Aldo Leopold: The Man and His Legacy*. Ankeny, IA: Soil Conservation Society of America.

Taylor, Steven T. 1994. *Sleeping with the Industry: The U.S. Forest Service and Timber Interests*. Washington, DC: Center for Public Integrity.

Thomas, Jack Ward, with Harold K. Steen, ed. 2004. *Jack Ward Thomas: The Journals of a Forest Service Chief*. Durham, NC: Forest History Society.

Tucker, Edwin A. 1989. *The Early Days: A Sourcebook of Southwestern Region History*. Book 1. Cultural Resources Management Report No. 7. Albuquerque, NM: USDA Forest Service, Southwestern Region. Book 2 printed in 1991 and Book 3 in 1992.

Tucker, Edwin A., and George Fitzpatrick. 1972. *Men Who Matched the Mountains: The Forest Service in the Southwest*. Item #781–388. Albuquerque, NM: USDA Forest Service, Southwestern Region.

Tweed, William C. 1980. *Recreation Site Planning and Improvement in National Forests 1891-1942*. FS-354. Washington, DC: USGPO. Reprinted, c.1989, as *A History of Outdoor Recreation Development in National Forests 1891–1942*. Clemson, SC: Clemson University, Department of Parks, Recreation, and Tourism Management.

Twight, Ben W. 1983. *Organizational Values and Political Power: The Forest Service Versus the Olympic National Park*. University Park: Pennsylvania State University Press.

USDA Forest Service. 1990. *The History of Engineering in the Forest Service (A Compilation of History and Memoirs, 1905–1989)*. EM-7100–13. Washington, DC: USDA Forest Service, Engineering Staff.

USDA Forest Service, Northern Region. 1944. *Early Days in the Forest Service*. Vol. 1. Missoula, MT: USDA Forest Service, Northern Region. Vol. 2 was published in 1955, Vol. 3 in 1962, Vol. 4 in 1976.

U.S. General Accounting Office. 1984. *Report to the Secretaries of Agriculture and the Interior: Program to Transfer Land between the Bureau of Land Management and the Forest Service*. GAO/RCED-85–21 (December 27). Washington, DC: USGPO.

Wengert, Norman, A. A. Dyer, and Henry A. Deutsch. 1979. *The "Purposes" of the National Forests—A Historical Reinterpretation of Policy Development*. Fort Collins: Colorado State University.

West, Terry L. 1992. "Centennial Mini-Histories of the Forest Service." Washington, DC: USDA Forest Service.

West, Terry L. 1993. "Forest Service Centennial History Bibliography, 1891–1991." Washington, DC: USDA Forest Service.

West, Terry L. 1993. "Social Science and the Forest Service." *History Line* (Spring): 24–29.

Williams, Gerald W. 1992. "John B. Waldo and William G. Steel: Forest Reserve Advocates for the Cascade Range of Oregon." In *The Origins of the National Forests: A Centennial Symposium*, ed. Harold K. Steen, pp. 314–332. Durham, NC: Forest History Society.

Williams, Gerald W. 1992. *Judge John Breckenridge Waldo: Diaries and Letters from the High Cascades of Oregon, 1877–1907*. Roseburg and Eugene, OR: USDA Forest Service, Umpqua and Willamette National Forests.

Williams, Gerald W. 1999. "Social Science Research in the Forest Service: An Increasing Emphasis." In *Forest and Wildlife Science in America: A History*, ed. Harold K. Steen, pp. 318–353. Durham, NC: Forest History Society in cooperation with the USDA Forest Service.

Williams, Gerald W. 2002. "Aboriginal Use of Fire: Were There Any 'Natural' Plant Communities?" In *Wilderness and Political Ecology: Aboriginal Land Management—Myths and Reality*, ed. Charles E. Kay and Randy T. Simmons, pp. 179–214. Logan: University of Utah Press.

Williams, Gerald W. 2004. "American Indian Use of Fire in Ecosystems: Thousands of Years of Managing Landscapes." Washington, DC: USDA Forest Service.

Williams, Gerald W. [2000] 2005. *The USDA Forest Service—The First Century*. FS-650. Washington, DC: USDA Forest Service.

Williams, Gerald W., and Stephen R. Mark. 1995. *Establishing and Defending the Cascade Range Forest Reserve: As Found in Letters of William G. Steel, John B. Waldo, and Others Supplemented by Newspapers, Magazines, and Official Reports 1885–1912*. Portland and Crater Lake, OR: USDA Forest Service, Pacific Northwest Region and USDI National Park Service, Crater Lake National Park.

Wood, Nancy C. 1971. *Clearcut: The Deforestation of America*. Battlebook Series No. 3. San Francisco: Sierra Club.

Yaffee, Steven Lewis. 1994. *The Wisdom of the Spotted Owl: Policy Lessons for a New Century*. Covelo, CA: Island Press.

Zimmerman, Eliot W. 1976. *A Historical Summary of State and Private Forestry in the U.S. Forest Service*. Washington, DC: USDA Forest Service, State and Private Forestry.

Zon, Raphael. 1927. *Forests and Water in the Light of Scientific Investigation*. Washington, DC: USGPO.

Index

About the Author

GERALD W. WILLIAMS taught for two years at Indiana State University, then one year as recreation research director for the City of Eugene, Oregon. He started working for the Forest Service in 1979, focusing on social/policy analysis, long-range planning, and social impact analysis/socioeconomic assessment/human dimension at all levels of the agency. Williams retired from the Forest Service in 2005, and is currently living in Portland, Oregon, where he is a historical researcher, writer, and teacher. He has authored and compiled extensive works regarding the social sciences in the Forest Service. He has written several books, as well as numerous professional reports, papers, and journal articles.